FROMMER'S
EASTERN EUROPE
ON $25 A DAY™

by Morris H. Hadley
and Adam Tanner

1987-88 Edition

Sponsored by
 Lufthansa

Published by Prentice Hall Press
A Division of Simon & Schuster, Inc.
Gulf + Western Building
One Gulf + Western Plaza
New York, New York 10023

ISBN 0–671–60720–0

Manufactured in the United States of America

*Lufthansa German Airlines shall not be responsible for any errors,
faulty information, and/or printing errors of any sort.*

CONTENTS

MAPS

To
Celia

To Sarah B. Boyden

whose reporting in the Chicago of the Roaring Twenties,
her own traveling
and her love were an inspiration.

Acknowledgments

This book would never have been written without the culinary wisdom of Prof. James Shenton, the sage counsel of Prof. Richard Pious, and the business acumen of Glen Cowley, as well as help from Walter Wager.

Many thanks to the ever-watchful bastions of lexicographical purity, Marilyn Wood and Gloria McDarrah, whose reserve of infinite patience was sorely taxed. Also thanks to publisher Paul Pasmantier, who gave two kids an even break.

We would also like to thank the national tourist agencies of Bulgaria, Czechoslovkia, German Democratic Republic (East Germany), Hungary, Romania, Poland, Yugoslavia, Austria, and Turkey. We owe special thanks to Andrew Jablonowski of Orbis, Krzysztof Ziębinski of LOT, Marajana Zečevič and Mr. Bojkovsky of the Yugoslav National Tourist Office, as well as Kamil Muren of the Turkish Tourism Office. Our sincere gratitude to the many Eastern Europeans who patiently explained everything that needed explaining, twice.

We would like to thank our three travel "comerades": Greg Viscusi, who saw us through Poland; Willi Chandler, who always meets adventure and adversity face to face; and Consuelo Márquez, whose insights, warmth, and humor were priceless.

Inflation Alert

Most Eastern European governments don't publish statistics on inflation. Nonetheless, prices do rise from time to time. Fortunately, the dollar has also risen vis-à-vis most Eastern European currencies, offsetting many price changes. Occasionally, inflation outpaces the strength of the dollar in Eastern Europe, and especially in the second year of this book (1988), you may see slightly higher prices in real dollar terms than those quoted here.

A Disclaimer

Throughout this guide we have tried to provide the latest and most accurate information possible, but keep in mind that hours, addresses, prices, rules, and so on often change without notice or explanation in Eastern Europe, so maintain your patience and good spirits.

EASTERN EUROPE ON $25 A DAY

BY PICKING UP THIS BOOK you have made a good choice and a better beginning. Eastern Europe is one of the most fascinating and historically rich regions in the world. It is also largely unexplored by Westerners.

Eastern European society is far more complex and difficult to categorize than most people think. It's not the "Workers Paradise," as advertised, nor is it a prison peopled by mindless robot-servants of Communism. While in Eastern Europe you will have the opportunity to meet friendly people from a world very different from your own and see magnificent sights rivaling the great monuments of Western Europe.

In Eastern Europe you will find that locals appreciate your Western, especially American, citizenship with an intensity and depth found few places in the world. At the same time you'll often observe official proclamations referring to Westerners as "capitalists" or "imperialists," the traditional foes of Communism. Eastern Europe, in short, is unlike any other place you will ever visit. And for that reason alone it's worth visiting.

There are many other reasons as well. Here are a few:

THE REASON WHY: To many Americans, Eastern Europe is a vaguely defined region somewhere east of Paris, north of Greece, and south of Sweden. Eastern Europe is seen as uniform, uninviting, and off-limits to tourists. Though it operates under a very different, and often conflicting, system from that of the United States, Eastern Europe has some of the most beautiful landscape, fascinating history, and friendly people in all of Europe. It is also substantially less expensive, in most cases, than many of the Western European countries that are such popular destinations today.

But what is there to see in Eastern Europe? Well, from the top of the snow-capped Tatra Mountains in Poland and Czechoslovakia to the deepest gallery of the fantastic Postojna caves in Yugoslavia, from dark forests in Poland to the wide beaches of the Bulgarian Black Sea coast, there is enough to make one of the finest vacations on the European side of the Atlantic. Some of the most fascinating places are world renowned; others we've found and will tell you about are less well known but equally rewarding:

- Kraków, Poland, a truly magical city with winding medieval streets where the great Wawel Castle and cathedral still dominate the Old City.
- Prague, the beautiful 18th-century capital of Czechoslovakia, which has managed to emerge unscathed from the two World Wars as the most splendidly preserved capital in Europe.

- Weimar, in the southeast corner of East Germany, the symbol of the greatest artistic achievements of German literature and music, and once home to Goethe, Schiller, Bach, and Liszt.
- Dubrovnik, aptly called the pearl of the Adriatic, whose crystal-clear waters make Yugoslavia's entire Dalmatian coast a summertime mecca.
- Budapest, strategically situated on the Danube, which still boasts the lively sidewalk cafés and baroque buildings that recall the glory days of the Austro-Hungarian Empire.
- Bulgaria's Black Sea coast, where towns that were ancient Greek colonies dot an appealing shore that also affords the latest in modern sports activities to active vacationers.
- And the monasteries of Moldavia in Romania, painted with frescoes whose brilliant colors depict what might be called a living Bible.

You can do what you want in Eastern Europe for so much less. A liter of some of the finest beer in the world for 47¢? Sounds incredible, but in Czechoslovakia, home to both the original Budweiser (Budvar) and pilsner (the most popular kind of beer, worldwide, today), you'll come to think that those prices are actually high! Some of the best wild boar hunting in the world is to be found in Poland and the fishing opportunities are just as good. How about tennis courts for less than $1.50 an hour or windsurfing for $2 an hour? It's all at Lake Balaton, Hungary's sun-drenched, aquatic playground.

But what about the Berlin Wall, the police and the repression and the hostile governments that you may encounter in Eastern Europe? Well, for starters, things have changed substantially in the last 20 years. Second, politics are rarely a problem for Western tourists. Now, more than ever before, Eastern European governments need tourist dollars and are going out of their way to cater to visitors. This means that getting a visa and traveling into and around Eastern Europe is much easier than it ever has been—even five years ago.

The good citizens of Paris, Rome, and London have seen plenty of Americans and they probably will see a lot more. Western Europeans don't hate tourists, but they are so commonplace that Western European attitudes toward visitors, especially Americans, have become fairly blasé. Not so in Eastern Europe. In every country we visited, Americans are looked upon with, at the very least, interest. Most Eastern Europeans were very eager to meet and talk with Americans—we were exotic, new, different. Curious and very polite at first, people would befriend us with a sincerity and depth that we had rarely experienced in our travels anywhere.

ABOUT THIS BOOK: This is a guide for the traveler who cannot simply ignore costs, who wants to get away from tours, away from the crowds, to *see* the country and *meet* the people. But above all, this is a practical guidebook. We hope that with this book in hand you will be able to avoid many of the mistakes that most travelers make.

This guide was initially planned to cover the Warsaw Pact nations of Eastern Europe: Poland, Czechoslovakia, East Germany, Hungary, Romania, and Bulgaria. But then we felt that a country so beautiful and varied as Yugoslavia, which borders three countries covered in this guide, simply had to be included. So it is the geography and great tourist attractions—not political unity—that brings Yugoslavia together with the rest of Eastern Europe in this book. As Yugoslavia parted ways with the Warsaw Pact in the late 1940s, it is a very different society, albeit still socialist, from the rest of Eastern Europe. Most of the comments in this introductory chapter are geared to the other six nations of Eastern Europe.

One country left out of the guide deserves coverage, at least geographically, in a guide to Eastern Europe: Albania. However, the Albanians do not allow Americans into their country. We tried several times to obtain permission to visit Albania, and each time we were turned down. The *Albania News*, a publication of the U.S.-Albania Friendship Association, explained in a recent newsletter that no U.S. travelers are allowed into Albania since the U.S. and Albania "have no state-to-state relations, and [because] the U.S., as one of the great superpowers in the world, represents a serious and genuine threat to the security and independence of Albania." We suspect that one day the virgin beaches and pleasant countryside of Albania will slowly open to Americans; as of now, however, it is virtually impossible to get into Albania. If you want to find out more information about this enigmatic country, ask for the latest *Albania News* from the U.S.-Albania Friendship Association, P.O. Box 2534, Gary, IN 46403 (tel. 219/938-0209).

ABOUT THE AUTHORS: We feel we make a good travel team because we disagree on so many things. Any item that we included has had to pass the stringent requirements of one and then be subjected to a determined probing by the other. But we both agree on one thing: Eastern Europe has some of the friendliest people, who welcome and respect Americans like no others in the world.

We are not residents of the countries we visited, though we do speak several languages useful in Eastern Europe. We are not chums with the senior directors of the government tourist monopolies; we dealt with the same officials, maps, hotels, trains, and everything else that you will encounter in Eastern Europe. We describe the process of getting a visa in detail, we walk you through Customs, we point you toward the best rooms for your money—in short, we cover the nuts and bolts of getting to and getting around Eastern Europe. We can't promise that we'll solve all the problems you may encounter, but we believe that this book will help you avoid most of them, leaving you free to do what, we feel, is most important during your visit to Eastern Europe: Enjoy your stay.

READING SUGGESTIONS: By far the most useful book we have come across on the evolution of the current societies in Eastern Europe is *Communism in Eastern Europe*, edited by Teresa Rakowska-Harmstone (Indiana University Press). Although not for the casual reader, this absorbing work gives country-by-country historical, political, and economic background in a detailed, informative manner.

For planning your travels, you may find it useful to obtain a copy of *Thomas Cook's Continental Timetable*, a map and listing of train routes in Europe. Although all local trains are not included in this 400-page book, it does detail major international train and ferry routes and times, an invaluable aid in plotting out your journeys. In the U.S. the guide is sold (for $15.95) only by the Forsyth Travel Library, P.O. Box 2975, Shawnee Mission, KS 66201 (tel. 913/384-3440). Since a new edition is published every month, sometimes you can convince a local travel agency to give you an old copy for free. In England (where it's published), it costs a more reasonable £4 (about $6) at 45 Berkeley St., London W1A 1EB (tel. 01/499-4000).

For travelers visiting Eastern Europe by car, we suggest *Roadbook Europe*, by Rune Lagerqvist, published by the British Automobile Association.

This thick guide contains hundreds of maps and brief descriptions of the cities along the road, a must for the automotive traveler. Larger bookstores in the U.S. sometimes stock this guide; if you can't find it, write to the Automobile Association, Fanum House, Basingstoke, Hampshire, England RG 21 2EA.

$25 A DAY—WHAT IT MEANS: As we were preparing this guide, many friends incredulously asked us whether it was really possible to spend *only* $25 a day and travel well in Eastern Europe. Sure it is—Eastern Europe provides some of the best value for your travel dollar in the world today! In fact, in many cases you can spend even less than $25 a day. This figure allows for about $10 for food and $15 for accommodations, but *excludes* transportation, museum fees, and various other expenses. However, with Eastern European museum entrance fees costing just spare change, and domestic transportation running a few dollars for a lengthy journey, you can often spend less than a *total* of $25 a day.

In many cases you'll fork out as little as $10 to $15 a day in Eastern Europe, provided you stay at rooms in private homes. Budget-conscious travelers can consistently spend less than $25 a day in two countries in particular, Hungary and Bulgaria, where private accommodations are widely available, food and transportation are inexpensive, and no minimum daily exchange requirement exists (see "Currency and the Black Market" in Chapter I). If you prefer hotels to private accommodations in Hungary and Bulgaria, you'll spend closer to $25 a day. Yugoslavia is a close third in amazing vacation value, offering a wide variety of handsome private rooms and excellent inexpensive cuisine.

In Poland and Czechoslovakia, due to a compulsory daily minimum dollar exchange and fewer private rooms, you're likely to spend closer to $25 a day. Again, enterprising travelers may be able to bring expenses down below the $25 mark if they can find private rooms.

East Germany and Romania will cost more than $25 a day. In East Germany, in order to get a visa, you must reserve and pre-pay rooms from a select group of markedly expensive hotels; thus you'll spend closer to $30 to $35 a day, at least getting an attractive hotel in the deal. In Romania by contrast, even the worst facilities are expensive. The government has actively lowered the local rate of exchange against the dollar, causing prices to rise for Westerners. And since you can't rent private rooms in Romania, you'll probably spend $25 to $30 a day for basic living.

You can save a lot of money by traveling with a companion in Eastern Europe. Most hotels charge almost as much for one as for two, so the savings can be considerable. In countries such as East Germany and Romania, not traveling alone can mean the difference between being able to afford a visit or not.

SOME DISCLAIMERS: No restaurant, inn, hotel, guesthouse, or shop paid to be mentioned in this book. What you read are personal recommendations—in many cases, proprietors never knew their establishments were being investigated.

A word of warning: Unfortunately, prices change, and they rarely go down.

Always, when checking into a hotel, inquire about the price—and agree on it. This policy can save much embarrassment and disappointment when it comes time to settle the tab. In no circumstances can you invariably demand to be charged the price quoted in this book, although every effort has been made to state the accurate tariff as much as it was foreseeable when this guide was published.

AN INVITATION TO READERS: Like all the $$$-A-Day guides, *Eastern Eu-*

rope on $25 a Day hopes to maintain a continuing dialogue between its authors and its readers. All of us share a common aim—to travel as widely and as well as possible, at the best value for our money. And in achieving that goal, your comments and suggestions can be of tremendous help. Therefore, if you come across a particularly appealing hotel, restaurant, store, even sightseeing attraction, please don't keep it to yourself. The solicitation for letters applies not only to new establishments, but to hotels or restaurants already recommended in this guide. The fact that a listing appears in this edition doesn't give it squatter's rights in future publications. If its services have deteriorated, its chef grown stale, its prices risen unfairly, whatever, these failings should be known. Even if you enjoyed every place and found every description accurate—that, too, can cheer many a gray day. We can't promise to answer each and every letter, but we will read them with appreciation. Send your comments to Morris H. Hadley and Adam Tanner, c/o Frommer Books, Prentice Hall Press, 1 Gulf + Western Plaza, New York, NY 10023.

The $25-A-Day Travel Club—How to Save Money on All Your Travels

In this book we'll be looking at how to get your money's worth in Eastern Europe, but there is a "device" for saving money and determining value on *all* your trips. It's the popular, international $25-a-Day Travel Club, now in its 24th successful year of operation. The Club was formed at the urging of numerous readers of the $$$-a-Day and Dollarwise Guides, who felt that such an organization could provide continuing travel information and a sense of community to value-minded travelers in all parts of the world. And so it does!

In keeping with the budget concept, the annual membership fee is low and is immediately exceeded by the value of your benefits. Upon receipt of $18 (U.S. residents), or $20 U.S. by check drawn on a U.S. bank or via international postal money order in U.S. funds (Canadian, Mexican, and other foreign residents) to cover one year's membership, we will send all new members the following items.

(1) *Any two* of the following books

Please designate in your letter which two you wish to receive:

Europe on $25 a Day
Australia on $25 a Day
Eastern Europe on $25 a Day
England on $35 a Day
Greece including Istanbul and Turkey's Aegean Coast on $25 a Day
Hawaii on $45 a Day
India on $15 & $25 a Day
Ireland on $30 a Day
Israel on $30 & $35 a Day
Mexico on $20 a Day (plus Belize and Guatemala)
New York on $45 a Day
New Zealand on $35 a Day
Scandinavia on $50 a Day
Scotland and Wales on $35 a Day
South America on $25 a Day
Spain and Morocco (plus the Canary Is.) on $40 a Day
Turkey on $25 a Day (avail. Sept. '87)

Washington, D.C., on $40 a Day

Dollarwise Guide to Austria & Hungary
Dollarwise Guide to Belgium, Holland, & Luxembourg (avail. June '87)
Dollarwise Guide to Bermuda & The Bahamas
Dollarwise Guide to Canada
Dollarwise Guide to the Caribbean
Dollarwise Guide to Egypt
Dollarwise Guide to England & Scotland
Dollarwise Guide to France
Dollarwise Guide to Germany
Dollarwise Guide to Italy
Dollarwise Guide to Japan & Hong Kong
Dollarwise Guide to Portugal, Madeira, and the Azores
Dollarwise Guide to the South Pacific (avail. Aug. '87)
Dollarwise Guide to Switzerland & Liechtenstein
Dollarwise Guide to Alaska (avail. Nov. '87)
Dollarwise Guide to California & Las Vegas
Dollarwise Guide to Florida
Dollarwise Guide to New England
Dollarwise Guide to New York State (avail. Aug. '87)
Dollarwise Guide to the Northwest
Dollarwise Guide to Skiing USA—East
Dollarwise Guide to Skiing USA—West
Dollarwise Guide to the Southeast & New Orleans
Dollarwise Guide to the Southwest
Dollarwise Guide to Texas
(Dollarwise Guides discuss accommodations and facilities in all price ranges, with emphasis on the medium-priced.)

A Shopper's Guide to Best Buys in England, Scotland, and Wales
(Describes in detail hundreds of places to shop—department stores, factory outlets, street markets, and craft centers—for great quality British bargains.)

Bed & Breakfast—North America
(This guide contains a directory of over 150 organizations that offer bed & breakfast referrals and reservations throughout North America. The scenic attractions, businesses, and major schools and universities near the homes of each are also listed.)

Dollarwise Guide to Cruises
(This complete guide covers all the basics of cruising—ports of call, costs, fly-cruise package bargains, cabin selection booking, embarkation and debarkation and describes in detail over 60 or so ships cruising the waters of Alaska, the Caribbean, Mexico, Hawaii, Panama, Canada, and the United States.)

Dollarwise Guide to Skiing Europe
(Describes top ski resorts in Austria, France, Italy, and Switzerland. Illustrated with maps of each resort area plus full-color trail maps.)

How to Beat the High Cost of Travel
(This practical guide details how to save money on absolutely all travel items—accommodations, transportation, dining, sightseeing, shopping, taxes, and

more. Includes special budget information for seniors, students, singles, and families.)

Marilyn Wood's Wonderful Weekends
(This very selective guide covers the best mini-vacation destinations within a 175-mile radius of New York City. It describes special country inns and other accommodations, restaurants, picnic spots, sights, and activities—all the information needed for a two- or three-day stay.)

Motorist's Phrase Book
(A practical phrase book in French, German, and Spanish designed specifically for the English-speaking motorist touring abroad.)

Swap and Go—Home Exchanging Made Easy
(Two veteran home exchangers explain in detail all the money-saving benefits of a home exchange, and then describe precisely how to do it. Also includes information on home rentals and many tips on low-cost travel.)

The Fast 'n' Easy Phrase Book
(French, German, Spanish, and Italian—all in one convenient, easy-to-use phrase guide.)

Travel Diary and Record Book
(A 96-page diary for personal travel notes plus a section for such vital data as passport and traveler's check numbers, itinerary, postcard list, special people and places to visit, and a reference section with temperature and conversion charts, and world maps with distance zones.)

Where to Stay USA
(By the Council on International Educational Exchange, this extraordinary guide is the first to list accommodations in all 50 states that cost anywhere from $3 to $30 per night.)

(2) A one-year subscription to *The Wonderful World of Budget Travel*

This quarterly eight-page tabloid newspaper keeps you up to date on fast-breaking developments in low-cost travel in all parts of the world bringing you the latest money-saving information—the kind of information you'd have to pay $25 a year to obtain elsewhere. This consumer-conscious publication also features columns of special interest to readers: **Hospitality Exchange** (members all over the world who are willing to provide hospitality to other members as they pass through their home cities); **Share-a-Trip** (offers and requests from members for travel companions who can share costs and help avoid the burdensome single supplement); and **Readers Ask . . . Readers Reply** (travel questions from members to which other members reply with authentic firsthand information).

(3) A copy of *Arthur Frommer's Guide to New York*

This is a pocket-size guide to hotels, restaurants, nightspots, and sightseeing attractions in all price ranges throughout the New York area.

(4) Your personal membership card

Membership entitles you to purchase through the Club all Arthur Frommer publications for a third to a half off their regular retail prices during the term of your membership.

So why not join this hardy band of international budgeteers and participate in its exchange of travel information and hospitality? Simply send your name and address, together with your annual membership fee of $18 (U.S. residents) or $20 U.S. (Canadian, Mexican, and other foreign residents), by check drawn on a U.S. bank or via international postal money order in U.S. funds to: $25-A-Day Travel Club, Inc., Frommer Books, Gulf + Western Building, One Gulf + Western Plaza, New York, NY 10023. And please remember to specify which *two* of the books in section (1) above you wish to receive in your initial package of members' benefits. Or, if you prefer, use the last page of this book, simply checking off the two books you select and enclosing $18 or $20 in U.S. currency.

Once you are a member, there is no obligation to buy additional books. No books will be mailed to you without your specific order.

Chapter I

ABOUT EASTERN EUROPE

1. A Brief History
2. Planning Your Travels
3. What to Take Along
4. Food and Lodging
5. The Facts of Life in Eastern Europe

IN THIS CHAPTER, we'll give you a bit of background on Eastern Europe, as well as some advance information on how to plan for your travels and what to expect when you get there.

1. A Brief History

There are many misconceptions about Eastern Europe, perhaps the greatest being that it is a single, homogeneous region. The history of Eastern Europe is one of vast human migrations, long wars, ancient kingdoms, and the earliest universities of Europe. In fact, the term "Eastern Europe" covers a territory so diverse and composed of so many different cultures that it has almost no value as a description at all—that is, until after World War II when the area, to all appearances, was "unified" under Communism. But while Communism has altered life to a great degree, Eastern Europe's culture and traditions, despite the Soviet presence, are still very much alive.

In this section we use the term "Eastern Europe" in a strictly geographical sense—not a political one—to cover the eastern half of the area between Portugal and the Soviet Union (not the Warsaw Pact lands, which is what we mean by Eastern Europe elsewhere in this book).

THE FIRST EASTERN EUROPEANS: The Slavs are believed to have entered Europe from the vast Priapet Marshes in west-central Russia. Invasions by Germanic tribes from northern Europe and the Magyars and others from the east divided the Slavs into several distinct groups: the Eastern Slavs (Ukrainians and Russians), Southern Slavs (Slovenes, Serbs, Croats, and Bulgars), and the Western Slavs (Poles, Pomerani, Czechs, and Slovaks).

The Romans conquered much of present-day Hungary and the region southward to the Mediterranean Sea by the 1st century B.C. Under Roman rule cities and roads were built, and the Roman influence permeated such fields of knowledge as astronomy and medicine as well. While the indigenous tribes had their own flourishing cultures, Roman rule united the territories. However, as

the Empire began to lose its power, Eastern European territory was left open to new waves of invasion. Both Germanic and Slavic tribes, inspired by population pressures and the prospect of rich plunder, fought the Romans in increasingly desperate battles. By the 4th century A.D. a virtual parade of invaders worked their way across what is now Poland and Czechoslovakia down through the Balkans.

The major ethnic groups living in Eastern Europe today had settled in the area by the 8th and 9th centuries. Those Slavs who had originally entered Eastern Europe with the Germanic tribes settled principally where the central Slavic states—Poland and Czechoslovakia—exist today. The Romanians, descended from the Romans, were longtime residents of the Danube Delta region. The Bulgars, who emigrated from the steppes of southern Russia, were on the scene by about A.D. 675. They moved south till they came to the borders of the Byzantine Empire. The Magyars, the tribe historically considered the progenitors of the Hungarians, came to Eastern Europe around A.D. 895 but did not settle permanently until late in the 10th century.

EXPANSION AND EMPIRES: Every country in Eastern Europe has undergone a period of imperialist expansion. There has been, for example, a greater Poland, a greater Hungary, and so on, and each of these empires overlapped, to a degree. To sort out the numerous dynasties and kingdoms would require a library—sufice it so say that borders in the areas were in constant flux. From the 11th century on the Germans, who had crossed the Elbe and moved into Poland, exercised control over the northern part of Eastern Europe. This control lasted until the end of World War II.

To the south, the influence of the Byzantine Empire held back Bulgarian expansion. The Byzantine emperor Basil II, called the slayer of the Bulgarians, subjugated the Bulgars, who had carved out a sizable kingdom, in the 10th century. In turn, the forces of the Ottoman Turks eventually conquered the Byzantine Empire in the 15th century. The Ottoman Turks built an even-larger empire that was not challenged until the early part of the 18th century by the Hapsburgs. Much of the Balkan peninsula remained under the Ottoman Empire until the end of the First World War.

EASTERN EUROPE TODAY: As we've noted, Eastern European history has been shaped by the territorial expansions of the Germans from the north and west, the Byzantines from the south, and to a lesser extent, other Slavs from the east. Because of their competing national interests and the pressure of their larger neighbors to the west and south, none of these political entities achieved lasting size or importance.

Today, Czechoslovakia and Yugoslavia are countries which did not even exist as true nations until the 20th century. Poland and Romania were independent states, but until recently were composed of so many different ethnic groups as to be almost confederacies. Bulgaria and Hungary existed as states and had a fair degree of ethnic homogeneity, but were dominated by foreign invaders for much of their history. East Germany is a post–World War II product of U.S.–Soviet rivalry.

The establishment of Communist governments in Poland, Czechoslovakia, Hungary, Romania, Bulgaria, and East Germany that are supported by the Soviet Union is perhaps the single most important event in modern Eastern European history.

POLITICS AND YOUR TRIP: Communist governments have not so changed the Eastern European countries that they are no longer recognizable. The Berlin Wall, the secret police, the spectre of Soviet repression are images which may be conjured up by some Americans when they think of Eastern Europe. But, rest assured, these countries want American dollars (and other hard currencies) and therefore you'll find that you're treated in as friendly a way as possible. Unless you are in fact a spy, a smuggler, or you trade currency on the black market, the official state police will have no interest in you at all. Ordinary people whom you encounter, like most of us, don't think much about politics unless a situation is forced on them. The Polish flower grower, the Slovak mountaineer, and the Hungarian cab driver have little to do with the political workings of their countries. They talk about flowers, they talk about climbing, or they speak of the traffic jams—and everything else that the average person is preoccupied with the world over.

The bywords for Eastern European travel—which hold true for travel anywhere—are to be discreet, keep your ears and eyes open, think before you speak, and you'll have the opportunity to meet fascinating people from a world very different from your own.

2. Planning Your Travels

You should begin planning your trip by contacting the North American offices of the national tourist agencies of the countries you want to visit, or the country's embassy or United Nations mission. (Their addresses and telephone numbers are listed in the introductory chapter on each country.) They can provide you with pamphlets and maps, give you updated visa information, and answer any questions you may have about their country.

It's generally a good idea to buy maps and guidebooks before you go to a city, especially if you're arriving on a Saturday or Sunday. Many tourist offices are closed on weekends and maps may be impossible to find. With maps already on hand, you can immediately orient yourself and avoid the hassle of searching for information while you're bogged down with luggage.

NECESSARY DOCUMENTS: All North American travelers will need certain basic documents (passport and visa) in order to enter Eastern European countries, and others may end up being very useful to you (driver's license, student ID card). Here are the details:

Passport

You'll need a passport to travel in each country listed in this book. If you don't have one, or you need to renew it, go or write to your nearest passport office several months in advance so that you'll have time enough to procure the necessary Eastern European visas. If you are getting a new passport and plan on visiting several Eastern European countries, we suggest asking for a 48-page passport (the many visa stamps of Eastern Europe will soon fill up a normal 24-page passport). For more information on passports, write for the pamphlet "Your Trip Abroad" from the Bureau of Consular Affairs, U.S. Department of State, Washington, DC 20520.

When in Eastern Europe, carry your passport with you at all times. You'll need it to check into hotels, to exchange Western money for local currency, and to book certain services at tourist offices. When you check into a hotel, your passport will usually be held by the hotel for a few hours (during which time you'll be unable to exchange money; if you need local currency, exchange money as you check in). Except for these few hours, try to keep this important document with you in a secure place at all times. Be careful—your passport is a very valuable document and should be closely guarded. Keep your visa with your passport, as you may occasionally be asked to show the visa as well.

If you are a dual national, or might be considered one by an Eastern European government (if, for example, you are now a U.S. citizen but you or your parents were born in Eastern Europe, or if you married a citizen of that country), write for a free pamphlet "Tips for Travelers to Eastern Europe and Yugoslavia," available from the Office of Passport Services, Department of State, Washington, DC 20524. This booklet outlines basic tips as well as information on special precautions dual nationals should take before traveling to Eastern Europe.

Visas

In order to enter each country covered in this guide, American, Canadian, and British visitors must obtain a visa (a special entry permit) specifying the duration of their stay (one exception—British subjects do not need a visa to visit Yugoslavia). Without a visa stamped in your passport, you will not be permitted to enter the country. You must procure the visa before you arrive at the border, except for Yugoslavia and Romania, where you may obtain a visa at the border crossing. However, we strongly recommend that visitors to Romania get their visas before traveling there.

If you plan on crossing through one Eastern European country en route to another, you will also need a transit visa. You must obtain Czech, Polish, Hungarian, and Bulgarian transit visas before arriving at the border.

We urge you to obtain all your visas before you leave North America. Just to be sure, allow several weeks to be granted a visa. If you plan on visiting several countries in Eastern Europe, the sooner you start on the visa process the better.

It is possible to procure certain visas from the country's embassy when you're in Western European capitals, but by waiting until the last minute you risk not getting into a country at all if complications arise. Hungarian and Czech visas are fairly easy to obtain in any European capital within a day or two. Bulgarian and Polish visas always seem to take longer to get than those of other countries, so be sure you have these before you head off to Europe.

For complete details on the visa requirements of each country in Eastern Europe, refer to the "Rules and Regulations" section of each introductory country chapter in this guide.

If you lose your visa when in Eastern Europe, you will be required to remain in whatever country you're in for the four or five working days it will take for reissuing an exit visa. Local authorities tend to be strict regarding official documentation.

Driver's Licenses

It's a good idea to bring along both your national driver's license and an international driver's license. Only Poland, Hungary, and East Germany require the international driver's license in addition to your national license, but in Eastern Europe, two documents are always better than one. You can easily obtain an international driver's license from your local American Automobile Association (AAA) upon presentation of your national license, two passport-size photos, and $5.

Student Cards

Eastern Europe offers many attractive discounts for students, if you have the correct documentation. To start out, get the **International Student Identity Card (ISIC)**, available to all high school and college or university students at your local student office. When you arrive in Eastern Europe, go to the local student organization (addresses are listed in each introductory country chapter) and purchase the International Union of Students (IUS) card, the equivalent of the ISIC and the only one consistently recognized in Eastern Europe. With the IUS card, you can get discounts on international transportation, as well as at some museums and hotels.

If you are not a student but are less than 26 years of age, then the **Federation of International Youth Travel Organizations (FIYTO)** card is the next best thing to a student card. Available in the West at your local student office, the FIYTO card offers young people discounts at select hotels, at museums, and on certain forms of transportation. You'll find the FIYTO card of most use for hotels and museums in Yugoslavia, for ferries on the Baltic Sea to Poland, and for accommodations in the "gateway cities" (Berlin, Vienna, and Istanbul) to Eastern Europe.

Anyone (students as well as others) who plans on staying in youth hostels should invest in a youth hostel card, which offers discounts at youth hostels across Eastern Europe. The card costs $10 for those under 18 and $20 for those over 18. Buy this card at any student office or from **American Youth Hostels, Inc.,** National Headquarters, 1332 I St. NW, Washington, DC 20005 (tel. 202/783-6161). This office also sells the *International Youth Hostel Handbook,* Volume 1, *Europe and the Mediterranean,* a sage investment as it includes a listing of all of Europe's youth hostels.

Safekeeping Your Documents

In societies highly reliant on lots of paperwork, you'll want to be sure that nothing happens to your passport, visas, and other documents. But just in case, you can save some hassle and lost days by photocopying your passport, visa, driver's license, etc., before you go and put these in a safe place in your luggage. We suggest that you also record your passport and visa numbers in another secure place, away from the original documents.

CUSTOMS: The Customs officials will be your very first direct contacts with Eastern Europe. As an American, you will probably be searched thoroughly at least once as you cross Eastern European borders. The job of the Customs official is to control the flow of goods and people in and out of the country. This involves examining you and your luggage, and also asking questions as to the length of your stay, the purpose of your visit, the location of your residence, and other related matters. You must allow Customs officials to examine anything they ask to see, and you must answer their questions. This procedure is not exclusive to Eastern Europe, but the Customs officials there are just more particular about it.

Prohibited Materials—Contraband

All of the following items are strictly illegal in Eastern Europe, and you should not attempt to bring any of them into any Eastern European country:

Narcotics and other controlled substances: Over-the-counter and prescription medications are permitted, but you should have your prescriptions with you. Any narcotics or other controlled substances without prescriptions will likely subject you to arrest.

Weapons: Weapons other than hunting weapons are prohibited. Hunting weapons of any sort will need special permits (requiring long application times) in order for you to bring them into the country.

Pornography: Any publication showing any skin at all is grounds for confiscation, and even fashion magazines may be considered pornographic. It seemed to us that some Customs officials are pleased to catch someone with a fashion magazine—they can easily sell the magazines, and there are no stiff penalties if they are caught. So be certain that more than one guard oversees the confiscation of your *Vogue;* that way you can make certain it's an official confiscation.

Written materials that are in any way damaging to the State: This is one of the hardest conditions for Westerners to endure, and one of the broadest. Consequences are usually no worse than confiscation, although denial of entry is the ultimate penalty. Anything can be categorized as antistatist, and the definition changes with each new day and every different Customs official. If you are bringing a lot of printed material with you, you may have a long wait—it is possible that the border guard will scrutinize every single page. (We sometimes waited endlessly at borders as the Customs officials leafed through every page of our notes and the tourist brochures of the Eastern European country we had just left.)

Registration/Declaration

It's a good idea to declare and register all jewelry or other items of an expensive, antique, or otherwise valuable nature. All electronic equipment and electrical appliances should be registered. Remember that things like portable short-wave radios, scientific calculators, automobile radar detectors, camera equipment, portable cassette players, and similar items are of interest to Customs officials. Audio cassettes are sometimes a problem to get into the country; video cassettes are even more difficult to import. (We heard of a 15-year-old who wanted to bring his portable computer along on his parents' vacation to give him something to do. While we don't know specifically what a Customs official would do if you suddenly whipped out a personal computer, it's safe to say that there would be considerable complications.)

In short, any obviously provocative literature, computer equipment, or similar objects should be left home unless they are absolutely essential to the nature of your trip. You might stroll by the first Customs official but most likely you'll be caught by the next one.

Dealing with the Customs Official

Customs officials and border guards are fairly low-level bureaucrats who, for a (hopefully) very short period of time, have an amazing amount of control over your travel plans. However, we have noticed that some travelers do not have as much trouble as others. Why? The answer is simple—they look trustworthy.

Appearance is everything. This is not a judgment of any particular way of behaving or dressing; it's simply advice on how to minimize hassles at the border. Ragged clothes and skimpy shorts or bathing suits generally do not impress Customs officials; the opposite extreme—formal wear, outrageous New Wave or punk clothing, or loads of jewelry—doesn't help much either. We generally wore clean, comfortable clothing that was conservatively cut and in no way flashy or attention-grabbing. We got the best results by never pretending to be friendly or in any way ingratiating, but by being relaxed and yet reserved. Don't be haughty or look down your nose at a border guard; treat them civilly and respond courteously to their requests and your time at the border crossing will likely be shorter.

You'll find Customs easier at the airport, a walk-through checkpoint, or any other situation in which you approach the Customs officials. The more intrusive situations are train or car searches, where the Customs officials come to you.

3. What to Take Along

LUGGAGE: You'll find few porters in Eastern Europe, and occasionally few taxis as well. Since you may end up carrying your luggage all the way to your hotel, you should travel lightly.

Wheeling luggage is a great help in alleviating these inconveniences. The simplest and cheapest device is a metal-frame luggage wheeler: you pile on the baggage and then push it along easily. The drawback to wheelers is that once your luggage has been strapped on, it's inconvenient to undo the bags to carry them up or down stairs.

An amazing piece of luggage called the **SkyValet** overcomes these problems. The SkyValet is a hang-up bag with two wheels on the bottom, a handle on top, and two pop-out legs on the bottom that can hold a second bag. When you get to stairs, you pick up the second bag, pop the legs in, and continue on. At the foot of the stairs, the legs pop back out in two seconds, you load on the other bag, and you're wheeling effortlessly along again. SkyValet is expensive, but it's a sound investment for the frequent traveler. Contact the Executive Gallery for a catalog at 970 Dearborn Dr., Columbus, OH 43085 (tel. toll free 800/848-2618, 800/282-2630 in Ohio).

If you prefer shoulder bags or backpacks, consider the bags offered by **Eagle Creek Travel Gear.** Write or phone for their catalog: 143 S. Cedros Ave. (P.O. Box 651), Solona Beach, CA 92075 (tel. 619/755-9399, or toll free 800/874-9925 outside California).

WHAT TO PACK: Now that you have your luggage, what should you pack? In general, pack lightly, with only the most basic clothes. People dress casually in Eastern Europe, so you don't need to bring along your sharpest clothing.

At the risk of going against our own advice by weighing down your luggage, we suggest you consider bringing along the following items, which we found particularly useful in Eastern Europe:

Batteries: If your camera, flash, or other appliances run on batteries, bring an ample supply along. Certain types of batteries don't exist in Eastern Europe, and those that do often don't last very long.

Calculator: Many travelers find it useful to figure out foreign-exchange rates on a calculator. We suggest a credit-card calculator, which fits snugly into your wallet or purse.

Camera: You'll probably want to take a great many photos of Eastern Europe's beautiful sights, so make sure to bring along your camera, plus lots of fresh film and extra batteries for the camera and flash attachment. The AAA and many other battery sizes that are standard in the U.S. are impossible to find in Eastern Europe, and the film there is of poor quality. If you don't bring these along, you risk missing a lot of great shots.

Cash: We've found it good to have a supply of small-denomination U.S. bills ($1s and $5s) to use in hard-currency stores, to buy international train tickets, for tips, etc. The hard-currency stores never seem to have the right change, and thus you may lose out without some "petty cash" on hand.

Electric Current Adapter: If you bring any appliances, remember that the electricity in Eastern Europe is 220 volts A.C., not the standard 110 volts of North America. A 110-volt appliance will soon burn out when attached to an unconverted 220-volt plug. Contact the Franzus Company, 352 Park Ave. South, New York, NY 10010 (tel. 212/889-5850), and ask for their short pamphlet, "Foreign Electricity Is No Deep Dark Secret."

Electric Razor: Although this is a splurge item for men, we single it out because on occasion in Eastern Europe you'll be without hot water or a mirror, or you may be on a night train which does not permit shaving, or find yourself in a number of other circumstances in which an electric razor will come in handy. A rechargeable shaver overcomes all of these hardships.

Filmshield: If you plan to travel through any Eastern European airports, we highly recommend Filmshield, a small, lead-lined, malleable pouch that prevents powerful X-ray machines from ruining your camera film. Without such a device the film may look foggy when developed.

Gifts: Though many Western products are now available in Eastern Europe, if you want to bring gifts from the West to friends in the East, we suggest electronics, such as a pocket calculator, an LCD watch, or a stereo Walkman. Postcards and mementoes from the West are always popular (a few summers ago we brought a bag of "I Love New York" buttons to the Soviet Union—small gifts, but they amused their recipients). For women, consider bringing makeup or perfumes. Don't bring too many of any one item lest you create suspicion at the border.

Language Tools: One of Eastern Europe's big challenges is communicating with the local people, since their languages are so different from our own. To help overcome difficulties, you might invest in phrasebooks before you go—you won't find them once you're in Eastern Europe.

If you are interested in learning an Eastern European language in more detail, we recommend the cassette courses produced by Audio Forum. They offer courses in Bulgarian, German, Hungarian, Polish, and Serbo-Croatian. In each course you listen to native speakers on a cassette and follow along in a textbook. You can contact Audio Forum for their catalog at 96 Broad St., Guilford, CT 06437 (tel. toll free 800/243-1234).

Langenscheidt Publishers offers a useful "German Quick and Easy" course on two cassettes, available through your local bookstore or from Langenscheidt at 46–35 54th Rd., Maspeth, NY 11378 (tel. 718/784-0055).

Liquid Soap: If you're planning to stay in private accommodations and budget hotels, liquid soap is another useful item to have. We suggest soap in a plastic container because it's less messy than a bar of soap.

Medical Products: Bring *all* toiletry supplies you are going to need, and any specific prescriptions—you won't find them in Eastern Europe. Those travelers who wear contact lenses should be sure to bring enough cleaning solution, as well as a spare pair of glasses.

Money Belt: A money belt is especially helpful when you have many documents to carry around (as you always do in Eastern Europe). The best one we found is made by Eagle Creek Travel Gear, 143 Cedros Ave. (P.O. Box 651), Solona Beach, CA 92075 (tel. 619/755-9399, or toll free 800/874-9925 outside California).

Short-wave Radio: News junkies who don't want to lose touch with what's going on back home will find a short-wave radio invaluable. Other than in Hungary and Yugoslavia, you're unlikely to find any Western newspapers or magazines besides the *Daily Worker.* Tuning to the BBC or the Voice of America is the only way to keep up on the news. A useful book in finding the right frequencies at different times of day is the *World Radio TV Handbook,* available from Watson-Guptill Publications, 1515 Broadway, New York, NY 10036.

Toilet Paper: A roll or two can come in handy, especially if you plan on staying in private accommodations—the newspaper in the bathroom isn't always for reading. Though there is toilet paper in East Germany, travelers might consider bringing their favorite Western brands to avoid the "sandpapery" local brands.

Travel Alarm: Many hotels don't have a wake-up service, and so for the traveler following a schedule, a small, reliable alarm clock is a necessity.

Traveler's Checks: These are *essential*. Since it's difficult to change Eastern European currencies back into dollars, bring your traveler's checks in small to medium denominations ($10, $20, or $50) to change a little bit at a time, so as not to be left with a lot of local currency. To be on the safe side, be sure to copy down the check numbers in two places, just in case something happens to the checks.

Woolite Powder: Coin-operated laundromats are nonexistent in Eastern Europe, so you'll need to hand-wash smaller items of clothing. We recommend Woolite powder in small packets (the liquid kind inevitably seems to spill all over our luggage).

Writing Materials: A pocket-size loose-leaf notebook is extremely useful in any country where you do not speak the language. You can write down the names of unpronounceable streets or sights, show the notebook to local people, and then let them indicate directions in your notebook. You can write down the departure time, destination, and class of a train that you want and show it to the clerk at the railroad ticket window; the clerk can then write down the ticket price and/or other, better trains to take, and so forth. The list of uses for a notebook in Eastern Europe can be endless.

4. Food and Lodging

You're probably wondering what kind of facilities you'll get for your money in Eastern Europe. Here's a brief description of the hotel and restaurant choices in the region.

HOTELS: Throughout this guide, we recommend second category or Class "B" establishments as the best budget value for your money. Not only do these hotels provide a good buy, in many cases they prove more appealing than Class "A" and deluxe hotels, the two categories ranking above the "B" category. The fact is that, with surprisingly few exceptions, the modern expensive hotels in Eastern Europe are unappealing government-run enterprises that mop up your dollars without offering substantially better facilities or services. In many cases we found that Class "B" hotels had more helpful staff and the same size rooms as top-category facilities.

A far better buy for your money are smaller, less expensive hotels. With the added benefit of many Eastern European guests, these hotels also offer a far more interesting ambience.

The one facility you do often lose in second-category establishments are private bathrooms. Eastern Europe does not have the extensive plumbing that most Americans are accustomed to. The budget hotels of Europe, both East and West, usually feature public bathrooms and showers on each floor rather than private facilities. In cases where the public bathrooms of a hotel proved less than pristine, we've indicated this quality in our review, listing the hotel only for more carefree budget travelers. Another money-saving suggestion is to take a room with a poor view; some hotels, especially at the seaside, offer discounts for rooms in the back of the building.

In each chapter we also suggest hotels above the $25-a-day price range. Usually, these are 19th-century or early 20th-century hotels which we think offer an especially good value for your money.

In general, we've found that you save money by paying directly in the country for your hotel room. The national tourist offices of the Eastern European countries in the U.S. will be more than happy to book you into their modern expensive hotels, but on the whole these tourist offices do not deal with the smaller budget establishments listed in this guide. To reserve at these (and there are definitely a few towns that we recommend reserving in; see each country chapter for suggestions), write directly to them with specific dates of arrival and departure well ahead of time and hope for the best.

Note on Registration: Most Eastern European countries require that all foreigners register their whereabouts on a day-to-day basis. In practice, your hotel will usually register you; if you stay in a private room arranged by a travel agency, the agency will register you. If, however, you stay with friends, you should register with the local tourist police (addresses are listed in this guide). If you're in a city whose registration address is not listed, ask at the local tourist office.

RESTAURANTS: Throughout this book, we list the best restaurants in any

price category, which the budget traveler fortunately can almost always afford. We fondly remember many delicious Eastern European meals served by waiters in black tie as a violin or piano played in the background, all for just a few dollars! Some of these restaurants do charge more than the budget traveler usually spends. Our advice? Go to these restaurants, but order selectively. Wine and alcohol are always expensive, and hors d'oeuvres and side dishes bring up the tab rapidly. So for restaurants that have excellent food at slightly more than budget prices, order an entree (usually a filling meal in and of itself). We feel that one excellent meal of an entree and soup, for example, is a much better buy than a tableful of mediocre food.

Hotels house many of Eastern Europe's best restaurants. Strange though that may sound to Western ears, it's true because more food and better resources are allocated to the large hotels. By contrast, smaller restaurants often offer just a few dishes (don't be fooled by the length of the menu; many items are not available). Although the hotels are well stocked with food, the decor usually features architecture that might have looked modern in the 1950s. In each section we try to list both quaint local places and the hotel restaurants that offer some of the region's best food.

If you are sitting in a restaurant at a table that has a few extra seats, don't be surprised if someone asks to join you. Usually they won't engage you in conversation, unless you start talking. They just want a seat where they can dine.

Another novelty of Eastern European restaurants is live music. Most restaurants offer a live band each evening. In some countries such as Hungary, the local folk and gypsy music add to the charm and enjoyment of the evening.

5. The Facts of Life in Eastern Europe

CURRENCY AND THE BLACK MARKET: In the countries of Eastern Europe

many rules apply to the national currencies. To begin with, you may neither bring in nor take out the currency of the Eastern European country you are visiting. Then, once in the country, you may only change money at the bank, at your hotel, or in tourist offices. In several countries (Poland, Czechoslovakia, and Romania) you must change a set amount of currency every day, usually a reasonable $10 to $15 daily.

Since currency-exchange rates are set by the government, all travel agencies and hotels offer the same rate as a bank (in Yugoslavia, some travel agencies may add a nominal service fee). Since banks are often crowded, we suggest that you avoid them altogether and break all of the Western European "rules" of savvy currency exchange by using travel agencies and hotels.

In countries such as Poland, East Germany, Czechoslovakia, and Bulgaria, you will probably be approached several times by locals who want to change currency for your dollars—at a much better ratio than the official rate. You might be approached by a student on the street, a taxidriver in a cab, or a waiter in a restaurant. Many Western visitors do change money and get between two and six times the official rate, depending on the country. But because some of those who approach you may be government agents or informers, exercise extreme caution (locals say that the only way to trade safely is among friends). Best of all, for tranquility of mind and body, you should avoid these transactions. Every country in Eastern Europe maintains strict penalties for black-market dealings, ranging from expulsion to imprisonment.

We recommend that when you do exchange money in official bureaus you only exchange the minimum amount at a time, as it's quite difficult to get dollars back for Eastern European currencies, despite government claims to the contrary. We have "donated" our remaining funds on several occasions to supposedly charitable causes at the international frontier.

And perhaps most important of all: *never* throw away any currency-exchange or sales receipts before you leave the country. You'll need these receipts to show that you have complied with the daily minimum exchange, to try to get back dollars for your leftover Eastern European currency, and to pass Customs.

HARD-CURRENCY STORES: Each of the six Warsaw Pact nations covered in this guide operates a chain of stores that will accept only Western (or "hard") currencies. In Poland the stores are called **Pewex;** in Czechoslovakia, **Tuzex;** in Hungary, **Intourist shops;** in Romania, **Comturist;** in Bulgaria, **Corecom;** in East Germany, **Intershop.** In these stores you can buy such Western products as chocolate, cigarettes, alcohol, and other items to remind you of home. Although these stores are an unusual concept for Westerners (can you imagine a store in the U.S. that accepts only Japanese yen?), they do offer Western-made items for reasonable prices.

MAIL: Most Eastern European postal systems are not as efficient as their Western counterparts. Therefore we suggest that you have any important mail sent to the Western gateway city you plan to arrive at or leave from. If you'll be passing through Berlin or Vienna, have your mail sent to you c/o **American Express** there. In Berlin, the address is American Express, Kurfürstendamm 11, Berlin W. 15, West Germany (tel. 882-75-75); in Vienna, it's American Express Europe Limited, P.O. Box 288, Kärntnerstrasse 21/23, 1010 Vienna 1, Austria (tel. 52-05-44). American Express cardholders receive their mail for free; others pay a nominal fee.

If you must receive mail within Eastern Europe, most **U.S. embassies and consulates** will hold mail for a short time. Their addresses and telephone numbers are:

Bulgaria: American Embassy, 1 Alexander Stambolijski Blvd., Sofia (tel. 88-48-01 to 88-48-05).

Czechoslovakia: American Embassy, Tržiště 15, Prague 1, Malá Strana (tel. 536-641).

German Democratic Republic: American Embassy, Kirchstrasse 4–5, Neustaedtische, 108 Berlin (tel. 220-2741).

Hungary: American Embassy, V. Szagadság tér 12, Budapest (tel. 124-224, 329-374, or 329-375).

Poland: American Embassy, aleje Ujazdowskie 29/31, Warsaw (tel. 283-041 to 283-049); American Consulate, Chopina 4, Poznań (tel. 595-86 or 595-87); American Consulate, Stolarska 9, Kraków (tel. 29764 or 21400).

Romania: American Embassy, Strada Tudor Arghezi No. 9, Bucharest (tel. 12-40-40, 12-40-48, or 12-40-49).

Yugoslavia: American Embassy, Kneza Milosa 50, Belgrade (tel. 645-655); American Consulate General, Brace Kavurica 2, Zagreb (tel. 444-800).

MEASUREMENTS: Eastern Europeans use the metric system, and usually denote time on a 24-hour clock, beginning at midnight (for example, 12 hours is noon, 16 hours is 4 p.m., and 22:45 is 10:45 p.m.). Here are some basic metric equivalents:

1 kilometer (km)	= 0.62 mile
1 meter	= 3.28 feet (about a yard)
1 kilogram	= 2.2 pounds
1 liter	= 0.26 gallons (about a quart)

Temperature: To convert degrees Centigrade to degrees Fahrenheit, multiply the Centigrade temperature by 1.8 (or multiply by 9, divide by 5) and add 32. To convert degrees Fahrenheit to degrees Centigrade, subtract 32 from the Fahrenheit temperature and divide by 1.8 (or multiply by 5 and divide by 9).

PHOTOGRAPHY: Although most Eastern European governments proudly pronounce that you can photograph anything you want to, except military sights, in practice you should refrain from photographing the following: all military installations and personnel; police; all transportation facilities such as harbors, bridges, train stations, and airports; and borders and border stations. "No Photography" signs—a camera in a red circle with a red slash across it, à la *Ghostbusters*—are often posted in front of particularly sensitive areas.

PRICE OVERCHARGES: If you have a disagreement with a waiter, a hotel clerk, a cab driver, or anyone else over a bill, stand for your rights then and there. Beware that in Eastern Europe, as in many other countries across the globe, some people see Americans as prime targets to earn extra money. In a restaurant, ask to have every item on the bill matched up with the menu if you think something is wrong. In a hotel, ask to see the price chart that all hotels have. If the disagreement continues, you can ask to see the manager, but often they are administrative bureaucrats unsympathetic to your plight. Hold your ground and try to reach a compromise.

In the end though, remember that the adage "the customer is always right" is a strange, radical thought, foreign to the Eastern European mentality. Unfortunately, in the end there is little that you can do to fight petty overcharges. If you have been overcharged a gross sum of money, you can turn to the local legal system, but results won't be soon in coming.

We don't mean to worry you about all transactions. Very few at most will result in the unpleasant situations described above. We jot down these thoughts because it's best to be prepared for whatever might happen.

Chapter II

GETTING THERE

1. Transportation Options
2. Gateway Cities

GETTING TO EASTERN EUROPE on a budget requires some advance preparation and planning. Many of our specific suggestions on getting there are given in each country's introductory chapter, but below is a general overview of the transportation choices you'll have.

In this chapter we're also including basic information about three "gateway cities"—Berlin, Vienna, and Istanbul. Travelers from North America may well want to consider flying first to one of these gateways and then continuing on to Eastern Europe. It can be a lot cheaper than flying to Eastern Europe directly, and since these cities are also world capitals, a few days in any one of them would make your trip to Eastern Europe even more rewarding.

1. Transportation Options

The one good piece of advice that applies to all transportation is this: buy your tickets ahead of time whenever possible to take advantage of cheaper advance purchase fares, to avoid last-minute lines, and to ensure your place on board. This is especially true for travel within Eastern Europe.

BY AIR: For convenient connections, competitive fares, and comfort in the air, the North American traveler can't make a better choice than Lufthansa German Airlines. Lufthansa serves 16 gateway cities in the U.S. and Canada: Anchorage, Atlanta, Boston, Calgary, Chicago, Dallas/Ft. Worth, Houston, Los Angeles, Miami, Montreal, New York, Philadelphia, San Francisco, San Juan, Toronto, Vancouver, and (starting April 1, 1987) Washington D.C. From each gateway, Lufthansa's wide-body jets fly nonstop or direct to Frankfurt— the most efficient connecting point in Europe, according to seasoned travelers. And from Frankfurt, Lufthansa provides frequent connecting flights to every capital in Eastern Europe: Belgrade, Bucharest, Budapest, Prague, Sofia and Warsaw. Lufthansa also flies from Frankfurt to Leipzig, East Germany, and Zagreb, Yugoslavia.

You can fly Lufthansa to Eastern Europe via Munich as well. Especially if your journey starts in New York, Boston, Chicago, or Los Angeles, you may find it most advantageous to do so. Daily Lufthansa flights speed from New York to Munich nonstop; from Boston, Chicago, and Los Angeles direct. From Munich, Lufthansa's connecting flights go on to Belgrade, Bucharest, Budapest, Sofia, and Zagreb. They're all nonstop flights, and most fly on a daily basis.

Lufthansa deserves exceptionally high marks for dependability, punctuality, and in-flight comfort—important considerations when you are flying to Eastern Europe. The national flag carriers of some Eastern European countries also offer flights from North America, and some U.S. airlines fly to certain cities in

Eastern Europe too. Space does not permit listing all the possibilities, but your travel agent can easily fill you in.

If you have never traveled to Eastern Europe before, we suggest you ask your travel agent to show you *The Lufthansa Holiday Collection.* This handsomely illustrated brochure, published by Lufthansa, may give you some helpful ideas when you plan your itinerary. It includes several tour programs that visit Eastern Europe, some at land prices that do not vastly exceed the $25-A-Day standard of this book. For the less experienced traveler, such programs can provide an easy, carefree introduction to Eastern Europe's special attractions.

For readers who decide to fly first to a gateway city in Western Europe, the Lufthansa airfares from the U.S. to Germany, Austria, and Turkey are given in this chapter. For the airfares from the U.S. to any Eastern European country, see the chapter devoted to that country. We list a complete range of fares, from the most expensive to the cheapest, so you can make your own comparisons.

Keep in mind that all fares cited here were valid as of Fall 1986, so there are likely to be changes by the time you read them. For updated information, exact details of low, shoulder, and high seasons, and a full explanation of ticket restrictions, consult your travel agent or Lufthansa directly.

Fares to Germany

The following chart shows round-trip fares to Germany in U.S. dollars. The fares to Frankfurt apply also to Bonn, Cologne, Düsseldorf, Hamburg, and Stuttgart; those to Berlin/Munich apply also to Bremen, Hannover, Münster, Nürnberg, Saarbrucken, Bayreuth, and Hof. All fares are subject to change without notice.

First Class and Business Class Fares: These fares are applicable all year. Unlimited stopovers are allowed.

Tourist Class Fare: More economical than First Class or Business Class, this fare allows no stopovers.

Holiday Fare: This special fare permits no stopovers, has advance purchase and minimum/maximum stay requirements, and also carries a penalty for cancellation that must be complied with. Tickets must be purchased 21 days in advance and are valid for 7 days to 3 months.

All fares are subject to a $3 departure tax plus a $5 Custom User Fee.

BY TRAIN: Most of Europe's major cities connect up by train to Eastern Europe's capitals. Over the years we've visited Eastern Europe by train from Berlin, Vienna, Rome, and several other cities. From Berlin a train takes about nine hours to Warsaw, or about seven hours to Prague. From Vienna a train takes six to seven hours to Prague or four hours to Budapest.

Many of these routes feature day as well as night service. Although we have a great fondness for overnight trains where you sleep away your traveling hours in a couchette, we must point out that when you cross international frontiers, passport and Customs officials will wake you several times.

A final tip: Remember that you will need transit visas if you are just passing through a country. Czech, Polish, and Bulgarian transit visas will not be issued at the border and *must* be obtained beforehand.

BY BUS: Although bus is a common means of transportation in many Eastern European countries, it is not a practical means of getting there. Exceptions are the Vienna–Bratislava (in Czechoslovakia) bus route, and bus connections between Turkey and Romania and Bulgaria.

Round-trip Fares to Germany

| From | To: | Applicable All Year | | Tourist Class | | | | 7 Day-3 Month-Stay Holiday Fare | | | | | |
| | | | | Sept. 15–May 14 | | May 15–Sept. 14 | | All Week | | May 1 to 31 Sept. 15 to Oct. 31 | | June 1 to Sept. 14 | |
		First Class	Business Class	Mid Week	Week End	Mid Week	Week End	Nov. 1 to Dec. 16 Dec. 25 to Feb. 11 Feb. 18 to April 30	Dec. 17 to Dec. 24 Feb. 12 to Feb. 17	Mid Week	Week End	Mid Week	Week End
New York	*F	$3212	$1724	$941	$991	$1190	$1240	$399	$499	$652	$702	$756	$806
	B/M	3250	1776	972	1022	1223	1273	429	529	692	742	811	861
Anchorage	F	4122	2338	1379	1429	1628	1678	836	936	1062	1112	1194	1244
	B/M	4162	2390	1410	1460	1661	1711	866	966	1102	1152	1246	1296
Atlanta	F	3212	1918	1073	1123	1328	1378	485	585	694	694	774	774
	B/M	3250	1970	1104	1154	1360	1410	515	615	734	734	829	829
Boston	F	3194	1714	931	981	1151	1201	394	494	647	697	734	784
	B/M	3232	1766	962	1012	1182	1232	424	524	687	737	786	836
Chicago	F	3606	2088	1034	1084	1269	1319	465	565	719	769	823	873
	B/M	3642	2140	1065	1115	1300	1350	495	595	759	809	876	926
Dallas/Houston	F	3606	2152	1063	1113	1230	1280	492	592	613	613	713	713
	B/M	3642	2204	1094	1144	1263	1313	522	622	653	653	768	768
Los Angeles/San Francisco	F	4162	2338	1124	1174	1373	1423	582	682	835	885	939	989
	B/M	4200	2390	1155	1205	1406	1456	612	712	873	923	991	1041
Miami	F	3480	2132	1049	1099	1286	1336	485	585	730	780	836	886
	B/M	3518	2184	1079	1129	1317	1367	515	615	769	819	888	938
Philadelphia	F	3374	1838	965	1015	1197	1247	415	515	668	718	771	821
	B/M	3412	1890	996	1046	1228	1278	445	545	708	758	823	873

*F=Frankfurt and common rated points Bonn, Cologne, Düsseldorf, Hamburg, and Stuttgart
B=Berlin M=Munich and common rated points Bayreuth, Nürnberg, Bremen, Hanover, Hof, Münster, Paderborn, and Saarbrucken

BY BOAT: You can go to Poland or East Germany by ferry from Scandinavia, or to Yugoslavia from Italy. You can also take a hydrofoil from Vienna to Bratislava or Budapest (for a pricey $60). See the description in these countries for full details. No regularly scheduled boats service the Black Sea coast of Romania and Bulgaria.

For specific details on ferry service see the chapter on the appropriate cities.

BY CAR: Some basic information on car rentals may also be of use. In Eastern Europe you're not going to find those $99-a-week deals that are offered in the U.S. Except in Hungary and Yugoslavia, car-rental rates are fixed by the government and are uniformly high regardless from whom you rent. In Poland, Hungary, East Germany, and Yugoslavia, a basic car with unlimited mileage begins at about $200 a week. Prices begin at $245 in Bulgaria, $270 in Czechoslovakia, and $295 in Romania. When calculating expenses, remember to add insurance ($20 to $35 a week) and tax. Hungary, Czechoslovakia, and Yugoslavia tax 14% or 15%; the other countries featured in this guide do not tax car rentals.

Drive with caution in Eastern Europe. In many cases the major "highway" will be a two-lane road crowded with horsecarts, tractors, and other slow-moving vehicles. Patience is the watchword. You must wear seatbelts, and drinking while driving is forbidden. Try to keep the tank topped off—gas stations are few and far between in much of Eastern Europe.

If you bring your own car, buy Green Card insurance, which provides full insurance coverage in foreign countries (inquire at your insurance agency). If you rent a car, you can get insurance at the rental agency.

If you decide to rent a car while in Eastern Europe, you may find it convenient to reserve via an American company. **Avis** (tel. toll free 800/331-2112); **Hertz** (tel. toll free 800/654-3131); **Dollar,** called **Interrent** abroad (tel. toll free 800/421-6868); and **National,** called **Europcar** abroad (tel. toll free 800/CAR-RENT)—all operate in at least several of the countries covered in this guide.

Usually drivers must have had their license for at least a year to rent a car.

2. Gateway Cities

Many experienced visitors to Eastern Europe prefer to fly to a city in Western Europe first, then continue to Eastern Europe, usually by surface transportation. Because of the high volume of tourist traffic to Western Europe, airfares to Western European cities are often less expensive than they are for direct services to Eastern Europe.

The cities most frequently chosen as gateways to Eastern Europe are Berlin, Vienna, and Istanbul. Not only are they good transportation hubs, but they are fascinating travel destinations in themselves.

FARES TO VIENNA AND ISTANBUL: The following chart shows Lufthansa's round-trip fares to Vienna and Istanbul in U.S. dollars. All these fares are subject to change without notice.

First Class and Business Class Fares: These fares, applicable all year, allow unlimited stopovers.

Excursion Fare: More economical than First Class or Business Class fares, Excursion fares allow no stopovers.

APEX Fare: This special fare permits no stopovers, has advance purchase and minimum/maximum stay requirements, and also carries a penalty for cancellation that must be complied with. Tickets must be purchased 21 days in advance and are valid for 7 days to 3 months (Austria) and 7 days to 6 months (Turkey).

All fares subject to a $3 departure tax plus a $5 Custom User fee.

Round-trip Fares to Vienna and Istanbul

From	To:	First Class All Year	Business Class All Year	7 Day-1 Yr. Exc. (V) / 10 Day-317 Exc. (I) Sept. 15–May 14	May 15–Sept. 14	7 Day-3Month APEX (V) / 7 Day-6 Month APEX (I) Nov. 1–Dec. 7 Dec. 25–Apr. 30 Midweek	Weekend	May 1–31 Sept. 15–Oct. 31 Dec. 8–24 Midweek	Weekend	June 1–Sept. 14 Midweek	Weekend
New York	V	$3446	$1864	$1039	$1289	$659	$719	$719	$779	$844	$904
	I	4650	2710	1519	1725	889	939	939	989	999	1049
Anchorage	V	4572	2786	1477	1727	1097	1157	1157	1217	1282	1342
	I	5776	3632	1957	2163	1327	1377	1377	1427	1437	1487
Atlanta	V	4134	2252	1167	1417	787	847	847	907	972	1032
	I	5338	3098	1647	1853	1017	1067	1067	1117	1127	1177
Boston	V	3446	1864	1039	1289	659	719	719	779	844	904
	I	4650	2710	1519	1725	889	939	939	989	999	1049
Chicago	V	4096	2308	1149	1399	769	829	829	889	954	1014
	I	5300	3154	1629	1835	999	1049	1049	1099	1109	1159
Dallas/ Houston	V	4178	2194	1167	1417	787	847	847	907	972	1032
	I	5382	3040	1647	1853	1017	1067	1067	1117	1127	1177
Los Angeles/ San Francisco	V	4808	2774	1222	1472	889	949	949	1009	1027	1087
	I	6012	3620	1702	1908	1072	1122	1122	1172	1182	1232
Miami	V	3888	2186	1185	1435	805	865	865	925	990	1050
	I	5092	3032	1665	1871	1035	1085	1085	1135	1145	1195
Philadelphia	V	3666	2028	1102	– 1352	722	782	782	842	907	967
	I	4870	2874	1582	1788	952	1002	1002	1052	1062	1112

V = Vienna   I = Istanbul

To help you get oriented, we include some basic orientation information for each of these three cities.

BERLIN: Former capital of Germany and a divided city in a divided nation, Berlin has become the symbol of the U.S.-Soviet conflict. A vast tract of land, more than 200 square miles, remains under Western control and includes lakes, farms, and forests as well as glittering modern buildings and an international airport. The Berliners still exhibit the remarkable strength and staying power that have kept them free from Soviet control; today Berlin is one of West Germany's most innovative and exciting cities. The many young people here, its culture and history, and the fantastic nightlife make West Berlin one of the hottest European vacation attractions.

We do not have the space to include in-depth coverage of Berlin. We just include basic information to help orient you when you arrive here as part of your continued itinerary to Eastern Europe.

Getting to West Berlin

You can get to West Berlin by plane, by bus or car, or by train relatively easily from the Federal Republic of Germany (West Germany). Traveling to the city from Eastern Europe is much more difficult. Getting to West Berlin from points in Eastern Europe is covered in the chapters on East Germany.

By Air: U.S., British, and French airlines fly to West Berlin's Tegel International Airport from their respective countries. While no German airline is permitted to fly into West Berlin, Lufthansa's international flights arriving in Frankfurt and Munich connect with Pan Am's internal German services to West Berlin.

Interflug, the East German national airline, flies into Schönefeld International Airport in East Berlin, as do most of the other Eastern European airlines.

By Car: Since the 1972 inter-German treaty and the 1974 official U.S. recognition of East Germany, the border check has relaxed considerably. There are three major access roads from the Federal Republic of Germany to West Berlin. The shortest is via Helmstedt, a town east of Hannover, which takes around two hours on the autobahn; the two others are Bad Herzfeld in the south and Rudolphstein in the north of Berlin.

The border costs are 10 DM ($3.50) for a road visa, 6 DM ($2.10) for mandatory insurance, and an additional 5 DM ($1.75) per person for a transit visa. When in the German Democratic Republic *do not* speed, *do not* drive with even a trace of alcohol in your blood, but *do* drive carefully on the poorly maintained international access routes. The access routes are crawling with East German traffic police, all with a real "go ahead, make my day" attitude. Don't leave the autobahn unless you have the proper visa—not just a transit visa—the police *will* spot you and you will be subject to arrest. All these police patrols may seem excessive, but they come in very handy if you ever have a breakdown. If you do have car trouble, flag down a police car or use one of the many emergency call boxes along the road. Do *not* leave the highway under any circumstances to look for a phone or garage.

By Train: Getting to West Berlin by train is almost as easy as by plane, and much less expensive. There are extremely informal border checks on the train and a 5-DM ($1.75) visa charge, but remember that once you cross the border, till you reach West Berlin you are in the German Democratic Republic. The train ride from Frankfurt is less than eight hours long. A second-class ticket

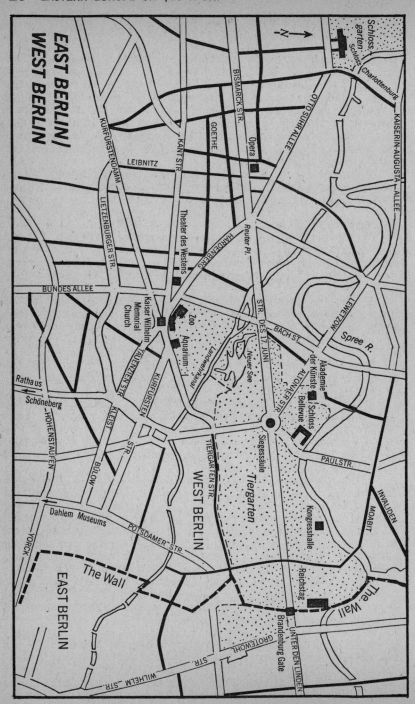

MILEAGE BETWEEN EUROPEAN AND EASTERN EUROPEAN CITIES

Distance in Miles

	Amsterdam	Athens	Belgrade	Berlin	Bucharest	Budapest	Frankfurt	Geneva	Istanbul	London	Paris	Prague	Rome	Sofia	Stockholm	Vienna	Warsaw
Amsterdam	—	1,748	116	428	1,507	893	285	645	1,724	217	316	564	1,097	1,358	837	701	756
Athens	1,748	—	732	1,265	763	1,016	1,624	1,674	744	1,996	1,897	1,370	880	539	2,368	1,178	1,432
Belgrade	116	732	—	651	453	248	856	905	589	1,283	1,128	601	818	191	1,668	422	670
Berlin	428	1,265	651	—	974	397	347	707	1,401	546	701	205	949	893	583	409	360
Bucharest	1,507	763	453	974	—	527	1,116	1,215	434	1,600	1,488	911	1,333	254	1,507	713	1,116
Budapest	893	1,016	248	397	527	—	614	806	831	1,035	967	360	837	484	980	167	422
Frankfurt	265	1,624	856	347	1,116	614	—	366	1,438	396	360	310	812	1,078	868	453	688
Geneva	645	1,674	905	707	1,215	806	366	—	1,488	601	341	645	589	1,066	1,234	637	961
Istanbul	1,724	744	589	1,401	434	831	1,438	1,488	—	1,885	1,705	1,172	1,401	366	2,257	973	1,203
London	217	1,996	1,283	546	1,600	1,035	396	601	1,885	—	254	812	1,060	1,525	918	856	890
Paris	316	1,897	1,128	701	1,488	967	360	341	1,705	254	—	620	868	1,345	1,135	818	1,066
Prague	564	1,370	601	205	911	360	310	645	1,172	812	620	—	800	843	1,674	186	911
Rome	1,097	880	818	949	1,333	837	812	589	1,401	1,060	868	800	—	1,035	1,674	707	1,135
Sofia	1,358	539	191	893	254	484	1,078	1,066	366	1,525	1,345	843	1,035	—	1,910	645	911
Stockholm	837	2,368	1,668	583	1,507	980	868	1,234	2,257	918	1,135	1,674	1,674	1,910	—	1,246	260
Vienna	701	1,178	422	409	713	167	453	637	973	856	818	186	707	645	1,246	—	428
Warsaw	756	1,432	670	360	1,116	422	688	961	1,203	890	1,066	911	1,135	911	260	428	—

from Frankfurt costs around 180 DM ($63). The main station in West Berlin is near the zoo (Zoologischer Garten) and is sometimes referred to as the Bahnhof Zoo.

Getting Around West Berlin

Berlin is oddly shapèd: the city is divided right through its old center by the Wall. The main street, **Kurfürstendamm** (called Ku'damm by Berliners), runs roughly east and west.

The subway, or **U-bahn,** and the elevated train, or **S-bahn,** in West Berlin radiate out from the old city center and are connected by circular lines, some of which run through East Berlin. There are also numerous **buses,** and a few even run at night. Public transportation hours of service are from 4:30 a.m. to 1 a.m. Fares cost less than 2 DM (70¢), 1 DM (35¢) for students.

Taxis are readily available, though expensive. The meter starts at 3 DM ($1.05) and you can easily spend $5 to $7 on a ride.

Information in West Berlin

The main **Berlin Tourist Information Office** (tel. 782-30-31) is in the Europa-Center, open every day from 7:30 a.m. till 10:30 p.m. There's also an office in the main lobby at Tegel Airport, open from 8 a.m. till 10:30 p.m.

The **American Express** office (tel. 882-75-75) is at Kurfürstendamm 11 and is open from 8:30 a.m. till 5:30 weekdays, on Saturday from 9 a.m. till noon; closed Sunday. Mail can be sent here, though if you don't have an American Express card you'll have to pay 50¢ or so to pick up your mail.

The **American Consulate** is at Clayallee 170 (tel. 832-40-87). Open generally during business hours, the consulate can help you in some emergencies but is not a tourist information office. The Berliners already have a very good one.

Hotels

The following listing of budget accommodations will be useful in case you arrive late or have no time to stop off at the tourist office. Otherwise we recommend that you inquire there first.

The **Astor Hotel,** at Grolmanstrasse 40 (tel. 881-7087 or 881-7088), is located just off Kurfürstendamm. It's an excellent bargain, with singles for 39 DM ($13.50).

Hotel Charlottenburger Hof, Stuttgarter Platz 14 (tel. 324-4819), has singles for 25 DM ($8.75) and doubles at 40 DM ($14). To get to the hotel, take the S-bahn to the Charlottenburg stop.

The **Hotel Pension Cortina,** at 140 Kantstrasse, has doubles for 55 DM ($19).

The **Hotel Gotland,** at Spreewaldplatz 4/6 (tel. 618-2744 or 612-2094), has singles for 25 DM ($8.75) to 35 DM ($12.15) and doubles for 45 DM ($15.65) to 65 DM ($22.50).

There is also a **room-finding service (Zimmervermittlung)** that can direct you to pensions with vacancies (tel. 791-4997). There's another room-finding service in the Europa Center on Kurfürstendamm (tel. 262-6031).

VIENNA: The heart of the old Austro-Hungarian Empire, Vienna controlled the fate of Eastern Europe for many decades. The city's great imperial past has left a legacy of huge royal palaces, elegant opera houses, and great museums. At the same time, however, Vienna boasts a vibrant modern life with everything from bustling shopping malls to exciting discos. As Vienna lies geographically farther east than either Prague or Berlin (with the Czech border an hour away, and Budapest only four hours away), Eastern European travelers often include the city on their itinerary. Although in-depth coverage of Vienna is beyond the scope of this book, we include some very basic information to help you get around when you arrive.

Transportation to and from Vienna

Lufthansa flies from Frankfurt to Vienna several times a day, and from Munich daily. Lufthansa's transatlantic arrivals in both cities also connect with frequent Austrian Airlines flights.

Travelers arriving at the airport can take a bus to the Wien-Mitte (Central Vienna) train station in the center of the city. For information or assistance while in Vienna, contact Lufthansa at: Kaerntner Strasse 42 (tel. 5-88-35).

If you are changing trains in Vienna to Eastern Europe, remember that there are a number of different train stations in the city. Thus be sure to double-check from which station your train connection leaves. Students can purchase discount tickets at **Transalpino,** Opernring 7 (tel. 54-44-95).

Information Office

Vienna's **Tourist Information Office,** in Opernpassage, the pedestrian underpass near the opera (tel. 43-16-08), is one of the best run in all of Europe. Even if you arrive in town with no information at all, don't worry; this office can provide a virtual hill of useful pamphlets. In particular, we recommend that you ask for their pamphlets "Live" (a reprint from the Viennese magazine *Falter,* which gives very useful reviews of Vienna's most inexpensive hotels, restaurants, nightspots, etc.), "Wien Programm" (for cultural listings), "Hotels in Wien" (for a useful map of where hotels are located), "Restaurants Wien" (divided by national specialty—Chinese, German, etc.), "Museums Vienna," and for rugged travelers, "Camping in Vienna" (which includes a listing of youth hotels). And of course, don't forget to pick up a city map. They can also sell a tourist ticket for public transportation which allows you to ride on any line for three days for only 83 schillings (about $4.75); one ticket alone costs 18 schillings (about $1). The tourist office is open from 9 a.m. to 7 p.m.

We strongly recommend that travelers to Eastern Europe receive their mail in Vienna rather than any Eastern European country. So tell your friends to write you care of **American Express,** Kärntnerstrasse 21/23 (P.O. Box 288), 1010 Wien 1, Austria (tel. 52-05-44). This is a complimentary service for all American Express cardholders; for others there's a small charge.

For further information about Vienna before you go, contact the **Austrian Tourist Office,** 500 Fifth Ave., Suite 2009, New York, NY 10110 (tel. 212/944-6880).

ACCOMMODATIONS: Inexpensive accommodations are hard to find in Vienna. The tourist offices in the train station and at the airport can assist you in finding a hotel room; otherwise, try calling one of these budget hotels, each located fairly near to the center:

Zu den Drei Kronen, Schleifmöhlgasse 25 (tel. 57-32-89), charges $17 to $18 for a single and $22 for a double.

Kugel, Siebensterngasse 43 (tel. 93-33-55), has singles at $12 to $20.50, and doubles at $17 to $27.

Altwienerhof, Herklotzgasse 6 (tel. 83-71-45), offers singles ranging from $13 to $22; doubles cost $15 to $24.

Zipser, Lange Gasse 49 (tel. 42-02-28), asks $12.50 to $23 for its singles and $16 to $25 for its doubles.

Columbia, Kochgasse 9 (tel. 42-67-57), charges only $11 to $12 per single and $14 to $15 for a double.

Acion, Dorotheergasse 6–8 (tel. 52-54-73), has singles for $15 to $20 and doubles for $21 to $32.

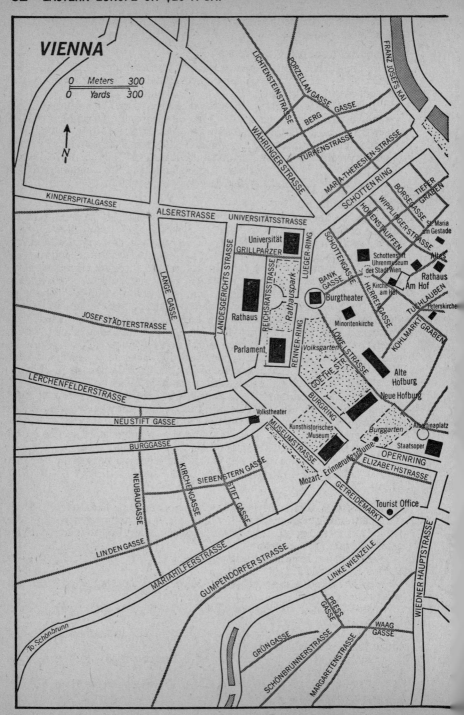

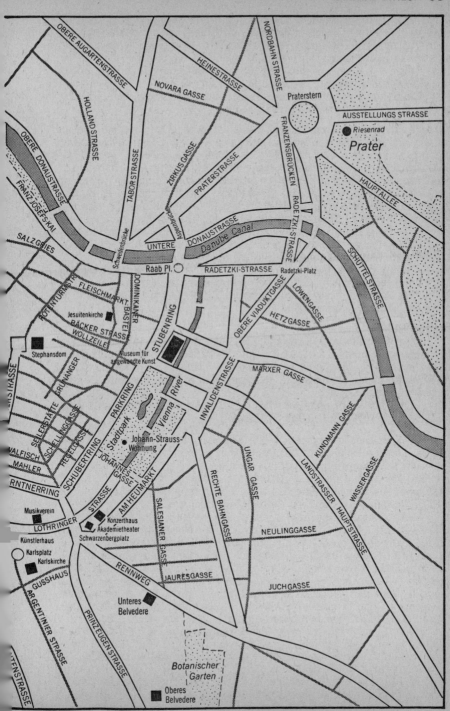

DINING: If you've just come from a stay in Eastern Europe, you may look forward to an exciting change of pace in your dining. If so, try **Da Pasquale,** Neustiftgasse 47 (tel. 96-19-21), open from 6 p.m. to midnight (closed Sunday and holidays), or **Pizzeria Da Peppino,** Lerchenfelderstrasse 65 (tel. 96-17-17), open from 6 p.m. to midnight (closed Monday). Both serve superb Italian cuisine at moderate prices, which you won't find in the East.

And if you prefer good Chinese food in a pleasant garden, make your way to **Chinatown 7,** Burggasse 67 (tel. 93-52-80).

ISTANBUL: Any traveler to the Balkans should try to include Istanbul on his or her itinerary. Why mention Istanbul in a guide to Eastern Europe? First, with mosques and minarets towering over the skyline, exotic spice markets and covered bazaars, and other Middle Eastern exotica, Istanbul is truly a must-see-at-least-once-in-your-lifetime metropolis. Second, Istanbul serves as a convenient and often inexpensive gateway to the Balkans. Third, the history of much of Eastern Europe is closely linked with the history of the Ottoman Empire, and signs of 500 years of Turkish rule are still evident across Eastern Europe in everything from the mosques and Muslim population of Sarajevo to the Hungarian castles that were destroyed by the Turks. In a visit to Istanbul, you can see the history of the region from the Turkish point of view, a history which in Turkish eyes was marked by greatness, a view not shared in many Eastern European countries where Ottoman rule was considered foreign oppression.

What follows is some quick information for getting to and from Istanbul and for a brief stay in this mystical city.

Getting There

By Air: Travelers to Bulgaria and Romania often choose to fly first to Istanbul. These two countries are less accessible from the West than the other countries discussed in this book, and Istanbul—farther east—offers a natural gateway. Lufthansa provides daily connections to Istanbul from either Frankfurt or Munich.

For information or assistance while in Istanbul, contact Lufthansa at: Cumhuriyet Caddesi 179-185 Sisli (tel. 1-46-51-30-34 or 1-46-84-41).

By Land: The most romantic way of arriving in Istanbul from Eastern Europe is on the *Orient Express.* As most of us don't want to spend $5,000 to take the newly refurbished *Orient Express,* the best choice is the old *Tauren Orient Express.* The truth of the matter is, though, that nothing makes the *Tauren Orient Express* any different from other trains. The 11-hour trip from Sofia to Istanbul is rather pricey, costing about $70 without couchette.

We have discovered a great starvation-budget way of traveling from Bulgaria to Istanbul, but it requires the most adventurous, happy-go-lucky sort of reader. From Sofia, Plovdiv, or any other city in Bulgaria, make your way over to Svilengrad (a town in southern Bulgaria near the border) by train or bus (the fare from Sofia to Svilengrad is only a few dollars) or hitchhiking. From Svilengrad, take a taxi to the Bulgarian-Turkish border at Kapitan Andreevo (for less than $8). Walk through Customs at the border. On the Turkish side you can change money into Turkish lira (at very good rates), and after you've left the last frontier, you'll find a bus that goes to Edirne, a 20-minute ride for 50¢.

If you're tired by this point, you may want to spend the night in Edirne, a large town with several interesting mosques and markets. From Edirne, buses leave frequently on the four-hour route to Istanbul at a cost of only $2 (ask for directions to the bus station).

The plan may sound far-fetched, but it does avoid the very high surcharge the Bulgarians add onto all international transportation tickets (note how much

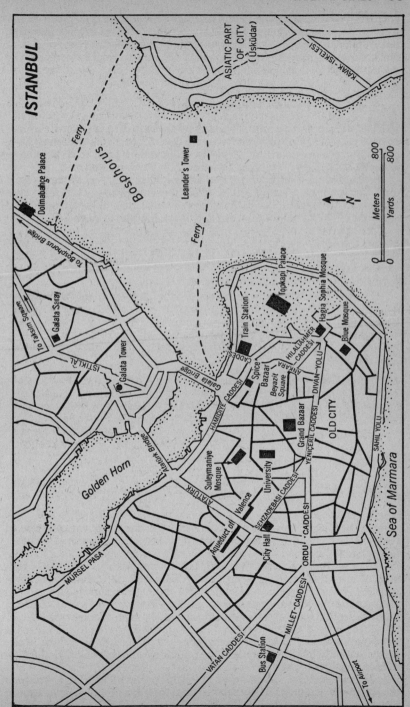

ISTANBUL

ASIATIC PART OF CITY (Üsküdar)

KAVAK-İSKELESİ

Bosphorus

Ferry

Ferry

Dolmabahçe Palace

To Bosphorus Bridge

Leander's Tower

Meters 800
Yards 800

N

To Taksim Square

Galata Saray

Galata Tower

İSTIKLAL

Topkapi Palace

Train Station

Galata Bridge

HAMIDIYE CADDESI

Spice Bazaar

Beyazit Square

Hagia Sophia Mosque

HILALIAHMER CADDESI

ANKARA CADDESI

Blue Mosque

DIVAN-YOLU

OLD CITY

Golden Horn

Atatürk Bridge

ATATÜRK

Suleymaniye Mosque

University

Grand Bazaar

YENIÇERIL CADDESI

SAHIL YOLU

Sea of Marmara

Valence

Aqueduct of

ŞEHZADEBASI CADDESI

MURSEL PASA

City Hall

ORDU CADDESI

MILLET CADDESI

VATAN CADDESI

Bus Station

To Airport

cheaper fares are *from* Istanbul to Bulgaria). Most important of all, this complicated way of getting to Istanbul actually works. We did it in the summer of 1985, and saved about $60 each over the price of a train ticket! Because of the rigorous nature of the many transfers, we recommend following this itinerary only if you have a lot of energy and time but little money.

Getting to Eastern Europe from Istanbul

By Air: From Istanbul, **Turkish Airlines,** at 131 Cumhuriyet Caddesi (tel. 145-7055 or 457-055 for reservations, and 454-208 for information), flies to all the Eastern European capitals. These flights are most attractive for travelers under 26 years of age, as they receive a 25% discount on flights to Eastern Europe and a 60% discount on flights to other destinations. The Istanbul–Bucharest or Istanbul–Sofia plane fare runs $116 (or $89 for students).

BalkanAir, the Bulgarian national airline, offers flights to Varna on the Bulgarian Black Sea coast for $30 to $35. You can buy these tickets from the BalkanAir office in the U.S., or in Istanbul at Taksim Gezi Dükkanlari (tel. 145-2456), open from 9 a.m. to 1 p.m. and 2 to 6 p.m. Monday through Friday.

By Land: The train from Istanbul to Sofia costs about $22, but those under 26 pay only $11. Several companies operate buses to Bucharest in Romania. The trip takes a tiring 17 hours, but the fare is a truly economical $15.

Orientation

Turkish Airlines operates buses between the airport and **Meşrutiyet Caddesi,** one of the major streets in the center of town. The **bus station** (Topkapi Otobüs Terminali) is located a fair distance from the city center, so your best bet is to take a taxi (they're fairly inexpensive by Western standards) to your destination. The **train station** (tel. 270-050) is centrally located near the Blue Mosque and Hagia Sofia.

Information and Hotel Reservations: Your first stop in town should be at one of the four helpful **Ministry of Tourism Information Offices.** They can provide you with a large quantity of useful materials on Istanbul, and they can also make hotel reservations in whatever price category you desire. The main office is at Meşrutiyet Caddesi 57, in the Galatasaray district (tel. 145-3032); there are also offices at the airport (tel. 573-7399), in Sultanahmet Square near Hagia Sofia (tel. 522-4903), and in the Maritime Station in Karaköy (tel. 149-5776). These offices stay open from 9 a.m. to 5 p.m. seven days a week.

For further information about Istanbul before you go, contact the **Turkish Tourist Office,** 821 U.N. Plaza, New York, NY 10017 (tel. 212/687-2194).

Dining

Although many travelers are unfamiliar with Turkish food, you can actually eat well in Istanbul. Just so you don't go astray, here are four good, moderately priced restaurants:

The **Four Seasons** (Dört Mevsim), İstikal Caddesi 509, Tünel (tel. 145-8941), offers excellent, delicately prepared Turkish specialties in an elegant dining room. Open from noon to 3 p.m. and 6 to 11 p.m.; closed Sunday.

For good pasta dishes and cheap wine, go to the small **Ristorante Italiano,** Cumhuriyet Caddesi 6 (tel. 147-8640). Open from 9 a.m. to midnight seven days a week.

Hotel Kalyon, Sahil Yolu, in Sultanahmet, a few blocks behind the Blue Mosque (tel. 520-1302), serves tasty meat and fish dishes at slightly splurgey prices. Open from noon to 3:30 p.m. and 6:30 to 11 p.m.

For a more simple local place with good Turkish fare, drop by **Haci Baba,** İstikal Caddesi 49, in the Taksim district (tel. 144-1886). Open from noon to midnight seven days a week.

Part One

POLAND

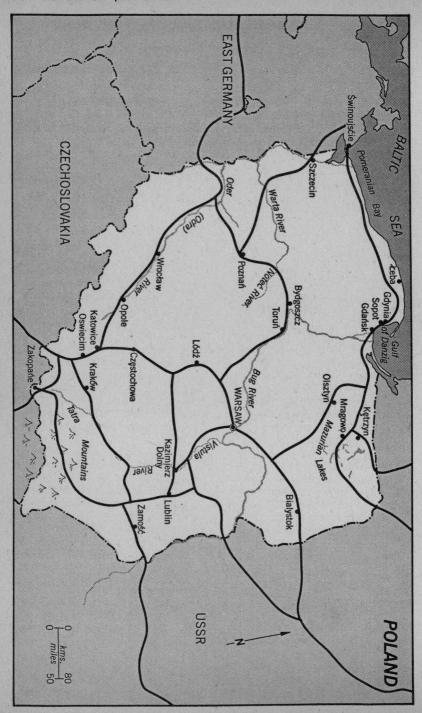

Chapter III

INTRODUCING POLAND

1. About Poland
2. Rules and Regulations
3. Getting There
4. Getting Around
5. Accommodations
6. Food and Drink
7. The ABCs of Poland

MOST AMERICAN TRAVELERS still haven't discovered Poland, and the few pioneers who have ventured over are Polish-Americans visiting family and friends. Your first thought might be similar to our own sentiment when, in 1979, we heard that a relative was traveling to Poland. "Why would anyone want to visit Poland?" we asked. What we've learned since then is that Americans don't appreciate the diversity of Poland. Let us share a little-known secret: if you enjoy rich collections of art and architecture, moving historical sights, and stunning natural landscape, then Poland is the place for you!

You can find everything in Poland. Picturesque Kraków in southern Poland stores centuries of priceless royal treasures in a fairytale castle; Gdańsk preserves the atmosphere of a medieval trading town, with its old cobblestone streets and richly decorated homes. Warsaw, now completely rebuilt from the destruction of World War II, is graced with one of Europe's most charming old market squares, not to mention a diverse museum collection. The spellbinding natural beauty of the Tatra Mountains in the Zakopane area will impress even the most blasé visitor. And those seeking peace and relaxation will find the Mazurian Lake region in the northeast of the country, with its thousands of lakes and forests, a unique outpost of nature.

Despite what you might think, for tourists the political situation in Poland is one of the most relaxed and unmenacing in all of Eastern Europe. Once there, you will be fascinated by this socialist country, without ever feeling oppressed by it. Most of the people you meet have a deep admiration for the West, and they will extend very friendly smiles to their rare Western visitors. The preservation of old customs, and a life centered around the family make for a peaceful, orderly society. Sons and daughters well into their 30s often still live with their parents, and together the families devote Sunday to churchgoing and family outings.

Few Western tourists means few dollars to build the Polish tourism infrastructure. As a result, Poland's travel industry has not developed to Western standards. At times your ingenuity and ability to improvise will be tested as you find that the bureaucracy seems devoted to making life difficult. But fear not. Although you may have to wait a little longer to buy a train ticket, or repeat yourself a few more times to make yourself understood, you should enjoy a fascinating vacation in Poland. We hope that with a little patience, and this chapter to guide you, any possible problems will be reduced to a minimum.

SUGGESTED ITINERARIES: If you have only a week to spend in Poland, we recommend dividing your time as follows: three days in Warsaw, which will serve as a good introduction to the history, politics, and culture of Poland; one day in Częstochowa, Poland's mecca where hundreds of thousands of religious faithful visit every year to see the sacred Black Madonna; two days in Kraków, Poland's most charming town, and a center of art and architecture, as well as one of the few Polish cities to escape World War II without damage; and a day in Zakopane, the center of the breathtaking Tatra Mountains. If you have more than a week to spend in Poland, we recommend adding another day in Kraków to visit Auschwitz, the former concentration camp nearby; spend two days in the Baltic port town of Gdańsk, an attractive old town and modern political center; and finally, add another day in Toruń, a pretty medieval town where Copernicus was born.

1. About Poland

THE PEOPLE: The Polish people are among the most intellectual as well as the bravest and most able in all of Europe. Day-to-day talk doesn't linger on the weather or sports, but on religion, politics, and current issues. The Poles boldly discuss these topics with great interest and fervor. Although Poland has been devastated by wars over and over again, the people endure and continue to hope that life will soon change for the better.

After you have spent some time among the Polish people you may wonder how Polish jokes ever emerged in America. They are based on the stereotype of the early 20th-century Polish immigrants to America. During that era, many stout, uneducated peasants made the long journey to a new life. But as you'll soon see, today's urban Poles are vastly different. As further proof, reflect on some of the best-known Poles in history, among whom are Mikolaj Kopernik (Copernicus), Marie and Pierre Curie, Joseph Conrad, and Frederic Chopin.

The Polish Złoty
Despite official claims to the contrary, inflation does diminish the value of the Polish złoty each year. At the same time, however, you can expect the złoty to devalue against the dollar, so prices remain fairly constant in real-dollar terms. The prices in this guide were calculated at 159 złoty = $1 U.S.; thus 10 złoty = about 6¢ U.S., or $10 = about 1,600 złoty. You may receive quite a bit more when you visit, but you may also see higher złoty prices than those listed here. Rely mainly on the dollar figures as your guideline.

A CAPSULE HISTORY: European wars have raged in Poland for hundreds of years, resulting in the partitioning of the Polish state and the destruction of its cities several times over.

The first Polish state was established in either A.D. 963 or 966 (historians aren't quite sure of the exact date), when Slavic tribes unified and broke away from German authority. Frequent battles with the Teutonic Knights, the German military and religious order, marked the next several hundred years. In 1226 the Knights occupied Poland and it was not until 1410, a date that is still remembered today, that the Poles decidedly defeated them in the Battle of Grunwald. The years that followed until the late 17th century make up Poland's Golden Age, a time of relative peace and prosperous development. All Golden Ages come to an end of course, and Poland's was no different. Beginning in the late 17th century and continuing throughout the 18th century, life became more difficult for the Pole. Starting in 1772, Prussia, Austria, and Russia began to conquer and divide up parts of Poland, and by 1795 nothing was left. The Polish state had simply ceased to exist. Poland did not appear again on European maps for 123 years, until it was reestablished in the Treaty of Versailles at the end of World War I.

Although the independent nation began to prosper in the middle 1920s, there was widespread unemployment in the depression of the 1930s. Not long after, Poland was to be scorched by the vast destruction of modern warfare, the likes of which no other European country had ever known. In March 1939 Adolf Hitler demanded that the Poles cede the Free State of Danzig to the Germans. They refused, and on September 1, 1939, Germany invaded western Poland. Some 2½ weeks later the Soviets attacked eastern Poland, in accordance with the secret Nazi-Soviet pact. Over the next six years, six million Poles were killed, three million of whom were Jews. Almost every Pole you meet lost a relative in World War II. In 1945 the boundaries of Poland were moved west in accordance with the Big Power agreements, and 3½ million people were forced to move out of the eastern Polish territories that were incorporated into the Soviet Union. In 1944 a socialist government was established in Poland.

Poland's postwar years have been marked by great reconstruction: today, many of the cities that were completely destroyed in World War II exist again. The past 40 years have also been marked by economic problems and worker unrest, most notably in 1956, 1970, and 1980–1981. The details of the 1980–1981 unrest are the best known: after months of domestic strikes and protest, the government concluded the Gdańsk Agreement in August 1980 with the representatives of the trade union Solidarity. This agreement allowed free and independent trade unions the right to strike, and respect for freedom of publications, among other things. In December 1981 the government, under the leadership of General Jaruzelski, imposed a state of martial law to quash the continuing unrest in Poland. In 1983 martial law was lifted, and in recent years the economic situation has improved somewhat.

RELIGION: In an officially atheist country, 95% of the Poles claim to be Roman Catholic. Of this 95%, many have a genuine devotion to the church, and great feelings for the Polish pope, John Paul II. Our trip to Poland in June 1983 coincided with the pope's second visit to his homeland after assuming the papacy. On the day he arrived in Warsaw, a crowd estimated at one million Poles lined the main street for miles. As the faithful waited, dressed in their best clothes, no one spoke above a whisper, thus creating a vast silence over Warsaw's streets. As the pope's car neared, the great silence ended as the crowd began to roar with wild cheers, and spontaneously to sing Polish songs such as "Sto Lat." Although the pope doesn't visit Poland every day, the people's religious devotion remains strong. If it is at all possible, we highly recommend that you visit Poland during a religious holiday. You will be certain to see some very moving ceremonies.

THE GOVERNMENT: The Polish Parliament (the Seym) holds the political authority in Poland's socialist system. The Seym also appoints two higher bodies, the Council of Ministers (which is the chief executive body) and the Council of State.

LANGUAGE: For English-speaking people the Polish language appears impossible to decipher at first glance, and it still may in subsequent glances! We have found, though, that once you learn the sounds of the various letters and consonant clusters, the language becomes progressively easier, and you can actually pronounce street names and ask basic questions. You can pick up the phonetic sounds of Polish letters from a book, but an easier way to learn is through a class or a cassette course. For those who want to learn Polish in some detail, we recommend the excellent eight-cassette course offered by Audio Forum (call them toll free at 800/243-1234, or write Audio Forum, Foreign Language Department, 96 Broad St., Guilford, CT 06437, for a catalog). And of course don't forget your Berlitz *Polish for Travelers*, an indispensable aid to help you through all sorts of situations. Only a few stores actually stock this book, so if you don't find it at bookstores, either ask Orbis (the Polish National Tourist Office), or Berlitz, 866 Third Ave., New York, NY 10022 (tel. 212/702-7986), if they can locate one.

If you make no progress in your rudimentary Polish, all is not lost. Most Orbis and hotel staff speak some English, although in smaller towns such personnel become increasingly rare. Some Poles speak German and French. Russian, although detested by most, is widely understood, if not spoken.

DEALING WITH THE BUREAUCRACY: Expect service generally to be poor in Poland and you won't be disappointed. Most workers have little incentive to work harder as neither promotion nor demotion is likely, whatever they do. No one is obliged to assist you with your requests or problems. Therefore, when you approach service professionals, kindness or generosity may help to get better service. Save anger for extreme circumstances, but sometimes a raised voice will shock a bureaucrat into action.

2. Rules and Regulations

The cheerful and helpful staff of the Polish national tourist offices abroad, **Orbis,** can assist you with valuable advice, visa forms, money exchange vouchers (which all tourists must have), and reservations for cars and Orbis hotels. When you arrive in Poland, the national offices can provide information, sell transportation tickets, and extend other services. Alas, the domestic Orbis offices are not so eager to please as their foreign offices, so we recommend taking care of all of your tourist needs in as few visits to domestic Orbis offices as possible, to avoid long lines and sometimes frustrating service.

In America, Orbis has its home at 500 Fifth Ave., New York, NY 10110 (tel. 212/391-0844 or 730-1978), or at 333 N. Michigan Ave., Chicago, IL 60601 (tel. 312/236-9013). Elsewhere in the U.S. you can call Orbis toll free at 800/223-6037. In England, their office is at 82 Mortimer St., London W1N 7DE (tel. 637-4971/3).

VISAS: All visitors to Poland must obtain a visa, but a special twist slightly complicates the process. As in Czechoslovakia and Romania, you must exchange a certain amount of money for each day you spend in Poland. The twist, however, is that you must exchange these monies *before you go,* otherwise you won't be issued the visa. As soon as you determine the length of your stay in Poland, you should then go to Orbis and give them the minimum daily sum for each day you'll be in Poland. In return you will receive a Polish złoty voucher which you can exchange for złoty when you arrive at the Polish border.

Most tourists must make a minimum daily currency exchange of $15. Those exempted from this rate are students (who have an ISIC card) and those under 21, as well as those of Polish descent (remote Polish relatives are usually enough to qualify); these travelers must exchange only $7 a day. Finally, travelers who pay Orbis beforehand for hotels and other services need not exchange any daily minimum.

Now (and only now!) are you ready to apply for the necessary Polish visa. In addition to the exchange voucher, mail or take your passport, completed application form, two photographs, and a visa application fee in cash, certified check, or money order (find out what the latest fee is from the Polish Embassy or Orbis) to your nearest Polish consulate. Although it usually takes about two weeks to approve the visa, you should send in the application early just in case. There are Polish Consulate Generals at 233 Madison Ave., New York, NY 10016 (tel. 212/889-8360), and at 1530 N. Lake Shore Dr., Chicago IL 60610 (tel. 312/337-8166). The consular division of the Polish Embassy, 2224 Wyoming Ave. NW, Washington, DC 20008 (tel. 202/234-3800), also issues visas. In Canada, write to the Polish Consulate General at either 1500 Pine Ave. West, Montréal, Québec H3G 1B4 (tel. 937-9481), or at 2603 Lakeshore Blvd. West, Toronto, Ontario M8V 1G5 (tel. 252-5471). If you go in person to any of these offices, allow a good deal of time—at least an hour. The lines here will be your first introduction to the worst aspect of Poland.

The whole process does sound pretty confusing. Actually, it's not that bad. First get your voucher from Orbis, then get your visa from the Polish consulate. Ask Orbis any additional questions you might have.

If you decide to extend your visa once you are in Poland, go early in the morning to one of the police stations listed in the important addresses section of each city. These people will change more money for you and then extend your visa. Most of these offices are open only from 9 a.m. to noon, and the bureaucrats have little sympathy for those who arrive late.

3. Getting There

BY AIR: From 16 gateway cities in the U.S. and Canada, the dependable, comfortable route to Warsaw is Lufthansa's connecting service via Frankfurt. From New York, you also can fly nonstop to Warsaw with LOT, the Polish national airline. For information or assistance while in Warsaw, contact Lufthansa at: Hotel Victoria-Intercontinental, Krolewska 11 (tel. 27-78-19 or 27-54-36).

Fares to Warsaw

The following chart shows Lufthansa round-trip fares (subject to change without notice) in U.S. dollars. First Class and Business Class fares allow unlimited stopovers. The Excursion fare is limited to two stopovers in each direction for a charge of $25 each. The APEX fare permits no stopovers and has a 21-day advance purchase requirement and a $75 penalty for cancellation. All fares are subject to a $3 departure tax plus a $5 Custom User fee.

Round-trip Fares to Warsaw

From:	All Year First Class	All Year Business Class	10 Day–3 Month Excursion		7 Day–3 Month APEX					
					Nov. 1–Mar. 31		Apr. 1–May 31 Sept. 16–Oct. 31		June 1–Sept. 15	
			Sept. 15 May 14	May 15 Sept. 14	Mid Week	Week End	Mid Week	Week End	Mid Week	Week End
New York	$3446	$1962	$1061	$1277	$749	$799	$799	$849	$899	$949
Anchorage	4572	2884	1499	1715	1187	1237	1237	1287	1337	1387
Atlanta	4134	2350	1189	1405	877	927	927	977	1027	1077
Boston	3446	1962	1061	1277	749	799	799	849	899	949
Chicago	4096	2406	1171	1387	859	909	909	959	1009	1059
Houston / Dallas-Ft. Worth	4178	2292	1189	1405	877	927	927	977	1027	1077
San Francisco / Los Angeles	4808	2872	1244	1460	932	982	982	1032	1082	1132
Miami	3888	2284	1207	1423	895	945	945	995	1045	1095
Philadelphia	3666	2126	1124	1340	812	862	862	912	962	1012

BY TRAIN: Since there are few charters and discount flights to Poland, you might consider flying to a city in Western Europe and then continuing on by train via Berlin or Vienna. Trains from either city take between 9 and 10½ hours. (Note that if you're coming by train from Vienna, you must obtain a Czech transit visa beforehand. You may be turned back at the border if you don't have it! If you're coming from Berlin, the East German transit police will issue you a DDR transit visa right on the train.) You can try to sleep away these long hours by reserving a couchette on an overnight train, but be aware that border guards have little respect for your slumber, and will awaken you several times during the night as you cross international frontiers.

BY SEA: A number of inexpensive ferryboats connect several cities in Scandinavia with Poland's Baltic Coast. Travelers from Copenhagen or the Swedish port of Ystad can sail to the unpronounceable Polish port of Świnoujście (try Sveen-ow-oo-scheh) near Szczecin. The ride from Copenhagen is nine hours long, and it costs about $25 for passage and $6 to $32 for a bed. Tourists from the distant port of Helsinki can take the slow boat to Gdańsk, which takes 41 hours and costs about $47 to $60 for passage and $25 to $50 for a bed. Students with the ISIC ID card get a 10% to 50% reduction on these prices, depending on the route.

For sailing times and exact prices, write one of the following **Polferries** agents and be sure to ask for a Polferries timetable: Gdynia America Shipping Lines Ltd., 238 City Rd., London EC1 V2 (tel. 01/253-9561), or Vindrose Rejser I/S, Nordre Tolbold 18, 1259 Copenhagen K, Denmark (tel. 01/154-647).

For those with the desire (and wallet) to sail to Poland in style, the ocean liner *Stefan Batory* crosses the Atlantic several times a year to Gdynia on the Baltic Sea coast via Montréal, London, and Rotterdam. For information, write to McLean Kennedy Passenger Services, 410 St. Nicolas, Montréal, PQ H2Y 2P5 (tel. 514/849-6111).

4. Getting Around

BY AIR: LOT flies from Warsaw to a number of Polish cities, including Gdańsk, Szczecin, Poznań, Wrocław, and Kraków. Flights are moderately priced, costing, for example, about $35 from Warsaw to Gdańsk. Students flying standby get 50% off (no one at LOT will confirm this discount, but if you press them at the airport you'll usually get the savings).

BY TRAIN: The trains of the Polish rail system (known by its initials, PKP) operate at three different speeds: express *(expresowy)*, the fastest trains which require a seat reservation; fast *(pospieszny)*, slower but cheaper trains which do not require seat reservations; and stopping or normal trains *(osobowy/ normalne)*, the cheapest and most common trains, which also are the slowest. All trains are divided into first and second class (first class costs 50% more). The passengers in first class can relax in cabins with six seats, not eight as in second class.

Here are some sample fares from Warsaw to Gdańsk:

	Normal	Fast	Express
1st class	469 złoty ($2.90)	694 złoty ($4.35)	922 złoty ($5.80)
2nd class	303 złoty ($1.90)	462 złoty ($2.90)	618 złoty ($3.90)

We recommend that you always take the fastest trains possible, and treat yourself to an occasional first-class seat, because the difference in price is very slight (on the Warsaw–Gdańsk line, the difference is less than $2). You can reserve seats up to two months in advance through Polorbis at the train station, or at Orbis in town. On the day of departure, however, you can only purchase tickets at the train station.

Orbis also sells a **Polrail Pass,** which entitles you to travel as much as you want on any Polish train (express trains too), and make seat reservations for free. These passes cost $40 for 8 days, $50 for 15 days, and $60 for 21 days. They probably won't save you any money (after all, Polish trains are very cheap!), but they can save you lots of time waiting on ticket lines.

When checking out departure *(objazdy)* times in the train station, look for the yellow schedules on the walls. White schedules, by contrast, show train arrival *(przyjazdy)* times.

BY BUS: In general, you're not going to want to use Poland's slow bus system (known by its initials, PKP). One exception is the Kraków–Zakopane route, since the train toils its way very slowly through the mountains. You may also have to take a bus to get to smaller towns where trains don't run.

BY CAR: In a country with some of the most picturesque landscape in Europe, driving is a unique pleasure. As you cruise along the Polish country roads, you'll marvel at peasants leading a horse-driven carriage carrying lumber, farmers working their fields with pitchforks and sickles, or even peasants with horse and plow! The price you pay for these memorable sights is narrow roads. Even on the major roads two-way traffic shares two lanes. Nonetheless, we recommend driving to all who can afford it. *Note:* The same things that delight by day are perilous by night; roads and unmotorized vehicles are usually not lit, making horse carriages and other vehicles difficult to see. Exercise extreme caution when driving at night.

Orbis rents cars in conjunction with several Western companies, including Hertz and National. The cheapest cars cost $235 a week with unlimited mileage from April 1 to October 31, and $200 a week at other times. Inquire at Orbis for more details. To drive in Poland, all foreigners (with a rented car or their own vehicle) need an international driver's license (issued in the U.S. by the American Automobile Association) and an international insurance card (the Green

Card), which can be purchased at the frontier or at the Orbis bureau when you rent a car.

TAXIS: Similar to other means of transportation in Poland, taxis are very economical. As of this writing, the meter starts at 30 złoty (19¢) and slowly inches its way up by increments of 5 złoty (3¢). Between 11 p.m. and 5 a.m. a night surcharge of about 50% of the meter figure is added. The final cost is increased slightly according to a government-issued price chart, but is *not* affected by the number of passengers.

Since taxis are so inexpensive, you can use them frequently. The traveler on a medium budget can rent a taxi for a few hours to explore the countryside, and even the budget traveler can use Polish taxis for trips of undreamed-of lengths (at least in the West). Short rides across the city cost less than $1, and even a lengthy ride into a nearby suburb will cost only 200 to 300 złoty—less than $2!

The taxi driver may be a source of valuable advice and assistance, especially outside Warsaw where they seem to be friendlier. Since American tourists are a rarity, the driver may be amiable if you speak a common language. Some taxi drivers also act as a source of information, tour guide, and room finder! For example, a friendly driver will often be willing to accompany you into a hotel or office to help with both the language and regulations. If you do find such a helpful driver, of course, tip him generously.

Unfortunately, with all these advantages over their Western counterparts, taxis in Poland can be hard to find. You can try to wave one down, or go to a taxi stand, but expect long lines. As with so many other things in Poland, patience is a prerequisite. Once you have found a taxi, it's usually worthwhile to have the driver wait during all the short stops you may make. The taxi meter does not run while waiting, though you should compensate the driver with a larger tip.

A word of caution does apply, however. Some drivers view American passengers as a chance to get rich and may ask for considerably inflated rates. Beware, for example, taxis that wait in front of large hotels. Keep in mind that the meter should always be turned on after you enter the taxi, and a slight increase in the price is allowed according to the government chart, but ask or signal to see the chart so that the driver does not "invent" the tariff. It's always a good idea to carry change to avoid any upward rounding-off of the fare by the driver.

HITCHHIKING: Believe it or not, the Polish government actually encourages hitchhiking! But there is a price for their liberal attitude. They ask you to buy little hitchhiking tickets, which you flash at passing cars. When you get a ride, you give some tickets to the driver, and those drivers with the most coupons win a bonus at the year's end. In reality, though, you don't really need these tickets at all to get a ride. If you look like a Westerner—or best of all, an American—you're likely to get a ride more quickly than an average tourist with hitchhike tickets!

5. Accommodations

As you know well from reading this guide, your goal as a $25-a-Day traveler is to spend about $15 a day on accommodations and the rest on food. Unfortunately, many Polish hotels cost more than these guidelines. But despair not! Some budget hotels do exist for the bargain hunter.

HOTELS: Hotels in Poland are divided into deluxe, four-, three-, two-, and one-star categories. Orbis holds a monopoly on the deluxe and four-star hotels, so you should be looking for the cheaper three-star hotels and downward.

Throughout Poland lower category hotels approach the quality of the Orbis hotels, both in the size of their rooms and in the helpfulness of their staff, so you might as well save by staying at a two-star hotel! The only amenity that you lose in a two-star hotel is a private bathroom, which is a rarity in Polish budget hotels. In our descriptions of hotels, we are careful to describe the state of the public bathrooms, which range from perfectly clean to those that can be used by only the least fussy traveler.

We recommend that you reserve a hotel room at least for Warsaw, Częstochowa, and Zakopane, because these cities often have large tour groups crowding the hotels. Write directly to the hotels listed here, as Orbis will reserve only expensive Orbis hotels. When you check into a hotel, the reception clerk will ask for your passport and hold it for a while to complete registration procedures. When you pay the bill, you'll have to present your currency-exchange slips to prove that you legally changed money for the room.

One final tip on using hotel services: Throughout this chapter we provide telephone numbers of Polish restaurants, organizations, etc., where English may not be spoken. We recommend that you give any number you want to call to your hotel receptionist and ask him or her to call for you.

PRIVATE ROOMS: In many Polish towns you can rent a spare room in a private house, usually owned by a retired couple or elderly woman. These are usually spacious, inexpensive rooms with clean bathrooms, and a boon for all budget travelers! If you intend to stay in private rooms in Poland, we recommend that you bring a roll or two of toiletpaper, as not every bathroom in Poland is always well stocked. If you're unsure how long you want to stay, you can pay for one or two nights at the local tourist office (addresses are listed in each city description), and then either return another time to the bureau or make a deal with the apartment owner.

HOSTELS AND CAMPING GROUNDS: Some 1,200 youth hostels sprinkle the map of Poland, so we advise those who want to stay in a hostel to buy the *Youth Hostel Handbook,* available from the **Youth Hostel Federation (MTSM** are the Polish initials), at ul. Chocimska 28, Warsaw (tel. 49-83-54). Those with a Youth Hostel Federation card will receive a 25% discount per night. In summer, student hotels help bargain hunters with another inexpensive housing option. Inquire at the local **Almatur** office (which we list under "Accommodations" throughout this section).

Outdoor campers can pitch a tent at numerous camping grounds across Poland. A camping map *(Polska Mapa Campingow),* which you can buy in Poland, indicates where they are; you can also inquire at Orbis.

6. Food and Drink

Poland's cuisine has gotten a bum rap in the West. For the past three summers after we returned from Poland, it seemed that the first thing people always asked was "How's the food situation in Poland?" or "I guess you had a lot of awful food." To the contrary! If you know where to go, Poland offers visitors a plentiful supply of delicious food.

The country certainly did suffer through some grim years of erratic food supplies in the early 1980s, and all of their problems are not yet over. For example, you'll still see to this day that many smaller restaurants offer more selections on the menu than they can provide (we vividly remember how overwhelmed and indecisive a Polish friend was when she came to visit America and we told her at lunch that *all* of the items on the menu were available). Luckily, Poland's first-class hotel restaurants remain largely immune to these lapses in supply (the government wants to be sure to impress its foreign visitors), and so you'll always be able to get a good meal in the country's best hotels. You may react by saying, "What! I never eat in hotel restaurants at home or abroad!" But this is Poland, and here hotel restaurants maintain and serve the best quality and quantity of food while smaller restaurants on the whole cannot compete.

Your next reaction might be: "I can't afford to eat in hotel restaurants!" Although Polish hotels do charge Westerners five or six times more than Poles pay for a bed, Poles and Westerners alike pay the same price at restaurants. Thus you can eat in a fine restaurant for about $5, and enjoy a really fancy meal for less than $10. A simple lunch or dinner often runs as low as $1 or $2. It's as though you died and woke up in budget traveler's heaven!

You may lament the uninteresting decor many hotel restaurants offer. It sometimes seems as though in Poland you have to choose between good food in a sterile hotel ambience or mediocre food in an attractive local place. Whenever possible, however, we recommend those few nonhotel restaurants that combine excellent food with an appealing atmosphere.

POLISH SPECIALTIES: What does Polish food taste like? As with other Eastern European cuisines, meat dishes, often prepared with rich sauces or garnished with spices, provide the staple of the Polish diet. Russian, German, and Hungarian cuisine have all influenced Polish cooking, and such ingredients as dill, caraway seeds, mushrooms, and sour cream often make an appearance. Favorite Polish entrees include **bigos,** a sauerkraut and sausage or smoked pork dish; **beefsteak Tatare,** raw hamburger meat served with raw egg, chopped onion, pickle, and seasonings; **kotlet Schabowy,** the ubiquitous pork cutlet; and **roast duckling** with an apple. A delicious soup always begins the Polish meal, and our favorites include **barszcz,** a beet-flavored soup; **botwina,** a cold beet soup with vegetables that's often served in the summer; and **chłodnik,** a cold soup of garden vegetables such as cucumbers, scallions, horseradish, and onions. As a side dish or entree, **pierogi** (potato-, cheese-, or meat-filled dumplings) make rib-sticking fare that will see you through an afternoon of sightseeing. In the not-to-miss-at-all-costs category are Polish **mushrooms,** the most buttery and tasty we've had anywhere in all of Europe or America.

As you can see, your stomach has a lot to look forward to in your Polish travels! Perhaps the one legitimate gripe about Polish cuisine is that few vegetables are served with your meal, the exception being cucumbers, which you'll see all too often.

Another category we can't omit in discussing Polish cuisine is drink. Poles feel that a good meal must be accompanied by good drink, and you know they're talking about alcohol. It's not by chance that the Poles are listed in the *Guinness Book of World Records* as the world's number one alcohol consumers! Naturally, Poland offers a wide variety of vodkas, their drink par excellence. These include **Zytnia,** a rye vodka; **Żubrówka,** a vodka flavored by bison grass; **Myśliwska** (Hunter's Vodka), flavored by juniper berries with a gin flavor; **Pieprzówka,** pepper-flavored vodka; and **Wyborowa,** vodka "classic." You may also enjoy Polish beer **(Zywiec).** Just beware that Poland imports almost all of its wine and fruit juices, so budget-conscious travelers should avoid them for maximum savings.

RESTAURANTS: Polish **restaurants** are divided into several categories. Most Orbis hotels earn an S (superior) rating, followed by first category for good restaurants, second category for simpler restaurants, and third category for peasant restaurants in small towns. Besides restaurants, a **bar** or **bar mleczny** (milk bar) serves simple meals and snacks; a **kawarnia** (café) offers pastries and coffee, and a **winaria** usually serves only wine.

When you go to local restaurants, don't be surprised if someone asks to join you if there's an empty seat at your table. Local custom dictates that all available seats be filled. Your tablemates won't strike up a conversation unless you want to, but it's usually to your gain if you try.

A final note: Outside of the large hotel restaurants, you'll often see menus only in Polish, so we've put a menu translation showing typical menu offerings at the back of this book.

7. The ABCs of Poland

AUTO REPAIR: Should you be in the unfortunate position of needing automotive care, do not despair! The **PZM Automobile Tourism Office** assists motorists in need. They maintain automobile help stations *(pomoc drogowa)* throughout Poland that will help you on the spot or tow you to the nearest service station. Their main office is at al. Jerozolimskie 63, Warsaw (tel. 286-251 or 294-550). In most cities you can get emergency help by calling 981. Other regional emergency service numbers are listed in the city descriptions.

BLACK MARKET: Over and over during your travels in Poland, someone will quietly approach you, his eyes darting to see that no one is coming, and then ask, often in heavily accented English: "Change money?" If you agree to change money with him, he will give you three to five times the official rate of złoty for your dollars.

There are basically four reasons why Poles are willing to risk imprisonment to change their złoty for your dollars: First, they want to shop at the Pewex stores, which sell everything from fine chocolate to appliances, but for dollars only. Second, dollars give the Pole a leverage in both legal and under-the-table business dealings. For example, the government offers special deals whereby the fortunate Pole with dollars can avoid a long wait (up to 14 years at present for an apartment) and promptly purchase a telephone, car, or apartment. Third, many Poles are anxious to travel to the West, but they must exchange their worthless-outside-Poland złotys before they leave. Fourth, many people believe that it's better to put their savings in dollars, rather than in the inflation-prone złoty.

You may feel sympathetic to those who want to trade illegally on the black market after reading all these reasons. However, you must remember that you are breaking the law by exchanging money outside official bureaus, and you risk expulsion, a fine, or up to five years in prison. Many Western observers and Poles in and outside Poland have told us that the government seems to turn a blind eye to these transactions because Poland desperately needs hard currency. But *we advise extreme caution.* You never know when the government will decide to crack down on black-market activities.

CIGARETTES: Polish cigarettes are strong, somewhat like French brands. Fortunately, the hard-currency Pewex stores sell popular Western brands at prices lower than in the West, so you don't need to stock up before you come.

CLIMATE: Poland has a generally cool northern European climate, with temperatures averaging 68°F in the summer, and 26°F in the winter. Winter begins early, toward the end of October or the beginning of November, and lasts until March. From March to May variable weather reigns—in some years warm, and in others cool. During the summer the weather can still be cool on occasion. For example, June temperatures average only 62.2°F in Warsaw, and cooler days are sometimes experienced throughout the summer.

CLOTHING: Anyone familiar with northern Europe knows that you need to bundle up for much of the year. Our advice is to dress warmly; even in June you often need a sweater, and if you plan on going to the mountains in the Zakopane area, you may need a sweater and jacket during summer. Also bring along sufficient rain gear (such as a waterproof jacket, galoshes, and umbrella) as it rains frequently.

CREDIT CARDS: Although larger hotel and Orbis restaurants may accept credit cards, you'll find that most establishments prefer to do business in cash.

CRIME: Most criminals in Poland seem to prefer breaking into apartments to street mugging, so the streets are generally safe at all hours. Avoid drunkards in the street, however, for they are sometimes combative.

CURRENCY: Poles conduct their economic affairs in the złoty ("gold" in Polish), which is subdivided into 100 groszy per złoty. Banknotes are issued in 10-, 20-, 50-, 100-, 200-, 500-, 1,000-, 2,000-, and 5,000-złoty denominations. As of this writing, $1 equals 159 złoty, but past trends have shown that the złoty devalues quickly, and so you should get quite a bit more when you visit. At the same time, inflation is likely to cancel out any extra buying power of your dollars. The import or export of Polish złotys, as with other Eastern European countries' currency, is illegal.

In most Western European countries you pay a heavy service charge to change money in a hotel. In Poland, however, exchange rates are uniform everywhere so you don't get more money by changing in a bank. Therefore we recommend that you change money at your hotel or at Orbis, where the process is far quicker. Always keep all your exchange papers in case you want to change złotys back into Western currency. If, however, you haven't managed to spend all of your minimum daily exchange, you must deposit the remaining money at the border, where the kindly guards supposedly hold the money for you for up to one year!

CUSTOMS: When you arrive at the frontier or at the airport, the Customs agent will ask you to fill out a form declaring the amount of cash and traveler's checks you have. Then another Customs agent will closely inspect your bags. You can bring in personal possessions as long as they do not seem to be in excess quantity (like five radios) and gifts as long as their market value does not exceed 6,000 złoty ($37.75). Polish law forbids you to bring in narcotics, antisocialist literature, and pornography. For complete guidelines on what you can take, inquire at Orbis.

Export regulations change frequently, so if you intend to make any large purchases, we strongly recommend that you ask your embassy for advice first. In general, purchases in hard-currency stores can be brought out duty free, as can folk costumes. Other items can also be taken out duty free if their value does not exceed 1,000 złoty ($6.25). Items made or printed before 1945 usually require special permission. If you have to pay duty on an item, the rate ranges from 20% to 300% of the purchase value. Antisocialist items (for example, old Solidarity manifestos) are subject to confiscation.

DRIVING AND TRAFFIC REGULATIONS: On open roads, the speed limit is 90 km/h (54 mph), and 60 km/h (37 mph) in town limits. Other local speed limits are posted on the roadside. Inside city limits, you are not allowed to blow your horn, and wherever you are, drinking and driving is forbidden.

ELECTRICITY: The power supply is 220 volts, 50 cycles, A.C.

EMBASSIES AND CONSULATES: While we hope you won't have need of their services, in case of emergency here are the embassy and consulate addresses and telephone numbers in Poland:

The **U.S. Embassy** is in Warsaw at al. Ujazdowskie 29/31 (tel. 28-30-41 to 28-30-49), and there are U.S. consulates in Poznań at Chopina 4 (tel. 595-86 or 595-87) and in Kraków at Stolarska 9 (tel. 297-64 or 214-00).

The **Canadian Embassy** is in Warsaw at al. Matejki 1/5 (tel. 29-80-51).

The **British Embassy** is in Warsaw at al. Róż 1 (tel. 28-10-01 to 28-10-05).

EMERGENCY PHONE NUMBERS: In most cities you can call 997 for police, 998 for fire, and 999 for first aid.

ETIQUETTE: Hospitality seems to flow naturally from Poles, and they will often invite guests over for dinner. If a Polish family invites you over for some hearty Polish home-cooking, repay this kindness by bringing flowers to the lady of the house. And when the proper time comes, cheerfully toast the health of your hosts!

FIRST AID: Poland extends free medical care to citizens of Great Britain, but Americans and Canadians must pay for any treatment they receive. If you are ill, call the American Embassy or Consulate for advice (they have a list of recommended physicians) or ask at your hotel. We list emergency numbers in each of our city chapters.

GAS: Oil-poor Poland has been forced to ration its limited gas supplies; as a foreigner, though, you can get as much gas as you want, but you must buy gas coupons in hard currency at Orbis. Most gas stations are open from 6 a.m. to 10 p.m., and can be spotted from the road by the fair-size lines trailing out of them throughout the day. On Sunday, gas stations close at 3 p.m.

HOLIDAYS: January 1, New Year's Day; Easter Monday; May 1, Labor Day; Corpus Christi (usually in early June); July 22, Polish National Day; November 1, All Saints Day; and December 25–26, Christmas.

Special events during the year include the Highland Carnival in February in the Tatra Mountains; the National Student Song Festival in Kraków in April; the International Short Film Festival in Kraków, the International Poster Fair on even years in Warsaw, and the International Poznań Trade Fair in June; the lively Dominican Fair in Gdańsk, or the International Song Festival in Kraków in August; the International Old Music Festival in Toruń; and a jazz festival in Warsaw in October.

INFORMATION: Offices with **it** *(informacja turystyczna)* written in the window give local tourist information to foreigners.

MAIL DELIVERY: Our experience is that mail is both slow and censored. If you still want to try your luck with the Polish post, direct your mail c/o the U.S. Embassy at al. Ujazdowskie 29/31, Warsaw, Poland.

MOVIES: Most movies are shown in the original language with subtitles.

NEWSPAPERS AND MAGAZINES: Western periodicals and magazines are usually not available in Poland.

OFFICE HOURS: Offices usually open at 8 or 9 a.m. and close at 3 or 4 p.m.

PACKAGE TOURS: We recommend package tours for those who are anxious to see Poland but fearful of engaging in the occasional bureaucratic struggles of living and traveling there on their own. A tour will shield you from such problems. If you're interested in a package tour, inquire at Orbis, or look in your local newspaper "Travel" sections and in travel magazines.

If you travel on your own, though, you can see Poland on your terms, at your speed. Also, by venturing forth alone you are more likely to meet Poles. Although you do sometimes encounter small problems when traveling alone, you'll probably find it a more active, exciting way to see Poland!

PHOTOGRAPHY: Aside from military or transportation sites (for example bridges, train stations, etc.), you can click away freely in Poland.

POST OFFICES: Post offices (*poczta* in Polish) are usually open every day except Sunday from 8 a.m. to 8 p.m. You can also buy stamps at newsstands.

RECOMMENDED READING: There are a lot of good books on Poland. We recommend the following: *God's Playground: A History of Poland,* by Norman Davies, perhaps the best and most exciting history on Poland, in two volumes; and *The Polish August* by Neal Ascherson (Penguin Books, 1982), an absorbing postwar history of Poland that culminates in the rise of Solidarity. You say you don't want to read serious history books? Then try James Michener's *Poland,* a novel that chronicles Poland's history in a light, very readable drama.

REGISTRATION: If you stay in a private home and the arrangement was not made by a public bureau, Polish law requires you to register with the police within 48 hours.

SHOPPING: No other Eastern European country relies so much on hard-currency shops for quality products as does Poland. Poland's hard-currency shops, known as **Pewex** (pronounced Pev-ex), sell Western goods for dollars or other Western currencies at prices often far less than in the West. These stores carry quality cigarettes, chocolate, and alcohol. Excited Polish shoppers usually crowd the larger Pewex stores, so for smaller purchases go to the Pewex desks in the larger hotels.

Aside from the Pewex stores, Polish folk objects provide an excellent value for gift-buying splurges. Some interesting gift possibilities include embroidery, lace, dolls in folk costume, prints and engravings, amber, pottery, and woodcarvings. You'll find many of these objects in the national **Cepelia** shops.

SPORTS: Sportsmen will revel in Poland's great outdoors. Hearty voyagers can hike during the summer in the Zakopane area and in several other mountain ranges, and change their boots for skis in winter. Those who love camping and fishing should trek over to the Lake Mazurian area of northeastern Poland. If these activities pall, you can brave the waters by boat and canoe, or confront the wild outdoors and go hunting. Beach resorts on the Baltic coast offer a selection of summer sports, and across Poland you can go horseback riding on one of Poland's two million horses. For more information, inquire at Orbis; they have special pamphlets on these sports.

STORE HOURS: Grocery stores are usually open from 6 or 7 a.m. until 6 to 8 p.m.; other stores are open from 11 a.m. until 7 or 8 p.m. On Sunday stores are closed.

STUDENT TRAVEL: The Almatur offices across Poland provide students with a variety of discounts (especially for museums, and for youth hotels in summer), and they also sell the socialist IUS (International Union of Students) card which you need to get these discounts. Students with the IUS card get a 25% discount on international trains to other socialist countries. We list local Almatur offices in the city descriptions.

TELEPHONE AND TELEGRAPH: Ready for the challenge of using a Polish phone? Actually it's not all that hard—at least not for local calls. To make a local call, place a 2- or 5-złoty coin on the coin holder (some phones accept only a 2-złoty coin; others accept both 2- and 5-złoty coins), dial the number, and push the coin into the slot only after someone picks up. For local information, dial 913.

Long-distance calls within Poland are a little trickier. Uniform area codes don't exist in Poland, and Warsaw, for example, has different area codes depending on where you're calling from. Ask your hotel to help you find the area code of the city you are calling, gather up many 5-złoty coins, and then you're ready to call. To give you an idea of phone rates, a three-minute call from Warsaw to Kraków costs about 130 złoty (82¢).

Calls to North America are even more difficult. Your hotel will gladly try to place an international call for you, but at the cost of $3 to $4 a minute if the call actually goes through. You can spare your wallet a bit by attempting to call from the public post office, but you may have to wait around all day.

TIME: Poland's clock ticks seven hours ahead of Eastern Standard Time in North America.

TIPPING: Waiters should be tipped about 10% of the check. Bartenders should also get 10%. A bellhop should get a few coins, and a rest room attendant gets 5 or 10 złoty. A 10% or 15% tip will be welcomed by a taxi driver.

WHERE TO MEET THE POLES: As we've mentioned before, Poles extend a warm welcome to their visitors; they make a special fuss about Americans. A popular joke illustrates the great Polish sympathy for America: "The only difference between people in the U.S. and in Poland is that in the U.S. not everyone supports Ronald Reagan!"

Before you leave home, ask your friends if they know a Pole in Poland or even one in America (we mention American Poles because they will always refer you to one of their relatives in Poland). You'll be surprised by the great hospitality these contacts often provide. If your search for a Polish friend of a friend turns out to be fruitless, be amiable as you travel. Talk to people on trains, in restaurants, etc. Once you know one Pole, you're likely to meet many more. If you are unfortunate enough not to meet anyone during your stay, you'll be missing one of the most memorable aspects of a visit to Poland!

Chapter IV

WARSAW

1. Orientation
2. Accommodations
3. Dining
4. Nightlife
5. The Sights
6. Side Trips from Warsaw
7. The ABCs of Warsaw

THE CAPITAL OF POLAND for almost 400 years, Warsaw offers some of the country's greatest collections of art, architecture, and historical sights. But Warsaw is not only a relic of Polish history. It continues to act as the vibrant intellectual, cultural, and political center of Poland.

To any observer of Warsaw in 1945, the rebirth of the city seemed impossible. At the conclusion of World War II Warsaw was reduced to a vast field of smoldering rubble, with a few building façades standing among the ruins. But that rubble has long since been cleared away and the city rebuilt. Home to a charming Renaissance market square, two royal palaces set in lush parks, and many fine museums, Warsaw today is definitely worth including in your travel plans.

A CAPSULE HISTORY: According to legend, Warsaw (Warszawa in Polish, pronounced Var-shava) was founded when a mermaid ordered two fishermen, Wars and Zawa, to form a city. In reality its position as a bustling trade center established Warsaw as an important town in the 15th century; merchants traveling across Europe would usually come through Warsaw. In recognition of the city's growing stature, King Sigismund III moved the Polish capital from Kraków to Warsaw in 1595, and Warsaw has been at the center of Polish affairs ever since.

Soon after it became Poland's capital, Warsaw was an obvious target for invading armies, including the Swedes in the 17th century. The city was controlled by Russian czars from the 18th century until World War I. From 1919 to 1939 it again became Poland's capital.

Warsaw survived many battles and conflicts, but its darkest days came during World War II, when the brutality of the Nazis crushed the bravery of the Varsavians. From the first day of World War II on September 1, 1939, when the Nazis dropped bombs on the city, the Germans continued a policy of terror until Soviet troops entered the city in January 1945. The Poles resisted the Nazi occupation rule despite great losses and suffering. Most heroically, the remaining 40,000 Jews in the Warsaw Ghetto rose up against the Nazis in 1943 in an all but fruitless resistance. The Germans responded by exterminating the participants and razing the Ghetto to the ground. A year later in the Warsaw Uprising, 18,000 soldiers and 150,000 civilians lost their lives in 63 days of bitter fighting. After these unsuccessful attempts to overthrow the invaders, Warsaw was systematically devastated by the Nazis. Over the course of the war, 800,000 Varsavians lost their lives, and 85% of Warsaw's buildings were completely destroyed.

In the years immediately after the war, town planners gathered old prints, photographs, and plans, and they rebuilt the city to appear as it was before the war.

1. Orientation

AIRPORTS: If you are flying into Warsaw from abroad, you'll arrive at **Okęcie International Airport,** on Zwirki i Wigury Street. It's not far from the town center, and bus 175 takes you to Krakowskie Przedmieście, Warsaw's main street in the center of town. Bus 175 gives you the best airport bus value we've found anywhere in Europe. The half-hour ride will cost you 3 złoty, less than 2¢! At this price you can ride between Warsaw's airport and the center of town 350 times and still spend less than one airport fare from New York City to JFK Airport! If you want to telephone the airport for international flight information, call 46-17-31 or 46-96-63.

Domestic flights leave from a second airport at 17 Stycznia St., near the Okęcie International Airport. Bus 114 will take you to the center of Warsaw. For domestic flight information, call 46-11-43, 46-97-65, or 46-96-70.

TRAIN STATIONS AND INFORMATION: Warsaw sometimes confuses visitors with its two major train stations. **Warszawa Centralna,** the central railway station on ulica Jerozolimskie, is near the center of town, and about a 15- to 20-minute walk to the Old Town center. If you arrive here, you can follow our orientation walk (described below). The second train station is **Warszawa Gdanska.** From Warszawa Gdanska, take trams 15, 31, and 36, or buses A, 116, 122, and 132 to reach the city center.

Four different levels make up the Warszawa Centralna station: On the first, trains arrive and depart. The second has bus and taxi connections, and baggage lockers are located here. On level three, the station's largest area, you can buy tickets for that day's departures. Windows 1 to 11 are for reserved tickets to certain specific destinations; windows 12 to 16 are for reserved tickets to any destination, and so the lines are longer and move slower. Before you stand on lines 1 to 11, look at the list of destinations above the ticket window. If your destination is not listed, you're in the wrong line. We recommend that you write down your train departure time, destination, and class to show to the ticket seller. On level four of the train station you can buy tickets for up to two months in advance.

To avoid the long lines of Warsaw's train station, we strongly suggest that you purchase all tickets from the Orbis office at the corner of Królewska and Marszałkowska Streets. The tickets will cost only 5% to 10% extra; in return you'll find English-speaking personnel and shorter lines. They're open Monday through Friday from 8 a.m. to 7 p.m., on Saturday to 3 p.m.; closed Sunday. When this office is closed, you can buy train tickets in the Metropol Hotel on Marszałkowska Street (tel. 29-69-28). You can also purchase tickets in advance from the POLRES train office at al. Jerozolimskie 44.

For train information (but only in Polish), call 20-62-61/9, or 3-19-16/8 for domestic trains and 20-45-12 for international trains.

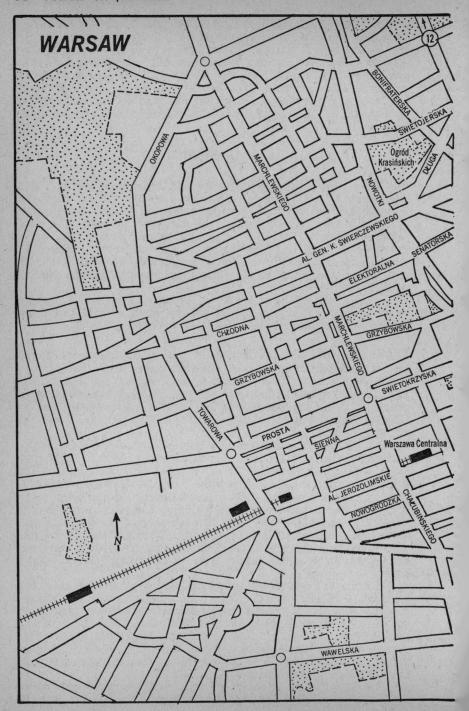

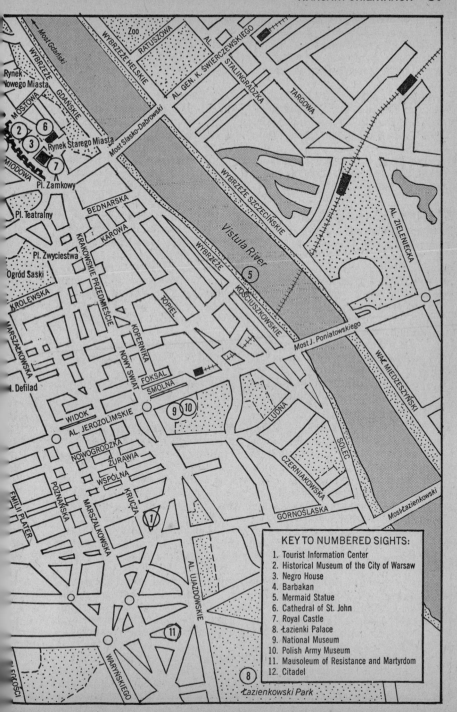

KEY TO NUMBERED SIGHTS:
1. Tourist Information Center
2. Historical Museum of the City of Warsaw
3. Negro House
4. Barbakan
5. Mermaid Statue
6. Cathedral of St. John
7. Royal Castle
8. Łazienki Palace
9. National Museum
10. Polish Army Museum
11. Mausoleum of Resistance and Martyrdom
12. Citadel

TOURIST INFORMATION: For tourist information, call 27-00-00; they should speak English. The **Tourist Information Center**, at ul. Krucza 16 (tel. 25-72-00/ 1, 28-80-51/2), should be open 24 hours for assistance. An it information desk at Castle Square (Plac Zamkowy), at the entrance to the Old Town (open 8 a.m. to 9 p.m.), can also answer your questions (tel. 25-72-01 ext. 12, or 25-72-03 after 4 p.m.).

Other places to go for information include the department of individual tourism of **Orbis**, at ul. Marszałkowska 142, across from the Ogrod Saski park (tel. 27-36-73 or 27-80-31), and the central Orbis office at ul. Bracka 16 (tel. 26-02-71). In addition, any Orbis hotel should also be able to answer any query you might have.

Finally, the **Centralny Osrodele Informacji Turystycznej** at Mazowiecka 7 publishes many English-language tourist pamphlets, and can provide you information on both Warsaw and other parts of Poland.

GETTING AROUND WARSAW: Warsaw's unbelievably inexpensive system of **buses and trams** conveniently links up the entire city. Tickets cost 3 złoty (2¢) for normal buses, but 10 złoty (6¢) for express buses (these have letters and not numbers, like bus "B"). Students and seniors pay 1 złoty 50 groszy (less than 1¢) for normal buses and 5 złoty (3¢) for express buses. You can buy tickets at newsstands (you'll see a sign *ruch* on them). If you can't find an open ruch, ask someone at the bus stop to sell you a ticket. Often, they'll give you a ticket and refuse payment. If you are caught on a bus or train without a ticket, you'll be fined 600 złoty ($3.35). When you get on the bus, cancel your ticket by putting it in the slot and pushing downward on the knob.

Taxis in Warsaw, as elsewhere in Poland, are inexpensive. A ride from the train station to the Old Town costs 150 złoty (95¢) to 200 złoty ($1.25). For a radio taxi, dial 919.

You can **rent cars** from Orbis at ulica Parkingowa, behind the Forum Hotel (tel. 21-13-60), or at the international airport.

FINDING YOUR WAY AROUND WARSAW: Although Warsaw is a large city, it's not very difficult to find your way around, and many of the city's sights are within a compact area. You will begin learning most of Warsaw's major streets if you walk from the main train station to the Old Town.

From the train station, walk down **aleja Jerozolimskie,** a wide avenue lined with stores. As you start your walk, you pass the huge Palace of Culture (Warsaw's tallest and, according to locals, ugliest building, a gift of "friendship" from the Soviet Union after World War II). Continuing on aleja Jerozolimskie, you soon pass the tall Forum Hotel on the right side of this noisy, busy street, and Warsaw's major department store, Centrum, on the left side. This intersection forms a major public transportation hub, and we'll refer to it later in this chapter.

Three blocks farther along, aleja Jerozolimskie intersects with Warsaw's principal street, the **Royal Way,** named for the elegant houses that once graced the avenue. At this point, the Royal Way goes by the name of **Nowy Świat** (pronounced Novi Svi-at). Turn left onto this main pedestrian and shopping avenue. Soon the street's name changes to **Krakowskie Przedmieście** (pronounced Kracov-ski-eh Pred-me-scheh). After about 15 minutes, the street ends and you arrive at the **Old Town,** Warsaw's historic center. Walking straight one block and then left for a few minutes, you reach the nucleus of the Old Town, the charming **Marketplace,** where Poles have traded and shopped for hundreds of years. If you've successfully navigated the way here, you have at least a nodding acquaintance with Warsaw's major streets, and you're on your way to knowing your way around!

The Wisła River flows to the northeast side of the Old Town. Across the Wisła you'll find the Praga district. It was the least damaged area of Warsaw during World War II, and is largely a residential area today.

2. Accommodations

Finding a good budget hotel in Warsaw will provide you with the first challenge of your visit. To start your search, you can either call the hotels listed here, or you can go to the sometimes (and only sometimes) helpful visitors' bureau in the **Orbis** Grand Hotel. During July and August, students and adventurous travelers under 35 can rent an inexpensive room in a student hotel; **Almatur** offices listed in this chapter will give you more details. Finally, you can avoid all the difficulties of finding a hotel by going directly to Warsaw's private room-finding service. Details for all these options follow.

HOTELS: The central reception office for foreign tourists at the Orbis Grand Hotel, ul. Krucza 16 (tel. 29-50-51), can help you find a hotel room, but often they won't send you to the cheapest hotels. Either try to scout out hotels on your own, or ask them to call the cheaper hotels listed here. You'll reach this office in about 10 or 15 minutes from the train station by walking down aleja Jerozolimskie for six blocks and then turning right at ulica Krucza. They can also provide you with tourist information on Warsaw.

Hotels in the Center

The **Dom Chłopa** (pronounced Dome Hope-a, which means "House of Peasants"), Plac Powstańców, Warszany 2 (tel. 27-92-51; Telex 816701), is—you guessed it—where many Polish peasants stay. But don't worry, you won't see anyone carrying bags of potatoes through the lobby. In fact, should you stay here you'll have found one of Warsaw's best deals. Small clean singles with a sink cost 2,810 złoty ($17.75), and doubles with private bathrooms cost 4,500 złoty ($28.30). It has a nice location as well, two blocks from Nowy Świat and about a 15-minute walk to the Old Market Square.

You can do no better in Warsaw than to stay at the **Pensjonat Zgoda,** at ul. Szpitalna 1 (tel. 26-80-31). This little-known place offers only six rooms, but at an incredible value. A simple, clean single room with private bathroom will cost you only 2,000 złoty ($12.60)! The pensjonat is located in the small office building in the center of town that also houses the Eastern European bureau of *Time* magazine.

If a relaxed atmosphere is what you're looking for, then stay at the **Hotel Saski,** Plac Feliska Dzierżyńskiego 1 (tel. 20-46-11/5 or 20-27-46). As you awaken early in the morning, the quiet of the hotel is punctuated by birds singing in the courtyard; as you open your windows, light floods the room. Singles cost 2,340 złoty ($14.75) to 3,170 złoty ($20) without a bathroom, and 2,890 złoty ($18.25) to 3,720 złoty ($23.50) with bath but no toilet. Doubles without bath range from 3,580 złoty ($22.50) to 4,130 złoty ($26). The public toilets are fairly clean; showers cost 40 złoty (25¢) extra. You can't do better on location either. The hotel is just five minutes from the opera, and a ten-minute walk from the Old Town Square. To get to the Saski, take any tram from in front of the large Centrum department store three stops in the direction of the Old Town.

As you first approach the **Hotel MDM,** Plac Konstytucji 1 (tel. 21-62-11 or 81-48-71), you might worry that you've chosen a rundown hotel at a noisy traffic intersection. Once you get inside, however, you'll find comfortable rooms, many facing a quiet courtyard. From the hotel you can walk to aleja Ujazdowskie, an extension of Warsaw's main shopping street Krakowskie Przedmieście, in just five minutes. The trams in front of the hotel conveniently link you up with the Old Town. Singles cost 3,510 złoty ($22) with sink only, 4,260 złoty ($27) with toilet and no shower, and 4,640 złoty ($29.25) with complete bathroom. Doubles with bathroom cost 6,390 złoty ($40.25).

The oppressive, tall Stalinist exterior of the **Warszawa Hotel,** Plac Powstańców Warszawy 9 (tel. 26-94-21; Telex 269421), may not appear to be Warsaw's most graceful building façade, but if you stay here you'll be right smack in the middle of town, just two blocks from Nowy Świat, Warsaw's main shopping street, and a ten-minute walk from the Old Town. The 190 small rooms here cost 4,100 złoty ($25.75) for singles with bathroom, and 5,700 złoty ($35.85) for doubles with bathroom. Try to get a room facing the courtyard; it will be much quieter.

The Polish teachers' union operates a hotel called the **ZNP** (House of Teachers), Wybrzeże Kościuszkowskie 31/33 (tel. 27-92-11/3). The hotel is supposed to accept only teachers as guests, but exceptions have been made. If you wish to try your luck here (and it's an outside chance), singles will cost only 1,730 złoty ($10.90) without bathroom and 2,490 złoty ($15.65) with private bathroom; doubles cost 2,450 złoty ($15.40) without bathroom and 3,110 złoty ($19.50) with.

One of Warsaw's best-known budget hotels is the **PTTK Dom Turysty, ul.** Krakowskie Przedmieście 4/6 (tel. 26-30-11 or 26-26-25), but we feel obliged to put you on your guard unless you are an Indiana Jones ready-for-adventure traveler. Although the rooms are tolerable, the state of the public bathrooms could cause consternation among the more faint-hearted. Singles cost 2,300 złoty ($14.50), or 2,700 złoty ($17) with a bath only. Doubles cost 1,600 złoty ($10) per person, or 1,900 złoty ($12) with a bath only.

Hotels Slightly Outside the Center

Despite the dreary-sounding name of the **Hotel Druh,** ul. Niemcewicza 17 (tel. 22-19-13 or 22-48-68/9), you will be hard-pressed to find a better budget buy in all of Warsaw. The clean rooms and adequate public bathrooms attract a large student crowd. Doubles with bathroom cost 1,385 złoty ($8.75) per person, and triples without bathroom cost 688 złoty ($4.35) per person. You'll need to use public transportation to get here, since the hotel is located outside the town center. Take tram 7, 8, 9, or 25 three stops from the train station.

The **Syrena Hotel,** ul. Syreny 23 (tel. 26-32-41 or 32-12-57), named after the mermaid that symbolizes Warsaw, is a standard hotel in the Wola district, a worker's residential area. The standard rooms are quiet and of medium size. Singles without private bathroom cost 2,340 złoty ($14.75); doubles cost 3,580 złoty ($22.50) without a bathroom and 4,410 złoty ($27.75) with a private bathroom. A shower costs 50 złoty (30¢) extra. Bus 109 from the train station stops here.

Nowa Praga, Bertolda Brechta 7 (tel. 19-82-35 or 19-50-01), a 15- to 20-minute bus ride from the center, offers sunny budget rooms equipped with telephone and radio. Singles cost 2,710 złoty ($17) without bathroom and 3,680 złoty ($23.15) with bathroom; doubles cost 4,150 złoty ($26.10) without toilet and 5,120 złoty ($32.25) with. Take bus D from Krakowskie Przedmieście or from the central train station bus stop on ulica Marchlewskiego, the street farthest from the tall Palace of Culture.

PRIVATE ROOMS: Looking for other budget ways to stay in Warsaw? We highly recommend private rooms. You won't find a better value for your money! You can rent a basic, though centrally located, room at the **Syrena Private Ac-**

commodations Bureau, Krucza 17 (tel. 28-75-40)—not the Syrena office across the street (make sure the number is 17). Singles cost 1,750 złoty ($11) a night, and doubles cost 2,710 złoty ($17). The bureau is open from 8 a.m. to 8 p.m. seven days a week.

If you're planning on staying in Warsaw for more than a week, why not rent a small apartment? You can get details on short-term rentals from **PUMA,** ul. Świętokrzyska 36 (tel. 20-99-41 or 20-99-62).

STUDENT ACCOMMODATIONS: As we've mentioned before, students can stay at inexpensive student hotels with two to four beds per room during July and August. For information on all student hotels in Poland, go to **Almatur** on Kopernika 15 (tel. 26-23-56). Here you can buy tourist vouchers (for $7 if you have the ISIC or IUS card, or $10 if you don't have either card but are under 35 years old) to pay for one night in most university dormitories across Poland. Don't be worried about buying one or two vouchers too many; unused vouchers *can* be refunded. If you buy nine vouchers, you get one extra free. This office will provide a list of the summer's youth hotels across Poland—which is crucial, since they change every year. If you don't have vouchers you can stay in these hotels anyway, but it will cost about $13. Reservations for student hotels across Poland aren't needed if you arrive before 2 p.m. If all this sounds slightly confusing (as things of this nature often are in Poland), ask to see Maria Kiminska, a very helpful staffer who speaks English well.

Starvation-budget student travelers can also stay at the very basic **youth hostel** at ul. Smolna 30 (tel. 27-89-52), near the Polish national museum. From the central train station take any tram three stops in the direction of the Forum Hotel. Bring your International Youth Hostel card. Rooms cost 140 złoty (just 88¢!) the first night, and then 120 złoty (75¢) from then on. You get what you pay for, though. Public toilets are rather ugly with no seats, and 15 beds crowd each room. You can't stay between 10 a.m. and 5 p.m., and you must return by 10 in the evening. Similar arrangements exist at ul. Karolkowa 53A (tel. 32-88-29). Take tram number 1 or 24 from the train station.

3. Dining

TOP CHOICES: Our favorite restaurant in all of Warsaw is the **Canaletto,** in the Hotel Victoria Intercontinental, Królewska 11 (tel. 27-80-11). At the Canaletto you dine in elegance, to the accompaniment of piano and harp music, and are served by skilled waiters in bow tie, working at a Western pace! The excellent specialties are in a class by themselves. Just picture the choices: roasted snails in garlic butter at 290 złoty ($1.80); delicious baked mushrooms with bread; a surprisingly light and tender pork cutlet Warsaw in a flavorful mushroom sauce; wild boar; smoked, fried, or baked fish; and a wide variety of other dishes for $2 to $6. Don't ignore your sweet tooth either; for dessert you can savor a rich ice cream or crêpe delight. Your wallet won't suffer too much, but you'll find a full meal somewhat splurgey. If you don't want to break the bank, however, avoid wine and alcohol, the most expensive items on the menu. Year after year, we have dined well, and so we recommend the Canaletto highly. Reserve; open 1 p.m. to midnight. (The attractive tavern-style Hetmanska restaurant next door in the hotel may catch your eye as you walk by, but you'll find service much slower and less professional at the same prices, so we prefer the Canaletto for our money.)

Although it's not as swank as the Canaletto, you can hardly find a better second than **Bazyliszek-Hortex** (pronounced Baz-ill-eash-ek), Rynek Starego Miasta 7/9 (tel. 31-18-41). In fact, many locals assert that the Canaletto has met its match in Bazyliszek! You'll enjoy the attractive decor, which includes rich paintings and decorations on the walls, and the smartly dressed clientele. Glamorous Warsaw waitresses add to the appealing ambience. Excellent specialties include smoked eel with garnish for 797 złoty ($5), wild boar, and various meat dishes. Entrees range in price from 504 złoty ($3.15) to 908 złoty ($5.70); a good selection of wine and stronger drink is also offered. Open noon to midnight; reservations are a must, as this is a very popular place, and we also recommend it highly.

You'll find another good hotel restaurant with unexceptional decor but excellent food and efficient service in the **Restaurant Maryla,** inside the Hotel Forum, ul. Nowogrodzka 24/26 (tel. 28-03-64). You can choose from a wide selection of Polish specialties, including wild boar with potatoes and pickled mushrooms for 480 złoty ($3), half a roast pheasant with potatoes and cranberries for 700 złoty ($4.40), and roasted pig and mixed salad for 750 złoty ($4.70). Open 7 a.m. to 10 p.m. Try to reserve; the maître d' seems to take a perverse delight in making you wait even if there are free tables, should you not have a reservation.

LOCAL FAVORITES: If you're looking for something more casual, try **Pod Krokodyl,** Rynek Starego Miasta 19, an intimate restaurant with brick walls and low ceilings. Despite the decor, lively crowds of Poles often celebrate here. During our visit, a group of Poles stood up and sang "Što Lat" in commemoration of someone's name day (the birthday of a saint with your name). You'll have to struggle with a Polish language menu, but it includes such tasty dishes as roast chicken and apple (kurcze pieczone i jablko pieczone) for 238 złoty ($1.50). Music plays during the evening—for which you must pay a 300-złoty ($1.90) entrance fee per person. Open 1 p.m. to 3 a.m.

At the end of ulica Szeroki Dunaj (no. 9/11) in the old city is the restaurant **Rycerska.** Old weapons adorn the walls, and a large boar's head grimaces over the dining room entrance. A suit of armor stands guard in the hall, and after an extended game of charades with the proprietor, we managed to determine that the armor was over 350 years old. The fare is hearty Polish home-style cooking. Pork is the common entree with an occasional lamb dish making an appearance, and there are interesting soups too. For restricted diets there's a vegetarian menu (Oblady Lekkostrawne) for no more than 200 złoty ($1.25). The waiters here will test your powers of communication as they speak only Polish. Open from 10 a.m. to 10 p.m.

The **Gdanska Restauracja Pod Rytmanem,** at ul. Bednarska 9 (tel. 26-87-58), is better appointed than the average Warsaw restaurant. The interior is slightly nautical with pictures of the old city of Gdańsk-Danzig on the walls. Upon entering the Gdanska you encounter the city's coat-of-arms and a largish restaurant with about 150 seats in a sectioned hall. The appetizer specialties are several types of smoked fish for around 40 złoty (25¢), and chlodnik z jajkien, a cold cucumber-and-egg soup. In the summer there is also rubarbarowa z nakar, a delicious rhubarb compote with noodles. Main dishes range from about 200 złoty ($1.25) to 300 złoty ($1.90); try the mintaj Gdanska, fish cooked with black currant juice, wine, and spices. The most popular specialty of the house is not a food but a drink: napej rajeow Gdanski, loosely translated as the drink of the Deputies of Gdańsk. It's a wine drink with black currant juice, plums, sugar, and assorted spices at 79 złoty (50¢) a glass. They don't speak much English here, but after a few Gdanskis it really won't matter. Open from 11 a.m. to 10 p.m.; closed Sunday.

AT WILANÓW: Outside the Wilanów Palace you'll find the appealing **Wilanów Restaurant** (tel. 42-18-52). Modern, polished hexagonal wood tables are offset by the antlers and animal pelts that adorn the walls. Red-jacketed waiters provide reasonably quick service in one of the more expensive restaurants in Warsaw. Your meal will get off to a rousing start with 30 grams of the finest black caviar at 1,900 złoty ($12). You're sure to enjoy the schab pieczony, roast pork with plums, reputedly the favorite dish of John III Sobieski, one of the early residents of Wilanow. Most main dishes cost 500 złoty ($3.15) to 800 złoty ($5). The bar does carry some Western liquors for those yearning for a taste of home. The restaurant opens at 1 p.m. and shuts down a bit before 11 p.m., every day. It's always best to call first to reserve.

Another choice near Wilanów is the **Kuznia** (blacksmith) **Restaurant** (tel. 42-31-72), just a short walk (50 yards) north of the palace. A large brick fireplace is usually kindled in the winter as well as on cold, wet summer days. Bunches of herbs, onions, and old smithy tools adorn the walls. The very international clientele relaxes in well-constructed wooden furniture. The cost of a main dish runs from about 300 złoty ($1.90) to 450 złoty ($2.85). Try the farm turkey or pork à la Marysienka, and end the meal with pears in chocolate sauce or peaches in mulled wine.

ETHNIC (FOREIGN) CHOICES: For those who wish to try something other than Polish cuisine while in Warsaw, the **Szanghaj**, ul. Marszałkowska 55 (tel. 28-70-27), is an obvious possibility. Open from noon to midnight, this two-story establishment has a bar on the first floor, and the restaurant is upstairs. At first glance there is a decidedly Oriental character to the interior. But with a second look those seemingly "Chinese" wall patterns are really traditional Polish floral motifs cunningly Orientalized; even the roosters have an Eastern cast about them. Fresh flowers adorn the windows and tables; woodwork and cane walls complete the picture. Some English is spoken here. Deciphering the menu is very simple: bambusuwa, consum à la Szanghaj, and Seczuanskim ryz translate as bamboo soup, Shanghai consommé, and Szechuan rice, in that order. Pork and lamb dishes are about 350 złoty ($2.20); chicken runs about 50 złoty (30¢) more than pork and fish dishes: 400 złoty ($2.50) to 600 złoty ($3.75). Whether the coffee à la Szanghaj, with sherry and milk, was ever served in a Shanghai coffee den is debatable, but in Warsaw it does take the chill off a wet evening. A band plays Polish music most nights but there's no dancing.

The **Cristal Budapest,** at ul. Marszałkowska 21 (tel. 25-34-33), just down the street from the Szanghaj, is open from 1 p.m. to 2 a.m. High-backed wooden chairs and long wooden tables are the hallmarks of this Polish restaurant, which has two large rooms off a central foyer. A large bar takes up most of one wall and in the room to the right a five-piece band plays Polish favorites as well as requests. Weavings and pottery adorn the walls. If you order the delicious goulash or any other soup, it is brought to the table in a huge steaming cauldron. Main entrees give you a fine taste of hearty Hungarian fare, and for this reason we strongly recommend the Cristal Budapest as an exciting alternative to Polish cuisine. Almost no English is spoken here. The average main-dish price is about 350 złoty ($2.20) to 400 złoty ($2.50).

The **Habana**, at Piękna 28 (tel. 21-37-16), features Cuban music, food, and atmosphere. The decor is highlighted by wicker ceiling lamps and modern art. The atmosphere does have a Cuban feel about it, although as far as we could tell, no one speaks any Spanish. The fare leans heavily on pork: one tasty version is schab "Havana Special" for 475 złoty ($3), a pork steak in a delicious piquant sauce. Much of the other fare is standard Polish cuisine; the well-prepared kuroza duszone po kuransku at 154 złoty ($1), however, stands out as an offering not usually found in the Polish kitchen. It's a chicken dish both light and very spicy by Polish standards that makes an excellent lunch. The cocktail bar under the restaurant is open from 5 p.m. and serves a variety of liquors, including Cuban vodkas and a good selection of fine Hungarian wines. A Cuban-style band plays every evening, sometimes with a cover of 300 złoty ($1.85) to 475 złoty ($3). Although the band is definitely not from Cuba, they do manage to get a pretty good beat rolling. The Habana is open from 10 a.m. till 2 a.m., with dancing from 5 p.m.

FOR AN EVENING OUT: Night owls will especially enjoy **Semafor, ul.** Wysockiego 10 (tel. 11-68-44): it offers a romantic setting with dim lighting and lots of plants, and it remains open until 1:30 or 2 a.m. (except Wednesday when it closes at 8 p.m.), a genuine rarity in Warsaw! During the evening a loud band plays (which costs you a steep 550 złoty, or $3.50), and as the hours grow late, the restaurant becomes an active nightspot (at least by Polish standards). The eel appetizer for 313 złoty ($2) is a specialty. Unfortunately the restaurant often offers more good cheer than food, due to problems in supply. Prices run fairly high by Polish standards, but it's worthwhile if you want to enjoy a typical Polish evening out. Reserve for Friday or Saturday night.

STUDENT RESTAURANTS: Warsaw's students are often conversant in a foreign language, and thus student hangouts are a good place to meet locals if you have absolutely no command of Polish. Students in socialist countries (and the world over) are eager to meet and talk to foreigners, especially Westerners. In Poland, Americans receive the warmest of receptions.

At ul. Krakowskie Przedmieście 8 you'll find the restaurant **Staropolska,** a favorite of students. The scholarly types at the University of Warsaw also hang out next door at the milk bar **Uniwersytecki.** Both are open from 7 a.m. to 8 p.m.; closed Sunday. Just south of the milk bar off ulica Krakowskie Przedmieście on ulica Oboźna is the PTTK (Polish Tourist Society Hotel), host to the **Café Harenda,** where you can meet Polish students as well as visiting students from other socialist countries. The café is open from 11 a.m. to 10:30 p.m., with dancing most nights from 6 p.m. to closing.

Warsaw does have a few establishments that cater to the Polish equivalent of young upwardly mobile types; one we liked near the Barbakan at ul. Freta 18 is called **Hacjenda.** It's lit with brass lamps and the atmosphere is private and subdued, sort of an upscale local bar. The specialties are pizza and some other fast foods. The pizza is served in single-serving sizes (about six inches) and there are three varieties: serem (cheese) pizza at 269 złoty ($1.70), kielbasa (sausage) pizza at 325 złoty ($2), and lozosiem (salmon) pizza for 321 złoty ($2). Although not up to Italian or Chicago pizza standards, both make a decent late lunch. The bar owner has his own reel-to-reel tape machine and a reasonable selection of Western pop and rock hits. Hacjenda is open from 1 p.m. to 1 a.m.

BUDGET BETS: You'll find a simple restaurant with a few dozen tables and excellent budget value in **Kamienne Schodki** ("The Stone Stairs"), at 25 Rynek Starego Miasta. You can only order one specialty here—a basic but flavorful roast duck with apple and vegetables, for a bargain 588 złoty ($3.70). (When is the last time you had a good roast duck dinner in North America for anywhere near that price?) A jukebox plays Italian and American songs. Open from 9 a.m. to 10 p.m.

For the ultimate in bargain eating, try the **Bar Mleczny,** near the Barbakan. The food is not gourmet—primarily noodles, chicken, potatoes, and soups— and all very inexpensive. Absolutely no English is spoken and the food is served quickly by several stern-looking women. Given the rush at lunchtime, it's best to have your order written out or memorized. Popular house specialties include jajecznica ze szczypiorkiem, a very tasty egg soup, for 31.50 złoty (20¢); marka-rod z huszczem, chicken with noodles, at 24 złoty (15¢); and kasza gryczana z pieczarkami, noodles and mushrooms. Hot and filling, the food here provides the best ballast for the buck we found, and combined with the central location, it's the best budget eatery in Warsaw. Unfortunately these same qualities have attracted most of the budget-conscious populace of the city. At the milk bar you'll find workers rubbing elbows with students, mothers with five children sharing a table with some recruits home on leave—in short, the bulk of Warsaw. Bar Mleczny is open Monday through Saturday from 7 a.m. till 8 p.m., on Sunday from 9 a.m. to 5 p.m.

SPECIALTY CLUBS: For traditional Russian specialties such as shashlik (grilled lamb) for 309 złoty ($1.95), and several caviar dishes, try the **House of Soviet Culture** at Foksal 10 (downstairs from the Soviet Cultural Community Center). Tall carved and painted chairs, crude wooden tables, and cheerful Soviet guests create a pleasant Russian folk atmosphere.

Also on Foksal (which is off Nowy Świat), you'll find the **Journalist's Club** at Foksal 3/5, and the **Architect's Club** at Foksal 24, both of which are specialty clubs that serve food. They usually let foreigners in, although they officially cater to Poles only.

FOR DESSERT: Those with a sweet tooth will want to visit **Borut,** on ulica Freta (a street just north of the Old Town), a restaurant and bar, but above all an ice cream parlor. Boruta is a Polish national demon (yes, they have attempted to nationalize just about everything in Poland) and the ice cream, reputed to be the best in Warsaw, will tempt you. Unfortunately, a potential patron risks not only the sin of gluttony, but of taking the Lord's name in vain (and several others) as the line tests the mettle of even the sternest consumer. The bright side of the whole affair is that you'll sweat off all the calories that you're about to put on. It's open Monday through Saturday from 10 a.m. to 6 p.m., though they may close earlier due to a lack of ice cream.

A more reserved and dignified establishment is **Nowy Świat,** at the corner of Swielokrzyska at Nowy Świat 17. The interior of the café consists of one large room with columns along one wall; in the back, a grand piano presides over the dignified clientele who quietly sip coffee and mixed drinks, and eat pastries and ice cream. The café's homemade ice cream is seasonal: in the summer, fruit flavors, and in the winter, chocolate and vanilla are the staples. In the pastry department, don't miss the krem sultanski, a crème pastry, always tops at the Nowy Świat.

4. Nightlife

Those who envision a Western- or American-style nightlife will be disappointed in Warsaw. Private parties are sometimes thrown in Warsaw with lots of drinking and revelry, but alas, you cannot enjoy this popular form of nightlife unless you know some locals. So why not spend the evening as the Poles do? Linger several hours over dinner with much drinking and talking. As you can see, the pleasure of nightlife for Poles comes from being with friends, not from the atmosphere.

BARS AND CAFÉS: Many Vasavians also spend their evenings in one of the city's hundreds of cafés or milk bars. In these establishments you can enjoy snacks as well as beer and wine; you might also meet some locals while you're there. Two of our favorites are **Pod Herbami**, at ul. Piwna 21/23, near the Old Town Square, a small though lively beer hall in the evening, and **Winiarna Fuk-**

ier, 27 Rynek Starego Miasta (the Old Town Square), a famous 300-year-old wine cellar that is very popular among students.

CLUBS AND DISCOS: For those who insist on a more active nightlife, here are some recommended clubs and discos.

Hybrydy, Kniewskiego 7/9, is a much-frequented student club and disco. You'll find it behind the Centrum department store.

One of Warsaw's most popular student clubs, **Park,** at al. Niepodległości 196, is located inside a small park. The club stays open on Friday and Saturday from 11 p.m. until 3 a.m., and from 6 to 10 p.m. on Sunday. Students pay 50 złoty (30¢); others pay 350 złoty ($2.20). To get here, take one of the trams and buses in front of the central train station on Tytusa Chałubińskiego Street.

Jazz and modern music fans will enjoy the **Akwrium,** ul. Emilii Plater 49, Warsaw's only jazz hangout.

Black Cat, on the lower level of the Hotel Victoria Intercontinental, Królewska 11, is open from 10 p.m. to 4 a.m. and plays low-key romantic music to a 30-and-over crowd.

5. The Sights

Begin your sightseeing in Warsaw by strolling around the charming **Old Market Square** (Rynek Starego Miasta) and the few blocks surrounding it. As mentioned before, this entire Old Town area was completely destroyed in the Warsaw uprising during World War II, but thanks to an outstanding reconstruction job, the Old Market Square once again looks as it did in the 17th and 18th centuries, when it bustled with traders and merchants. Be sure to make a stop or two at one of the square's good restaurants and bars, as well as the fascinating **Museum of the City of Warsaw** (see our restaurant and museum descriptions elsewhere in this chapter). Next to the Museum of the City of Warsaw, at the **Negro House,** 36 Rynek Starego Miasta, you'll see a statue of a black slave; the original owner of this building was a dealer in slaves.

If you leave the square by Nowomiejska Street (the street along the Warsaw Historical Museum), you come upon the **Barbakan,** Warsaw's fortified town walls, first built in the 16th century. On the right side of the walls, you'll notice the **statue of a mermaid,** the symbol of Warsaw.

If you walk in the other direction toward Krakowskie Przedmieście from the Old Market Square you'll pass the **Cathedral of St. John** to your left, one of Warsaw's oldest churches. First built in the 13th and 14th centuries, the church was badly damaged in 1944 and rebuilt in 1956. Many of Poland's great events have taken place here, including the coronation of Poland's last king and the proclamation of the country's first constitution in 1791.

One block farther along you reach a large open square, Plac Zamkowy. On this square stands the **Royal Castle,** where the king of Poland made his home, and where the Polish Parliament discussed issues of life and death from 1596 until the end of the 18th century. Sadly, this building lost some of its royal splendor when it was rebuilt in 1971.

Warsaw's **Royal Way** begins at Plac Zamkowy. This noble name commemorates the many royal residences, manors of the nobility, and other important houses that stood here during the Polish monarchy. Today shoppers and strollers still parade up and down the avenue to check out the latest goods in the stores and faces in the street. As if one name isn't enough to remember, the Royal Way's name changes several times as you move farther away from the Old Town. It begins as Krakowskie Przedmieście, then Nowy Świat, and then it's aleja Ujazdowskie.

If you follow the Royal Way away from the center of town, you'll eventually arrive at two of Warsaw's most interesting sights. The first is **Łazienki Park,** on aleja Ujazdowskie, which many consider to be Poland's most beautiful palace and park complex. Poland's last king, Stanisłaus Poniatowski, built up this romantic park in the second half of the 18th century. The royal grounds consist of several ornate buildings and palaces, including the Orangery, which houses a sculpture garden, and the White Cottage (where the king's family lived during the summer) and the neoclassical Palace on the Lake (where the king himself lived). Chopin concerts are held on summer Sundays at noon and at 5 p.m. at Łazienki Park's monument to the great composer. The palace is open from 10:30 a.m. to 3:10 p.m. every day except Monday. You can take almost any bus leaving from the Old Town on Krakowskie Przedmieście and Nowy Świat.

You'll find the beautiful, baroque **Wilanów Palace** a fair distance farther down the road on ulica Wiertnicza. The legendary Polish King John III Sobieski (who is famous for helping the West finally defeat the Turks at the gates of Vienna in 1683) built Wilanów, and used the palace as his summer residence in the late 17th century. The equally famous King August the Strong next resided here in the 18th century. The palace and park grounds are still impressive today, with the rich baroque details typical of palaces built during the time of Louis XIV. Although the Nazis plundered the estate in World War II, its great splendor and rich art have been completely restored. Distinguished foreign guests are still accommodated in one of the wings of the palace, but the rest of the building is open as a museum. The interior is open from 10 a.m. to 2:40 p.m., except Tuesday, Thursday, days following public holidays, and the first Sunday of every month. Take bus B from the Forum Hotel, or bus 193 on Nowy Świat to the last stop; the palace is 300 yards down the road from here.

Next to the Wilanów Palace is the **Poster Museum,** open Tuesday to Sunday from 10 a.m. to 4 p.m. On the other side are two good restaurants (see our restaurant descriptions).

MUSEUMS: Be sure to visit the **Historical Museum of the City of Warsaw,** on the Old Market Square at Rynek Starego Miasta 20 (tel. 31-02-51). This museum shows an incredible movie that depicts Warsaw's utter destruction in 1945 and the extensive restorations that were made in the postwar years. The film plays in several languages a day, but you should see it regardless of language, for the images are really outstanding. The museum is open Tuesday and Thursday from 12:30 a.m. to 7 p.m., on Wednesday, Friday, and Saturday from 10 a.m. to 3:30 p.m., and on Sunday from 11 a.m. to 4:30 p.m.; closed Monday.

The **National Museum,** al. Jerozolimskie 3, houses the Polish national art collection, with displays of everything from ancient Egyptian, Greek, and Roman art to modern Polish art. It's open on Tuesday from 10 a.m. to 8 p.m., on Wednesday, Friday, and Saturday from 10 a.m. to 4 p.m., on Thursday from noon to 6 p.m., and on Sunday from 10 a.m. to 5 p.m.; closed on Monday and the day after a public holiday.

If you step next door, you'll find the **Polish Army Museum,** which displays a fascinating collection of weaponry from medieval times until the Second World War. History buffs will especially enjoy the extensive World War II collection. Open Monday, Thursday, and Saturday from noon to 5 p.m., on Wednesday from 1 to 7 p.m., on Friday from 10 a.m. to 5 p.m., and on Sunday and public holidays from 10:30 a.m. to 5 p.m.; closed Tuesday and days after public holidays.

Many museums in Warsaw detail the horrors of World War II. These include the **Jewish History Institute,** al. Świerczewskiego 79, which documents the plight of the Jews in Poland during World War II. It's open daily from 9 a.m. to 1 p.m.; closed Sunday and holidays. The **Mausoleum of Resistance and Martyr-**

dom, al. I Armii Wojska Polskiego 25, was the former Gestapo headquarters during the war. Today documents display the brutality of the Nazis during the occupation of Poland. Hours are Tuesday, Wednesday, Friday, and Saturday from 9 a.m. to 3 p.m., on Thursday to 4 p.m., and on Sunday and public holidays from 10 a.m. to 4 p.m.; closed Monday and the days following a public holiday.

We also recommend that you visit the town **Citadel** in the Żoliborz district (down the riverbank from the Old Town), an impressive sight often overlooked because it receives little publicity, perhaps due to its anti-Russian implications. The Russians built the Citadel Fortress in 1832–1834 to demonstrate their great power over their new territory. Inside, the Russians maintained a prison and rooms of torture and execution. Today you can visit these halls and also see some fascinating paintings by Alexander Sochaczewski, a Polish artist who was interned in Siberia for 22 years. His paintings depict the horrors of gulag internment with a very anti-Russian tone to them. Open most days from 10 a.m. to 4 p.m., on Wednesday to 6 p.m., and on Saturday from 9 a.m. to 3 p.m.; on Monday and the day after a public holiday, the museum is closed. Take bus 118 or 185 from the street on the riverbank, Wybrzeże Gdańskie.

On a more upbeat note, the **Chopin Museum,** in the Ostrogski Palace at ul. Okólnik 1, celebrates the life of the great Polish composer with displays of his personal belongings. It's open from 10 a.m. to 2 p.m.; closed Sunday and holidays.

MORE SIGHTS: You'll find another interesting sight in the **Warsaw Nike,** across from the Grand Theater on Plac Teatralny. This huge 1964 statue of a woman, with both hands raised up holding a sword that points downward behind her back, pays tribute to the heroes of Warsaw during World War II. During the early 1980s many demonstrations in support of Solidarity were held on the square in front of this monument.

The outspoken priest Jerzy Popiełuszko gave his weekly Sunday sermons at **S.W. Stanislavska Kostki** on Jana Kozietulskiego. Today he lies buried on the church grounds following his clumsy and brutal murder by the Polish secret police in 1984. You won't be the only one visiting the church; many Poles visiting Warsaw come here to pay tribute to this modern-day martyr. Symbols of the labor union Solidarity continue to flourish here, perhaps the only place you'll still find them publicly displayed. The current pastor discusses the role of religion and nationalism in Poland on the last Sunday of each month at 7 p.m. in a very popular "national" mass. Take bus A, J, 116, 132, or 157 or tram 6, 15, 31, or 36. Get off at Plac Komuny Paryskiej and then ask for directions (it's only two blocks away from there).

Finally, for an impressive aerial view of all of Warsaw, go to the top of the **Palace of Culture,** Warsaw's tallest building, on Plac Defilad.

6. Side Trips from Warsaw

Those interested in Polish folk art should visit **Łowicz,** a center of regional folk tradition 50 miles west of Warsaw. In addition to a charming small town, there's a worthwhile ethnographic museum of folk costumes and other objects. The best time to visit Łowicz is on the holiday of Corpus Christi (which is held ten days after Pentecost) when the townspeople wear original folk costumes and put on an elaborate pageant. Inquire at your hotel or Orbis for bus or train connection information from Warsaw.

Fans of Frederic Chopin may be interested in visiting the great composer's birthplace at **Żelazowa Wola,** 32 miles west of Warsaw. A museum in town documents the life of Żelazowa Wola's most famous son with a collection of Chopin mementos. Each Sunday from May to October noted musicians give concerts at 11 a.m. and 3 p.m. You can only reach Żelazowa Wola by bus or car from Warsaw. Orbis also sponsors half-day trips with an English-speaking guide for 1,110 złoty ($6.90).

7. The ABCs of Warsaw

AIRLINE OFFICES: Lufthansa, Pan Am, and LOT all maintain offices in the Hotel Victoria Intercontinental, at ul. Królewska 11. **Lufthansa** (tel. 27-54-36) is open from 9 a.m. to 5 p.m. Monday to Friday and 9 a.m. to 1 p.m. on Saturday. **Pan Am** (tel. 26-02-57) is open from 8:30 a.m. to 4:30 p.m. Monday to Friday and 8:30 a.m. to noon on Saturday; LOT is open from 8 a.m. to 4 p.m. Monday to Friday and 8 a.m. to 2 p.m. on Saturday.

For **LOT** tickets, go to LOT's main ticket sales and reservation office at ul. Waryńskiego 9, off Plac Konstytucji (tel. 21-70-21). Shuttle buses leave this office for both the international and domestic airport every half hour between 5:20 a.m. and 7:45 p.m. LOT has another ticket office at Jerozolimskie 44 (tel. 27-25-78). For LOT reservations, call 28-24-31 for international flights or 28-24-38 for domestic flights.

BOOKSTORES AND POSTERS: You can find some good English-language guidebooks, as well as colorful artbooks and biographies of Pope John Paul II, in the many bookstores (called *Dom Ksiazki* in Polish) on Nowy Świat. One English guide we strongly recommend is *A Guide to Warsaw and Environs,* a helpful city guide by Janina Rutkowska that also contains an excellent city map of Warsaw. Newsstands also sell guides to Łazienski Park, Wilanów, the Royal Way, and other sights in Warsaw.

If you want some good English guides to all of Poland, go to the **Interpress** office at Bagatela 7. The guides they sell include Adam Bajcar's *Poland,* Krzysztof Wichrowski's *Poland: A Guide for Young Tourists,* and Tadeusz Wojnowski's *A Polish-American's Guide to Poland.*

BUS TERMINALS: If you take a long-distance bus from Warsaw, you'll probably leave from the **main bus terminal** at the Warszawa-Zachodnia train station (on aleja Jerozolimskie). You can reach this terminal by taking the suburban railway two stops from the main train station. If you're leaving for the northeastern part of Poland, however, you'll depart from the **Stadium Coach Terminal** on Zamoyskiego, near the Stadion Dziesieciolecia (the Tenth Anniversary Stadium on the other side of the river, built from World War II rubble), which you can reach on tram 25 from the center.

CONCERTS: Warsaw offers frequent concerts, theater, film, and other cultural performances. For information, ask at your hotel, go to the **Syrena** office at ul. Krucza 16 (tel. 25-72-01), or to **Orbis.** Or you can buy the weekly publication available at newsstands called *Informator Kulturalny Stolicy* for 25 złoty (15¢), which tells you what's going on in Warsaw's opera, theater, concerts, movies, etc.

SPATiF, at al. Jerozolimskie 25 (tel. 28-06-22), sells tickets to many theater, film, and other performances. The **National Philharmonic** at ul. Sienkiewicza 12 also sells concert tickets at their box office.

CRIME: In Warsaw's train station, one finds a few confidence men, pickpockets, and purse snatchers now and again. On the whole, however, there is less street crime in Warsaw than in most European capitals.

DRY CLEANING: Although they don't provide next-day service, they do dry clean at the **Praznia-Chemiczna,** at ul. Chmielna 98, open from 11 a.m. to 9 p.m. You can find this store right across from the central train station, off ulica Złota.

EMBASSIES: Should you be so unfortunate as to lose your visa, passport, or wallet, or should you fall seriously ill, call your embassy. The **U.S. Embassy** is at a1. Ujazdowskie 29/31 (tel. 28-30-41 to 28-30-49). The **Canadian Embassy** is at ul. Matejki 1/5 (tel. 29-80-51), and the **British Embassy** is at a1. Róż 1 (tel. 28-10-01 to 28-10-05).

GAMBLING: You can gamble on horses on Sunday afternoons during the summer at a racetrack near the airport. The track is called Teren Wyscigow Konnych, and can be reached by taking tram 4 or bus A.

HORSE-AND-BUGGY RIDES: What could be a more romantic way of seeing Warsaw's old town? You can ride much like Warsaw's old aristocrats did, starting from the Rynek Starego Miasta (the Old Market Square). A 15-minute ride costs about 1,000 złoty ($6.25).

HOSPITAL: Daily newspapers list which hospitals care for what ailment. Ask at your embassy or hotel for assistance. For emergency service, call 999 or 28-24-24 at ul. Hoża 56.

PHOTOS: If you need photos (including passport photos), you'll find a photography store, **Polifoto,** in the underground arcade of the central train station. Remember that Eastern European developing is not compatible with that of its Western counterparts. Open from 7 a.m. to 9 p.m.

POLICE: To extend your visa, go early in the morning to ul. Stefana Okrzei 13 in the Praga district, on the other side of the river. Take any tram or bus from the Old Town across the Ślasko-Dąbrowski bridge. If you need to register (if you're staying with friends or family), call 26-75-67. For a police emergency, call 997 or 26-24-24.

POST OFFICES: Here are the addresses of four central post offices: Ulica Świę-tokrzyska 31/33, the main station, open 24 hours a day; Krakowskie Przedmieście 11, near the Old Town; Rynek Starego Miasta 15, in the Old Town Marketplace; and Warszawa Centralna (central train station), porta n. 120. These last three post offices are open from 8 a.m. to 8 p.m.

SHOPPING: Our favorite places to stroll and shop are **ulica Marszałkowska** (in front of the Place of Culture), where you'll find the large Centrum department stores, Wars and Sawa; **ulica Rutkowskiego** (behind the Centrum department store), a smaller street with quaint shops that sell used watches, a few antiques, and other goodies; **aleja Jerozolimskie,** a large avenue that intersects the Royal Way; and **Nowy Świat** and **Krakowskie Przedmieście,** Warsaw's Royal Way and main shopping avenue with a wide variety of stores.

Bargain-hunters will delight in the bustling outdoor **flea market** in the Praga district at Targowa 50/52, open from 7 or 8 a.m. until 7 p.m.; closed Sunday. You can find a wide variety of things such as food (including Russian caviar), clothes, old coins, medals from World War II, and various odds and ends. Very few tourists venture to this market, so beware of pickpockets. Take tram 13 or 26 from outside the Old Town or tram 25 from in front of the Forum Hotel.

STUDENT TRAVEL: The main youth travel bureau, **Almatur,** located at ul. Ordynacka 9, a small street off Nowy Świat (tel. 26-84-04), is open from 9 a.m. to 4 p.m. Monday to Friday. They can sell you the IUS socialist student card, and can also give you advice on planning your travels. A few doors down at Kopernika 15 you can get information on student hotels.

TELEPHONE AND TELEGRAPH: Warsaw is the only city in Poland from which you have any hope of getting an international call through to North America. You can try from the main post office at ul. Świętokrzyska 31/33, but you may have to wait for many hours.

TOURS: Orbis sponsors a four-hour sightseeing tour of Warsaw conducted by an English-speaking guide. Tours depart from the Forum, Grand, Victoria, and Europejski Hotels, and cost 900 złoty ($5.65). Inquire at your hotel reception, at Orbis, or at one of the four hotels from which the bus leaves.

TRAVELER'S CHECKS: There is no American Express office in Warsaw, so if you lose your traveler's checks, one hopes they'll be Thomas Cook checks, as they have an office at ul. Nowy Świat 64 (tel. 26-38-67 or 26-47-29). It's open Monday to Friday from 9 a.m. to 4 p.m., and on Saturday from 9 a.m. to 2 p.m.

Chapter V

KRAKÓW AND SOUTHERN POLAND

1. Kraków
2. Częstochowa
3. Sights in Silesia
4. Zakopane and the Tatra Mountains
5. Lublin
6. Side Trips from Lublin

NO TOUR OF POLAND would be complete without a visit to Kraków and some of the cities in southern Poland. Why Kraków? Kraków embodies everything you'd expect from a medieval capital of an important kingdom. A large castle filled with treasures sits on a hill just outside the center of town. At Kraków's large town square, merchants sell their wares and locals rendezvous throughout the day. And as you stroll the cobblestone streets of this city—one of the few in Poland that escaped large-scale destruction in World War II—you'll find the atmosphere of the past is still maintained.

North of Kraków in Częstochowa, thousands of pilgrims and tourists arrive every day to pay tribute to the Black Madonna, said to be the second most sacred Catholic shrine in the world after the Vatican.

South of Kraków, visitors don skis or hiking boots and make for the breathtaking Tatra Mountains around Zakopane.

And in the surrounding areas near Kraków, around Lublin and in Silesia, towns far older than the U.S. continue to delight visitors with their old town squares, churches, and medieval fortifications.

In all, Kraków and southern Poland truly show the best of Eastern Europe.

1. Kraków

Ancient royal capital, medieval university, modern metropolis with over 800,000 inhabitants—Kraków is all of these things. In no other Polish city will you find the undamaged wealth of history and culture that is here. With its Gothic churches, cobblestone streets, rich museums, and a great castle overlooking the city, you're sure to find that few cities in Eastern Europe can rival Kraków for sheer timeless beauty.

Legend has it that Kraków was founded well over 1,000 years ago, aptly enough, by Prince Krak; certainly written documents show that the city was established by the 9th century A.D. The excellent defensive position of Wawel Hill and Kraków's location on a main north-south trade route contributed to the growth of the town. Merchants from southern Europe traveling to the north in search of Baltic amber and from Western Europe en route to Byzantium and Ruthenia converged on Kraków.

The first surviving written mention of the town's name occurs in the A.D. 965 chronicles of a traveler from Cordova, Ibrahim ibn Yaqub. The city was finally consolidated when it was granted foundation privilege in 1257 by Boleslaus the Bashful. The foundation privilege was the basis for an urban plan that has been part of the city for the last 700 years. Recently UNESCO recognized the Stare Miasto (old city) of Kraków as a "world heritage."

In 1038, during the reign of the Piast Dynasty, the royal capital was transfered from Gniezno to Kraków. For over five centuries, until the capital was transfered to Warsaw in 1596, Polish kings were crowned and laid to rest here. The Wawel Castle and Cathedral, and the treasures they contain, are the two most important relics from this era in Polish history.

But Kraków is not just a city of kings; it is also the site of the Jagiellonian University, one of the oldest formal centers of learning in Europe. Founded in 1364 by King Casimir the Great, the oldest part of the university, the Collegium Maius, had among its many distinguished scholars the astronomer Nicolaus Copernicus.

ORIENTATION: Kraków is roughly circular in shape, with the Wisła (Vistula) River running along the southern edge of the city. There is an excellent tram system, but since most of the points of interest are inside the once-walled old city, they're easily accessible on foot. When the capital of Poland was moved from Kraków to Warsaw in the late 16th century (a topic that is still debated between residents of the two cities), the city walls were torn down. This, in effect, made Kraków an open city, nearly impossible to defend, thus assuring Warsaw's preeminence. Where the old walls once stood there is today a beautiful green park, called the **Planty,** that encircles the old city and protects it from much of the noise and clutter of modern life.

The **Rynek Główny,** the large Main Market Square, lies at the heart of the old town. **Wawel Castle and Cathedral,** Kraków's most noted monuments, are situated a five-minute walk south on Grodzka Street.

The better hotels, with a few exceptions, are located inside or close to the old city. Less expensive hotels are on the boulevards in the newer section. Kraków was hardly damaged during World War II, and the old city retains its winding intricateness with the newer development spread around it in broad ring boulevards.

Getting into Town

If you arrive by train or plane, here are some tips for getting into (and leaving) Kraków.

From the Train Station: Although several buses run from the railroad station to the city center, taxis are so inexpensive in Poland that it's always a good idea to grab one. As you exit the main railway terminal building, you'll see a taxi stand to the right. After a train arrives, a line often develops at the stand; so if you're traveling with a group, have someone walk ahead to get a taxi. If you aren't burdened with a lot of luggage, you might just walk straight ahead as you exit the main station building; and you'll be in the old town in about 15 minutes.

When you want to buy tickets for your departure, go to windows 1 and 2 for

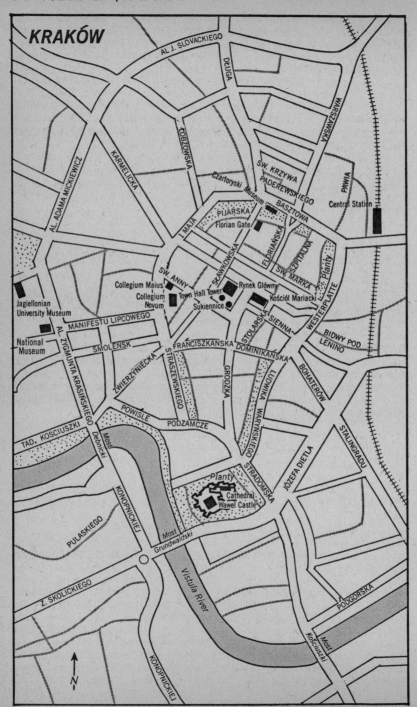

KRAKÓW

AL. J. SLOVACKIEGO

DŁUGA

WARSZAWSKA

ŁOBZOWSKA

KARMELICKA

AL. ADAMA MICKIEWICZ

SW. KRZYWA

PADEREWSKIEGO

Czartoryski Museum

BASZTOWA

PAWIA

Central Station

PIJARSKA

Florian Gate

FLORIANSKA

SZPITALNA

1 MAJA

SŁAWKOWSKA

SW. MARKA

Planty

Westerplatte

SW. ANNY

Collegium Maius

Rynek Główny

Collegium Novum

Town Hall Tower

Kościół Mariacki

Jagiellonian University Museum

Sukiennice

STOLARSKA

SIENNA

BIDWY POD LENINO

National Museum

MANIFESTU LIPCOWEGO

FRANCISZKAŃSKA

DOMINIKAŃSKA

AL. ZYGMUNTA KRASIŃSKIEGO

SMOLEŃSK

ZWIERZYNIECKA

STRASZEWSKIEGO

GRODZKA

LUDWIKA WARYŃSKIEGO

BOHATERÓW

STALINGRADU

POWISLE

PODZAMCZE

TAD. KOSCIUSZKI

Most Dębnicki

STRADOMSKA

JÓZEFA DIETLA

Planty

Cathedral Wawel Castle

KONOPNICKIEJ

PULASKIEGO

Most Grundwaldski

Z. SKOLICKIEGO

Vistula River

PODGORSKA

Most Kościuszki

KONOPNICKIEJ

N

international tickets, or 3 through 7 for tickets inside Poland. If a problem develops and you want to see the manager, you'll find him at window 8. At windows 9 to 14 you can buy tickets for local trains that run within a 50-mile radius of Kraków. You can deposit your bags around the clock at either of two spots—one in the main station hall and the other near platform 2. For further information, go to the *informacja krajowa*, near the exit.

From the Airport: The airport is 16 km (10 miles) from Kraków in a town called Balice. The LOT airline office in Kraków, at ul. Basztowa 15 (tel. 250-76 or 270-78), can sell you tickets and tell you where and when to catch the airport bus (they do speak some English).

Tours and Tourist Information
The **Informacia Turystyki**, ul. Pawia 6 (tel. 22-04-71 or 22-60-91), sponsors tours in English of Kraków, Auschwitz, and other points of interest in the area (see "Kraków Side Trips" for descriptions of these towns). They also give out maps and tourist information, but unfortunately they don't make hotel reservations. Sometimes Turystyki's rates are cheaper than Orbis, though they don't have the same range of tours that Orbis offers. You'll find both offices opposite the train station, open around the clock.
If the Informacia Turystyki doesn't offer the tour you want, try **Orbis**. Their bus tours leave from the Holiday Inn at 10 a.m. and at 3 p.m., and from the Hotel Krakówia at 10:15 a.m. and 3:15 p.m. Standard bus tour prices are 900 złoty ($5.65) to Wieliczka and 1,100 złoty ($6.90) to Oświęcim (Auschwitz).

Important Addresses
PZM, the Polish Automobile Association that helps motorists in need, runs an office at ul. Sławkowska 4 (tel. 202-15).
To extend your visa, go to the **police station** on ulica Józefitów.

ACCOMMODATIONS: Our choices in Kraków range from a splurge hotel (well worth the price) to some basic student accommodations. If you haven't booked a room in advance, head for one of the two regional tourist offices, called **Wawel Tourist**. Private rooms can be reserved at ul. Pawia 8 and hotel rooms at ul. Pawia 6 (tel. 22-15-09; Telex 0325355). Because tourist accommodations are in such great demand in the summer, it's a good idea to reserve in advance at the Wawel Tourist Office in Warsaw for your stay in Kraków.

A Splurge Choice
On the north side of the city and about a five-minute walk from the station, the **Hotel Francuski**, at ul. Pijarska 13 (tel. 251-22; Telex 0322253), is modeled on French themes. The interior is one of the most pleasing in Kraków; somewhat dark, it is nevertheless a refreshing change from the ever-present "Polish Modern" style of most Orbis hotels. A single room costs about $36 per night, and a double room runs $50, including breakfast. We feel that this is the only luxury hotel that is substantially different from most American hotels—and therefore worth a splurge—in Kraków. The hotel restaurant, the Paryska (Paris), is considered one of the best in Kraków (see our dining recommendations). After a tiring day of touring, a very distinguished maître d' will usher you into the lobby where you can relax and have a drink at their well-stocked, very cozy bar.

Kraków's Budget Hotels

The **Wawel Tourist** office, ul. Pawia 6 (tel.22-15-09; Telex 0325355), controls all of the budget hotels that we recommend in Kraków. We particularly like the **Monopol Hotel,** ul. Waryńskiego 6 (tel. 227-626 or 227-666); it's one of Wawel Tourist's better hotels. Another good choice is the **Warszawski,** at ul. Pawia 6 (tel. 220-622 or 227-114). The **Polski Hotel,** at ul. Pijarska 17 (tel. 221-144, 221-426, or 221-327), has been closed in recent years. Remodeled and cleaned up, it should be open for business in 1987. The **Europejski Hotel,** ul. Lubicz 5 (tel. 228-925), is clean but only has small showers. The noisy **Polonia,** at ul. Basztowa 25 (tel. 221-621 or 221-661), is to be avoided if you have the choice. The **Pod Złota Kotwicą,** at ul. Szpitalna 30 (tel. 221-243, 221-044, or 221-128), is not very clean and has few private baths.

The prices of Wawel Tourist's hotel rooms range from 3,000 złoty ($18.90) to 4,600 złoty ($29) for a single, and 4,350 złoty ($27.35) to 5,420 złoty ($34) for a double. Subtract about 800 złoty ($5) to 1,000 złoty ($6.25) for rooms without private bath.

Wawel Tourist takes the reservation, then you go to the hotel and pay for the room. Check-out time is noon, and any vacancies open soon after. They usually have rooms early in the day, but by the afternoon all their rooms may be taken as Kraków is a big tourist center. If they don't have anything, ask them to call around for you; their job is to try and find you a room somewhere.

Private Rooms

If you're interested in a room in a private home, try the **Wawel Tourist** office at ul. Pawia 8 (tel. 22-19-21 or 22-16-40). They're open from 7 a.m. to 9 p.m. and do a brisk business, so it's best to arrive early. Unfortunately, in the summer things tighten up and they don't always have free rooms. A private room costs 1,800 złoty ($11.30) per person, though it increases as the summer progresses, usually by 10% to 15%.

Very little English is spoken at Wawel Tourist, so bring a dictionary and patience. Most of the rooms are not near the city center; ask for bus or tram connections. A large wall map facilitates this explanation. And since there is no Telex number, you must write or call if you wish to reserve in advance.

Starvation-Budget Lodgings

The amazing appearing/disappearing student dorms! Because of poor planning, student hotel availability is an unknown factor until the summer arrives. This year the dorm will be "perhaps" at ul. Piastowska 6. Your best bet is to ask **Almatur,** the student travel agency, at Rynek Główny 7 (tel. 22-63-52 or 21-51-30; Telex 0325214), after student dorms open on July 15 (the dorms stay open until the end of August). Though a visit to Almatur is very confusing and time-consuming, they can help you find cheap housing during the summer. A bed in Almatur lodgings costs between 500 złoty ($3.15) and 800 złoty ($5) per night.

Although you will often be told that Almatur's student hotels are booked, don't give up. Americans are a rarity, and if you are patient and polite, and above all very insistent, they'll try to help. Since this office, like the Wawel Tourist office, is the main clearinghouse for all student housing, don't bother looking for official student housing on your own. Even if you do manage to find the student dorm, you'll probably be sent back here to register. Almatur has rooms for relatively short stays of one, two, or three nights.

A second major student housing bureau is the **Biuro Krwater Studentckich** at Rynek Główny 15. They have rooms available for tourists, primarily young people, from July 15 to September 15. A bed works out to about 500 złoty ($3.15) to 750 złoty ($4.75) per person per night, depending on which dorm you're assigned and how large the room is. Things are a confused jumble sometimes as the traditionally underpaid and overworked staff tries to sort out the influx of foreign tourists. Be patient and get here as early in the morning as possible.

The **PTTK Hotel,** ul. Westerplatte 15/17 (tel. 22-95-66; Telex 0322210), is an inexpensive place, but it's very crowded with absolutely no privacy. There is also a very inexpensive self-service restaurant. Though the PTTK is supposed to be for all travelers, it is overwhelmingly patronized by young people and student groups. The rooms are small but clean, with a radio that will sometimes squawk if you turn it on. Though the place is something of a zoo in the daytime, it quiets down at night. The lobby is large and well lit, but done in a very chintzy plastic-and-glass style. There are no private baths and few private rooms, but they do have a luggage room where you can leave your things when you go out for the day. The English-speaking staff is sometimes short-tempered because of the hordes of Polish schoolchildren that flow through the lobby. They recommend that you reserve ahead, or call the reception desk after 10:30 a.m., when they learn of possible vacancies. One person who worked there told us that you can "sometimes" make reservations through Almatur in Warsaw. The rare single is 2,420 złoty ($15.25) without a bathroom or sink; a double room costs 1,740 złoty ($11) per person; in the larger rooms a bed costs 860 złoty ($5.40) per night.

There is **camping** at Ośrodek Turystyczny Krak, at ul. Radzikowskiego 99.

DINING: In Kraków, unlike many other Polish cities, hotel restaurants don't have a monopoly on the best food. We lead off our recommendations with the one we feel stands out above the rest.

Our Top Choice
We like the **Restauracja Wierzynek,** on the second floor of Rynek Główny 15 (tel. 298-96), so much that we're willing to go out on a limb and say you won't find a better restaurant in all of Poland! Everything about the restaurant is elegant. Upon entering, you'll pass two shining suits of armor; upstairs in the main dining room, sharp-looking waiters sporting bow ties will seat you in antique chairs underneath elegant wood ceilings and brass chandeliers. You'll be given a ten-page menu, and even more surprising for a restaurant in Poland, almost every item on the menu is available!

Your many appetizer possibilities include zurek polski (a rich, flavorful broth garnished with sausage and egg), Polish beetroot barszcz soup, or a choice of ten other soups at a cost of only 40 złoty (25¢) to 93 złoty (60¢). For an entree you can select one of several carp, trout, or salmon dishes, roast duck with apples for 610 złoty ($3.85), roast goose for 664 złoty ($4.20), roast pheasant for 518 złoty ($3.25), or dozens of other scrumptious specialties for only $3 to $5! To really live it up, order the buttery and altogether-amazing sautéed mushrooms at 133 złoty (85¢) in addition to your entree. Extensive dessert offerings such as chocolate or poppy-seed cake or ice cream finish off the meal in memorable style.

The menu boasts that guests are entertained in a regal manner, and after spending only $4 to $8 for a complete and superb meal in a sumptuous setting, you certainly will feel like a king! You must reserve here; if you want a table for two, request the romantic window tables overlooking the town square. Open from 9 a.m. to 11 p.m. daily.

Other Local Favorites

At the restaurant **Staropolska,** at ul. Sienna 4 (tel. 258-21), you'll find an attractive and relaxing clean, white-painted interior. The drapes are usually drawn during the summer so the interior is pleasingly cool and shady. If you like cold drinks, the cola and mineral water are sufficiently chilled, American style. The specialties of the Staropolska are the ryba po żydowska, fish "Jewish style," which makes a delicious light snack or appetizer, and the Polish barley soup, for 25 złoty (15¢).

Since the Staropolska is not in the Orbis chain they get the second pick of meats. This doesn't mean that the meat is of inferior quality; in fact, the owner probably tries harder to get the best meat since he doesn't have guaranteed patronage like the Orbis restaurants. In any event, when we visited there was a meat shortage, but they did have a delicious lamb steak for 347 złoty ($2.20) and kuropatwa pieczona, fried partridge with cranberries, for 744 złoty ($4.70). For vegetarians the waiter recommended naleśniki z serem at 144 złoty (90¢), pancakes with cottage cheese which makes a good light meal, especially in hot weather. There are very few fresh greens because of distribution difficulties. Luckily the dessert menu hasn't suffered as the jablka w cieślie z sokiem, apple pie with fruit sauce for 119 złoty (75¢), is always in stock.

Most of the waiters speak some English and are reasonably attentive. Open from 9 a.m. to 11 p.m.

One of the better values on the Rynek Główny main square is the restaurant **Hawełka** (tel. 22-47-53), a spacious room divided by columns; on weekends locals and soldiers on leave frequent the Hawełka in large numbers. The waiters and waitresses force their way through the crowds and clouds of cigarette smoke with an amazing dexterity. The Hawełka, though a tad raucous, is easy on the wallet with solid if not exciting food. The ragoût baranie of lamb at 179 złoty ($1.15) is good, both filling and tender; there is also stek barani pieczarki frytki, fried lamb with mushrooms and a salad, for 370 złoty ($2.30). The Hawełka suffers from shortages from time to time, so check with the waiter to see if the dish you want is in fact available. It's open from 8 a.m. till 10 p.m.

Hotel Restaurants

Located in the Hotel Francuski, ul. Pijarska 13 (tel. 251-22 or 252-70), the restaurant **Paryska** specializes in French cuisine. The restaurant consists of several rooms which can be opened or closed off, depending on the crowds, so there's no vast dining-hall expanse that you sometimes experience in large restaurants. Shields decorated with the coats-of-arms of various French provinces adorn the walls. Fresh flowers brighten the tables and the service is reasonably fast. There's an extensive menu, but as in other Kraków establishments, shortages plague the restaurant. It's always wise to stay away from the complicated foreign dishes and eat local specialties. You're not going to leave the Paryska for less than 700 złoty ($4.40) to 900 złoty ($5.50) per person; the best budget bet meal is the daily menu—if it's available.

We found the food well prepared but not exceptional, though many of our acquaintances in Warsaw spoke fondly of the Paryska even after absences of ten or more years! The restaurant is open from 7 a.m. to midnight, and the bar stays open another hour. There is dancing every night except Monday, from 8 p.m. till 1 a.m.

The restaurant of the **Orbis Holiday Inn,** ul. Marsz. Konicwa 7 (tel. 754-44), is quite true to the Orbis standard. Despite the average hotel decor, as one of the premier Orbis restaurants in the city it receives the best available foodstuffs. It is filled almost entirely with tourists and tour groups, with an occasional businessman looking conspicuous in a dark three-piece suit. There are also families with children out for a big feed. In short, the atmosphere is not romantic or intimate. Service is slow, though you can eat here till 11 p.m. most nights. The Orbis Holiday Inn serves good food at top prices; for example, the beef fondue costs 1,098 złoty ($6.90) per person. There's a full menu with a wide selection of meat and fish dishes, and, in season, pheasant, duck, and other game. There are also many foreign dishes for those looking for a change from Polish cuisine. The average main dish is 650 złoty ($4.10).

Starvation-Budget Dining

For the budget-conscious, a self-service restaurant is the place to go. The **PTTK self-service** at ul. Westerplatte 15/17 provides solid food for very little. If you like eggs, you can get a very filling meal for less than 150 złoty (95¢). Entrees include pirogi at 41 złoty (25¢), a quite delicious cottage cheese plate with egg and tomatoes for 83 złoty (50¢), and the staple of all cafeterias worldwide, the mystery-meat cutlet smothered in mushrooms, at 97 złoty (60¢). Though the food is not gourmet and the soups are a bit thin, the atmosphere here should send you right back to good ol' P.S. 101 or wherever.

NIGHTLIFE: If you're in Kraków in June, you can enjoy the famous **Dni-Krakówa** (Days of Kraków), a festival with folk music, dancing, and local rock bands. Generally most of the music takes place in theaters and in the House of Culture. The festivities are marked by the entry of the Lajkonik (raftsman) dressed in a colorful costume. The legend, dating from around 1240, tells of a young raftsman who, upon spotting an approaching Tartar horde, gathered up some of his buddies and routed the enemy. To celebrate their victory, they donned the clothes of the defeated Tartar chief and rode into the main square of Kraków. Some of the events also take place by the Wistła (Vistula) in the shadow of Wawel Castle.

If you understand Polish you might consider an evening at **CRICOT 2,** a theater at ul. Szezepanska 27 that is the home of many avant-garde productions. The chief director is Tadeusz Kantor, but he's usually away on extensive foreign tours. In the summer the main company is generally on tour, so there aren't as many performances, but several of the experimental groups keep the boards smooth.

Bars

The jazz club **Jaszczury,** on the Rynek Główny, is known as the premier music spot in Kraków. A stage with two large speakers dominates the room. The high ceiling is composed of delicately arched stone, though a relatively unattractive shade of red paint has been slapped over the interior. The furniture is low set and comfortable. In the daytime it's a good place to plop down and relax after a full sightseeing program. In late afternoon and evening the room fills with university students, and at night there's usually music and dancing. Since this is primarily a student bar, it's a good place for you to find foreign language speakers—put that high-school or college French to work! The drinks are generally pretty bad, with frequent shortages. Sometimes the front door is closed and guarded for reasons no one is quite sure of. The official reason is that there isn't enough room. In any case, don't try to crash the place as the bouncer, Alex, a national judo champion, is often on guard.

For those looking for a quiet and dignified place to take their refreshments, the **Polish Literary Club,** at ul. Kanonicza 7, is the place. Through the large, arched stone doorway and on the left at Kanonicza 7 is the small public room.

The larger room in the back is for club members only. Open from 11 a.m. till 9 p.m., it's an interesting little bar, good for intimate, quiet conversation. Music and any loud or unseemly behavior are frowned upon.

THE SIGHTS: There are over 1,000 buildings of historical and architectural note within Kraków's city limits. The best place to begin a tour of the city is in the Rynek Główny (Main Market Square) in the center of the old town.

Rynek Główny

Over 200 yards on a side, the square is one of the largest in Europe. It's divided by the huge, arcaded **Sukiennice** (Cloth Hall), which was built as a commercial center in the 13th century and is still used for that purpose. A row of shops running the length of the arcade sell a variety of souvenirs and folk art, all handcrafted. The second floor houses the **Gallery of Polish Painting.** The collection, dating primarily from the 18th and 19th centuries, includes works by famous Polish painters. The gallery is open from 10 a.m. to 4 p.m. Friday through Monday and Wednesday, and from noon to 6 p.m. on Thursday; closed Tuesday.

Towering above the Rynek Główny are the uneven towers of **Kościół Mariacki** (St. Mary's Church), built in the 13th and 14th centuries. The interior of this splendid Gothic church contains a magnificent wooden altar carved between 1477 and 1489. The altar, besides being a work of art in its own right, is a valuable historical record: the sculptor carved the faces of the saints in the likenesses of the current town fathers. At noon every day a single bugle sounds from the church towers. The call begins, repeats, and then is cut short. Broadcast throughout Poland, this bugle call honors a bugler who kept blowing the warning that saved the city from a surprise Tartar attack. The bugler kept to his post on the city walls until his clarion alarm was cut short by a Tartar arrow that pierced his throat.

The church is balanced on the other (west) side of the square by the slender, single remaining tower of the **Town Hall,** which was destroyed in 1820. The tower is a fine example of lay, medieval Gothic architecture. Not far from the tower is a stone slab marking the spot where Tadeusz Kościuszko declared open rebellion against the Russians on March 24, 1794.

Around the Old Town

Heading south on the narrow, partly cobbled ulica Jagiellońska, we reach the **Collegium Maius** on ulica Św. Anny. Established in 1364, this is the oldest part of the Jagiellonian University. The stunning Gothic buildings house the **University Museum.** The **Czartoryski Museum,** the current branch of the Polish National Museum, has an impressive collection of early weaponry and foreign paintings. The most famous painting in the collection is Leonardo da Vinci's portrait *Lady with an Ermine.* Nearby is the beautiful baroque **St. Anne's Church.**

On the northern end of the old city on ulica Floriańska is the **Florian Gate,** over 37 yards high. The core of this original town fortification was built in the 13th century and the cupola was added in the 17th century. The other major remnant of the once impregnable outer works is the **Barbican.** A circular fortification representing the pinnacle of medieval defensive architecture, the Barbican was once linked to the Florian Gate by a covered passage and surrounded by a moat. The road from the Florian Gate down ulica Floriańska, through the Rynek Główny and to ulica Grodzka, is known as the **"Royal Route."** Here, kings returning from war or travel held a procession before returning to Wawel Castle.

Wawel Castle and Cathedral

Wawel Castle and Wawel Cathedral are two of the most important historical treasures in all of Poland. The royal residence was built in the 16th century by Italian masters brought in by King Sigismund the Old of the Jagiellons. The Polish Renaissance is reflected in the gardens and colonnaded courtyard of the Royal Palace. The 71 rooms of the castle display literally thousands of priceless works of art in the **State Art Collection,** including the world's only collection of Flemish tapestry. These tapestries were ordered expressly for the royal chambers by Sigismund Augustus the Jagiellon. He supervised the work during the more than 20 years it took to complete the weaving. When King Sigismund Augustus died, the collection numbered 356 tapestries of the highest quality. Unfortunately, only 136 pieces have survived; as can be expected, the tapestries and other pieces of the royal treasury were the primary goal of any plunderer and most of the once-fantastic royal collection has disappeared. However, the Szczerbiec, the sword used for coronations since 1320, remains in the castle. Other surviving treasures include an impressive array of arms and knightly armor, and a collection of Middle and Near Eastern artifacts accumulated, as one tour guide managed to phrase in a magnificent understatement, "through the years of not always peaceful contacts with the Middle East." The State Art Collection of Wawel Castle is open from 10 a.m. to 3 p.m., except Monday. During the summer, the museum remains open until 6 p.m. on Wednesday, Friday, and weekends.

The **Wawel Cathedral** was built in the early 14th century and marked the end of an era in Polish history. After its completion, practically all Polish kings were crowned and buried here. The nave, filled with the tombs of many Polish kings, is surrounded by Gothic, Renaissance, and baroque chapels. The most spectacular is the **Sigismund Chapel** (1519–1539), designed by the Florentine Bartolomeo Berrecci. High in the tower is the church bell **Zygmunt.** Cast from captured cannon in 1520, its powerful toll echoes off the surrounding hills and far out to Kraków's suburbs.

Below the Wawel is a cave reputed to have been the home of a dragon with the usual epicurian tastes. Though the consumption of maidens is standard for all dragons, this one must have enjoyed particularly delicious fare, as the maidens of Kraków are known for their uncommon beauty. The tale of how the dragon met his end is best told by a native, though make sure you hear it in a pub or other location where drink is handy. There is an actual fire-breathing dragon on view—though well constructed, it is merely a metal rendition (spouting fiery butane jets) by the sculptor Bolesław Chromy.

KRAKÓW SIDE TRIPS: On a side trip from Kraków, you can visit the site of an infamous concentration camp or see what a salt mine is really like.

Auschwitz (Oświęcim)

The sun may shine, birds may gracefully sing, and cows may quietly graze in the distance as you walk through the campgrounds, but a visit to the concentration camp at Auschwitz will certainly be one of the most deeply felt experiences of your Polish travels. Opened in June 1940, Auschwitz proved to be the ultimate in Nazi insanity. Up to 60,000 could be killed in a single day, and at this pace the Germans exterminated some four million people of 28 different nationalities in five years.

Located 38 miles west of Kraków just outside the industrial town of Oświęcim (pronounced Ausch-vien-chim), the Konzentrationslager Auschwitz consisted of two main camps and 40 smaller subcamps. Visit two in particular,

Auschwitz and Birkenau. Auschwitz itself today houses a grisly museum. Begin your visit here by viewing a graphic film shot on the day the camp was liberated, January 27, 1945. The film runs every half hour in different languages, but there is no need to wait around for the English version—you will understand well enough. After passing under the gate with the infamous slogan *Arbeit Macht Frei* ("Work Will Set You Free") written above, you'll find that the sights in the museum challenge the mind's capacity to believe: a large room full of human hair, a display case of thousands of eyeglasses, another case full of empty tins of Cyclon B, the chemical used to gas prisoners. Perhaps the most moving display comes from the long rows of prisoners' portraits, thousands of them, spread among several museum buildings. They were all killed in Auschwitz.

After viewing the Auschwitz museum, continue on the 20- to 30-minute walk down the road to Birkenau (Brzezinka, in Polish), the huge main camp of the Auschwitz complex which has essentially been left as it was during World War II. Note the seemingly endless rows of prisoners' barracks, all in different states of decay. In contrast to the Auschwitz museum, the wide fields of Birkenau are virtually free of tourists. Within the camp grounds, surrounded to this day by barbed-wire fences and tall watchtowers, you can wander alone for hours, visiting the barracks and other buildings that made up the world's greatest death factory in history. Some barracks still have bowls lying around; in others you can still read the German regulations printed on the building's wooden frame: "No Smoking! Keep Yourself Clean!" In the front of the camp lie the tracks of the trains which transported the arriving prisoners, and at the back of Birkenau stand several crematoria, as well as a large vat where the Nazis attempted to make gasoline from human excrement.

The museum complex is open daily except Monday, from 8 a.m. to 7 p.m. in June, July, and August, to 6 p.m. in May and September, to 5 p.m. in April and October, to 4 p.m. in March and November, and to 3 p.m. in December, January, and February. On the way in to the museum at Auschwitz, you can buy the museum guide as well as the incredible memoirs of Rudolf Höss, the Nazi commander of the camp.

Travel to these two camps either by train or by bus from Kraków. Then take a taxi or bus from the front of the train station to the Auschwitz Museum.

Wieliczka Salt Mines

Another interesting side trip takes you just seven miles from Kraków. The 900-year-old Wieliczka Salt Mines are a memorial to the ingenuity and religious devotion of the Poles. Salt miners have carved out some 90 miles of tunnels, chambers, and most amazingly, a number of religious chapels with saints and other decorations dating back to the 17th century. In addition to these moving chapels, you'll see a large chamber where the Germans operated an airplane factory in World War II, and you'll even find a modern-day tennis court! A museum carved into the salt rock also documents the history of the mines.

The mines are open to the public from 7 a.m. to noon and 2 to 7 p.m. from April 1 to November 1; the rest of the year they are open from 8 a.m. to 4 p.m. You must go with a guide, however, so inquire at Orbis or Almatur (if you're a student) in Kraków for information on tours that depart directly from Kraków. If you're willing to chance it, you can go by bus to Wieliczka and wait at the entrance to the mines to join the first group that comes along (to get here from the railroad station, follow the signs reading *do kopalni*).

2. Częstochowa

Famous as the site of the Jasna Góra monastery, which houses the sacred Black Madonna, Częstochowa (pop. 250,000) contains a collection of Catholic religious and historical artifacts as important as any in Poland, including the Royal Wawel Cathedral in Kraków.

THE BLACK MADONNA: Częstochowa's monastery was founded by Władysław Opolczyk (Ladislaus, Duke of Opole) in 1382 in the name of Louis of Hungary. In 1430, growing in reputation and power, the monks built a church to accommodate the increasing number of pilgrims who journeyed to the monastery. After a fire in 1690 that destroyed much of the complex, it was again rebuilt and has survived remarkably intact.

The monastery, standing on the Jasna Góra (Bright Mount), is a veritable codex of building styles. The baroque restorations and additions blend harmoniously with the Gothic core of the monastery. The stucco and frescos of the interior were added between 1680 and 1740. The lavishly rich interior of the monastery refectory (1696) and the library (1739), the latter containing over 3,500 metric tons of priceless historical documents, attest to the power that the monastery once held.

The Jasna Góra monastery was fortified by King Zygmunt II in the first half of the 17th century. Once built, the walls were put to good use: the monastery was beseiged by Swedish armies from November to December in 1655, but did not fall. In fact Częstochowa was one of the few Polish towns to successfully resist the first and only Swedish attempt at empire building; Częstochowa's stand was a turning point in the war. Later, in September 1770, Kazimierz Pułaski (also a hero of the American Revolution) repulsed a Russian assault on the monastery.

The greatest treasure of the Jasna Góra monastery is the holy icon of Our Lady, also known as the Black Madonna. Probably brought to the monastery by its founder, the icon is believed to have been painted on a cypress plank at the dawn of the Christian era in Jerusalem. Later seen in Byzantium, it was offered to the Pauline Monks at Jasna Góra in the 14th century. During a particularly successful attack on Częstochowa by Hussites in 1430, the attackers managed to break in and slash the face of the Madonna. Desecrated, stolen, and later abandoned, it was allegedly retrieved and restored. However, because of the very unusual style of the work and the perfection of the restoration itself (the restoration was so good that it was hailed as little short of a miracle in its time), some experts feel that the present picture is a copy ordered by King Władysław Jagiełło. According to this theory, the scars are merely burn marks carefully made to resemble the Hussite sword slashes.

There is a good guide to the Jasna Góra monastery and the old town available in the monastery bookstore. Otherwise, ask at the Orbis office at ul. Aleja 40/42 (tel. 420-56 or 417-69), right near the city center, or at the Orbis desk in the Hotel Patria (tel. 470-01).

ORIENTATION: The aleja Najświętszej Marii Panny, the Avenue of Our Lady, bisects the town from east to west and runs from the foot of the Jasna Góra monastery through the center of town. The railroad station is just south of aleja Najświętszej Marii Panny on ulica Świerczewskiego. To reach the monastery, turn left (north) as you exit from the station and walk till you reach the first cross street; this is aleja Najświętszej Marii Panny. Turn left (west) and the Jasna Góra monastery is not more than a 15-minute walk away.

Travelers who do not have a map can find a large public city map on the corner of aleja Najświętszej Marii Panny and aleja Wolnosci.

A CAPSULE HISTORY: The main street, aleja Najświętszej Marii Panny (Avenue of Our Lady), was once a road that joined the two separate villages of Częstochowa and Częstochowka. The earliest records of these settlements date from 1220 when both were barely more than farming communities. Around 1370 the larger one, Częstochowa, was granted municipal rights. Situated on the left bank of the Warta River, Częstochowa sat astride the "Royal Road" between central and southern Poland, which gave it the impetus to grow as a trading center.

Częstochowka, on a hillside above the river, commanded a view over much of the surrounding region. The ruler of the area, Władysław Opolczyk (Ladislaus, Duke of Opole), founded the Jasna Góra monastery in the name of Louis of Hungary in 1382.

Both Częstochowa and Częstochowka continued their independent development. Częstochowa was older and more prosperous; Częstochowka, on the other hand, remained a small settlement clustered around the monastery.

History was not kind to the two villages. The 17th century was a time of fire, plague, and lawlessness for the towns, but even worse was the Swedish invasion of 1655. After the invasion, a period of decline set in and it was not arrested till the arrival of the Warsaw–Vienna railroad in the 19th century.

Eventually, the two towns were joined, and the united city became a leading industrial center. The rich iron ore deposits and metallurgical manufacturing make Częstochowa an industrial as well as a religious center.

ACCOMMODATIONS: Tourists and pilgrims often crowd Częstochowa's few hotels; during any religious festivals, accommodations are harder to get than an audience with the pope. Thus it's a very good idea to reserve rooms ahead of time in Częstochowa, or better yet, to stop there for a day and continue along to another, less famous (and less crowded) town to spend the night. As Częstochowa is located along the main route between Kraków and Warsaw, this is not difficult to do.

A Splurge Choice

On the outskirts of Częstochowa along the highway to Warsaw lies the **Orbis Motel**, ul. PPR 181 (tel. 556-07), a single-story building in the "Polish Modern" style, which would not seem out of place along an American interstate. The motel is far enough removed from the highway traffic to be quieter than its American counterparts. Clean and reasonably airy, the motel has a restaurant, an apéritif bar, and gas pumps, as well as limited auto-repair capability. Tour groups of Catholic pilgrims from West Germany and Italy often fill up the hotel, so the staff understands the expectations of the Western traveler, and English is spoken here. The rooms are clean and well maintained, but very expensive. A single with private toilet and shower costs 7,470 złoty ($47), and a double runs 8,750 złoty ($55). During a religious festival the motel will put extra beds in a room at around 200 złoty ($1.25) per person. In any event, this motel is often filled with tour groups, so make a reservation.

Budget Hotels

For a better value, try the **Turysta Motel** (tel. 522-36, 522-69, or 522-80), just off highway E-16 three kilometers north of Częstochowa. You can enter the motel only from the southbound lanes of the E-16, and it's a very sharp turn at that. The hotel receptionist speaks English and is very familiar with groups of visiting foreign pilgrims. The 30 rooms are reasonably clean and the beds have mattresses from the last five-year plan so they're still firm. A small shower and toilet are crammed into the tiny but clean bathrooms. Windows look out across rather pastoral southern Polish landscapes; in all, the Turysta makes a pleasant change from the bustle of the city. A single costs slightly over 1,000 złoty ($6.30)

per night; a double, 1,500 złoty ($9.45). The hotel restaurant offers some of Czę-
stochowa's better dining, with a good if limited menu and no main dish over 300
złoty ($1.85).

For those not able to pay the high price for Orbis quality, there are several
budget hotels on ulica Świerczewskiego just south of alejo Najświętszej Marii
Panny. Cleanliness and modernity are definitely not the strong suits of these
establishments, but for the stranded budget traveler without reservations in
Częstochowa, they are really the only alternative.

The **Centralny,** at ul. Świerczewskiego 9 (tel. 440-67), is the southernmost
of the hotels on that street. Inside the bare green-painted lobby, you'll see many
pilgrims milling about. The receptionist does not speak English. The rooms are
clean if somewhat rundown, and the beds are reasonably firm. As most rooms
do not have a private bath, you'll have to go to the end of the hall, behind the
sign marked *wanna* for an often lukewarm shower. There is one shower per
floor and the separate toilets have seen better days, but the chambermaids assured us that they clean them frequently. A single costs 2,640 złoty ($16.60) per
night; a double, 4,030 złoty ($25.35). As the Centralny is often packed with pil-
grims, plan ahead and make reservations or be prepared to pay a few dollars'
"tip" to the clerk to help "find" you a room.

A couple of doors north is the **Hotel Dworcowy,** ul. Świerczewskiego 1 (tel.
421-80), a real budget hotel. Less English, if possible, is spoken than at the
Centralny, but the Dworcowy is cleaner. The Dworcowy charges 538 złoty
($3.70) per bed. There are no singles; single travelers may have to share a room
with as many as four strangers unless all beds in a room are paid for. A double
room costs about 1,000 złoty ($6.30) and the beds are firm and clean. The only
staff I saw was a friendly, if monoglot receptionist-cum-porter who controls the
key to the three baths (no showers) upstairs. The toilets were probably taken
from one of the nearby castles. The warren-like hallways are not overly clean.
This hotel should not be a first choice unless you're looking for the ultimate bargain. To sum up: you get what you pay for.

RESTAURANTS: The restaurant of the **Hotel Patria,** ul. Starucha 1 (tel.
470-01), is said to be the best in Częctochowa. The main dining room has a few
token military ornaments on the walls, perhaps reminiscent of an armory. A
grand piano on a riser at one end adds a nightclubby atmosphere in the evening.
The waiters do not speak English, though not through lack of effort; luckily,
English menus are available. There is a wide selection of cold meat appetizers
including schab na zimno at 258 złoty ($1.60), a plate of cold roast pork and
almost a meal in itself. Another fine choice is the ever-present zurek, or Polish
country soup, for 43 złoty (27¢); here the cook has decided to make it a vegetable soup heartily laced with beef. The house specialty is juk Ułański, a pork
cutlet Ulan style, for a modest 370 złoty ($2.35). For vegetarians there's an
omlet z pieczarkami, a mushroom omelet for 133 złoty (85¢). This restaurant
also features an unusually large selection of vegetables, including fresh French
beans, fasolka szparagowa at 43 złoty (27¢) as well as ćwikła, a tart but refreshing red-beet salad at 20 złoty (15¢), and the old favorite sałatka z pomidorów, a
tomato salad, at 51 złoty (30¢). Because of the number of tour groups that come
through, a larger than normal tip, especially at the beginning of your stay, may
aid in obtaining a waiter. During mealtimes, patience is the watchword. The
restaurant is open from 1 till 10 p.m.

Many locals also consider the restaurant at the **Orbis Motel,** ul. PPR 181
(tel. 556-07), to be one of Częstochowa's best. The dining room is large and
modern with quite conventional wooden chairs contrasting with the decor; the
clean restaurant's large windows let in abundant sunlight. Because this motel is

reserved almost entirely for foreigners, service is better—but with the corresponding rise in price—than many local restaurants. Tour groups of elderly Italian, German, and English voyagers are a standard sight and tend to absorb most of the waiters with their demands. Consequently, an individual is at a slight disadvantage, but once you manage to attract a waiter's attention, he becomes more helpful. Because of the volume of tour traffic the menu resembles a collection of international favorites. The kotlet schabowy panierowany at 256 złoty ($1.60) is basically a wienerschnitzel, a well-prepared but common German favorite. A better bet is the mushroom soup, and the tasty house specialty, Polędwica po rzymsku, at 438 złoty ($2.75), a grilled, diced pork dish topped with a yellow cheese. Different from standard Polish cooking and quite delicious, it's not at all Italian despite the cook's best intentions.

Starvation-Budget Dining

For those interested in getting out of the tourist rut and meeting an authentic Częstochowian, try restaurant **Kosmos** (tel. 561-58). A real restaurant of the proletariat, Kosmos offers no frills. The fare is limited to omelets and a few different kinds of pork sandwiches, all priced about 50 złoty (30¢) to 100 złoty (65¢). The sausage sandwich, at 76 złoty (50¢), is the best sandwich option; the tried-and-true pieczarkowa z makaroncm (mushrooms and noodles), at 44 złoty (30¢), will stave off hunger for pennies. The food is not high quality, so come here only if you want to break out of the Orbis monopoly system. Poles seem to be here at all hours, and despite the sign that cautions against drinking during working hours, the boys at the Kosmos enjoy a liter or two with lunch. To reach this spartan establishment, take tram 1 north; look out the right side of the car till you see the restaurant, which is clearly marked.

NIGHTLIFE: Most of the official nightlife in Częctochowa is found at the night bar of the **Hotel Patria.** The tourist must remember that, above all, this is a religious town, and the construction of a gambling casino, disco, or such establishment is unlikely to happen in the near future. There is, however, an old and prestigious university in Częstochowa, and the students have managed to find some ways to divert themselves. Given the number of students wandering around on a Friday or Saturday night, it's not unlikely that you may bump into a group looking for the proverbial 14th member.

Begin your quest for student nightlife at the **Vacans Club,** just north of the main square, Bieganskiego, at ul. Racławicka 2. Officially, the Vacans offers not just recreation, but serious activities as well: poetry readings or some structured political discussion, for example (no alcohol). Visiting the Vacans can not only introduce you to organized Polish student activities, but may also offer the possibility of meeting some locals who often move on later to a local disco or a party at someone's home. Try a few opening lines like "I'm an American." And if that doesn't seem to have any effect add "Here's a bottle of scotch" (usually available at the hard-currency shop in the Hotel Patria). These two openers will generally get you a most heartfelt and warm invitation to the group. Younger students hang out here and the place closes up at 7 p.m. or so. The Vacans is usually closed on weekends.

The more adventurous can try **Tunal,** on ulica Dekabrystów, an east-west street north of the Bieganskiego main square, for dancing. To get there, walk north on alejo Kościuszki past alejo Lenina to ulica Dekabrystów, then turn west. About 100 yards down the road are some student houses numbered 1 through 5; inside you'll find Tunal and **Rival,** two good, cheap places for drinks.

Most student clubs keep irregular hours but are rarely open past 11 p.m. on any given night, and are always closed on Sunday.

If you're not thrilled by the Hotel Patria bar or student nightlife, you'll enjoy the quiet of this well-preserved Polish town and get a good night's sleep.

3. Sights in Silesia

Almost 10% of the Polish population comes from Silesia, although the region itself accounts for only 2.1% of Poland's total land area. Rich in coal and iron ore, it is one of the most industrialized and urbanized areas of Poland. Its main cities are Katowice, Opole, and of course, Częstochowa. Archeological finds, including burial grounds and settlements, indicate that this area was probably settled around 2,500 B.C. Silesia was subject to what the Poles refer to as "Germanization," but this area was heavily settled by Germanic tribes and later Germans, until they were forcibly expelled at the end of World War II.

AROUND LAKE GOCZAŁKOWICE: The artificial Lake Goczałkowice is the center of an area with several interesting towns. Foremost among them, **Pszczyna** has several 18th-century structures including a 19th-century magnate's château, converted from an old castle. Nearby are a beautiful arboretum, and a reserve for European bison in Jankowickie forest. South of Lake Goczałkowice is the fabric-manufacturing city of **Bielsko,** and to the south of that are some of Poland's most beautiful villages. **Bestwina,** with its 16th-century church, is one of the most picturesque. To the west on the Polish-Czechoslovak border, the town of **Cieszyn** is known for its many architectural monuments, including an 11th-century Romanesque rotunda, a parish church containing many sarcophagi of the old rulers from the Piast Dynasty, and the remnants of a 14th-century castle.

KRAKÓW-CZĘSTOCHOWA UPLAND: To the north is an area known as the Kraków-Częstochowa Upland, a stretch of rolling, forested land interspersed with interesting rock formations. Concealed within the forests are the ruins of over 20 **castles** that once constituted a defensive system called the Eagles' Nests. Take a train to **Olsztyn,** seven miles from Częstochowa, a good jumping-off point for walks in this region and expeditions into the beautiful rolling hills flatteringly called the Sokole Mountains. From Olsztyn you can also visit the village of **Ostrężnick,** which is adjacent to a forest reserve and the ruins of a castle hewn out of living limestone rock.

4. Zakopane and the Tatra Mountains

At the bottom of the map of Poland, wedged between two jutting strips of land that belong to Czechoslovakia, lies a small area, 50 miles wide, where the Tatra Mountains encircle Zakopane. Although it may look insignificant on a map, this is the most awesome, inspiring landscape in all of Poland. Steep peaks towering 6,000 feet into the clouds, gushing waterfalls, snow-covered hills, completely placid lakes, and a wild animal population that includes bears, lynxes, and soaring golden eagles make up the amazing Tatra Mountains; even those city slickers who protest that they are not awed by scenes of natural grandeur will be astonished!

The appealing small mountain town of Zakopane has been a frequented resort area since the end of the 19th century, when some Polish scientists declared that the healthy Tatra Mountain air could cure tuberculosis, among other ailments. Today it is one of Poland's most-visited tourist spots with some three million visitors a year, in a town of just 30,000 inhabitants. As a result, Zakopane has become a fairly cosmopolitan town dotted with hotels, restaurants, stores, and tourist offices. Yet just beyond Zakopane's hilly streets begins the wild outdoors of the Tatra Mountains. Visitors include dedicated hikers with thick leather boots, khaki shorts, and hiking sticks, carefree Polish ski bums, noisy Polish schoolchildren, and quiet couples. If you, too, want to see the Tatras, find a hotel in Zakopane to serve as your mountain base, and then continue your explorations (or skiing, if you come during the winter).

If you are interested in skiing in the Tatra Mountains, contact Orbis in the U.S. or England. They can arrange a package deal including hotel, meals, rental of ski equipment, and cable-car tickets.

ORIENTATION: Most travelers have more trouble getting here than finding their way around after arrival, so we'll begin with . . .

Getting to Zakopane

Most travelers arrive in Zakopane via Kraków, and we offer only one piece of advice for those coming this way: Don't take the train; it takes five hours. Your best bet is the bus, which covers the distance in half the time. If, however, you are taking a long overnight train ride from some distant city, you won't want to lose sleep over a bus connection, and so it makes sense to stay on the train.

The bus and train stations are situated right across from each other on the intersection of ulica Kósciuszki and ulica Jagiellońska, just a few minutes from the center of Zakopane. The **bus station** (tel. 46-03) has a baggage check open from 7 a.m. to 7 p.m. daily. To buy your return ticket, go to window no. 4 for connections to Kraków and Warsaw. The bus to Kraków—210 złoty ($1.30)— leaves from stand 6.

The **train station** (tel. 45-04), across the street, maintains a baggage check office from 5:30 a.m. to 10:30 p.m. every day, and charges 100 złoty (65¢) per bag. You can buy return tickets at windows 4 and 5. If they are closed, go to window 2, where you can get seat and couchette reservations as well.

Useful Information

For a map of Zakopane and information about hiking trails, go to the **Tatra Tourist Information Center** at ul. Chałubińskiego 44 (tel. 43-43).

Orbis, at ul. Krupówki 22 (tel. 50-51 to 50-55, or 48-12), can assist you with your other travel needs.

Should you need to send a communication down the mountain, you'll find the **Telephone and Telegraph Headquarters** on ulica Zaruskiego, across from the Hotel Gazda. It's open from 7 a.m. to 9 p.m. weekdays, from 9 a.m. to 2 p.m. on Saturday, and from 8 a.m. to noon on Sunday and holidays (Christmas too!).

For emergency aid in the mountains, the **Mountain Volunteer Rescue Team (GOPR),** ul. Krupówki 12 (tel. 34-44), stands ready to help. For **emergency** service in Zakopane, call 999, ul. Szpitalna 21.

If your difficulties are not life-threatening but of an automotive nature, call **PZM** at 27-97, or go to their office on ulica Droga na Bystre.

After a hard day of hiking, you might want to bring a shirt, jacket, or other article of clothing to be cleaned; if so, the **Pralnia** at ul. Krupówki 16, open from 8 a.m. to 6 p.m., will do a fine job.

ACCOMMODATIONS: Visitors to Zakopane can choose to stay either in a hotel or in a small rustic pension run by Orbis; bargain-hunters can also rent private rooms, Zakopane's most inexpensive form of accommodations. Finally, the most adventurous travelers can rough it at spartan PTTK hotels in the middle of the mountains. Let us stress again that if you reserve a room in only one Polish city, reserve in Zakopane, for all the hotels are booked solid in the high season. Complete details for all your overnight options follow.

Hotels

Travelers in a splurgey mood should consider the three-star **Hotel Orbis Giewont,** ul. Kościuszki 1 (tel. 20-11 to 20-15; Telex 0322270). This hotel is the center of Zakopane looks much like a New England mountain lodge. It offers 48 quaint, narrow rooms with high ceilings and carpeting, a place in which you'll feel snug falling asleep at night after rigorous trekking in the mountains. Singles cost 4,220 złoty ($26.50) to 5,270 złoty ($33.15); doubles cost 6,330 złoty ($39.80) with bathroom and 4,190 złoty ($26.35) without—which is by far the best budget value of the hotel.

You'll quickly notice that the glass exterior of the **Hotel Gazda,** ul. Zaruskiego 2 (tel. 50-11; Telex 0325304), makes the hotel uniquely modern in a town of rustic chalets. Fans of modernity will find each of the 63 pleasant rooms framed by three large windows, which bring in lots of mountain air and light. Singles will cost you 2,880 złoty ($18.10) without bathroom, and 3,910 złoty ($24.60) with; doubles with bathroom cost 5,120 złoty ($32.20).

You'll find the **Morskie Oko,** ul. Krupówki 30 (tel. 50-76 to 50-78), a simple hotel with 43 rooms, an excellent buy. Large but bare rooms rent for 1,700 złoty ($10.70) for a single without bathroom, 2,800 złoty ($17.60) for a double without bathroom, and 3,200 złoty ($20.15) for a double with bath but no toilet.

Low-budget travelers can save money by staying at the **Dom Turysty PTTK,** Zaruskiego 5 (tel. 32-81 to 32-84), a large sturdy stone-and-wood chalet. On the way to your room you pass through a long, spacious lobby. In your room you'll also have plenty of space to stretch out, and most come with large bathrooms with vintage plumbing. Singles with bathroom rent for 2,840 złoty ($17.85); each person in a double with bathroom pays 1,910 złoty ($12) per night, or 1,800 złoty ($11.30) per person in a double without bathroom.

Student Lodgings

During July and August students can stay at the **Juventur Hotel** at ul. Słoneczna 2A (tel. 20-53 or 20-54). A private cubicle for one with a sink will cost you only 1,104 złoty ($6.95), a real value for Zakopane.

For information on other student lodgings, inquire at **Almatur,** ul. Marusarzowny 15 (tel. 57-06); they're open from 8 a.m. to 4 p.m. Monday to Friday, and to 1 p.m. on Saturday.

Pensions (Pensjonats)

Orbis coordinates the rental of Zakopane's dozen pensjonats, small inns which serve three meals a day in addition to housing you in quaint two- or three-story wood chalets. In order to rent one of these charming rooms, go either to the Orbis desk at the **Giewont Hotel,** ul. Kościuszki 1, or to the **Orbis** bureau at ul. Krupówki 22 (tel. 48-22 or 50-51), on the second floor. Upon reserving and paying for your room, you'll receive a voucher and a small map to guide you to your new home. From December 20 to January 6, full room and board costs $23 for a single, and $43 for a double; from January 7 to April 15 and from June 1 to September 30, room and board costs $21 for one person and $36 for two; and from April 10 to May 31 and October 1 to December 19, prices drop to $16 for a single and $29 for a double.

Although all the pensjonats seem to exude charm, we suggest that you ask Orbis for a room in one of the following three, as they are the most centrally located and serve the best food: **Lipowy Dwór,** an old wooden house from 1937 that offers a fine view of the mountains; **Orion,** a small stone-and-wood house; and **Rzymianka,** a small stucco building in a quiet area of Zakopane. We highly recommend pensjonats for outstanding comfort at a good price.

Private Rooms

Since prices for hotels run fairly high throughout Zakopane, and the pensjonats rapidly fill up, you should definitely consider renting a private room from the **Tatra Regional Tourist Office** at ul. Kościuszki 23A (tel. 21-51), open from 8 a.m. to 8 p.m. Rooms are divided into three classes and priced accordingly: single rooms cost 700 złoty ($4.40) to 1,460 złoty ($9.20), and double rooms cost 1,150 złoty ($7.25) to 2,240 złoty ($14). From April 6 to May 5 and from October 1 to December 19, a special off-season discount applies to these prices.

DINING: Those tired of having to go to frequently mediocre hotels for their food will delight in finding **Jędruś**, ul. Świerczewskiego 5 (tel. 31-73). Colorful ceramic plates adorn the walls, the waitresses wear bright, ornate folk dress, and the tables and chairs are carved in a traditional mountain-chalet style. What price do you pay for these pleasant surroundings? A fine beefsteak with tomatoes, potatoes, and vegetables costs only 350 złoty ($2.20). Add a hearty soup with meat, croutons, and vegetables for 130 złoty (80¢) and you've bought yourself a very tasty and filling lunch for only $3. When we visited the Jędruś, a traditional wedding celebration of a Zakopanian couple further enhanced the folk atmosphere. As you can see, this excellent restaurant maintains a charming ambience, serves good food, and celebrates many Zakopanian ceremonies in style. If only more restaurants in Poland were as pleasant as the Jędruś! Open from 9 a.m. to 8 p.m.

Some locals assert that the restaurant in the **Hotel Giewont**, ul. Kościuszki 1 (tel. 20-11), is "the only decent place to eat" in Zakopane. Although we can't agree that it's the *only* decent place, we must admit that you do eat quite well. Specialties include really superlative mushrooms, and a crispy, tender, buttery, and altogether mouthwatering chicken cutlet Giewanta! An attractive large dining room, with very tall ceilings and ceramic chandeliers, complements the fare in this highly recommended restaurant. A full meal can often be enjoyed for less than $5 at the Giewont.

Real mountaineers will savor the atmosphere of the **Obrochtowka**, ul. Kraszewskiego 10A (tel. 30-69), a small restaurant with log cabin walls on one side and cavernous stone on the other. The place caters to Poles, some of whom come to eat such specialties as chicken shish kebab for 300 złoty ($1.90); others just to drink and talk. Obrochtowka serves food from noon to 9 p.m., but remains open later to serve drinks.

You'll find another good restaurant, **Polska,** in the Kasprowy Hotel, at Droga Junakow, Polana Szymoszkowa (tel. 40-11). Located in one of most pleasant Orbis hotels in Poland, the Polska offers such traditional Polish specialties as a tender, tasty roast duck with an apple for 393 złoty ($2.50), roast rabbit for 560 złoty ($3.50), and roast mutton with noodles and beet roots for 369 złoty ($2.30). For dessert, you can choose among delightful Western sweets such as ice cream and cakes! The modern interior decoration is nothing special, but you can gaze at the beautiful mountains from the large restaurant windows. In all, the Polska offers a fine meal at very reasonable prices.

WHAT TO SEE AND DO: Having come all the way to Zakopane, you must take at least one hike into the mountains to enjoy the incredible beauty at close range. An adventurous raft river trip or an outing to nearby picturesque towns are other touring options in the region.

Mountain Excursions

We highly recommend a half- or full-day visit to **Morskie Oko** (which translates as "eye of the sea"), the largest of several lakes (86 acres) high in the mountains, 4,570 feet above sea level, right near the Czech border. Take the hour bus ride from the center of Zakopane (for 110 złoty, or 70¢) even if you have a car, as only buses are allowed all the way up the mountain to within a fair walking distance of the lake. Even the most jaded city dweller will marvel at the view, with jagged rock mountains, covered in snow even in the summer, reflected perfectly off a still lake.

Hikers will definitely want to continue walking around the lake and then up the hill on the left. It's a strenuous climb, but at the top you'll find another beautiful lake, **Czarny Staw** ("Black Pond") at 5,182 feet above sea level, where you'll observe a breathtaking panorama of Morskie Oko and the surrounding mountains.

Hiking often works up a big appetite, so your next stop might be the **Jadłospis** restaurant at the foot of Morskie Oko lake. Located inside a small wooden lodge, the Jadłospis offers hearty, though not exceptional, fare from 9 a.m. to 6 p.m. When we visited, we enjoyed an inexpensive, large plate of bigos which warmed us up after our mountain hike.

Another journey we recommend is a ride by cable car to the **Kasprowy Wierch** (6,510 feet above sea level). This 20-minute ride above the mountains will prove to be a spellbinding journey both for trekkers who want to get to the top quickly to begin their explorations, and those who just want to enjoy the ride, dine leisurely in the restaurant at top, and then return, again by cable car. To get to the cable-car station at the foot of the mountain, take a bus from Zakopane to Kuznice.

If you intend to take hikes in the Tatra Mountains other than these short treks we've outlined, definitely invest in a *Mapa Turystuczna*, which gives detailed information on the trails and lodgings up in the mountains. You can buy this helpful map at ul. Krupówki 22 (tel. 50-51 to 50-55) in Zakopane. With this map and a lot of energy, you can trek up to the highest Tatra Mountains which mark the border with Czechoslovakia. In fact, at certain points small signs delineate this border between socialist nations. As we've hinted before, real outdoors people can continue through the mountains for days, and eat and lodge at the various PTTK hotels scattered in the high Tatra area.

Side Trips

Those interested in visiting an older, more picturesque town in the mountains should visit **Nowy Sącz**, slightly to the northeast of Zakopane. Originally developed because of its importance on the "Hungarian Trade Route," Nowy Sącz, and its sister town, Stary Sącz, look as they did hundreds of years ago. For private room rentals, go to Rynek 15 (tel. 218-78), and for tourist information, go to ul. Romanowskiego 4A (tel. 218-78 or 200-00).

Those looking for more fast-paced adventure than summer hiking can ride a raft (made from a hollowed tree trunk) down the River Dunajec in the nearby **Pieniny National Park.** The three- to four-hour ride passes through beautiful, sometimes rugged, territory beneath steep rocks as high as 1,300 feet above the river. The ride is an invigorating experience that you're not likely to forget soon. Book your excursion (from May to September only) through Orbis in Nowy Sącz, Zakopane, or Kraków. Rides cost about $12 per person.

5. Lublin

Political events that took place in **Lublin** (pop. 300,000) determined the course of Polish history for hundreds of years. In 1569 an agreement signed in Lublin united Poland and Lithuania, thus forming the largest state in Europe. Poland consequently entered into the most prosperous years in its entire history. More recently, when Poland was fighting for survival in 1944 Lublin served as the country's provisional capital while the Allied forces fought back the Nazi occupier.

Lublin has evolved from a great political center into an educational and cultural capital. There are two universities in Lublin (more than in any other city in Poland), one of them Poland's only private institution of higher learning, Catholic University. Although many buildings have been erected in Lublin since World War II, the small Old Town, one of the most ancient city quarters in all of Poland, retains the picturesque atmosphere of the Middle Ages, with its Gothic castle and Renaissance houses on the main square. Just outside Lublin, the Nazi death camp Majdanek provides testimony to the horrors of World War II.

Despite its charms and majestic past, Lublin is a small city which can be seen in a day; enthusiastic travelers could even make it a day trip from Warsaw, but the two-hour drive each way (for the 100-mile journey) necessitates an early start.

ORIENTATION: Travelers arriving by train will find themselves at Plac Wojtowicza 1 (tel. 202-19), about a 15-minute walk from the center. From the station, follow ulica 1 Maja and then ulica Mariana Buczka to the Old Town. This route is rather long and may be confusing, so consider either taking bus 50 from in front of the station to Krakowskie Przedmieście, or taking a taxi to your hotel. You'll find an information desk in the station open around the clock to assist you (with breaks from 9 to 9:20 a.m. and 2 to 2:20 p.m.). To buy tickets for your departure, go to windows 2 to 6 (you'll see *bilotowe* above them). Line 1 answers questions about ticket costs, and the *biuro obsługi* across from the ticket windows sells seat and couchette reservations.

Once you reach Lublin's center, you'll find it very easy to get around by foot. The modern section of town centers around **Krakowskie Przedmieście,** and if you follow this street eastward, you arrive at the gates of the **Old Town,** a walk which we describe in the "Sights" section.

Useful Information

After checking into your hotel, you should make your way to the **Tourist Information Office** at Krakowskie Przedmieście 78 (tel. 244-12). They can give you a number of English-language pamphlets on Lublin, and they can sell you a short guide to the city for 20 złoty (15¢). They're open Monday to Friday from 8 a.m. to 8 p.m., to 3 p.m. on Saturday and Sunday (from October to June the office is closed on Sunday). Don't be put off if the office looks dark during these hours; go in anyway—they're open, but just saving on electricity expenses.

Should you require the services of **Orbis,** you'll find the main office at Krakowskie Przedmieście 25 (tel. 278-48 or 289-16). They work Monday through Friday from 9:30 a.m. to 5 p.m.

Students looking for the summer student hotel should inquire at **Almatur,** ul. Langiewicza 10 (tel. 332-37 or 332-38).

Motorists in need of assistance should contact either **PZM** (the Polish Automobile Federation) at ul. B. Prusa 8 (tel. 342-05), or **Polmozbyt** at ul. Wojciechowska 40 (tel. 320-41).

Finally, to extend your visa, go to Okopowa 2.

ACCOMMODATIONS: We highly recommend the large **Hotel Victoria,** ul. Narutowicza 56/57 (tel. 270-11; Telex 0642349), which caters to Lublin's Western visitors. You'll find it well maintained and clean, qualities not always present in Lublin hotels. In the small but pleasant rooms, you'll get a radio and telephone, as well as hygienic bathrooms. If you are lucky enough to have a room on one of the top floors of the hotel, you can also marvel at the fine view of Lublin from your window. Singles cost 3,750 złoty ($23.60) with private bathroom, and 2,730 złoty ($17.15) without. Doubles with bathroom cost 4,900 złoty ($30.80). An added bonus is a helpful receptionist, Anna Krawczyk (pronounced Crav-chick), one of the few people in Lublin who speak English. Downstairs you'll find a Pewex store, and a good, inexpensive restaurant—with entrees costing 189 złoty ($1.20) to 385 złoty ($2.40)—that many consider Lublin's best. Open noon to midnight.

If the Victoria is full, try the **Motel PZM**, ul. B. Prusa 8 (tel. 342-32; Telex PZM 3192), just a ten-minute walk to the Old Town. You'll find the rooms quite pleasant, with a plant, radio, telephone, and lots of natural light. The public bathrooms are also pleasantly clean. Single rooms rent for 3,280 złoty ($20.60) with a shower, 2,950 złoty ($18.55) without. Doubles cost 4,800 złoty ($30.20) for a complete bathroom, and 4,020 złoty ($25.30) for a shower only. In the off-season (from September 9 to June 1) prices fall 25% from these rates. A decent restaurant downstairs (open from 9 a.m. to midnight; closed Monday) serves simple dishes like goulash for 100 złoty (65¢) and roast chicken for 200 złoty ($1.25).

Starvation-budget travelers might consider staying at the **PTTK Dom Wycieczkowy** on Lublin's main street, ul. Krakowskie Przedmieście 29 (tel. 239-41). Many Polish students rent the clean, pleasant rooms here, but you should note that the public toilets are a big drawback (Mr. Clean would not be at all happy!). Fortunately, you'll find the showers much tidier. Singles with sinks in the room cost 2,400 złoty ($15), doubles cost 1,400 złoty ($8.80) to 1,560 złoty ($9.80) per person, and triples cost 1,240 złoty ($7.80) per person.

DINING: The restaurant in the **Hotel Orbis-Unia,** al. Racławickie 12 (tel. 320-609), stands out from all the others in Lublin: it's the only one to provide its foreign guests with an English-language menu! Its decor is standard hotel style —paneled wooden walls, a large expanse of windows, and a small stage (where musicians play light dinner music beginning at about 9 p.m.). Specialties include a veal steak for 500 złoty ($3.15), and a tender Chateaubriand with sauce béarnaise, served with potatoes and vegetables, for 1,008 złoty ($6.35). We also recommend the light and buttery mushroom soup, served with small bits of mushrooms. In addition to the good food, you'll be served promptly and courteously. Open from 1 p.m. to 1 a.m.

You'll find a nice, simple place for lunch in the **Restaurant Europa,** Krakowskie Przedmieście 29 (tel. 220-12). Cloth wallpaper provides a pleasant setting, and a band occupies a stage in the back of the restaurant during the evening (but not during the day). We recommend the Europa for lunch because the waiters are quick to serve, ensuring enough time for afternoon sightseeing. Prices will please the budget-hunter, with entrees running from 90 złoty (50¢) to 500 złoty ($3.15). We enjoyed a slightly oily, but tasty chock-full-of-mushrooms omelet here for only 96 złoty (60¢), as well as tasty, crispy fries for 58 złoty (35¢).

THE SIGHTS: Begin your sightseeing with a walk through Lublin's **Old Town** (Stare Miasto). As you enter the Old Town from the Krakowskie Przedmieście, you pass under the 14th-century **Kraków Gate.** The interior of the Kraków Gate serves as the **Regional Museum,** with objects from Lublin's long history; you also have a nice view of the city. It's open from 10 a.m. to 4 p.m. Monday to Saturday, to 5 p.m. on Sunday.

Continuing on the main road past the gate, you'll soon arrive at the **Rynek** (the Old Town Square), which once served as the center of business, political, and religious affairs in Lublin. At this square you can still see the Gothic 14th-century **Old Town Hall,** which is also known as the Tribunal, in reference to its use from the 16th century onward.

If you turn right at the Old Town Square, you reach the **Dominican Church and Monastery,** a 14th-century "must see" built by King Casimir the Great. Closely inspect the beautiful frescos dating back to the 17th and 18th centuries in the church's chapels. Monastic buildings are connected to the church on the side.

After you leave the core of the Old Town away from the modern center, you'll come to the impressive 14th-century **castle,** at ul. Zamkowa 9, also built by King Casimir the Great, but greatly restored in the 19th century with a flamboyant, almost Arabic façade. During the Middle Ages important political meetings were often held in the castle, and the Polish king frequently received visitors and foreign envoys here. During World War II the Nazi occupiers used the castle as their regional headquarters, where they interrogated and tortured some 400,000 prisoners in five years. Today the castle museum displays Polish paintings and folk art. Open Tuesday, Thursday, and Friday from 10 a.m. to 4 p.m., on Wednesday and Sunday to 5 p.m., and on Saturday to 3 p.m.; closed Monday.

Four kilometers (2½ miles) away from the center of Lublin, you'll find the concentration camp **Majdanek** (on Męczennikow Majdanka Road), which was second only to Auschwitz among concentration camps in Poland in the number of deaths. Today the camp remains much as it was more than 40 years ago when 360,000 people from 30 countries were murdered. We especially recommend that you see this sight if you won't have a chance to visit Auschwitz—it is unforgettable. Open Tuesday to Sunday from 8 a.m. to 6 p.m. from May 1 to September 15, and 8 a.m. to 3 p.m. the rest of the year. Take bus 7 or 23, or trolleybus 58 from the center of Lublin to get here.

TRANSPORTATION FROM LUBLIN: Travelers continuing on to Kraków, Częstochowa, or other cities to the southwest will need to take a bus from the **bus station** at al. Tysiąclecia 9, on Nowy Plac Targowy (tel. 266-49), as no direct rail connections exist. Buses depart once a day for Zakopane, and about a dozen times daily for Kraków and Warsaw. You can check your bags here from 6 a.m. to 7:30 p.m.; look for the sign reading *przechowalnia bagazu.*

You'll also find a colorful outdoor food market in the square in front of the station where local peasants sell their produce, so you can stock up on fruits and vegetables before your journey.

6. Side Trips from Lublin

The day-tripper from Lublin can choose between two of Poland's most charming little towns: **Kazimierz Dolny** and **Zamość.**

KAZIMIERZ DOLNY: Those who enjoy quaint towns with cobblestone streets, few cars, and a spacious town square with a large water well in the middle are sure to appreciate **Kazimierz Dolny,** less than half an hour's drive from Lublin (25 miles away). Small houses and narrow streets built in the late Renaissance style, along with the impressive remains of a 14th-century castle reigning above the city, all add to the charm of this picturesque town on the Vistula River banks. From the top of the castle (built by King Casimir the Great), you'll marvel at the breathtaking view of the town and the surrounding lush countryside. Previously, as many as 30,000 Jews lived in Kazimierz Dolny, but today there are none—they were all killed in World War II.

Orientation

Take the bus from Lublin to Kazimierz Dolny; it will deposit you within a block of the Town Square (Rynek). Upon arrival, go to the **Tourist Information Office** in the main Town Square at no. 27 (tel. 46); they sell a booklet in English called "Kazimierz Dolny and the Countryside."

Accommodations

Should you become so enchanted with Kazimierz Dolny that you want to spend the night, the rustic **PTTK Murka Tourist House,** ul. Krakowska 29 (tel. 36), has decent rooms but borderline public bathrooms. Singles with bath but no toilet cost 3,560 złoty ($22.40), and a double with bath but no toilet costs 2,400 złoty ($15) per person.

The town also has another basic PTTK hotel, the **Dom Wycieczkowy,** at ul. Czerniary 37 (tel. 96), and two camping sites as well.

Dining

Kazimierz Dolny will delight all with a sweet tooth; the town's unique culinary specialty is gingerbread animals (Kazimierzowski kogut). If you go to **Piekarnia,** at ul. Nadrzeczna 6 (a block away from the Town Square), you can choose among a large gingerbread chicken, alligator, and other animals for only 60 złoty (35¢) each.

For a full meal, go to **J. Michalski's** house at Nadrzeczna 616. He runs an *obiady domowe,* a unique and increasingly rare Polish treat that brings together travelers and a local family to serve you, along with a few other guests—Polish home-cooking in a genuine Polish home!

ZAMOŚĆ: Over the past few hundred years the decayed old buildings of Europe's cities have been replaced by modern structures and new streets, thus greatly altering the original town plans. In fact, in all of Europe only one humble town, **Zamość,** an enjoyable half-day trip from Lublin, retains its original Renaissance layout! An Italian architect designed this small attractive town in the 16th century, and today you can still enjoy the original charm. The architectural features include a very spacious main square with a symmetrical and tall town hall at the center, and a covered passageway circling the entire square. The effect is so authentic that you might even expect a messenger to ride into this beautiful town square and read a royal pronouncement to the townspeople! Zamość is only about an hour away from Lublin (53 miles) by train or bus.

Accommodations

If you want to spend the night, the best choice is the **Hotel Renesans,** ul. Grecka 6 (tel. 20-01). Here you'll rest in very pleasant rooms just a few minutes away from the Renaissance market square. From June to August, singles with bath but no toilet cost 2,650 złoty ($16.65), and doubles cost 4,110 złoty ($25.85); prices are lower at other times of the year.

PTTK also runs a hotel in Zamość, but we cannot recommend it as the public bathrooms are not clean.

Dining

A simple town like Zamość doesn't offer fancy dining, but by frequenting the **Hetmanska,** ul. Staszica 7 (tel. 25-63), you can enjoy a good meal in an attractive local place with vaulted ceilings and wooden tables. Meals are very inexpensive, with no entree above 200 złoty ($1.25). For instance, simply prepared lamb cutlet or pork steak costs 199 złoty ($1.25). Open from 10 a.m. to 10 p.m.

Chapter VI

THE BALTIC COAST AND NORTHEAST POLAND

1. Gdańsk
2. Sopot
3. Gdynia
4. Baltic Coast Excursions
5. Szczecin
6. The Mazurian Lakes Region

MUCH OF WHAT WESTERNERS KNOW about Poland's Baltic Coast relates to politics. When Winston Churchill announced the presence of an "Iron Curtain" in Eastern Europe, it began "from Stettin in the Baltic." In more recent years, when Poland suffered through internal division due to the rise of Solidarity, the new trade union had its headquarters in Gdańsk.

With all of this momentous history in their minds, visitors often overlook the great charms and beauty of the area around Poland's Baltic Sea coast. Gdańsk preserves the picturesque atmosphere of an important seafaring town of hundreds of years ago. And Gdańsk forms only one part (albeit the largest and best known) of the Baltic's Trojmiasto or Tri-City (a grouping of cities much like New York City's five boroughs) of Gdańsk, the resort town Sopot, and the largely industrial town of Gdynia. You can visit Sopot in just 15 to 20 minutes by car or train from Gdańsk, or Gdynia in just 30 to 40 minutes, so your visit to Gdańsk combines three cities for the price of one.

In addition to Gdańsk, the Baltic Coast offers attractive beaches and sleepy fishing towns. Although Szczecin (formerly Stettin) lost many historic structures in World War II, the smaller towns in the area boast old defensive walls and castles from the Middle Ages as well as impressive Gothic churches.

Finally, those interested in getting away from the modern world will greatly enjoy a visit to the Mazurian Lake region, located to the east of Gdańsk. Here the visitor can do everything from swimming, fishing, boating, to just plain nothing but relaxing among an unspoiled chain of beautiful lakes.

We first detail Gdańsk, Sopot, and Gdynia, followed by some suggested side trips. Then we swing west to Szczecin, followed by a visit back east to the Mazurian Lakes.

1. Gdańsk

You can hardly find a more charming enclave in all of Poland than Gdańsk's Main Town, where 18th-century Gdańsk still lives in the blocks now closed off to traffic. Tall, narrow buildings with peaked roofs and decorative façades, each painted a different color, line the wide cobblestone streets. Church bells ringing throughout the day add to the bustle of the streets filled with shoppers and strollers. Even though most of the area's Renaissance buildings were reconstructed following World War II, they look surprisingly authentic, as though they had not been touched for hundreds of years. As you walk to the old port, the houses on the canal at the edge of the Main Town may remind you of Amsterdam. One or two houses on the port are so narrow that only one window fits on each floor!

At the same time, significant contrasts mark Gdańsk, most notably in the areas where its role as a major Polish industrial center is evident. The cranes of the famous Lenin Shipyards are visible throughout the city, and squalor characterizes the area near the shipyards. So the Gdańsk of today embodies the great charm of an old seafaring town, as well as the problems of a major industrial center. In sum, the city provides a fascinating glimpse into the past alongside the present, an interesting contrast you won't want to miss.

HISTORY: A Polish settlement was recorded in Gdańsk as early as A.D. 999, and for hundreds of years thereafter Gdańsk served as a fishing and trading outpost. The city has not always been Polish; it changed hands between the Poles and Germans six times, and for three periods it maintained an independent status. Gdańsk dates its importance back to the 13th century, when it joined the Hanseatic League, a group of merchants in northern Europe. Starting in the prosperous 16th century under Polish rule, Gdańsk enjoyed a meteoric development as it became the city through which all of Poland's maritime trade was transported. With the partition of Poland in 1793, the city went back into Prussian hands; its name was again changed to the German Danzig, and its trading importance rapidly declined.

After World War I and the Treaty of Versailles, Gdańsk was declared the "Free State of Danzig." Poland had limited rights in the city, such as permission to run the local post office and Customs bureau, but throughout the between-war years, Polish-German relations were strained over Danzig. In August 1939 many healthy German male "tourists" visited Danzig, and the German battleship *Schleswig-Holstein* paid a "courtesy" visit to the port. Days later on September 1, this battleship started shelling the Polish garrison at Westerplatte, and World War II began.

The war destroyed 90% of Gdańsk's town center, and extensive restorations were undertaken immediately after the war. Gdańsk's postwar history has been marked by turbulence, and numerous workers' uprisings have taken place. Most notably, Gdańsk spawned the Solidarity trade union in 1980; even today many Poles still consider the town the spiritual center of Solidarity.

ORIENTATION: Several different districts make up the city of Gdańsk, though the **Main Town (Głowne Miasto)**, where Gdańsk's historic buildings and sights are concentrated, will be of most interest. The medieval arrangement of the streets in the Main Town makes it easy to find your way around; all the major avenues lead to the port, and the small streets link up these major avenues. The main avenue to the port is **Długi Targ** ("The Long Market"), which we discuss in depth in the "Sights" section, along with a description of the adjacent area.

If you arrive by train or bus, the Orbis and tourist information office are directly across a busy highway, ulica Podwale Grodzkie (see important addresses). You'll find the beginning of the Main Town to your right, about a ten-minute walk down ulica Podwale Grodzkie.

If you fly to Gdańsk, you'll arrive at the Rębiechowo Airport (tel. 41-52-51 or 41-31-41), 14 miles from the center. Take bus 131 or 162 to the Main Town, or the LOT bus (if it's functioning). To get to the airport, a special LOT bus leaves one hour before LOT flights from Targ Węglowy (the square in front of Długi) and the Hotel Monopol (in front of the train station). Make sure to ask Orbis if these buses are running as scheduled, so you don't risk missing your flight.

Important Addresses

Our nomination for the most helpful worker in the entire Orbis organization is Wojciech Łygaś, who can be found in the main **Orbis** office across from the train station at ul. Heweliusza 22 (tel. 31-49-44, 31-45-44, or 31-40-45). Not only does Mr. Łygaś speak English well, but he's also happy to give helpful information and advice, with no strings attached. If you desire, you can also book a four-hour guided tour of the city from him.

You'll also find a **Tourist Information Center** down the street at ul. Heweliusza 8 (tel. 31-03-38), but, alas, they don't give you the same service that the Orbis office does; they may not even speak English, depending upon who's working when you visit.

You'll find the main **LOT** office at Długa 79/80 (tel. 31-40-26), and the **Almatur** office at ul. Długi Targ 11 (tel. 31-78-01 or 31-78-18).

The main **post office** (open 24 hours) is located at Długa 22.

If you're searching for some good in-depth English-language guides to Gdańsk, go to the **Dom Ksiazki** at Długi Targ 62/63.

For car troubles, call **PZM** (tel. 323-550, 21-05-22, or 981), with an office at Kartushka 187.

ACCOMMODATIONS: Gdańsk does not offer many budget lodgings. First try to find a private room. If that fails, either rent a room in one of the following hotels, or consider staying in Sopot.

Hotels

Exhausted train travelers will welcome the proximity of the three-star **Hotel Orbis-Monopol,** Plac Gorkiego 1 (tel. 31-68-51; Telex 0512238), to the main train station—it's right across the street. The Monopol may seem somewhat old, though, and in fact the Orbis-Monopol is conspicuously absent from Orbis's glossy brochures which proudly list information and photos of all their hotels. Nonetheless, you can rent one of 125 medium-sized rooms containing a radio and phone at $22 for a single without bathroom, and $30 for a single with. Doubles rent for $33 without bathroom, and $41 with. Because it's a bit pricey, we recommend the Monopol only if you are dead-set against staying in Sopot.

Hotel Jantar, ul. Długi Targ 19 (tel. 31-62-41), on Gdańsk's most appealing street, in an area of decorative Renaissance buildings with a king's palace right near by, appears to be a perfect solution to where to stay. Unfortunately, it's too good to be true: most travelers will find the public bathrooms rather unsavory. From July 1 to September 31, the two-star Jantar charges 3,350 złoty ($21) for singles without bath, 4,250 złoty ($26.75) to 4,730 złoty ($29.75) for a double without bath, and 5,680 złoty ($35.75) for a double with a large bathtub only. Prices for the 56 rooms drop 17% to 25% in other times of the year. Only travelers who will accept spartan accommodations for a great location and a view from their rooms should choose the Jantar.

Private Accommodations

You'll be hard-pressed to find anything cheaper or more pleasant than the private accommodations in Gdańsk. You can arrange to rent a large, clean room near the center for only 1,750 złoty ($11) for a single or 2,440 złoty ($15.35) for a double at the **Biuro Zakwaterowania,** in Gdańsk's Tourist Office at ul. Elżbietańska 10/11 (tel. 31-26-34 or 31-38-49), across from the train station.

As you walk toward the office, you may notice someone in front of the mail box on the Gdańsk Tourist Office's façade. He (or she) is mailing a letter, you say? No, chances are that that person wants to offer you a private room. We've found that most of these freelance operators are honest, but you always take a slight risk in renting from someone not screened by the bureau. If you decide to strike your own private room deal, don't forget to register at the Militia Registration Office for Foreigners at Okopowa 9 (tel. 31-62-21).

DINING IN GDAŃSK: If you're looking for an old seaport's ambience, where a salty captain with a corn-cob pipe in his mouth might down some brew with local shipowners, visit the **Tawerna Restauracja Bar,** ul. Powroźnicza 19/20 (tel. 31-41-14). Those who love the sea can admire the pictures of old sailing ships that cover the restaurant's attractive wood-paneled walls. The unique atmosphere makes the Tawerna one of Gdańsk's most-frequented restaurants, and you'll find a smartly dressed crowd sipping drinks at the long bar that stretches across the length of the restaurant. You can enjoy an excellent meal at the Tawerna for only a few dollars an entree, which may include a simple, delicate chicken cutlet for 370 złoty ($2.35), or a tasty fried steak with mushrooms and fries for 477 złoty ($3). You'll find other specialties, including roast duck, mutton, and several beefsteak dishes, at similar prices. The waitresses serve with speed and efficiency, and they can also help translate the Polish-only menu. Need we say more? Go to soak up the atmosphere and devour the food!

Another of our favorites is **Pod Łososiem** ("Under the Salmon"), ul. Szeroka 54, a posh restaurant which has been visited by the richest patricians and foreign merchants for hundreds of years. First opened as an inn in 1598 during Gdańsk's golden years, the restaurant made and served its own liquor. Although it closed down in World War II, in 1976 it opened again with all its former elegance. Hand-holding romantics should make their way over immediately. On entering, you pass through an elegant Renaissance parlor room. Inside the restaurant, a dark-stained wood ceiling supported by large beams, brass chandeliers hanging from the ceilings, and paintings of old Gdańsk on the walls surround you. Best of all, there are candles on the tables, and as far as we can predict, this is likely to be your only candlelit meal in all of Eastern Europe, so enjoy! Baltic Sea fish is the specialty here, and you can choose among boiled trout, salmon, eel, and other fish from the day's catch for $4 to $5. Those in a really splurgey mood can order the "Sailor's Plate," a selection of trout, salmon, eel, and other fish in one giant dish, all for 2,259 złoty ($14.20). If you don't want to eat fish, other options include roast duck with apples, boar steak, and pheasant. Prices are higher than in most Polish restaurants, so count on spending about $10 a person for a memorable meal. Open 11 a.m. to 11 p.m.; try to reserve.

In the Wrzeszcz District

Bargain-hunters with a large appetite will find excellent value in the **Cristal Restaurant,** at ul. Grunwaldzka 105, in the Wrzeszcz district of Gdańsk, heading toward Sopot. A basic complete meal, such as a hot plate of bigos and boiled potatoes, or beef, carrots, and potatoes costs only 100 złoty (65¢) to 200 złoty ($1.25). When you enter this cafeteria-style restaurant, go up to the glass counter and point to the food you want; then go to the separate area to order your beverages. You're likely to find that the food tastes just as good as in many restaurants, except that you can eat right away without waiting. Most buses and trams going toward Sopot from in front of the train station pass the Cristal.

Those desiring a more leisurely, quieter lunch in the area should visit the **Newska,** ul. Grunwaldzka 99/101, just down the block from the Cristal. The interior suggests an old country tavern, with folk woodcarvings and decorative tapestries on the walls. The Newska gives excellent budget value, and you can sample such dishes as tender lamb steak with tomatoes and fries (stek barani) for 327 złoty ($2), roast chicken with fries and cabbage (kurczak pieczony) for 430 złoty ($2.70), and various soups for less than a dollar. It's open from 10 a.m. to 10 p.m. The restaurant may be a bit hard to find as it's on the second floor, so ask for directions.

NIGHTLIFE: American students looking to find their Polish counterparts should not fail to visit the lively **Interclub ZAK** at Wały Jagiellońskie 1, on the second floor above the Leningrad moviehouse. The ZAK runs an entertainment program that you could call avant-garde for Eastern Europe. Huge posters and words of praise for such rock masters as Jimi Hendrix cover the dance floor walls. When the disco is not in session, the club screens movies like James Bond classics (if you consider that English spy Bond's traditional enemy is SMERSH, a division of the KGB, then you'll understand why films of this nature constitute "provocative Western propaganda," and are thus rarely shown). ZAK stays open from 8 p.m. to 2 a.m. on Friday and Saturday, until 1 a.m. weekdays.

Farther from the town center you'll find the **Bar Eda,** on ulica Startowa in the Oliwa district, another good place to meet Polish students. The club offers a bar on one side and a dance floor on the other. It's open from 6 p.m. to 4 a.m. every day except Wednesday. If you grow bored at the Eda, go next door to the **Romantica,** ul. Startowa 31, the most modern-looking club in the entire Tri-City area, with chrome fixtures and hi-tech lighting throughout. A more mature crowd in their 30s comes to dance on the small floor and drink at the bar near the entrance. The Romantica's owner, Stefan Matkowski, set up an excellent sound system when he opened the club in 1984, but you pay a price for this modernity: a bottle of Gran Cinzano spumante costs about $20! The club is open from 8 p.m. to 4 a.m., seven days a week.

Music lovers who prefer to take in their music at a concert hall can attend performances at the **State Baltic Opera and Philharmonic,** at al. Zwycięstwa 15 in the Wrzeszcz district. Inquire at Orbis for the current program.

THE SIGHTS: Begin your sightseeing of the Main Town from Plac 1 Maja, just a few blocks to the right of the train station. Starting from this square toward the Renaissance port, you pass the **High Gate** and then the **Golden Gate,** two historic entrances to the city. After these gates, Gdańsk's **Royal Road** (ulica Długi) begins, the street where the Polish king used to greet the locals during his annual visit. After a few blocks you'll pass the 14th-century **Town Hall,** which currently houses the **Gdańsk Historical Museum,** open Tuesday, Wednesday, and Friday from 10 a.m. to 4 p.m., on Thursday from 11 a.m. to 6 p.m., on Saturday from

10 a.m. to 2 p.m., and on Sunday from 11 a.m. to 4 p.m. You can also enjoy a fine view of Gdańsk from the top of the tall Town Hall tower.

Continuing on past the Town Hall, you'll notice that the street widens and **Długi Targ** ("The Long Market") begins. This area has served as the town's main center and marketplace for hundreds of years, and each year during August, the Long Market comes alive again in **St. Dominic's Fair.** At this fair, you can buy colorful folk crafts and artistic works, as well as enjoy theatrical and musical performances.

Immediately on your left after the Town Hall, you can photograph the famous 17th-century symbol of Gdańsk, the **Neptune Fountain** (yes, the one that spurts water from the sea god's pitchfork). Behind the fountain lies one of Gdańsk's most elegant buildings, the **Artus Manor** (Dwor Artusa), built during the 15th to 17th centuries in the Renaissance style. Local patricians often met and reveled here in days of yore; today the manor displays modern art exhibitions. The richest traders and nobility lived in the other 16th- to 18th-century buildings on this street, as Długi Targ was the "in" place to live. Even the king stayed on Długi Targ when he visited. His house, known as the **Green Gate,** is found at the end of the street just before the port.

Passing under the king's Green Gate, you now find yourself at the **Old Port** embankment. You'll probably agree that these Renaissance riverfront buildings make up one of Poland's most charming sights. In the distance you're sure to notice the distinctive Gothic **Harbor Crane,** a very large Dutch-looking wood building from 1444 with a bright-orange roof which curves over the waterfront. This crane (the oldest of its kind in Europe) was used to hoist up masts and unload cargo from boats as they pulled into the Gdańsk harbor. The Harbor Crane houses the **Maritime Museum,** at ul. Szeroka 67/68, open Tuesday, Wednesday, and Friday through Sunday from 10 a.m. to 2 p.m., and on Thursday from noon to 6 p.m.; closed Monday. Displays document the history of Gdańsk's merchant marine and seafaring tradition.

Across the Motława River on the embankment lies **Granary Island** (Wyspa Spichlerze); during the height of Gdańsk's importance as a shipping power, some 175 granaries stored grain, one of Poland's major exports at the time. Today you can still spot traces of World War II damage in the area as quite a few buildings (including a number of the old granaries) remain in rubble.

After walking along the embankment, return to the town center on **ulica Mariacka,** a quiet cobblestone street with charming houses. Memorable sculptures and great ornaments adorn the fronts of these homes, each of which has a large staircase leading up to the parlor floor. Note the drainpipes of these buildings: the water, instead of exiting through a plain tube of metal from the roof, comes through sculptures of dragons and angry gargoyles.

At the end of ulica Mariacka, turn right and then take the first left and you will reach the Gothic **Church of Our Lady** (Kościół Mariacki) on ulica Piwna. It's Poland's largest church (and indeed, the largest brick church in the world!) and can hold up to 25,000 people at a time. It was erected in the 14th century but greatly reconstructed after World War II.

The Gdańsk Shipyards

The **Monument to Shipyard Workers** outside the Lenin Shipyards, one of Gdańsk's most noted monuments, is less than a decade old. Unveiled in December 1980 after only four months of work, the immense monument (130 feet high) of three crosses and an anchor commemorates the 28 workers who died in the unrest of 1970. In many ways it serves as a symbol of the Solidarity trade union, and in fact the construction of the monument came thanks to the demands of the outlawed trade union in August 1980. During the heyday of Solidarity from December 1980 to 1981, Polish workers often demonstrated around this monument. The bronze bas-reliefs at the base show scenes of Polish workers, and you'll even see one inscription with the word Solidarity which the authorities have decided to let stand.

The **Lenin Shipyards** (Stocznia Gdańska im Lenina) do not allow individual travelers to visit; however, you may be able to go on an Orbis-arranged tour. Apply at Orbis at least a week beforehand. Even if you don't get into the shipyards, you'll see the massive ship cranes (which help build boats and then put them into the sea) dominating the Gdańsk skyline. If you let your imagination run wild (and ours always does), each crane looks like a massive arm with the elbow facing the sky and the forearm reaching back to the earth.

To reach the shipyards, take trolleybus 9 or 10 from Plac 1 Maja at the end of ulica Długi, and get off at ulica Jana Z Kolna (you'll see the huge monument on this square). If you continue walking in the shipyards area, especially away from the town center, you'll see some unglamorous worker's quarters.

Westerplatte

At Westerplatte, located at the mouth of Gdańsk's inland ports, a garrison of 182 Polish soldiers held out in the fighting against 4,000 Germans for one week in September 1939 as World War II began. Only 15 Poles died in the futile fighting, which starkly contrasts with the some 400 German deaths. Today a memorial, a small exhibition, and a few burnt-out barracks stand in the area. The sight can be interesting for history buffs, but otherwise there's little to warrant a visit.

To reach Westerplatte, take bus 106 from Plac 1 Maja, or take the one-hour scenic boat ride from the port at the town center's Green Gate.

More Sights

Celebrity-seekers on the lookout for Gdańsk's most famous personality, Lech Wałęsa (pronounced Wa-vensa in Polish) should go to the **Šw. Brygidy** church at ul. Profesorska 17 in Stare Miasto on Sunday morning. The former shipyard electrician regularly attends the church ceremony, along with many other shipyard workers. On the Sunday we visited, the crowd of worshippers overflowed into the rain outside; they continued to pray and participate in the service despite the downpour. To determine the best time, try to find out when the "national mass" (in the name of Poland) takes place. Both locals and tourists usually find this mass the most moving of the day's ceremonies.

Those with a taste for art shouldn't miss the **National Museum,** housed in a former Franciscan monastery at ul. Rźeznicka 25. The major piece is the Flemish master Hans Memling's *Last Judgment;* the museum also displays Gothic, Renaissance, and baroque art, as well as some furniture built in the distinctive Gdańsk style. May 16 to September 15 the museum is open from 9 a.m. to 2 p.m. Wednesday to Friday and Sunday, and from 11 a.m. to 7 p.m. on Tuesday and Saturday; the rest of the year it's open Wednesday, Thursday, and Sunday from 9 a.m. to 3 p.m., on Tuesday from 10 a.m. to 6 p.m., on Friday from 10 a.m. to 3 p.m., and on Saturday from 9 a.m. to 2 p.m.

Another impressive sight in the Oliwa district consists of the Gothic **cathedral** (off ulica Armii Radzieckiej) that was first constructed in the 13th century. Notice the distinctive façade with a very tall, narrow front marked by two thin turrets on both sides. Inside you'll see one of the largest and most impressive organs in all of Europe (from the 18th century). Before the days of electricity, seven men were needed to operate the bellows that pump air into the organ's 6,300 pipes! You can hear organ concerts here Tuesday evenings during July and

August. Take tram 2 or 6 from in front of the train station in the direction of Sopot.

2. Sopot

Poland's crème de la crème have visited the Polish Baltic's premier resort town since early in the last century, and until World War II visitors to Sopot enjoyed beautiful unspoiled beaches by day and a wild nightlife that centered around a large casino. Since then, the casino burned down (in World War II) and the industrial waste from Gdańsk and Gdynia has polluted the town's sea water. Nonetheless, Sopot remains one of Poland's most lively and appealing resort towns (albeit without swimming and gambling!): Victorian architecture lines the streets and a wide variety of cultural activities take place throughout the year. We recommend a visit to Sopot during your sojourn in Gdańsk; you might even stay in a budget hotel here and travel to Gdańsk by day.

ORIENTATION: Most of Sopot's major streets run parallel to the sea; the town's foremost shopping and tourist promenade, **Monte Cassino,** however, is perpendicular to the sea. From the train station, walk to your left down the small hill; when you come to Plac Konstytucji 3 Maja, turn right onto the beginning of Sopot's famous and picturesque pedestrian mall. Should you want to leave luggage behind at the train station, you'll find the baggage depot open at all hours.

If you prefer not to take the commuter train from Gdańsk to Sopot, Poland's amazing taxis will charge (rather, *should* charge) only about 300 złoty ($1.90) for the 15-minute ride.

Important Addresses

Orbis is at ul. Bohaterów Monte Cassino 49 (tel. 51-41-42). There's a **Tourist Information Center** at Monte Cassino 31 (tel. 51-06-18).

To extend your visa, go to ul. 20 Października 736.

ACCOMMODATIONS: You want to see Gdańsk, so why in the world should you stay in Sopot? We've come up with several good reasons. First, Gdańsk offers only a few budget hotels, which often fill up so you may be forced to look for a hotel elsewhere. Second, the larger number of hotels in Sopot gives you a better chance to find a good budget buy. And finally, Sopot sponsors more cultural events than Gdańsk, ranging from opera in the woods to punk rock, so after a day of sightseeing in Gdańsk you can enjoy an evening of fun near your hotel in Sopot.

In the Center

If you want to be in the center of Sopot, you can hardly do better than at the **Hotel Dworcowy,** ul. Konstytucji 3 Maja no. 2 (tel. 510-034 or 511-525), a 28-room hotel right across from the train station and just five minutes from the beach. They have informed us that prices will rise substantially, so we can only estimate that rooms without bathrooms will cost about $18 for a single, and $25 to $30 for a double. You'll also find that they maintain the public facilities well.

A Splurge Choice

We think the **Hotel-Orbis Grand,** ul. Powstańców Warszawy 8/12 (tel. 51-00-41 to 51-00-49; Telex 051360), is so special that we have to include it even though it costs far more than the average budget hotel. This 1926 hotel on the beachfront maintains a very stately demeanor. It reminds us of the Des Bains hotel in Venice, where the aging Mr. Aschenbach stayed in the film version of

Death in Venice. The building resembles a huge royal palace from the outside with its long noble façade and red-tiled roof. Inside, the 156 huge rooms are equally impressive. Turn-of-the-century details, such as old brass faucets and gigantic tubs in the bathrooms, as well as wood-and-mirror closets and period furniture, ornament the interior. The rooms facing the beach offer a great view in addition to everything else. It's no wonder that visiting dignitaries, from the Shah of Iran to Charles de Gaulle, have stayed here. From June 1 to September 31 the Grand charges $32 for a bathless single, and $46 for a single with bathroom; doubles rent for $49 without bathroom and $65 with. In the off-season, prices fall to $20 to $28 for a single and $30 to $38 for a double. We like this hotel so much that we unhesitatingly recommend it as one of Poland's most pleasant.

Visitors in Sopot speak of the Grand's restaurant downstairs as Sopot's best; offerings include roast turkey with tasty (not oily) fries, Chateaubriand, and a flavorful cherry soup with rhubarb. Entrees cost $3 to $5. Try to sit at one of the romantic window tables overlooking the Baltic Sea.

Outside the Center

If you have a car, consider staying at the budget **Hotel Bałtyk,** Bieruta 83 (tel. 51-62-69, 51-57-51, or 51-32-95), a motel made up of several different buildings with separate entrances for each room. A double with bath rents for only 1,755 złoty ($11), and a triple rents for 2,430 złoty ($15.30). You can find the Bałtyk by heading in the direction of Gdynia from Sopot.

Although located near Gdynia, the **Pensjonat Maryla,** al. Sępia 22 (tel. 510-034), offers 25 nice but narrow rooms with clean bathrooms at a reasonable price. Singles rent for 2,880 złoty ($18.10) without bathroom and 3,540 złoty ($22.25) with; doubles without bath cost 3,910 złoty ($24.60). It's just a two-minute walk to the beach from the hotel.

Private Rooms

The organization that can help you find a private room is the **Biuro Zakwaterowan,** on your right about half a block down the street from the train station at ul. Dworcowa 4 (tel. 51-26-17). They charge slightly more than the Gdańsk bureau does: 1,910 złoty ($12) for a single and 2,910 złoty ($18.30) for a double. They're open from 7 a.m. to 9 p.m. Don't be surprised if almost everyone in front of the bureau also attempts to rent you a room.

DINING: As you first walk into the **Restaurant Ermitage,** ul. Monte Cassino 23, you'll see an uninspiring shade of green on the walls, but after a while the decor will grow on you. Silky window shades allow subdued light to filter in, highlighting the green walls and the many plants in the restaurant. Even if green's not your favorite color, the chefs will see to it that you still enjoy some tasty standard Polish specialties prepared with a light and practiced hand. Try the flaczki sopocis z piecz, a slightly muddy-looking chicken soup with a touch of spice at 169 złoty ($1), and one of the chicken dishes, perhaps the roast chicken (kurcze piezone) for 445 złoty ($2.80). In the evening, music accompanies your meal.

For good budget fare, try the restaurant in the basement of the **Pensjonat Irena,** ul. Chopina 36 (tel. 512-073), where you can feast on quality home-cooking. The small dining room only holds a dozen tables and so every item is individually prepared when you order. During our meal we were treated to a creamy tomato soup for 27 złoty (15¢) and a simple but tasty chicken cutlet for 209 złoty ($1.30).

NIGHTLIFE: Sopot offers a richer cultural program than Gdańsk, especially in the summer. We particularly enjoy the summer **Opera in the Woods** (Opera

Lesna), ul. Moniuszki 10, which performs such classics as *Carmen* and *Aïda*. You can find out the latest program and buy tickets at the Sopot Orbis office or at the BART office at ul. Kościuszki 61. Tickets for this memorable evening only cost 200 złoty ($1.25). And you will indeed find the opera theater outdoors in the woods; you can get there by walking on Monte Cassino away from the sea, but you may find it easier to take a taxi. Call 51-44-43 for further information.

If the weather isn't suitable for an outdoor evening, why not see a film? Several theaters on Monte Cassino show American and English films in the original language. A two-hour movie will only cost you about 120 złoty (75¢).

If you want to check out the local scene, go to **Spatif,** at Monte Cassino 54. Actors, musicians, and local artists all come here to enjoy the café and night-club. You see much drinking here, but no dancing.

THE SIGHTS: Sopot is a 20th-century resort town, and the main areas to visit are the pedestrian mall, Monte Cassino, and the park at the end of the mall. A 1,680-foot pier extends from the park out to sea; you can catch ferries from the pier to Gdańsk, Westerplatte, Gdynia, and Hel for less than a dollar each way.

To see what Sopot might have looked like in its glory days before the war, wander on ulica Westerplatte, a few minutes' walk from Monte Cassino.

3. Gdynia

Gdynia makes up the third part of the Polish Tri-City. Although Gdynia's industry plays an important role in the Polish economy, the city offers little to the average traveler. It was first built up after World War I when the Poles felt that the so-called Free State of Danzig was not serving Polish shipping interests, and so in the 1920s Gdynia rapidly grew into a major port and shipping town.

Orbis is at ul. Świętojańska 36 (tel. 20-18-50).

DINING: You can dine and dance at the **Maxim,** ul. Bohaterów Stalingradu 15, one of the Tri-City's most expensive places. Choose from the Maxim cutlet of breaded pork with vegetables and cabbage, a sautéed trout dish, or many other entrees for about $5 each. A mixed crowd of Poles and foreigners comes to relax in Maxim's, with dim lighting and soft music playing in the background. In the bar in the backroom there are tables where you can have drinks. The scantily dressed waitresses are a most unusual sight for Eastern Europe. The Maxim is open from 8 p.m. to the forbidding hour of 5 a.m., every day!

THE SIGHTS: Even a Polish printed pamphlet admits that "Gdynia has no his-torical monuments of architecture." Those interested in maritime affairs may, however, want to visit one of three museums in Gdynia. The **Oceanographic Museum and Aquarium,** al. Zjednoczenia 1, displays living and model speci-mens of marine life. The threatening warship in the harbor, the *Błyskawica,* which fought in World War II, now houses a small **ship museum,** open May 1 through October 15 from 10 a.m. to 1 p.m. and 2 to 5 p.m. on Tuesday and Sunday only. To the left of the pier lies the town **Naval Museum,** on Bulwar Szwedzki, open Tuesday through Sunday from 10 a.m. to 5 p.m.

4. Baltic Coast Excursions

TO THE BEACH: Just because the beach in the Gdańsk area has been polluted doesn't mean you won't be able to get in some swimming while in Poland. You'll find a number of beaches on the nearby Baltic Coast that are both unspoiled and relatively uncrowded. We especially recommend the following.

Hel

Many travelers enjoy Hel, a peninsula that juts out into the Baltic Sea above the Tri-City area. Little fishing villages and small forests dot the 21-mile peninsula, so explore around a bit to find a beach to your liking. Boats leave from Gdańsk, Sopot, and Gdynia every morning and return in the evening for about $1 each way. Inquire at Orbis for more details.

If you decide to stay in Hel, go to the **PUT Biuro Zakwaterowan** at ul. Stefanskiego (tel. 178).

Łeba

Many Gdańsk locals prefer Łeba, 62 miles west of the Tri-City area. It's a small fishing town with clean beaches and fewer visitors than Hel. Łeba is noted for its shifting dunes, which give the sand a desert-like appearance. In World War II the Nazi Afrika Korps trained at Łeba and V1 and V2 rockets were fired at London from here. Today, desert movies are filmed on the beach from time to time. You can get to Łeba by bus from Gdańsk. The **PTTK** office on ulica Kościuszki can give you information upon your arrival.

Krynica Morska

Perhaps the least crowded beaches can be found on the **Amber Coast** (so named because of the rich supply of amber that has been found here) near the Soviet border to the east. Those journeying by car or bus will take in some beautiful views of the Polish forest and placid lakes on one side and the sea on the other. On the way you will also pass the former Nazi concentration camp, **Stuthoff** (Sztutowo). The beaches along the way are undeveloped and rugged, ending in thick dunes which look somewhat like Fire Island off New York's Long Island.

Many vacationers settle in **Krynica Morska,** the most developed beach town on this strip of land. It's a one-hour ride to Krynica Morska from Gdańsk; buses run from 5:30 a.m. to 10:30 p.m.

If you feel daring and want to go even closer to Soviet territory, you're likely to find a strip of beach all to yourself, as Poles apparently don't want to annoy their big brother.

You can get tourist information at Krynica Morska's **PTTK** office (tel. 16).

HISTORIC TOWNS: Those who prefer to sightsee in Gdańsk's environs will find plenty of fascinating historic sights, including the massive Teutonic castle at Malbork (33½ miles south of Gdańsk), and Copernicus's former home in the quaint medieval village of Frombork (64 miles to the east).

Malbork

The Order of the Teutonic Knights, the persistent and mighty enemy of Poland, set up their headquarters (in a castle, naturally) in Malbork in the last half of the 13th century so that they could rule the northern Baltic territories. These impressive Knights kept on expanding their fortifications until they were finally defeated by the Poles in the 15th century. The entire Gothic castle still survives (with some restoration work done in the 19th century) on such a scale you might have thought was only possible in fairy tales. The castle complex is made up of three large sections—the low, middle, and high castle—which all are divided from the outside world by moats and drawbridges. Of course, the entire complex is also protected by high defensive walls and watchtowers.

Today the Malbork castle houses an extensive collection of amber art and jewelry, as well as displays on the history of this defensive bastion, and on medieval weaponry. It's open May 1 to September 30 from 8:30 a.m. until 5 p.m. During the rest of the year, the castle receives visitors from 10 a.m. to 4 p.m. Monday through Friday, to 7 p.m. on weekends. The train from Gdańsk to Warsaw (and vice versa) stops in Malbork, so we recommend a stop to see this amazing citadel before continuing on to your final destination.

If you need further information during your stay in Malbork, go to the **PTTK Tourist Information Office** at ul. Hiberna 4 (tel. 26-77), open from 8 a.m. to 3 p.m.

Frombork

Between 1512 and 1543 Copernicus made his home in the small medieval town of Frombork, just ten miles from the present-day Soviet border. In Frombork, Copernicus paved the way for modern astronomy with his classic work, *On the Revolutions of Celestial Bodies,* which postulated that the earth moved around the sun and not the other way around!

The town boasts an attractive 14th-century cathedral where Copernicus was buried, as well as the 14th-century castle where the astronomer lived and did his research. A museum in the Palace of the Bishops of Warmia documents Copernicus's life and shows replicas of the instruments he used to conduct his experiments; it's open Tuesday through Sunday from 10 a.m. to 4 p.m.; June 15 to August 31 the museum remains open until 6 p.m.

Travelers can get to Frombork by bus from Gdańsk or by ferry from Krynica Morska.

5. Szczecin

One of Poland's major ports, Szczecin served as the central port of Berlin prior to World War II. In fact, for most of Szczecin's history the city has been controlled by either quasi-independent nobles depending on the sea trade for their livelihood or by German-speaking peoples.

ORIENTATION: Situated on the left bank of the Odra River, Szczecin is actually quite far from the North Sea. Only about 30 miles from East Germany, Szczecin is at the south end of a large inland bay and river system called the Stettiner Haff, making it a safe and well-protected anchorage.

The railway station is about a 15-minute walk south of the city center. As you leave the station, turn right (north) and walk across Ratuszowy and up the hill on ulica Staromiejska. Across aleja Wielka is the old town; you can see the old Ducal Palace on the hilltop.

THE SIGHTS: The most famous historical relic in Szczecin is the **Castle of the Pomeranian Dukes,** built at the end of the 13th and 14th centuries. Destroyed and rebuilt often, the castle has been turned into an art gallery, photography exhibition hall, and open-air concert hall. Nearby, the Gothic **St. John's Church,** built in the 13th and 14th centuries, overlooks the Odra River.

The once-stunning Gothic 15th-century **Town Hall** was seriously damaged during World War II, and has the look of a restored building about it. It stands alone now, but looking at this single structure you can imagine a whole town constructed in a similar style. There are also several scattered 15th- to 18th-century buildings, including the **Professors' Houses** on Żołnierza Polskiego Square. There are many beautiful buildings in Szczecin, but unfortunately they have not been restored as extensively as the buildings in Gdańsk.

ACCOMMODATIONS: The **Hotel Gryf,** at ul. Wojska Polskiego 49 (tel. 340-35 or 36-37-38), is one of Szczecin's better buys. A small establishment (67 rooms) with a bar well patronized by local townspeople, the Gryf offers single rooms for 3,470 złoty ($21.80) per night with bath and 2,640 złoty ($16.60) without. A double room costs 4,720 złoty ($29.70) per night with bath and 3,890 złoty ($24.50) without. About 70% of the rooms do not have a private bath. The rooms are very large and airy, with surprisingly attractive furnishings. After several nights in two-tone rooms it's a relief to be in a room with patterned rugs and a high ceiling. No English is spoken here.

Student Lodgings

The student dorm **Akademik Politechniki Szczecińskiej,** at al. Piastów 24 (tel. 49-48-58), will try your patience and communication skills to the utmost. The office is behind the first building, and though it's officially open 24 hours a day, don't bet on it. The business office keeps hours from 7 a.m. to 3 p.m. and closes down on weekends. The "only for groups" restriction sometimes in effect here may be the first response (if any) you'll get from the receptionist. Officially, half of the dorm is reserved for foreign students, so just keep trying. It's difficult enough to gain admission if you are a student; for those readers who have graduated, it's unlikely that you'll be able to stay here.

The rooms are organized as suites around a central bathroom. The facility is clean and well maintained, and is a good place to meet students from other Communist countries. A bed costs around 300 złoty ($1.90) per person per night. The complex has a bar but no restaurant.

At this place perseverance is *really* important; even with 160 beds, on rare occasion they actually do run out of spare beds. If things look really bleak, ask one of the student residents if you can camp on the floor for a night. Although not really illegal, it is frowned on by the management.

To reach the Akademik Politechniki Szczecińskiej, take tram 4 from the railroad station. The dorm is on the left side of the tram as you're heading out.

DINING: In the old Ducal Palace at Rycerska 3 is the **Kawiarnia Zamkowa** (tel. 386-23). The high-vaulted ceilings and waitresses in long skirts and embroidered blouses seem very appropriate in this restored palace. A glass case filled with antique ceramics and glassware stands against one wall. There is music and dancing most nights from 7:30 p.m. until closing. In addition to standard Polish specialties at moderate to expensive prices, you can enjoy a fresh assortment of cakes baked daily for 91 złoty (55¢), as well as quite good Turkish coffee (kawa po' Turecku) at 184 złoty ($1.15). Closed Monday, the Kawiarnia is usually open from 10 a.m. till midnight during the week and till 3 a.m. on Saturday.

A NIGHTCLUB: Black-jacketed waiters greet a very young crowd at the **Dance Bar U Wyszaka** (tel. 351-18), on Plac Rzepićhy 1. Built in the cellar of the restored old Town Hall, the U Wyszaka is something that you won't find in the United States. The beautiful, arched stone-and-brickwork vaults give this nightclub an almost Gothic atmosphere. Young laughter echoes off pillars where the town fathers of Szczecin once plotted and governed the city. The only light comes from large wax candles in wrought-iron candlesticks. The candlelight flickers off the old stone, creating plenty of shadows among the vaults and pillars of the establishment. Sitting on wooden benches and drinking hot mulled mead at 127 złoty (80¢), one could almost pretend to be relaxing after an audience with the Pomeranian dukes. The only modern features are a well-stocked bar and a large fish tank at one end of the bar. The service is very polite and efficient. No hot food is served here, though they do offer some cold meats and bread, so stop here after dinner. As dancing is what the U Wyszaka is all about, there is an obligatory band donation of 400 złoty ($2.50) at the door. There is dancing every day except Wednesday, from 9 p.m. till sometimes 5 in the morning. A real night-owl establishment!

SZCZECIN SIDE TRIPS: There are some stunning landscapes, both inland and on the coast, in the vicinity of Szczecin. Northeast of Szczecin, near the airport, is **Goleniów,** an old fortified town on the Ina River surrounded by dense forests. In Goleniów you can see the Wolińska Gate and other remnants of the old defensive works, as well as the reconstructed Gothic church. You can reach this town by taking the bus to the airport and from there a local bus into town, or you can go by railroad.

Due east of Szczecin is one of the region's most picturesque towns, **Stargard Szczeciński.** Since this is an important rail junction, it's easy to reach. There are many examples of the once-impressive defensive works, such as the Młyńska, Pyrzycka, and Wałowa Gates, and many towers. You'll enjoy the Church of St. John, which has one of the tallest towers in Poland (over 300 feet).

To the north is the **Wolin National Park** and the small islands south of the Przytorska Mierzeja. This is a "cure resort" where many ailing Poles come to rest in these beautiful natural surroundings. The whole area is connected by rail so it's not difficult to reach. For all accommodations ask (during working hours) at the Bałtyk Hotel at ul. Armii Czerwonej 5, or call the tourist information center (tel. 22-11 or 37-66).

At the very end of the rail line from Szczecin (56 miles away) is the extremely well-preserved **Kamień Pomorski,** the former capital of Western Pomerania. The town boasts a 12th-century cathedral and a fantastic 17th-century baroque organ. There are frequent concerts throughout the summer as well as a chamber music festival.

Some of the most unspoiled countryside in all of Poland can be found near the town of **Drawno.** Located by the Drawa River, Drawno acts as a limited wildlife reserve that, according to one pamphlet, contains one of the "least contaminated rivers in all of Poland." The terrain here is interesting as the forests are occasionally broken by cliffs and glacial rock formations. The Drawa River is home to a rarity in Europe these days, a spawning ground for salmon, sea trout, and live sponges. Its purity and tight governmental controls have made this river one of the premier fishing spots in Poland with trout, eel, pike, and a very rare species of cottid.

MOVING ON: For ferry journeys abroad, contact **Polferries,** ul. Wyszyńskiego 28 (tel. 359-45; Telex 0422533), open from 11 a.m. till 4:30 p.m. Their ships sail only from Świnoujście and not from Szczecin. To get to Świnoujście, you must take a short boat ride 37 miles by sea to the north at a cost of 400 złoty ($2.50) per person, one way. At Świnoujście you then change to the larger ocean-going ships.

If you are planning to leave Poland, you will of course need all the proper papers, as well as your passport. (See "Getting There" in Chapter III for sample fares).

On Sunday you can try your luck by taking the short-haul ferry up to the terminal at Świnoujście and see if there are any free places on a ferry, but this is not recommended. You should make the effort to reserve and pre-pay for a berth on the ship.

6. The Mazurian Lakes Region

If you ask a Pole what section of the country he or she most enjoys visiting, chances are the answer will be the Mazurian Lake Region in northeast Poland.

Known as the "Land of 1,000 Lakes," the area in reality boasts some 3,000 lakes set into lush forests, an outdoors person's dream. In July and August you can swim in the lakes' clean, pure waters, but unless you grew up in the Arctic you'll probably find it too cold even in June and September. During the rest of the year you can fish for trout, crayfish, eel, or pike; you can go in the woods and hunt for bison, lynx, deer, and fox; and if you're in a less predatory mood, you can sail or canoe in many of the lakes which connect up through small canals.

Keeping in mind that one of the Mazurian Lake Region's most attractive features is its undeveloped natural beauty, expect few tourist facilities in the area. The paucity of hotels in the region leads one official Polish guide to conclude that "the best way to visit this area is by car with one's own trailer, camper, or tent." If roughing it appeals to you, inquire at Orbis for information on camping sites and boat rentals. If you prefer to check into a hotel rather than pitch a tent, remember that Mazurian Lake hotels are often more basic and sometimes not so clean as the usual tourist facilities. They do not cater to foreigners, so you won't wallow in luxury with or without a tent.

Whether or not you travel with tent in hand, you are likely to pass first through the unexceptional town of Olsztyn on your way to the Mazurian Lakes. Then you can travel on to our favorite towns in the region: Mrągowo, and Giżycko on Lake Niegocin.

OLSZTYN: We think Olsztyn just doesn't measure up to the fascination of other Polish cities—town "sights" include the Monument of Gratitude to the Red Army, and the Monument for the Heroes Who Fought for the Social Liberation of Warmia and Mazury—and you too may find that it offers little to the visitor. However, as the largest city in the Mazurian area (pop. 130,000), the former Prussian capital of Olsztyn offers a few hotels to those who can drive to the lakes during the day. Also, the train makes its last stop to the east here, so you'll have to change to a bus if you don't have a car (the bus station is just to your left as you exit from the train station).

You'll find Olsztyn's **PTTK Tourist Information Office** at Wysoka Brama (the High Gate), off ulica Staromiejska (tel. 227-38), open from 9 a.m. to 5 p.m. **Orbis** is at ul. Dąbrowszczakow 1 (tel. 57-91). Both of these offices can provide information on accommodations and sports in the Mazurian Lakes. If you are a student, go to the **Almatur** office, ul. Kortowo DS 2 (tel. 286-53); they can give you information on the large student center at Lake Mamry.

For **visa extensions,** go to Dąbrowszczakow 42, Room 12. The **main post office** is located at ul. Pieniężnego 21, and the local **PZM** office (for motorists in difficulty) is at ul. Pstrowskiego 28 (tel. 303-61).

Where to Stay

The town's two basic budget hotels are the 156-room **Hotel Warmiński, ul.** Głowackiego 6 (tel. 241-51), and the 100-room **Hotel Relax,** ul. Zołnierska 13A (tel. 344-22 or 377-28). It will take you about ten minutes to reach either hotel by foot from the town center, and about the same amount of time from the train station.

MRĄGOWO: We recommend Mrągowo to those who prefer a quiet resort town with fewer visitors than elsewhere in the lake region.

The budget traveler doesn't have a choice in hotels, for there is only the 26-room **Hotel Miejski,** a very basic one-star hotel at ul. Warszawska 10A (tel. 25-74).

For tourist information, go to **Mazur-Tourist** at ul. Kościelna 1 (tel. 24-04), or to one of two **"it"** offices, one at the Hotel Miejski, the other at ul. Ratuszowa 8 (tel. 20-51).

GIŻYCKO: You'll enjoy Poland's water sports capital, a popular and crowded lake resort town that offers canoeing, sailing, yachting, and more to the visitor. You can set up base in one of two two-star hotels, the **Wodnik** at al. 1 Maja 7 (tel. 39-57), or at the **Motel,** ul. Moniuszki 1 (tel. 26-46).

You'll also find the **Almatur Student Center** at ul. Moniuszki 22A (tel. 39-71). For **tourist information,** go to ul. Dworcowa 3 (tel. 37-12), or to **Orbis,** ul. Obrońców Stalingradu 11 (tel. 36-50).

HISTORIC SIDE TRIPS: Two sites in particular will fascinate history buffs traveling in the Mazurian Lake region: Hitler's wartime headquarters at Kętrzyn and the historic battlefield of Grunwald.

Kętrzyn

During World War II Adolf Hitler decided that he and his highest commanders (including Goering, Bormann, and others) could best direct the campaign against the Soviet Union from the **Wolf's Lair** (Wilczy Szaniec in Polish) in the woods of what then comprised the German territory of Prussia. The complex (called Wolfschanzer in German) consisted of many huge concrete-and-steel bunkers, one bunker per commander, camouflaged and spread out over several miles. With the Russian advance of 1945 they abandoned the headquarters, and the last Nazi commander to leave the premises pushed the "self-destruct button," destroying everything except the bunkers (it's rather difficult to demolish thick concrete-and-steel walls, although they were displaced and cracked by the blast).

The Wolf's Lair was also the site of the only nearly successful attempt on Hitler's life during the war. On July 20, 1944, Count Claus Schenk von Stauffenberg, a General Staff colonel, placed a bomb inside a briefcase which he left at a meeting that Hitler was chairing. Several people died in the blast, but Hitler somehow survived, and that evening he gave a radio address to assure the German people that all was well.

Today you can visit these historic sites, including Hitler's own bunker, which is covered by a 30-foot-thick ceiling. Although you may think that the five- to seven-hour trip is too long to warrant a visit from Gdańsk or Warsaw, you should definitely consider it if World War II intrigues you and you're already in the Mazurian Lake region. You can reach the complex by taking the bus from Olsztyn or the resort town of Giżycko to Kętrzyn (pronounced Kentchin); get off at Wilczy Szaniec (the Wolf's Lair), six miles east of the town center. If the bus stops only in central Kętrzyn, you can catch a public bus to the Lair. If you experience difficulties, the **Mazur-Tourist** office at Plac Wolności 1 (tel. 24-07), or the **"it"** office at ul. 1 Maja 20 (tel. 29-78), can answer your questions.

Grunwald

After hundreds of years of bitter struggle, the Poles finally managed to defeat the menacing Teutonic Knights at Grunwald in 1410. Today a huge monument and a museum commemorate this historic battle that Poles still recall; one inscription in the museum reads "Grunwald 1410, Berlin 1945." The museum is open in summer from 10 a.m. to 5 p.m.

For history trivia buffs, note that German Chancellor Hindenburg (Hitler's predecessor as leader of Germany) was initially buried just outside Grunwald, in tribute to his role in defeating the Russians in 1914 during World War I. His remains were later transferred to the Rhineland. You won't find his sepulchral monument in the area, however; the Soviet Red Army destroyed it as they advanced in World War II.

You can take the bus to Grunwald from Olsztyn, a 25-mile journey.

Chapter VII

WESTERN POLAND

1. Toruń
2. Poznań
3. Łódź
4. Wrocław

MANY FIRST-TIME TRAVELERS to Poland leave the western part of the country off their travel itineraries, for they think that the area appeals only to those with specialized interests. For example, many businessmen from both Eastern and Western Europe meet annually in Poznań at the large trade fair that promotes international commerce. Clothing manufacturers visit the textile warehouses of Łódź, a large factory city from the 19th century. Others visit western Poland to see the birthplace of their ancestors, often in and around Wrocław.

In addition to these specialized sights, however, western Poland offers several appealing tourist destinations. Toruń, in the northern half of Poland, is one of Poland's most charming medieval towns and birthplace of the astronomer Copernicus. And both Poznań and Wrocław offer attractive old town squares that illustrate what all of Europe was like hundreds of years ago.

In between these large cities in western Poland you'll find dozens of quaint peasant villages seemingly unaffected by modern times. In these sleepy areas that largely escaped the damage of World War II, the arrival of a Westerner is a big event. It's an appealing place to see Poland at its everyday best, away from the main tourist path. To fully enjoy the small towns and big cities, we recommend that visitors to western Poland rent a car.

We'll begin our tour in magical Toruń, and then move to Poznań, Łódź, and Wrocław.

1. Toruń
If you found Kraków interesting and you want to visit another picturesque medieval Polish town, then make Toruń your next stop. Like Kraków, Toruń (pop. 180,000) escaped World War II with very little damage, so you'll see buildings virtually untouched since the Middle Ages and the Renaissance.

Toruń was first established in 1233 to handle Poland's trade with Western Europe. Over the years, especially after Poland finally defeated the Teutonic Knights, Toruń developed into a rich and prosperous city with many special privileges granted by the king. During these golden years many ornate buildings were erected, and of these, some 350 Gothic structures still remain. The scientific work of Copernicus, who was born here in 1473, furthered the fame of Toruń throughout the world.

Toruń continues to maintain the academic tradition established by Copernicus. Today several academic institutions, including the Nicolaus Copernicus University, dispense knowledge to a large student population. In sum, you'll find that Toruń, with its impressive historical sights and lively élan vital, certainly merits at least a day's visit.

ORIENTATION: You'll most likely arrive at Toruń Główny, the **main train station** across the river from the Old Town center. Take tram 4 two stops to the center. If you've arrived with a lot of luggage that you don't want to carry around, no problem: the baggage check is open around the clock. Go to windows 1 to 5 to buy tickets to your next destination after Toruń.

If you've taken the bus to Toruń, you'll find the **bus station** considerably closer to the center of town, on ulica Dąbrowskiego. Walk down ulica Uniwersytecka one block, walk right one block and then left one block, and you'll reach the **Old Town Marketplace.** You'll find that the center of Toruń is fairly small so you'll soon know your way around without difficulty.

Important Adddresses

You'll find **Orbis** at ul. Żeglarska 31 (tel. 261-30 or 228-73), and the **visa extension bureau** at ul. Bydgoska 39. **Almatur** is located at ul. Gargarina 21 (tel. 204-70), and the summer student hotel is usually located nearby. For emergency car repair, call **Polmozbyt** at 954; it's office is at ul. Dabrowskiego 26.

ACCOMMODATIONS: The **Hotel Pod Orłem,** at ul. Mostowa 15 (tel. 250-24; Telex 862734), right in the Old Town center two blocks from the main square, offers typical two-star accommodations: slightly worn, but quiet rooms with clean public toilets. We recommend this hotel as it gives you a good value in a very central location. Singles without bathroom cost 2,300 złoty ($14.50) to 2,560 złoty ($16.10); doubles rent for 3,670 złoty ($23) without bathroom and 4,840 złoty ($30.45) with private bathroom.

You'll find another good choice in the **Hotel Polonia,** Plac Armii Czerwonej 5 (tel. 230-28; Telex 862734), a two-star hotel just a three-minute walk from the Old Town Marketplace. The hotel shows some wear and tear from years of use, but is very well maintained, and the public bathrooms appear exceptionally clean for a hotel of this category. Singles cost 2,560 złoty ($16.10) without bathroom and 3,320 złoty ($20.90) with; spacious doubles without private bathroom rent for 2,940 złoty ($23).

The **Hotel Pod Trzema Koronami,** ul. Stary Rynek 21 (tel. 260-31; Telex 862734), offers an unbeatable location, right on the Old Town Marketplace overlooking Toruń's most charming sights. Unfortunately, the rooms are not so impressive, and the public bathrooms could use more frequent cleaning. But then again, a room facing the Old Town Marketplace may make you forget the hotel's other shortcomings! The hotel charges 2,560 złoty ($16.10) for a single without bathroom and 3,670 złoty ($23) for a double.

The **Zajazd Staropolski,** ul. Żeglarska 12/14 (tel. 260-61 to 260-63), offers very pleasant large rooms with white stucco walls and clean private bathrooms, all for half of what Orbis might charge. A single with bath rents for 4,470 złoty ($28.10), and a double with bath rents for 6,020 złoty ($37.85). Ask for the corner doubles; they're larger and have more windows. You'll find the hotel just minutes from the Old Town Marketplace. Guests can also dine in style in the restaurant downstairs (see the description below).

DINING: You'll find a charming Gothic-style restaurant that serves good food at the **Zajazd Staropolski,** ul. Żeglarska 12/14 (tel. 260-61 to 260-63) in a setting of old stone floors, a high wooden ceiling, and exposed brick walls. An elevated wooden walkway serves as an entrance into the hotel behind the restaurant. Although you'll sit on high-backed uncomfortable wooden chairs, you can enjoy good Polish and Central European specialties such as goulash soup for 111 złoty (70¢), a creamy, delicious tomato soup with macaroni, several steak dishes for 260 złoty ($1.65) to 350 złoty ($2.20), and for lighter eaters, a good omelet with jam. Many locals consider this Toruń's best fare; the one difficulty you might have here is in reading the menu—it's only in Polish or French.

Our choices in town for good hotel restaurants include the **Restaurant Orbis-Kosmos,** ul. Portowa 2 (tel. 289-00), a modern place with a 20th-century stained-glass window. Specialties include beefsteak with vegetables and fries for 301 złoty ($1.90), and a tasty veal cutlet à la Suisse (with breadcrumbs on the outside and butter and cheese on the inside) for 374 złoty ($2.35).

Or try the **Restaurant-Helios,** ul. Kraszewskiego 1/3 (tel. 250-33), also in another modern hotel. It has the exact same menu as Orbis-Kosmos but the setting is different: windows covered by a light curtain, a carpet hanging on one wall, and a painting of Toruń on another.

Lighter Fare

Delicious culinary treats to sample in Toruń are **spice cakes and ginger-bread men,** a Toruń specialty since the Middle Ages. You can find these goodies at ul. Szczytna 3, among other places.

For a snack or a drink, go to the charming **Kawiarnia Markiza,** ul. Kras-zewskiego 23. You'll sit on small footstools, and waitresses will serve your coffee or tea in a turn-of-the-century ambience highlighted by chintz-covered walls. Open from 10 a.m. to 10 p.m.

THE SIGHTS: As you might guess, the town's major sight is the **Old Town Mar-ketplace** (Rynek Staromiejski) and the area in the immediate vicinity. In the middle of this square stands the **Town Hall,** which was first built in the 13th century and was rebuilt in the 16th and 17th centuries. During the Polish monarchy, kings and distinguished guests stayed in the Town Hall. Today the building houses a collection of church art from the Middle Ages, including some interesting 14th-century stained-glass windows. You can also enjoy a panoramic view of the entire town from the top of the 14th-century bell tower. The museum is open on Tuesday, Wednesday, and Friday from 10 a.m. to 4 p.m., on Thursday from 11 a.m. to 5 p.m., and weekends from 10 a.m. to 3 p.m.; closed Monday.

Just off the Old Town Marketplace is the huge **Church of Our Lady** (Sw. Marii), an impressive Gothic brick church from the 13th century. Another Gothic church worth visiting just a few blocks away is **St. John's Church** (Sw. Jana), which was first built in the 12th century and offers a beautiful collection of Gothic frescos.

If you continue toward the river from the Old Town Marketplace, you'll find the **House of Copernicus** at ul. Kopernika 17, just two blocks away. The great astronomer who first advanced the theory of the heliocentric universe was born here in 1473, and inside you can visit a museum of Copernicus's life. It's open the same hours as the Town Hall museum.

Continuing on to the riverbank, you can see the impressive **defensive walls** which protected the very rich city of Toruń from attack. The walls stood undamaged until the 19th century when the Prussian occupiers of Toruń deemed them ugly and tore many of them down. The walls at the river were allowed to remain, and they provide a fascinating glimpse of 13th- to 15th-century city fortifications. Inside the defense walls near ulica Podmurna you can also see the ruins of a Teutonic **castle** from the 14th century.

2. Poznań

Poznań, the site of Poland's annual International Trade Fair, suffered heavily during the war. Rebuilt, it's now one of the main business centers of Poland. Tall glass buildings, flickering neon signs, and the beautifully reconstructed old square make Poznań one of Poland's more cosmopolitan cities.

A CAPSULE HISTORY: Poznań (pop. 560,000) began as a small settlement clustered around a wooden castle on the island which was subsequently called Ostrów Tumski early in the 9th century. Under Prince Mieszko I, the town became the capital of the surrounding area. By the 11th century the town was strong enough to leave its island cradle, and in 1253 Przemysł I chartered Poznań on the left bank of the Warta River and granted the town municipal rights.

Poznań was renowned for its large marketplace and (at that time) large geometric avenues. As the town grew, defensive walls were erected. The excellent geographical position of Poznań, astride the main trade routes, contributed to its growth; the town was familiar to foreign merchants as early as the 14th century.

When the Black Death scythed across Europe in the Middle Ages, Poznań enjoyed her most prosperous years. By the 16th century most of the Kingdom of Poland's east-west trade passed through Poznań. However, the Swedish invasion and subsequent political upheaval brought bitter fighting and much adversity. Worse, under the partition of Poland in 1793, Poznań fell to Prussia, which retained control for the next 125 years.

During the Second World War over 50% of the city was destroyed, along with much of the Old Town. Reconstruction, especially the restoration of the Old Town, was accomplished speedily and with remarkable success considering the damage.

ORIENTATION: The Poznań **Trade Fair complex** lies to the west of the train station and the **city center** is about a 20-minute walk to the east. Bus and tram connections are in front of the station and tickets cost 4 złoty (3¢). Buy your tickets from the kiosk near the stop.

The **railroad station** at Poznań is split into two parts, connected by an underground passage. The main station building is on the east side of the tracks and contains ticket windows, reservations, information, and the baggage check. The smaller building on the west side of the tracks is primarily for local train travel. The baggage claim is open 24 hours, every day of the year. One backpack or medium-sized piece of luggage should cost 100 złoty (65¢) for the day.

The information window at the Poznań station presents some problems, since you must often wait in line about 15 to 30 minutes. When buying tickets, be certain that you're standing in the correct line. Remember that the reservation windows are divided by city. English is not usually spoken at these windows, so have your destination, time constraints, and any other concerns written out. If you are going to a very small town, ask at the information window which line you have to stand in. Again, if you're not sure that you're in the correct line, ask your neighbor. A phrase book and pad and pencil come in handy.

Orbis, at ul. Armii Czerwonej 33, also sells advance train tickets.

Buses leave from the **airport** to the LOT office at ul. Armii Czerwonej 69 (tel. 528-47). Buses to the airport leave from the LOT office 45 minutes prior to departure.

ACCOMMODATIONS: Rooms are nearly impossible to get without reservations during the annual Trade Fair, so note the date of the fair (it changes annually but is usually in June) and plan accordingly.

The **Przemysław Accommodations Bureau,** at ul. Głogowska 16 (tel. 603-13; Telex 0412677), is an office for both private and hotel rooms. Open 24 hours every day of the year, they control rooms in the Lech, Poznański, and Wielkopolka Hotels. The office is clean and well lit with one person on duty and the rest listening to jazz. During the Trade Fair only, you'll find someone who speaks English in this office. In Przemysław's private rooms, singles with bath cost 2,300 złoty ($14.45) per night and a double room costs 3,600 złoty ($22.65) per night. The hotel rooms rent for approximately 5,400 złoty ($34) for a single and 7,400 złoty ($46.50) for a double per night; subtract about 1,400 złoty ($8.80) per night for rooms without a private bath. All the hotels are reasonably close to both the city center and the Trade Fair. They are clean and well maintained, and are often full.

Starvation-Budget Accommodations

At ul. Stalingradzka 32/40 is **Hostel Number "I,"** an impressive state building that appears uninhabited. Don't despair; enter the front door, turn left, and walk down the hallway and up the four flights of stairs till you reach the top. Walk down the hall, straight ahead and to the left, and you'll find the hostel. The office door is unmarked. There is no official telephone number, but if you're desperate, there is a phone that is sometimes answered after 5 p.m. (tel. 549-25 to 549-27). Anyone can stay here, and when we visited at the height of the Trade Fair it was packed with business types. If you're a student your Western International Youth Hostel (IYHF) card is valid here. The cost per bed, per night, is 230 złoty ($1.45), 300 złoty ($1.90) if you're over 21 years of age. If you bring your own bedding, subtract 100 złoty (65¢).

There's a total of 55 beds in the hostel, but no room has more than six beds. There is a common bathroom at the end of the hall, as well as one bathtub, one slightly partitioned shower, and six sinks for the whole hostel. The bathing is mixed and the facilities are dirty and crowded. The beds are extremely small and the rooms have small garret windows. If you can, get one of the smaller rooms, which are cleaner and have larger windows. The outer doors to this place close at 10 p.m., so it's early to bed at Hostel Number "I."

The **Almatur** office at ul. Obornicka 84B, upstairs (tel. 204-709 or 232-497), is open all day. They have 80 rooms available throughout the year, and in late June the MHS Student Hotel opens up and adds "hundreds" of beds.

To get to the **MHS Student Hotel,** take bus 78 from the west side of the station for about four kilometers (2½ miles). These rooms are for everyone, not just students, and only at the height of the Trade Fair do they fill up. The standard student dorm room holds two or three people and is very clean. Everything is painted a depressing shade of institutional green, the walls are thin, and the bathrooms vary greatly in cleanliness. A bed in a double room costs 1,200 złoty ($7.55) per person per night; a triple costs 1,000 złoty ($6.30) per person. Most of the receptionists speak some English, but ask for Krzysztof, who speaks the best English.

The **hostel,** at ul. Berwinskiego 2/3 (tel. 636-80), is protected by a large outer door with a green triangle (the mark of the student hostel) imprinted upon it. When you enter, you are faced with a forbidding locked door and a buzzer. Buzz—the office is straight ahead. There is someone in attendance in the morning between 6 and 8 a.m. and in the evening between 5 and 10 p.m.; otherwise your buzz may not be answered. Beds, sheets, and registration total 270 złoty ($1.70) for the under-21 set; the rest of us pay an additional 50 złoty (30¢). This place is filled with grade-school groups and is not very clean. The prison atmosphere, the noise, and the lack of cleanliness make this a last choice in the starvation-budget category.

RESTAURANTS: Be warned that, especially during the big Trade Fair, many restaurants in Poznań have their larders cleaned out by hungry visitors. Not that the restaurants run out of food, but the menus become extremely limited as the evening progresses. It's our advice to have an early dinner when you are in Poznań during any of the big conventions.

The **U-Della,** at Stary Rynek ("Old Square") 37/39 (tel. 517-76), is a restored older place with arches, painted in a dull gold, separating the rooms. On the ceiling are thin, darkly stained beams that probably do not support the floor. Pictures of princes and queens that are oddly reminiscent of playing-card portraiture adorn the walls. The food is good and filling, with the average main dish running less than 300 złoty ($1.85).

An Evening Out

We are certain that Liberace is alive and well, even behind the Iron Curtain, as the restaurant and disco **Adria,** on ulica Głogowska (tel. 208-485), will attest. Not far from the entrance of the Trade Fair, it's also only a short walk away from the railroad station. Done in tones of flaming red, the restaurant is open from 8 a.m. till 7 p.m., with dancing and floor shows from 8 p.m. till 2 a.m. In the afternoon the Adria is open to the ordinary Pole, but in the evening it's the playground for Poznań's upper class and their guests. Prices are higher than almost everywhere else in Poznań. The sautéed trout at 508 złoty ($3.20) is delicious, as is the rest of the fare, but you will not enjoy yourself here for less than 600 złoty ($3.75) per person. On Friday and Saturday there's a cover charge of 600 złoty ($3.75), which entitles you to watch the floor and strip shows. There are also occasional animal acts, plenty of crooners, and even Ragiz the fire eater. The Adria has been around for about 20 years, but the proprietor tells us that "it has never been as nice." Very little English is spoken, so ask your receptionist to make reservations; it's a must on weekends.

For Dessert

Despite the sign that says "cocktail bar," **Hortex,** at ul. Głogowska 29, is a place to abuse sugar, not alcohol. Hortex is part of a Polish ice cream and confectionery chain and is where you go if you've already eaten lunch but it's too early for dinner. There are a variety of different sweets ranging from pastries at 57 złoty (35¢) to pieces of multilayer cake at 110 złoty (70¢) but the strongest suit of Hortex is their *lody,* or ice cream, served in what look like large scotch tumblers. There are several flavors along with fruit toppings and nuts. There is also very good tea for those not up for a heavy dessert. Downstairs is the self-service counter, usually with a real wait. The café upstairs is tastefully done in green and is somehow comfortably intimate without being overcrowded. Hortex is a good place to make plans before plunging into the tourist whirl or as a fortifying pause before embarking on a train. It's open every day from 9 a.m. to 8 p.m.

THE SIGHTS: After all the effort that went into the reconstruction of the **Stare**

Miasto, it's only fair that you begin any tour of Poznań there. In the very center of the marketplace stands the Renaissance **Town Hall,** designed by the architect Jean Baptiste Quadro of Lugano. Begun in 1550 and finished five years later, the façade is adorned with a splendid three-story loggia and three turrets; the central one has a coat-of-arms and a clock. When the clock strikes noon, a bugle is heard and the famous heraldic goats of Poznań appear. Inside the Town Hall is the perfectly preserved Grand Lobby from 1555, with its magnificent coffered ceiling.

In front of the Town Hall you'll also see a rococo fountain of Persephone as well as a more painful relic of the good old days: a **pillory** where wrongdoers were once flogged. Another point of interest near the Town Hall is the **Museum of Musical Instruments,** at Stare Miasto 45. Here you can observe instruments from all over the world, including some of Chopin's personal pianos. This museum is said to be the fifth most valuable of its kind in the world. It's open from 9 a.m. to 6 p.m. Tuesday through Saturday, from 10 a.m. to 3 p.m. on Sunday; closed Tuesday.

The Stare Miasto is but a stone's throw away from the island of **Ostrów Tumski,** where Poznań was first settled. There is a beautiful, restored 14th- or 15th-century **cathedral** that burned during the Soviet occupation in 1946. The cathedral vaults contain relics from earlier churches dating from the 10th and 11th centuries. Of special note is the 19th-century Golden Chapel, built in the ornate Byzantine style. In the chapel are the tombs of Prince Mieszko I and King Boleslaus the Brave.

3. Łódź

Łódź (pronounced Wooch), Poland's second-largest city (pop. 800,000), became prominent in the 19th century when it emerged as the country's largest producer of textiles and cloth goods. Today it still serves as an important industrial center, and its streets remain a mix of 19th- and 20th-century industrial architecture. For most people this doesn't sound like an interesting place to visit, and Łódź's critics have called it "Poland's ugliest city." However, we include a short entry on the city for three types of travelers: automobile travelers from Wrocław to Warsaw, or Toruń to Kraków, who may be passing through town; business people who are interested in checking out what goods Łódź has to offer; or history and architecture buffs who want to see a vintage 19th-century industrial town.

ACCOMMODATIONS: Those in a splurgey mood should definitely stay at the **Hotel Orbis Grand,** ul. Piotrkowska 72 (tel. 399-20 to 399-30), a building with turn-of-the-century elegance and details in the rooms, such as very high ceilings, huge bathrooms, and a bed area separated from the rest of the room by a thick curtain. Singles cost $39 with bathroom and $29 without; doubles cost $55 with bathroom, $44 without.

The slightly rundown but very centrally located **Hotel Polonia,** ul. Narutowicza 38 (tel. 287-73), rents more basic rooms with private bathroom for 3,600 złoty ($22.65) in a single and 4,490 złoty ($28.25) in a double.

Finally, those who seek more rustic surroundings during their stay in Łódź, or just better prices, should rent a room at the **Zespol Domków Turystycznych,** ul. Skrzydlata 75 (tel. 787-93). The spartan rooms, located in log cabins right in the middle of the forest, cost 1,646 złoty ($10.35) for a single with bathroom and 2,298 złoty ($14.45) for a double. Take bus 56 to reach the hotel.

DINING: You'll find an elegant 19th-century dining room with small cherubs crowning neoclassical columns and lofty ceilings at the **Hotel Orbis Grand** restaurant. In addition to the appealing decor, you'll enjoy a good, standard selection of Polish specialties for $2 to $5 an entree.

Travelers who don't want to eat in a big hotel will enjoy the **Zajazd Na Rogach,** ul. Łupkowa 10/16, a popular local eatery in a simple wooden building on the outskirts of town. Although the menu only offers a few dishes, you can dine on tasty meat entrees for only 170 złoty ($1) to 336 złoty ($2.10). Since it's a bit tricky to find, take a taxi. Open from 8 a.m. to 9 p.m.

THE SIGHTS: Łódź's **Art Museum,** ul. Więckowskiego 36, houses a broad selection which starts with early icons and religious art and moves up to interesting modern paintings, including works by Paul Klee, Max Ernst, Picasso, Fernand Léger, and others, including some Polish avant-garde artists. It's open on Tuesday, Wednesday, and Friday from 11 a.m. to 5 p.m., on Thursday from noon to 7 p.m., on Saturday from 9 a.m. to 5 p.m., and on Sunday from 10 a.m. to 4 p.m.; closed Monday.

A former factory from the beginning of the 18th century serves as the **Textile Museum,** ul. Piotrkowska 282. Early textile-manufacturing equipment, fabrics, and other articles associated with the history of the textile industry are on display. Open on Tuesday and Thursday from 10 a.m. to 5 p.m., on Wednesday and Friday from 11:30 a.m. to 7 p.m., and weekends from 10 a.m. to 3 p.m.

To view some of the ornate and detailed architecture of the 19th century, with buildings ranging from those quite aesthetically pleasing and even charming to those rather ugly, walk along **ulica Piotrkowska,** where merchants, politicians, and others lived in Łódź's heyday. For a view of some typical industrial architecture, visit the **Poltrex** factory at Ogrodowa 17, and the factory at Piotrkowska 242/250.

IMPORTANT ADDRESSES: You'll find the **Orbis** office at Plac Wolności 6 (tel. 334-82), **Almatur** at ul. Piotrkowska 59 (tel. 361-12), and **PZM** (for car problems) at ul. Traugutta 5 (tel. 264-10, 355-03, or 390-00). The **Tourist Information** desk is located in the Hotel Centrum, at ul. Narutowicza 27/29 (tel. 472-01), open from 8 a.m. to 10 p.m.

Most buses and trains arrive at ulica Armii Ludowej right in the center of town. Call 655-55 for train information and 265-96 for bus information.

4. Wrocław

It would be difficult to say that Wrocław has always been a Polish city. Certainly there have always been Poles living in Wrocław, but from the 14th century until the end of the Second World War the town was controlled by Bohemians, the Hapsburgs, Prussians, and finally, Germans. Most of the older structures still left in the city, once called Breslau, are of Hapsburg or Prussian origin.

During World War II Wrocław was declared a fortress city by Nazi soldiers. It was bitterly defended for several months in early 1945. The resulting fighting destroyed two-thirds of the city and earned Wrocław the dubious distinction of being, after Warsaw, the most devastated city in all of Poland. Wrocław is perhaps best remembered by an earlier generation as the site of the 1948 World Congress of Intellectuals, including such giants as Frédéric Joliot-Curie, Pablo Picasso, Ilia Ehrenburg, Jaroslaw Iwaszkiewiecz, and hundreds of others. Today it is a major industrial center and one of Poland's five largest cities.

ORIENTATION: Wrocław was at one time a beautiful city, but it suffered severe damage during the war. Only the reconstructed main square, **Rynek Główny,** is reminiscent of the prewar Wrocław; the rest is quite modern.

The **train station** is on the south side of the city center. To reach the center, walk east on ulica Świerczewskiego till you reach ulica Świdnicka. Turn right (north) and continue till you cross Plac Kościuszki; then simply keep following the road north into the main part of town. It's not more than a 20-minute walk. Practically all of the sights are clustered around the old town or north of it along the Odra River.

Important Addresses

The **Orbis** office in Wrocław, at ul. Świerczewskiego 62, is always crowded with Poles buying tickets for foreign travel. If you want to buy a ticket in advance, you must get here early. Because of the crowds and lines, it's best to stop at a hotel Orbis desk for maps and information. Orbis organizes tours of the city in English most Tuesdays and Fridays during the summer. The office is open from 8 a.m. till 4 p.m.

There is another Orbis office on the Rynek Główny which specializes more in international travel, though they don't speak English. German is very helpful, French almost useless, and Russian not as helpful as one would think.

ACCOMMODATIONS: Wrocław has plenty of inexpensive hotel rooms; unfortunately, most are grabbed up by the hordes of businessmen that convene here. For price value as well as cleanliness, we recommend the Polytechnic Hotel and the Europajski Hotel, even though they're almost always full. So that you have the best chance of finding someplace with a free room, we've included all of the good hotels we found.

The **Polytechnic Hotel,** on ulica Stwosza, three blocks west of Plac Dzierzyńskiego (tel. 44-27-51), is a great deal. The rooms are clean with a TV, radio, and shower. A single room costs 2,300 złoty ($14.50) per night, a double room costs 3,600 złoty ($22.65), and a suite runs 5,000 złoty ($31.45). If possible, reserve a room; sometimes an empty room can still be found when you arrive, perhaps for a few dollars at the desk. Be very, very careful if you try this tactic—if the clerk says yes, you could displace a Socialist Bloc businessman, who will be only too glad to "blow the whistle" on such dealings. You really can't blame him if he does; after all, it was his room. Otherwise the desk clerk will direct students to the existing student hostel, wherever it might appear.

The **Europajski Hotel,** at Świerczewskiego 90 (tel. 310-71), is one of the better bargains in Wrocław. Little English is spoken, but the receptionist is friendly and patient. A single costs 3,620 złoty ($22.75) per night and a double runs 5,030 złoty ($31.65). There are only 40 rooms here so it is difficult to find a space. Breakfast is not included in the room price.

The **Hotel Odra,** ul. Stawowa 13 (tel. 375-60; Telex 0715157), is through the same arched passage as the Europajski; continue through to the next street, then make a left and walk one block west. The 46 rooms here open up after noon and are usually filled by 2 p.m. Unlike many hotels, the prices are clearly posted: a single room costs 2,350 złoty ($14.75) per night, and a double room, 4,410 złoty ($27.75); subtract 150 złoty (95¢) per night for rooms without a private bath. The Odra also has rooms for three and four people, at 3,760 złoty ($23.65) and 4,080 złoty ($25.65) respectively. No English is spoken here, but they do have a Telex so it's easier to make reservations in advance.

The **Grand Hotel,** ul. Świerczewskiego 100/102 (tel. 360-71; Telex 0712-457), isn't the best hotel in Wrocław, but you can find a good clean room here. Again rooms are hard to come by, so it's a good idea to make reservations. The rooms are done in a flat green floral print and are small. A single room costs 4,090 złoty ($25.75); a double room, 5,350 złoty ($33.65). The common bathrooms leave a lot to be desired, so if they're available, spend the extra money for a room with a private bathroom. The rooms on the south side of the hotel are sunny but noisy.

Student Lodgings

The **Almatur** office, at Noicinzlei 34 (tel. 44-30-03 or 44-39-51; Telex 0712-783), is the best place to look for private rooms or student accommodations. The office is in the left-hand corner of the courtyard (past some repair work) and under a sign marked, strangely enough, "Almatur."

Almatur runs an International Student Hotel from July 1 till September 30. A bed costs 500 złoty ($3.15) per night, and most of the rooms contain two or three beds. Every four rooms share a bathroom. During the summer of 1985 the student hotel was at Olszewskiego 25 (tel. 48-10-91), but it may not be there in following summers. The student hotel usually has rooms, and the Almatur people say that if you call two to three days in advance, then it's "absolutely certain" that you'll get a place.

You'll find the Almatur workers friendly and helpful if you wait a bit. They should be able to find you something either in the student hotel or a private room. Almatur also organizes day and city tours with English-speaking guides.

Starvation-Budget Accommodations

At ulica Kołłataja 20 is a **House of Culture** where students can find a place to sleep. "Just walk in," we were told by an old woman who remembered the German presence when Wrocław was once called Breslau. She was kindly and patient, but spoke no English. There are 30 beds in two rooms—one room for 20 people and the other for 8 (how 8 and 20 make 30 is a question you'll have to save for the proprietress). It's a seemingly vast complex, clean and somewhat spartan. A bed for the night is 320 złoty ($2), with each additional night a scandalous 200 extra złoty ($1.25). The bunkbeds are very flimsy, the toilets are not very clean, and there are no showers. This place is open all year and has a couple of beds free almost all the time, so it's the best starvation-budget solution to lodging in Wrocław.

DINING: Wrocław is a city of kawiarnia—coffeehouses. An institution not common in the United States, the kawiarnia is a meeting place, a common room where news and gossip are exchanged, but above all, a place to drink and eat in the company of friends. For the hungry there are several restaurants of about the same quality near the center of town on the Rynek Główny (Main Square) or just off it on ulica Kościuszki. There seems to be more food in Wrocław than in Kraków, as evidenced by greater availability of menu listings in the restaurants. There are also occasional street vendors; try ulica Świerczewskiego, across from the train station.

After a long climb up a barren and somewhat forbidding stairway, you'll find the **Polonia Restaurant** at ul. Świerczewskiego 66 (tel. 310-21). Open from 8 a.m. until 2 in the morning, the Polonia has a small menu with offerings that range in price from 150 złoty (95¢) to 400 złoty ($2.50). Three large iron chandeliers hover over the open conference hall–like dining room. An enclosed stage at one end is the stomping ground of a dance band that plays most nights from 9 p.m. till closing. Primarily a dance hall, this is a good place for a vigorous evening on the dance floor.

The kawiarnia of the **Europajski Hotel,** at ul. Świerczewskiego 94/95 (tel. 44-41-40), is one of the more popular local places, open from 8 a.m. till 9 p.m. You enter the place through a narrow mirrored entryway off the street and not through the hotel. The faded biege interior, the well-worn floor, and a blue miasma of cigarette smoke attest to this place's popularity. To get to the hotel, don't go through the kawiarnia (you can, but the door is so cleverly camouflaged as to be next to impossible to detect). Go around to the hotel sign; you'll see the hotel entrance there.

The kawiarnia **Reduta,** ul. Piotra Skargi 16A (tel. 44-76-04), adds a new twist to the coffeehouse scene with a large colonnaded dance floor (the large tables are arranged around the dance floor, with the bandstand at one end). The ceiling is a fading red with small, rather insecure stars scattered around it; the carpet is also red. There are a few fresh flowers on some of the tables. Arrayed in a glass case are several appealing cakes. There are some dinner entrees, but most of the food is cold. Sardines for 120 złoty (75¢), cold chicken for 130 złoty (80¢), sausages, and salads are the standard fare. There are some Western drinks available here, but as usual, such drinks are very expensive.

At Rynek Główny (Main Square) 19 is the kawiarnia **Herbowa.** The vaulted ceilings, stone-flagged floor, fine wooden furniture, and wood trimmings give this well-restored kawiarnia a pleasing old-world feeling. A glass of tea here costs 150 złoty (95¢) or almost the same price as four glasses of Hungarian wine (40 złoty, or 25¢, each). This is not to promote alcohol consumption, but keep in mind that a warming cherry cordial costs no more than a glass of tea. There are also light foods such as omelets at 93 złoty (60¢) and cakes. Beware, the waitresses have a tendency to bring non-Polish-speakers the most expensive items on the menu. Alcohol is served only after 1 p.m. Open from 10 a.m. till 9 p.m.

Also on the Rynek Główny is the **U Prospera Café** (tel. 44-85-89). Located on the second floor, the U Prospera's height gives the coffee drinker a good view of the square. Open from 10 a.m. till 10 p.m., this brightly decorated kawiarnia is one of our favorites in town. The fiery griffons and cavorting unicorns brighten up the place even on rainy days (though certainly there'll be few of those on your vacation). A younger crowd enjoys weekend coffee here, and the establishment is mercifully freed from the oppressive weight of piped-in music. There is a small fee—4 złoty (2½¢)—for use of the rest rooms.

There's a good cheap **pizza place** right next to the Orbis office at Rynek Główny 46, open from 10 a.m. till 9 p.m. You too can join the hundreds of Poles eating slices of pizza as they hurry back to their work places.

NIGHTLIFE: Next to the Almatur office is the **Pałacyk** student club. This place really doesn't get started till the evening, usually after 7 p.m., and it's an excellent place to meet Polish students. There are endless goings-on here: movies, music, sometimes a big dance and poetry readings. If you do come here, don't be put off by the dark, poorly stained wooden interior. Wander around and ask people until you find someone who speaks English. Upstairs is a surprisingly appealing ballroom despite its ugly shades of green.

There are two other recommended student clubs, **Implus** and Igloo. Implus on Plac Berna, right by the university, is not a large establishment but a great place to meet students and young people. There is dancing most nights. **Igloo** is a long ride outside town in the Novotel. It's nothing more than the hotel bar, but it is the late-night joint of Wrocław, open from 8 p.m. till 3 in the morning on the weekends.

THE SIGHTS: In the heart of town at the reconstructed **Rynek** (Marketplace) are Renaissance and baroque burghers' houses as well as the splendid **Old Town Hall.** Built initially in the 13th century, it was refinished, damaged, and rebuilt until it was finally finished in the 16th century. Inside, you can visit the **Wrocław**

Historical Museum, open Tuesday through Friday from 10 a.m. to 2:30 p.m. and 11 a.m. to 5 p.m. on weekends; closed Monday. The **Ostrów Tumski** (Minister Island) in the middle of the Odra River holds the reconstructed Gothic **Cathedral of St. John the Baptist,** begun in the 12th century, and the **Church of the Holy Cross,** begun approximately 100 years later in the 13th century. The Piast tombs are to be found in the fine old **Church of St. Clare.**

Part Two

EAST GERMANY

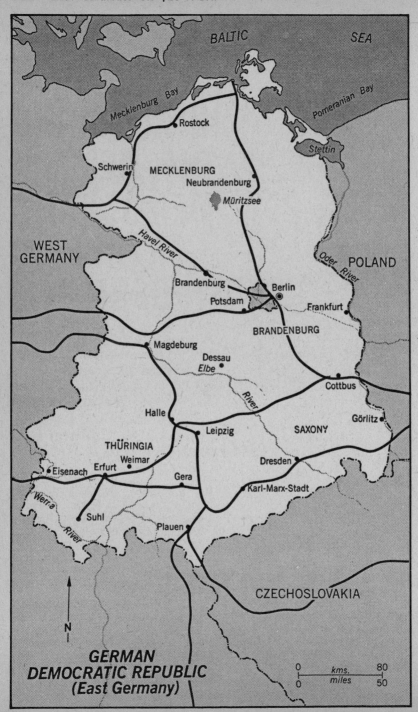

BALTIC   SEA

Mecklenburg Bay

Pomeranian Bay

Rostock

Stettin

Schwerin

MECKLENBURG

Neubrandenburg

Müritzsee

Havel River

WEST
GERMANY

Oder River   POLAND

Brandenburg

Berlin

Potsdam

Frankfurt

BRANDENBURG

Magdeburg

Dessau

Elbe

River

Cottbus

Halle

Görlitz

Leipzig

SAXONY

THÜRINGIA

Weimar

Dresden

Eisenach   Erfurt

Gera

Werra

Karl-Marx-Stadt

River

Suhl

Plauen

CZECHOSLOVAKIA

N

**GERMAN
DEMOCRATIC REPUBLIC
(East Germany)**

| 0 | kms. | 80 |
| 0 | miles | 50 |

Chapter VIII

INTRODUCING THE GERMAN DEMOCRATIC REPUBLIC (EAST GERMANY)

CREATED OUT OF THE SOVIET ZONE of occupation at the end of the Second World War, the German Democratic Republic (GDR) was once one of the most forbidding Eastern European countries. More recently the government has relaxed its attitude and tourism is now encouraged.

There is much to see in East Germany. When Germany was partitioned after World War II, some of the finest historical and cultural monuments were in the Soviet Zone. There is also a very beautiful countryside, ranging from the stark Baltic shoreline in the north to the dark Thüringer Wald (forest) in the south.

You can travel from West Germany to East Germany in less than 15 minutes. As you pass the Wall that divides Germany, remember that the two parts of the country share a common past. In East Germany the people have the same cultural and historical roots as those on the western side of the Wall. The only difference is that they have been living under a Communist form of government for over 40 years.

With a total area of 67,000 square miles, the German Democratic Republic is packed with points of historical and cultural interest. Weimar, Erfurt, Leipzig, Dresden, and many other towns, now in East Germany, were home to some of the luminaries of European history—Martin Luther, Bach, Goethe, and Wagner, to mention just a few. Dresden, long the jewel in the Imperial German crown, is still a cultural and historical masterpiece. There are numerous well-preserved medieval towns, such as Erfurt and Weimar, throughout the country. And of course we can't forget the cultural and historical wealth of East Germany's capital, Berlin.

SUGGESTED ITINERARIES: We recommend that you spend at least a week in East Germany. East Berlin (called just Berlin in East Germany), capital of the German Democratic Republic, requires at least two days, especially if you wish to explore the outlying neighborhoods. Potsdam, where Truman, Churchill, and Stalin met to decide Germany's fate in June 1945, is a city worth at least an entire day. However, given its attraction, the hotels can fill up. We recommend that you stop off and see Potsdam on your way south to Weimar and Erfurt.

Weimar and Erfurt are each worth a day's visit. They are only about 45 minutes apart by train and one can easily be reached from the other. Leipzig is a beautiful old town with numerous interesting buildings. Dresden was once one of Europe's most beautiful cities and still has some of the most impressive baroque structures in Europe. You can easily spend a few days at the charming resort towns of Oberhof and Suhl in the Thüringer Wald. To the north, on the Baltic Sea, are the old (though heavily reconstructed) Hanseatic cities of Rostock and Stralsund. These two towns are off the beaten track, so we recommend stopping off if you are en route to or from Scandinavia.

1. About the German Democratic Republic

A CAPSULE HISTORY: Under the terms of the 1945 Potsdam Conference, Germany was to be temporarily divided into four sectors administered by the four Allies—the Americans, British, French, and the Soviets. As a result of the postwar break-up of the "Big Three" (as the wartime alliance of England, the Soviet Union, and the United States—respectively under the leadership of Churchill, Stalin, and Roosevelt—was known), Europe was divided between the Western Allies and the Soviet Union. The German Democratic Republic was created out of the Soviet Sector of occupied Nazi Germany in June 1945.

Disintegration of the Alliance

Postwar tensions rose to a fever pitch with the Soviet efforts to regain control over all of Berlin. In 1948 the Soviets cut off all land access to the city and the United States was forced to begin a massive airlift in order to provide for the people in the Western sectors of Berlin. By this time the Western European nations and the United States had agreed to tie West Germany, economically, with the rest of Europe. The Soviet-supported Eastern European countries formed their own alliance. East Germany was created in the new atmosphere of a divided Europe. Some attempts were made to reunite Germany in 1949, but the outbreak of the Korean War in 1950 effectively ended all attempts at negotiation.

The Creation of East Germany

With the completion of the constitution on May 30, 1949, a new government was established. Three years later, although the Soviet Military Authority still retained supervisory control, they formally transferred the right to self-govern to the new government. However, it was not until March 25, 1954, that the Soviet Union gave the country complete autonomy. But the heavy burden of paying war reparations to the Soviet Union, widespread shortages of all essential goods (food, fuel, medicines), and the repressive Soviet occupation caused widespread discontent among the populace.

In the wake of Stalin's death in March 1953, confusion and uncertainty reigned throughout the Soviet Bloc. In an attempt to bolster faltering production, the East German government instituted a longer work week. Strikes and rioting soon followed in East Berlin and in over 250 places across East Germany. Soviet forces returned to East Germany to quell the worst disturbances. With their return, many people felt that escape to the West was the only option left open to them. Between 1945 and 1961 it is estimated that 2.5 million people left the German Democratic Republic and crossed over into West Germany.

The Mass Emigration to the West

Many of the reasons for the mass defections, which averaged somewhere around 20,000 people a year, were economic. At the beginning of the new Five Year Plan in 1960 the Communist government began an intensified program of collectivization. In 1960–1961 over 350,000 people, many of them highly trained specialists in their most productive years, left East Germany, attracted by the promise of "the good life" in the West. The people who left, the "Flüchtlinger," exacerbated East Germany's already-grim economic situation. The creation of "The Wall" is rightly seen as an act of desperation by the Communist government, but it was successful.

Creation of the Wall

Efforts to curtail the flow of people to the West began as early as 1952 with the establishment of a cleared, guarded, three-mile-wide corridor along the intra-German border. In 1961 a new series of barriers were constructed along the frontier, stopping most of the traffic across the border. With this route gone, people began to leave East Germany by literally strolling into West Berlin.

To close the West Berlin "escape hatch" once and for all, the Communist government, with the support and aid of the Soviet Union, began to isolate West Berlin from East Berlin and the surrounding countryside. On August 13, 1961, a wall was hastily thrown up around West Berlin and all the border areas cleared by force. Today the barriers range from elevated guard towers covering barbed-wire fences in the countryside to the 12-foot-high concrete "Berlin Wall" which divides the former capital of Germany.

Détente and the German Democratic Republic Today

In an attempt to reduce international tensions, both the Soviet Union and the United States pressed the two Germanys to find some way to coexist on a number of issues, especially West Berlin. With the exit of Chancellor Konrad Adenauer and the arrival of Willi Brandt and his "Ostpolitik," treaties with East Germany were concluded in 1973. Ever since, the German Democratic Republic has been opening up to the West, albeit slowly. While East Germany maintains restrictive internal policies, tourists were never as seriously affected. Contact, especially with West Germany, is increasing, as is the opportunity for West Germans to travel to East Germany. On the whole this is probably the best time there has ever been to travel to the German Democratic Republic.

THE WALL: The Wall that now separates East and West Berlin was put up by the East German government to stem the flow of people to the West. It also serves to keep out ideas unacceptable to the Communist regime. The Wall is

The German Mark

The mark is the unit of currency for both the German Democratic Republic (East Germany) and the Federal Republic of Germany (West Germany), and the exchange rate against the dollar is the same for both the eastern and western versions of the mark. The prices in this guide were calculated at 2.85 marks = $1 U.S.; thus 1 mark = 35¢ U.S., or $10 = about 28.5 marks.

basically the same along the entire frontier of Eastern Europe—a barrier of fences, mines, and sensors guarded by soldiers, dogs, and tanks.

When questioned today about the Wall, many East Germans accept it philosophically. There has been a Communist government in East Germany for over 40 years, and many of the younger people enjoy, or at least tolerate, the system. One thing the Wall did bring that was welcomed by many in the German Democratic Republic, was stability.

THE PEOPLE: The land area comprising East Germany has traditionally been known as the German heartland. Though their influence has varied, German-speaking peoples have long been established in much of Saxony and Prussia—what is today the German Democratic Republic. Thus the citizens of East Germany are just as "German" as the citizens of the Federal Republic to the west.

Living conditions in the German Democratic Republic, materially speaking, are perhaps the best in the Soviet Bloc: East German citizens enjoy the highest per capita standard of living in Eastern Europe (in fact, it's higher than in the Soviet Union itself). With no other major natural resource than brown coal, East Germany is now ranked in the top 15 industrial nations in the world.

Most East Germans are just as proud of their economic achievements as are their Western counterparts. There even seems to be a current of smugness in any discussion of the postwar reconstruction; many East Germans feel that their achievement was greater than the West German recovery because their "economic miracle" took place with the added burdens of the Soviet Union's war reparations and restrictive economic policies.

GOVERNMENT: The German Democratic Republic is a Socialist People's Democracy. The legislative body is the People's Chamber, whose members, elected every five years, represent all the legal political parties. The Council of Ministers, headed by General Secretary Erich Honecker, is the highest governmental body in the country.

LANGUAGE: The official language is German. More English is spoken and understood in East Germany than in other Eastern European countries. However, English-speakers are not nearly as common in the German Democratic Republic as in the Federal Republic to the west. French and, to a lesser extent, Russian are useful languages as well.

SPORTS: The East German national identity rests to a great degree on excellence in sports. Extensive sports participation is mandatory for most of the population, and star athletes are groomed and trained with the utmost dedication and intensity. There is an abundance of swimming pools, sports facilities, and playing fields—most of which are open to the public. Generally, when the facilities are not closed for races or other special events, Western tourists can use them for a small fee.

GEOGRAPHY: East Germany has three major regions: the Baltic Coast in the north, the eastern part of the North German Plains, and the forested Harz Mountains in the southwest. In and around the slopes of the Harz Mountains is the beautiful, dark Thüringer Wald (forest). There are numerous small and medium-sized lakes scattered throughout the north and central parts of the country. East Germany is not large enough to contain the kinds of national parks and vast nature reserves that are found in the U.S. There are, however, many parks and reserves such as the forests of the Seenplatte north of Berlin and the Müggelheim preserve to the east of Berlin.

2. Rules and Regulations

TOURIST INFORMATION: There is no government-sponsored tourist bureau of the German Democratic Republic in the United States. The requirements for any Western tourist traveling in East Germany are complicated and best completed before you go. You can either contact the Koch organization in New York or write directly to the East German travel bureau (see below).

What's in a Name?

Most North Americans casually refer to the divided Germanys as "West" Germany and "East" Germany, and to the divided city of Berlin as "West" Berlin and "East" Berlin, and in this guide we have generally followed this usage for ease of the reader's understanding. But the governmental officials of the German Democratic Republic ("East" Germany) will probably not be so accommodating, and will likely react much more positively to your concerns or questions if you use the geographic designations accepted within their country. So in your dealings with these officials—whether they be Customs officers, policemen, tourist information office staff, or other government bureaucrats—we suggest that you call the country by its official name, the **German Democratic Republic** (Deutsche Demokratische Republik, or DDR), and that you refer to its capital as **Berlin–Hauptstadt der DDR** (Berlin, capital of the DDR), or simply **Berlin.**

The only travel bureau in the U.S. that specializes in travel to the German Democratic Republic is **Koch Overseas Company,** 157 E. 86th St., New York, NY 10028 (tel. 212/369-3800).

If you have a flexible schedule, you can wait until you reach Berlin before you make your travel plans. The **Reisebüro der Deutschen Democratishen Republik** (Travel Bureau of the German Democratic Republic), Generaldirektion, Alexanderplatz 5, DDR-1026 Berlin, DDR (tel. 21-50; Telex 114648), can make the necessary arrangements, usually in a morning.

VISAS: In order to enter the German Democratic Republic you will have to submit a day-by-day itinerary of every location where you will spend the night. The only exception is a day visa from West Berlin to East Berlin (see Chapter

IX). The types of visas and their requirements depend on whether or not you plan to stay with friends or relatives in East Germany.

If you plan to stay in any type of accommodation other than an officially managed hotel for foreign tourists, you'll have to get an **entry permit.** If you plan to stay only in state-managed hotels for foreigners, and not stay with friends or relatives at any time during your visit in the German Democratic Republic, then you need only submit your itinerary and pre-pay all hotel costs.

Only transit visas between the Federal Republic of Germany and West Berlin are issued at the border. You must get *all* other visas in advance—*no* visas are issued at the border.

Visas for Visitors Staying Exclusively in State-Run Accommodations

If you are planning on staying in hotels, you'll join the average tourist in this category. You must present an itinerary, including arrival and departure dates and length of stay, and must indicate the category of hotel you wish to stay in. (In the German Democratic Republic hotels are ranked—a five-star hotel is the most luxurious, and a one-star the least.) You must also pre-pay all hotel costs and collect your hotel vouchers, which serve as both receipts and proof of reservations.

Planning an itinerary and selecting hotels with no prior knowledge may seem a bit daunting. However, we feel that this mandatory planning will make your actual visit to East Germany much simpler. Note that the sooner you start the visa application process, the more likely it is that you'll get the hotel you want.

Visas for Visitors Staying in Non-State-Managed Accommodations

If you plan to spend even one night of your stay with family or friends in East Germany, you will have to submit a day-by-day itinerary as well as the name(s) and address(es) of the people you'll be staying with. If you'll be staying in state-run hotels for part of your visit, you must pre-pay all hotel costs and get your hotel vouchers. Once you have submitted your intinerary (along with a $20 registration fee) and pre-paid for your hotels (if any), you should receive your entry permit in about six to nine weeks. Given the amount of time it takes, this procedure can only be done long in advance.

Since one of the principal reasons the East Germans want you to visit is for your Western currency, there is a minimum exchange for all visitors for every night they don't stay in state-run accommodations. The minimum exchange for adults is 25 marks ($8.75), 15 marks ($5.25) for senior citizens, and 7.50 marks for children ($2.65) per day. This sum is exchanged, in advance, at the border. Tourists staying exclusively in state-run hotels do not have a minimum exchange requirement. They can also get all the paperwork done in a single morning in East Berlin without the wait.

Because of the complexity and the time involved we recommend that you contact the Koch Overseas Company, which will do all the paperwork for you. It costs $45 per person for an entry permit and $20 for tourists who plan to stay exclusively in state-run accommodations.

Where to Get Your Hotel Vouchers

If you are staying exclusively in state-run establishments, you can get your hotel vouchers directly from the Reisebüro der DDR by writing them from the United States. This will take some time (six to eight weeks), however. A better bet, if you don't have a firm schedule or are unwilling to commit yourself to an East German vacation months in advance, is to go to the main office of the Reisebüro der DDR at Alexanderplatz 5 in East Berlin. You can reach the office in about an hour from West Berlin on a day visa (detailed in Chapter IX). Here, on the second floor, you can submit your itinerary and, in about 20 minutes to an hour, pay for and collect your hotel vouchers. The office is open daily from 10 a.m. to 7 p.m.

The friendly staff will try to get you the hotels in the cities you want. If all the hotels in a particular city are full, you may have to spend the night in another, nearby, town.

Again, if you're planning to stay in private residences, you'll have to get your hotel vouchers in advance by mail from the Reisebüro der DDR or through Koch Overseas Company in New York.

Getting Your Visa

Though it may seem like a long process, it takes about the same amount of time as for most of the other Eastern European countries. To get your visa, bring your passport, hotel vouchers, and—if you are *not* staying exclusively in state-run accommodations—an entry permit. There is an information card that will have to be filled out, but you get this along with your vouchers at the Reisebüro der DDR or the Koch agency. Go to any international border-crossing point and present these documents plus another 15 West German marks ($5.25) to the guard and you'll get a visa as well as a stamp in your passport. Keep your visa and all your hotel vouchers on your person while you're in East Germany.

CUSTOMS: The primary job of the East German Customs official is the security of the German Democratic Republic. The second most important aspect of their job is to speed as many Westerners (and their accompanying hard currency) as possible into East Germany. Understand that the guards are not there to keep you out. Be helpful, but never chummy or ingratiating. Assume that your bags will be opened, and behave as if they will. Sometimes if you appear as though you're ready to go through with a search, it happens less often. And if they do search you, it's much more casual and the guards are much more polite.

On a day trip, keep your baggage, especially all printed material, to a minimum. Do *not*, no matter what kind of rates you get in the West, attempt to import East German marks—it's strictly illegal. All other Customs restrictions (as detailed in Chapter I) apply at the border of the German Democratic Republic.

Gifts of no more than 200 marks ($70) per day of visit in East Germany, to a maximum of 1,000 marks ($350), may be brought in duty free, per person.

Cars

State insurance is mandatory unless you have the International Insurance Card (Blue or Green Card). Insurance costs 45 marks ($15.75) for one to ten days and 90 marks ($31.50) for any more time. There are also road tolls of varying rates, depending on how much driving you plan to do in East Germany. These tolls should not run more than $25 for an average one-week stay.

REGISTRATION: All visitors to the German Democratic Republic must register within 24 hours of their arrival. Most of the larger hotels will do this for you, but occasionally in some of the smaller hotels and in private accommodations you have to do it yourself. To register yourself, go to the nearest main police station (not a local branch office). This sometimes means a good half-hour wait, though the actual process is no more complicated than having your passport stamped. Note that in East Germany every time you enter a new district (Bezirk) you have to register again. Dresden, Leipzig and Weimar, Erfurt, East Berlin and Potsdam are in separate districts.

3. Getting There

One of the easiest and cheapest ways for North Americans to get to East Germany is through West Germany.

BY AIR: Prices for direct plane connections from New York to East Berlin's **Schönefeld International Airport** are very expensive—upward of $850 one way. We recommend flying via Lufthansa into the Federal Republic of Germany and then traveling by train to Berlin. You can stop over for a night or two in West Berlin, make all your visa and entry arrangements, and then travel into East Germany.

There are several airlines that fly from Frankfurt International Airport to East Berlin for around $160. Another good way we found was to take advantage of some of the discount fares offered well in advance to cities in the north of West Germany. For example, Lufthansa has a low Holiday Fare (see chart to Germany on page 24) from New York to Hamburg, West Germany. Hamburg is less than six hours and $45 away from Berlin by train, or you can fly there for about $95. On low fares to Berlin, there are several restrictions, the worst of which is availability. Therefore, it is recommended that you make reservations in February for a flight in May or June.

BY TRAIN: The three major entry points from the Federal Republic of Germany are detailed in Chapter IX in Section 2 on the day visa from West Berlin. The most likely routes for visitors from Eastern Europe are Prague, Czechoslovakia, in the southeast and Warsaw, Poland, in the east. A less-traveled route is from the northern Scandinavian countries.

From Czechoslovakia, the train trip is through Dresden and then East Berlin; counting the border formalities, the trip takes around six to seven hours. The Warsaw–Berlin train is a true endurance test of over eight hours, with a border check that always seems to occur at night. The best starting point is West Berlin; and train arrivals are detailed in Chapter IX.

BY CAR: Most tourists coming from West Germany drive to the German Democratic Republic. The rental packages in East Germany are not competitive with the Western ones, so we recommend sticking with East Germany's excellent train system.

BY BOAT: All of East Germany's ports are in the north, on the Baltic Coast. The two principal international ports are **Rostock** in the western part and **Sassnitz** in the east. In summer five daily ferries link Sassnitz with the Swedish port of Trelleborg; the trip takes four hours. Rostock and the port of Warnemunde are linked with the Danish port of Gedser, not far from Copenhagen. The whole trip by ferry and train from Copenhagen to East Berlin is more than 11 hours, with the border formalities.

4. Getting Around

BY AIR: Air travel around East Germany is not worth the expense, as any trip that begins in Berlin is no more than six hours from almost all of the major points of interest. There are commercial airfields near Leipzig and Erfurt in the south, and several smaller, limited-access airfields in the north. Air travel runs around $60 for a flight from East Berlin to the north on Interflug, the East German state airlines.

BY TRAIN: Train is by far the most economical and convenient way to get around. The train ride from East Berlin to Erfurt takes less than four hours, and the new express line from Berlin to Dresden has shortened the trip to under three hours. Prices are low and any International Student Identity Card (IUS, the Eastern European student card) holder is entitled to a 25% discount on certain train routes within the German Democratic Republic.

BY CAR: You drive on the right and obey the standard European rules-of-the-road in the German Democratic Republic. The speed limit on highways is 120 km/h (75 mph); on other roads, 95 km/h (60 mph); and in built-up areas, 55 km/h (35 mph). Pedestrians have the right of way in "zebra crossings" and when turning at road junctions.

The consumption of alcohol, sleeping pills, and any other debilitating drugs and medicines by the driver is absolutely prohibited. The East German police are very strict about enforcement and there are stiff penalties for offenders. Other auto-related rules in East Germany: three-point (shoulder harness) seatbelts must be worn by everyone in the front seat of a vehicle; no children under the age of 6 are allowed in the front seat; all motorcycle riders and passengers must wear crash helmets; in populated areas you may use your horn only to avoid accidents.

In case of accidents involving any injury and/or serious damage, you must notify the emergency service immediately. In all other instances it's sufficient to exchange insurance numbers and notify the police within 24 hours of the accident.

HITCHHIKING: Hitchhiking, though reasonably safe, is frowned on by the authorities. East Germany is one place where single women travelers have reported few problems, either on or off the road. In any event, proper caution should be exercised and any admonition by the local police to take the train should be heeded.

5. Food and Lodging

ACCOMMODATIONS: In East Germany, **hotels** are ranked by the international system of stars: five stars is the most luxurious and one star indicates the most basic and inexpensive accommodations.

Since all your accommodations must be pre-selected before you enter the German Democratic Republic, choosing a hotel is often done for you. When making your itinerary, indicate which hotel you wish to stay in. The people at the Reisebüro der DDR will call the hotel for you. If a particular hotel is full, you'll have to accept another (the Reisebüro's) choice. The categories are structured primarily by price, so that often will be the deciding factor on where you will stay. Not all the hotels are for foreigners and true budget selections are harder to find in East Germany.

Hostels are for organized student tour groups only, and not for the individual, private traveler.

You can only get **camping** permits at the main office of the Reisebüro der DDR. Camping permits are handled much the same way hotel reservations are: you must pre-pay for a particular campsite and then you receive a voucher. Either make reservations at the main office of the Reisebüro der DDR in East Berlin or write them, adding "Direktionsbereich AAT" to the given address.

FOOD: East German food is heavy and filling, often with several starchy dishes. We recommend that you try small local places, and then order the special of the day. This is both the tastiest and most inexpensive way to eat. If you need a change from "blue-plate dining," try some of the Socialist international restaurants, such as Hungarian or Cuban. If they are run by actual natives of those countries you'll get a much higher quality of international-style cuisine than is available in the larger hotels.

There are many different sorts of sausages *(wurst)*, such as Halberstäder würstchen and the Thüringer rostbratwurst. Both are usually served with klössen, a kind of dumpling. The specialty in many of the finer restaurants in Saxony and the southeast is roast duck *(entenbraten)*. A favorite everywhere is eisbein mit sauerkraut (pigs' knuckles and pickled cabbage).

Communism has not diluted any of the traditional "bierkultur," and emptying a mug is often a cure for the heaviest of thoughts. Try any of the local beers, especially Radeberger beer. There are also several different kinds of schnapps and fruit brandies available.

6. Cultural Life

Perhaps one of the best reasons to visit East Germany is the wealth of music and theater performances. Bach, Handel, and Schütz (a famed choirmaster in Dresden) all lived in what is today the German Democratic Republic. The government has gone to great lengths to preserve the churches, theaters, concert halls, and other buildings associated with the numerous famous historical figures that are a part of German history.

There are several annual music festivals which feature numerous international ensembles and many of the East German state orchestras. The Gewandhaus Concert Hall in Leipzig, the State Opera House in East Berlin, and the recently (1985) opened Semper Opera House in Dresden are restored historical monuments where some of the international festivals are held. There is everything from Bach concerts throughout Thüringia in March, chamber music at Potsdam-Sanssouci Palace in June, to accordion concerts in Vogtland in May. There are usually many performances and the ticket price for excellent seats is less than $7, though most seats are available for less than $5.

The Reisebüro der DDR offers numerous tours that range from an afternoon of opera in the State Opera House in Berlin to a five-day tour of all of Bach's major haunts. For more information on Music Tours in the German Democratic Republic, write: Musik Information Zentrum, Leipziger Strasse 26, DDR-1086 Berlin, DDR.

7. The ABCs of the German Democratic Republic

AUTO REPAIR: All auto repair is handled through the police, though you can contact emergency repair facilities at most gas stations.

BLACK MARKET: The police are reasonably efficient and the fines, if you're caught, are very stiff. Most souvenir items are already very inexpensive and there is no way around the minimum exchanges and pre-paid hotels. The black market is not worth it.

BANKS: As with most Communist countries, there is little need to go to a bank as the exchange rates are the same at all Reisebüro der DDR offices and state-run hotels.

BUSINESS HOURS: Most stores and businesses in East Germany are open from 9 a.m. to 6 p.m., except in East Berlin where things open and close an hour later. Only the largest stores are open Saturday morning from 9 a.m. until 11 a.m., and everything closes on Sunday.

CLIMATE: You'll find typical northern European weather: often rainy and cool in summer, but with milder winters.

CRIME: There is crime in East Germany, but it's extremely rare. Single women should be cautious, but there should be no difficulty for any woman traveling alone.

ELECTRICITY: The electric current in the German Democratic Republic is 220 volts, 50 cycles, A.C.

EMBASSIES AND CONSULATES: The U.S. Embassy is in East Berlin at Neustadtische Kirchstrasse 4/5 (tel. 220-27-41), just north of the Unter den Linden and about four blocks from the Friedrichstrasse station. Though the embassy personnel are always ready in an emergency, most routine inquiries and questions about U.S. citizens in East Germany can be answered by the U.S. Consulate staff in West Berlin, at Clay Allee 170 (tel. 832-40-87). There are no U.S. Consulates in the German Democratic Republic.

The British Embassy is in East Berlin at Unter den Linden 32-34 (tel. 220-2431).

EMERGENCY: In an emergency, dial 110 for the police or 115 for an ambulance.

FIRST AID: Everyone will be taken care of in a medical emergency, though unless they have special insurance, all Western tourists will have to pay.

GASOLINE: There are no restrictions on how much gas a Western tourist may purchase. All gas must be purchased with coupons that come in 5-, 10-, and 20-mark denominations. You can get these coupons at all Reisebüro der DDR offices or at Intertank, the specially designated international service stations.

HOLIDAYS: The official public holidays in the German Democratic Republic are: New Year's Day on January 1, Good Friday, Easter Sunday, May Day (the international Communist holiday) on May 1, the founding date of the German Democratic Republic on October 7, and Christmas on December 25–26.

NEWS AND MEDIA: You can get West German television and radio in practically every part of East Germany except the southeast corner (around Dresden). No printed news from the West is available.

POST OFFICE: All post offices are open weekdays from 9 a.m. till 5 p.m. and Saturday mornings; closed Sunday.

SOUVENIRS: Intershop is the state-run chain of stores in the German Democratic Republic. Anything that you buy in these stores you can bring out duty free.

East Germany has some excellent classical music albums (though their selection of everything else is pretty thin) of good quality for usually under $3 per album, often less than that. Excellent art and other coffee-table-type picture books are also available for a fraction of their cost in the West, though they are of course printed in German. Certain editions of classic German authors are available in fine hardcover editions for the German-speaking bibliophile.

The less literarily inclined or those who left their reading glasses at home can exult in the good selection of Meissen porcelain in most larger Intershops.

TELEPHONE, TELEGRAPH, AND TELEX: Telephoning back and forth across the two Berlins between large state offices is now quite easy. In fact you can call the Reisebüro der DDR from any telephone booth in West Berlin. Otherwise, calling across the Atlantic is an expensive and often lengthy process. We recommend waiting and calling from West Berlin if possible.

Telegrams are rarer in East Germany than in the United States. We recommend sending Telexes for all important messages within Eastern Europe (not just East Germany), as a Telex provides a hard copy for both the sender and receiver.

Chapter IX

EAST BERLIN AND POTSDAM

1. Orientation
2. The Day Visa from West Berlin to East Berlin
3. Accommodations in East Berlin
4. Dining in East Berlin
5. The Sights of East Berlin
6. The ABCs of East Berlin
7. Potsdam

NO OTHER CITY IN THE WORLD has occupied a more pivotal position in 20th-century history than Berlin. Former capital of Imperial Germany and the Third Reich, Berlin now stands in the very center of Europe as the symbol of the Cold War. To compare the two halves of Berlin is unavoidable. West Berlin is indeed a mecca of consumer wealth and political freedoms so broad that it has become the haven for the most outspoken elements of both ends of the political spectrum in West Germany. East Berlin can boast of great cultural resources that are a must for Western visitors.

Many of the largest art and historical collections in the city fell in the Soviet zone at the end of World War II. Fischer's Island (Fischerinsel), now known as Museum Island (Museuminsel), has two of the largest ancient and medieval history museums in the world, the Pergamon and the Bodemuseum. There are also two major art galleries, the National Gallery and the Altes Museum, both with extensive post-18th-century collections.

The Alexanderplatz, showcase of the German Democratic Republic, is a vast concrete expanse dominated by the huge Radiotower (Funkturm) looming over the beautiful Church of St. Mary (Marienkirche).

After visiting the many museums, we suggest that you leave the center and take the metro or elevated train to the suburbs. There you'll see fewer officials and have an opportunity to meet the locals. Just outside the city center are the most appealing cafés and the best home-style restaurants. The city has some of the most interesting people and vibrant cultural life, but you must look past the concrete façade to find the true heart of East Berlin.

A CAPSULE HISTORY: In 1987 Berlin will celebrate its 750th anniversary. The city began as two small settlements in 1237, one called Cöllin on Museum Island, and the other, on the east bank of the Spree River, called Berlin. Later the communities merged, and as a result of their advantageous position on both river and land trade routes, quickly grew in both size and importance. By the 14th century Berlin was a bustling center of commercial activity with a large population of artisans producing numerous goods.

This period of prosperity ended with the outbreak of the Thirty Years' War (1618–1648), which left central Europe a shambles. On a percentage basis, the destruction and loss of life throughout central Europe was greater than during World War II. The German Empire at the end of the Thirty Years' War suffered 5 million dead out of a total population of about 15 million. Following the war, banditry, famine, and fanatic delusions of witchcraft and sorcery were rampant throughout Europe. But northern Germany recovered quickly under the German Princes of Brandenburg and Prussia.

The Union of Brandenburg and Prussia

The Brandenburgs were a powerful dynasty that reached their pinnacle of power during and following the Thirty Years' War. In 1470 the Electors of Brandenburg had made Berlin their seat of government. Though both Brandenburg and Prussia were under the House of Hohenzollern, they were not effectively united until the late 17th century. The man most often associated with Prussia, the religious and ascetic Friedrich Wilhelm I (The Great Elector), was determined to "govern his lands well." He demanded total obedience from his subjects, contending that "the soul is God's, all else is mine."

Through the efforts of Friedrich Wilhelm I, power was removed from the numerous petty lords and concentrated in a government which had much greater control over the realm. This new centralization gave the Hohenzollerns the ability, among other things, to raise great armies and keep large numbers of troops ready at all times. Berlin became the capital of this new union with the coronation of Friedrich III there in 1701. Known as Prussia's courtly "Baroque King," he also began the construction of many of Berlin's major buildings.

The Imperial Court in Berlin

Friedrich III's coronation added to an already vigorous building boom in Berlin. The famed architects Eosander and Andreas Schlüter designed much of the Royal Court, including the Zeughaus, the Royal Palace (Schloss). Under the patronage of Queen Charlotte, both the Academy of Art (1698) and, following a suggestion by the philosopher Leibniz, the Academy of Sciences (1701) were built. Prussia expanded under Friedrich der Grosser (the Great), and though a brilliant stratagist, he could not prevent the entry of Russian armies into Berlin in 1759. Following the Seven Years' War (1756–1763) Prussia emerged as a major European power with Berlin as its capital.

The Establishment of the German Nation-State

Germany existed as several independent principalities until late in the 19th century. Count Otto von Bismarck united Germany under Prussian control between 1866 and 1871. His philosophy of "Realpolitik" gave precedence to foreign, rather than domestic policy, including the use of war as the ultimate instrument of politics. With the Franco-Prussian War of 1870 and the subsequent Prussian victory, Berlin became the capital of a united Germany. Greater Berlin was established with the merger of eight smaller cities, 59 rural communities, and 27 farming townships and villages.

Post–World War II Berlin

After World War II Berlin became an occupied city with four sectors: the American, British, French, and Soviet. The city had been severely damaged and the former center of Hitler's government was totally destroyed. The city has remained divided to this day, as the three Western powers joined their sectors and the Soviets retained control over the eastern part of the city. There was very little communication between the two German governments following the war, though the situation was improved with the signing of the Four Power Agreement on September 3, 1971.

Berlin Today

The two halves of the city have different titles, embodying the two very different positions each occupies in their respective eastern and western spheres. Though West Berlin is not officially a part of the Federal Republic of Germany, it is intimately linked to the West politically, militarily, and economically. East Berlin is officially known by the Communist government and the Soviet Union as Berlin, capital of the German Democratic Republic. The Federal Republic of Germany and West Berlin have promised never to move the seat of government from Bonn to Berlin until the country is reunited.

1. Orientation

To begin with, Berlin has a 45-mile-long, 12-foot-high Wall that divides the city in half. Since Berlin was built as a whole, not a half city, the Wall has caused some peculiarities in the mass-transit system. The old city centered around the Brandenburger Tor. Now there are two city centers: in East Berlin it's the **Alexanderplatz,** three S-bahn stops from the Friedrichstrasse station (in West Berlin the center is at the east end of the Kurfürstendamm).

The main street in East Berlin is the **Unter den Linden,** which proceeds east to **Marx-Engels Platz** (square) on Museum Island and then across the River Spree. The street continues as **Karl Liebknecht Strasse,** which runs along the north end of the new heart of Communist Berlin, the Alexanderplatz. Most of the museums are located in the area north and west of Marx-Engels Platz.

ARRIVING IN EAST BERLIN: You may arrive in East Berlin as a stopover on some Eastern European national airline or as the beginning of your visit to the German Democratic Republic. You can get to the city by car or train, but Berlin remains the only city where one can actually cross an international border by mass transit.

By Air

Schönefeld International Airport in East Berlin is where most flights from other Eastern European countries will land. There is an entry check for everyone exiting the aircraft and then another border control to actually enter the German Democratic Republic. You don't need to get a visa in advance to go from Schönefeld to West Berlin. After you go through the first check, follow the arrows to the bus to West Berlin. There, for an additional 5 marks ($1.75) you can get a direct transit visa to West Berlin. If you can, bring in your own Western Deutsches marks or you'll lose about 30% to 50% on the exchange. However, for these small amounts it almost isn't worth the hassle. Buses to the West Berlin border cost 2 marks (70¢) and, if you have a visa, the bus to the Funkturm costs 7 marks ($2.45).

By Car

There are three main international highways that run through Berlin: the E15 runs north and south from Berlin to Prague, the E8 runs almost due east and west from Hannover to Berlin and east to Warsaw, and the E6 connects Sweden (via ferry) to Munich. Driving between the Berlins is the same as crossing a national boundry. Driving from West Berlin to the German Democratic Republic is covered in Section 2, below.

By Train

Train fares from the West are not expensive—about $60 per person from Frankfurt, for example. From Warsaw the train fare is about $35, and from Prague, less than $25.

There are three train stations, all located on the S-bahn line. The **Ostbahnhof** is closest to the city center and is only four stops from Friedrichstrasse. The train station where you catch many of the south-bound trains is **Schöneweide.** To get to the Schöneweide train station, take the S-bahn from Friedrichstrasse and change at the Ostkreuz S-bahn stop for the S-bahn heading toward Königs Wusterhausen (south) for four stops. The Schönefeld Airport train station is one stop past the Schöneweide train station farther outside the city center, on the same line. At the Schönefeld Airport station you can go directly from plane to train or vice versa.

By the Metro and Elevated Train

At first it may seem a bit strange, just popping in to East Berlin on the S-bahn (the elevated train) or the metro. In fact there are several West Berlin metro and S-bahn lines that run under or over parts of East Berlin, but only the Friedrichstrasse is open to international traffic. The Friedrichstrasse station is by far the easiest way to get into East Berlin and the German Democratic Republic. And it has the added advantage of being part of both halves of Berlin's mass-transit system.

TOURIST INFORMATION: There are two major offices of the **Reisebüro der DDR,** one at Alexanderplatz 5 (tel. 21-50) and the office in the base of the Funkturm (tel. 212-46-75). The office in the Funkturm is one of the easiest offices to find, as the spire is visible from over 20 miles away on a clear day. The Reisebüro der DDR office in the Funkturm, just south of Alexanderplatz, deals mainly with tourism in Berlin. Here you can get a map of the city center (though not the outlying districts) and directions. The office is open on Monday from 1 to 6 p.m., Tuesday to Friday from 9 a.m. until 6 p.m., and weekends from 10 a.m. until 6 p.m.

The main Reisebüro der DDR office at Alexanderplatz 5 handles everything else—travel in East Germany, tickets for concerts and theater performances, all other information, and tours. All services for foreigners are open weekdays from 8 a.m. until 8 p.m. and weekends from 9 a.m. until 6 p.m.

GETTING AROUND EAST BERLIN: The best idea for all visitors to East Berlin is to get a day pass to the S-bahn and metro for 1 mark (35¢) or a pass to all the East Berlin mass transit for 2 marks (70¢). There is a ticket office in the lower (street-level) section of the Friedrichstrasse station.

Buses and Trams

Buses and trams are well kept and plentiful, but most of the city can be reached by the clean and very safe S-bahn. There is also a metro system, but our attitude is: Why burrow when you can fly? Almost everything closes down at

11:30 p.m., though a few lines remain open until midnight. One advantage the buses have is that they do not "go down" like the electrically powered S-bahn system, a problem not uncommon in East Berlin.

You can get a map of the system at any of the Reisebüro der DDR offices. The mass-transit system is oddly shaped because of the Wall that divides the city. It runs due east and then arcs in a semicircle both north and south. To get to any suburb you must first go east to the Ostkreuz S-bahn station and then change trains.

Taxis

There are more taxis in central East Berlin than in many of the other Eastern European capitals. You must wait in line at the taxi stand, but the lines at the taxi station near Friedrichstrasse station are usually so long that walking becomes a real alternative. Because the city center is so compact, you probably won't need a taxi. If you plan to go to the suburbs, the S-bahn is the quickest and most inexpensive way to go. You can also call for a taxis at 36-46.

2. The Day Visa from West Berlin to East Berlin

THE REQUIREMENTS: One of the easiest ways to see East Berlin from West Berlin is with a day pass. The day pass, or *Tagesaufenthalt* (as it's known in German), is also called the "Cinderella Pass" because it expires, just as the heroine's magic did in the tale by the Brothers Grimm, at midnight. The day pass is sold between 7 a.m. and 9:30 p.m. daily and is good from 7 a.m. till midnight for one day.

For a day trip only, you'll need a valid passport, 5 DM (West German marks) ($1.75) for the visa, and a 25-DM ($8.75) minimum exchange, and if you are driving, your Green (international insurance) Card. There is a map on the back of the pass showing the extent of the area in which day visa bearers are allowed. Leaving this area makes you subject to arrest.

You are not allowed to bring East German marks across the border in either direction. However, as you leave East Berlin you can exchange any leftover East German marks you have for a voucher. When you return, after again exchanging the mandatory 25 West German marks ($8.75), you can cash in the voucher for your East German marks. Also, be careful of changing any more currency beyond the minimum required exchange. Although the official policy states that it is easy to convert any East German marks above the minimum exchange back into Western currency, in practice it isn't.

WHERE TO CROSS THE BORDER: The Freidrichstrasse is one of the easiest and quickest ways to enter East Berlin for either a day trip or a prolonged stay. It's a large public transportation intersection connecting both East and West. Border formalities move quickly and with fewer problems than at Checkpoint Charlie.

After you exit the S-bahn or metro, follow the signs to the border-crossing point, *Grenzübergangstelle*. All citizens of other countries—*Burger anderen Staaten*—(not West Berliners or other German nationals) go to line 1 at the far left. After this, there is a Customs check that's usually, though not always, perfunctory. On a day trip, keep your baggage to a minimum. Printed materials often bog down the process more than bulky luggage. To avoid an exchange surcharge, have your 30 DM in West German marks ($10.50) ready.

If you are driving you'll have to use the border crossing at the corner of Friedrichstrasse and Zimmer Strasse, better known as Checkpoint Charlie. It's open 24 hours, though the latest you can get a day pass is 9:30 p.m.

3. Accommodations in East Berlin

There are no budget accommodations in East Berlin. All hotel rooms cost upward of $35 per person per day. There are no hostels and no private rooms, so it's wise to stay in West Berlin (see Chapter II) and visit East Berlin on a day visa. We include one hotel here, the Hotel Unter den Linden, as it's the least expensive of all the hotels in East Berlin.

The lobby of the **Hotel Unter den Linden,** at the corner the Unter den Linden and Friedrichstrasse (tel. 220-03-11; Telex 112036), is small by luxury hotel standards. With rock music pounding perhaps slightly too loudly in the background, the otherwise comfortable lobby is always filled with a mix of business people. The small bar is stocked with Western liquors as well as some interesting East Berliners. The hotel is also where many foreign musicians stay. Some Hungarian rock groups and an American jazz band were checking in when we visited.

All the rooms are clean and have private bath. The hotel restaurant is standard, with a slightly overpriced menu.

4. Dining in East Berlin

The influx of Western business people is now a normal and accepted phenomenon in East Berlin and has been since the mid 1970s. Establishments in East Berlin that offer better quality get more Western visitors and consequently more Western currency. Slowly East Berlin is developing several excellent restaurants. However, East Berlin's single greatest advantage still remains its low prices.

Tipping is officially a thing of the past. However, we found that no one objects to 10% left behind after a meal. In fact tipping is almost expected of Western tourists. Be careful about tipping people in East Germany with West German marks—it's illegal, though appreciated.

Leaving one's coat at the door is a custom that has been universally and very seriously adopted throughout East Germany. In some places it's mandatory, so be aware and ask for the coat check (*die Garderobe).*

DINING IN CENTRAL EAST BERLIN: On Friedrichstrasse right off the Unter den Linden, the **Metropol Grill** (tel. 220-42-72) is one of the better restaurants in East Berlin, but it's usually quiet in the daytime. The dining room has a chair/table arrangement that simulates booths, and the windows are lined with blue curtains. The cooking is done directly behind the bar by several efficient cooks. If you're in a hurry you can sit right at the bar on diner-style stools and enjoy excellent grilled platters. A lighter lunch dish is chicken paprika with butter at 10.80 marks ($3.75) or the specialty of the house, beef filet with mushrooms, at 20.60 marks ($7.20). The Metropol Grill is open daily from 11 a.m. to midnight.

The **Lindencorso Restaurant,** at Unter den Linden 17 (tel. 220-24-67), has five different, very spacious dining rooms. The room to the right as you enter usually serves only a daily menu (Tagesmenu), averaging 8 marks ($2.80) to 10 marks ($3.50). Despite its size, reservations are recommended at the Lindencorso, especially on weekends (on Sunday the pace and the service slow down). The management requests that you check your coat, though the Garderobe is difficult to find.

Even the most expensive dinner should not set you back more than 35 marks ($12.25), and most of the filling dishes here cost less than 25 marks ($8.75). The restaurant is open from 9 a.m. to midnight on weekdays, until 1 a.m. on weekends. Upstairs is the Koncert Café, which opens up at 7 p.m.; the first band begins playing at 8 p.m., and the music continues until the café closes around 2 a.m.

The huge **Palast der Republik** in Marx-Engels-Platz has three different restaurants offering good food: the Palastrestaurant, the Spreerestaurant, and the Lindenrestaurant. All have the same menu, featuring such dishes as Ukrainian soljanka soup for 1.90 marks (65¢), schnitzel for 6.25 marks ($2.20), and filet steak with pineapple for 11 marks ($3.85). The Palast, a long and spacious restaurant with large glass windows overlooking an old church, is the most elegant of the three. It's a popular place to go before those cultural events that are held in the Palast der Republik. All three restaurants are open from 11 a.m. to midnight. Note that on Monday, Tuesday, and Wednesday one of the three restaurants is closed.

The **Markisches Restaurant** has an attractive interior with brick walls and wooden tables. Specialties include braised beef marinated in red wine at 13 marks ($4.55) and roast duckling with plum sauce for 24.80 marks ($8.70). There is also a selection of fish and poultry. Open from 6 a.m. to midnight.

The **Ratskeller,** in the Rathaus on Rathausstrasse (tel. 212-53-01), is a decent budget restaurant that attracts many young people and workers to its pleasant dining room with brick walls and wooden tables. Hungarian goulash soup costs only 90 pfennigs (0.90 marks, or 30¢), the chicken with fries and toast in sauce runs 3.30 marks ($1.15), and steak with cucumbers and onions is 5.40 marks ($1.90). It's open from 11:30 a.m. to midnight.

The **Weinrestaurant Moravia,** at Rathauspassagen 5 (tel. 212-32-92), has good Czech specialties, including gulasova polevka (goulash soup) for 1.30 marks (45¢) and pantientes schweineschnitzel (a tender schnitzel with butter and cheese on top) for 8.85 marks ($3.10). For dessert, try the Czech pancakes, called palacinky, for 4.20 marks ($1.50). The simple Czech decor is appealing, with plates on the walls, Zodiac tablecloths, and country-theme salt shakers.

In the TV tower in Alexanderplatz (from the bottom it looks like a tall smokestack with a huge metal golfball on top) is a rotating restaurant (in the golfball) called the **Telecafé** (tel. 210-42-32). The food here is not very good, but the view is impressive. Many East Germans come here, and the long line for the elevator to the top can be a good place to meet them. As you enter the TV tower, go to the left side to get to the café and to the right to go to the observation deck. It costs 5 marks ($1.75) to go up. A typical entree of beefsteak costs 8.75 marks ($3.05), but you can have just an ice cream dish for about 3 marks ($1.05). The café is open from 9 a.m. to 11 p.m.

EAST OF ALEXANDERPLATZ: The **Haus Budapest** restaurant, at Karl-Marx-Allee 91 (tel. 436-21-87), is one of East Berlin's best foreign specialty establishments. It's officially a Hungarian restaurant, though the Hungarian staff doesn't arrive until 6 p.m. During the day the waiters are Germans with some guest workers from Bulgaria. The Haus Budapest serves primarily German-style cooking with some Hungarian specialties. The portions are small and served à la carte, so ask for salads. Try the pork steaks for 8 marks ($2.80), which are spicy and quite good. The chicken, for 7.05 marks ($2.45), is solid fare though it could be spicier. Very much like German cooking, it's different enough to make an

appetizing change. To get here, take the metro toward Tierpark (east) and get off at the Marchlewski Strasse stop; then walk back (west) on Karl-Marx-Allee about two blocks. The Haus Budapest restaurant is open from 11 a.m. until midnight.

A favorite of old Berlin hands is the **Restaurant Moskau,** at Karl-Marx-Allee 34. This spacious restaurant with large picture windows looking over the street is patronized by business people and tourists. In the '60s and early '70s most of the Soviet European Command is supposed to have raised vodka glasses here. Today the military presence has dwindled, leaving the clean white table linens and excellent Russian specialty dishes to the civilians. We enjoyed an excellent meal of hearty borscht for 4.90 marks ($1.70) and chicken cutlet garni for 13.40 marks ($4.70).

ROCK-BOTTOM DINING: Those with barely two coins to rub together should try the fast-food *(Schnellimbiss)* booths at the foot of the Funkturm. They often are not very fast at lunchtime, as all of East Berlin seems to line up for the cheap, filling food available here.

CAFÉS: **Club Metropol,** right off the Unter den Linden on the corner of Friedrichstrasse, is a very spacious, well-appointed café with a gilded white piano in the window. Decorated in light green with a green-and-white marble floor, the café has large windows that let in abundant light. For those needing a sugar fix, this café has a large selection of delicious ice creams, and there are strong coffees for chasers. For those who need to take the edge off the day there is some excellent Czech pilsner beer for 4.20 marks ($1.45). The Club Metropol is open daily from 8 a.m. until 9 p.m.

The **Koncert Café,** above the Lindencorso restaurant, opens its doors at 7 p.m. and live bands begin to play at 8 p.m. and stop around 2 a.m. For 35 marks ($12.25) each you can order the most lavish banquet here. There is also a goodly selection of Eastern European wines and liquors, including Russian champagne and assorted Hungarian wines. The Koncert Café is visited by many tour groups, including Russians or East Germans from other cities who enjoy a meal and the music here.

The **Mocca-Milch Eis Bar,** at Karl-Marx-Allee 35 (tel. 436-22-76), is the soda shop where some of East Berlin's milkshake set hangs out. There are some insidiously good ice cream dishes, smothered with homemade whipped cream for 2.55 marks (90¢) to 5.20 marks ($1.80), depending to what depth you want to sink. The Eis Bar is open from 9 a.m. until midnight, with the disco pounding on for at least another two hours.

Outside the Center

Once you leave the city center, the Funkturm blurs a little in the mist and becomes a bit harder to see. Away from Alexanderplatz there are far fewer police and far more "real" Berliners—students, peaceniks, children, old people, families, workers, and oddballs—who are lacking in the showcase center. By eating in local restaurants, you'll spend less money but run into more variable quality and availability (food distribution is a problem in Eastern Europe, though less so in the German Democratic Republic).

Many of the houses on Schönhauser Allee are old and dusty, and in need of repair. But on the side streets there are still beautiful prewar buildings, occasionally pockmarked with bullet holes. Old bits of baroque façade, some statuary peeking out of an old garden, and a faded mural in a small local pub are all part of East Berlin's older suburbs. We recommend several cafés in the Schönhauser Allee area.

The **Wiener Café,** at Schönhauser Allee 68 (tel. 448-57-22), has a somewhat gloomy appearance that's merely a disguise for the modish interior. The walls are covered with large images (blowups) of Viennese street scenes. There is a good selection of cakes. In the evening artists and students come to talk. The Wiener Café is for those interested in meeting "real" East Berliners. It's open from 2 p.m. until midnight. There's also a disco on weekends from 8 p.m. until 2 a.m. To reach the Wiener Café, take the S-bahn or metro to Schönhauser Allee and walk a couple of blocks west down Schönhauser Allee.

One of our favorite finds in East Berlin is the **Café Flair,** at Stargarder Strasse 72 (tel. 448-34-88). The café is done in shades of purple and violet, with prints and slightly overbright lamps, but with a very pleasant atmosphere overall. One would expect to find a place like this in West Berlin. There is a very intellectual, well-dressed crowd, though you might find the waitress is a bit overdressed. The bartender wears an elaborate moustache. The Café Flair is an excellent place to meet the Berlin intelligensia. Open from 10 a.m. until 6 p.m., the Café Flair has hours suited only to the tourist or the full-time intellectual. The café is located right off Schönhauser Allee, about two blocks south on Stargarder Strasse.

5. The Sights of East Berlin

The cultural heart of Berlin, Museum Island, as well as Alexanderplatz (the former main square), now lies in East Berlin. The best place to begin any tour of East Berlin is Alexanderplatz.

ALEXANDERPLATZ: Some people may remember the Alexanderplatz of Werner Rainer Fassbinder's movie epic—a large square with baroque buildings, cobbled courtyards, and ornate ironwork. After World War II the rubble of the old Alexanderplatz was bulldozed away and replaced with the vast concrete plain that is here today (there was no effort made to reconstruct the old Alexanderplatz). The principal prewar monuments are the Marienkirche, the old Berlin Town Hall (Berliner Rathaus), and the St. Nicholas Church (Nickolaikirche). The new Alexanderplatz has the Hotel "City of Berlin" on one corner and the spire of the Television Tower or Funkturm at its very center. Now bounded on the north by Karl-Marx-Allee and on the east by Lenin-Allee, Alexanderplatz was once the crossroads of the German Empire.

Just after World War II Karl-Marx-Allee was called Stalin-Allee, and before the war it had been Frankfurter Allee. The housing projects along this stretch of road were where the first strikes broke out in 1952, which later escalated into the full-scale civil unrest of 1953, suppressed only by the return of Soviet tanks and troops. Though nothing could be done about the name of the street while Stalin lived, soon after he died the name was changed to Karl-Marx-Allee in an attempt to mollify the Berliners.

Funkturm

The very center of Alexanderplatz is marked by the tall Television Tower, or Funkturm as it's known in German. The Funkturm is widely recognized as the first great postwar project. Completed in 1969, it rises 357 meters (1,170 feet) into the Berlin sky and is clearly visible from all parts of the city, both East and West. There is a viewing platform and a revolving restaurant at the 800-foot level. The Funkturm is an impressive engineering accomplishment, as Berlin's bedrock lies hundreds of feet beneath the surface. The Funkturm has become the symbol of East Berlin.

Marienkirche

Standing at the foot of the Funkturm, but not in its shadow, is the exquisite Church of St. Mary (Marienkirche), the second-oldest church in Berlin. The choir dates from the middle of the 13th century, though the tower was added in the 15th century. One of the most haunting frescos to be seen anywhere is *Der Totentanz* (the Dance of Death), painted at the end of the 15th century. Covered up for many years, it was revealed in 1950 during the postwar restoration. It depicts a hideous, grimacing Death cavorting with everyone from the most powerful noble to the poorest farmer—an allegory of the primacy of death.

Nikolaikirche

The Church of St. Nicholas (Nikolaikirche), on Spandauer Strasse, built in the 12th century, is Berlin's oldest building. Unfortunately, it was so damaged by bombs as a result of the air raids in World War II that only the red brick walls are left standing. Some restoration work is proceeding despite the condition of the remains.

Just across Spandauer Strasse from the Nikolaikirche is the **Berlin Town Hall (Berliner Rathaus),** also known as the Red Town Hall (Rotes Rathaus). Red long before the Communists arrived in Berlin, the Rotes Rathaus was built in 1861–1870 out of the same red-tinged stone as the Nikolaikirche.

UNTER DEN LINDEN: "Under the Lindens" is the name of Berlin's most famous east-west avenue. Along the street the war-damaged lindens are slowly growing back.

As you stroll along the avenue you'll pass the **State Opera House (Staatsoper),** at Unter den Linden 7. Built in 1742, it is being restored using the original plans of its architect, Georg Wenzeslaus von Knobelsdorff. Inside are restored portraits of (as the official guides proudly proclaim) "the heros of the War of Liberation."—the sturdy Prussians Geneisenau, Scharnhorst, and Blücher, and the stolid Englishman, the Duke of York, who sent Napoleon packing in 1813–1814.

Farther along the Unter den Linden is the **Armory (Zeughaus),** now a memorial to the Victims of Fascism. While honoring the memory of the fallen is a laudable goal, we found the armed, goose-stepping guards a grotesque parody of the ideals the memorial supposedly stands for.

At the end of the Unter den Linden is the **Brandenburger Tor (Brandenburg Gate).** Built as a triumphal monument in 1788–1791, the gate consists of a colonnade surmounted with a four-horse chariot bearing Victory. The gate is constructed entirely in the classical Athenian style. The Brandenburger Tor was so heavily damaged that it had to be reconstructed using a West Berlin replica as a building guide. The gate is located at the easternmost border of East Berlin.

MUSEUMINSEL: Located in the very heart of Berlin, where the Unter den Linden meets Karl-Liebknecht-Strasse at Marx-Engels-Platz, Museum Island holds the art and historical artifacts accumulated during hundreds of years of Imperial rule. There are three museums: the Pergamon, which houses one of the world's greatest collections of classical antiquities; the Bodemuseum, which contains one of the world's largest Egyptian collections, as well as over 25,000 ancient documents; and the National Gallery, which holds an immense collection of 19th- and 20th-century artworks.

The Museums

The **Pergamon Museum,** built in 1912–1930, has a collection of classical antiquities matched only by the British Museum in London or the Louvre in Paris. The museum is best known for the Pergamon Altar (184–159 B.C.), a huge (104- by 98-foot) structure that depicts the struggle between the gods and the giants. There is also the impressive Babylonian Gate of Ishtar (580 B.C.) and a reconstruction of the ritual procession avenue of the gods Nabu and Marduk (600 B.C.). The Pergamon is open daily from 9 a.m. to 6 p.m.

The **Bodemuseum** contains an enormous collection of ancient Egyptian relics, one of the largest collections in the world. If you don't have much time, be certain to see the huge Sphinx of Hatshepsut (1490–1480 B.C.). There is also a fascinating section with detailed descriptions of many ancient burial customs. The museum is open Wednesday through Sunday from 9 a.m. to 6 p.m.

The **National Gallery,** the oldest of the three museums (1867–1876), contains a large collection of works from the 19th century to the present. Among numerous masterpieces are works by Liebermann, Slevogt, and Cézanne, as well the Berlin masters Menzel, Schadow, Rauder, Kollwitz, and Nagel. The National Gallery is open from 9 a.m. to 6 p.m. Wednesday through Sunday.

Marx-Engels-Platz

Marx-Engels-Platz on Museuminsel was the site of the former royal palace but is now (if possible) an even less attractive concrete monument than Alexanderplatz. Karl-Marx-Platz is the site of a foreign ministry, the State Council Building, and the rebuilt St. **Hedwig's Cathedral,** Berlin's first Roman Catholic church to be built after the Reformation—a Catholic cathedral not more than 40 miles from Wittenburg, the birthplace of Protestantism.

THE CHANCELLERY OF THE THIRD REICH: The Soviets completely destroyed Hitler's command bunker after stripping it and using much of the recovered stone to build (among other things) the War Memorial in Treptow Park. Located in the "Death Strip" created by the Wall, just south of the Brandenburg Gate, the Chancellery, with the bunker below, is no more than a grassy knoll.

NIGHTTIME ACTIVITIES: While the bar scene is infinitely more active in West Berlin, there's a lot going on right here in East Berlin. We recommend seeing at least one concert or opera during your visit.

The **State Opera (Staatsoper),** Unter den Linden 7 (tel. 205-40, ext. 456), has numerous performances, and you can call or drop by to get a detailed schedule. Most tickets are less than $5, and the best seats (if they're available) cost less than $10. The ticket window is open from noon till 5:45 p.m. most weekdays. The opera closes in the late summer.

There is the **Comic Opera (Komische Oper)** at Behrenstrasse 55/77 (tel. 229-25-55), with modern, realistic, and (of course) comic operas. There are also several theaters, including the **Berliner Ensemble** (tel. 282-31-60), on Bertolt-Brecht-Platz; it was founded by the famous playwright Bertolt Brecht. And many other theaters are home to excellent theater ensembles, all of which deserve some time.

It's easiest to get tickets to all performances at the main Reisebüro der DDR office at Alexanderplatz 5.

6. The ABCs of East Berlin

AUTOMOBILES: Most emergency repair and towing is handled through the police. There is a 24-hour towing service (tel. 559-25-00).

CRIME: One beneficial result of all the Volkspolizei (People's Police) is that East Berlin is an extremely safe city. The usual precautions should be observed, but we heard no traveler complain of crime problems.

EMBASSIES AND CONSULATES: The U.S. Embassy is in East Berlin at Neustadtische Kirchstrasse 4/5 (tel. 220-27-41), just north of the Unter den Linden and about four blocks from the Friedrichstrasse station. Though the embassy personnel are always ready in an emergency, most routine inquiries and questions about Americans in East Germany can be answered by the U.S. Consulate staff in West Berlin at Clay Allee 170 (tel. 832-40-87). The **British Embassy** is at Unter den Linden 32-34 (tel. 220-2431).

EMERGENCY: You can always reach the People's Police (Volkspolizei) by telephone at 110, the fire department at 112, and an ambulance at 115.

MAIL AND TELEPHONE: The international telephone exchange (tel. 181 or 183) can aid you with any international calls you need to make. We recommend for all international calls to the West, and all mail, that you cross back to West Berlin—it's simply cheaper and more efficient.

TIPPING: Most cab drivers, doormen, and other people in the East German service economy expect some sort of gratuity. Depending on the quality of service received, you can tip 1 or 2 marks (35¢ to 70¢) for coat checks and bellboys, or 10% for more extensive services.

TOURS: There are several tours of East Berlin organized both by the West Berliners and the Reisebüro der DDR. From West Berlin there are **Berlin Bären City Tours** (tel. 883-60-02), **Berolina Stadtrundfahrt** (tel. 881-68-57), and **Severin + Kühn** (tel. 883-10-15). All three tours are run by West German operators and depart from various points along Kurfürstendamm in West Berlin.

If you wish to see East Berlin from the **Reisebüro der DDR** viewpoint, there are several English-language tours available. Contact the Reisebüro der DDR at Alexanderplatz 5 or the office in the Funkturm; both have tours through the city center. There are also **cab tours** (tel. 246-22-55) of East Berlin lasting 40 minutes to 2½ hours. Usually the shorter rides don't cost more than 25 marks ($8.75) and give you a good idea of the city's layout.

7. Potsdam

Potsdam, a stunning city of palaces and lakes, retains much of its grandeur from the days when it was the summer retreat of Brandenburg and Prussian nobility. It is remembered today as the site of the postwar conference of the same name, between England, the Soviet Union, and the United States. Though the city center was bombed during World War II, the royal summer palace, Sanssouci, was not seriously damaged. Former summer hideaway of the Hohenzollerns, Potsdam is a city on the very edge of West Berlin. Though it's the ninth-largest city in East Germany, Potsdam today is quiet and peaceful, a perfect place to stroll among the many palaces and formal parks.

A CAPSULE HISTORY: There are traces of Neolithic and Roman settlements in and around the Potsdam area. The first recorded mention of the area was in A.D. 993 when King Otto III made a gift of Poztumimi and Geliti (as Potsdam and the neighboring district of Geltow were then known) to his Aunt Matilda of Quedlinburg. Surrounded by numerous lakes and rivers, the area became an independent township in 1317. By 1573 the town had a population of over 2,000, despite plagues and a major fire. Following the horrors of the Thirty Years' War (1618–1648) the town numbered fewer than 700 souls.

With the arrival of the Brandenburgs and Prussians in Berlin, Potsdam's fortunes changed. In 1660 Friedrich Wilhelm the Elector ordered the construction of several country palaces, and later, in 1701, Potsdam was officially known as the country residence of the Prussian kings. A period of prosperity followed and by 1747 there were nearly 12,000 people living in Potsdam. The Sanssouci Palace was built (1745–1747), Voltaire spent some time there (1750–1753), and despite an Austrian occupation during the Seven Years' War (1756–1763), the city prospered. The numerous wars sparked the buildup of a large garrison in Potsdam. Voltaire described Potsdam as a city where there were "an astonishing number of bayonets and few books. The King has certainly improved upon Sparta but has brought Athens only to his study." The rise of Napoleon and his victories over the Prussians led to the French occupation of Potsdam in 1806. Potsdam under Napoleon was turned into a giant stable with over 6,000 soldiers and twice that many horses. Ironically Napoleon's forces were routed in 1813 by a force of mounted Russian Cossacks.

Following the defeat of Napoleon, Potsdam again flourished and soon became a leading industrial city. In the period between 1825 and World War I Potsdam was home to numerous scientific research centers and academies: everything from the Institute of Astrophysics (1877) to a Zepplin airfield (1911). Following World War I there was much social unrest, and during World War II the city center was seriously damaged in an air raid.

From July 17 to August 2, 1945, the leaders of Great Britain, the Soviet Union, and the United States met at Cecilienhof Palace in Potsdam to decide the fate of Germany. It was decided to rebuild Germany with the three (and later a fourth, the French) major powers guaranteeing that Germany would never again threaten world peace. Germany was also to be united, but united under what political system? The answer to that question has become one of the fundamental divisions of the postwar world.

ORIENTATION: Historic Potsdam is bordered on the south by the Templiner and Tiefer Sees (Lakes), on the west by the Sanssouci Palace, and on the northeast by the Cecilienhof. Most of the sights in the old city are within easy walking distance of one another.

You can reach Potsdam from East Berlin by train in under an hour. From the railway station (tel. 46-61), take any S-bahn eight stops to the city center or six stops to the Sanssouci Palace. If you walk to Lenin Allee you can catch bus F to Cecilienhof. A day pass to all public transportation costs 1 mark (35¢) and can be purchased at a small kiosk right by the tram stop at the railroad station.

There is a 24-hour baggage office at the railroad station. It costs 80 pfennigs

(0.80 mark, or 30¢) to leave an average-sized suitcase here for each six-hour period.

Information

From the tram stop in the center of town, the main **information center** is south one block, right next to the Church of St. Nicholas (Nikolaikirche), on Friedrich-Ebert-Strasse 5 (tel. 2-31-85 to 2-31-88 or 32-92-17). They are extremely friendly here, but English-speaking personnel are not always available. They also run out of tourist materials and maps late in the summer. However, you can buy any one of several guides to Potsdam with excellent maps in most of the bookstores.

A Warning

Though Potsdam is not far from East Berlin, it's *outside* the area you are allowed to visit on a West Berlin day pass. It's not difficult or overly expensive to spend the night in Potsdam or anywhere else in East Germany, so don't risk visiting Potsdam on your day pass.

THE SIGHTS: There are few towns as attractive to visit as Potsdam. The major sights are set in parks or surrounded by formal gardens, and are conveniently spaced within walking distance of each other. The two major sights in Potsdam are the Sanssouci Palace and the Cecilienhof, though there are several interesting baroque buildings in the city center.

Sanssouci Palace

Built on what was known as the Desert Mountain (actually a small hummock of sand) in front of Potsdam's Brandenburg Gate, Sanssouci Palace stands as one of the premier rococo structures extant. In 1744, on the orders of King Friedrich II, chief engineer Diterichs dug and terraced the Desert Mountain (Wüste Berg) into a beautiful vineyard. A year later von Knobelsdorff began construction of the Sanssouci Palace on the site. The palace, unlike other Prussian undertakings, was not designed to reflect the might of the state. Instead it was to be a place where Prussian rulers could retire in pleasant surroundings and be perfectly content and at peace. So the palace was named Sanssouci ("without cares" or "free from worry"), a place where kings could slip off their responsibilities and attend to their private lives.

The Sanssouci Palace is actually a complex of buildings that includes the **Picture Gallery** (Bildergalerie), built a few years after the main palace by Johann Gottfried Büring, and the **Orangerie,** built in 1859. At the southwestern end of the park is the **Charlottehof Palace,** built in a much more subdued style in 1825 by Karl Friedrich Schinkel for King Friedrich Wilhelm III as a gift to his son, the crown prince. The largest structure on the grounds is the **New Palace** (Neues Palais), built at the end of the Seven Years' War (1763–1765). Begun by Büring and completed by Carl von Gontard, the New Palace served as the summer residence of the entire royal family and some of the court. Today, concerts are held in the main hall.

The Sanssouci Palace (tel. 2-39-31) is open throughout the year. From March to September its hours are 9 a.m. till 5:15 p.m. During October and February the palace closes an hour earlier. The New Palace (tel. 9-31-43) has the same hours as the Sanssouci Palace, except it's closed every second Monday in the month. All the other buildings are open daily between May and October from 9 a.m. till 5:15 p.m.

The New Garden and Cecilienhof

The **New Garden** (Neuer Garten) was built after the Sanssouci Palace as a pastoral retreat rather than an opulent summer palace. Between 1787 and 1791 over 13,000 trees from various parts of the empire were transported and planted in the New Garden, making it an interesting place indeed for any botanists. The **Cecilienhof** was begun in 1913 and completed during World War I in the style of an English manor house. In July 1945 it was the site of the Potsdam conference. Furnishings from many other manors and palaces were gathered together in order to accommodate the delegations headed by Truman, Stalin, and Atlee. The Cecilienhof (tel. 2-25-79) is open daily between April and October from 8 a.m. to 5:30 p.m.; in winter it closes an hour earlier. To get to the New Garden, take bus F toward Höhenstrasse.

In 1909 Orville Wright demonstrated his remarkable flying machine on Bornsteader Field, about a 20-minute walk due west of the Cecilienhof.

FOOD AND LODGING: There are very few accommodations for the budget traveler in Potsdam. Our pick is the **Hotel Jägertor,** on Am Jägertor (tel. 2-18-34). It's a small hotel (67 beds) with some private baths. The receptionist doesn't speak English, though the hotel is clean and otherwise pleasant. The hotel is somewhat noisy as the little Wartburg cars race around the Jägertor during the day. The restaurant is also good but expensive. Try the delicious wild pig with mushrooms and salad (in season) for 17 marks ($6). There is also a good selection of Hungarian wines as well as a curious concoction called kaffee Baltimore, coffee with egg yolk.

The **Restaurant Bolgar,** at Klement-Gottwald-Strasse 35-36 (tel. 2-25-05), is considered one of the best in Potsdam. An average meal here costs about 8 marks ($2.80), with a ham omelet for 5.90 marks ($2) and the filling Bulgarian grillplatter for 8.25 marks ($2.90). For desert there is a fresh fruit salad for 3.90 marks ($1.35). The Restaurant Bolgar is open from 11 a.m. until midnight Tuesday through Thursday, on weekends from 11 a.m. until 1 a.m.; closed Monday.

The **Klosterkeller,** at Friedrich-Ebert-Strasse 94, is a perfect place for a light meal. The Klosterkeller serves smaller proportions of beefsteak with red cabbage, or goulash with potatoes and mushrooms, for about 3.70 marks ($1.30). For those who are hungry there's also a grill serving full dinners: a hearty schnitzel for 8.15 marks ($2.85) and the entrecôte with béarnaise sauce and vegetables for 20.95 marks ($7.35). The tastiest dish the Klosterkeller serves is pikantes hühner (spicy chicken) ragoût for 6.55 marks ($2.30). Breakfast is served from 7:30 a.m. until 11 a.m.; lunch, from 11 a.m. until 3 p.m.; and dinner, between 3:30 and 9:30 p.m.

Cafés

The **Café Heider,** at Friedrich-Ebert-Strasse 29, is frequented by both students and professors. The café is conveniently located near the center of town. A surprising number of long-haired youths enjoy their afternoon coffee here. The modish set is a refreshing change from the thousands of "regulation" East German citizens one sees throughout the country. A veritable constellation of pastries and cakes are offered for about 1 mark (35¢) to 2 marks (70¢) apiece. Even if the café seems full (and in the afternoon it usually is), feel free to ask if you can sit wherever there's an extra seat.

The **Café Rendevous,** at Friedrich-Ebert-Strasse 114 (tel. 2-30-63), is a good place to meet. Every Monday and Friday there's live singing and cabaret acts of a sort. The program begins at around 9 p.m. and runs to midnight. The entrance fee is 10.50 marks ($3.70). You must buy your ticket in advance at the Potsdam Information Center (behind the shoe store on Friedrich-Ebert-Strasse). The songs range from romantic airs to old favorites to *very* mild political commentary. The café is open Monday through Friday from 2 p.m. until midnight, with a break from 6 to 7 p.m.; weekends they stay open an hour later.

THÜRINGIA AND SAXONY

OF ALL THE OLD GERMAN PROVINCES, Thüringia and Saxony remain almost intact in the German Democratic Republic. These two provinces were once part of the very heart of the old German Empire and produced some of Germany's greatest scholars and statesmen. Today Thüringia and Saxony are a treasure trove of towns rich in history and culture: Dresden, the former capital of Saxony; Weimar, where Goethe and Schiller lived and wrote; and the dark Thuringian Forest, dotted with castles and manors.

We list the cities roughly from east to west. Dresden and Leipzig are in Saxony and all the other cities are in or near Thüringia. This area, about 150 miles long and 50 miles wide, is literally packed with historical towns and charming country hamlets. The excellent train and bus connections make it easy for the budget traveler to get around. We recommend making a base in Erfurt or Weimar and exploring Thüringia in a series of day trips. The larger cities deserve a day to themselves. Don't let the relatively small area fool you—there's a wealth of things to see and do in Thüringia and Saxony.

1. Dresden

"It's been over 40 years since Dresden sank into the soot and ashes. It seems hardly believable that the city would ever live again." There has been very little written about Dresden and its destruction. Perhaps one of the best eyewitness accounts of the bombing is the novel *Slaughterhouse Five,* written by an American author, Kurt Vonnegut. Dresden is still one of the most beautiful baroque cities in Europe. There are numerous structures that were rebuilt and extensive art collections that escaped destruction. The characterless new sections of the city are balanced by the many reconstructed prewar buildings. You can still see the effects of the bombing—the Frauenkirche is a grass-covered pile of rubble—but don't let that stop you from visiting Dresden. The city is eminently worth visiting, both for its historical wealth and for the promise of new beginnings that its reconstruction embodies.

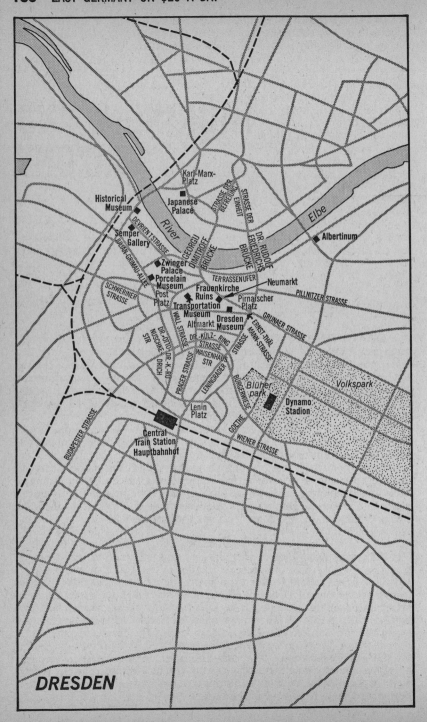

Karl-Marx-
Platz

Historical
Museum

Japanese
Palace

STRASSE DER BEFREIUNG

STRASSE DER EINHEIT

Elbe

River

Semper
Gallery

DEVRIENT STRASSE

JULIAN-GRIMAU-ALLEE

Albertinum

GEORGIJ
DIMITROFF
BRÜCKE

DR. RUDOLF
FRIEDRICHS
BRÜCKE

Zwinger
Palace

Porcelain
Museum

TERRASSENUFER

Neumarkt

PILLNITZER STRASSE

SCHWERINER
STRASSE

Post
Platz

Frauenkirche
Ruins

Transportation
Museum

Pirnaischer
Platz

Altmarkt

Dresden
Museum

ERNST-THÄL-
MANN-STRASSE

GRUNAER STRASSE

WALL STRASSE

DR.-OTTO-DR.-K.-RU
NUSCHKE-DRICH
STR

DR.-KÜLZ-
RING
STRASSE

WAISENHAUS
STR

STRASSE

PRAGER STRASSE

LENINGRADER

BÜRGERWIESE

Blüher
park

Volkspark

Dynamo
Stadion

BUDAPESTER STRASSE

Lenin
Platz

Central
Train Station
Hauptbahnhof

GOETHE

WIENER STRASSE

DRESDEN

A CAPSULE HISTORY: The first recorded mention of Dresden appeared in 1206, and the city was granted municipal rights ten years later. Following the Thirty Years' War (1618–1648) the German Empire fractured into some 300 autonomous states. Samuel Pufendorf (1632–1694), a scholar of international law, referred to this mass of competing petty states as a "monstrosity." Enterprising families found this postwar chaos the perfect time to consolidate and lay the foundations of new kingdoms.

The House of Wettin in Saxony, under Elector Friedrich August II, called August the Strong (1694–1733), forged a personal union with the Kingdom of Poland in the early 18th century. This union and adroit political maneuvering gave Saxony control over Bohemia, Moravia, most of Austria, and parts of Switzerland. As a result of these gains August II was able to commission the architect Matthaus Daniel Pöppelmann (1622–1736) to build magnificent baroque palaces and churches in Dresden. Pöppelmann's masterpiece is the Zwinger (forecourt) Palace, which is still considered the finest extant example of the late baroque period.

During this Golden Age some of the world's finest jewelry was produced by Dinglinger; exquisitely toned, powerful organs were crafted by Gottfried Silbermann; and the alchemist Böttger worked on creating the fabled Philosopher's Stone. Saxony's preeminent position ended at the close of the Seven Years' War (1656–1663) and Prussia emerged as a major European power. The Imperial capital moved to Berlin and Dresden's Golden Age came to an end.

Not heavily industrialized during the 19th century, Dresden has been known as a city of museums and universities since the 18th century. Since it was neither an industrial nor transportation center, Dresden remained unscathed for most of World War II. Then, in early February 1945, in support of the Soviet Marshals Zhukov and Konyev, the decision was made to bomb Dresden. On the night of February 13–14, when Dresden was packed with refugees fleeing the successful Soviet advance from the east, several hundred American and British bombers dropped a mix of incendiary and high-explosive bombs which ignited a firestorm that virtually destroyed the city. It is estimated that 80% of the city was leveled and over 130,000 people died—nearly twice as many as were killed in the bombing of Hiroshima six months later.

Dresden has been slowly restored, albeit with rather unimaginative modern "socialist" architecture that does little to complement the Old City. You can cross the Elbe and luxuriate in the glory of the Altstadt (Old City). The light Saxon sandstone of the Zwinger is beautifully complemented by the Kreuzkirche (Church of the Cross) just across the Altmarkt (Old Market Square). The Kreuzkirche is the home of the Kreuz Choir, an internationally famous boys' choir. Right across from the Zwinger is the restored Hofkirche, where you can hear the magnificent organ built by Silbermann in the 18th century. Take a look around the city, and don't miss a leisurely stroll around the Altstadt and along the Elbe.

ORIENTATION: The center of town is the modern **Prager Strasse** (Prague Street) pedestrian mall. The **Altmarkt** (Old Market Square) is the historic center of the city, where most of Dresden's sights are located. The Zwinger Palace and the Albertium museum complex are nearby. Across the **River Elbe** is another attractive pedestrian mall, the **Strasse der Befreiung.**

Getting Around Dresden

The city has a convenient **tram** system. But before you start traveling by tram, buy a large city map showing all the routes, and tickets, which are sold at newsstands.

If you want a **taxi,** phone 812.

Important Addresses

The helpful **Dresden Information Office,** at Prager Strasse 11 (tel. 495-50-25), is open Monday through Saturday from 9 a.m. to 8 p.m., on Sunday and holidays to 2 p.m. They have information on Dresden's cultural events, and sell tickets to performances as well. They also have information on boat tours in Saxony. The **Reisebüro der DDR** is at Ernst-Thälmann-Strasse 22.

The **main post office** is at Otto-Buchwitz-Strasse 21/29, past the Strasse der Befreiung. It's open Monday through Thursday from 8 a.m. to 6 p.m., on Friday to 7 p.m., and on Saturday to noon. There's also a post office on Prager Strasse, open Monday through Friday from 8 a.m. to 6 p.m.

ACCOMMODATIONS: Note that in Dresden, unlike other East German cities, the hotel will give your passport to the police (who will stamp your passport and register you), and then return it to you in the morning.

The **Hotel Gewandhaus,** Ringstrasse 1 (tel. 49-62-86; Telex 2527), is a smaller hotel that the Reisebüro der DDR doesn't always promote, but it's certainly Dresden's best buy. It has a central location across from the Town Hall, and is minutes away from the old ruins and the Zwinger museums. Ask the Reisebüro specifically for this hotel, or write ahead of time to reserve (write to Hotel Newa Dresden, BT Hotel Gewandhaus, 8012 Dresden, DDR, PSF 101 und 150—and state clearly that you want to reserve at the Gewandhaus) and then pay at the Reisebüro once you have a written confirmation. Singles cost 35 marks ($12.25) without private bathroom and 47 marks ($16.45) to 57 marks ($20) with bath; doubles with bath cost 65 marks ($22.75) to 75 marks ($26.25).

There are three hotels on Prager Strasse, the main pedestrian street in front of the train station. The **Hotel Konigstein** and the **Hotel Lilienstein** share a telephone and Telex number (tel. 485-60; Telex 2221). They are both three-star hotels where a single with private bath costs about $25 and similar doubles run about $35. The four-star **Hotel Newa,** Leningrader Strasse 34 (tel. 496-271; Telex 26067), is the first hotel on Prager Strasse to the right from the train station. The fairly modern rooms with private bath cost $36 for a single and $50 for a double.

Motel Dresden, Münzmeisterstrasse 10 (tel. 448-51; Telex 2442), is the most distant motel from the center of town. From the train station, take tram 26 to the end of the line (it takes about ten minutes) and then walk for a few minutes following the tram tracks toward the motel. Aside from its location, it's a nice, one-story motel where singles cost 70 marks ($24.50) and doubles run 110 marks ($38.50).

The **Hotel Astoria,** at Ernst-Thalmann-Platz 1 (tel. 441-71; Telex 2442), is about a ten-minute walk down Strehlener Strasse from the train station. Tram 16 also comes here. The rooms are small and without private bathrooms, and the public bathrooms are mediocre. Singles cost 62 marks ($21.70) to 77 marks ($27) and doubles are 118 marks ($41.30) to 128 marks ($44.80). Unfortunately, this is one of Dresden's worst buys.

DINING: One of our favorite restaurants in Dresden is **Szeged,** Ernst-Thälmann-Strasse 6, where Hungarian specialties are accompanied by live Hungarian music. Two complete dinner menus are offered at 11.20 marks ($3.90) and 15.90 marks ($5.55), including soup, pork steak or rumpsteak, and dessert. If you prefer to order à la carte, specialties include gulyas soup for 1.70 marks (60¢) and a large selection of delicious meat dishes for 5 marks ($1.75) to

10 marks ($3.50) each. Warm food is served from 10:30 a.m. to 2:45 p.m. and from 3:30 to 11 p.m.

The **Kugelgen Haus,** on Strasse der Befreiung, is a small, attractive restaurant with a quiet atmosphere and a smartly dressed clientele. Old prints decorate the walls. The food here earns rave reviews from most locals, and entrees are moderately priced from 6 marks ($2.10) to 12 marks ($4.20). For instance, the mixed grill plate with pork and steak costs 11.45 marks ($4). Service is from 11 a.m. to 2:45 p.m. and 4 to 11 p.m.

Aberlausitzer Töppl, Strasse der Befreiung, is a lively local place with a wood roof, stalls and tables surrounded by a white brick wall, and modern stained-glass windows. Traditional German specialties are prepared at moderate prices. The meat is tender, but the dishes are nothing exceptional. Nonetheless, this is an attractive place. Hours are 10 a.m. to 9:30 p.m.

The **Ratskeller,** in the City Hall (Rat der Stadt) basement at Dr.-Kulz-Ring 19 (tel. 495-25-81), is an elegant long corridor restaurant with painted ceilings. A typical German menu is offered at good budget prices: entrees cost no more than 7 marks ($2.45). In the evening an unexceptional band plays, for which you must pay a 1.60-mark (55¢) cover charge. The Ratskeller is open Sunday through Friday from 11 a.m. until midnight, on Saturday to 1 a.m.

Restaurant Ostrava, at the intersection of Fetscherstrasse and Borsbergstrasse, is a popular and inexpensive Czech restaurant with good Bohemian offerings. The decor is simple, with wooden wheel-shaped chandeliers and tables contained within wood stalls. Specialties include gebaktes beefsteak, a pork steak served with bread dumplings and a rich mushroom sauce, for 5.20 marks ($1.80). In keeping with the Czech tradition, a lot of beer is served for very little money, about 1.25 marks (45¢) for a half liter, though service is slow. The Ostrava is open Monday through Friday from 10 a.m. to 5 p.m. and 6 p.m. to midnight, on Saturday and Sunday from 10 a.m. to midnight. Try to reserve; the restaurant is often full. To get here, take tram 10 or 15 from in front of the train station to Borsbergstrasse.

The **Restaurant Wrocław,** on the second floor at Prager Strasse 15 (tel. 495-51-34), serves Polish specialties, including bigos at 7.20 marks ($2.50), veal and pork dishes, and braised pork knuckles for 8 marks ($2.80). A large selection of Eastern European wines is also offered. The Wrocław is open daily from 11 a.m. to midnight; there's live music from 6 to 11:30 p.m.

A nice place for lunch is the **Café Prag Speisebar,** in the Altmarkt. It's a small restaurant with grilled specialties prepared behind a marble bar. Only a handful of dishes are offered, but at 3 marks ($1.05) to 5 marks ($1.75) each for meat, french fries, and a small salad.

For a quick, cheap meal, go to the outdoor food stands called **Dresdner Ausspanne,** on Wallstrasse off Postplatz. Here a decent bowl of meat and potato soup costs 2 marks (70¢), and a roast chicken costs about twice that.

Dresden's best ice cream is served at **Eiskafe Kristal,** a large café at the beginning of Strasse der Befreiung near the Georgij-Dimitroff-Brücke (bridge). Open 9 a.m. to 10 p.m. weekdays.

THE SIGHTS: The major sights of Dresden are centered around the Altmarkt (Old Market Square), so that's where we'll start, with the top sightseeing attraction—the Zwinger Palace.

The Zwinger Palace

Constructed between 1709 and 1728, the majestic Zwinger Palace is a "must see" for all students of art and architecture. Built around a huge courtyard with many ornamental fountains, the Zwinger offers one of the finest examples of German baroque architecture of the 18th century. The palace architect Matthias Pöppelmann incorporated some of the greatest architectural elements he had seen on journeys to Rome, Paris, Vienna, and Prague; you can notice stylistic features from each of these cities across the palace.

The palace had just undergone a restoration from 1924 to 1936 when it was almost completely destroyed in the 1945 bombing. Thanks to research done for that restoration, many detailed photographs and prints of the palace were available for architects to reconstruct the palace after World War II.

Ever since 1728, festivals and important ceremonies have been staged in the Zwinger; the palace has also housed a world-famous museum collection. Most noted is the impressive **Semper Gallery of Old Masters,** with rich holdings of Italian, Dutch, and Spanish masterpieces. Highlights of the collections include Raphael's *Sistine Madonna,* an illustration of the Renaissance ideal of perfect grace, and Giorgione's *Sleeping Venus,* a vivid example of Renaissance harmony between man and nature. You'll also see many works by Titian, Veronese, Rembrandt, Rubens, and van Dyck. Other interesting works are Canaletto's paintings of 18th-century Dresden, similar in style to his portraits of Venice. The Semper Gallery is open Tuesday to Sunday from 9 a.m. to 6 p.m.; closed Monday.

Across from the entrance to the Semper you'll see the **Historical Museum.** Here you can see a rare collection of ornamental weaponry (weapons used for pageants and other events but not battle) that includes armor, helmets, and a wide selection of swords and spears. It's open Thursday to Tuesday from 9 a.m. to 5 p.m.; closed Wednesday.

At the other end of the Zwinger Palace sits the **Porcelain Museum,** the second-largest collection of porcelain in the world. Started in the early 18th century by Augustus II, the collection displays everything from early Chinese pottery to baroque works from the nearby Meissen factories. Open Monday through Thursday from 9:30 to 4 p.m., on Saturday and Sunday from 9 a.m. to 4 p.m.; closed Friday.

The Albertinum Palace

Dresden's second most famous museum complex is the 19th-century Albertinum Palace, down the riverbank from the Zwinger on Brühl Terrace. Of most interest in the museum is the **Green Vault** (Grünes Gewölbe) of the Saxon kings. Now we usually don't spend much time admiring gems, but this collection is truly dazzling. The rooms here are literally filled with precious stones, starting with gold, silver, and ivory, and moving on to emeralds, rubies, sapphires, topaz, pearls, and best of all, diamonds. Be sure to note the *Court of Delhi on the Birthday of the Great Mogul Aurungzebe,* a phenomenal work of 137 gold figures studded with some 3,000 diamonds, rubies, emeralds, and pearls.

Other museums of interest in the Albertinum are the **Modern Art Museum,** which displays 19th- and 20th-century works by such artists as Monet, Manet, Renoir, and Van Gogh, and the **Sculpture Museum,** consisting of mostly ancient Roman pieces.

All the museums in the Albertinum are open Friday through Wednesday from 9 a.m. to 6 p.m.; closed Thursday.

Other Museums

Those interested in Dresden's past should visit the **Museum of Dresden,** Ernst-Thälmann-Strasse 2. Here you'll find historical displays including photos of Dresden in 1945 after the bombing and during its reconstruction. Open Monday to Thursday from 10 a.m. to 6 p.m., on weekends to 4 p.m.; closed Friday.

The **DDR Military History Museum,** Dr.-Kurt-Fischer-Platz 3, is East Germany's only military museum, but a complete and compelling one. The museum is divided into three sections: 1400–1917, 1917–1945, and a postwar collection. The World War II collection is particularly interesting. The museum also shows two five-minute films that should not be missed: one is footage of the Red Army marching in Moscow to celebrate the defeat of Germany in World War II in 1945, and the second film, with action and music worthy of James Bond, is footage of the Soviet army in sea, land, and air attack maneuvers. Ask the person at the information desk to show these films for you. Take tram 7 or 8 from Prager Strasse and get off three stops after the Platz der Einheit after you cross the river. The museum is open Tuesday and Wednesday from 9 a.m. to 7 p.m., Thursday through Sunday to 5 p.m.

Those interested in old trains, streetcars, and other modes of transportation that kept Germany moving in the past should stop in at the **Transportation Museum** (Verkehrsmuseum), on Neumarkt. It's open Tuesday to Sunday from 10 a.m. to 5 p.m.; closed Monday.

World War II Ruins

Several areas of Dresden continue to show the legacy of the 1945 firebombing. The ruins of the **Frauenkirche** (Church of Our Lady) in the Neumarkt square are quite moving and certainly worth visiting. Once one of Dresden's finest churches, today the Frauenkirche consists only of two standing fragments and a huge pile of rubble.

There are still several blocks of relatively untouched war ruins between the **Sophienstrasse and Schlosstrasse.** Among these buildings is the former royal residence where the "Green Vault" (Grünes Gewölbe) held the treasures of the Saxon monarchy (today, these impressive treasures are housed in the Albertinum Museum; see above). Most of the buildings in this area have their ornate 18th-century façades intact, while their interiors have collapsed. One interesting detail (right off the Dimitroff-Platz) is a decorative covered passageway on the second floor (which appears green and black from the firebombing) that connects the restored 18th-century Dresden Cathedral (which also has a beautiful façade) with these ruins. On Sophienstrasse (across the street from the Zwinger Palace), you'll see several elegant façade ruins with royal crests or statues of guards atop the buildings.

Sights Outside Dresden

Three popular destinations near Dresden are **Pillnitz,** 12 km (7¼ miles) to the east, home to a beautiful baroque palace designed by M. D. Pöppelmann, the architect who designed the Zwinger; **Meissen,** 25 km (15 miles) away, a charming medieval town where elegant porcelain is produced; and **Moritzburg,** 14 km (8½ miles) northwest, site of a large hunting lodge also designed by M. D. Pöppelmann that houses a baroque museum.

The Dresden Information Office, Prager Strasse II (tel. 495-50-25), has information on these towns as well as train and boat departure times.

CULTURE AND NIGHTLIFE: Dresden offers a rich cultural program including an annual music festival in May and June, and concerts in the courtyard of the Zwinger Palace in the summer. The **Dresden Information Office** has schedules as well as tickets. The Hotel Bellevue, at Kopckestrasse 15, also sells concert tickets. Note, however, that both sell tickets at a higher price than the box office, so you might want first to see whether the theater box office has any tickets left over.

Two important concert halls are the impressive, newly restored **Staatsoper** (the Semper Opera House), at Theaterplatz 2 (tel. 484-20), where opera and theater are performed, and the **Kulturpalast,** in the Altmarkt (tel. 486-60), where the Dresden Philharmonic plays. For a complete listing of events in Dresden, buy the *Dresden Informationen Veranstaltungen* at the Dresden Information Office or at newsstands.

SHOPPING: For good maps, postcards, and guidebooks to East Germany, go to **Volksbuchhandlung Heinrich Mann,** next to the Hotel Konigstein on Prager Strasse. It's open on Monday and Tuesday from 9 a.m. to 6 p.m., on Wednesday from 9:30 a.m. to 6 p.m., on Thursday from 9 a.m. to 6:30 p.m., on Friday from 9 a.m. to 7 p.m., and on Saturday from 9 a.m. to 1 p.m.

Perhaps the only place to buy the *International Herald-Tribune* in all of East Germany is at the modern **Hotel Bellevue** at Kopckestrasse 15, across River Elbe from the city center.

If you have many long train rides ahead, perhaps you'd like to invest in a chessboard or some playing cards. The **Ultenberger Spielfarten,** at Obergraben 2, off Strasse der Befreiung, has portable chess boards for only 14 marks ($4.90).

2. Leipzig

Leipzig is a lively metropolis with a population of 600,000, making it East Germany's second-largest city. Although it lacks the small-town charm of Weimar or the rich art and monuments of Dresden or Berlin, Leipzig offers good concert music, 18 varied museums, two exciting fairs a year, some interesting historical sights, and the usual mix of modern socialist buildings.

Since the 18th century Leipzig has been host to Germany's largest goods fairs, and the city maintains that tradition with its biannual Leipzig Fair. Today the fair (which is usually held during the second or third week of March, and the first week of September), displays mostly industrial and electronics goods.

ORIENTATION: At the **Tourist Information Center** (Zentraler Informations-Service) at Sachsenplatz 1 (tel. 795-90), you can get maps of Leipzig, and concert information and tickets. A publication sold here, "Treffpunkt Leipzig," details Leipzig's monthly cultural program. To get here from the train station, cross the little park in front of the station, go one block to the right, and then walk down Hallischen Tor. At the end of this small street you'll arrive at this large office. Open Monday to Friday from 9 a.m. to 8 p.m., on Saturday from 9:30 a.m. to 2 p.m., and on Sunday from 10 a.m. to noon. During the Leipzig Fair the office is open every day from 8 a.m. to 8 p.m.

The main **Reisebüro der DDR** office, at Katharinenstrasse 1-3, is open Monday through Friday from 9 a.m. to 12:30 p.m. and 1:30 to 4 p.m., on Saturday from 10 a.m. to noon.

During the Leipzig Fair, you'll find the **Foreign Visitors Center** at Universitatsstrasse 7.

ACCOMMODATIONS: If you ask the Reisebüro to find you the absolute cheapest hotel, you'll probably be placed in either of the following three-star hotels.

The **Hotel International,** Trondlinring (tel. 718-80 or 73-86; Telex 51559), is an older hotel with 110 large clean rooms with private bathroom. It's just three blocks from the train station. Singles cost 78 marks ($27.30) to 86 marks ($30) and doubles are 140 marks ($49) to 179 marks ($62.65). There's a good restaurant downstairs.

The **Hotel Zum Lowen,** on Rudolf-Breitscheid-Strasse (tel. 77-51; Telex 51535), is a three-star hotel right across from the train station and just down the block from the Hotel Astoria. Rooms are fairly small and basic, and priced about the same as at the Hotel International.

Sometimes you'll also be put up in one of the town's slightly more expensive four-star hotels, which include our next three choices.

Hotel Stadt Leipzig, on Richard-Wagner-Strasse (tel. 28-88-14; Telex 51426), is directly in front of the train station behind a small piece of park. Petit box singles here cost 87 marks ($30.50) to 96 marks ($33.60), and the much nicer doubles cost 212 marks ($74.20).

The **Hotel Astoria,** Platz der Republik (tel. 717-10; Telex 51535), is an older hotel across from the train station on the right side and just minutes from the center of town. Singles with private bathroom cost 80 marks ($28) to 155 marks ($54.25), and doubles cost 170 marks ($59.50) to 211 marks ($73.85).

The **Hotel Am Ring,** on Karl-Marx-Platz (tel. 795-20; Telex 51559), is about a ten-minute walk from the left side of the train station down the Goethe-Strasse. The rooms here are small, but clean and modern.

During the Leipzig Trade Fair, usually held in the early summer, **private rooms** and small (and less expensive) hotels are also available for the foreign visitor. There is a special fair package deal. You buy a fair ticket for about 50 marks ($17.50)—which everybody must buy anyway during this time to visit Leipzig—and with this ticket you will get your visa at the border. When you arrive in Leipzig, you can then go to the Reisebüro and find a hotel or private room. Private singles cost 30 marks ($10.50) to 50 marks ($17.50), and doubles cost twice that. You can also reserve a private room for this time through the Reisebüro before you arrive.

DINING: At Grimmaische Strasse 2/4 in the Madler passage, **Auerbachs Keller** (tel. 20-91-31), is recorded in Goethe's epic *Faust* as the place where Dr. Johann Faust and Mephistopheles meet. The dimly lit restaurant with vaulted ceilings has attractive paintings on the wall depicting Faustian scenes. Many locals consider Auerbachs Keller to be Leipzig's best restaurant. Specialties include Mephistofleisch (the meat of Mephisto, for those who dare), which is really strips of beef and pork with paprika and pepper, and fillettopf fasskellerart, beef and pork filets with fries and cauliflower, for 11.80 marks ($4.15). It's an appealing and popular restaurant, so reservations are necessary. Open 10 a.m. to midnight, daily.

Falstaff, Georgiring 9 (tel. 28-64-03), is an elegant restaurant with Persian rugs on the floor and a well-dressed clientele. The house specialty is "2 kleine schweinesteaks und grillwurst mit pommes frites angerichtet" ("2 small pork steaks and grilled wurst with french fries") for 11.45 marks ($4). There is also a large wine selection, including the delicate Tokaj Aszu dessert wine from Hungary. The restaurant is not far from the train station. Open seven days; try to reserve.

Barthels Hof, Markt 8 (tel. 20-09-75), right off the old town square, is a lively tavern restaurant with vaulted ceilings and wood benches and tables. A traditional German menu is offered at very reasonable prices. This is a popular local place with large tables, so expect others to sit at your table during your meal. It's open from 11 a.m. to midnight; closed Sunday.

Stadt Kiew, in the Messehaus am Markt at Petersstrasse (tel. 29-56-68), has Russian specialties such as chicken and pork Kiev, borscht, and blinis, all at reasonable prices. The best part about this restaurant is the outdoor tables which overlook the old town square and the majestic Thomas Church. Open daily from 11 a.m. to midnight; warm dishes are served until 11 p.m.

A Splurge Choice

The **Vietnamesisches Restaurant,** Grosse Fleischergasse 4, off Richard-Wagner-Platz (tel. 29-52-83), is the only Vietnamese restaurant in all of East Germany, and quite a good one at that. There's an attractive interior with paper lamps, vases, little Oriental figurines, and best of all, a little goldfish pool with a ceramic frog presiding as you walk in. There is a set complete menu at a cost of $10 to $15. The food is excellent—this is a nice splurge. It's open from 4 to 7 p.m. and 8 p.m. to midnight. Reservations are needed as it's a small restaurant.

For the best ice cream, go to the **Pinguin Bar,** Katharinenstrasse 4, open Monday to Friday from 9 a.m. to 11 p.m. and on weekends from 3 to 11 p.m. Should you want a cup of tea, the **Teehaus** across from the Thomas Church is an attractive little place with an 18th-century look. It's open Tuesday to Thursday from 10 a.m. to 6 p.m., on Friday to 7 p.m., and on Saturday to 1 p.m.

CULTURE AND NIGHTLIFE: The **Gewandhaus** (tel. 713-20) and the **Opernhaus,** both on Karl-Marx-Platz, are hosts to frequent operas, concerts, theater, ballets, and other cultural events. The modern Gewandhaus, which opened in 1981, usually has concerts Monday through Friday at 8 p.m., on Saturday at 3 p.m., and on Sunday at 6 p.m., including frequent recitals on the huge organ. Both theaters are very popular, and the performances are frequently sold out. Tickets and concert schedule information are available through the Leipzig Information Office, the Hotel Merkur (at Gerberstrasse 15; tel. 79-90), and the theater box offices. The box offices always hold back a few tickets, even for sold-out events, but it's a real challenge to get them. Note that the Gewandhaus is closed all of July and August.

For those who want a more active night out, try the **Cottbuser Postkutsche,** Strasse am Brunl 64, a nightclub and disco; **Eden Tanzbar,** Petersstrasse 34, a popular student disco (open Sunday through Thursday from 7 p.m. to 1 a.m., on Friday and Saturday to 3 a.m.); or the **Esplanade,** at Richard-Wagner-Strasse 10.

WHAT TO SEE: You are likely to see one of Leipzig's most awesome sights as soon as you arrive. The **train station,** on Platz der Republik, is the largest train terminal in Europe, a huge steel frame several blocks long covered with translucent glass. This impressive station was built between 1909 and 1915, and shows the grandeur of turn-of-the-century Europe.

You should continue your sightseeing in the picturesque Renaissance Market Square, site of the Old Town Hall built in 1556. Inside is the **Museum of the History of the City of Leipzig,** Markt 1, which has displays on the city's political and cultural history. It's open Tuesday through Sunday from 9 a.m. to 5 p.m.

Just one block away is the **Thomas Kirche,** a Lutheran church built in 1212. In 1539 Luther preached here, in 1723 Bach was chosen to be the church choirmaster (he continued to serve until his death in 1750), in 1789 Mozart played the organ here, and in 1813 Richard Wagner was baptized here. The St. Thomas boys' choir performs motets here every Friday at 6 p.m., and motets and cantatas on Saturday at 3 p.m.

The **Grassi Museum complex** at Johannisplatz 5/11 houses several interesting museums, including the **Ethnographical Museum (Museum für Volkerkunde),** at Taubchenweg 2, which has an intriguing exhibition on the diverse peoples of the Soviet Union. It's open Tuesday through Friday from 9:30 a.m. to 6 p.m., on Saturday from 10 a.m. to 4 p.m., and on Sunday from 9 a.m. to 1 p.m. At the end of the Grassi building at Taubchenweg 2E is a fascinating **Musical Instrument Museum,** which has old pianos, lutes, and horns from the

16th to 19th centuries. This museum is open Tuesday to Thursday from 2 to 5 p.m., on Friday and Sunday from 10 a.m. to 1 p.m., and on Saturday from 10 a.m. to 3 p.m.; closed Monday. On Sunday some of the musical instruments are demonstrated.

The **Modern Art Museum (Museum der bildenden Kunste)**, at Georgi-Dimitroff-Platz 1, has a good collection of 19th- and 20th century artworks. It's open weekdays from 9 a.m. to 6 p.m. (on Wednesday to 9 p.m.).

If you're interested in seeing the older, prewar areas of Leipzig, wander behind the old town center, on **Nürnberger Strasse**. Some of the buildings are in ruins from the war, but others show rich architectural detail.

Outside the center of town, past the fairgrounds at Leninstrasse 210, is the **Monument to the Battle of Nations.** Built in 1913, this impressive monument is 300 feet tall and celebrates the great defeat of Napoleon's armies by the combined forces of Russia, Prussia, and Austria not far from Leipzig in 1813. Take tram 15 from in front of the train station.

German Political Museums

There are four politically oriented museums in Leipzig honoring figures or events in recent German history. The **Georgi Dimitrov Museum,** at Georgi-Dimitroff-Platz 1, was the site of the famous Reichstag Fire trial of 1933. Dimitrov, a Bulgarian Communist leader, the chief defendant at the trial, was interrogated by German Interior Minister Hermann Goering. The museum is open Tuesday through Friday from 8 a.m. to 5 p.m., on weekends to 2 p.m.; closed Monday.

The **Lenin Museum,** at Rosa-Luxemburg-Strasse 19/21, is open Tuesday through Saturday from 9 a.m. to 5 p.m., on Monday from 1 p.m.

The **Karl Leibknecht Museum,** Braustrasse 15, is where the German revolutionary was born. It's open weekdays from 9 a.m. to 4 p.m.

The **Iskra Museum,** Russenstrasse 48, celebrates the spot where Lenin secretly published *Iskra,* a Bolshevik newspaper, in 1900. The Iskra Museum is open Tuesday through Saturday from 9 a.m. to 5 p.m., on Sunday to 1 p.m.

SHOPPING: For used classical records, music scores, and books about great composers (in German), go to the **Musikalien Antiquariat** at Thomas Kirchof 16, open Monday through Thursday from 9 a.m. to 6 p.m., on Friday to 7 p.m., and on Saturday to noon. Next door is a small Bach museum.

3. Magdeburg

Magdeburg, a city on the River Elbe with a population of 300,000, is interesting for those who have some extra time and a special interest in visiting East Germany in more depth. It is off the usual track of tourist towns visited by Westerners. Most of Magdeburg was destroyed in World War II, so today the city itself combines a few art and architectural gems with many ugly modern apartment houses. The sights include some beautiful old churches and elegant details on some of the prewar homes.

ORIENTATION: From the train station, Wilhelm-Pieck-Allee leads to the Old Market Square. On the way there, you should stop at the International Hotel, across the park from the station, to buy a useful city map for 1.50 marks (50¢).

The **Magdeburg Tourist Information Office** is in the Old Market Square at Alter Markt 9 (tel. 353-52; Telex 31667). It's open Monday and Friday from 9 a.m. to 3 p.m., on Tuesday to 6 p.m., on Thursday to 5 p.m., and on Wednesday from 10 a.m. to 5 p.m.; it's closed every day for lunch from 12:30 to 1:30 p.m. The **Reisebüro der DDR** is at Wilhelm-Pieck-Allee 14 (tel. 328-91 to 328-95).

ACCOMMODATIONS: There are two conveniently located two-star hotels where foreigners can stay. The **Grüner Baum,** at Wilhelm-Pieck-Allee 40, is a slightly rundown hotel just one block to the left of the train station.

The **Hotel Gewerkschaftshaus,** at Julius-Bremer-Strasse 1, is just one block from the Alter Markt (Old Market Square). From the train station, walk down Wilhelm-Pieck-Allee until you get to Karl-Marx-Strasse; turn left, and the next street after the Old Market Square is Julius-Bremer-Strasse. The hotel is just to your right.

DINING: At Leiterstrasse 6, **Postkutsche** (tel. 319-12) is considered by many to be one of the town's best restaurants. The specialty is a veal cutlet with mushrooms, for 13 marks ($4.55). Try to reserve, as the restaurant is often full.

Bordegrill, Leiterstrasse Block 3A (tel. 327-10), is a clean, attractive place with plain white stucco walls framed by stained wood. The specialty here is gegrillter bordespeiss flambiert, a very tasty shish-kebab-type dish, cooked in butter and served flambé with french fries and a sauerkraut salad, for 17 marks ($5.95). The Bordegrill is open from 11 a.m. to midnight.

The **Ratskeller,** in the Town Hall basement at Alter Markt 15, is also a good choice. The stone columns down here are old, but everything else is modern. The house specialty is braumeistersteak, a pork steak with ham and eggs, for 7.55 marks ($2.60). The basement is open daily from 11 a.m. to midnight.

WHAT TO SEE: The **Magdeburger Dom,** on Domplatz, is one of East Germany's most charming churches. Begun in 1209 but not completed until 1520, it was also the first church in Germany to have a completely Gothic façade. Inside are tall, bare stone walls and long Gothic arches, plus a few statues and interesting architectural details.

The **Kloster Unser Lieben Frauen,** at Regerungsstrasse 4/6, is a beautiful, tranquil cloister built in the 11th and 12th centuries in the Romanesque style. The courtyard is always open; visiting hours for the interior of the cloister are Tuesday through Sunday from 10 a.m. to 6 p.m. There are also frequent music concerts in the basilica area here.

The **Alter Markt** (Old Market Square) is a reconstructed square typical of the Middle Ages, with the Town Hall at one end and a fountain in the middle.

The **Kulturhistorisches Museum (Cultural History Museum),** at Otto-Von-Guericke-Strasse 68/73, has a varied historical collection, the most intriguing part of which is the collection of medieval paintings and sculpture. One interesting piece is the first German equestrian statue (built in 1240) since antiquity. The museum is open Tuesday through Sunday from 10 a.m. to 6 p.m.

The **Ruine Johanniskirche,** behind the Alter Markt toward the Elbe, is the tall remains of an elegant church destroyed by World War II bombing. Today only the outside walls still stand, and the long Gothic arches contrast boldly against the blue sky, as there is no roof or interior to the building. A postwar sculpture in brass on the façade illustrates the horror of war. The church remains are open Monday through Friday from 1 to 5 p.m., on weekends from 10 a.m. to 5 p.m.

4. Weimar

Weimar was the center of German classical literature and the site of the first German democracy. The decline of the Weimar government and the rise of Adolf Hitler in 1933 ended both. Not seriously damaged in World War II, the city has been restored and now has several excellent museums. Surrounded by several Renaissance palaces and with a beautiful promenade in the center of the old town, Weimar also has a stunning city park.

A CAPSULE HISTORY: Some old gravesites dating from between the 5th and 7th centuries A.D. were found along what is now Cranachstrasse in the center of Weimar. In A.D. 957 the town of Wimare or Wehmare was first mentioned in surviving records. Later, in the 10th century, under King Otto II, the city was officially made the residence of the Counts of Weimar. Between the trade cities of Erfurt and Leipzig, Weimar was not established as a municipality until 1373 under the control of the Counts of Thüringen.

The small, quiet town on the banks of the meandering River Ilm was thought of as a backwater town by people in the 16th century. In 1552 one of the principal painters of the Reformation, Lucas Cranach, came to Weimar and spent his last few years living here. The 17th century saw much growth in the town. The Wilhelmsburg Palace, the Opernbuhnen, and several other of Weimar's famous buildings were constructed. In 1775 as the American Revolution was brewing, the young Johann Wolfgang von Goethe visited Weimar. The beauty and peace of Weimar were such that he decided to make the town his home. Later Friedrich Schiller came to live in the town and the two became friends. The literary work of Goethe and Schiller form the heart of German classical literature.

Weimar's prominence as a town of high art continued throughout the 18th century. Many of the famous Bauhaus artists and philosophers lived in Weimar, as well as Wassily Kandinsky and Paul Klee. It was partially because Weimar was said to hold the very essence of German humanism that it was chosen as the site of the first democratic convention in 1919. The ill-fated Weimar Government, as it came to be known, could not hold Germany together in the face of the new mass ideologies, Communism and National Socialism. Adolf Hitler also enjoyed Weimar and visited the town several times. Luckily, the town was not heavily damaged during World War II.

Today Weimar offers a glimpse of a world that has almost entirely vanished. You may have to do a lot of reading between the lines, but the essence of Weimar has managed somehow to survive—at least for the tourist.

ORIENTATION: The city center is only about a 15- to 20-minute walk from the train station along Leninstrasse and then Karl-Liebknecht-Strasse. Or you can take bus 4 or 7 to Goethe-Platz. Bus tickets cost 20 pfennigs (0.20 mark, or 7¢), and should be bought at a newsstand beforehand.

The **Weimar Information Office** is at Marktstrasse 4 (tel. 21-73). It's open on weekdays from 9 a.m. to 12:30 p.m. and 1:30 to 5 p.m. (on Monday from 10 a.m.), and on Saturday from 8:30 a.m. to noon. They can give you a helpful monthly publication, *Wohin in Weimar,* which lists concerts and cultural events as well as museum and other important addresses.

The **Reisebüro der DDR** is located in the green-and-white Stadthaus on the Marktplatz (tel. 26-82). It's open on Monday, Tuesday, Wednesday, and Friday from 8:30 a.m. to 4 p.m., on Thursday to 6 p.m.

There is one central office where you need to buy tickets to all of Weimar's museums, the **Zentralkasse,** at Frauentorstrasse 4, open Monday through Friday from 8:30 a.m. to 12:45 p.m. and 1:30 to 4:30 p.m., on Saturday and Sunday from 8:30 a.m. to 12:45 p.m. and 1:45 to 4:30 p.m. A ticket for all of Weimar's museums costs 3.05 marks ($1.05); tickets to the individual museums cost 0.50 mark (17¢) to 1 mark (35¢) each. They also sell postcards here.

ACCOMMODATIONS: The Hotel Elephant, Am Markt (tel. 614-71; Telex 618961), is Weimar's nicest hotel and has been a favorite of visitors to Weimar for hundreds of years. Guests have included J. S. Bach, Franz Liszt, Richard

Wagner, Leo Tolstoy, Thomas Mann, and Adolf Hitler. (Hitler was a frequent guest; in 1944 he spoke from the hotel balcony here to declare that Germany was winning the war.) Today the interior is clean and modern. Single rooms without bath don't cost much more than in Weimar's other hotels: 60 marks ($21). Doubles without bath are a much steeper 130 marks ($45.50), and rooms with private bath are a very expensive 140 marks ($49) to 200 marks ($70). Downstairs is a very good, though expensive, restaurant, open from 6:30 a.m. to midnight Sunday through Friday, to 1 a.m. on Saturday.

The **Hotel International,** Leninstrasse 17 (tel. 21-62 or 21-63), and the **Hotel Einnert,** Brennerstrasse 42 (tel. 36-75), are both right across from the train station and 15 minutes to the town center by foot. Both are slightly rundown, but they're the cheapest hotels close to the center. Singles cost 52 marks ($18.20) and doubles run 70 marks ($24.50). Of the two, the Einnert may be the better buy, for its rooms have a private toilet without shower while the International has neither. On the other hand, the Hotel International has a good restaurant downstairs with live classical music from 4 to 6 p.m. every night except Monday and Tuesday.

The **Hotel Am Ettersberg,** Auf dem Ettersberg (tel. 22-26), is about eight kilometers (five miles) outside Weimar. We asked the Reisebüro der DDR to find us Weimar's cheapest hotel, and we were put here, in a decent hotel with large rooms. Only later did we learn that this building was once a casino and officers' club for SS men from Buchenwald; in fact the hotel is just two minutes away from the camp itself. There's bus service to and from the city center every hour. Think twice about whether you want to stay here before you ask the Reisebüro to find the cheapest hotel in Weimar.

DINING: Weimar offers the following good restaurants, and you should reserve at all of them:

The **Gaststatte Alt-Weimar,** on the corner of Steubenstrasse and Preiler Strasse (tel. 20-56), is widely considered Weimar's best restaurant (along with the restaurant in the Hotel Elephant). Many artists associated with the National Theater have been frequent guests here, including Franz Liszt and Richard Strauss. Even today artists, actors, and musicians come here, and the reason is clear: the food is excellent and the prices are low. We recommend the Ukrainian soljanka, a soup with meat and vegetables, for 1.65 marks (58¢), and the schweinesteak mit feinem wurzfleisch, a tender, juicy pork steak with cheese, fries, and vegetables, for only 4.95 marks ($1.75). The kitchen is open from 4:30 to 9:30 p.m., but once here, you can stay until 11 p.m.; closed Monday and Tuesday.

Gastmahl des Meeres, on Herderplatz (tel. 45-21), is an attractive fish restaurant. The simple interior has white vaulted ceilings and a few nautical maps on the walls. One specialty is edelfischplatte mit pommes frites, a mixed plate of three different fish and fried potatoes for 7.25 marks ($2.55). Other entrees cost around 5 marks ($1.75). Another rare plus about the restaurant is the self-service salad bar. You can add a fine bottle of Hungarian white wine to your meal for 9.75 marks ($3.40) to 11 marks ($3.85). The restaurant is open from 11 a.m. to 8 p.m. weekdays only. *Note:* Smoking is forbidden in the restaurant.

The **Ratskeller,** in the basement of the Stadthaus in Markt (tel. 613-31), has excellent food at reasonable prices, albeit with slow service. Some specialties are feuerfleisch (roast beef served with potatoes) for 6.50 marks ($2.25), and steak with eggs (schweinsteak mit kesselgulasch) for 7.55 marks ($2.65). It's open Tuesday through Saturday from 10:30 a.m. to 11 p.m.; closed Sunday and Monday.

For good breakfast pastries, go to **Backerei Seidenschwanz,** at Karl-

Leibknecht-Strasse 10A, open from 7 a.m. to 1 p.m. Monday through Friday and from 6:30 to 10 a.m. on Saturday.

Cafés

Locals love to spend hours at the town's cafés. Here are our favorites.

The **Goethe Café,** at Wielandstrasse 1, off Goethe-Platz (tel. 34-32), is Weimar's most elegant, with frosted-glass windows, an attractive wooden bar, and a dozen tables. Here you can have a large variety of coffees, cakes, pastries, ice cream, and crêpes. It's open Tuesday through Saturday from 10 a.m. to 8 p.m., on Sunday from 2 to 6 p.m.; closed Monday. Smoking is not permitted.

The **Café Esplanade,** Schillerstrasse 18, is known affectionately by locals as Coca (short for concert café) because this is the place to go after the theater. The upstairs is the nicest part of the two-story café. Here you can get coffee and cake, or mixed drinks, served by waiters in black tie. Hours are 9 a.m. to 5 p.m. downstairs, 2 to 11 p.m. upstairs.

Eis Kaffee, at Abraham-Lincoln-Strasse 9, has the best ice cream in Weimar. Choices include a wide variety of sundaes and ice cream with wine. It's open Monday through Thursday from 10 a.m. to 5 p.m. and on Sunday from 1 to 5 p.m.; closed Friday and Saturday. When walking down Abraham-Lincoln-Strasse, note that no. 5 is the central Soviet command headquarters in Weimar, and you can see officers of the Soviet army wandering around.

CULTURE AND NIGHTLIFE: The **National Theater,** on Wielandstrasse, is the cultural center of Weimar. In front of the theater is a schedule of events ranging from plays to opera—even rock ballets. The program changes almost daily, but in July and August the theater is closed. The box office is open Tuesday through Saturday from 10 a.m. to 1 p.m. and 4 to 6 p.m., on Sunday and holidays from 10 a.m. to noon, as well as evenings one hour before showtime. Opera and ballet tickets cost 4 marks ($1.40) to 10 marks ($3.50); other events cost 2 marks (70¢) to 8 marks ($2.80).

The National Theater is also an important historical monument. It was here in 1919 that the national meetings to establish the Weimar Republic were held.

Nachtclub Bajadere, in the Hotel Elephant on the Marketplace (tel. 614-71), is Weimar's most avant-garde nightspot attracting a very diverse crowd, including gays, transvestites, couples, and singles in their 20s to 60s. It's open Tuesday through Saturday from 8:30 p.m. to 3 a.m. You should call to reserve a table.

THE SIGHTS: At the **Goethe Haus,** Am Frauenplan, exhibitions show the development of the writer's life (1749–1832), including sample works and other displays on the celebrated author of *Faust.* Every week there's a reading from Goethe's works, and on his birthday, August 28, there's a big party in the back garden. The museum is open from 8:30 a.m. to 12:45 p.m. and 1:30 to 4:30 p.m. Behind the museum is an attractive, un-museum-like café with a light-green decor and marble floors, open from 9 a.m. to 12:30 p.m. and 2 to 4:30 p.m. weekdays only.

The **Schiller Haus,** at Schillerstrasse 12, is a memorial to the poet Friedrich Schiller's life. Old books (such as that of his most famous drama, *William Tell),* letters, clothes, and other mementos are displayed on the second floor. The third floor is the apartment where Schiller lived from 1802 to 1805. The museum is open from 9 a.m. to 1 p.m. and 4 to 6 p.m.; closed Tuesday.

The art collection in the **Schlossmuseum,** at Burgplatz 4, features paintings by the 16th-century artist Lucas Cranach, but there are also paintings by Veronese, Tintoretto, Rubens, Monet, and others. Open Tuesday through Sunday from 9 a.m. to 1 p.m. and 2 to 5 p.m. (on Friday from 10 a.m.); closed Monday.

Stadtmuseum Weimar, at Karl-Leibknecht-Strasse 7, chronicles the history of the city of Weimar. It's open from 9 a.m. to 1 p.m. and 2 to 5 p.m. Sunday through Thursday; closed Friday and Saturday.

The **Church of Sts. Peter and Paul** (also known as the Herder Church), in Herderplatz, is a flamboyant Gothic structure built in 1500. An altarpiece here was begun by Lucas Cranach and finished by his son. The church is open Monday through Friday from 10:30 a.m. to 1:30 p.m.

Across from the National Theater is a modern art gallery, the **Kunsthalle Am Theaterplatz,** where there are new shows every month or two. It's open Tuesday through Sunday from 9 a.m. to 1 p.m. and 2 to 6 p.m.; closed Monday. Admission is 1.05 marks (37¢) for adults, 0.25 mark (9¢) for students. In Theaterplatz is a statue of Goethe and Schiller shaking hands.

Goethe Park (or Park an der Ilm) is a long strip of park parallel to the stream that runs through town. It's unusually wild for an urban park, and very tranquil. You might, as we did when we visited, see a shepherd leading his sheep to pasture. Goethe's small summer house (Gartenhaus) is in the center of the park, and Liszt's house is on the edge of the park on Marienstrasse.

Buchenwald

In July 1937 a concentration camp was set up outside Weimar to hold the enemies of the Nazi Party. Unlike Auschwitz and most other German camps, Buchenwald was a work camp, not a death camp. Thus in relative terms the number of the dead in Buchenwald was small as concentration camps went: 56,000 prisoners from 18 countries died here (four million died at Auschwitz). But Buchenwald remains one of Nazi Germany's most notorious legacies because of the intense perversity of what went on. In the Buchenwald **museum** you can see the shocking examples of these atrocities in the form of shrunken heads and lampshades made from tattooed human skin, among other displays.

In addition to the museum and the remains of the camp at Buchenwald, there is also a modern **memorial.** The Communist regime has attempted to turn Buchenwald into a showcase of anti-capitalist propaganda. The result is a disturbing indication that the lessons of Buchenwald have already been forgotten by many.

The museum is open Tuesday through Sunday from 8 a.m. to 4:30 p.m.; closed Monday. A bus leaves from the city center near the train station every hour to the entrance to the camp.

SHOPPING: The **Musikalienhandlung Franz Liszt,** at Schillerstrasse 11A, has the best selection of classical records and tapes in Weimar. Records are inexpensive—about 12 marks ($4.20) for a Liszt album—though cassettes are almost twice as much. The shop is open Monday through Friday from 9 a.m. to 1 p.m. and 3 to 6 p.m. (on Tuesday from 10 a.m.). There's another record shop at Graben 45.

You can find nice old pocket watches, for 200 marks ($70) to 400 marks ($140), and other antiques at **Fachgeschaft,** Am Frauenplan 19. Technically, you aren't supposed to bring antiques out of East Germany, but with an old pocket watch, in the words of one antique dealer in East Berlin, "it would be hard for the authorities to know" whether you already owned the watch. It's open Monday through Friday from 10 a.m. to 1 p.m. and 3 to 6 p.m., plus every fourth Saturday in the month from 9 to 11 a.m.; closed other Saturdays, on Sunday, and every second Monday in the month.

5. Eisenach

Eisenach is the birthplace of J. S. Bach and is where the young Martin Luther began his studies. At the very northwestern corner of the Thüringer Wald (Thuringian Forest) and only about ten miles from the West German border, Eisenach is one of East Germany's most picturesque towns. Martin Luther translated the Bible from Latin into vernacular German here, and J. S. Bach spent his youth in Eisenach. Since the early Middle Ages Eisenach has been the site of the **Minnesang,** a form of lyric poetry that originated in Germany at this time. Eisenach's tie with the poetic art was so strong that Wagner set a mythical contest of Minnesangers in his opera *Tannhäuser* at the Wartburg Castle.

THE SIGHTS: Eisenach is best known for **Wartburg Castle** (tel. 30-01 or 30-02), which sits on a hill overlooking the town. The hilltop has been fortified at least since the 11th century during the reign of King Henry IV. By the end of the 1200s the fortified hill and the town around it were an important center of German culture. Many famous medieval poets sang and composed in the court of Baron Hermann I in the 13th century. In 1521 Martin Luther was banished to the castle by Saxon nobles while he was being sentenced by the Council of Worms. Not one to remain idle for long, he translated the Bible during his stay at Wartburg. In 1777 Goethe stopped briefly at the castle. Today the well-preserved castle remains one of Thüringia's most stunning and beautifully restored castles. The castle is open daily from 8:30 a.m. until 4 p.m.

Luther lived in many places in northern and central Germany. The **Luther Haus,** at Lutherplatz 8 (tel. 49-83), is one of the better preserved in the country. It's open from 9 a.m. until 5 p.m. Monday through Saturday, on Sunday from 2 until 5 p.m.

The **Bach Haus,** at Frauenplatz 21 (tel. 37-14), is well worth visiting. The Bach household was a large one and J. S. Bach spent many years of his childhood here. There is a good museum and an excellent collection of period instruments, some of which were probably played by J. S. Bach himself. The Bach Haus is open from 9 a.m. to 5 p.m. weekdays, on Saturday from 9 a.m. to noon and 1:30 to 5 p.m., and on Sunday from 10 a.m. until noon only.

Right on Predigerplatz is the **Dominican Cloister.** Dating from 1240, the cloister was often used as a school, and J. S. Bach learned the basics of reading and writing here. Today it is home to the **Museum of Medieval Art.**

HOTELS: Eisenach's best hotel is the **Parkhotel,** at Wartburg Allee 2 (tel. 52-91), just a skip and a jump from the train station. Western tourists are warmly received here. A double with bath costs $29. The hotel restaurant has dancing daily from 7:30 p.m. until midnight every night except Monday and Tuesday. The restaurant has a varied menu, with nothing more expensive than 9.05 marks ($3.15) and a decent schnitzel for 7.60 marks ($2.65). The Parkhotel is clean, quiet, and centrally located. When we visited, the restaurant was empty except for the local police celebrating their 40th anniversary of the People's Police.

RESTAURANTS: Housed in the old tower which was built in 1040 are two of Eisenach's most popular restaurants. On weekends reservations are a must at the Turmklause.

Turmschanke is an old, excellent restaurant loved by all those who are in the know. They serve delicious and very inexpensive local wines as well as hearty traditional, if slightly overpriced (for East Germany—$10 for a complete meal) food. Considered the "best" restaurant in Eisenach, the Turmschanke is open only for dinner and dancing, from 7 p.m. until 2 a.m.; closed Wednesday and Thursday.

In the basement of the Turmschanke is the **Zwinger** restaurant, a good place for inexpensive dining. Though it's generally crowded at lunchtime, you can eat breakfast here for less than 4 marks ($1.40). Lunches run less than 5.50 marks ($1.90), and for dinner, try the wild rabbit for 5.35 marks ($1.85). The Zwinger restaurant is open from 8 a.m. until 11 p.m., on Sunday to 9 p.m.

The **Wartburg Hotel Restaurant,** on the Wartburg (tel. 51-11), is a large indoor restaurant with a smaller, yet comfortable terrace. Remodeled, the hotel restaurant is a relatively pleasing pastiche of plastic modern and old Thüringer hunting lodge. The specialties are roastbraten (pork roast) for 6.50 marks ($2.30) and wild game, in season.

For nighttime fun, try the **Ho-stadt Café**, at Karlstrasse 33-35 (tel. 30-54). There is a bar and café with a revue on Friday and Saturday nights that runs from 8 p.m. to 3 a.m. The show we saw involved two men and a woman, all scantily clad and all wearing huge white fur boots with an odd dance routine set to "socialist modern music"—not anything like the other side of the border. You can nevertheless get comfortably tight in the company of several other Eastern European business types for less than 75¢ a drink.

6. Thüringia

These sights were suggested by some of our well-traveled East German friends. Though we can't guarantee that the establishments are as described, our sources are responsible, educated travelers with an eye to the problems an English-speaker could face. So without further ado we introduce . . .

RUDOLSTADT: Rudolstadt is the home of a 12th-century castle which was once the seat of the Counts of Orlamünde and was later the seat from which much of the surrounding area was ruled. There is also an 18th-century theater where Richard Wagner composed in 1834.

The **Interhotel in Rudolstadt,** Zum Löwen at Markt Strasse 5 (tel. 20-59 or 20-60), was built in the 1950s and has modern, comfortable rooms with large baths.

SCHWARTZBURG: The nearby town of Schwartzburg is a picture-postcard town. One of our East German friends stated that the town looks as if it were inhabited "only by little garden gnomes." Unfortunately, on sunny weekends the town is often crowded with East German tourists.

To get here you can catch the bus from either Saalfeld or Rudolstadt.

SAALFELD: Just south of Rudolstadt (one stop by train or less than 20 minutes by bus) is the town of Saalfeld. Here, a very pure spring, known as the Feegrotten, produces waters used to brew an excellent local beer. The Feegrotten has proved to be such an inspiration that Saalfeld is dotted with numerous beer halls, generally open from 9 a.m. till midnight.

You can munch bread and sausages as you drink your beer in any of the beer halls, or you can try the **Loch** (Hole) restaurant. The Loch has a good "farmer's kitchen," as the locals call the solid home-style food.

ARNSGERUTH: A few miles southwest of Saalfeld on Hwy. 281 is the hamlet of Arnsgeruth. With not more than 150 houses, Arnsgeruth is a quiet country town, but it has an exceptional collection of mechanical pianos, organs, music boxes, and a mechanical symphony. The collection is privately owned so hours are whenever the proprietor is home and willing to let anybody in. The admission charge is officially 10 marks ($3.50), but the owner will often admit visitors for some cigarettes at all reasonable hours. Remember that it is a private house so he is under no obligation to let anybody in. Arnsgeruth is so small that you should not have any difficulty finding the museum—just ask for the "Privat Museum."

STADTILM: About 12 miles south of Erfurt on a winding country road is the town of Stadtilm. Though there's not much here of historical significance, Stadtilm is a relaxing country town.

For perhaps the most authentic home-cooked food in all of East Germany, try the old **Scharfe-Ecke** (Sharp Corner), right by the train station. It has a new name now, but everybody still refers to it by its old title. All the food is raised locally, from the succulent pork to the corn-fed barnyard chicken. In the kitchen the three elderly matrons sometimes sing as they peel potatos and prepare the simple but hearty fare. The average meal, with the good-sized beers, will not cost more than 12 marks ($4.20).

PLAUE: The town of Plaue in the Arnstadt district is known for its restaurant inside the ruin of the old Customs castle, Ehrenburg. The restaurant has a good selection of well-prepared local dishes and a good view. (By all means do not go to the Ehrenburg restaurant in the town of Plaue proper, a place that serves food on plastic plates.)

Plaue is two stations south of Arnstadt and about six miles south on Hwy. 4.

SINGEN: About two miles north of Stadtilm is some of the rarest and best-tasting beer in all of East Germany. Singen is home to a one-man **brewery** (tel. 25-56), open only on weekdays during "normal work hours." The Braumeister will sometimes show people around if he's not busy and "feels like it."

Part Three

CZECHOSLOVAKIA

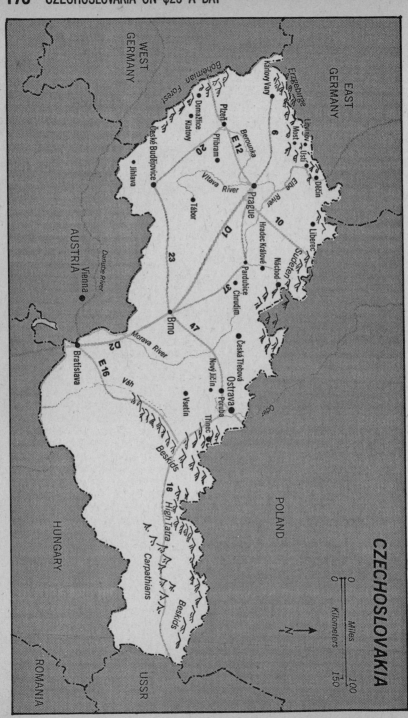

Chapter XI

INTRODUCING CZECHOSLOVAKIA

1. About Czechoslovakia
2. Rules and Regulations
3. Getting There
4. Getting Around
5. Accommodations
6. Food and Drink
7. The ABCs of Czechoslovakia

CZECHOSLOVAKIA MAY BE ONE of the most surprising countries for North Americans. Unexplored by Westerners, Czechoslovakia has practically become a synonym for all that is unknown and distant; we even use the word "bohemian" to describe our offbeat friends. For all this mystery, nothing could be farther from the truth. Unravaged by war and time, Czechoslovakia is a virtual living museum and natural park. Unlike any other European country, Czechoslovakia has not had a major battle fought on its territory for hundreds of years. Deep in pine forests and serviced by sleepy little spur rail lines, the timeless Slovakian hamlets remain practically unchanged. Seemingly on every hilltop or mountain pass stands a castle or fort. The number of intact historical monuments rivals that of any other country in Europe: there are over 2,500 castles, manors, and palaces in Czechoslovakia today.

There are few cities that can rival Prague, the capital of Czechoslovakia, in the opulence and splendor of its historical buildings. Those who saw the motion picture *Amadeus* will know the streets of Prague—the movie was filmed almost entirely in Prague and other locations in Czechoslovakia. Prague's old city (Staré Město) is one of the best preserved and largest in Europe.

Most beer consumed throughout the world today is a light brew called pilsner. This golden, flavorful drink originates in the Czechoslovakian town of Plzeň. If you take time to put down your beer glass, there are the incredible natural wonders of the High and Low Tatra Mountains and East Slovakia or "Slovak's Paradise." Snow-capped peaks, glittering waterfalls, and some of the wildest and most mountainous country in Eastern Europe lies in central Bohemia and Slovakia. There's so much to see in Czechoslovakia that you run a serious risk of exhaustion if you try to see it all in one trip. Therefore we offer the following suggestions for planning your itinerary.

SUGGESTED ITINERARIES: Czechoslovakia has so much of interest—

palaces, museums, parks, galleries, and picturesque villages—that there is no way the average stay will be enough to see it all. You could easily spend two weeks in Czechoslovakia and still not see all you might like to in the country!

Prague
Try to spend at least four days here. Though some may try to pack most of the major sights into three one-day programs, it's a blistering pace. Therefore we recommend staying at least four days in the capital. While you're staying in Prague there are several impressive sights in the vicinity of the city. Some, but by no means all, of these sights are the magnificent castles Karlštejn, Konopiště, and Český Šternberk; the town of Kutná Hora, a baroque and Gothic gem; as well as Lidice, the symbol of the suffering endured during World War II. You should allow at least a day for sightseeing excursions from Prague, so a five-day stay in the capital would be even better.

Bohemia
West of Prague are the old Austro-Hungarian cities and spa towns of Karlovy Vary (Karlsbad) and Mariánské Lázně (Marienbad), as well as Plzeň, the hometown of the light beers popular today. These 18th- and 19th-century resort and spa towns are well worth a day's visit. To the north of Prague is Děčinské stěny, a wooded area with numerous fantastic rock formations and beautiful trails, all centered around the town of Děčín. To the south of Prague are countless beautiful baroque and Renaissance towns including Tábor, the old Hussite stronghold, and České Budějovice. Both towns are worth visiting, but there are also many other beautifully preserved towns of historical note, so plan to stay for two days in southern Bohemia.

Moravia and Slovakia
In Moravia there are also many appealing towns, such as Telč and the Moravian capital Brno, throughout the forests and vineyards. Farther east, the High Tatras (Vysoké Tatry) demand a day's hike and another day to explore the local hamlets and numerous 17th-century wooden churches in the area. On the Soviet border at the eastern end of the country is a hilly, wooded region known as the "Slovak's Paradise." The eastern Slovak towns of Košice and Levoča, and the Slovak capital of Bratislava to the west, need three days to explore and enjoy.

Obviously not everyone can spend two weeks in a country, but understand when you visit the capital, Prague, that it's only the beginning of the numerous wonders that Czechoslovakia has to offer.

1. About Czechoslovakia

A CAPSULE HISTORY: The first major settlers in this region were the Celtic tribes, the Boii (from which the name Bohemia is derived), in the 5th century A.D. Archeological evidence indicates that the Boii lived peacefully among the various German and other tribes that were already established in the area. There were several early attempts to unify the various tribes, some moderately successful. In 626 Samo, a Frankish merchant, organized the Czech and Moravian tribes to defeat the Avars, a tribe from the East Asian steppes that had moved into the area. After Samo's death the state became a tributary of Charlemagne's empire in the early 9th century (805).

The Moravian Empire and the Division of the Czechs from the Slovaks

After Charlemagne died the Holy Roman Empire began to crumble. The Czechs, under the princes of the royal House of Přemsyl, carved out a significant holding in the second half of the 9th century. Mojmir (Moymir) I, who ruled from 830 to 846, and his nephew, Rastislav (who ruled in 846–870), established the Great Moravian Empire. Under Rastislav, Christianity flourished. He was responsible for having Catholic masses said in Slavic rather than the traditional Latin, for translating the Bible into Slavic, and for sponsoring the creation of the first Slavic alphabet. Intense internal feuding plus growing German pressure from the north signaled the decline of the Moravian Empire. The final blow came in 906 when Hungarian armies ravaged the countryside and added most of eastern Moravia and Slovakia to their country. This separation of the Czech and the Slovak people was of major historical importance. The separation continued until the country was reconstituted at the end of World War I. For a period of almost 1,000 years the Czech (western) part of the country and the Slovak (eastern) part existed independently.

The Přemyslid Dynasty

From this chaos rose the Přemyslids, the first and only indigenous Czech dynasty. They had long been rulers in the environs of Prague, but under King Ottokar II, who ruled from 1253 to 1278, and his son, Wenceslas (Václav) II (ruled 1278–1305), the Přemyslids amassed a vast empire. Their influence extended as far south as the Adriatic and to the Baltic in the north; they even mounted two crusades to Prussia. Oddly enough, in order to consolidate their power in the newly conquered territories, the Přemyslids encouraged German immigration. The German peasants in Saxony had developed a system of farming that greatly increased food production and so were considered valuable additions to any lord's fiefdom. Ottokar II actively supported the Teutonic Knights, who named their capital Königsburg (1225) after the Czech king. With the addition of much of Austria to the Kingdom of Bohemia, Ottokar II ruled at the pinnacle of Czech power. The Přemyslids' reign ended in 1306 with the assassination of Wenceslas III on his return from Poland. Thereupon the Bohemian nobles elected John of Luxembourg to the throne. He ruled until 1346, when he fell in battle (drowned in a swamp) fighting under the French banner against the English at Crécy. Fortunately his son, who had also participated in the battle, remained on firmer ground and survived to become one of Bohemia's greatest kings, Charles IV.

Charles IV and the Golden Age of Bohemia

Between 1346 and 1378 Charles IV transformed Prague into one of the major political, cultural, and religious centers of Europe. He relocated the capital of his entire empire, including much of the old Holy Roman Empire (known also as the German or Roman-German Empire) to Prague. Under Charles IV the country entered the "Golden Age of Czechoslovakia." A lavish patron of the arts as well as Roman Catholicism, Charles IV secured an archbishopric for Prague and St. Vitus' Cathedral as its seat. He established the first university in Central Europe in 1348—appropriately named the Charles University. Especially significant in this period of artistic expansion was the evolution of the typical Bohemian architectural style that graces the skyline of Prague to this day.

Jan Hus and Religious Reformation

The rapid introduction of the Roman Catholic church in Bohemia, because of Charles I's generous support, aroused strong opposition. Soon after

Charles's death, there were accusations of widespread corruption in the Bohemian Catholic church. Further tensions came from the German sections of the empire. In 1402 John Hus was appointed to the Bethelehem Chapel pulpit in Prague. He was so outspoken on the issues of church corruption and controversial church practices (the sale of indulgences) that the Pope forbade him to preach in the Bethelehem Chapel. Hus's constant demand for reform finally brought the church to excommunicate him.

The Hussite Wars

Acting with Sigismund, King of the German Empire and the brother of the King of Bohemia, Wenceslas IV, the pope in 1414 called a council in Constance to discuss the charges of heresy and general disobedience against Hus. Although traveling under a safe conduct order from Sigismund, Hus was imprisoned in the winter of 1414. In the spring of 1415 the council offered him freedom in exchange for signing a formula of abjuration (essentially a confession). Hus refused, and on July 6, 1415, was burned at the stake. Following the death of Wenceslas IV in 1419, Sigismund, supported by Czech and German Catholics, assumed the Bohemian throne. Sigismund's aversion to Protestantism and his condemnation of Jan Hus to die at the stake enraged the Hussites. In 1419 Hussites hurled envoys of the Catholic church and Sigismund out the windows of a palace and declared outright rebellion against the Roman Catholic church. The Bohemian peasantry, low clergy, merchants, and lesser nobility under the leadership of Jan Žižka (nicknamed the Rhino) and Prokop Holý (Procopius the Bald) proved to be an unbeatable combination. They defeated five papal crusades, including the combined armies of Sigismund, the pope, and several German princes, sent against "heretical" Bohemia.

The End of the Bohemian Empire

With the common enemy vanquished, the Hussite factions resumed their feud, culminating in the fratricidal battle of Lipany (Lipan) in May 1434. Sigismund's death in 1437 intensified this struggle for power, which continued until the whole area was conquered by the Polish King Matthias Corvinus in 1466. Bohemia was then ruled by the Jagiellonian kings of Poland in an uneasy peace that lasted until the Lutheran Reformation 30 years later. In 1526 the last of the Jagiellonians, King Louis II of Hungary, was killed at the battle of Mohács fighting against the Ottoman Turks, leaving no heir.

Hapsburg Rule

From the death of Louis until the end of World War I (1526–1918) the Hapsburgs controlled most of Czechoslovakia. Initially the Hapsburgs appeared sympathetic to the Czech cause. However, a division in the Hapsburg Empire and the rise of Archduke Ferdinand spurred suppression of the Hussites. Disgruntled Bohemian nobles, both for religious and political reasons, rebelled against the Hapsburgs. Demonstrating their contempt for the empire, in 1618 Bohemian nobles threw the imperial envoys out of the chancellery windows in the Hradčany (Prague castle). This is known as the Second Defenestration of Prague.

The Thirty Years' War

The Second Defenestration sparked the horrendous bloodletting known as the Thirty Years' War (1618–1648). On November 8, 1620, the rebellion was crushed at the Battle of White Mountain. As a result of this defeat, many Bohemian leaders were executed or exiled, and their lands distributed to foreigners. By the end of the Thirty Years' War one-third of the population in Bohemia was killed or starved to death. Though not directly involved in European wars, Bohemia suffered tremendous manpower and financial burdens imposed by the Hapsburg Empire. In the mid 16th century, to appease growing social unrest, Empress Maria Theresa (1740–1780) began widespread reforms, carried out by her son, Joseph II. Among these reforms were the abolishment of serfdom, a reinstatement of religious freedom, and land reform.

The Rise of Czech and Slovak Nationalism

In the hope of creating a more sympathetic government, the Czechs, along with the Slovaks, who were suffering similar injustices under Hungarian rule, allied. During this period three key figures—Josef Dobrovsky, Josef Jungmann, and František Palacý—emerged as champions of the suppressed Czech culture, language, and history. They eventually became the symbols of the entire revival movement. Although a reluctant Emperor Franz Joseph I eventually acquiesced to the revival movement, entrenched legal prejudices against the Czechs and Slovaks prevented any substantial progress toward independence.

World War I

At the outbreak of war, the Czech leaders grasped the opportunity to achieve complete independence from the Hapsburg Empire. When Austria-Hungary joined with the Central Powers, Czech soldiers defected and fought with the Entente in Russia, Italy, and France. Although an active war effort was never organized, the Czechs were notorious for their passive resistance to the Hapsburg Empire. Both hilarious and biting, Jaroslav Hašek's brilliant antiwar novel *The Good Soldier Schweik* (Svejk) is one of the best portrayals of the Czech resister. Following the defeat of the Central Powers in 1918, Tomáš Masaryk, Czechoslovakia's first president, signed a declaration of independence on October 26, 1918, in (appropriately enough) Philadelphia's Independence Hall.

The First Republic (1918–1935)

As a result of the Paris Peace Conference, the newly independent state inherited tremendous economic resources and industry from the old Hapsburg monarchy as well as territory which had not shared history with the Czechs or the Slovaks, such as Carpathian Ruthenia, which is today in northeast Hungary. Antagonism between these ethnic groups became a major problem. Czechs and Slovaks only comprised 67% of the total population. A large contingent of Germans (27%), Hungarians (5%), and Poles (0.5%) refused to become part of the new state, and agitated for minority rights; some even advocated union with their various motherlands.

Depression and Munich

The economic problems of the Great Depression in the 1930s were compounded by the constant meddling in Czech domestic affairs by Germany and Hungary. The ultimate goal of Czechoslovakia's neighbors was not only to incorporate their own nationals, but the destruction of the "synthetic" Czech state. Fearing another world war, Britain, France, and Italy, at the Great Powers conference in Munich (August 29–30, 1938), agreed to Hitler's demand to cede all Czech counties that were more than 50% German to Germany, effectively "selling Czechoslovakia down the river." Poland and Hungary followed Germany's lead and claimed their disputed territory. The Great Powers' appeasement of Germany was to no avail: on March 15, 1939, Hitler invaded Czechoslovakia.

World War II

In many ways the Czechs responded to this war the same as they had responded to World War I. With the exception of a few isolated incidents, the Czech people again used passive resistance against their occupiers. However, Hitler was determined to completely "assimilate" Czechoslovakia into Germany and brutally proceeded with a systematic suppression in Bohemia and Moravia. He played upon Slovak desires for an independent state, and during the war Slovakia existed as a quasi-independent part of the Third Reich. By the end of the war more than 250,000 Czechoslovaks had died as a result of the Nazi occupation.

Postwar Czechoslovakia

Though there was a coalition government in Czechoslovakia for a few years, dissatisfaction with the West (based in large part on the Munich betrayal) resulted in a landslide Communist victory in 1948. Most of Czechoslovakia's vast industrial capacity was still intact at the end of the war. But mismanagement and extensive Soviet "reparations" led to inflation, low productivity, and social discontent in the 1950s. In response, in 1960 the government changed the name of the country to the Czechoslovak Socialist Republic (ČSSR) and proceeded with careful reforms.

The Prague Spring

In 1968, despite ominous warnings from fellow Warsaw Pact members, Alexander Dubček began to dramatically liberalize political controls on the economy and human rights. Censorship was eased, political prisoners were rehabilitated and released, and a movement was started to decentralize industry. Known as "The Prague Spring," this rapid liberalization eventually displeased Czechoslovakia's mighty neighbor to the east. On August 20, 1968, Soviet troops and a few token brigades from other Warsaw Pact forces crossed the Czechoslovakian frontier and entered Prague, ending the Czech experiment in applied socialism. Today the Czechoslovak government is one of the more rigidly dogmatic in the Warsaw Pact. Waste, mismanagement, and the worsening economic situation has left the Czechoslovakian economy in a sad state. Nevertheless there has been a rise in the standard of living over the years and limited forms of private enterprise have been introduced with some success.

THE PEOPLE: There are three geographic regions of Czechoslovakia: Bohemia, Moravia, and Slovakia. In the 10th century the Hungarians controlled Slovakia, while the German-dominated empires to the west also dominated Bohemia and Moravia. This division led to independent development and a distinct difference between the two cultures and languages. In the 1978 census there were 15 million people: 66% were Czech and 28% were Slovak, with a scattering of Hungarians, Polish, Germans, Ukrainians, and other minorities. Over half of the Czech population lives in the country or in small villages of 5,000 people or less.

But statistics can hardly describe the Czechoslovakian people. Energetic and friendly, the Czechs boast some of the highest productivity in Eastern Europe. The more traditional Slovaks live in the mountains and forests to the east, priding themselves on their hospitality to the traveler.

GOVERNMENT: The Czechoslovakian Socialist Republic (ČSSR) is a federation of the Czechs in Bohemia and Moravia with Slovakia. The government is closely modeled on that of the Soviet Union, and Czechoslovakia is the only other Eastern European country that claims to have reached the Communist ideal of "scientific socialism." The country has been led since 1968 by President and First Party Secretary Dr. Gustav Husák.

LANGUAGE: There are two closely related Slavic languages in Czechoslovakia: Czech and Slovak. German is spoken by many of the older people in Bohemia and in the northern part of Moravia. English is not widely understood, but it's the preferred language of many students, so sometimes younger, educated people will speak some English.

SPORTS: The two most popular sports in Czechoslovakia are soccer and ice hockey. The Czechoslovakian national hockey team is usually one of the top contenders in the Olympics. There is a national athletic association which claims 1.8 million members. In 1985 the government organized a vast display of the nation's finest in the Spartakiada, a "mass unison exercise." For those unaccustomed to 140,000 people exercising together, there are numerous trails and nature reserves to lose yourself in.

The Czechoslovakian Koruna

The official currency of the ČSSR is the Czechoslovakian crown, the Koruna (Kčs), made up of 100 hellers. The Koruna is circulated in 10-, 20-, 50-, 100-, and 500-Kčs notes, as well as 1-, 2-, and 5-Kčs coins. The prices in this book were calculated at 11.81 Kčs = $1 U.S. Thus 1 Kčs = about 8½¢, or $10 = about 118 Kčs.

NATURAL FEATURES: Czechoslovakia is composed of five major geographical regions with the three largest—the Bohemian massif in the west and the two spurs of the Carpathians—making up the bulk of the countryside. There are many national parks and reserves including most of the Tatra Mountains in the northeastern part of the country. These parks offer plentiful opportunities for hiking and climbing. The High Tatras are steep enough to provide challenging climbs for the experienced mountaineer.

SPAS: Czechoslovakia is gifted with more spas than practically any other country in Europe; certainly they are more famous. The spa towns of Karlovy Vary (Karlsbad) and Mariańské Lázně (Marienbad) have been resorts and recuperation centers for centuries, and the Czechs have restored and modernized the old resorts. For drinking as much as bathing, the mineral waters that are found throughout the country are an integral part of Czechoslovakian life.

2. Rules and Regulations

TOURIST INFORMATION: In the beginning there was one tourist bureau in Czechoslovakia, called Čedok. Unfortunately, as tourist organizations go, it's not one of the best in Eastern Europe. Since it's the main tourist bureau in the country and because it does have several tours and package deals worth considering, we recommend using Čedok (pronounced *Che*-dauk) only for specific requests or short periods of time (try to avoid entangling yourself in their bureaucracy as much as possible). For package tours or special information (youth groups, sport groups, hunting, etc.) you may write the Čedok people. Their only American office is in New York: **Čedok,** Czechoslovak Travel Bureau, 10 E. 40th St., New York, NY 10016 (tel. 212/689-9720).

For motoring information and campsite reservations, contact the **Autoturist** people in Prague, at Opletalova 29 (tel. 22-35-44 to 22-35-47).

For the sportsman, contact **Sport-Tourist** at Prague on Národní 33 (tel. 26-33-51). They handle all reservations and travel arrangements for budget accommodations, ski and hiking tours, and tickets to major sporting events in Czechoslovakia.

VISAS: Getting into Czechoslovakia is not difficult at all. The only two things you need to enter the country are a valid passport, with at least seven months till it expires, and a Czechoslovakian visa. There are *no* visas issued at the border. To get the visa you will need an application form, two passport photos, and $12. To get your visa in the United States, you can write the Czechoslovakian Embassy: Czechoslovak Embassy, 3900 Linnean Ave. NW., Washington, DC 20008. In Canada, write to the Consulate General of Czechoslovakia, 1305 Pine Ave., West Montréal, PQ H3G 1B2, Canada.

Rather than shipping things through the mail and waiting for weeks (it takes at least six weeks to get a visa through the mail) we prefer to get our visas in person while traveling in Europe. You can get your visa at any of the Czechoslovakian consulates in Europe. The requirements are the same (remember those two photos!), but the process will take less than a morning at most. There are consulates in Vienna, West Berlin, most Western European capitals, and the capitals of every other Eastern European country. All visa sections are open only in the morning, so show up around 8:30 a.m. to beat the rush.

Extending your visa once you have entered Czechoslovakia is a problem, so always sign up for a few days more than you think you'll actually stay—but not too many extra days as there is a minimum daily currency exchange.

The Minimum Daily Currency Exchange

Like granny's castor oil, the minimum daily currency exchange is the Eastern European cure-all remedy for economic distress. For every day you spend in Czechoslovakia, you must exchange $12 per adult; children between 6 and 15 years of age need exchange only half that, and children under 6 need exchange nothing. This minimum exchange cannot be re-exchanged back into Western currencies. The Customs officials will accept practically anything—credit cards, cash, any traveler's check, even personal checks (though it's wise not to risk it)—for the minimum daily exchange. You receive Czechoslovakian currency in return, and a voucher which you should keep with you until after you have exited the country.

CUSTOMS: There are usually few problems on the Czechoslovakian border, though the guards tend to be as dogmatic as their East German neighbors to the north. The only requirement is that you make the minimum daily currency exchange. The usual rules apply for entering Czechoslovakia. Keep all printed materials to a minimum. You are allowed to bring $60 worth of gifts into the country and export $30 worth out, duty free. On all items, except for goods purchased in the state-owned Tuzex shops—which are duty free—there is a 100%-of-value duty. For more information you can write the Czechoslovakian government or any consulate or Čedok office. There is an information sheet that lists all prohibited export items including, among other things, infantwear, hand towels, and textile underwear.

Do *not*, under any circumstances, attempt to smuggle narcotics in or out of Czechoslovakia; the *minimum* penalty is two years in jail.

You do not need a special health permit to enter Czechoslovakia.

Any traveler who was once a Czechoslovakian national or could be considered as such should take special care to abide by the regulations. Former nationals should consult the Czechoslovakian Embassy in Washington, D.C., and the American Department of State.

Cars

You must have valid international insurance (the Green Card) in order to drive, as well as *both* an American and an international driver's license. If you don't have insurance, there is another $10 charge for mandatory collision insurance. Studded tires are prohibited in Czechoslovakia.

REGISTRATION: Once you have entered Czechoslovakia you must register with the police within 48 hours of your arrival. Almost all hotels will do this for you during your first night in the country. Otherwise, ask the proprietor of your hotel where the nearest police station is. In Prague there is a police station at Bartolomeska 14, open daily from 9 a.m. till 3 p.m. (on Wednesday until noon).

3. Getting There

With Germany and Poland to the north and west, Austria and Hungary to the south, and a common border with the Soviet Union in the east, Czechoslovakia is in the very center of Central Europe. If you travel through Eastern Europe at all, you'll probably have to cross Czechoslovakia at least once. From the West, Czechoslovakia is best reached through either Austria or the Federal Republic of Germany (West). If you're arriving from other Communist countries your travel options are much greater.

There are *no* visas issued on the border.

BY AIR: There are still few really inexpensive ways to fly directly to Czechoslovakia from the United States. Probably your best bet is Lufthansa's Super APEX fare from your U.S. gateway to Prague, via Frankfurt. Certainly it is the most dependable and comfortable way. CSA, the Czechoslovakian State Airlines, also offers weekly flights to Prague from New York's Kennedy International Airport. For information or assistance while in Prague, contact Lufthansa at: Parizska 28, 11000 Praha 1 (tel. 2-31-75-51).

Flying to Prague

Tourist and Business Class fares in the chart below allow unlimited stopovers. Excursion fares are limited to one stopover in each direction, for a charge of $25 each. The Super APEX fare permits no stopovers and has a 21-day advance purchase requirement and a $75 penalty for cancellation. All fares (which are subject to change without notice) are also subject to a $3 departure tax plus a $5 Custom User fee.

Round-Trip Fares to Prague

From:	All Year First Class	All Year Business Class	10 Day–3 Month Excursion		6 Day–3 Month Super APEX	
			Sept. 15– May 31	June 1– Sept. 14	Sept. 15– May 31	June 1– Sept. 14
New York	$3042	$1450	$ 958	$1136	$ 610	$ 750
Anchorage	4168	2372	1396	1574	1048	1188
Atlanta	3730	1838	1086	1264	738	878
Boston	3042	1450	958	1136	610	750
Chicago	3692	1894	1068	1246	720	860
Houston / Dallas-Ft. Worth	3774	1780	1086	1264	738	878
San Francisco / Los Angeles	4404	2360	1141	1319	793	933
Miami	3484	1772	1104	1282	756	896
Philadelphia	3262	1614	1021	1199	673	813

All fares are subject to change without notice.

BY TRAIN: There are express trains to Prague from Wrocław and Kraków in Poland, Berlin, Munich in the Federal Republic of Germany (West), and Vienna. The trip from Vienna to Prague takes about five hours and passes through some of the most beautiful countryside of both lands. From Berlin you must first get a transit visa to cross East Germany.

BY CAR: We strongly recommend bringing a car to Czechoslovakia. Since the rental packages in Prague leave something to be desired, you might consider renting a car in the West. All the major routes into Czechoslovakia center on Prague: the E15 from Berlin to Budapest via Bratislava and Prague, and the E12 from Warsaw to Nürnberg and Munich. There are no major roads that run the direct length of Czechoslovakia. The shortest route from the Soviet Union is the E85 via Brno.

4. Getting Around

The trains may be a little slow and the roads narrow, but whichever route you take you'll pass through some of Europe's most beautiful scenery.

BY AIR: For those with more cash than time, flying is an alternative. However, if you travel by plane you'll miss some of Czechoslovakia's finest sights, the small towns and castles tucked away in the hills and forests. There are air connections to Bratislava in the south, Brno in the central part, and the High Tatras and Kosice in the east.

BY CAR: Of all the countries in Eastern Europe, Czechoslovakia is where you will want a car most of all. Many of the most fascinating sights and grandest castles are outside the major cities and are extremely difficult to reach by public transportation. The small, uncrowded towns, the hunting lodge deep in the forest, are attractive partially because of their very remoteness.

Czechoslovakian roads are generally two lane and narrow, and often carry many different kinds of nonmotor traffic—horse-drawn vehicles, foot traffic, and an occasional tank. Obey the traffic regulations (standard European driving rules) as the police are empowered to levy 100-Kčs ($8.45) to 500-Kčs ($42.35) on-the-spot fines. If you don't want to pay, you can schedule a court appearance. Remember when entering villages that the speed limit is always 60 km/h (35 mph), whether posted or not.

The national car-rental company is **Pragocar**, with offices in most major towns in Czechoslovakia; the main office is in Prague, at Štěpánská 42 (tel. 24-

84-85, 24-00-89, or 12-26-41). You can rent a Skoda, a domestic Czechoslovakian car, for $310 a week. But on Czechoslovakia's winding, hilly roads we recommend the more powerful Renault 13 GTL for an extra $46 a week. For $402 a week you can rent the top-of-the-line Pragocar, a Ford Sierra. These prices are not competitive with many of the fly-drive car-rental packages offered in Western Europe, but when you add insurance, taxes, and border fees, the contrast is not so obvious.

BY TRAIN: Czechoslovakian trains seem slower than many of the other Eastern European national rail services. Therefore we recommend buses in Czechoslovakia rather than trains for most short hauls.

Train travel in Czechoslovakia is ridiculously inexpensive, about $7 from Prague to Poprad (gateway to the High Tatras), second class. In summer the crowds are such that we recommend splurging on a first-class ticket, especially on all longer train rides. *(A word of warning:* Avoid all the local trains if possible; at one point we were certain that a farmer and his horse, plowing the fields next to the tracks, were making better time than our local train.) By express train, the travel times from Prague are: to Plzeň, two hours (90 miles); to České Budějovice, three hours (95 miles); to Brno, four hours (156 miles); and to Poprad, over nine hours (for a distance of less than 350 miles).

BY BUS: The bus is a reasonable alternative in Czechoslovakia if you don't have a car: many of the castles and smaller villages are only accessible by road. Most buses leave in the morning, so the earlier you start the more connections are available. We recommend getting your bus tickets and a reservation at least a day in advance. When you exit the bus at a new town, go directly to the bus office and get your next ticket and reservation. Bus prices range from $1 to $3 depending on the length of the journey. Since buses are far less comfortable than trains, you should take buses on all local routes and trains only for long distances or on express lines.

HITCHHIKING: In the western part of the country there are more automobiles, but our Slovak acquaintances assure us that, since they are friendlier, your chances of getting a ride are about the same throughout Czechoslovakia. Only about 40,000 Americans visit Czechoslovakia every year, and 90% of those never leave Prague. Try to appear as Western and as American (exotic) as possible in order to capitalize on your rarity. All these good feelings not withstanding, hitchhiking is often a slow business in Czechoslovakia. Women alone should exercise caution, but generally there are few problems for the single female traveler in Czechoslovakia.

5. Accommodations

HOTELS: The Czechoslovakian tourist bureau uses the following hotel rating system: A de Lux, A*, A, B*, B, and C classes. The A classes are generally outside the range of the $25-a-day traveler. B* hotels are less expensive but of almost the same quality as the A class. B hotels are generally acceptable and cost between $13 and $17 per person per night. C hotels are not usually recommended, but are included for the rock-bottom traveler. They average around $9 to $12 per person per night, though sometimes less.

MOTELS: There are two classes of motels which fall into the auto-camping category. They are usually modern, with additional camping facilities right nearby. Class A motels have private baths and Class B do not; otherwise they're about the same.

CAMPING: Most camping spots in Czechoslovakia are auto campsites. There are a few foot-traffic-only campsites in some of the national parks, but overwhelmingly you will have to share your tentsite with motor trailers. There are two classes of campsites—A and B. Most campsites are Class A and have good shower and toilet facilities; Class B camps often do not have hot running water. Most of the campsites are open only from April or May until September or October.

YOUTH HOSTELS AND STUDENT TRAVELING: All youth travel is handled by **CKM (Cestovní Kancelář Mládežw)**. The main office is in a large modern building in Prague not more than five minutes southwest of Václavské náměsti at Žitná 12. Their address is Žitná ulice 12, 12105 Praha (tel. 29-99-41 to 29-99-49; Telex 122299).

CKM provides student services as well as an excellent network of decent budget hotels. The friendly management makes CKM one of Czechoslovakia's best-run tourist bureaus, though they still have problems. If you're spending more than a week in Czechoslovakia, stop by the office in Prague and make reservations in CKM hotels for the towns you plan to visit. There are three categories of CKM accommodations: B+, B, and C. Prices are based on full or half board (we recommend only the half-board options). In a Class B hotel, half board and room cost $16.40 per person per day. If you make advance reservations before entering Czechoslovakia, this cost counts against your minimum exchange.

6. Food and Drink

Typical Czech food is hearty, and pork specialties abound. Prague ham is rightly world famous, and you'll consider yourself lucky if you ever have the opportunity to sample the farm fresh sausages of a local butcher. Cheese making was an ancient part of Bohemian culture and the Slovaks pride themselves on their fine sheep's cheese. Dumplings, crêpes, cakes, and gingerbread are a few of the delicious Czechoslovakian excursions into baking. But far and away the greatest Czechoslovakian contribution to the world comes from the plains of central Bohemia, Moravia, and southern Slovakia. Here, some of the finest hops are grown and brewed into the world premium beers.

FOOD: Prague ham, Slovak sausages, Moravian smoked meats, liver sausage, and pâtés are just part of the traditional Czechoslovakian artistry in pork. These are often accompanied by dumplings or, in Slovakia, *halushky* (homemade pasta). Cheese from Tábor, a creamy Roquefort type, is justly famous, as are *oštiepok, brynza,* and *parenica,* Slovakian sheep's cheese. Just as important as the pig, the goose occupies a primary place in the Czech menu. Served in its own juices with dumplings and cooked in a special oven to make it light but not greasy, roast goose and duck are dishes you cannot miss in Czechoslovakia. To go along with the meals is the array of Czechoslovakian pickled gerkins onions, sauerkraut, and peppers. To end the meal there is usually a choice of strudels, numerous cakes, and other pastries, as well as the traditional gingerbread.

DRINK: The light, flavorful pilsner beer, the most common beer in the world today, originated in Czechoslovakia. Even that most red, white, and blue of beverages—Budweiser beer—originates from the Budvar breweries in southern Bohemia. Yet as you expectantly eye a dewy glass of Pilsner-Urquell or wipe the creamy foam of a Budějovice Budar from your lips, remember that practically every town in central Bohemia and Moravia and southern Slovakia has its own brewery. The numbers of fantastic local beers are seemingly endless, and disputes as to which is the better are settled daily by residents with extensive sampling.

The Czechs also grow a mean grape. The flow of good local burgundies from Bohemia has steadily increased since Emperor Charles introduced the vine. There are also numerous fruit liqueurs, but by far the rarest drink can only be found at traditional Moravian weddings. Here, the father of the groom will carefully broach a cask of mead that he has been carefully tending since the bridegroom was born. The wedding party will sample the mead—the drink, according to legend, that gave the ancient Slavs their strength.

7. The ABCs of Czechoslovakia

AUTO REPAIR: In Prague, **Autoturist,** at Opletalova 29 (tel. 22-35-44 to 22-35-47), handles all emergency repairs and towing. Throughout the country it's easiest to contact the police or a service station for these services.

BANKS: The exchange rates in Interhotels and other large hotels are the same as at the banks, and the hotels are usually more efficient.

BLACK MARKET: You will almost certainly be exposed to the black market during even the briefest of visits to Czechoslovakia. While trafficking in currency on the black market is strictly illegal, it is also quite commonplace. You will probably be offered at least three times the official exchange rate for your dollars, sometimes more. Remember that black market dealing is risky, though the local citizen is likely to suffer much stiffer penalties than you are; in any case, living expenses in Czechoslovakia are so low that it's really not worth the risks involved. You may, however, legally give dollars to a Czechoslovakian citizen as a gift, but that person must then exchange the Western currency for Tuzex coupons within 15 days.

BUSINESS HOURS: Post offices and most other government offices are open from 8 a.m. to 6 p.m. Shops open around 9 a.m. and close up at 6 p.m. weekdays; on Saturday they may be open until noon.

CLIMATE: Czechoslovakia is frequently showery, but not as wet or nearly as cold as the northern European countries. Bring good raingear as well as some warm clothing. The highest average summer temperature is 87° Fahrenheit, and the lowest average winter temperature is 41°.

CREDIT CARDS: The following credit cards are valid at participating businesses in Czechoslovakia: ACCESS, American Express, BankAmericard, Carte Blanche, Diners Club, Eurocard, MasterCard, and VISA. You may *not* use these cards at banks or businesses to obtain cash advances.

CURRENCY: The official currency of the ČSSR is the Czechoslovakian crown, the **Koruna (Kčs),** made up of 100 hellers. The Koruna is circulated in 10-, 20-, 50-, 100-, and 500-Kčs notes, as well as 1-, 2-, and 5-Kčs coins. The prices in this book were calculated at 11.81 Kčs = $1 U.S. Thus 1 Kčs = about 8½¢, or $10 = about 118 Kčs.

ELECTRICITY: The electric current in Czechoslovakia is 220 volts, 50 cycles, A.C.

EMBASSIES AND CONSULATES: The U.S. Embassy is in Prague at Trziste

15 (tel. 536-641). The **Canadian Embassy** in Prague is at Mickiewiczova 6 (tel. 32-6941), and the **British Embassy** is at Thunozska 14 (tel. 53-3347).

EMERGENCY: For the police, call 158; for an ambulance, call 155.

FIRST AID: Everyone is entitled to emergency first aid in Czechoslovakia, although unless your insurance specifically covers accidents in a Communist country you may have to pay for any such treatment.

GASOLINE: There are two grades of gasoline sold: Special (90 octane) and Super (96 octane). You can buy gasoline only with coupons available at most Tuzex shops and Interhotels, as well as at the border. There is no rationing in effect for Westerners.

HOLIDAYS: Czechoslovakian national holidays are January 1 (New Year's Day), Easter, May 1 (May Day, the international Communist holiday), May 9 (the Communist national independence day), and December 24–25 (Christmas).

HUNTING: For more information about hunting and fishing opportunities, as well as permits, write to Čedok, Foreign Travel Division, Department VI–Hunting, at Na příkopě 18, 111 35 Praha 1, Czechoslovakia.

INFORMATION: Tourist information on Czechoslovakia is handled primarily by Čedok, the Czechoslovak Travel Bureau, which has offices in most major towns.

NEWS AND MEDIA: You won't find any Western publications in Czechoslovakia, and any Western literature is regarded with suspicion by the border guards.

POST OFFICE: Mail to North America from Czechoslovakia is very inexpensive (usually not more than 25¢ for airmail), and generally the mail services are not bad. Post offices are open weekdays from 8 a.m. to 6 p.m.

SHOPPING: There are numerous excellent buys in Czechoslovakia, especially Bohemian crystal and worked glass. The still-vital peasant culture produces worked-leather and wood items, such as the nativity scenes from the northern Czech-Moravian borderlands, as well as handmade jewelry and cloth.

STUDENT TRAVEL: All youth travel is handled by **CKM (Cestovníí Kancelář Mládeže)**, whose main office is at Žitná ulice 12 in Prague (tel. 29-99-41 to 29-99-49; Telex 122299).

TELEPHONE AND TELEX: For the public phones you need a 50-heller (½-Kčs, or about 6¢) coin. To reach information in Prague, dial 120; for the rest of Czechoslovakia, dial 27-55-51.

Telexes can be sent conveniently from most of the Interhotels, which, for a small fee, will also hold all replies.

TIME: Czechoslovakia is on Central European Standard Time, which is seven hours ahead of Eastern Standard Time.

Chapter XII

PRAGUE

1. Orientation
2. Accommodations
3. Dining on a Budget
4. What to See
5. Evenings in Prague
6. The ABCs of Prague
7. Excursions from Prague

"IF PRAGUE WERE BY THE SEASIDE, it would be too lovely to believe," wrote F. R. de Chateaubriand. To see the spires and turrets of the Prague Hrad (castle) rise out of the morning haze or reflect the last red glimmers of a sunset is an experience to be treasured. The beauty of the Hrad and St. Vitus Cathedral is such that they seem to soar over the city. The Staré Město (the Old City) is an arched, cobblestoned mystery. Its old churches, buildings, and fountains are time worn but intact, seemingly untouched by the passage of centuries. Between the Hrad on the west and the Staré Město on the east flows the Vltava (Moldau). Delicately framing the river with its 14th-century spans is the Karlův most (Charles Bridge), the very symbol of Prague.

Wander down some narrow street and stop for a beer in an establishment that may once have been frequented by Bohemian and Hapsburg nobility. Stand in the middle of the Staroměstské náměsti (Old Town Square) near the statue of Jan Hus. It was here, in 1420, that religious war was unleashed and the power of the Roman Catholic church was challenged. Stroll along the Vltava and up to the Hradčany (castle district), where perhaps you'll find a quiet bench in an alcove that was old when Columbus set sail to discover the New World. The appeal of Prague goes beyond beautiful buildings and hospitable people. There is an attraction and a misty glory to Prague which will inspire you the first time you visit and remain with you when you leave.

A CAPSULE HISTORY: Unchanged for centuries, Prague's remarkable state of preservation is the result of war. Prague was the powerful capital of an aggressive feudal coalition in the 14th and 15th centuries. The religious war that began when Jan Hus was burned at the stake resulted in continuous bloodshed for over seven years and culminated in the internecine battle of Lipan in 1431. The battle of Lipan, between rival Hussite factions, prevented the Bohemian nobility from creating a successful nation-state. Trade routes that once centered on Prague moved elsewhere and much of the surrounding territories was absorbed by land-hungry neighboring nobles. As a result, from the early 17th century onward, much of the fighting and resulting destruction bypassed Prague.

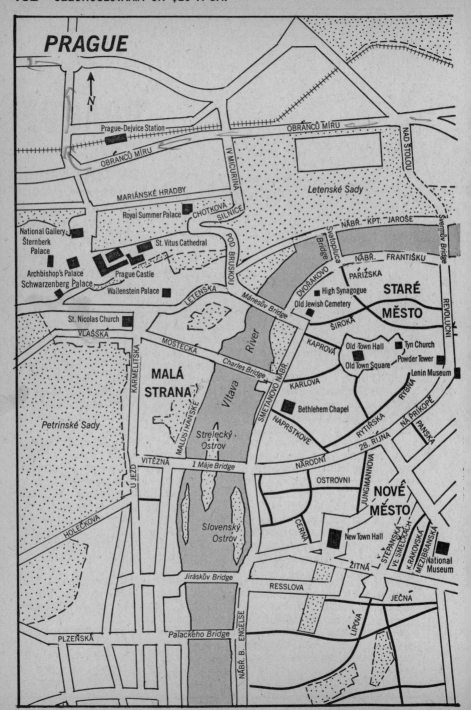

PRAGUE

N

Prague-Dejvice Station

OBRÁNCŮ MÍRU

OBRÁNCŮ MÍRU

NAD STOLOU

MARIÁNSKÉ HRADBY

Letenské Sady

IV MICURINA

Royal Summer Palace

CHOTKOVA SILNICE

NÁBŘ.- KPT. JAROŠE

National Gallery
Šternberk
Palace

St. Vitus Cathedral

POD BRUSKOU

Svatopluca Bridge

NÁBŘ. FRANTIŠKU

Švermův Bridge

PAŘÍŽSKA

STARÉ
MĚSTO

Archbishop's Palace
Schwarzenberg Palace

Prague Castle

DVORAKOVO

High Synagogue
Old Jewish Cemetery

REVOLUCNI

Wallenstein Palace

LETENSKA

Mánesův Bridge

ŠIROKA

St. Nicolas Church

VLAŠSKÁ

MOSTECKÁ

River

KAPROVA

Old Town Hall
Old Town Square

Tyn Church

Powder Tower

Lenin Museum

KARMELITSKA

Charles Bridge

Vltava

KARLOVA

RYBNA

MALÁ
STRANA

MALOSTRANSKÉ

SMETANOVO NÁBŘ.

Bethlehem Chapel

NA PŘÍKOPĚ

PANSKÁ

Petrinské Sady

Strelecký
Ostrov

NAPRSTKOVE

RYTIRSKA

28. ŘIJNA

VITĚZNÁ

1 Máje Bridge

NÁRODNI

U JEZD

OSTROVNI

JUNGMANNOVA

NOVÉ
MĚSTO

HOLEČKOVÁ

Slovenský
Ostrov

CERNA

New Town Hall

ŽITNA

ŠTEPANSKA
VE SMECKACH
K. RAKOVSKA
MEZIBRANSKÁ

National
Museum

Jiráskův Bridge

RESSLOVA

JEČNA

LIPOVÁ

PLZEŇSKÁ

Palackého Bridge

NÁBŘ. B. ENGELSE

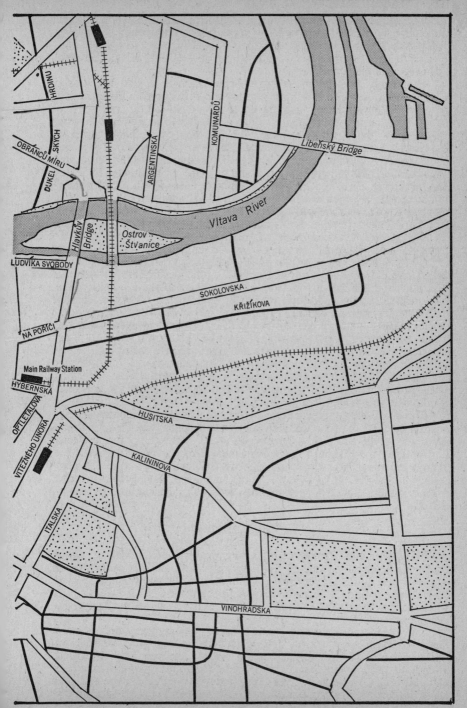

First settled by Slavic people moving in among the resident German tribes in the 5th century A.D., Prague became the principal town of a fierce tribe known as the Czechs. Headed by the Přemysl Dynasty, the Czechs gained control over much of central Bohemia and parts of Moravia. Prague's Golden Age did not arrive until the reign of Charles IV.

Thoroughly schooled in France, the new king was at first viewed as a foreigner—and he was. Yet Charles's constant contributions to Bohemia and the capital, Prague, actually created the distinct architectural style you see today. Though many of the buildings, such as the Old Town Hall (1338), were constructed before Charles IV's reign, he began the most ambitious projects. The Hrad was conceived and constructed in his day, and the whole city was enlarged under Charles's masterplan. He called together some of the best urban planners of the day, Mattias of Arras and later the brilliant Peter Parler of Gmünd in Swabia. The Hrad was rebuilt along the lines of French castles and a new cathedral was begun. Charles procured an archbishopric for Prague and in 1344 built a huge Gothic cathedral as its seat. The new building was dedicated to St. Vitus and has not been radically altered since the 14th century.

With the fall of the Luxembourg Dynasty and the Hussite Wars in the 15th century, Prague passed into the hands of the Hapsburg Empire. By the mid 16th century Prague was in the middle of a Renaissance-style building boom imported from Italy by the Hapsburgs. Painted and other decorations as well as the Renaissance garden clashed with Gothic Prague. It was not until "a compromise between native traditions and imported style," as the official history so delicately puts it, was reached that the new Renaissance styles were incorporated. Prague's beauty lured even a few of the Hapsburg monarchs away from Vienna. Prague experienced more prosperity when Emperor Rudolf II made the Hrad his permanent residence. His passion for the arts as well as alchemy and sorcery fed the flowering of Renaissance Prague, but also attracted numerous tricksters and hustlers. The bid by Rudolf's successors for control of the empire culminated in the defeat at White Mountain in 1620. This defeat ended the ascendancy of Prague, and in effect left it a provincial town.

This defeat did not prevent Prague from wholeheartedly adopting the baroque style, symbol of the Counter-Reformation. Under the Catholic Hapsburgs this style achieved a preeminence far outreaching the previous Renaissance period. Though Prague remained a backwater city, it was not left out of the cultural and artistic flow of events. Its manpower and wealth were used by the empire, but no wars were fought in Prague, leaving the city free to develop without any of the catastrophies most other European capitals endured.

1. Orientation

LAYOUT: "Prague is a golden ship majestically sailing on the Vltava," wrote Guillaume Apollinaire (1880–1918), a French poet of Polish extraction. Once you are in the city center every view includes the wide **Vltava.** The mighty Hrad (castle) and St. Vitus Cathedral on the west bank and the Church of our Lady of Týn and the Staroměstské náměsti (Old Town Square) on the east bank could almost be the bulkheads of some mighty ship.

There are four major parts of the city center: the **Hradčany,** the castle district; the **Malá Strana,** the lower or lesser town on the west bank of the Vltava; the **Staré Město,** the Old City; and the **Nové Město,** the New Town. The Malá Strana is at the foot of the Hradčany. From the Hradčanské náměsti, the center of the Hradčany (castle district) is a long stairway (Nové zámecké schody) leading to the central throughfare of Malá Strana, **Mostecká ulice** (Bridge Street).

The Mostecká ulice is appropriately named as it connects with Prague's most famous bridge the **Karlův most** (Charles Bridge). Across the Vltava are the twisted narrow streets of the Staré Město (Old Town). From the Karlův most, the **Karlova ulice** leads directly to the Staroměstské námĕsti (Old Town Square). South of the Staré Město is the Nové Město, or New Town, though it was built in the 14th century.

This string of roughly east-west-running streets connects the most important parts of Prague and also acts as a general base line. Except for the Nové Město to the south, most of Prague's sights are not far from this route. The principal subway line (Line C) also follows this route to a degree, further aiding the sightseer. You probably won't have to leave the four central districts, all of which are within walking distance of one another, though the Hradčany is at the top of a substantial hill.

ARRIVING IN PRAGUE: Geographically one of the primary transportation hubs of Central Europe, Prague is the logical point to begin any tour of Czechoslovakia.

By Air

You may fly into Prague from another Eastern European country. The **airport is** located on the outskirts of town at Ruzyně and is about an hour away from the city center by bus. Buses leave from the five major Prague Interhotels —the Parkhotel, Esplanade, Jalta, Ambassador, and the Panorama—at three-hour intervals between 8:45 a.m. and 6:15 p.m. A ticket costs $4 and can be purchased at any of the Interhotel receptions or at ticket window 29 at Ruzyně airport.

By Train

Prague's **main railroad station** (Praha hlavní nádraži) is a modern well-laid-out building resembling an airport terminal. It's about a 15-minute walk east from the Staroměstské námĕsti (Old City Square), or you can take the metro south to the museum stop and than change to Line C and go two stops north (toward Leninova).

By Bus

For national bus travel information, you can go to the Čedok office or the Florenc **main bus station** (autobusové nádraži) on Vítĕzného února. The Florenc station is about a five-minute walk, or one metro stop, north of the main railway station.

By Car

As noted above, Prague is one of Czechoslovakia's central transportation hubs. The Staré Město (Old Town) is closed to all motor traffic unless you have accommodations there. Parking is generally not a problem as there are several parking lots on the outskirts of the Staré Město.

TOURIST INFORMATION: The main tourist information center and room-finding service in Prague is managed by Čedok, at Na příkopě ulice 18 (tel. 22-42-51 to 22-42-59; Telex 121109, 121809, or 122233). Open weekdays from 8 a.m. until 4 p.m., weekends from 8 a.m. until noon, this office handles everything except accommodations. You can buy train tickets and reservations or get tourist information and guides, but you'll have to endure particularly poor service. Arrive early in the morning if possible, and avoid buying tickets of any sort through this office as prices seem to increase at least 15% for no corresponding rise in quality. For a more relaxed and professional atmosphere, try any of the Čedok booths in the large Interhotels, such as the Ambassador on Václavské náměsti 5.

Just around the corner on Panská ulice 5 is the **accommodation office** (tel. 22-56-57 or 22-70-04), open from 9 a.m. until shortly before 5 p.m. This office is detailed under "Accommodations" in the next section.

GETTING AROUND: Getting around Prague is extremely easy. There are now three **subway** lines serving almost all of "tourist Prague," as well as an extensive **bus** and **tram** network. To ride the metro, just drop a 1-Kčs (8¢) coin into the box. If you don't have any change, there is an automatic change maker on the walls that will change 2-Kčs and 5-kčs coins. For trams the price is the same (1 Kčs), though you must buy your tickets in advance from any newsstand adjacent to a bus or tram stop. The transportation network closes down at 11 p.m. except for a few tram and bus lines.

For our comments on **taxis,** see "The ABCs of Prague."

2. Accommodations

There is an abundance of budget-type accommodations, though you may not find a room in the city center. With a little legwork and some luck you can find decent budget accommodations at practically any time of the year. As the subway lines are perfectly safe and extremely efficient, a place that seems far from the center is probably not inconvenient if it's within walking distance of the subway.

HOTELS: Prague still suffers from chronic shortages of hotel space due to the influx of visitors from other Eastern European countries. The size and fervor of the Russian tour groups, who come to shop (not to sightsee), have led people jokingly to call them the second Russian offensive (after the 1968 intervention). We have listed almost 40 budget hotels in this section. Many of these hotels are quite similar, with almost no interior decoration to speak of. They are generally in the B category, with Class C hotels included only with the provision that they be considered if everything else is full. Most of the hotel staffs do not speak English, so a phrasebook is a must. There are enough budget hotels in Prague so that if one pick is full there are several more in a given area.

In the Staré Město (Old Town)

The **Hotel Centrál,** Rybná 8 (tel. 231-92-84), has small, time-worn double rooms for 426 Kčs ($36.10) with ugly green walls and large bathtubs in the private bathrooms. The advantage of this hotel, as its name suggests, is that it's right in the town center, just minutes from the Old Town Square.

Hotel U Haštala, Haštalská náměsti 16 (tel. 231-10-42), is a Class C hotel with an amazing location, just three minutes from the Old Town Square. This little-known hotel (it's never listed in the master list of hotels in Prague) has decent rooms for a C hotel. Unfortunately, the public spaces are not as well maintained. The corridor walls are plastered and not painted, and the public bathrooms are pretty sloppy; as such, we can only recommend this hotel to the most adventurous travelers who require little comfort. Singles are 154 Kčs ($13); doubles are 233 Kčs ($19.75) and triples run 337 Kčs ($28.55).

On Václavské náměsti

The **Grand Hotel Europa,** Václavské náměsti 25 (tel. 26-39-05), is one of Prague's most beautiful hotels, at a accessible price for the budget traveler. Here you get the flavor of a turn-of-the-century "grand hotel." The large rooms have old-style furniture such as wooden closets with mirrors on the doors and a bed partially recessed into the wall; the large bathrooms have huge tubs. The public space is also very ornate, with brass gates and fancy furniture, and there's a beautiful dining room in the restaurant downstairs. Not everything in the hotel is in top shape, however, and that's why the Grand has only a B* rating and a lower price. A single without bath is 230 Kčs ($19.45) and a double without bath costs 426 Kčs ($36.10). Many groups fill up this hotel, but every so often there are some spare rooms for individuals.

Adria, Václavské náměsti 26 (tel. 26-86-22), is an older Class B hotel with small rooms, some in need of painting and plastering. However, the rooms are well lit by day, and are quiet on the back side of the hotel. Bathless singles go for 162 Kčs ($13.70), and doubles cost 244 Kčs ($20.65).

The **Hotel Družba** ("Friendship"), Václavské náměsti 16 (tel. 24-05-16), is a somewhat rundown and used-looking B* hotel. The advantage and explanation of the high price is the prime location. Singles without bath are 203 Kčs ($17.20); doubles cost 305 Kčs ($25.80) without bath and 426 Kčs ($36.20) with.

Hotel Tatran, Václavské náměsti 22 (tel. 24-05-41), is a B* hotel similar to the Hotel Družba, perhaps slightly nicer, but also more expensive: singles with bathroom are 304 Kčs ($25.75) and doubles run 466 Kčs ($39.45).

East of Václavské náměsti and North of the Train Station

Hotel Palace, Panská 12 (tel. 26-83-41), is one block from the Václavské náměsti and four blocks from the train station. This is one of Prague's nicer B* hotels, and it has the kind of details—stained-glass windows and brass bannisters on the public stairs—that you associate with a top-class hotel. Singles cost 218 Kčs ($18.45) without bath, 259 Kčs ($21.95) with a shower, and 299 Kčs ($25.30) with a bath and toilet; doubles run 355 Kčs ($30) without bath, 395 Kčs ($33.45) with a shower, and 456 Kčs ($38.60) with bath and toilet. *Note:* These rates also include breakfast.

Hotel Hybernia, Hybernská 24 (tel. 22-04-31 or 22-04-32), is just minutes from the bus and train stations, and about a 10- to 15-minute walk from the Old Town Square. Here you'll find fair-sized, clean rooms with nice public bathrooms as well. Singles without bath are 162 Kčs ($13.70); doubles run 244 Kčs ($20.65) without bath, 305 Kčs ($25.80) with a shower, and 365 Kčs ($30.90) with a bathroom. The Hybernia is a highly recommended budget choice, but, unfortunately, it's often full with tour groups.

Just down the street from the Hybernia is the **Hotel Meteor,** Hybernská 6 (tel. 22-42-02), a standard Class B hotel that is slightly rundown but has clean public bathrooms. Singles without bath cost 218 Kčs ($18.45) and doubles with shower only run 305 Kčs ($25.80).

East of the Staré Město

Hotel Atlantic, Na poříči 9 (tel. 231-85-12), is a 10- to 15-minute walk from both the train station and the Old Town Square. All rooms have phones. The large singles are 162 Kčs ($13.70) without bath; doubles run 244 Kčs ($20.65) without bath and 365 Kčs ($30.90) with.

Hotel Centrum, Na poříči 31 (tel. 231-01-35), is not exactly in the center, but it is located on a major shopping street. Tram 5 takes you from here to the beginning of Václavské náměsti and the Můstek metro stop. The medium-sized Class B* rooms are 244 Kčs ($20.65) for a single with shower but no toilet; doubles cost 205 Kčs ($25.80) without bath, 365 Kčs ($30.90) with a shower, and 426 Kčs ($36.10) with a full bathroom.

Right across the street is the **Hotel Axa,** at Na poříči 40 (tel. 24-95-57), which has large bare rooms that are overpriced: singles cost 203 Kčs ($17.20) without bath and 284 Kčs ($24.05) with; doubles go for 305 Kčs ($25.80) without bathroom and 426 Kčs ($36.10) with. One American couple who stayed here told us that the staff was not as scrupulous in preparing the bill as one might hope.

Hotels Farther East

The **Hotel Opera,** Těšnov 13 (tel. 231-56-09), is a good budget hotel located on a noisy highway intersection, so try to get the courtyard rooms here. Singles are 162 Kčs ($13.70) without toilet and 244 Kčs ($20.65) with shower only; doubles run 244 Kčs ($20.65) without toilet and 365 Kčs ($30.90) with shower only. Use of the public showers costs 41 Kčs ($3.50). The public toilets are clean. Trams 133 and 207 along the river take you within a block of the Staroměstka metro stop.

Across the street is the similar **Hotel Merkur,** at Těšnov 9 (tel. 231-68-40), which has bathless singles for 162 Kčs ($13.70), doubles for 244 Kčs ($20.65), and triples for 305 Kčs ($25.80). Use of a public shower costs 41 Kčs ($3.50).

Hotels in the Nové Město

The **Hotel Moráň,** Na Moráňi 15 (tel. 29-42-53), is a good Class B hotel value, with clean, small modern rooms. There's also a helpful staff here. Singles cost 162 Kčs ($13.70) without bath, 244 Kčs ($20.65) with a shower; doubles go for 244 Kčs ($20.65) without bathroom and 276 Kčs ($23.35) with a shower. Use of the public shower costs 41 Kčs ($3.50). Trams 14, 15, and 24 are just two stops to the Václavské náměsti.

Hotel Ametyst, Makarenkova 11 (tel. 25-92-56), is a nice Class B hotel with quiet rooms and clean public bathrooms. The only drawback to the Ametyst is its residential neighborhood location: it's about a 10-minute walk to the I. P. Pavlova metro stop, or a 20- to 25-minute walk to the town center. Singles without bath are 162 Kčs ($13.70), and doubles cost 244 Kčs ($20.65).

The **Hotel Union,** Jaromirova 1 (tel. 43-78-58 or 43-78-59), is the most remote of the hotels in Nové Město, but trams 18 and 24 are only six stops from the Václavské náměsti. The rooms are of medium size, with old-style bumpy-glass windows. Bathless singles are 162 Kčs ($13.70), and doubles run 244 Kčs ($20.65). Use of the public showers cost 32 Kčs ($2.70). The Union is a decent budget hotel value if you don't mind taking the tram.

Near the I. P. Pavlova Metro Stop

The **Hotel Lunik,** 2 Vin. Londynska 50 (tel. 25-66-17 or 25-27-01), has small bare rooms, and the public bathrooms get only a "fair" rating. Even the concierge here admitted that the hotel is basic with "no comfort." Singles without bath cost 162 Kčs ($13.70) and doubles run 244 Kčs ($20.65). Showers cost 34 Kčs ($2.90). The Lunik is near both the námesti Miru and the I. P. Pavlova metro stops.

Hotel Krivář, náměsti I. P. Pavlova 5 (tel. 29-33-41), is a recommended budget hotel. Although it is now somewhat rundown, it looks as though it was once an elegant hotel. It also has a convenient location, right across the street from the I. P. Pavlova metro stop. Singles without bathroom run 174 Kčs ($14.75), or 256 Kčs ($21.70) with a bathtub but no toilet. Doubles are 268 Kčs ($22.70) without bath and 389 Kčs ($32.95) with tub only. Use of the public showers is 41 Kčs ($3.50) extra.

Hotel Beránek, Bělehradská 110 (tel. 25-45-44), just one block from the I.

P. Pavlova metro stop, is a B* hotel with a modern "socialist" lobby and long plain rooms. Singles are 203 Kčs ($17.20) without bath, 244 Kčs ($20.65) with shower, and 284 Kčs ($24) with complete bathroom. Double rooms with the same facilities cost 305 Kčs ($25.80), 365 Kčs ($30.90), and 426 Kčs ($36.10) respectively. Use of the public shower costs 50 Kčs ($4.25). The Beránek is a little overpriced and not up to the standards of the other Class B hotels, so you might look elsewhere for a Class B room first.

West of the Hradčany

The **Hotel Savoy**, at Keplerova 6 (no telephone), has an excellent location —just to the west of the Hradčany and at the top of the hill leading to the Malá Strana. This clean, well-run establishment offers double rooms without bath for 375 Kčs ($31.75) a night. With a quiet location, good service, and an English-speaking staff, the Savoy is often filled up.

South of the Malá Strana

The **Praga Hotel** is not in the best of condition, but its out-of-the-way location generally means that there are rooms available here. The dark, worn lobby has a gravel terrace behind it. The rooms and bathrooms are usable, but rundown and dark, though the beds are reasonably firm. Without a private bath, single rooms rent for 203 Kčs ($17.20) and doubles go for 285 Kčs ($24.15). While the large numbers of Russian tour groups generally don't go this far south, they have left the Praga to the tour groups of their Polish allies.

Starvation-Budget Hotels East of the Train Station and the Old Town

Národni Dŵm ("The People's House"), Bořivojova 53 (tel. 27-53-65), is the best of the area's Class C hotels. The building has an interesting, if worn, façade. The rooms are bare, but the public bathrooms are okay. Singles cost 122 Kčs ($10.35), doubles go for 203 Kčs ($17.20), and triples run 305 Kčs ($25.80). Use of the public showers costs 32 Kčs ($2.70) extra. Trams 9, 10, 21, and 26 pass within half a block of the hotel.

Hotel Ostaš, Orebitská 8 (tel. 27-28-60), is a used and battered-looking hotel with very basic rooms. The private bathrooms are borderline, and so this place is only for the young and adventurous. Singles cost 122 Kčs ($10.35), doubles run 203 Kčs ($17.20), and use of the public bath is 41 Kčs ($3.50). The Ostaš has the same tram connections as the Národni Dŵm.

BOTELS: As the name indicates, these are hotels in old river boats permanently tied to the riverbank. The *Albatros*, near the Staroměstské náměsti, and the *Racek* are on the east bank of the Vltava. The *Admirál* is just across the river from the Nové Město south of the Malá Strana. All are well maintained and quiet, though they tend to be slightly more expensive than their landlocked counterparts.

The *Admirál* **Botel**, on Hořejší nábřeži (tel. 54-86-85 or 54-74-45; Telex 123568), is reserved for Western tour groups, though sometimes they have a few extra rooms that they'll rent to individual tourists for short periods of time. The lobby is unspectacular but comfortable, with a nautically themed décor. The cabins are well maintained and cozy, though the showers are extremely small. The *Admirál* has only double cabins, with private showers, for 406 Kčs ($34.40) a night. There is a restaurant and a nightclub with a dance floor about the size of a large table. The cramped interior is offset by a very pleasant outdoor dining deck. The botel's location, about five minutes east of the Lidicka metro stop on the new line, or by tram 14 or 15 to Václavské námĕsti, is not the best, but it's quiet.

The *Albatros,* nábřeži Ludvika Svobody (tel. 231-36-34 or 231-36-06; Telex 121721), is a long boat that gently rocks in the river. The *Albatros* has small doubles with tiny bathrooms, and everything is in modern ship-shape. It's a fun hotel; make sure you get a room facing the river and not the parking lot. In July and August the rooms are sometimes hot and stuffy, however. It's just a ten-minute walk to the Old Town Square. Doubles cost 406 Kčs ($34.40). From December 18 to 29, the botel is closed so that the decks can be swabbed and the boat can be cleaned up.

The *Racek* ("Gull"), Podoli, Na Dvoreckelonce (tel. 42-60-51 to 42-60-55; Telex 122202RAC), is similar to Prague's other botels, except that it's not as near to the center as they are. (But Tram 21 quickly links you up with the center.) The area around the hotel is beautiful, and from the boat you can see swans, gulls, and boat races originating from the rowing club across the river. Upstairs is an attractive restaurant and bar on the terrace. Double rooms with bathrooms cost 400 Kčs ($33.90).

ROOM-FINDING SERVICES: At Cestovni Kancelař, U Obecniho Domu 2, a little sidestreet off námĕsti Republiky about a ten-minute walk from the train station, **Pragotour** (tel. 231-72-00, 231-72-34, or 231-72-81) has private rooms at 108 Kčs ($9.15) for a single and 155 Kčs ($13.10) for a double—but there is a three-night minimum. Most of the rooms are located outside the city center, but are easily accessible by public transportation. Pragotour can also find you an inexpensive hotel room for one or two nights. If you want to make sure you'll get a room, reserve ahead of time by mail (July to September is the most crowded time). The office is open Monday through Friday from 7:30 a.m. to 9:45 p.m., on Saturday to 8 p.m., and on Sunday to 3:25 p.m. (from December to February the office is open Monday through Saturday from 7:30 a.m. to 7 p.m.; closed Sunday). Try to arrive early—the line for private rooms seems to grow according to the lateness in the day.

Just around the corner from the main Čedok office, about a five-minute walk from the train station at Panská ulice 5, is the **Čedok Accommodation Office** (tel. 22-56-57, 22-60-17, or 22-70-04), open from 9 a.m. until shortly before 5 p.m. From May to September there's a three-night minimum for private rooms. As with Pragotour, rooms are mostly in residential areas (such as Districts 4 and 10). Čedok can also help you find a hotel room, but they usually work with the more expensive hotels, so you're best off going to Pragotour or on your own.

This Čedok office has some of the more unsympathetic types we encountered in Czechoslovakia. By no means accept any verdict from this office as final. Also, you might be accosted outside the office by pensioners offering private rooming deals. Use judgment, but usually these offers are on the level.

FINDING PRIVATE ROOMS ON YOUR OWN: Since there is a large influx of socialist visitors to Prague we have listed most of the budget accommodations, but in Prague private rooms are certainly an option. There are many people who rent out a room in their house. Usually these accommodations are excellent and inexpensive, but since such dealings are done unofficially you must exercise some caution. If a hotel is full, ask the proprietor if he or she knows of someone willing to rent out a room. Always look at the rooms before you accept, but overwhelmingly we found that private rooms are a good bet. These unofficial rooms should cost around 100 Kčs ($8.45), with 10 Kčs (85¢) or so to whoever helped you find it. Remember that if you are staying in private accommodations, you will have to register with the police (see "Police" in Section 6, "The ABCs of Prague").

3. Dining on a Budget

In Prague you can eat in all but one or two of the finest restaurants and still remain comfortably within your budget. There are three main areas where you'll find the most restaurants: the Staré Město, the Malá Strana, and the Hradčany. There are many other good restaurants in other areas, but these three districts have the greatest concentrations.

DINING IN STARÉ MĚSTO: The Staré Město is a veritable maze of twisting cobblestone streets with basement restaurants and small, unmarked beer halls. Street addresses for some of the establishments included here are of limited value. You'll have to explore with a map and ask directions, but be assured that if you miss one place you'll be almost certain of finding another where the food is just as delicious and the beers just as large as the place you were looking for.

The **U Červéncho Kolá** ("At the Red Wheel"), at Anezska 808/802 (tel. 231-89-41), has several small intimate dining rooms with white vaulted ceilings. A quiet place with only two or three tables in a room, the U Červéncho Kolá is the perfect place for a tête-à-tête or small party. There is also an appealing garden out back for fair-weather dining. The specialties are beefsteak with mushrooms for 66.50 Kčs ($5.65) and beefsteak with cranberries for 68.50 Kčs ($5.80). Come to the U Červéncho for a relaxed lunch, though it's best to reserve for dinner. Open from 10 a.m. until 10 p.m.; closed Monday.

Just south of the Staroměstské náměsti, at Spálená 41, is the **Vinarna U Šupů** (tel. 29-93-10), an intimate, very relaxed place featuring some Chinese-style Czech dishes. This is definitely the place where upwardly mobile loving couples come to coo to the soft strains of '50s-style romantic tunes. The prices are reasonable: 25.60 Kčs ($2.15) for Pekingské-maso (pork with vegetables), and 27 Kčs ($2.30) for švej-ča-žou (veal in a wine sauce). The U Šupů is a pleasant change from the more bustling Czech beer factory.

The **U Pinkasů,** at Jungmannovo náměsti 15 (tel. 26-18-04), is a good, cheap beer bar with one or two very solid blue-plate specials for around 13 Kčs ($1.10). A few of the waiters can actually speak some English, but not because they get many tourists. Workers, soldiers, and rowdy students meet here to exercise their drinking arms in this genuine local bar. The U Pinkasů is a place where you can buy a liter of beer (6.30 Kčs or 55¢) for less than six ounces of mineral water, and find good company to drink with.

Just minutes from the Old Town Square you'll find **U Golema,** at Maislova 8 (tel. 26-18-98). Perhaps the most distinctive feature of U Golema is its subdued, quiet ambience, making it popular with couples and European visitors. Dark-wood walls and ceilings and one white stucco wall make up the attractive interior; subdued lighting adds to the romantic flavor. The limited menu features carp, trout, and several beef dishes for 22 Kčs ($1.85) to 42 Kčs ($3.55). They also serve delicious crispy french fries.

U Anežky, areál Anežského Kláštera 12 (St. Agnes Convent) (tel. 231-42-51, ext. 35), is a moderately priced restaurant with a modern wood interior located a few minutes from the Old Town Square (walk up Dlouhá street on the northeast corner of the square). The specialty here is the "Monk's Pocket," a dish of cheese and sausage wrapped in a pork cutlet. The service is friendly and efficient; there are also tables for two here, so you don't have to worry that others may join you during your meal. It's open from 11 a.m. to 11 p.m.; closed Monday. Warm meals are served only till 8:15 p.m.

For a typical regional lunch, consider **Staropražská Rychta,** Václavské náměsti 5 (tel. 22-13-51), a lively German-Czech cellar restaurant on Prague's main street. Cheerful waiters serve specialties such as goose or duck for 43.90 Kčs ($3.70) or pork cutlet Bohemia with mushrooms and cream sauce for 38.50 Kčs ($3.25). You don't need to make reservations at Staropražská Rychta; you'll just be seated at free places at one of the hall's long tables. Service is from 11:30 a.m. to 11 p.m. seven days a week.

Theater-goers frequent **Klášterni Vinária,** at Národni 8 (tel. 29-48-63), located just a block from the National Theater. Although much of the restaurant appears somewhat faded, some elegance from years past continues to shine through, such as the chandeliers on the ceilings. The typical Czech specialties cost 17 Kčs ($1.45) to 49 Kčs ($4.15). For dessert, don't miss the rich palačinky pancakes served with jam, peaches, and whipped cream. Open from 11 a.m. to 2 a.m.

An Italian Restaurant

If one of these evenings you feel that you want a change of pace, consider the **Viola Trattoria,** Národni tr. 7 (tel. 26-67-32). This small restaurant features roughly stuccoed white walls and a relaxed Mediterranean atmosphere. The menu, with several pasta dishes for 14.60 Kčs ($1.25) to 20.10 Kčs ($1.70), is written in Czech and Italian. Although the fare may not be totally authentic, it does provide a nice change from the homogeneous fare of Prague's restaurants. It's open from 11:30 a.m. to 3 p.m. and 5:30 to 11 p.m.

A Wine Cellar

U Zlaté Konvice, Melantrichova 20 (tel. 26-21-28 or 26-21-17), is a wine cellar far beneath the ground, but not far from the Old Town Square. Here you go down past cold stone walls and tall ceilings lit by candles; finally you arrive at the cavernous dining area where beer barrels separate the tables. In this eerie atmosphere there is cimbalom music—for which you must pay a 10-Kčs (85¢) music charge. This restaurant serves only cold food and wine, so it's good for a snack or after-dinner relaxing. Open from 5 p.m. to 2 a.m.

Splurge Choices

Not far from the railroad station at Washingtonova 19 (tel. 22-52-52) is the **Hotel Esplanade restaurant.** The black-jacketed waiters will seat you and tempt you with a well-laden platter of hors d'oeuvres. You can begin the meal with the delicious stuffed mushrooms for 21.50 Kčs ($1.80) or the lobster cocktail for 27.90 Kčs ($2.35). For the main course there's a fine duck with dumplings for 50 Kčs ($4.25) or succulent veal with vegetables for 86.90 Kčs ($7.35). For the light eater there's a very tasty chicken-liver omelet at 18.30 Kčs ($1.55). A huge Morano-style glass chandelier dominates the black-marble columned dining room. The restaurant Esplanade is open from noon to 3 p.m. for lunch and from 6 to 10 p.m. for dinner.

Opera Grill, Divadelni 24 (tel. 26-55-08), is a cozy restaurant that seats only 24 people in an atmosphere reminiscent of an elite club of the 1920s or 1930s in Europe. There are ornate chairs and old porcelain pieces over a small fireplace. After 8 p.m. a pianist plays classical Czech music. The delicious specialty is "steak à la kitchen chef," a beef dish with asparagus and mushrooms, french fries, and vegetables, for 94.50 Kčs ($8). This is an elegant place to spend a leisurely evening out. The grill is open from 7 p.m. to 2 a.m.; closed Saturday and Sunday. You must reserve.

For Prague's most charming view, dine at the **Zlata Praha,** located on the eighth floor of the Intercontinental Hotel at náměsti Curieových 5 (tel. 28-99, ext. 824). As you eat, you can admire beautiful vistas of Prague's rooftops and spires through the restaurant's large windows, a sight especially dramatic at sundown. The menu features both international and Czech specialties, with a large selection of fish, pork, veal, and steak. Zlata Praha is one of Prague's most expensive restaurants and the service is slow, but the great view makes this a worthwhile splurge.

MALÁ STRANA:
The Malá Strana, on the west bank of the Vltava, is the second-oldest part of Prague. The district extends from the Vltava River up the hill to the foot of the Hrad (castle). While small, it has a great number of excellent restaurants and beer halls scattered throughout its winding streets and staircases.

Practically in the park, the **Lobkovická Vinarna,** at Vlássaka 17 (tel. 53-01-85), is one of the better restaurants in Prague. As officers' quarters, the 200-year-old building once shook to the tramp of imperial boots. Now the subdued lighting and the cosmopolitan English-speaking headwaiter complement the excellent food. A limited but very appealing menu is offered. Try the trout miller's style, grilled with buttered potatoes and fresh asparagus, for 34.50 Kčs ($2.90), or the thick beefsteak for 54.60 Kčs ($4.60). Perhaps before the meal you might wish to try some of the delicious locally grown mushrooms, served in a variety of ways for 15 Kčs ($1.25). The owner gets a full-flavored wine from a small vineyard at Melnik, where the Vltava (Moldau) and the Elbe meet. The Lobkovická is recommended.

Almost at the top of the hill is the **U Černého Vola** ("Black Ox"), on Loretánské náměsti (tel. 53-86-37). An old-fashioned beer hall with long wooden tables and benches, it also has a good selection of local wines and even some Russian champagne. Only cold snacks are served, so come here to quench your thirst after a hard day's sightseeing. The building was built in the 1500s though the pictures of beer steins and hunting horns on the walls were painted by a local only about ten years ago. At 6 Kčs (50¢) for a half liter of Czechoslovakia's finest brew, the U Černého Vola upholds the Prague beer-hall tradition of "the best for less."

Never fear if the hill seems too steep to climb. If you can make it to Nerudova 29 you'll have made it to **U Bonaparta,** one of the better beer bars in the Malá Strana. Napoleon may not have visited this establishment, but he could have used some of the excellent homemade grog—for 7.60 Kčs (65¢)—on his Russian adventure. If you tire of the beer for less than 6 Kčs (50¢) a half liter, then try some of the wine for 3.60 Kčs (30¢) a glass.

For those with a sweet tooth, the café **Malostranská,** at Malostranské náměsti 28 (tel. 53-94-24), serves a variety of pastries and ice cream as well as cold snacks. There are cold fruit drinks and wine, but no beer. The Malostranská Kavárna is a pleasant place for a mid-morning refresher or an afternoon rendezvous over wine. The ice cream is some of Prague's best, according to the five-year-old resident expert we interviewed.

A Splurge

Right under the tower on the west (Hradčany) side of the Charles Bridge (Karlův most) is the well-appointed **U Tří Pštrosu** restaurant, at Dražickétio náměsti 12 (tel. 53-61-51/2/3/4/5). The fine paneled interior and handsome fittings make the U Tří Pštrosu one of Prague's more elegant dining establishments. To begin the meal, the black-jacketed waiters will offer a tray of delicious hors d'oeuvres for about 20 Kčs ($1.70) for three pieces. The lunch entrees include a flavorful stuffed veal and asparagus for 28 Kčs ($2.35), or, if you have a hearty appetite, the beefsteak with dumplings for 31 Kčs ($2.60). In the evenings reservations are a must; lunchtimes are more relaxed and less crowded. The waiters speak English, and the food and service are excellent.

HRADČANY: The Hradčany area includes Loretánská street and the maze of streets to the west of the castles. Tucked away behind ministries and in little medieval buildings, the Hradčany has some delightful restaurants. Rather than walk back down to the Malá Strana or over to the Staré Město, wander west from the castle up Loretánská street.

On the more expensive side, the **U Zlaté Hrušky,** located behind the Hrad on Nový Svět 3 (New World street) (tel. 53-11-33), is one of the "in" restaurants in Prague, so reservations are a must. The restaurant's name has existed for more then 300 years though it has been located in this part of Prague for only the last 200, specializing in wild game and Moravian wines. You won't escape for less than 50 Kčs ($4.25) to 60 Kčs ($5.10) per person for a meal here. Cool in the summer, the thick-walled U Zlaté Hrušky is set in one of the city's most charming medieval sections. It's open all week from 6 p.m. till midnight, and is highly recommended.

FARTHER AFIELD: The Čínská restaurant, at Vodičkova 19 (tel. 26-26-97), is one of Prague's better specialty restaurants. Officially a Chinese restaurant, the decor is a curious, yet somehow pleasing, combination of the Orient and Bohemia. Carved-wood and cloth lamps shed soft light on the plush upholstered chairs. The duck with almonds for 50.90 Kčs ($4.30), the filet of carp for 25.80 Kčs ($2.20), and the roast chicken and rice for 26.90 Kčs ($2.30) are a few of the restaurant's specialties. The waiters speak English and the food is well prepared, though not, strictly speaking, Chinese. Despite the Czech cooks in the kitchen the Čínská is a nice break from Central European–style cooking.

If you're willing to venture outside the immediate center of Prague, **Myslivna,** on Jagellonská in District 5 (tel. 27-62-09 or 27-22-11), is an excellent choice. The restaurant features game on its menu and also on its walls, where you can admire a boar's head, horns, and furs. Enjoy such specialties such as venison pie for 9.80 Kčs (85¢), stag goulash for 27.50 Kčs ($2.35), and pheasant braised with bacon and stewed in red cabbage for 21.20 Kčs ($1.80). Fortunately, all of these exotic specialties are clearly listed on an English-language menu. Open from 11 a.m. to 11 p.m.; it's best to always reserve. You'll find Myslivna a five-minute walk from the Flora metro stop.

Originally a brewery from 1459, **U Fleků,** at Křemencova 11, is today Prague's most famous beer hall. Restorations have tried to create such details of the past as a decorated medieval wood ceiling in one room or a courtyard surrounded by columns in another area. U Fleků still produces its own beer, but it only makes enough to service its own restaurant, so you're in for a unique treat. In the large courtyard and several indoor rooms, guests eat and drink, many doing little of the former and much of the latter. The enthusiasm for U Fleků beer leaves many guests with a distinct glaze over their eyes. The cuisine served here is undistinguished. Open from 9 a.m. to 11 p.m. Tram 21 reaches the restaurant from Václavské náměsti.

As you walk into **U Pastýřky,** at Bělehradská 15 in District 4 (tel. 43-40-93), you might feel as though you're in West Virginia, with the log cabin walls and dried corn and other rustic objects on the walls. In reality, this is a good Czech restaurant with a high reputation among Prague locals. The moderately priced dishes here are tasty and tender, and the waiters are efficient as well. In the main dining room there is cimbalom music, for which you pay 10 Kčs (85¢) extra in the evening. It's open Monday through Saturday from 3 p.m. to 1 a.m.; closed

Sunday. Take tram 11 from behind the National Museum at the end of Václavské náměsti.

One of Prague's most popular restaurants is **U Kalicha,** Na Bojišti 12 in District 2 (tel. 29-60-17). In fiction, U Kalicha is visited by the Good Soldier Schweik in the novel of the same name by the Czech writer Jaroslav Hašek. In commemoration of this often-read novel, the walls boast drawings of characters from the book. Another novelty here is the orchestrion at the side of the main room, a seven-foot-high music box that plays the same piece of martial music over and over again as you eat. The music, drawings, and good wine and beer translate into a very lively crowd, which gets louder as the evening goes on. The kitchen at U Kalicha features traditional Czéch specialties, always tasty; entrees cost $2 to $4. We highly recommend that you visit at least one lively restaurant like U Kalicha during your stay in Prague. Open from 11 a.m. to 11 p.m., it's just a few minutes from the I. P. Pavlova metro stop.

As salads are rare, places that serve them are gems. The **Grill-Bar,** upstairs from the Můstek metro station (Line A), at the beginning of Václavské náměsti, is a Western-style café-restaurant which has a pseudo–salad bar offering tomatoes, cucumbers, peppers, and onions, with Italian dressing. Such salads are free with a rather inexpensive meal. The atmosphere and music attract a younger crowd (early to mid 20s).

DINING MISCELLANY: For starvation-budget diners, there are several self-service restaurants, called **Automat Samoobsluha,** on Václavské náměsti. The food at these places is average, but it's quick and inexpensive.

For a delicious American-style breakfast with ham and eggs for 20 Kčs ($1.70), go to the **Intercontinental Hotel** on the first floor at náměsti Curieových 5.

On the hill coming down from the Prague castle to the Charles Bridge at Gorkeho 11 is a fine cafeteria-style **pastry shop,** good for snacks at all hours. It's open Monday through Friday from 7 a.m. to 6 p.m., on weekends to noon.

The best **ice cream** we've found in Prague is at Vodičkova 4. Try the rich tartufo sundae with vanilla and chocolate ice cream with nuts, coconut, and raisins for 9.30 Kčs (80¢). A welcome rich, creamy treat after a full day of touring!

4. What to See

The flames of war have not been seen in Prague for hundreds of years; the city stands virtually intact from the 17th century. The Staré Město (Old City), on the east bank of the Vltava River, is one of the largest and most beautiful in all of Europe. In the Staré Město are the twin-towered Charles Bridge, Týn Church, and the Old Town Hall. There is the magnificent Hradčany (castle district), including St. Vitus Cathedral that dominates the skyline on the west bank of the Vltava, plus the St. Nicholas Church and the old university buildings as well as literally hundreds of other architecturally important structures.

There are two points that might logically begin any tour of Prague. The Staroměstské náměsti (Old City Square) in the heart of the Staré Město, and the Hradčanské náměsti (Castle Hill Square) in the very center of the Hradčany (castle district). Between these two points lie most of Prague's important sights. We suggest that you start at the Hrad and work your way down the hill. Also, on the first day you might spend most of your time walking, familiarizing yourself with the sights and simply enjoying the city. On the succeeding days, work in as many museums as you have time and energy for. In Prague, if you feel an itch, scratch it. If a street calls to be explored, explore it. If a restaurant door stands invitingly ajar, peek in to see if they're open. In Prague, do as the Praguers do and follow your heart.

HRADČANY: The very first thing that rivets the eye when you arrive, the Hradčany (castle district) is like a natural magnet for the tourist in Prague. The third oldest of Prague's districts, the first settlement arose on the hill in 1320. Charles IV considerably expanded and fortified it, though it was severely damaged by fire in 1541. Rudolf II rebuilt and again expanded the Hradčany in the early 17th century. Throughout the next 100 years the district was rebuilt in the baroque style, but it has not been significantly altered since then. To the west, behind the Hradčany, was the once poor quarter, Nový Swět (New World). Today its 16th- to 19th-century buildings form one of Prague's most charming old neighborhoods.

The array of spires belong to several important buildings: the Hrad (Prague Castle), the Cathedral of St. Vitus, the Summer Palace of Queen Anne (the Belvedere), the Archbishop's Palace, the Šternbek Palace, and the Loretto Palace. The **Cathedral of St. Vitus** (Katedrála sv. Vitá) is the largest of all Prague's churches. The Gothic cathedral that stands here today was begun in 1344 by Charles IV. He commissioned the famous architect Matthias of Arras to oversee the construction. But Matthias died before work was completed and Charles IV entrusted the cathedral to the then-unknown Peter Parler from the small German town of Gmünd. Most of the cathedral was completed under Parler, except for some of the façade and towers. Under the cathedral are the only remnants of the original 10th-century structure which contains the tomb of Charles IV as well as several other Czech kings. At the south end of the cathedral is the Chapel of St. Wenceslas, founded in 1362–1367 on the site of the saint's grave. The lower part of the chapel is encrusted with over 1,300 pieces of amethyst and jasper. The upper part is decorated with paintings from the middle of the 14th and 16th centuries depicting the life of the saint. The tomb of St. Wenceslas also dates from the 14th century, and the nearby ragstone statue of the saint was done by Parler's nephew, Henry, in 1373. Underneath this part of the cathedral is the royal treasury, with the fabulous gold crown of St. Wenceslas, weighing over four pounds.

The site of the **Hrad**, or **Royal Palace complex,** has long been the residence of Bohemian nobles. The cellar and parts of the ground floor are from Prince Sobĕslav's 12th-century palace. Built of timber, Sobĕslav's palace was replaced by the single story of the palace of Charles IV. At the end of the 15th century, following the Hussite Wars, the Polish King Vladislav Jagellon began the reconstruction and expansion of the Hrad. The Vladislav Hall (1486–1502) is the centerpiece of the palace. On special occasions, such as coronations, the knights would bring their chargers up here and stage jousting tournaments—tilting lance to lance right here in the hall! Through the northern portal is the Diet, where the king's advisors met and the supreme court was held. After 1918 it was also where Czechoslovakia's presidents were inaugurated. One floor down is the Bohemian Chancellery, best known as the site of the Second Defenestration. In 1618 two Imperial governors and their secretary were thrown out the window by enraged Bohemian nobles. They survived, but this affront to Imperial power let loose armies all across the European continent. For the next 30 years the bloodletting known as the Thirty Years' War (1618–1648) continued.

Across from the Royal Palace is the **Royal Summer Palace or Belvedere** (Královský letohrádek). Built in 1538–1563 for Queen Anne, wife of Ferdinand I, it is a remarkably pure example of Italian Renaissance architecture. The palace was used by the Swedes when they occupied Prague in 1648 at the close of the Thirty Years' War. The Swedes chose the Belvedere for its beauty, and were so taken with it that when they left they dragged as much of the interior as they could back north with them. The Renaissance garden is also a wonder, with the Singing Fountain (Zpívající fountánou) in the very center. Designed by the Italian Francesco Terzio and cast in bronze by Tomáš Jaroš of Brno in 1563–1568, the fountain makes delicate music as the water gently drips into the basin below.

The **Archibishop's Palace** (Arcibiskupský palác), at Hradčanské náměsti 16, is a baroque building with the façade redone in rococo style in the mid 17th century. Inside is an excellent collection of exotic tapestries woven in Paris between 1753 and 1756. The **Šternberk Palace** (Šternberský palác), next door, houses the **National Gallery.** The **Schwarzenberg Palace** (Schwarzenberské palác) today houses the Swiss Embassy and the **Military History Museum.**

Of all the later palaces, the most interesting is the **Loretto Palace** (Loreta), at Loretánské náměsti 7. Loretto is a town in Italy where the dwelling of the Virgin Mary was brought by angels from Palestine in the 13th century. After the Hapsburgs beat the Bohemians at the battle of White Mountain in 1620, the Loretto cult was chosen as the device for the re-Catholicization of Bohemia. More than 50 copies of the Loretto church were built, the most famous being this one in Prague, built between 1626 and 1750. The Prague master clockmaker, Peter Naumann, fashioned a complicated set of bells that can play several different melodies at once. The interior was done completely by Italian masters under the supervision of Giovanni Battista Orsi de Como, who completed it in 1631. The Loretto Treasury has a major collection of fabulous 17th- and 18th-century jewelry. The most impressive item in the treasury is a Viennese chalice (1699) of gold-plated silver and studded with over 6,200 diamonds.

Leading down to the river is the **Golden Lane** (Zlatá Ulička), so named because it was believed Rudolf II's alchemists transmuted lead into gold here. Actually, the castle gunners and goldsmiths made their homes in this curious narrow lane.

MALÁ STRANA:
Just down the hill from the Hradčány is Prague's second-oldest quarter, the Malá Strana (Lower Town). Founded by Ottokar II in 1257, the Malá Strana is perched on the hillside and was always a rich section of town. Damaged once, in the fighting between local Bohemians in the Malá Strana and the Imperials in the Hrad in 1419, it has remained basically intact since the 16th century. After the battle of White Mountain (1620) the Hapsburgs moved in and built many of the beautiful baroque buildings—at the expense of the equally beautiful Renaissance Bohemian structures—that are here today. If the practically uninterrupted rows of 17th-century baroque buildings are not enough, the Malá Strana is blessed with many formal gardens. These terraced gardens are a rarity in Europe and are truly extraordinary. Wander through the beautiful stairwells and narrow lanes or rest in the beautiful **Lobkovicova Zahrada park** above the town. In this park you have the Malá Strana and the rest of Prague spread out below with the Hrad towering above.

The principal sights of the Malá Strana are the **Church of St. Nicholas** (Chrám sv. Mikuláše) and the Wallenstein Palace (Valdštejnský palác). As the Cathedral of St. Vitus represents Gothic architecture in Prague so does the Church of St. Nicholas, on Malostranské náměsti, represent the pinnacle of the baroque Counter-Reformation. One of the most opulent baroque structures extant, it was begun in 1703 and work continued for almost 60 years (1760). The ceiling fresco of St. Nicholas by J. L. Kracker, took nine years to complete. Covering almost 4,275 square feet, it's one of the largest single frescos in Europe.

The **Wallenstein Palace**, at Valdštejnské náměsti 4, was the first baroque palace in Prague. It was built in 1624–1630 for a dubious nobleman, Albrecht Václav Eusebius of Wallenstein. Initially in the Protestant army, he betrayed his comrades and went into the service of Ferdinand. Under the Hapsburgs he amassed a vast fortune from the confiscated property of his former comrades. Titled and honored by the emperor, he began secret negotiations with the Protestant Swedish armies to depose the Catholic Hapsburg emperor and gain the crown himself. The emperor got wind of this plan and had Wallenstein assassinated in Cleb in 1634. Wallenstein spared no expense in his desire to rival the palace up the hill. A virtual galaxy of Italian masters worked on his palace at one time or another. The work of Baccio de Bianco can be seen in the main hall, covering two stories; its size is further heightened by mirrored windows. Bianco depicted Albrecht of Wallenstein as Mars, the god of war, in a triumphal chariot. The portrait says it all—nasty as he may have been, he had style.

THE CHARLES BRIDGE: The symbol of Prague, the Charles Bridge (Karlův most) is the oldest standing bridge in the city. Commissioned by Charles IV, work began in 1357 under the supervision of Parler and was not completed until the end of the century. Almost 1,500 feet long and 30 feet wide, the bridge is built of sandstone blocks and is designed both as a major thoroughfare and as an aspect of the city's defense; hence the two towers at either end. The bridge became one of the focal points of life in Prague—a marketplace, a lawcourt, a theater, and even tournaments were organized on the bridge. Here, in 1620, the crushed remnants of the Bohemian army retreated across it after the debacle at White Mountain; 18 years later the heavily armored Swedes shot and hacked their way across to finally occupy the former Imperial bastion of the Hrad. In the late 17th century the wonderful baroque statues that adorn the sides were added; the most recent addition was in 1938. Notice the odd contrast between the luxuriant baroque statuary and the severe Gothic lines of the bridge itself.

STARÉ MĚSTO: The oldest section of Prague, the Staré Město (appropriately enough, the Old Town) emerged sometime in the 10th century, situated at the site of a good fording point. A hundred years later it included a Jewish settlement and a German merchant quarter. In A.D. 965 the Arab-Jewish chronicler Ibrahim Ibn Jacob spoke of the Staré Město as a busy, growing trading center where food and goods were inexpensive. By the turn of the next century Prague was permanently on the map, with numerous public buildings and a stone bridge across the Vltava (Moldau). In 1338 the town was granted a charter and in 1348 Charles IV founded the city's first university. The Staré Město increased in importance with the Hussite Wars and continued to be the dominant section of the city until the Bohemian defeat at the hands of the Hapsburgs at the battle of White Mountain.

The **Powder Tower** (Prašná brána), on náměsti Republiky, is the late Gothic masterpiece of Matěj Rejsek, built in honor of the Polish King Vladislav Jagellon, who in 1475 brought peace in the wake of the Hussite Wars. This was originally an important gateway and a crucial part of the Staré Město's defense system. At the end of the 17th century it was used as a powderhouse, from which it gets its name. The **Old Town Square** (Staroměstské náměsti) was a marketplace and center of the Staré Město for over 1,000 years. It was here in 1621 that the mass execution of Czech rebel leaders took place. Occupying the center of the square is the monument to Jan Hus, who was burned at the stake in 1415. It was unveiled in 1915 to mark the anniversary of his death.

The largest structure by far on the square is the **Týn Church.** Founded in 1365 on the site of several earlier churches, the Týn Church had numerous alterations over the course of centuries; the fantastic towers were added in the second half of the 15th century, and there are pieces of the church by Parler,

Rejsek, and others. The Týn Church was where Jan Hus first heard the fiery reform oratory of Konrád Waldhauser and Jan Milíč that led to his struggle with the Roman Catholic church. The Týn Church was long the bastion of Hussite religion (until 1621). Of historical interest is the tomb of the famous astronomer Tycho de Brahe (1601), next to the high altar.

Prague once had a thriving Jewish community. During World War II the population was deported to concentration camps, leaving the old buildings of the **Jewish Ghetto** intact but empty. Perhaps the most famous is the **Old-New Synagogue** (Staronová synagóga), on Cervena ulice. No one is quite certain where the name comes from, but it's the oldest synagogue in Europe and one of the oldest Gothic structures in Prague (1270). Nearby is the **State Jewish Museum** and **Jewish Town Hall,** where there is a kosher commissary for Prague's few remaining Orthodox Jews. At the edge of the Ghetto, where Maisel and Karp streets intersect, a bronze cast of Franz Kafka commemorates the writer's birth here in 1883. Perhaps the saddest remnant of the once-thriving Jewish community is the **Old Jewish Cemetery,** on U starého hřbitova, the oldest Jewish cemetery to survive World War II: the earliest known gravestone is dated April 25, 1439. It marks the grave of the poet Abigdor Karo, who witnessed the pogrom of 1389 and wrote an elegy for the victims. There are an estimated 12,000 graves, in places over 12 deep. The multitude of gravestones arrayed so close together creates a powerful and lasting impression.

One of Prague's most important sights is the **Bethlehem Chapel** (Betlémská kaple), on Betlémské náměsti. Here, in 1402, Jan Hus began to preach his revolutionary ideas. The church remained a center of revolutionary activity and was extensively rebuilt in the mid 16th century. Following the battle of White Mountain the Jesuits bought the chapel. In 1786 the chapel was practically demolished and turned into an apartment building. After World War II a painstaking and extensive restoration was begun under the direction of architect Jaroslav Fragner.

MORE PRAGUE ACTIVITIES: Near the Prague Castle, you can see **historical fencing and medieval battles** between two men at 2 and 4 p.m. on select days. Many children go and enjoy the show as there is some dialogue (in Czech) and joking around. Look for signs on the street in front of the Prague Castle (called Loretánská street) posted on days of the performances.

It's interesting to visit a large **department store** here to see what the locals can and cannot buy. Try the large Prior store on náměsti Republiky, open Monday to Wednesday and Friday from 8 a.m. to 7 p.m., on Thursday to 8 p.m. and on Saturday to 2 p.m.

5. Evenings in Prague

"Prague nightlife—in comparison with most other European capitals—is of a more serious cast," ominously states the official guidebook to Prague. Actually, while things are not as lively as other capitals, there is a lot happening—and not all of it is serious. The number of discos and nightclubs is limited and the closing hours are much earlier than in the United States, usually around midnight or 1 a.m.

TICKETS AND INFORMATION: For the latest happenings around town, you can check at either one of the two **Sluna offices,** which handle most bookings for concerts, film, and theater. The office at Panská 4 (tel. 22-12-06) is right next to the Čedok Accommodations Office, in the rear right-hand side of the arcade; it's open from 9 a.m. until 6 p.m. weekdays. The other is in the Alfa Promenade, Václavské námĕsti 28 (tel. 26-16-02), open Monday to Friday from 9 a.m. until 5 p.m., with a break from noon to 1 p.m.

There is also a program **"Pruehled Kulturnich Pořadu v Praze"** for 2.50 Kčs (20¢), which has fairly comprehensive listings, in Czech, of theaters, film, galleries, clubs, new bands, etc. The "Přehled Kulturnich" is available at most newsstands, Interhotels, and at the two Sluna bureaus. There is also a publication called *Prague Cultural Summer '87*. Published in English, it's not always easy to find; try at the Sluna offices or at Čedok.

FILM: One film event that the Sluna offices do not sell tickets for is the **Magic Lantern,** a very popular multimedia production incorporating recorded images and song, along with live performances. You can only purchase tickets directly from the theater at Národni 40 (tel. 26-00-33).

CONCERTS AND OPERA: Of all the cultural events Prague has to offer, the classical concerts are perhaps the best. Czech opera, on the other hand, is not always captivating; it can be long and is sometimes underproduced. During the summer there are a number of cultural events held in Prague, including concerts in the Hrad. There are no hard-and-fast rules for performances, so often you'll have to take your chances. In no case will you have to pay more than $7 for good seats, and usually around $3 or $4.

NIGHTLIFE: For all its glory by day, Prague doesn't have much of a nightlife. It picks up a bit in summer, but is pretty dead the rest of the year. On the whole, people in Prague are well adapted to the philosophy "early to bed, early to rise." Still, in all fairness, there are a few worthwhile places to go:

Zlata Husa, at Václavské námĕsti 7 (tel. 214-31-20), is Prague's most appealing disco. Here a 20- to 30-year-old crowd enjoys a small dance floor with floor lights and a video playing. Off to the side are tables and seats. It's open from 7:30 p.m. to 2:30 a.m., and reservations are necessary. No jeans or sneakers are allowed.

The three hotels—the **Admirál,** on Hořejší nábřeži (tel. 54-86-85 or 54-74-45); the **Albatros,** nábřeži Ludvika Svobody (tel. 231-36-06 or 231-36-34); and the **Racek,** Podoli, Na Dvoreckelonce (tel. 42-60-51 to 42-60-55)—have small but popular discos.

CKD is a popular student disco at Na mŭstku 9, open from 9 p.m. to 4 a.m., and the **Klub U Konica,** at Staromĕstské námĕsti 20 (tel. 29-96-84), is a student club which sometimes has a disco and other times a theater production, etc. Either call or check in the "Přehled Kulturnich Pořadů v Praze."

Jazzklub Parknas, at Národni 25 (tel. 26-20-65), open from 9 p.m. to 1 a.m., has frequent jazz concerts. Check the posters on Prague's walls or in the Sluna offices.

6. The ABCs of Prague

BATHS: There are some well-run and spotlessly clean showers in the lower level of Prague's main railroad station (Praha hlavní nádraži), open from 8 a.m. to 8 p.m. A shower plus a clean towel costs less than $1. The station is about a 15-minute walk from the Staromĕstské námĕsti (Old City Square), or one stop north from the Muzeum metro station.

EMBASSIES AND CONSULATES: The **U.S. Embassy** is in Prague at Tržištĕ 15 (tel. 53-66-41). The **Canadian Embassy** in Prague is at Mickiewiczova 6 (tel. 32-69-41), and the **British Embassy** is at Thunozska 14 (tel. 53-33-47).

EMERGENCY: For the police, call 158; for an ambulance, call 155.

GUIDES: If you want to hire a private guide, go to the PIS office at Panská 4 (tel. 22-34-11, 22-43-11, 22-60-67, or 22-61-36). Give them a few hours' notice and later that day you'll have a private guide for 25 Kčs ($2.10) an hour.

LOST AND FOUND: There is a state-run lost-and-found agency in Prague at Kaprova 4 in the Staré Město (tel. 601-44). If you happen to lose something that no one else will need, check here.

POLICE: If you are not staying in a hotel or private room arranged through a bureau, or if you want to extend your visa, you'll have to visit the District 3 Police Station at Olsanská 2. Note that before coming here you should be sure that you have exchanged enough money to meet the minimum currency-exchange requirements for your entire stay (or for the extra days, if you plan to extend your visa).

To register, all you need do is show your passport and visa, and then fill out a form stating where you are staying.

To extend your visa, you must pay 30 Kčs ($2.55) for a one- or two-day extension, and 60 Kčs ($5.10) for three days or more. Be sure to bring your passport, visa, and currency-exchange receipts for your entire stay, including the extra days.

To get here, take the metro to the Flora stop, walk downhill parallel to the park (where Franz Kafka is buried), and take the first right. After a few minutes you'll arrive at the police station; go to entrance 2 (Vchod 2). The office is open on Monday, Tuesday, Thursday, and Friday from 8 a.m. to noon and 12:30 to 3:30 p.m.; closed Wednesday, Saturday, and Sunday.

TAXIS: Taxis are inexpensive in Prague. Based on our experience, however, Prague's taxi drivers are the most seasoned hustlers in all of Eastern Europe—and given the unscrupulous nature of some of Eastern Europe's cab drivers, this is really a dubious distinction. Here are some tips to avoid being ripped off:

(1) If you get into a taxi and the driver doesn't turn on the meter (a common trick), remind him within a minute. It should begin at around 6 Kčs (50¢).

(2) Make sure that the meter is visible. If it's covered with a newspaper, the driver's hat, or anything, ask the driver to remove the item so that you can see the meter.

(3) If the driver tells you that the meter is broken (which is almost always a lie), either agree on a price for the ride right away, or if you're feeling particularly feisty that day, pay him what you think is right when you arrive at your destination, for he is technically not supposed to drive with a broken meter.

(4) You should pay only the price indicated on the meter. Unlike the practice in some countries, there are no supplements to the fare (as of this writing).

The driver may become annoyed when you thwart his attempts to pilfer extra cash from you, but remember—you are in the right! As a last resort in an argument, you can threaten to call the police. When this happens the driver will almost always back down.

Note: Never exchange currency on the black market with a taxi driver; many also work as government informants.

TELEPHONE AND TELEX: Local calls from a public telephone require a 50-heller (½-Kčs, or 6¢) coin. To reach Prague information, dial 120; for the rest of the country it's 27-55-51. There's a long-distance telephone office in the Hrad (castle), open weekdays from 9 a.m. until 5 p.m.

Telexes can be sent conveniently from most of the Interhotels, which, for a small fee, will hold all replies.

TRAIN INFORMATION: Although you can buy domestic train tickets at the train station, the Čedok office at Na příkopě 18 (tel. 22-42-51 to 22-42-59) handles all international tickets and seat and couchette reservations. For international trains you pay in Czechoslovakian korunas to the border, and in hard (Western) currency for all travel after that. Couchettes must also be paid for in hard currency. Čedok is open Monday through Friday from 8:15 a.m. to 4:15 p.m.; June 1 to September 30 it's open on Saturday from 8:15 a.m. to 2 p.m., and during the rest of the year to noon.

Prague has two train stations, only about ten minutes apart. When you're getting train information, be sure you know from which station the train departs. A seat reservation is often a good idea as well; they cost about $1, but they ensure that you won't be standing on a long ride.

7. Excursions from Prague

Prague is not more than 50 miles from some of the largest and most impressive castles in Europe. Of the major castles in the area around Czechoslovakia's capital we list the three most impressive—Konopiště, Český Šternberk and Karlštein. And to the east of Prague is the stunning Gothic and baroque masterpiece, the town of Kutná Hora.

The easiest way to visit these sights is by car. You can rent one or you can hire a car and driver from Čedok for about $65 for the day. We recommend bargaining with one of the local cabbies instead, who may do your driving for $30 in Western cash. The transaction is legal as long as you give the money as a gift and the cabbie reports it within 15 days.

KONOPIŠTĚ: Less than 30 miles south of Prague, on the E14, the 17th-century Konopiště Castle was the hunting lodge of the Hapsburgs. It was here that the emperors and archdukes would relax amid the well-stocked hunting grounds that surrounded the castle. In 1887 the castle became the property of the Archduke Franz Ferdinand, whose assassination was to begin World War I. The interior and exterior provide excellent examples of ornate and costly baroque stonework. There is also an impressive collection of 15th- and 16th-century weapons, late Gothic statuary, and an amazing collection of hunting trophies, as well as many mementos of Ferdinand's world travels.

ČESKÝ ŠTERNBERK: Only about another ten miles off on a side road (head east at the town of Benešov), Český Šternberk was once one of Bohemia's most powerful fortifications. It was begun in the first half of the 13th century during the reign of King Wenceslas I, in the late Gothic style. The Hapsburgs added baroque elements to the castle and improved the defenses. The huge main hall and several smaller salons in the castle have some fine baroque detailing. Because of the forest and streams that surround Český Šternberk, it's a good place to escape the heat on a summer's day.

KARLŠTEIN: Karlštein, or Karlštejn as it's spelled in Czech, was founded on June 10, 1348, to display the wealth and power of the new emperor, Charles IV. This magnificent castle was constructed to house the crown jewels of the German Empire. Blessed by the archbishop of the newly created archbishopric that Charles IV had founded, and designed by Mattias of Arras, the architect Charles IV had commissioned, Karlštein was a fitting testament indeed. Karlštein was the most secure treasury and the most important archive of Bohemia. During the Hussite Wars the castle was controlled by Imperial forces. In 1422 Karlštein withstood Hussite artillery for more than seven months. The advance of gunpowder technology, however, soon made the castle obsolete. The Swedish armies quickly overcame the castle and wreaked great devastation in 1648. In 1887–1897 the castle was rebuilt and modified by the Hapsburg owners. Today it's a well-preserved example of Bohemian defensive architecture. There is also still a vast collection of medieval Bohemian paintings and a few pieces of Charles's vast treasures. The Karlštein castle is about 15 miles west and south of Prague.

KUTNÁ HORA: Money may not grow on trees, but printing the stuff can't hurt. In the 15th century Kutná Hora was a mint town and thus was one of the wealthier towns in the region. Today the whole town is one vast museum. There is the beautiful Hrádek (castle), dating from the late 15th century, and the Church of St. Barbara, built in the middle of the 16th century, is one of the more fanciful Gothic structures in Czechoslovakia. A longish drive, Kutná Hora is about 45 miles due east of Prague on Hwy. 333.

BOHEMIA AND MORAVIA

THE PROVINCES OF Bohemia and Moravia comprise the western half of Czechoslovakia. With much common history and a common language (Czech), the two provinces have some of Czechoslovakia's most important historical sights. The region is rocky and forested in the north, with broad fertile plains in the south. Little explored by Western tourists, the small towns and forested countryside remain much the way they were in the 18th century.

1. Introducing Bohemia

"Bohemian"—the very word conjures up the image of the unusual, different, the nonconformist. For most of Catholic Europe in the 15th century, Bohemian meant devil.

Though the balance of power often shifted in favor of their larger German neighbors to the north, the Bohemians have left a lasting mark on European history. Initially a Slavic tribe that peacefully settled the Vltava (Moldau) River valley, the Bohemians managed to develop an independent culture despite constant invasion and upheaval. In the late 13th century, during the reign of King Ottokar II, the Bohemian Empire included much of eastern Germany and Austria as well as parts of Poland and Hungary. A few years later a confederation of German princes took control of the empire from the Bohemians.

The history of the Germans and the Bohemians is inextricably combined. Ottokar II founded over 60 German towns in Bohemia, Moravia, and Slovakia, yet 28 years after he fell in battle against the Hapsburgs, Bohemia and Moravia were reduced to provinces of the German Empire. But Europe had not heard the last of the Bohemians. With the death of Jan Hus at the stake in 1415, Hus's followers threw Imperial and Catholic emissaries through the windows of the Prague palace in 1419. There began a violent religious war in which the numerically inferior Bohemians managed to defeat the combined armies of much of Christendom. Not content with a successful defense, the Hussite armies roared across Central Europe bringing both war and their new religious ideas. This violent upheaval took place 40 years before Martin Luther shook the Catholic church and set the stage for the Reformation.

Warring nobles, fluid boundaries, and profitable foreign trade have left the Bohemian countryside dotted with castles and manor houses. The rolling woodland hides countless hamlets seemingly untouched by the passage of time. Trade in silver and lumber, and native Bohemian industriousness, provided the wealth to build beautiful, imposing trade towns such as Česk´ Budějovice. The later Hapsburg presence added the fanciful baroque towns of Karlovy Vary and Mariánské Lázne, though they had been known as spa towns since the reign of King Charles IV in the 14th century. The list is endless.

TRANSPORTATION IN BOHEMIA: If you're in a hurry, *don't* take the train. The trains in southern Bohemia are excruciatingly slow, and cost slightly more than bus travel. The only drawback to the buses is the crowds. Buses are often sold out, so try to buy your ticket at least a day in advance.

2. České Budějovice

A town very different from Prague and the Hapsburg playgrounds to the north and west, České Budějovice is about as "down home" Bohemian as you can get. Near the head of the Vltava (Moldau) River, the town was founded by King Ottokar II in 1265 to protect the Crown's interests and the approaches to the southern part of Bohemia. The successive expansion of Ottokar's kingdom fueled rather than slowed the expansion of the town's fortifications. Wealth flowed into České Budějovice in the form of wine and salt extracted from Austria in the south. Despite the name of its main square (Žižka, a Hussite commander), České Budějovice was a bastion of Catholic reaction to the Hussites in the north. The town's Golden Age came during the Renaissance when local silver mines and a mint funded the construction of numerous edifices, including the huge marketplace. The catastrophic Thirty Years' War (1618–1648) flattened the town, and a fire in 1641 almost finished off what was left. In the 18th century, under the Hapsburgs, České Budějovice was reconstructed in the baroque style. Today the pace is relaxed and slow. Sometimes on a heavy summer's day, during the lunch hour, the locals say that you can hear the beer brewing in the nearby Budvar brewery.

ORIENTATION: The circular **old town** is surrounded by parks, the remnants of its once-mighty fortifications, and is centered on the huge Žižkovo náměsti (square). From the railroad and bus stations, located side by side on Nádražní (Station) ulica, walk west for ten minutes along maršála Malinovského to the central square, Žižkovo náměsti. Most of the points of historical interest are within easy walking distance of the Žižkovo náměsti.

INFORMATION: The Čedok office, right on the north side of the Žižkovo náměsti (tel. 357-51), is friendlier than most, if not better organized. Open from 9 a.m., they like to break early on a hot day, usually around 4 p.m. (or earlier).

The **emergency** number (police and ambulance) in České Budějovice is 158.

THE SIGHTS: The old town of České Budějovice is small enough to be comfortably seen in a single day. At the center of town is the broad Žižkovo náměsti, one of the largest squares in Central Europe. At the very center of the Žižkovo náměsti is the **Fountain of Sampson,** built in 1727 by Josef Dietrich. The ornate fountain was once the town's principal water supply. On one side of the square is the **Town Hall,** rebuilt in 1731, and nearby is the **Cerná věž (Black Tower),** the symbol of České Budějovice. Built in the 16th century and badly damaged in the Thirty Years' War, the main tower of the Černá věž commands an excellent view of the surrounding countryside. Perhaps the most important sight in České Budějovice is the 13th-century **Church of St. Nicolas.** Built around the time České Budějovice was founded, it is the symbol of the town's adherence to Catholicism in the face of the Hussites.

ACCOMMODATIONS: České Budějovice's distance from Prague and its proximity to some of southern Bohemia's most beautiful countryside make it a good base for exploring, so you might wish to stay over. There are several good hotels right near the Žižkovo náměsti.

The **Hotel Malše** (tel. 276-31), named after one of the local rivers, is run by an elderly woman who seemed proud of the few American visitors she had. There are usually some vacancies in this hotel right across from the railway station. The bathless singles cost 104 Kčs ($8.80) and bathless doubles cost 156 Kčs ($13.20); doubles with a bath go for 234 Kčs ($19.80). There are only two public bathrooms for the entire hotel of about 60 beds, so we recommend getting a room with a private bath if possible.

Right on Žižkovo náměsti is the **Hotel Zvon** (tel. 353-61). The reception is friendly but not well informed; English is not understood. The rooms facing the square are larger and generally have a private bath. A single with a bath costs 234 Kčs ($19.80); without bath, 104 Kčs ($8.80). Bathless doubles run 156 Kčs ($13.20); with a bath, 351 Kčs ($29.70). Though the Zvon is not exceptional, its location and price make it worth considering.

Our recommended choice in České Budějovice is the **Interhotel Slunce,** also right on the Žižkovo náměsti (tel. 367-55 or 387-61; Telex 144325). This hotel is usually filled with groups, but four rooms are kept for private tourists and are usually available. The rooms are well kept and the doubles with bath are very nice indeed. All the rooms facing the square have an excellent view and lots of light and air. The English-speaking clerk is friendly and extremely professional. Bathless singles (when available) run 119 Kčs ($10.10), but the doubles are a very reasonable 264 Kčs ($22.35); all prices include breakfast.

With all these fine hotels right near the center, to trudge all the way to the plasto-modern **Hotel Gomel** at Miru 14 (tel. 289-41; Telex 144446) may seem superfluous. However, the new 195-room hotel usually has vacancies and its high-rise views more than offset the walk (about 15 minutes from Žižkovo náměsti). Singles with a bath cost 254 Kčs ($21.50), doubles with bath cost 391 Kčs ($33.10), and bathless doubles cost 352 Kčs ($29.80). All the rooms are well kept, clean, and very new.

DINING: There are several good restaurants in České Budějovice. Our pick is **Masné Krámy,** at Května 23, just off the northwest side of the Žižkovo náměsti in a pleasing old building. Where many restaurants have shields adorning the wall, here beer-barrel tops testify to many an arduous (but usually successful) battle with thirst. Painted sheaves of barley and hops parade around the main hall and drinking "apses," highlighting the vaulted ceiling of the Masné Krámy. At night the cigarette smoke is overpowering, but in the day the cool interior is perhaps one of the best places to commune with the spirit of the Good Soldier Švejk (though, technically, he never lived here).

There are also several good local restaurants in the area. Try the **Hluboká u Vltava** restaurant in Hluboká, a small village about seven miles north of České Budějovice, or the restaurant **Lovecká Chata,** also in Hluboká (tel. 96-51-45), celebrated for its wild game specialties.

3. Tábor

Tábor was the center of the Hussite movement. Founded in 1420, the town was named by the fervent Hussites after the biblical Mount Tabor. Hard as it is to believe today, a relatively small group of people (maybe 15,000 soldiers) decided in 1420 that they had been commanded by God to break the temporal power of the Catholic church. The Taborites, as this sect of the Hussites was known, were led by the legendary Jan Žižka and routed the combined papal forces for over 16 years.

Needless to say, Tábor has quieted down in the intervening 567 years. The main sights, including several beautiful Renaissance houses, are clustered around the old town center. The late Gothic (1440–1515) Town Hall is now the **Museum of the Hussite Movement.** Inside are an interesting collection of Hussite relics and a droll Marxist interpretation of the Hussite movement. Politics aside, the Hussite commander, Jan Žižka, figured out an unbeatable combination against the mounted, heavily armored papal knights. Žižka teamed armored wagons with cannon, protected at close range by pikemen, and cut swaths through the cream of Imperial military might time and time again. Near the small town square, the principal **Gothic church** (1440–1512) has a Renaissance gable (added in the middle of the 16th century). Under the marketplace and extending around the old town, is a **tunnel complex** used by the Taborites during sieges.

TOURIST INFORMATION: Though the Čedok office is at Tr. 9 kvetná, we preferred the **Interhotel Palcát** (tel. 229-01 to 229-03), whose competent receptionist offers to help our readers. The hotel is the large modern building about a 15-minute walk from the station. Just ask the way to the "Palcát."

ACCOMMODATIONS: The **Slavia,** near the railroad station (tel. 228-28), is one of Tábor's better hotels. The clean lobby, comfortable rooms, and English-speaking staff are real pluses. A single with a bath costs 100 Kčs ($8.45); a double, 150 Kčs ($12.70). Bathless singles run 80 Kčs ($6.75) and bathless doubles cost 120 Kčs ($10.15). Unfortunately, because of its convenient location the Slavia is almost always full.

The next best choice is the **Interhotel Palcát** (tel. 229-01 to 229-03), a modern pile with clean if unexceptional rooms. All rooms come with a private shower and breakfast. A single costs 120 Kčs ($10.15); a double, 180 Kčs ($15.25); and a suite, 330 Kčs ($27.95).

The **Hotel Slavon,** at Tr. 9 kvetná (tel. 36-92 or 34-35), pushes the hotel classification system to the limit. Though it has all the official trappings of a Class B hotel—phones, radios (one channel), black-uniformed waiters, and so on—it is most certainly a Class C in every other respect except for the price: 109 Kčs ($9.25) for bathless singles. The young Czech couple "getting away from it all" comes here, but don't feel you have to unless everything else is full.

DINING: The restaurant in the **Interhotel Palcát** is considered to be the finest establishment in Tábor. The food is filling and very inexpensive—less than 35 Kčs ($2.95) for a full meal, including soup and salad.

The restaurant in the **Hotel Slavia** is one of our favorites. You can eat a hearty meal for less than 27 Kčs ($2.30) in a relaxed, friendly atmosphere.

4. Karlovy Vary

A famous spa and resort town of the Hapsburgs, Karlovy Vary (Karlsbad) was supposedly found accidentally by King Charles IV while he was out hunting. Since the springs were near the village of Vary, he named it Karlovy (Charles's) Vary, after himself. However, such large springs could scarcely have gone unnoticed for so long that Charles found them thousands of years after the area was settled. In fact, the name of the village, Vary ("Boiling Place"), gives the game away. Some of the world's greatest thinkers and statesmen have "taken the cure" (as bathing and imbibing the waters were once called) here over the last three centuries. Karl Marx and practically every other major European figure in the 19th century visited these famous springs.

There are over 12 main springs in this small valley alone, the most famous spring is the 162°F "Sprudel," which gushes up to a height of 25 feet or more.

The town is one delightfully gaudy building after another, all squeezed into a very narrow valley. Most of the architecture dates from the 19th century when the resort reached its heyday. Also of note is the impressive, modern Yuri Gagarin Promenade (named after the first man in space) in the very center of town. There is some nightlife in Karlovy Vary, but the best time to see the town is during the day. The mineral springs, the forested hillsides ending just above the rooftops of the nearest houses, and the overall festival air can bring you back to the prewar gaiety of Karlovy Vary, the premier resort in all of Europe.

GETTING THERE: With a reservation included, the bus from Prague to Karlovy Vary costs only 39 Kčs ($3.30).

TOURIST INFORMATION: The Čedok office (tel. 261-10 or 222-27) in Karlovy Vary, open from 9 a.m. until 6 p.m. weekdays, on Saturday until noon (closed Sunday), is friendly. They seem to know as much about Karlovy Vary and its environs as the average tourist, so have a plan in mind before you go in. They are of limited assistance as far as room finding is concerned.

THERAPEUTIC VACATIONS: If you wish to come to Karlovy Vary to "take the waters," it's best to make long-term advance reservations in Prague through **Balena,** Pařížská 11, 110 01 Praha (tel. 26-37-77; Telex 122215).

ORIENTATION: The town of Karlovy Vary is shaped much like a "T" at the confluence of the Tepla and the Ohre Rivers. The old city, arrayed along the Tepla River to the south of the Ohre, forms the stem of the "T." The bus and railroad stations are a ten-minute walk up Československé armády from the main promenade.

ACCOMMODATIONS: There are several hotels in Karlovy Vary, but they fill up with all sorts of people coming to sample the waters. However, there are enough accommodations for the private traveler who does not plan to make an extended stay. If you wish to "take the waters," see the previous section on therapeutic vacations.

The **Hotel Národni Dům,** at Československé armády 24 (tel. 249-52), is an establishment done in the best 19th-century style. The polite English-speaking clerks and its location (about five minutes from the stations) make it a solid bet. A bathless double rents for 176 Kčs ($14.90). The rooms are clean but the fixtures date from the '70s and are rather worn as a result. While it's quiet in the day, noise from neighboring nightclubs can be tiresome.

The **Atlantic,** at Tržiště 23 (tel. 247-15), is often full but it's very clean, well maintained, and quiet. A bathless single costs 125 Kčs ($10.60) and a bathless double, 187 Kčs ($15.85); a double with a bath costs 281 Kčs ($23.80). The hotel also has some nice views along the valley.

The pearl of Karlovy Vary is the vast **Grand Hotel Moskva,** at Mírové náměsti 2 (tel. 221-21; Telex 0156220). Founded in 1701, this imposing old hotel has seen better days, but its gilt and style, though faded, are still impressive. Set against the steep, wooded valleyside, it reminds one of a more prosperous time. A single with a shower runs 250 Kčs ($21.15); with a bath, 390 Kčs ($33). A double with bath costs 650 Kčs ($55). A veritable warren, the hotel offers several restaurants and a disco. The lobby is packed with German travelers, a common phenomenon throughout Karlovy Vary. Though the Hotel Moskva is a fine hotel, the proximity of so many other good and less expensive hotels does not make it a good splurge choice.

The **Hotel Adria**, Koněvova 1 (tel. 237-65), offers simple rooms in an excellent location right in the town center. Each of the small rooms has a private bathroom and an old radio. The rates are the same as at many of the town's hotels, but you do get the added bonus of a private bathroom. Singles cost 156 Kčs ($13.20) and doubles go for 234 Kčs ($19.80). You'll find a restaurant downstairs as well.

Also located on one of Karlovy Vary's main streets is the **Hotel Jizera,** Dimitrovova 7 (tel. 24-302). The rooms are much like those of the Hotel Adria except that they don't have private bathrooms. Fortunately, the public bathrooms are clean, and showers are free. The rates are identical to those of the Adria.

The **Hotel Tourist,** on Dimitrovova, in the center of town, is a decent Class C hotel that stands high above its "C" counterparts in Prague. Not only does it offer a central location near the main shopping streets, but the rooms here are also well kept and clean. Because the hotel only has 13 rooms, it is often full. Doubles without bathroom cost 156 Kčs ($13.20), and triples run 234 Kčs ($19.80). Showers cost 26 Kčs ($2.20) extra.

South of Town

On the southern outskirts of town are two budget picks that usually have room. The **Motel Auto-camp at Karlovy Vary,** on Slovenska (tel. 252-24 or 252-25), has clean, well-kept doubles with a private, somewhat fragile shower for 195 Kčs ($16.50), and three-bed bungalows with no shower for 186 Kčs ($15.75). The nearby camping area charges 15.50 Kčs ($1.30) to set up your tent, and an additional 21 Kčs ($1.80) for a car.

There's also a CKM Junior hotel about two miles south of Karlovy Vary. The **Junior Hotel Alice** (tel. 248-48) is spotless and set off the road in some beautiful woods, and all rooms have "showers" (actually, tiled compartments set into the wall). Doubles run 234 Kčs ($19.80) and triples go for 291 Kčs ($24.65). The CKM hotel "always" has something free, according to the reception; no English is spoken. To get here, take bus 7 four stops after you leave the town.

DINING: We heartily recommend the **Francouzska** ("French") restaurant in the Grand Hotel Moskva, at Mírové náměsti 1 (tel. 221-21). This elegant restaurant, with tall ceilings, several huge mirrors, and large chandeliers, is Karlovy Vary's best. There's a wide selection here, including a tasty (but un-Italian) spaghetti entree topped with thick melted cheese. For a light dish, try the trout with mushrooms, prepared in a butter sauce. For dessert there's palačinky or a variety of ice cream sundaes. You can eat here for less than $4 a person. The Francouzska is open from noon to 3 p.m. for lunch and from 6 to 9 p.m. for dinner.

NIGHTLIFE: There's almost no nightlife in Karlovy Vary. As one local told us, "The best you can do is find a good *vinaria* [bar] and stay there."

Concerts are presented occasionally at Spa (Sanitorium) No. 3, and organ concerts are given twice monthly at the Grand Hotel Moskva. Inquire at Čedok.

5. Plzeň —

Those who have enjoyed Pilsner-Urquell beer (and not one of its many imitators) almost all agree that no other beer is as smooth, thirst-quenching, or delicious. These words about Pilsner-Urquell come as no surprise. As many say, Pilsner-Urquell is the true king of beers!

The tradition of beer drinking here began hundreds of years ago, although in its early years Plzeň's beer was remembered for its bitter, disagreeable taste. This didn't keep a group of hearty men from coming together in the 16th century to form the town's first guild of beer drinkers. The group declared that the only way to live was to "sleep in daytime, drink, play, sing, love, and make merry by night!"

Although some citizens of Plzeň were happy with their beer in the 16th century, by the 19th century beer drinkers began to complain that the beer in Plzeň was inferior. It was neither tasty nor refreshing, they lamented. On a rebellious night in 1838, townsmen poured out 36 barrels in front of the Town Hall, having deemed the beer unfit for human consumption.

One of the town's home brewers got up and declared to the crowd: "Give us what we need in Plzeň—good and cheap beer!" It's not known how the crowd reacted, but it's likely that a roar of approval followed. Then he said, "Let the citizens holding boiling privileges join and build a brewery together." Everyone agreed, and the Plzeň factory was opened in 1842. From that time on, the factory made beer history.

The medium-sized town of Plzeň offers few sights other than the Pilsner-Urquell factory. Although the town sports some interesting turn-of-the-century architecture, Plzeň's many years of industry and pollution have grayed all beauty and added a noticeable smell in the air. Thus we recommend Plzeň only to those with a passion for beer.

ACCOMMODATIONS: Many international businessmen in town stay at the **Hotel Ural,** náměsti Republiky 33 (tel. 326-85 to 326-88; Telex 154399). Located right off the Old Town Square, the Hotel Ural is a modern building which has bathrooms with showers in every room. The reception is a bit distracted here, sometimes making guests wait a few minutes to get keys, but the cleaning staff is diligent. The attractive rooms all sport radios, telephones, and a small couch. Some also overlook the Old Town Square. The Ural charges 208 Kčs ($17.60) for singles and 312 Kčs ($26.40) for doubles. The hotel also houses a popular restaurant downstairs.

Another good, but more economical, pick is the **Hotel Slovan,** Smetanovy sady 1 (tel. 377-28, 375-92, or 322-38). The hotel recently celebrated its 100th birthday, and though it has aged over the years, some elegant touches still show through, such as a stately staircase. The reception is also quite friendly to Western guests. Singles rent for 133 Kčs ($11.25) with a sink but no bathroom; doubles cost 203 Kčs ($17.20) without a bathroom and 297 Kčs ($25.15) with. Each bath costs 31 Kčs ($2.60) extra. You'll find the Hotel Slovan a few blocks away from the Old Town Square in the direction of the train station.

Better located but more pricey, the **Hotel Continental,** Zbrojnická ulice 8 (tel. 304-71 to 304-73; Telex 154380), is just a block from the Old Town Square. It offers 40 spacious rooms with showers but no toilets—fear not, the public toilets are clean. A single runs 199 Kčs ($16.85) and a double goes for 305 Kčs ($25.85). You can also rent one of a few singles without shower for 137 Kčs

($11.60), or similar doubles for 211 Kčs ($17.85). A standard hotel restaurant, considered by locals to be one of the town's best, is located downstairs.

THE SIGHTS: As the only producer of what many consider the world's greatest beer, the **Pilsner-Urquell Factory** in Plzeň is a "must see" sight for dedicated beer drinkers. Every year this large factory produces 1,400,000 liters (350,000 gallons) of beer and exports much of it to some 64 different countries.

There are two ways to visit the factory. You can join a Čedok tour (it costs only 50¢, but inquire first in the Prague office at Na příkopě 18; tel. 22-42-51). If no tour is offered when you visit, either telephone (at 21-64) or go to the information desk at the factory gates at U Prazdroje and ask for Stanislav Frank, the distinctive company lawyer with long black hair and a Vandyke beard. He speaks decent English and can sometimes arrange a private tour of the factory.

At the beginning of the tour you'll see a short movie which professes to tell the "secret" of Pilsner-Urquell's taste. Then you're off to see the wondrous brewing facilities, many of which have hardly changed since the factory opened in 1842. In the first room, ground malt and water, beer's staple ingredients, are mixed into one of 20 huge copper vats, the start of the long road to brewing smooth beer.

As you wander through the factory, you'll see dozens of busy technicians in white jackets who look like laboratory scientists conducting an important experiment. In fact, they're supervising the whole operation of the vats and making sure the temperatures are just right. But if they let you look inside the vats, you'll see a swirling mass of water and steam that looks more like a witch's brew than anything else!

When the various brewing stages are over, the beer is piped down into underground fermentation vats. After the beer has fermented, it's pumped into large oak barrels spread out over some five miles of underground cellars. On occasion, guests are also taken down to see these cellars.

When you leave the beer factory, go to the **Prazdros Restaurant,** right outside the factory gates, open Monday to Friday from 10 a.m. to 10 p.m., and on Saturday, Sunday, and holidays from 11 a.m. to 8 p.m. In this humble, though lively, restaurant hall, you can eat lunch and drink Pilsner-Urquell with the spirited workers from the factory.

Afterward, you might also want to visit the **beer museum,** housed in a former malt house from the 15th century. The documents and displays on the history and evolution of beer will teach you all the trivia you want to know! It's open on Tuesday from 1 to 4:30 p.m., Wednesday through Sunday from 9 a.m. to 4:30 p.m.; closed Monday. Ask for a museum description in English as you walk in.

6. Moravia and Brno

MORAVIA: Moravia is the smallest region in Czechoslovakia. Where the Carpathians and the Bohemian highlands meet, the hilly north of Moravia gives way to the smiling plains in the south. Sandwiched between the two other republics, Moravia nevertheless has maintained a distinct cultural identity. The north is known for its mineral wealth and deep forests. Also known as the "steel heart" of Czechoslovakia because of the vast smelting complex here, the stern pagan god Ragegast is still said to live in the rocky, wild north Moravian hills. The south is a pleasant fertile land, home of some of the country's most beautiful folksongs and best wines. The fecundity of the land must have inspired even prehistoric man, as one of the earliest fertility symbols, the Věstonice Venus, was found in southern Moravia. Castles, forests, vineyards, and the traditionally friendly people will make any visit to Moravia memorable.

BRNO: Brno is the historical and cultural center of Moravia. Initially, it does not appear to be one of Czechoslovakia's lovelier cities. Yet if you spend a relaxed day here, the beauty of the city will slowly unfold. Explore the Špilberk Castle and the Gothic Cathedral of Sts. Peter and Paul, walk down the main streets, but be certain to spend time in the parks to the west of the city center.

Not far from Vienna, Brno is located at the confluence of the Svratka and Svitava Rivers. The city, first mentioned in documents in 1091, enjoyed its Golden Age in the 14th century. During this time the city walls and the Špilberk Castle were built. The Špilberk Castle has served many of Europe's conquerors: the Hussites held it in the 15th century, the Swedes controlled it for long periods during the Thirty Years' War, the Prussians found its commanding view excellent for their purposes, and the Nazis also tenanted Špilberk Castle. Today Brno is one of Czechoslovakia's largest trade centers and has a beautiful old city center.

The Sights

The main sights in Brno are the Špilberk Castle, the Cathedral of Sts. Peter and Paul, the Capuchin Cloister, the Dietrichstein Palace, and the Old Town Hall.

The **Špilberk Castle** has seen many masters, the latest and most terrible being the Nazis in World War II. Over 80,000 opponents of the Nazi regime were killed deep in the castle dungeons. Špilberk Castle was begun in the 12th century and rebuilt in the baroque style in the middle of the 18th century.

On the site of the old Přemyslid castle, the **Cathedral of Sts. Peter and Paul** was begun in the late 11th and early 12th centuries. It was rebuilt in the baroque style in 1743 and again just before World War I. This is one of the most architecturally interesting and unique of Czechoslovakia's baroque cathedrals. Both the castle and the cathedral are on hills clearly visible from most the city.

Across from the cathedral is the **Old Town Hall,** a hodgepodge of Gothic, Renaissance, and baroque styles. Above the lintel of the late Gothic entryway is a dragon and a wheel, the symbol of Brno.

About a block away from the train station and down the east side of the hill from the cathedral, the **Capuchin Cloister** (Kapucínský klášter) is famous for its mummies. The unique ventilation of the cloister preserved numerous bodies of Brno's most famous citizens, including Moritz Grimm, the architect who rebuilt the cathedral in the 18th century.

The **Dietrichstein Palace** was once where the Russian Marshal Kutuzov prepared for the battle of Austerlitz. Today it houses an art gallery and the Moravian history museum.

Information

The **Čedok** office, at Diadelní 3, is open from 9 a.m. to 6 p.m. weekdays, until noon on Saturday; closed Sunday.

Accommodations

All of the following hotels are located within a 10- or 15-minute walk of the bus and train station. *Note:* All prices are higher during the Brno Trade Fair.

Hotel U Jakuba, Jakubske náměsti 6 (tel. 229-91 to 229-93), offers 37 fair-sized, slightly worn rooms in which a curtain separates the bed from the rest of the room. Each room also sports a telephone, a one-channel radio, and a small bathroom. Singles with shower only (no toilet) cost 233 Kčs ($19.75), and similar doubles are 358 Kčs ($30.30). A double with toilet and bathtub costs 415 Kčs ($35.15). The public bathrooms are clean here.

At the **Hotel Avion,** near the city center about a ten-minute walk from the railroad station, you are likely to be greeted by a helpful, spirited, English-speaking receptionist. The rooms are small and old, but quaint. The Hotel Avion is often frequented by East Bloc guests. When we visited, a group of Soviet women had arrived at the hotel just as some East Germans were checking out. Singles cost 171 Kčs ($14.50) without bathroom, 202 Kčs ($17.10) with a shower, and 264 Kčs ($22.35) with a private bathroom. Doubles rent for 311 Kčs ($26.35) with a shower and 358 Kčs ($30.30) with a private bathroom. Unfortunately, the public bathrooms here are just passable.

A somewhat less expensive establishment is the **Hotel Morava.** Unfortunately, the reception knows that their prices are lower and seems to feel that they can offer decidedly unhelpful service. Each room sports a telephone, a radio, and a sink, but no bathroom. The public bathrooms can only be described as usable. Singles cost 140 Kčs ($11.85) if bathless and 171 Kčs ($14.50) with a shower. A bathless double rents for 217 Kčs ($18.35) or 311 Kčs ($26.35) with shower.

A Splurge Choice: If you don't want to deal with the shortcomings of Brno's budget hotels, check into the tall, modern **Hotel Continental** at Leninova 20 (tel. 75-31-21 or 75-07-27; Telex 62350). The A* category Continental offers modern rooms with refrigerators, private bathrooms, and balconies with appealing views of Brno. Singles cost 285 Kčs ($24.15), and doubles go for 434 Kčs ($36.75). Breakfast is included in these rates.

Dining
Asia Restaurant, in the Grand Hotel, Maje 18-20 (tel. 25-03-13), is a recommended splurge as it's one of Eastern Europe's better Oriental restaurants. A genuine attempt has been made to create an Oriental atmosphere: there are satin wall decorations, Oriental hanging lamps, screens dividing the tables, and fish tanks set into the walls. Entrees cost 25.60 Kčs ($2.15) to 46.40 Kčs ($3.95), and include chicken with pineapple and pork cooked with rice wine and mushrooms. Start off your meal with the tasty Japanese soba soup with pork, Chinese noodles, and seaweed for 12.40 Kčs ($1.05). Open from 5 p.m. to midnight; closed Sunday.

As you walk into the **Lucullus Restaurant** in the Hotel International, Husova 16, you'll be greeted by 1950s modern socialist architecture. The food at the Lucullus, however, is usually more digestible than the decor. Traditional Bohemian and Moravian regional specialties, such as a variety of steak dishes, are offered for 36.20 Kčs ($3.05) to 94.40 Kčs ($8). It's best to reserve; call 265-11 and ask for the restaurant. Open from noon to 3 p.m. and from 6:30 to 11 p.m.

Chapter XIV

SLOVAKIA AND THE TATRAS

1. Bratislava
2. Želina and the Low Fatras
3. The High Tatras

GRACED WITH GENTLE rolling plains in the west and rugged mountains in the central and eastern regions, Slovakia comprises the eastern third of Czechoslovakia. Since the Hungarians invaded Slovakia in A.D. 906 it has shared little history—or language or popular culture—with the rest of the region. It was not until after World War I that Slovakia was joined with the Czech lands to the west to form modern-day Czechoslovakia. Two of Czechoslovakia's largest mountain ranges, the Fatras and the Tatras, with peaks over 8,500 feet high, are in Slovakia. The forested, sparsely settled (for Europe) lands east of the mountains are known as the Slovak's Paradise. In Slovakia you'll find untouched peasant hamlets and sturdy mountain folk who try to keep the old ways alive and, as much as possible, to avoid the "comings and goings in the lowlands."

1. Bratislava

Just 75 miles east of Vienna, Bratislava, with a population of 400,000, is Czechoslovakia's third-largest city and the capital of the Slovak Socialist Republic. The city has had a long and distinguished history. Archeological finds indicate that the area was inhabited as long ago as 4000 B.C. The Romans fortified the area around Bratislava because it was an important spot on the Amber Route which went north to the Baltic Sea. The first Slavs migrated into this area in the 5th and 6th centuries, and by the 9th century a fortified castle was being built on one of Bratislava's hills.

From the 10th century until 1918 Bratislava was part of the Hungarian Empire. After the Turks threatened Budapest in the 16th century, the Hungarian capital was moved from Budapest to Bratislava, and between 1563 and 1830 some 19 Hungarian coronations took place here, including that of Maria Theresa. In 1918 Bratislava was incorporated into the new nation-state of Czechoslovakia.

Today Bratislava is a pretty city with a fairly active cultural life. Concerts and festivals are often held here, and nighttime activities are much more common here than in many other medium-size Eastern European cities. Despite Bratislava's rapid growth since World War II (spurred by great government investment) the city still has a small-town feel about it, an atmosphere fostered by pleasant squares in the center of town, an old castle, and many parks around the city. The relaxed pace, combined with some interesting sights, makes Bratislava a rewarding place to visit.

ORIENTATION: Bratislava is a large city with many residential districts, but the center of town is reasonably compact. One point of orientation is the **town castle,** which is perched up on a hill on the southwest corner of town, just off the Danube River which lies to the south. The town center lies immediately to the east.

The town's main pedestrian mall is **Poštová,** a street about five blocks from the castle. Poštová continues past the large traffic intersection at **Kyjevské náměsti.** To the south of this square runs **Stúrova,** another large shopping avenue. Right after Kyjevské náměsti to the west lies **Leningradská,** a narrower shopping street which leads to the quaint heart of old Bratislava near the castle.

Getting into Town

The new **main bus station** in Bratislava is at Mlynské Nivy, across from the "Ordrejský Cintorin," a cemetery (note that the bus station at Sovietské náměsti marked on most Bratislava maps no longer exists). Many public buses and trams go to the center from here, but if you prefer to walk, it will take you about 20 minutes heading toward Dunajská (ask to make sure you're going in the right direction). You can check your bags at the station from 7 a.m. to 6 p.m.

The **main railway station** (Hlavna Stanica) is at Dimitrovovo náměsti (tel. 469-45 or 482-75). Trams 1, 3, 6, and 8 go to the center from here. Some domestic trains arrive and leave from Bratislava Nové Mesto at Tomasikova (tel. 607-48). Take tram 6 to get to the center.

Public Transportation

Local **buses and trams** cost 1 Kčs (8¢). Tickets must be bought at newsstands before you get on the bus or tram. **Taxis** start at 6 Kčs (50¢) and go up 3.40 Kčs (30¢) per kilometer. If you want to rent a taxi for an hour, it costs 30 Kčs ($2.55). The rates vary slightly according to whether the taxi is a Škoda (a cheap car) or a Volga (an expensive car). You can call a taxi at 508-51 to 508-54.

Tourist Information

You'll find the efficient main **Čedok** office on a street east of Kyjevské náměsti at Dunajská 40. They're open Monday to Friday from 9 a.m. to 6 p.m., on Saturday to noon. They have a few private double rooms for 150 Kčs ($12.70), but it seems that not everyone in the office knows about these, so keep asking.

Some of Eastern Europe's friendliest clerks are in the **Bratislava Information Office** (BIPS–Bratislavska Informacna A Propagacna Služba), down the street in the other direction at Leningradská 1 (tel. 33-43-70, 33-37-15, or 33-43-25). In this organized, professional office you can get a wide variety of information on Bratislava. Also come here to get details on cultural happenings. *Kam V Bratislava,* a monthly Czech publication sold here for 2 Kčs (17¢), has a comprehensive listing of concerts, films, art exhibitions, and other events in town. It's open Monday through Friday from 8 a.m. to 6 p.m., on Saturday to 1 p.m.

Both Čedok and the Bratislava Information Office can give you information on **tour boats** that depart from Bratislava and sail the Danube. If you want a **private guide** to show you around, inquire at Červenej armády 7 (tel. 597-64), another street that runs northeast from Kyjevské náměsti.

Travel on to Vienna

If you're continuing on to Vienna, note that buses leave infrequently—only twice a day, as of this writing. Neither Čedok nor the CKM student office sells the tickets. You can pay for them—in hard (Western) currency only—as you're getting on board. It's best to have Austrian schillings, but other hard currencies are also accepted. It costs 74 Austrian schillings ($3.80); the driver has no change except for schillings (if you only have a $10 bill, you'll get no change, so try to get smaller bills before you go to the station).

ACCOMMODATIONS: Accommodations in Bratislava are more expensive than in other Czech cities since there is only one B category hotel. Here are your hotel options:

Our Best Pick

We recommend the **Hotel Palace**, at Poštová 1 (tel. 33-36-56 or 33-36-57). Not only is this hotel right in the center of town on Bratislava's most frequented mall, but it's the town's only class B hotel, and thus the best-priced establishment. The reception is friendly and welcoming to the rare Western visitors. The rooms do not have toilets, but public facilities are generally well maintained. A basic single costs 161 Kčs ($13.65), or 233 Kčs ($19.75) with a bathtub; doubles rent for 248 Kčs ($21), or 358 Kčs ($30.30) with a bathtub only. Try to reserve ahead of time for the hotel is often full.

A Student Bargain

The **Junior Hotel Sputnik,** Drienova 14 (tel. 82-10-10), is the most incredible bargain B* hotel in all of Eastern Europe—if you are a student with the IUS card (which you can easily buy at the local CKM office; see important addresses, below). The Sputnik is housed in a large modern six-story building with 60 rooms. Most distinctively, the building houses a large indoor atrium which stretches from the parlor floor all the way up to the top floor. In this large space, young people meet at a bar on the first floor throughout the day and night. Three of the hotel's floors have recently been redecorated, and so these rooms are modern and rather attractive. The two other floors are less appealing, but still a steal in price. Both sections rent single rooms to students with private bathroom for 27 Kčs ($2.30), and twice that for a double. Nonstudents can stay here as well, but for 156 Kčs ($13.20) to 182 Kčs ($15.40) in a single, and 186 Kčs ($15.75) to 273 Kčs ($23.10) in a double. Although these figures are a great deal more than the student prices, they still offer a good deal for Bratislava. Next to the hotel you'll find a small lake where you can swim on hot summer days. To get to the Sputnik, take tram 8, 9, or 12 from the center to within one block of the hotel.

Other Hotel Choices

Hotel Tatra, náměsti 1 Mája no. 5 (tel. 535-87, 512-78, or 514-64; Telex IHBTA 93444), is a nice B* hotel with a good central location right off the large Mierove náměstie. Although the public hallways show signs of wear, the rooms are large and nice. Singles are 197 Kčs ($16.70) without bathroom and 233 Kčs ($19.75) with private bathroom; doubles cost 303 Kčs ($25.65) without a bathroom, and 358 Kčs ($30.30) to 412 Kčs ($34.90) with a bathroom.

Hotel Krym, Šafárikovo náměsti 6 (tel. 554-71 to 554-73), has a good location at the end of one of Bratislava's main streets. It looks like a Class B hotel, but is priced as a B*: singles are 197 Kčs ($16.70) without bathroom and

270 Kčs ($22.85) with a bathtub only; doubles run 303 Kčs ($25.65) without bathroom and 412 Kčs ($34.90) with a bathtub.

A good, though slightly splurgy hotel pick is the **Hotel Carlton,** on the beautiful Hviezdoslavovo náměsti at no. 7 (tel. 33-18-51 or 33-51-41; Telex 093349), in the center of town. The Carlton has both A and B category rooms, with corresponding price differences. The class A rooms offer traditional furniture from 50 years ago, as well as a telephone, bathroom, and attractive view of one of Bratislava's most picturesque squares. The class B rooms are considerably less elegant, with just a sink in the room, but also far less expensive. Singles cost 353 Kčs ($29.90) in the A category and 207 Kčs ($17.50) in the B category; doubles rent for 541 Kčs ($45.80) in the A category and 305 Kčs ($25.85) in the B category.

Hotel Dukla, náměsti Ludových Milicii 1 (tel. 21-29-07 or 21-29-08), is a decent hotel choice about ten minutes from the town center. The 58 rooms here look like what was modern for the 1950s, with a plant, a radio, and a phone in the room. Doubles with bathroom cost 307 Kčs ($26), and triples go for 380 Kčs ($32.20). Thanks to the location just outside the town center, rooms are quiet at the Dukla.

Youth Hostels

If the Sputnik is full, students can stay in a town youth hostel. In July, the CKM hostel is at the **International College J. Hronca** on Bernolákova (tel. 441-57), near the Americhé and Sovietské náměsti. Rooms here have four beds and a bunk costs 25 Kčs ($2.10) with a student card. In August you can stay at the **College Družhba,** at Arm. General L. Svobodu place, about ten minutes by bus from the center. Check these two addresses at CKM or Čedok before going to either hostel, as every few years they change location.

Leave the **Hotel Bratislava,** Urxova 9 (tel. 29-35-23 or 29-56-41; Telex 092336), as one of your last picks, unless you have a car. The modern cement construction with a bright white-and-blue exterior offers pleasant rooms, but it's rather inconveniently located in a residential area of Bratislava. Because of the location, many tour groups traveling by bus stay here. In fact, the only Americans we saw during our stay in Bratislava, a large tour group, stayed in this hotel. Singles with bathroom rent for 270 Kčs ($22.85), and doubles are 422 Kčs ($35.75). Breakfast is included in the room price. Take tram 9 or 12 about ten stops from the city center.

DINING: Although Bratislava doesn't have many bargain hotels, it has probably the best lineup of restaurants in all of Czechoslovakia.

Restaurant Ukrajina, in the Hotel Kyjev, Rajska ulice 2 (tel. 563-41), is one of the best restaurants in the country. The dishes here are cooked with care and refinement. We recommend the well-prepared baked chicken stuffed with ham and cheese, with a crispy crust. The french fries are also excellent. There's a quiet hotel decor, and jazz music played by a pianist and violinist adds to the pleasant atmosphere. This is an expensive restaurant for Czechoslovakia— entrees cost 27.60 Kčs ($2.35) to 74.80 Kčs ($6.35) each—but the food is excellent, so we highly recommend the Ukrajina. It serves from 11:30 a.m. to 10 p.m.

Restaurant Stará Sladovna ("The Old Malt House"), Cintorinska 32 (tel. 511-51, 512-35, or 562-79), is a huge place with 1,600 seats. It's located in a former barley factory (in use from 1872 to 1976), with an attractive outdoor garden and two large halls inside. Each area has a separate menu. Slovak specialties are prepared on the first floor, Czech specialties on the second, and grilled foods are offered in the garden. Meals are inexpensive, with entrees in the 20-Kčs ($1.70) to 40-Kčs ($3.40) range. In all the restaurant offers some 100 different dishes. The Stará Sladovna is a lively place, with the loud hum of hundreds of people talking and drinking beer. The Revival Jazz Band adds to the lively atmosphere on the ground floor from 5 to 9 p.m. daily except Tuesday. The restaurant serves from 10 a.m. to 10 p.m. We offer one caution: there are many tables here and few waiters, so expect a leisurely meal.

Restaurant U Zlatcno Kapra, Přepostska 6, has two quiet dining rooms with attractive wood and white-painted walls. Tasty fish dishes are featured: our favorite is devinsky kapor, a buttery fresh fish filet with a light, crispy batter crust, for 23.50 Kčs ($2). This restaurant has varied offerings, a fine change of pace from the usual Czech meat dishes. Hours are 11 a.m. to 10 p.m. Monday through Saturday; closed Sunday.

Vinaren Velki Františkáni, Diebrovovo námĕsti 7 (tel. 33-30-73), is a good restaurant with three different dining areas: an indoor restaurant with a vaulted ceiling; a long, dimly lit cellar hall with gypsy band music (there's a 10-Kčs, or 85¢, cover charge per person); and a small courtyard. The courtyard is the nicest area, except that as it gets later in the evening, bacchanalian singing by some of the guests spoils the quiet, romantic atmosphere. Specialties include presporska pochutka obložena, a hot pork dish with pepperoni, for 30.90 Kčs ($2.60), and hovadzie file obložene, beefsteak in tomato sauce with paprika and cheese, for 32.80 Kčs ($2.80). The restaurant is open daily from 10 a.m. to 1 a.m.

Koliba Expo, in the Koliba Park (tel. 67-17-64), is a homey and relaxing place considered by many locals to be Bratislava's best restaurant. This chalet restaurant (a copy of a restaurant exhibited at the 1972 Montréal Expo) is located in the middle of a thickly wooded area. Grilled meats are the specialty, many of which are prepared at tableside. Entrees cost 25 Kčs ($2.10) to 50 Kčs ($4.25). In the evening a folklore band plays. The only problem with this wonderful restaurant is that it's five kilometers (three miles) outside town and hard to get to unless you have a car. It's a 25-minute walk down a road through the woods from the last stop of the no. 213 bus. The Koliba is open Tuesday through Friday from 6 p.m. to 1 a.m., on Saturday from noon to midnight, and on Sunday from noon to 10 p.m.; closed Monday.

The **Interhotel Devin,** at Riečna 4 (tel. 33-08-51 to 33-08-57), on the riverfront, has a nice Slovak specialty restaurant with a subdued atmosphere. Two delicious dishes are the thick, filling cabbage soup with smoked sausage, cream, and mushrooms, for 13.40 Kčs ($1.15), and the "Tatra Delicacy," spiced meat and vegetables rolled up in a crêpe, for 37.50 Kčs ($3.20). The excellent food here is complemented by efficient and courteous service. Hours are 11:30 a.m. to 10:30 p.m.

On top of Bratislava's bridge (Most SNP) is the circular restaurant **Kaviaren Bystrica** (tel. 513-45 or 503-92). The food is standard, but from here—280 feet up—there's an impressive view of the city. Come during the day, for at night the restaurant's lights reflect off the windows and block your view. Prices are moderate: entrees cost 20 Kčs ($1.70) to 60 Kčs ($5.10). It's open daily from 9 a.m. to 11 p.m., on Monday from 1 p.m. Always reserve.

There are also a lot of decent and very inexpensive stand-up cafeteria restaurants *(Samoobsluha)* in Bratislava. Try looking on the main street, Stúrova.

CULTURE AND NIGHTLIFE: During the summer there's a full program of concerts. For information on cultural events, go either to Čedok at Dunajská or to the **Bratislava Information Office,** at Leningradská 1 (tel. 33-43-70, 33-37-15, or 33-43-25). To buy tickets for any of these summer concert events, go to the **ticket office** (Predpredaj Vstupenick) at the back of the passageway at SNP 14 (beyond the Kino Slovan), open from 8 a.m. to noon and 2 to 4 p.m. Monday through Friday. Note that the Slovak Philharmonic is on tour and thus does not perform in Bratislava during the summer.

The rest of the year, for musical events, go to **Reduta** at Palackého ulice 2 (tel. 33-33-51). Tickets usually cost about 20 Kčs ($1.70). For opera and ballet, go to the **Slovak National Theater,** at Hviezgoslovovo náměsti (tel. 552-28), where tickets usually cost 20 Kčs ($1.70) to 50 Kčs ($4.25).

Those with a sharp memory for obscure trivia may recall that the television show "Saturday Night Live" had a popular skit featuring the "Wild and Crazy Czech Brothers" (played by Dan Ackroyd and Steve Martin) who came originally from Bratislava. Anyone who expects to relive their style of nightlife here will be disappointed. Nightlife centers largely around lengthy dinners. There are, however, three decent **discos,** mostly for students: one in the **Junior Hotel Sputnik,** Drienova 14 (tel. 82-10-10); another in the **Interhotel Devin,** at Riečna 4 (tel. 33-08-51 to 33-08-57), with a slightly older crowd; and a third called **Steps,** at Panenska 25 (tel. 308-65).

The local socialist youth club, **Dôm Ruh,** on náměsti Frantiska Zupku (tel. 615-38), has films, plays, jazz and pop concerts, and other events. The Bratislava Information Office can give you more details, or a monthly program.

THE SIGHTS: The first documented mention of the **Bratislava Castle (Bratislavsky Hrad)** was in A.D. 907, and since then it has served to fight off attacks by the Tartars, the Turks, and the Czech Hussites, among others. When Bratislava was the capital of Hungary, the Parliament met here and the crown jewels were stored here for a time. In 1811 much of the castle was destroyed by fire, and in 1953–1962 it was restored. Today the castle houses both archeological and historical exhibitions on Bratislava. It is open daily except Monday, from 9 a.m. to 5 p.m.

The **Town Museum (Mestske Muzeum),** at Primaciálne náměsti 1, in the Old Town Hall (Staroměstika Radnica), has displays on the history of Bratislava. It's open Tuesday through Sunday from 10 a.m. to 5 p.m.; closed Monday.

Seeing at least one Lenin museum is the key to any visit to Eastern Europe, so it might as well be the **Museum of V. I. Lenin** at ulica Obrancov mieru 25, open Tuesday through Friday from 8 a.m. to 6 p.m., on weekends from 9 a.m. to 4 p.m; closed Monday.

The **Museum of Bratislava Watches and Clocks,** at Zidovska 1, is open daily except Monday from 10 a.m. to 5 p.m.

The **Slovak National Gallery,** at Rázusovo nábrežie 2, displays everything from 15th-century Italian art to modern Slovak paintings. It's open daily except Monday from 10 a.m. to 5 p.m.

The **Slavin Monument** in Horsky Park is a tribute to the Soviet effort in World War II. A statue here symbolizes Victory in the form of a Soviet soldier. From the monument you have a fine panorama of all of Bratislava. It's also a nice place to go on a hot day as it's breezy and cool under the marble.

In summer the best place to go **swimming** is at the Zlate Piesky, a large lake about 15 to 20 minutes from the center of town. Take bus 106, 108, 110, or 114.

IMPORTANT ADDRESSES: The student **CKM Office,** at Hviezdoslavovo náměsti 16 (tel. 33-16-07), is open on Monday from 1 to 6 p.m. and Tuesday through Friday from 1 to 4 p.m. Here you can buy the socialist IUS student card.

The **main post office** is on Dimitrovovo náměsti.

You can make **international telephone calls** at Kolářova ulice 12 from 8 a.m. to midnight.

If you want a rental car, go to **Pragocar,** Hviezdoslavovo náměsti 14 (tel. 33-32-01).

2. Želina and the Low Fatras

After some fast-paced sightseeing in Prague and other large cities in Eastern Europe, consider a visit to the Low Fatras in northwestern Slovakia. Although not as awesome and overwhelming as the Tatra Mountains, the Low Fatras offer beautiful scenery in a quiet environment—a perfect place for a few days of relaxation.

Start your exploration of the Low Fatras from Želina, an option especially useful to those without an automobile (the hotels in the mountains are often obscurely located, and fully booked to boot, so you're best off leaving your luggage in Želina before heading for the mountains).

Želina is a pretty little city; although you won't find any famous sights in town, you'll feel a special air about the town from decades or centuries ago. For example, you might see peasant women shopping early in the morning with fresh bread sticking out of their bags, and street workers paving the road with a now-ancient coal-burning gravel mixer, the same method used 100 years ago. Even if Želina does not wildly excite visitors, it certainly calms them with its slow pace and easy-going way of life—a place you'll appreciate after an active day of hiking in the mountains.

ACCOMMODATIONS: The **Hotel Polom,** Olomoucka 1 (tel. 211-51, 211-52, 217-43, or 235-04), offers a great location for those day-tripping to the mountains: it's right across from the bus and train station. The Class B* rooms range in size from very small to moderate; each room features a small but clean private bathroom with shower. Singles rent for 187 Kčs ($15.85), and doubles go for 281 Kčs ($23.80).

If the Polom is full but you want that same location near the bus and train stations, try the **Hotel Metropol,** Hviezdoslavona ulica (tel. 239-00). The entrance to the hotel is a bit rundown, and off to the side you'll notice a restaurant that seems to attract many spirited locals. However, rooms in the back of the hotel are quiet, the public bathrooms are clean, and prices are slightly less than at the Hotel Polom.

Hotel Slovakia, náměsti V. I. Lenina (tel. 465-72 or 465-73; Telex 75606), is the city's best hotel. The 140 rooms are well lit and modern, with large bathtubs in the bathrooms. A large bust of Lenin guards the square in front of the hotel. In a major city this hotel would certainly be more expensive, but in Želina it's a real value. Singles are 234 Kčs ($19.80) and doubles run 312 Kčs ($26.40). It's about a 10- to 15-minute walk from the bus station. There is also a good restaurant downstairs (see our dining recommendations).

Grand Hotel, Sladkovičova 1 (tel. 232-91 or 210-56), located off the town square and about ten minutes from the bus station. This B hotel offers small rooms with sinks, but no bathrooms, at 104 Kčs ($8.80) for singles and 156 Kčs ($13.20) for doubles; triples with bathrooms cost 286 Kčs ($24.20). Light sleepers should go elsewhere, however: a variety program downstairs sometimes means late-night noise.

If the town's other hotels are full and you have to make your way to the **Hotel Slovan,** Safarikova ulice (tel. 205-56 or 208-74), brace yourself for your first encounter with the receptionist: she's often hostile to visitors. If you manage to work your way past her, you'll find standard B-category facilities for a very reasonable 104 Kčs ($8.80) for a single without private bathroom, and 156 Kčs ($13.20) for a similar double. Showers cost an additional 26 Kčs ($2.20).

A Starvation-Budget Choice

Readers traveling on a shoestring should check into the **Hotel Dukla,** Dimitrovova 3 (tel. 202-34). The Dukla slightly resembles a Western motel, since you enter the small basic rooms from an outdoor walkway on the second floor. Although the hotel is rated in the C category, the public bathrooms are usable, and thus better than most class C plumbing facilities. Singles with sinks cost 78 Kčs ($6.60), doubles run 150 Kčs ($12.70), and triples go for 180 Kčs ($15.25). Add 24 Kčs ($2.05) for each shower. You'll find the hotel just a few minutes from the Old Town Square.

DINING: Most locals consider the **Hotel Slovakia,** náměsti V. I. Lenina (tel. 465-72 or 465-73), as Želina's best restaurant. The decor here is unexceptional, with modern hotel wall decorations as well as large glass windows overlooking Lenin's huge bust in the square below (although you can only see the top of his balding head from the second floor of the restaurant, you can admire the fine work, complete with its reproduction of Lenin's signature on the base, more closely after your meal). You'll find a menu in English, and a large selection to choose from. We enjoyed the sautéed trout for about $3.50, but you can also dine on game such as venison, or beef, veal, or pork dishes, many prepared with local Slovak recipes.

IMPORTANT ADDRESSES: Čedok operates their office at Hodzova ulice 9 (tel. 207-74, 206-75, or 220-87). **Autoturist** helps motorists from their office at trieda Obrancov mieru (tel. 335-35).

SIDE TRIPS FROM ŽELINA: You'll probably want to visit the Low Fatras from your base in Želina. We suggest heading first for **Vratna,** in the heart of the mountains. Buses leave frequently from Želina, for 10 Kčs (85¢), and take less than an hour to get there.

Get off at the last stop in Vratna (at the Hotel Vratna). From here you can take a cable car 2,500 feet up **Chleb Mountain,** and then wander around admiring the beautiful landscape. Although you won't find snow in the summer, the weather can be brisk even in July, so dress warmly and bring hiking shoes.

If you want to set your sights on a fixed destination, consider the **Chalet pod Chlebom,** 30 minutes away, a mountain lodge that also serves food. Hard-core hikers can set their sights for **Medzihole,** about 3¾ hours away (you'll find the **Chata pod Rozsutcom** there), or for **Zazriva,** site of another tourist chalet 7¾ hours away.

Those who don't want to go hiking will still enjoy riding on the ski lifts, breathing the fresh air, taking in the mountains and forested landscape of the Low Fatras. You can also dine at the Hotel Vratna at the foot of Chleb Mountain, where the bus from Želina stops.

Those going up the mountain via cable car may find that lines are long going up, but virtually nonexistent coming down. From December until the end of March you can trade your hiking boots for skis and savor some downhill runs.

Low Fatra Accommodations

For those who want to complete their complete mountain experience by living in the mountains, we recommend the following hotels.

At the **Interhotel Vratna,** 01306 Terchova (tel. 952-23), 2,500 feet above sea level, you'll find quaint wood-cabin-style rooms without bathrooms. Singles run 172 Kčs ($14.55), doubles are 187 Kčs ($15.85), and triples go for 234 Kčs ($19.80). The management here recommends reserving six months in advance. There is a decent restaurant downstairs.

Chata na Gruni, 01306 Terchova (tel. 953-24), 3,200 feet above sea level, is for the hearty outdoors types only. Located in a tranquil area where sheep roam (you can get up here by cable car), it offers hostel-style rooms each sleeping three to six people. A bed for the night costs 65 Kčs ($5.50).

Hotel Boboty, 01306 Terchova (tel. 952-27 to 952-29; Telex 075314), is a fairly modern B* hotel with a sauna, swimming pool, restaurant, disco, and other facilities. It's good for those seeking simple relaxation. Every two of the hotel's 100 rooms share a shower. Singles are 187 Kčs ($15.85), doubles go for 281 Kčs ($23.80), and triples run 354 Kčs ($30). In addition to these rates, you must spend at least 105 Kčs ($8.90) per day in the hotel's restaurants.

You can also stay in private homes in the area. Inquire at SlovakoTour in Terchova (tel. 953-05).

3. The High Tatras

The crowning glory of Czechoslovakia are the Vyoské Tatry, or High Tatra Mountains. The High Tatras are truly stunning, boasting some of the highest peaks outside of the Alps.

Much of the area was settled by Saxons, who were invited in to defend the western provinces from Tartar attacks and to mine in the mountains. The Saxons stayed in this vicinity and formed a semi-independent province in the 13th century.

Numerous beautiful wooden structures, especially 18th-century churches, stand in the area east of the High Tatras.

There are great hiking opportunities in summer and good skiing in the winter months. Vacationing in the Tatras is much less expensive than in the Alps. We recommend the High Tatras for the tourist looking for some of Eastern Europe's most beautiful countryside to wander through.

ORIENTATION: Poprad is the major transportation hub servicing the High Tatras. There is an airport as well as rail connections. From Poprad, a narrow-gauge railway winds up to several small resort villages at the foot of the mountains. Running roughly diagonally from the southwest to the northeast for a distance of roughly 15 miles are the towns of Štrbské Pleso, Starý Smokovec, and Tatranská Lomnica, the three main resort towns of the High Tatras.

The Tatras are also shared by the Poles, and an overly vigorous hike can accidentally place you inside the territory of the People's Republic of Poland. Border officials in the area seem to be used to this sort of thing, however, and will do no more than point you back in the right direction toward your hotel and country.

The narrow-gauge railway runs from Poprad to all the towns about every 30 to 45 minutes between 6 a.m. and 8 p.m. from April to September. Tickets can be purchased inside the Poprad station for 3.50 Kčs (30¢) to Starý Smokovec. There are also several chair lifts and cable cars, even a cog-railway, that shuttle tourists up the mountainsides. Most cost less than 15¢ to ride and are open from 6 or 7 a.m. until 7 or 8 p.m.

Štrbské Pleso

Site of Czechoslovakia's ski-jump competitions, Štrbské Pleso comes alive in the winter with cross-country skiing and ice skating. In the summer it's the southwesternmost resort town in the Tatras. From here you can head up into several major valleys adorned with shimmering mountain lakes. There is also a lodge and restaurant at Popradské Pleso, up the slope about three miles away.

Tatranská Lomnica

At the other end of the Slovakian Tatras is the town of Tatranská Lomnica. In the winter Tatranská Lomnica has the best skiing opportunities, as well as bobsled runs and ice skating. In the summer you can take a cable car to the top of Lomnický peak (8,632 feet) for a fantastic view of the surrounding country-side and most of the Tatra range.

Starý Smokovec

Starý Smokovec, the largest town and the center of the High Tatra resort area, actually includes several smaller towns that have merged together for all practical purposes. With several hotels and the main railway station, it's a good place to begin any exploration of the Tatras. Since it's in the center of the mountain range you have the greatest choice of hiking routes in the summer and cross-country skiing trails in the winter.

TOURIST INFORMATION: There is a large and well-equipped Čedok tourist office in Starý Smokovec (tel. 24-16), and a smaller office in Tatranská Lomnica (tel. 96-74-28). The Čedok offices handle all plane connections and can help you with advance ticket purchases. The towns are small so you should have little difficulty finding the Čedok offices. You can exchange money in any Interhotel reception, and at the Čedok offices.

ACCOMMODATIONS: There are several good hotels and many excellent camping sites, though in July and August many of the budget hotels fill up. There are also some mountain huts, but they are packed year round. Since many of the hotels often fill up in the high summer months, it's best to arrive early in the morning and inquire at the Čedok offices. For rock-bottom-budget travelers we recommend stopping in at the CKM offices in Prague (see Chapter XII) and making reservations at any of the several youth hostels in the area. Finding spaces in these establishments without a reservation in the summer is often a disappointing task.

Štrbské Pleso

In Štrbské Pleso is the **Hotel Panoráma** (tel. 921-11), a ten-story concrete structure that has some excellent mountain views. It's an expensive choice: doubles cost $48 with a private bath and breakfast. There is a restaurant and café in the hotel, often filled with the very international crowd Štrbské Pleso attracts. The Hotel Panoráma is about a three-minute walk from the train station.

There's also a Class B establishment, the **Hotel Fis** (tel. 922-21 or 923-01), that has some triples without private bath for about $18 per person. There are no organized camping sites in Štrbské Pleso.

Tatranská Lomnica

Some of the best hotel and camping opportunities of all the towns are here. The modern **Hotel Horec** (tel. 96-72-61), about half a mile from the train station, is located well away from the other hotels. The double rooms with private baths cost $39 and, though small, are clean and quiet.

The **Hotel Mier** (tel. 96-79-36) is a real bargain, with doubles for $23. But it's almost always packed with tour groups.

Luckily, Tatranská Lomnica has several excellent campsites, the best of which is the **Eurocamp FICC.** The Eurocamp is the largest and most modern camp in the High Tatras, with hot running water and a restaurant and café. Camping spots cost less than $4. To get here, take the bus from the station or the train one stop back toward Poprad.

There are also four-bed cabins and a 90-bed youth hostel.

Starý Smokovec

Though the old **Grand Hotel** may not live up to its prewar standards, it's still a beautiful and relaxing place to stay. It is quiet and the oversize bathtubs are a blessing after a hard day's hiking. A double room runs $56 a day here without breakfast. The Grand Hotel usually has vacancies and is worth the splurge.

There are several other new hotels in the B category, but all are generally reserved for group use. Try the **Hotel Park,** which has large double rooms with private baths for $37. Horribly modern, it nevertheless is one of the better hotel values in Starý Smokovec.

Unfortunately, Starý Smokovec does not have the camping opportunities that Tatranská Lomnica has, so the pressure on the hotels is that much greater.

DINING: All the Class A hotels have good restaurants, but of particular note in the High Tatras is the **Zbojnícka koliba,** a typical wine restaurant in Tatranská Lomnica. About three or four minutes from the Hotel Praha, the Zbojnícka koliba is known for its grill specialties. Dinner won't cost more than 50 Kčs ($4.25). In the evenings a large crowd gathers, the beer flows freely, and a local folk band pumps out solid Slovak favorites to the delight of all.

In Starý Smokovec, about 15 minutes from the Grand Hotel is another folk-style restaurant with a good selection of wild game, in season.

If you go hiking, it's best to stop in one of the stores in Starý Smokovec or Tatranská Lomnica and pick up some bread, cheese, and sausage. The food at the high mountain chalets is very expensive and quite limited.

SHOPPING: The local folk art is known for its bright colors and excellent craftsmanship. From Zvolen come delicate lace and embroidery, and nearer to the Tatras are numerous peasant costumes of brilliantly dyed, homespun wool. Many of these handmade folkwares are available in the local Tuzex shops.

Part Four

HUNGARY

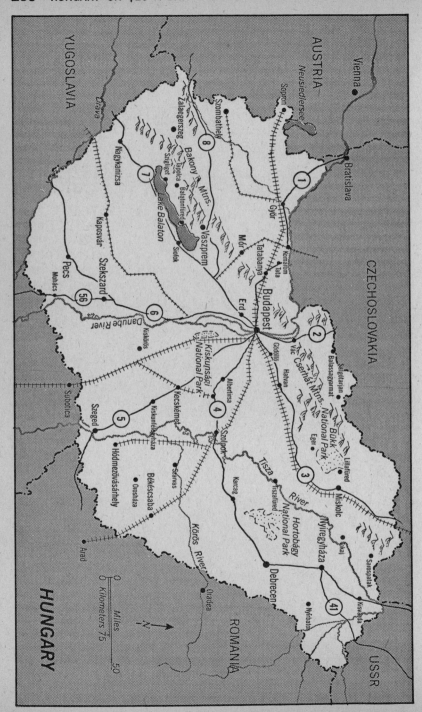

Chapter XV

INTRODUCING HUNGARY

1. About Hungary
2. Rules and Regulations
3. Getting There
4. Getting Around
5. Accommodations
6. Food and Drink
7. The ABCs of Hungary

A LAND OF RIVERS AND PLAINS, a history of vast empires ruled by the iron Magyar horsemen astride their fleet-footed steeds, Christianity tempered by Ottoman-Turkish influences, vineyards filled with juicy fat grapes ripening in the strong southern sun, small towns unchanged since the 18th century nestling in green valleys—all of this is Hungary.

A small country, about the size of Indiana (35,000 square miles), in the middle of Eastern Europe, Hungary has 11 million or so citizens, who speak a language not related to any other in Europe, except Finnish. Today Hungary boasts some of the most beautiful medieval towns in its western provinces. Lake Balaton, an inland sea that gives the country and the people a certain Mediterranean ambience, is a water-lover's paradise. Budapest, once the capital of the Austro-Hungarian Empire, has a legacy of fine baroque buildings and broad avenues. The Great Hungarian Plain or puszta, a short distance east of Budapest, reminds one more of the vast Asian steppes than of the more varied European geography. Hungarian cooking offers some of the most varied and delicious fare in the world. Elements of Eastern, Mediterranean, German, and French cuisine have been combined in Hungary to tempt and excite every palate. And Hungary is a country of natural and cultural wealth, with some of the most hospitable people in all of Europe.

SUGGESTED ITINERARIES: We recommend at least a week to see Hungary, but if you are just making a brief excursion to Hungary from Vienna, you should find the time to get to Budapest, once the other capital of the Austro-Hungarian Empire. Budapest is a fascinating city that will take at least two nights, even for the most hurried tour. In western Hungary are some of the most beautiful medieval towns you'll find anywhere: Köseg and Sopron are each worth a night's stay. Farther south in western Hungary is Lake Balaton, where you can spend a summer at the beach. Depending on how much work is needed on your tan, adjust the length of your stay accordingly; less than a night would be too bad. The great plain presents some challenges for the traveler without a car, but the towns of Pécs and Szeged on the southern edges of the plain are well worth a visit and are good base towns for further exploration. Eger, in the north, and the surrounding mountains are a hiker's dream and worth at least one night's visit.

1. About Hungary

A CAPSULE HISTORY: In the 3rd century B.C. Celtic tribes established themselves across much of the western part of Hungary, but it was the Romans who built the first chain of settlements and brought an excellent road system to the area. A few miles from Budapest the Romans built a major legion garrison which later developed into a city. In A.D. 106, Aquincum, as the settlement was known, was made the capital of Lower Pannonia, an area incorporating parts of modern Hungary, Yugoslavia, and Romania. Other Hungarian towns, such as Sopron, Szombathely, and Pécs, were initially the Roman settlements of Scarbantia, Savaria, and Sopianae, respectively.

Arrival of the Magyars

The Magyars, the tribe from which modern Hungarians are descended, entered modern-day Hungary about A.D. 896. Moving into the Danube Valley, they easily subjugated the established Slavic tribes. The Magyars were hard-riding horse people whose favored offensive tactic was to gallop around enemy forces and shower them with arrows. The successful conquest of the Danube Valley bred confidence, and the Magyars began to raid westward. By A.D. 924 they had crossed the Rhine and plundered as far as Champagne in what is now France. Thirty years later they rode through Burgundy, crossed the Alps into Italy, and returned after completing one of the more unsettling wine tours that the French and Italians had yet experienced. The Saxon noble, Duke Henry the Builder, checked the Magyar advance at Merseburg in A.D. 933. The Magyar expansion was finally halted when Henry's son, Otto the Great, defeated them at the battle of Lechfeld in A.D. 955.

The First Hungarian Kings

After that defeat the Magyars abandoned their westward expansion. Exactly 1,000 years after the birth of Christ, the Hungarians crowned their first Christian king, Stephen I. In 1222 the much-lauded Hungarian Golden Bull was drafted. Like the Magna Carta, the Golden Bull was a historic document that paved the way for reform. Nineteen years later Odgai, son of Genghis Khan, and his "Golden Horde" (better known as the Mongols) charged through. In the wake of the two-year Mongol rampage young King Béla IV began to rebuild his newly acquired kingdom. He granted a charter to the fledgling trading town of Pest on the east bank of the Danube. Béla IV also began the serious fortification of Buda Hill, a project which continued until the middle of the 19th century. Hungary, during Béla IV's reign, waxed powerful.

Dissolution of the Empire and the Ottoman Turks

Under Béla IV, Hungary expanded into territory that today is part of Romania, Yugoslavia, Poland, and Russia. With the end of the Arpad Dynasty in 1301 a series of foreign-born kings held sway over Hungary as enemies slowly whittled down the empire. Hungary experienced decline and stagnation until the threat of Ottoman (an empire that was centered in what is now Turkey) invasion in the middle of the 15th century galvanized the country. A Hungarian noble, János Hunyadi, led the Christian forces to a monumental victory over the Ottoman armies in 1456 near what is now Belgrade. The victory was so important to the defense of Europe that Catholics still celebrate it to this day with the joyous pealing of church bells. János Hunyadi's son, Matthias Corvinus, was crowned king in 1458.

The Reign of Matthias Corvinus

Under King Matthias Hungary experienced a golden age of artistic and intellectual development that lasted until his death in 1490. Many of the beautiful structures that grace Hungarian skylines, in particular the Matthias Church on Buda Hill, were constructed in this period. However, as you gaze, remember this: many of the churches were at one time also mosques. The church in the main square at Pécs was once a mosque, as was the Matthias Church in Budapest and many other churches throughout Hungary. The mosques and many baths that dot the countryside are all reminders of the successful Ottoman Turkish invasion in the 16th century.

The Ottoman Turkish Occupation

After the death of King Matthias scheming nobles and an unsuccessful peasant revolt in 1514, led by György Dózsa, severely weakened Hungary. The Ottoman armies again swept north up the Danube, and in 1526 routed the Hungarian forces in the battle of Mohács. After that victory the Ottoman armies again moved north, capturing the fortified city of Buda in 1541. In 1532 Hungarian troops under Capt. Miklós Jurisich staged a resistance in the town of Kőszeg that can only be described as fantastic. Hungarians boast that the 1,000 sturdy defenders of Kőszeg were all that stood between an Ottoman horde numbering 200,000 of the pasha's finest and the rest of Western civilization. In any event, the Ottomans were delayed and narrowly defeated at the very gates of Vienna. An Ottoman pasha reigned in Buda until a Hapsburg-led army defeated the Ottomans in 1686.

The Hapsburgs, Revolution, and the Two World Wars

Under the Hapsburgs, Hungary, and particularly the combined city of Budapest, experienced a period of rapid economic and cultural growth. It all came to an end with the major social and political upheavals caused by the First World War, the defeat of the Hapsburgs and the division of the empire, and the Great Depression that spread across Europe. In 1919 there was a 133-day Communist government under Béla Kun, followed by a Conservative regime under the regency of Admiral Horthy. Because of Hungary's initial alliance with Nazi Germany and the changing fortunes of war, Hungary was occupied by both Nazi and Soviet forces during World War II. As the battleground for some brutal last-ditch fighting in early 1945, Hungary was virtually in ruins at the war's close; more than 80% of the buildings in Budapest were damaged or destroyed.

Modern Hungary

The country's occupation by Soviet forces after the war led to the formation of a heavy-handed Communist-dominated government in Hungary, but in 1956 reformist currents throughout Eastern Europe encouraged increased Hungarian opposition to the continuing Soviet presence. On October 23 a mass meeting in front of the Budapest radio station was dispersed with gunfire. The result was the 13-day "Hungarian Uprising" which, in the early hours of November 4, was met by an armed force composed almost entirely of Soviet troops. About 2,000 people died in the uprising, and an estimated 200,000 Hungarians fled the country. After order was effectively (albeit brutally) restored, János Kadar, the new Soviet-supported leader, slowly began a course of reform, which has since led to Hungary's present position as one of the most prosperous and liberal of all the Warsaw Pact countries.

THE PEOPLE: Unlike many other Eastern European lands, Hungary has long been an ethnically homogenous country. The origins of the Magyars, as the Hungarians call themselves, are difficult to pin down. They were a nomadic plains people, neither Slavic nor Celtic in origin, though there has been intermingling with these two larger ethnic groups since the Magyars arrived in Europe. Over 95% of the population of 11.7 million call themselves Magyars. The remainder is made up of Germans, Jews, Gypsies, and other ethnic groups.

The Hungarian Forint

The official currency of Hungary is the Forint (Ft), made up of 100 fillers (something rarely seen). Banknotes are printed in denominations of 10, 20, 50, 100, and 500 Forints, and there are coins of 1, 2, 5, and 10 Forints. The prices in this book were calculated at 48 Ft = $1 U.S. Thus 1 Ft = about 2¢, or $10 = 480 Ft. Though this exchange rate will fluctuate a bit, the dollar amounts we have given should remain reasonably constant.

GOVERNMENT: Hungary is officially a Socialist democracy in which the citizens are represented by duly elected members of the National Assembly. The executive branch of government is composed of 14 ministers, presided over by János Kadar, who is also First Secretary of the Hungarian Communist Party.

LANGUAGE: The Hungarian language is different from every other European language except Finnish, to which it is distantly related. As you might imagine, Hungarian is very difficult for English-speaking people to pronounce, and you will probably have to write out street names or addresses in order for Hungarians to understand you. However, we feel that there is no language in which such basic courtesy words as "please" and "thank you" cannot be mastered. Hungarians recognize the problems their language causes for foreigners, and are usually quite patient with visitors who give Hungarian the old college try. In major centers you'll find that some English is spoken, but a phrasebook and a little practice will prove invaluable in the provinces.

SPORTS: Sports are an important part of the Hungarians' daily lives. National character and honor rest on every international competition, hometown pride is at stake in contests between any two municipalities, and so on down to competitions between rival squads on a soccer team. Sports are taken very seriously in Hungary.

For a landlocked nation Hungary has many water-oriented activities. The fishing is good, with numerous protected and stocked watersheds. Sailing on Lake Balaton is pursued with fervor. There are numerous rivers on which you can raft or canoe, and the Danube is the principal artery of communication in Hungary.

Hunting is also an important part of the Hungarian tourist scene. Although there were many "hunters" in the country in 1956, only 19 of them were registered; in 1983 some 15,000 registered "guest" hunters tried their luck in the Hungarian wilds. For more information write or phone MAVAD, the state hunting office, at 1014 Budapest, Úri utca 39, Hungary (tel. 532-358 or 161-688; Telex 225965).

Better yet you can go **hiking** almost anywhere you please on the numerous well-maintained trails. Some of the most beautiful areas are the Mátra Mountains in the north, the hills just west of Budapest, and some of the terrain north of Lake Balaton.

Hungarian history would have been much different if the Magyars had not been the consummate horse people that they were. This tradition of **riding** and superior breeds of horses lives on today. Practically the entire Great Plain is devoted to horse farms, and the spirited mounts and even more spirited riders were once Hungary's most valuable resource. The list of riding centers in Hungary is too lengthy to include here; almost every Hungarian town has some riding school or facility.

NATURE RESERVES AND PARKS: Some 5% of Hungary's total land area is protected by law. There are two major national parks. **Hortobagy** is a section of the vast Great Plain between the Tisza River in the west and Debrecen in the east. An area of marsh and forests, it's best known for the vast expanse of rolling grassland. Its flatness and the distances involved make this area better for riding than for hiking. The other national park is the **Bükk Plateau,** north and east of Eger, comprising some 70,000 acres of natural caves and forests. It's excellent for hiking and camping. There are hundreds of other reserves and protected areas throughout Hungary.

ART AND CULTURE: The Hungarians pride themselves on the fact that their small country has contributed such greats as Franz Lizst and Béla Bartók to the music world and their traditional revolutionary poets, including Endre Ady, Attila Józef, and Sándor Petőfi, the most romantic of all the 19th-century Hungarian poets, to the literary world. In the prose realm, Hungarians have contributed major works in every category from plays to the political philosophical works of Arthur Koestler (though you won't find *Darkness at Noon* for sale in Hungary today).

Folk Art

Hungary boasts relics from its rich peasant history and fine examples of contemporary peasant culture. A few of the centers of folk culture in Hungary are Buzsák, Mezőkövesd, and Kalocsa, but in practically every town there's a peasant or cultural history museum. Many of the Intourist shops carry folkcrafted items.

Spas

Spas are an integral part of Hungarian culture, not just for their curative benefits but their social ones as well. Hungary can boast a second "sea" besides the inland Lake Balaton—the underground sea of mineral water. The thermal and mineral springs are deemed effective cures for a variety of ailments from nervous disorders to gastric complaints. In Budapest alone there are 123 mineral springs, and there are extensive springs at Héviz, Bükfürdő, Hajdúszoboszlo, and Zalakaros, to name a few. The effectiveness of this form of treatment is not discussed here, but as one Eastern European said, "You Americans don't hold much for the mineral cure. You believe in pills. Here [in Eastern Europe] we are a spa-minded people."

Art and Culture Today

Hundreds of cultural events take place every year in Hungary. With concerts at Keszthely and Matonvásár, the series of events in the Budapest Spring Festival and the Budapest Music Weeks, the open-air concerts at Szeged, and over 500 other scheduled events, Hungary is alive with performing artists. If you visit Budapest you can pick up the free copy of *Programme,* a monthly listing of everything going on in Hungary in the arts. There's also a free "Events in Hungary" booklet that the IBUSZ people can send you.

2. Rules and Regulations

TOURIST INFORMATION: You can contact **IBUSZ**, the Hungarian National Travel Bureau, at their New York City office: IBUSZ Hungarian Travel Ltd., 630 Fifth Ave., Rockefeller Center, Suite 520, New York, NY 10020 (tel. 212/ 582-7412). For the IBUSZ office in England, contact Danube Travel Ltd., 6 Conduit St., London W1R 9TG U.K. (tel. 01/493-0263).

They are friendly and have a variety of different tours available. They can also help you reserve a room in any of the hotels that we mention, or even contact one of the private room services to rent apartments or rooms for extended periods.

VISAS: All U.S. and Commonwealth citizens must have a valid passport and visa to enter Hungary—no exceptions. Any U.S. citizen should be able to obtain a Hungarian visa within 48 hours of applying directly at any authorized Hungarian consulate, embassy, or IBUSZ office.

Single-entry, multiple-entry, and transit visas are available at varying fees. Transit visas permit a maximum stay of 48 hours. Regular tourist visas permit varying stays up to a maximum of 30 days.

When your visa is stamped, the number of days you'll be in Hungary should be indicated on it, as well as your entry date.

If you happen to come from an "infected area" of the world, you must also present a valid, yellow international vaccination certificate.

Visas are also issued at main road, *not* rail, border-crossing points and at the international airport in Budapest. We quote the U.S. Embassy: "Despite the availability of border visas, the Embassy's standard recommendation is that United States travelers obtain their Hungarian visas in advance of coming. Dual U.S.-Hungarian citizens and non-citizen legal permanent residents should particularly do so."

CURRENCY EXCHANGE: There is no minimum or mandatory currency exchange in Hungary.

CUSTOMS: Hungarian Customs officials are fairly relaxed as far as their dealings with Westerners are concerned. We heard no reports of problems on any of the Western border crossings.

You are allowed to bring no more than 400 Ft ($8.35) per person across the border. Anything above this limit is unconditionally and automatically donated to the Hungarian Border Patrol. There is no limit to the amount of hard (Western) currency you may bring in as long as the currency is declared. You can import small gift items up to a maximum of 5,000 Ft ($104) and you can bring out 3,000 Ft ($62.50) of Hungarian goods without receipts. Everything else is subject to duties.

Narcotics, anti-statist literature, pornography, explosives, and firearms are strictly forbidden. Hunting equipment and most electronic equipment (two-way radios, radar detectors, etc.) must have special permits.

Pets

Dogs and other animals must have rabies shots and accompanying certificates. Dogs must also have distemper shots.

Motor Vehicles

When entering Hungary with a car you must fill out a car data form. List the car's registration number and your insurance card number, and the name of the person, if different, who will drive the car back out.

REGISTRATION: All nonsocialist citizens must be registered with the police within 24 hours of their arrival in Hungary. Most hotels and pensions do this automatically, but if you're staying in private homes, be certain to register yourself. The head of the family can register for everyone.

3. Getting There

See the section in Chapter II on Vienna, a gateway to Eastern Europe; there we detail air travel to Vienna, which is generally much cheaper than any direct flight to Eastern Europe.

BY AIR: There is just one international airport that serves all of Hungary: Ferihegy International Airport (tel. 140-400) on the outskirts of Budapest. Lufthansa offers a choice of daily connections via Frankfurt, Munich or Dusseldorf.

For information or assistance while in Budapest, contact Lufthansa at: 1052, Vaci utca 19-21 (tel. 184-511).

Flying to Budapest

The First Class and Business Class fares in the chart below allow unlimited stopovers. Excursion Fare is limited to two stopovers in each direction for a charge of $25 each. The APEX fare permits no stopovers and has a 21-day advance purchase requirement and also a $75 penalty fee for cancellation. Fares are subject to a $3 departure tax plus a $5 Custom User fee and are subject to change without notice.

Round-Trip Fares To Budapest

	From:	New York	Anchorage	Atlanta	Boston	Chicago	Houston/ Dallas-Ft. Worth	San Francisco/ Los Angeles	Miami	Phila-delphia
First Class	All Year	$3446	$4572	$4134	$3446	$4096	$4178	$4808	$3888	$3666
Business Class	All Year	1978	2900	2366	1978	2422	2308	2888	2300	2142
10 Day-3 Month Excursion	Sept. 15–May 14	1060	1498	1188	1060	1170	1188	1243	1206	1123
	May 15–Sept. 14	1276	1714	1404	1276	1386	1404	1459	1422	1339
7 – 180 Day APEX	Nov. 1–May 31 Midweek	749	1187	877	749	859	877	932	895	812
	Nov. 1–May 31 Weekend	799	1237	927	799	909	927	982	945	862
	Apr. 1–Mar 31 Midweek	799	1237	927	799	909	927	982	945	862
	Sept. 16–Oct. 31 Weekend	849	1287	977	849	959	977	1032	995	912
	June 1–Sept. 15 Midweek	899	1337	1027	899	1009	1027	1082	1045	962
	June 1–Sept. 15 Weekend	949	1387	1077	949	1059	1077	1132	1095	1012

Midweek = Mon–Thurs
Weekend = Fri–Sun

BY CAR: The two major international roads that link Hungary with the West are the E5 from Vienna and the E15 from Berlin.

BY BUS: All international bus travel must be paid entirely in hard currency. There are two express buses daily to Vienna, one at 7 a.m. arriving just after 11:30 a.m. and another at 5 p.m. arriving at 9:35 p.m. The cost is 262 Austrian schillings ($11) for a one-way adult ticket. In the summer there's also an express bus to Munich (at 6:30 a.m.) as well as to Venice (at 6:20 a.m.).

BY TRAIN: There are numerous train connections into Hungary. Remember that you can *not* get a visa at the border when arriving by train.

BY BOAT: There is a scheduled **hydrofoil** service between Vienna and Budapest. For reservations and more information, in Vienna contact IBUSZ Wien, Kärntnerstrasse 26 (tel. 52-42-08 or 52-48-70), or DDSG on Mexiko-Platz 8; in Budapest contact MAHART, Belgrád rakpart (tel. 181-953), or any of the main IBUSZ offices. A one-way ticket on the hydrofoil costs approximately $50 from Vienna to Budapest.

4. Getting Around

BY AIR: There is no domestic air service in Hungary.

BY CAR: You drive on the right and obey the standard European rules-of-the-road. Hungarians try to keep things interesting by introducing carts, bicycles, pedestrians, even livestock on most of the major roads. Drive alertly.

The **speed limit** on highways is 120 km/h (75 mph); on other roads, 95 km/h (60 mph); and in built-up areas, 60 km/h (35 mph). Pedestrians have the right of way in "zebra crossings" and when turning at road junctions.

If you want to extend your stay in Hungary indefinitely (in other words, go to jail for a long time), imbibe any substance that will affect your ability to drive and then get behind the wheel. Alcohol, sleeping pills, drugs, and medicines of any sort must *not* be taken by the driver. The Hungarian police are very, *very* strict in this regard, and keep a sharp eye out for offenders.

A couple of more mandatory rules: Three-point (shoulder harness) seat-belts must be worn by everyone in the front seat of a vehicle; no children under the age of 6 are allowed in the front seat; all motorcycle riders and passengers must wear crash helmets; in populated areas you may use your horn only to avoid accidents (not if you're in a bad mood).

In case of accidents involving any injury and/or serious damage, you must notify the emergency service immediately. In all other instances it's sufficient to exchange insurance numbers and notify the police within 24 hours of the accident.

Gas stations are generally open from 6 a.m. to 10 p.m., but in large towns there's usually one 24-hour filling station. Normal (86 octane), Super (92 octane), Extra (98 octane), mixtures, and Diesel fuels are all available in Hungary.

Rental Cars

You may rent a car in Hungary if you are 21 or older and have had your driver's license for more than one year. The fee must be paid in hard (Western) currency and includes comprehensive insurance. Most major credit cards are accepted.

BY BUS: The bus station at Engels tér in Budapest is the home of **Volán,** the national bus company (tel. 172-562), open weekdays from 6 a.m. to 6 p.m., on Saturday to 4 p.m.; closed Sunday. They go almost everywhere in Hungary and are a practical alternative to the radial constraints placed on the traveler by a Budapest-centered railway system.

You can also buy an excursion ticket for one, three, or ten days. There are three categories for the ticket: all of Hungary, the Danube Bend region, and the Balaton region. An excursion ticket to all of Hungary will cost $12 for one day, $18 for three days, and $45 for ten days. The other categories are correspondingly cheaper. A good plan for the budget conscious could be the three-day excursion to Lake Balaton for $11.

BY TRAIN: Hungary has a good rail network that is centered on Budapest. You can buy tickets a maximum of 60 days in advance. If you interrupt your journey, your stamped ticket is good for a 24-hour period after the stamped date. Children under 4 travel free; children between 4 and 10 years of age travel half price. Students with the Socialist International Union of Students Card receive a 50% reduction. You can also purchase 10-, 20-, or 30-day continuous-ride tickets.

Tickets and information are available at the **MAV Central Booking Office** at Népköztársaság út 35 in Budapest.

BY BOAT: There's an extensive Danube ferry system that runs from the early spring to the late autumn, depending on the weather. Practically every large town on the river is in the network. There's also a ferry across Lake Balaton between Szántód-rév and Tihany-rév. Tickets are available right at the piers.

HITCHHIKING: Hitchhiking is reasonably safe, though frowned on by the authorities. Hungarian roads are poorly lit, so be very careful when hitchhiking at night.

5. Accommodations

HOTELS: In Hungary, hotels are ranked by the international system of stars, five stars being the most luxurious and one star indicating minimal and inexpensive accommodations. We recommend trying the two-star hotels first, and one-star establishments with a certain bit of caution. Three-star hotels and above are almost always of acceptable quality in Hungary.

CAMPING: All campsites are ranked with one to four stars. Four stars indicates deluxe accommodations, though to date there are none in Hungary. A single-star campsite is basically fenced-off, open ground with communal washing and toilet facilities. The average campsite is 45 square meters, or a square about 22 feet on a side. There are over 100 camping locations in Hungary, open from early May to early October. Most are really only suitable for motor camping, but it's possible to ask locals if you can pitch your tent on their land. Remember, ask first.

PRIVATE ROOMS: There are five classifications from deluxe to budget: a **home** is a private house; a **suite** is a detached unit with separate sleeping rooms, living room, bathroom, and sometimes a kitchen; **first-class rooms** are much like a studio apartment; **second-class rooms** have a private bathroom; and **third-class rooms** vary in size and number of beds, and rarely have a private bathroom.

6. Food and Drink

Our advice here is simple: Forget about your diet in Hungary. Paprika is only the beginning. Fish soup, chicken and paprika, fried bream, strudels, and of course, goulash are all so well prepared as to be irresistible. Could it be a plot to inflict every capitalist visitor with obesity? Not likely, as the Hungarians are eating right along with you and washing it all down with any number of fine Hungarian wines. The most notable are the full, red Egri bikáver and the very sweet, golden Tokay Aszu.

We recommend that you think of **paprika** as a light melody that weaves its way through Hungarian cooking rather than an ever-present theme. Certainly the orange-red spice is used with creativity and imagination in Hungarian cooking, but it has unfortunately become practically the sole thing that Americans think of when they think of Hungarian food.

There is the famous *gulyás* or goulash of Magyar plains origin, a hearty soup or a light stew. There seem to be about as many ways to prepare it as there are Hungarians with pots to cook it in. Add some chicken instead of beef or lamb and you have *pörkölt,* and add cream to that and the dish becomes *paprikás.* In restaurants along the Danube or on Lake Balaton you'll find *halászlé,* a fish soup that often contains more than one variety of fish. And don't forget the thick cabbage soup, *káposztaleves;* Hungarian cooks keep a pot of this bubbling on the back burner for any unexpected guests.

The Hungarians seem to have remembered only the tastier aspects of the Hapsburg legacy. The light, flaky *rétes* pastries are very similar to a torte, and the Hungarians have developed the perfect cream puff, called *indianfank.*

7. The ABCs of Hungary

AUTO REPAIR: All emergency auto repair is handled by the **Hungarian Automobile Club.** The breakdown service (tel. 152-212) operates daily from 7 a.m. to 10 p.m.

BLACK MARKET: It's not worth it! At most you'll get 75 to 80 Forints (about $1.50 officially) for your dollar, and the penalties are stiff if you get caught. The black market is here, but the exchange rate is already so good that the black marketeers are hard-pressed to do better.

CLIMATE: The climate in Hungary is very pleasant, cool in winter and warm in summer, with few temperature extremes. The annual mean temperature is 50° Fahrenheit, and summer temperatures rarely exceed 80° to 85°. There are over 2,000 hours of sunshine per year in sunny Hungary.

CREDIT CARDS: Most major credit cards are accepted for major purchases in the larger towns; otherwise, you'll need cash. Note that there are no cash advances given on credit cards in Hungary; you'll have to nip across the border to Vienna for that.

CRIME: Violent crime statistics are very difficult to come by in Communist countries, but crime is definitely not a major problem here—just take the usual precautions. Even single women traveling alone should have no difficulties. The police we talked to said that much of Hungary's criminal problem arrived with the tourists.

CURRENCY: The official currency of Hungary is the **Forint (Ft)**, made up of 100 fillers (something rarely seen). Banknotes are printed in denominations of 10, 20, 50, 100, and 500 Forints, and there are coins of 1, 2, 5, and 10 Forints. The prices in this book were calculated at 48 Ft = $1 U.S. Thus 1 Ft = about 2¢, or $10 = 480 Ft. Though this exchange rate will fluctuate a bit, the dollar amounts we have given should remain reasonably constant.

ELECTRICITY: The electric current in Hungary is 220 volts, 50 cycles, A.C.

EMBASSIES AND CONSULATES: The U.S. Embassy in Hungary is in Budapest at V. Szabadság tér 12 (tel. 124-224, 329-374, or 329-375). There are no U.S. Consulates in the country.

The **Canadian Embassy** is in Budapest at Budakeszi út 55/d (tel. 365-738, 365-728, 165-949, or 165-858).

The **British Embassy** is in Budapest at Harmincad utca 6 (tel. 182-888).

EMERGENCY: You can call for help at the same telephone numbers anywhere in the country: dial 07 for the police, 04 for an ambulance, and 05 to report a fire.

FIRST AID: "All foreigners visiting Hungary are entitled to first aid." So states the Hungarian Tourist Bureau. However, your insurance may not pay for it, so make certain before you go abroad that your insurance provides international coverage.

GUIDES AND INTERPRETERS: Guides and interpreters are available through IBUSZ and many of the other travel agencies. Most can be hired for only a day, but if you need an interpreter for the duration of your stay, contact IBUSZ.

HOLIDAYS: The official holidays in Hungary are: January 1 (New Year's Day), April 4 (Liberation Day), May 1 (May Day, or Labor Day), August 20 (Constitution Day), November 7 (Anniversary of the Great October Socialist Revolution), December 24-25 (Christmas).

NEWS AND MEDIA: Because of the language barrier most Westerners find Hungarian television programs difficult to follow. There's an English-language radio program, with weather reports, every morning.

In Budapest, Western newsweeklies are available at the larger hotels. For the socialist view of the world you can pick up the *Daily News,* free in large hotels in most parts of Hungary.

POST OFFICE: Office hours are 8 a.m. to 6 p.m. Monday through Saturday. In Budapest there are two 24-hour post offices: at Lenin krt. 105/107 and at Baross tér 11/c. Letter boxes are red and are emptied once daily.

STORE HOURS: Throughout Hungary stores are open Monday through Saturday from 10 a.m. to 5 or 6 p.m. (in Budapest, until 8 p.m.). Business offices keep about the same hours as in the West, sometimes opening and closing an hour earlier.

TELEPHONE, TELEGRAPH, AND TELEX: Making an international telephone call from Eastern Europe is difficult, but it's much less difficult in Hungary. Since most hotels tack on a healthy surcharge to your phone bill, we don't recommend making international calls from your hotel; almost every post office has a telephone capable of handling international calls. We advise doing all your international calling from Budapest, if possible.

If you want to call from Budapest to any other part of Hungary, first dial 06 and wait for a buzzing sound; then dial the local number. For international calls the procedure is the same, except that you first dial 00. There's a foreign-language information number (tel. 172-200) and information for foreign direct-dial calls (tel. 186-977).

TIME: Hungary is seven hours ahead of Eastern Standard or Daylight Time in the U.S.

TIPPING: Tipping is still a fact of life in Communist countries, especially where Westerners are concerned. For restaurants, generally tip 10% to 15%; for all other services, tip 10%.

Chapter XVI

BUDAPEST

1. Orientation
2. Accommodations
3. Dining on a Budget
4. The Sights of Budapest
5. Nightlife
6. The ABCs of Budapest
7. Excursions from Budapest

DESPITE MANY TRIALS, Budapest remains one of the most varied and beautiful European capitals. Its turbulent past gave the city its castles, forts, and tales of heroic deeds enough to strain the sides of its many history museums.

Budapest has not always been the present city that graces both banks of the Danube. Originally Buda and Pest developed as two independent towns divided by the River Danube. Joined physically in 1849 by the Széchenyi Lánchíd (Chain Bridge), the cities were politically united in 1873. Today the city, now connected by more than seven bridges, forms a unique modern metropolis.

Budapest is a city of contrasts. The Ottoman occupation gave Budapest large public baths and introduced Islamic culture into everything from delicately peaked window frames to the numerous, exotic spices found in an authentic Hungarian kitchen. The baths, begun under the Romans and expanded under the Ottomans, harness some of the 123 mineral springs in Budapest alone. The volume of "liquid health," as some Hungarians refer to the mineral waters, that bubbles to the surface is so great that it's called "the second river" (after the Danube, of course). The period of Empire left many of the imposing baroque buildings and stunning parks. Since 1968 new economic reforms led Hungary (and especially Budapest) to become one of the most prosperous regions in Eastern Europe. In all, the blending of both old and new lets the Western visitor experience a vibrant culture that is a colorful blend of its ancient history and present-day political orientation.

A CAPSULE HISTORY: In the Historical Museum of Budapest there is evidence that humans have been living in or near the city site for approximately half a million years. Buda, perched on the last ramparts of the Trans-Danubian hills, was fortified by Celts as early as the 3rd century B.C. In its long and turbulent history Budapest has been invaded and destroyed several times. Located on one of the major east-west axes of communication, it has been in the path of most major European invasions. Since Stephen I was crowned King of Hungary on Christmas Day in A.D. 1000, Hungarians have had to defend their country from Europeans, Muslims, and Asians. In 1241 the rampaging Mongol hordes

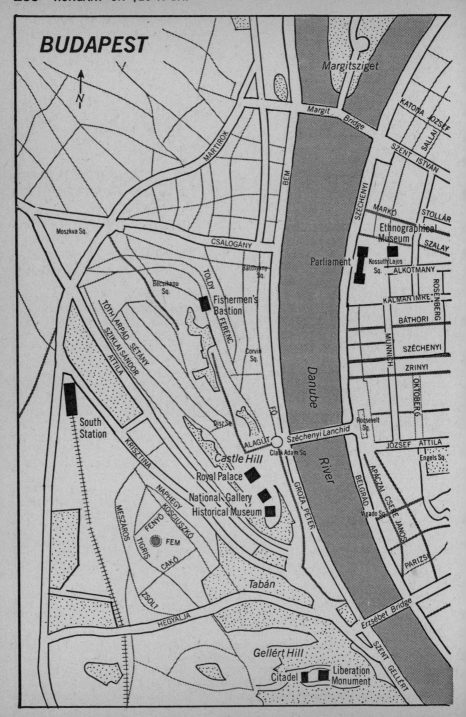

BUDAPEST

N

Margitsziget

Margit Bridge

KATONA JOZSEF

SALLAI

SZENT ISTVAN

MARTIROK

BEM

SZÉCHENYI

MARKÓ

STOLLÁR

Moszkva Sq.

CSALOGÁNY

Ethnographical Museum

SZALAY

Batthyany Sq.

Parliament

Kossuth Lajos Sq.

ALKOTMANY

Becsikapu Sq.

TOLDY

Fishermen's Bastion

KÁLMÁN IMRE

ROSENBERG

BÁTHORI

TÓTH ÁRPÁD SÉTÁNY

FERENC

SZÉCHENYI

SZIKLAI SÁNDOR

Corvin Sq.

MUNNICH

ZRINYI

ATTILA

Danube

OKTÓBER 6.

South Station

Disz Sq.

FŐ

Roosevelt Sq.

ALAGÚT

Széchenyi Lánchíd

JÓZSEF ATTILA

Castle Hill

Clark Adam Sq.

Engels Sq.

KRISZTINA

Royal Palace

River

BELGRÁD

APÁCZAI CSERE JÁNOS

National Gallery

Historical Museum

GRÓZA PÉTER

NAPHEGY

MESZAROS

KOSCIUSZKÓ

FENYO

Vágadó Sq.

FEM

TIGRIS

CAKÓ

PARIZS

ZSOLT

Tabán

Erzsébet Bridge

HEGYALJA

SZENT GELLÉRT

Gellért Hill

Citadel

Liberation Monument

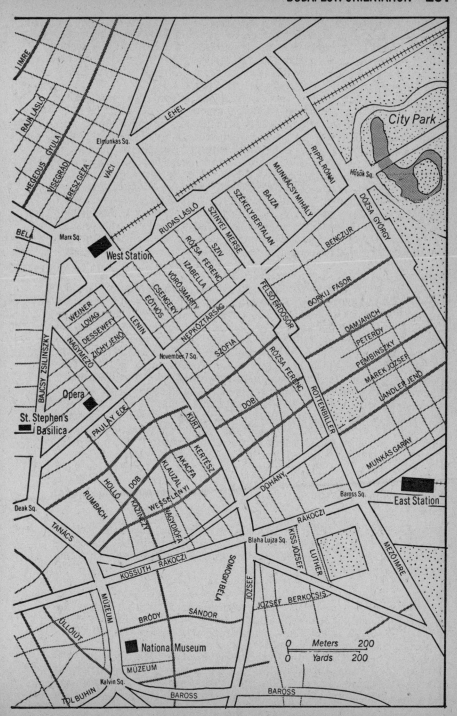

City Park

I IMRE

RAJK LASLO

HEGEDUS

VISEGRADI

GYULAI

KRESZ GEZA

VACI

Elmunkas Sq.

LEHEL

RIPPL RONAI

MUNKÁCSY MIHÁLY

BAJZA

SZÉKELY BERTALAN

SZINYEI MERSE

RUDAS LASLO

BÉLA

Marx Sq.

West Station

RÓZSA FERENC

SZIV

IZABELLA

VÖRÖSMARTY

CSENGERY

EÖTVÖS

WEINER

LOVAG

DESSEWFFY

ZICHY JENŐ

LENIN

NEPKÖZTÁRSASÁG

November 7 Sq.

SZÓFIA

BENCZUR

FELSŐERDŐSOR

GORKIJ FASOR

DAMJANICH

PETERDY

PEMBINSZKY

MAREK JOZSEF

LANDLER JENŐ

DÓZSA GYÖRGY

Hősök Sq.

BAJCSY ZSILINSZKY

NAGYMEZŐ

Opera

St. Stephen's
Basilica

PAULAY EDE

KÜRT

KERTÉSZ

AKÁCFA

KLAUZAL

HOLLÓ

DOB

RUMBACH

KAZINCZY

WESSELÉNYI

NAGYDIÓFA

ROTTENBILLER

RÓZSA FERENC

DOB

DOHÁNY

MUNKÁS GARAY

Baross Sq.

East Station

Deak Sq.

TANÁCS

Blaha Lujza Sq.

RÁKÓCZI

KISS JÓZSEF

LUTHER

MEZŐ IMRE

KOSSUTH

RÁKÓCZI

SOMOGYI BÉLA

JOZSEF

JOZSEF BERKOCSIS

MÚZEUM

ÜLLŐI ÚT

BRÓDY

SÁNDOR

National Museum

MÚZEUM

Kalvin Sq.

| 0 | Meters | 200 |
| 0 | Yards | 200 |

TOLBUHIN

BAROSS

BAROSS

under Ogdai, successor to Genghis Khan, overran and occupied Hungary for about two years. Though the Hungarians were constantly battling their neighbors, Buda and Pest were not destroyed by foreigners for a period of 300 years. In 1541, following the Hungarian defeat at Mohács, Ottoman armies took the fortified town of Buda. Much of the city was again destroyed when the Hapsburgs evicted the Turks in 1686, but reconstruction was swift.

Like most other European capitals, Budapest suffered little physical damage as a result of World War I. However, in the closing days of World War II the Germans fortified Budapest, demolishing all of the Danube bridges and digging into the Castle Hill. It took the Soviets seven weeks of brutal street fighting to finally take the city. Hungary, along with the rest of Europe, was in ruins; in Budapest more than 80% of all structures were damaged or destroyed. In 1956 reformist currents in Eastern Europe led to increased Hungarian opposition to Soviet occupation, centered in Budapest. On October 23, 1956, a mass meeting in front of the Budapest radio station was met with gunfire; the result was a 13-day uprising. During the Hungarian Uprising an estimated 2,000 Hungarians, primarily in Budapest, were killed by a Warsaw Pact force composed almost entirely of Soviet soldiers. Hundreds of buildings were damaged and not all of the bullet marks that can still be seen on side streets are from Nazi guns.

1. Orientation

Budapest is actually two cities: Buda and Pest. Because of its excellent defensive location **Buda** was first a city of forts and castles. Most of its museums and points of historical interest are arrayed along Castle Hill, a mile-long ridge paralleling the Danube. Forested and cool, with narrow roads that twist and coil around the hills, Buda, on the western side of the Danube, is primarily residential. **Pest** was not formally established until King Béla IV chartered the town in the late 13th century. However, people had been trading on the east side of the Danube long before then. Pest, though expansive, does not "sprawl" like many American cities. There is a definite city center contained by concentric ring avenues and sectioned by broad, radial boulevards that slice to the horizon. Always the trading center, Pest is now the commercial heart of the modern city. Founded on the remnants of the old Roman city of Aquincum, Óbuda is the third major section of Budapest that developed independently. Today it's mostly modern housing for the some 2.2 million inhabitants of greater Budapest.

About a day's river journey from Vienna, Budapest lies on the edge of the puszta, the Great Hungarian Plain. Though broken by the Moldavian hills in Romania, this plain eventually merges with the vast expanse of the Asian steppes.

ARRIVING IN BUDAPEST: Budapest is the capital and primary transportation center in Hungary. Since it is geographically and politically the center of the country, you will almost *have* to pass through Budapest at least once during your visit to Hungary.

By Air

Hungary's only airport open for regular commercial flights is **Ferihegy International Airport,** located well outside of Budapest (tel. 340-504, 477-973, or 477-974; Telex 224054). It is a link only with other countries, as Malév, the Hungarian flag carrier, has no domestic service.

For travel to Budapest from Ferihegy, inquire at the IBUSZ desk (tel. 474-353) at the airport, open from 7 a.m. to 9 p.m. Volán runs a bus from the airport to several points in the city, including the main bus terminal. The bus runs every day at half-hour intervals from 5 a.m. to 11 p.m. A one-way ticket costs 20 Ft

(40¢). A **taxi** ride to or from the city should not set you back more than 150 Ft ($3.15). Rock-bottom budgeteers can take bus 93 to the Kőbánya-Kispest metro station for 1.50 Ft (3¢) and then into Budapest.

By Bus

The bus station on Engels tér is the home of **Volán,** the national bus company (tel. 182-122 or 172-562), open weekdays from 6 a.m. to 6 p.m., on Saturday to 4 p.m.; closed Sunday. It's very near the city center and the Engels tér metro stop.

By Train

If you arrive by train from the West, you'll arrive at **Keleti pu.,** or the Eastern Train Station ("pu." is the official abbreviation for *pályaudvar,* or train station). Its attraction to the consumer-goods-starved Eastern European countries and its proximity to Vienna make Budapest one of the great meeting grounds of East and West. In Keleti pu. the hoards of Eastern and Western tourists, African exchange students, and Hungarian soldiers on leave combine to overwhelm much of the traditional gloom that cloaks other Eastern European train stations.

Keleti pu. has two main levels. On the upper level (constructed in the classic stone and iron-beam manner of most European train stations) are the tracks, international ticket counters, train information booths, and the IBUSZ office. The lower level, a modern, plastic-tiled cavern, echoes with the cries of newspaper vendors. There are ticket windows here for local trains, as well as some windows with no observable purpose. If you aren't certain whether you're standing in the correct line, go to the information or ticket window with the shortest line and pressure the ticket seller for directions. At all train stations in Hungary the yellow schedules are departures *(indulo vonatok)* and the white ones are arrivals *(erkezo vonatok).*

TOURIST INFORMATION: A telephone information service, **Tourinform** (tel. 179-800) reputedly can respond in all major languages, including English. We tried it several times and always talked with someone who spoke passable English. Services like Tourinform exemplify the quality that sets Hungarian tourist bureaus above their Eastern European counterparts. They provide up-to-date information on cultural events, museums, and accommodations (only major state-run establishments, however), as well as the weather. Dial 179-800 yourself or ask your concierge.

There are two **publications** you should pick up when you're in town. One is "Events in Hungary '87" (summer edition), which lists all program events, festivals, holidays, and tours throughout Hungary. The second is the monthly "Programme in Ungarn / in Hungary," which has comprehensive listings of events, primarily in Budapest, but it covers the rest of the country as well. Both publications are free and in English, and can be found in the lobbies of most better hotels or at major tourist offices.

GETTING AROUND: It's easy to get around Budapest. Public transportation in Budapest is quick, clean, and safe. There are three metro lines and numerous bus and tram lines, as well as taxis.

Buses and Trams

The bus lines open at 5 a.m. and close down at 11 p.m., though a few of the major bus and tram lines stay open a bit later. Blue tickets, at 3 Ft (6¢), are for buses; trams and omnibuses use yellow tickets, at 2 Ft (4¢). These tickets cannot be used interchangeably; however, no conductor will fine you for using a 3-Ft (6¢) bus ticket where a 2-Ft (4¢) tram ticket would have done. All fares are good for only one noncontinuous ride—no transfers. Tickets can be bought in the numerous kiosks that are adjacent to most stops. With such wallet-wrenching prices—about 4¢ a ride—there's absolutely *no* reason to risk a fine for not using a ticket.

The Metro

Budapest's three metro lines are spotless, not overcrowded, and perfectly safe at all times of the day. If you step over the safety guard line at the edge of the tracks, the personnel watching you by closed-circuit television will sound a buzzer to alert you. The transit network opens at 4 a.m. and closes down sharply at midnight. The fare has recently risen to 2 Ft (4¢); just drop the coin right in the machine.

Taxis

You can call a taxi by dialing 222-222. The base fare on the meter is 8 Ft (17¢), and rises 2 Ft (4¢) every half kilometer. There's no charge for waiting time, so you should add on about 2 Ft (4¢) or 3 Ft (6¢) per minute if you make the driver wait. Cabs may be flagged down on the street, but your best chance is to wait at one of the numerous cab stands, indicated by a "Taxi" sign and clearly marked on tourist maps. A vacant taxi will have the light on its roof lit.

Car Rentals

Budapest is not compact, but walking is, of course, the best option when you're touring a particular district, such as Castle Hill. IBUSZ will rent you a car, and a driver as well, if you want. Inquire at any of the large IBUSZ offices concerning prices and regulations.

2. Accommodations

During the two big trade fairs in Budapest (usually in late May and in September) accommodations are difficult to come by. Also, room rates can escalate an additional 20% if you're staying less than four days in a private apartment.

HOUSING SERVICES: The housing services in Budapest are some of the best-run agencies of their kind in Eastern Europe. They can find you private rooms as well as space in a hotel. Be sure to bring your passport, visa, and currency-exchange voucher (if you plan to pay in Forints).

In the summer there's also a student-run information desk in front of Track 7 at the Keleti pu. (Eastern Train Station) that offers some information on hotel vacancies. What the freshly scrubbed student staff lack in organization, they make up for in energy.

IBUSZ

The IBUSZ office at the Keleti pu., the Eastern Train Station (tel. 429-572), is open from 8 a.m. to 9 p.m. all week. (Keleti pu. is the train station where almost all traffic from the West arrives, so it will probably be your first stop in Budapest.) The IBUSZ office, in the northwest corner of the station (remember that the tracks run in from the east), is usually very crowded. However, if you can endure the lines, or you happen to come at an off-peak hour (mornings are usually better), it's a good bet. IBUSZ has exclusive "rights" to about 150 rooms, of which about 30% are in the center of town. For a single room in the city center you'll pay 160 Ft ($3.35) per night; a double costs 230 Ft ($4.80) to 280 Ft ($5.85). The rest of the rooms are no more than 25 minutes from the city center and run 180 Ft ($3.75) to 210 Ft ($3.40) for a double. All these rooms include access to a bath, but no breakfast. You must have your passport and visa with you, and if you want to stay in the center city, don't hesitate to say so. The staff here are friendly and speak English well. They can also reserve a room for you in another town. If there's a Telex link it will take only a few minutes; if they have to telephone it will take "hours at least."

The IBUSZ office at Petőfi tér 1 (tel. 185-707; Telex 224941) is open 24 hours a day, seven days a week. Located just south of the Duna-Intercontinental, the office is a five-minute walk from the Deák tér metro stop. Again, you must bring your passport and visa with you. In this office only, you must pay everything in hard (Western) currency with no discount. This is offset somewhat by the fact that they don't tack on any hidden costs. They can help you find hotel space as well as private rooms. Doubles cost 300 Ft ($6.25) and up; singles run 150 Ft ($3.10). Apartments must be reserved a minimum of ten days in advance. One-bedroom apartments are 400 Ft ($8.35) per day, and two-bedroom apartments are 600 Ft ($12.50). All apartments have a kitchen, and the price includes a cleaning person who comes once every couple of days. If you have changed money already and you have your exchange voucher, you may change half of it back for the express purpose of paying for your accommodations.

Budapest Tourist Office

The Budapest Tourist office, at Roosevelt tér 5 (tel. 181-453; Telex 225726), is open in the summer Monday through Friday from 8 a.m. to 9 p.m., on Saturday to 8 p.m., and on Sunday from 9 a.m. to 3 p.m. When you present your passport and visa the Budapest Tourist people will help you find hotel space as well as private rooms. Remember to request a location, for example, "as close to Castle Hill as possible." Rooms in or near the city center or Castle Hill tend to be hard to find and may cost more. In general we've found that private room services in Budapest almost always have vacancies, but rooms can be distant from the city center. A double costs 200 Ft ($4.15) to 330 Ft ($6.90); a single, 120 Ft ($2.50) to 160 Ft ($3.35) with a bath. The bath may be shared with a family or other occupant—be sure to ask. Suites cost 300 Ft ($6.25) to 400 Ft ($8.35) per person with a private bath. If you're alone and there are no singles available, you may have to share a room or pay the cost of a double to ensure your privacy.

Budapest Tourist can also make reservations for private rooms almost anywhere in Hungary. They charge 20 Ft (40¢) for the telephone call and 10 Ft (20¢) for the service itself, for a grand total of 30 Ft (60¢). In the summer it can be one of the best 30 Ft you'll spend. The amount of time it takes varies, but it's usually no more than a day. There's a 5% discount if you pay in hard currencies.

Cooptourist Office

The Cooptourist organization, Kossuth Lajos tér 13, north of the Parliament building (tel. 121-017), is open from 9 a.m. to 4 p.m. in summer, the rest of the year to 3 p.m. Cooptourist controls approximately 90 first-class private rooms, 10% to 15% of them in or near the city center. You must have your passport and visa with you, as well as payment in hard currency. A single costs $4 per night, and a double, $6. Bathrooms are usually shared with the owner. Cooptourist also has apartments—one-bedroom for $9 per night and two-bedroom for $12 to $13—but almost all the apartments are relatively far away from the center. You must rent the apartments for a minimum of one week, and they are very difficult to obtain in the high season (July and August).

Cooptourist will reserve private rooms for you in "any other city in Hungary" at no extra charge, but the service takes around 14 days. Don't expect Cooptourist to organize tours or assist in other tourist-oriented activity; they can't do much more than find you a room.

HOTELS: We've grouped our recommendations into two areas: Buda and Pest. Directions are included for those hotels not within walking distance of either the city center in Buda or Moszkva tér in Pest.

In the Buda Hills

A new find and privately run, the **Paradiso Pansió** opened in June 1985 and had no phone at this writing. Quite far from the city center, it's in a quiet residential neighborhood. There are four scrupulously clean double rooms without private bath for 600 Ft ($12.50) a night. Breakfast is 50 Ft ($1.05) extra. The café is open from 9 a.m. to 9 p.m. The restaurant looks out on a peaceful backyard and features a balanced and well-prepared menu. The meats and vegetables are purchased daily from private butchers and growers—and this, the cook modestly insists, is the reason for the freshness and quality of the food. The restaurant is open from noon till 2 a.m., and the bar till 4 a.m., every day. Though the bathrooms are shared, more showers and a sauna are under construction and should be completed by the summer of 1986. Reservations are a must, and in the summer it's nearly impossible to have an extended stay without at least five weeks' notice. Unfortunately Paradiso Pansió has no phone as yet, so to reserve call Citi-taxi at 228-855. Some foresight is needed since this process will take at least a day.

Paradiso Pansió is on Isten-Hegyi út, about 50 yards east from Orbán tér and up a substantial hill, so we strongly recommend a taxi for the first trip. Otherwise take local bus 21 (black lettering) five stops from Moszkva tér or the express bus 21 (red lettering) two stops.

North of Buda

The **Hotel Victoria,** at Dobrentei út 13 (tel. 154-888 or 155-455; Telex 227112), is Budapest's first privately owned hotel. The 13 founding fathers who opened this hotel in 1984 did an impressive job: potted palms decorate the lobby, and on the left as you enter is an attractive breakfast room. The Victoria has 32 double rooms with air conditioning (a rarity in Eastern Europe), private bathrooms, and a sauna downstairs. The rooms in the back of the hotel have oversize windows looking over a peaceful church garden. A double room (there are no singles) costs $36 per night. The Victoria fills up quickly, so call before you come out. Some English is spoken. If you're coming from the train station, take a taxi as the hotel is quite a distance away.

North-Central Buda, Nearer Castle Hill

Perched on top of a hill overlooking Pest, the **Hotel Ifjúság** (pronounced *If*-you-shag), at Zivatar út 1/3 (tel. 154-260), is a sight to behold. It has an orange-and-pink façade that has caused some locals to remark, with a sniff, that the colors seem to attract mainly Soviet tourists. Though the color scheme leaves something to be desired, the rooms are large and clean, and all have a private shower—some rooms even have a refrigerator. A single room costs 850 Ft ($17.70) per night, double rooms run 900 Ft ($18.75), and triples go for 1,050 Ft ($21.90). This hotel also fills up quickly, so call ahead; the reception speaks passable English.

To reach the Ifjúság, take bus 91 north from the Batthyány tér metro stop till the bus zigzags a short way up the hill.

South-Central Buda, Close to Gellért Hill

The **Hotel Express,** at Beethoven út 7/9 (tel. 158-891), is one of the better budget values in Budapest and, as a result, is packed with students. Airy, clean double rooms with a sink but no bathroom are 250 Ft ($5.20) per night. Rooms with three or four beds cost 320 Ft ($6.65) and 390 Ft ($8.15) per room per night respectively.

A Splurge Accommodation: Like a scaled-down version of Chicago's Marina Tower, the 280-room **Hotel Budapest,** on Petőfi Sándor utca (tel. 153-230; Telex 225125), is billed as the only round hotel in Budapest. All rooms are doubles with bath. Single occupancy is 1,725 Ft ($35.95); doubles cost 2,130 Ft ($44.40), and triples run 2,730 Ft ($56.90). Because of the circular design, the rooms are somewhat inconveniently shaped, but are well kept. Insist on an upper floor; all the rooms above the second floor have spectacular views of Budapest to the east and the Buda hills to the west. There is a sauna on the upper floors but no pool. A restaurant serving unspectacular cuisine is open from 7 a.m. to midnight. Since prices here are at the upper end of our proposed budget, use the Hotel Budapest only as a fall-back, in case other, cheaper hotels are filled.

To get here, take tram 18 or 22 from Moszkva tér west (toward the Buda hills) for about ten minutes. The tram stops directly in front of the only 18-story round building in Budapest.

Pest

The following hotels are clustered within a block of each other around the Blaha Lujza tér metro stop.

Of the Big Four hotels in this area, the **Hotel Metropol,** at Rákóczi út 58 (tel. 421-175; Telex 226209), is the best budget value. Come early in the day as the small, clean rooms are usually all taken by the afternoon. The concierge on duty when we visited was friendly and helpful, and conversant in six different languages—including English. Another plus for single travelers are the single rooms for 630 Ft ($13.15) without or 750 Ft ($15.65) with a bathroom. A double room without bath costs 1,030 Ft ($21.45) per night, 1,350 Ft ($28.15) with a bath.

The **Hotel Nemzeti,** at József krt. 4 (tel. 339-160; Telex 227710), was built in 1902 and still retains some of the grandeur of that era. A stately main staircase and ornate mirrors in some of the rooms seem sadly out of place in the rather worn decor. Doubles without a bath cost 955 Ft ($19.90) per night and doubles with a bath cost 1,230 Ft ($25.65) per night.

Though the **Palace Hotel** (tel. 136-000; Telex 224217) was built in 1911, only a few of the 91 rooms are graced with mirrors and antique furniture. Most rooms are spartan, though fairly spacious. A double without a bathroom costs 1,420 Ft ($29.60) and a double with a bathroom costs 1,840 Ft ($38.35) per night.

The last choice of the four is the **Hotel Emke,** at Akácfa út 1/3 (tel. 229-814; Telex 225789). The medium-sized double rooms with bathrooms cost 1,410 Ft ($29.40) per night.

If you're stumbling out of a train and don't want to move one step farther, the **Hotel Park,** off Baross tér 10 (tel. 131-420; Telex 226274), is for you. It's just across from the Keleti pu., ahead and on the left side as you exit at street level.

The rooms are bare but clean; the elevators are painfully slow. A single room without a bathroom costs 705 Ft ($14.70); with a shower, 855 Ft ($17.80). A basic double room without a bathroom costs 1,160 Ft ($24.15); with a bathroom, 1,510 Ft ($31.45).

A **Splurge Accommodation:** Slightly above our limit, the **Grand Hotel Margitsziget** (tel. 111-000; Telex 226682), on the Margitsziget (Margaret Island), is located in the middle of one of Budapest's most beautiful parks. The pleasingly furnished rooms have all the comforts of home, including a refrigerator. All rooms have terraces, many with stunning views of the Danube. If you can get a room without a private bathroom you can keep the costs within a reasonable limit. A single room without a bath costs $20, and with a bathroom, $30 per night; doubles cost $33.50 without a bathroom and $46 with. A hotel shuttle bus runs to and from the Hilton Hotel in the center of Pest four times daily. Otherwise you can take bus 26 to the Marx tér metro stop. Since Budapest's summer weather is so mild, the walk down the park and across the oddly bent Margit híd (Margaret's Bridge) to Marx tér is an enjoyable 20-minute stroll.

Rock Bottom in Budapest

On the other side of the coin are the absolute rock-bottom budget hotels. Budapest's ultimate no-frills spot is the **Hotel Citadel,** within the walls of the Citadel at Széntendréi út 189 (tel. 887-167). High above the city, this hotel has only 11 rooms with bathrooms for 454 Ft ($9.45) to 500 Ft ($10.40) and hostel rooms with seven to ten beds per room. A bed for one night in a hostel room costs 45 Ft—an amazing 95¢!

If the Citadel is full, then you have a long trip ahead of you to the **Hotel Lido,** at Nanasi út 67 (tel. 886-865; Telex 227350). Built in a former resort area outside Budapest, the hotel is in a northern suburb on the west side of the Danube. Take bus 134 from the west side of the Árpád híd for about 20 to 30 minutes north and ask the driver to tell you when you reach Széntendréi út. The rooms and public bathrooms are not overly clean, but the good news is that a single costs only 212 Ft ($4.40) per night, and a double room twice that.

3. Dining on a Budget

A couple of pointers before we launch into the gastronomic whirl of Budapest. It's a good idea to learn a few German menu and descriptive terms. Most **menus** in Budapest have an English translation, but in the smaller, family places and in the provinces, if there is a translated menu it's in German.

Live gypsy music is a feature of most Hungarian restaurants. For those who enjoy gypsy music, a good tip is 50 Ft ($1.05). For 100 Ft ($2.10) they'll play a selection for you, and if you give them 20 Ft (40¢) they'll go away. Regardless of your opinions of personalized live music, the musicians are always to be treated with respect. Though they may seem a bit intrusive by American standards, the attention that they give to the guests is considered an important part of the Hungarian dining experience.

There are **three main areas** where the bulk of Budapest's restaurants are to be found. Downtown Pest, which is convenient to the Felszabadulás and Deák tér metro stops; the Castle Hill; and a broader area on the Lenin krt., the major ring avenue, around Blaha Lujza tér. That doesn't mean that if a restaurant isn't in one of these three areas it isn't worth visiting. On the contrary, we found many excellent eating establishments scattered throughout the Buda hills or tucked down a sidestreet in Pest. The three areas just outline sections where you can easily prowl for a restaurant. We emphasize the smaller, less pretentious establishments rather than the more hackneyed choices on Castle Hill and the central Pest landscape. We've also tried to offer a balance between settings composed of stout wooden tables polished smooth by countless plates of hearty, steaming, home-cooked food and ones where the rustle of fine linen is accompanied by the melodious clink of crystal.

CENTRAL PEST: You can see how the **Apostolok** (Apostle) restaurant, Kigyó út 4–6 (tel. 183-704), got its name from the pictures of the 12 Apostles that adorn the walls. Handsomely decorated with fine stained glass, wood paneling, and oaken booths, the Apostolok has been a favorite Budapest eatery since 1902. The average meal here won't be more than 150 Ft ($3.15) with beer, though the crowds and the somewhat frenetic pace of the waiters may not be what you're looking for. The natives maintain that the crowds have no effect on what they refer to as the "best food in Hungary." The Apostolok is open daily from 10 a.m. to 11 p.m.

The **Bajkál** (Baikal), at Semmelweiss utca 1–3 (tel. 176-839), is named after a very deep lake in the eastern half of the Soviet Union. At night the modern bar, done mostly in plastic or plastic-like substances, is a good place for a drink (no English spoken), and the restaurant below serves food that the owner assured us is indeed "Soviet." They can prepare specialty dishes from most districts in the Soviet Union, including the delicious Armenian mutton goulash for 25 Ft (50¢), beef Stroganoff prepared at the table for 160 Ft ($3.35), and chicken Kiev stuffed with butter and honey for 85 Ft ($1.75). The staff is Hungarian, and if you start with some Danish caviar at 85 Ft ($1.75) and finish with some Armenian cognac, a truly Pan–Eastern European experience can be had. The Bajkál is open every day except Sunday, from 10 a.m. till 10 p.m.

The **Mátyás Pince,** at Március 15 tér 7 (tel. 181-650), one of the best-known restaurants in Hungary, feeds tourists of all nationalities. The waiters have had about as much practice ordering formations of visiting Germans (not to mention practically every other nationality) around as Bismarck ever did. The restaurant has a fascinating guest book: Russian generals, GDR delegations, Romanian trade ministers, and cosmonauts have left their mark in the book. Even Roger Moore signed in: "You'll make me fat—but I love it. The Saint." The cheapest entree here is Transylvanian goulash for 95 Ft ($2), with the average main dish at 150 Ft ($3.15). There are a couple of "for two" specialties ranging from 220 Ft ($4.60) to 450 Ft ($9.40). The food is excellent and the service is good, but you can find places where the pace is somewhat more relaxed. It's open from 10 a.m. till 1 a.m., and there is Gypsy and Hungarian music most nights till midnight.

The **Százéves** restaurant, at Pesti-Barnabás utca 2 (tel. 183-608), is one of the more interesting places we found. An incredible amount of bric-a-brac covers the walls—everything from old spice containers to the front page of a German newspaper from 1848. Those who wish to escape the history that adorns the restaurant can eat on the terrace out back. The Százéves is known as one of the oldest restaurants in Budapest; an inn known as "Buda-town" was built on the site in 1831 and people have been eating here ever since. The specialties are fish and game, notably quails and bacon at 280 Ft ($5.85) and braised haunch of venison at 290 Ft ($6.05). Open from noon to midnight, the Százéves is expensive for Budapest, but the excellent food and service are well worth it.

The **Szecsuan** restaurant, at Roosevelt tér 5 (tel. 172-502 or 172-407), is where the Gresham, a famous prewar restaurant, used to be. The cook is actually from the Szechuan province of China, which bodes well for this establishment. (In Eastern Europe it's sometimes believed that one need only change the name of an eatery to something vaguely Oriental and "poof," you have a Chinese restaurant.) The Szecsuan is decorated in tones of red and black, with a bar running the length of the dining room. Though they have some beef dishes the specialty here is pork, spicy in a variety of ways. A complete well-cooked dinner for two costs 600 Ft ($12.50); for four, 1,400 Ft ($29.15); and for six, 1,600 Ft ($33.35). The à la carte menu is decidedly more expensive. These prices may seem reasonable, but the portions are extremely small. In fact, be prepared —you may mistake your main course for your appetizer. We asked the waiter why the portions were so small. "Well," he replied, "it's the small plates that 'they' insist on using." The Szecsuan is open daily except Saturday, from 11 a.m. to 3 p.m. and 7 p.m. to midnight.

AROUND PEST: The **Hungária**, at Lenin krt. 9–11 (tel. 223-849), is open from noon to 3 p.m. and from 7 p.m. to midnight every day. Opened in 1894, the Hungária is one of the most famous of Budapest's restaurants, and rightly so. The beautiful, baroque interior practically groans under the weight of marble, mirrors, and exquisite woodwork. Dining at the Hungária will give you a taste of how Hapsburg royalty lived. Unfortunately, in the summer you'll find many, many fellow would-be courtiers "tasting" right along with you. The grill platter runs 240 Ft ($5), and you won't escape for less than 300 Ft ($6.75) per person for a full meal. We recommend lunch for a slightly less expensive experience, and reservations always.

Beautifully carved wood, antique furniture, and old paintings on clean white walls enhance the intimate atmosphere of the restaurant **Legradi Testverek**, at Magyar út 23 (tel. 186-804). The dish to have here is the deboned duck stuffed with liver, mushrooms, and herbs, for four. Open from 6 p.m. till midnight, the Legradi Testverek is a small establishment so you must reserve.

One of our favorites is the private **Kispspa Vendéglő** at Akácfa utca 38 (tel. 422-587). As you enter you are invited to view some of the finer specimens of the Danube Fogás fish swimming in the window tank. This delicious fish, a house specialty, is served grilled, sautéed, or fried to order. On the walls hangs a delightful and humorous collection of old Hungarian alcohol advertisements. The piano player is one of the best nonconcert performers we heard in Hungary, versed in everything from Bach to some of the more complex jazz chords, and he seemed genuinely to enjoy playing. The atmosphere is both interesting and relaxing, if slightly overlit in the evenings. The evening crowd is a mix of families and couples, both local and visiting. The waiters don't speak much English, but they're friendly and patient. Open Monday through Saturday from noon to 1 a.m. (closed Sunday), the Kispspa Vendéglő is about a 15-minute walk east from Deák tér.

IN BUDA: Castle Hill has many of the better restaurants in Buda, and the **Régi Országház**, at Országház utca 17 (tel. 160-225), is one of the better restaurants on Castle Hill. The long, narrow dining room is pleasantly done in brick and wood. In summer the thick walls keep it refreshingly cool, as well as warm in winter. There is a small courtyard with a single tree in the middle. Try the Paloc leves, a piquante soup for 24 Ft (50¢); there's also the Fogás fish cooked in a variety of ways for 130 Ft ($2.70) to 180 Ft ($3.75). For lunch the menu features well-prepared Hungarian staples for less than 100 Ft ($2.10). Like many of the other restaurants in this area the Régi Országház is open from noon till midnight, daily.

Opposite the Hilton Hotel, the **Halászbástya** ("The Fisherman's Bastion") has the most breathtaking view of any restaurant in Budapest. As you dine here you can see lower Buda and the whole of Pest through the arched Romanesque windows. The house specialties include filet of beef Kedvessy at 310 Ft ($6.45), a grilled filet of beef with paprika, mushrooms, and garnished egg dumplings, as well as the whole grilled pike perch at 300 Ft ($6.25) for an average portion. A proficient four-man gypsy band plays for your dining enjoyment every evening. The excellent food, service, and ambience have a price, but the view alone is more than worth it. The Halászbástya is very popular and reservations for dinner are always a must.

On Gellért Hill just to the south of Castle Hill (you can't miss it) is the **Citadel** restaurant (tel. 667-686 or 667-736). Here you can eat in the fortress that was once Budapest's primary defense. High above the city, the Citadel's view rivals that of the Halászbástya. The offerings in this restaurant are varied and well prepared. The specialty is veal, prepared in several different ways for about 210 Ft ($4.40), depending on the dish. Another attractive feature of the Citadel is its constant temperature, pleasantly cool all summer long because of its thick walls. Open from noon to midnight daily, the large dining room can fill up, so reserve for dinner. There's live music every night after 7 p.m.

The **Kislugas Vendéglő**, a little farther afield at Szilágyi Erzsébet fasor 77 (tel. 351-503), is a low-key and homey garden-terrace restaurant. Closing time varies, but is usually around 10 p.m. The Kislugas is the place to go for a very relaxed, unpretentious lunch for about 70 Ft ($1.45) to 100 Ft ($2.10). The food is home-cooked, slightly oily, but spicy and filling. Almost no English is spoken, but Ms. Éliás speaks some German.

A Splurge Choice

For a real splurge we suggest the **Vad Rósza** ("Wild rose") restaurant at Pentelei Molnar út 15 (tel. 351-118), one of the most expensive restaurants in Eastern Europe and, we feel, one of the region's five best. A visit here is a complete dining experience: you can enjoy the beautiful garden restaurant, the excellent jazz pianist, and above all, the delicious food. Among the numerous recommended specialties, the boned pike at 350 Ft ($7.30), served with a light flaky batter crust, has a subtle taste enhanced by buttery herb sauce. There are also several meat dishes, but you must sample the goose liver served with a piquant sauce and mixed vegetables at 440 Ft ($9.15). Reservations, a must, can be made after 3 p.m. Though you can spend a lot of money here, we feel it's worth it. A meal of this quality in the United States would cost enough to pay for your stay in Hungary. Though you can reach the Vad Rósza by bus 11, why not live it up and take a taxi? You can always take the bus back. . . .

In the Buda Hills

Budapest is the one Eastern European city that has been "discovered" by Western tourists in force, and their presence in central Budapest can be overwhelming. So if you're willing to go farther afield, we offer the following restaurants in the hills of Buda. In recent years many private and semiprivate restaurants have opened in this area, offering real competition to the larger state-run establishments. Most of the private restaurants offer inexpensive home-style cuisine in a relaxed atmosphere and they're frequented almost exclusively by locals. Some are difficult to get to, but we feel that they're all worth a visit.

The **Kikelet Vendéglő** ("Sunrise restaurant"), at Filler út 85 (tel. 155-511), is one of the better-run small local places. Kikelet has a comfortable terrace as well as a garden and rustic indoor dining. Immediately recognizable by his thick droopy mustache and curly hair, the manager, Miklos Gulyás, runs his place with a mischievous sense of humor. One sign on the wall promises "neither will we tell your wife what woman you were here with, nor will we tell you who your wife was here with." The accordion player is a veritable fountain of wit. Every now and then he stops and plays to allow the locals time for their hearty, well-cooked food. The entrees, priced from 70 Ft ($1.45) to 190 Ft ($3.95), include goose liver and turkey with mushrooms and cream. For dessert, try the scrumptious "delicacy of Somlo," a custard cake topped with chocolate and fresh whipped cream. To reach this lively spot, take bus 49 from Moszkva tér, four stops to the top of the hill. Open from noon till 11 p.m., the Kikelet Vendéglő is closed Tuesday.

At the **Kiss István** ("Silver Carp") at Nemetvolgyi út 96 (tel. 450-139), you can dine on a simple red-and-white-checked tablecloth underneath the trees in the garden, or inside if the weather is nasty. This homey restaurant also has fine fish and poultry dishes for under 150 Ft ($3.15), including a hearty gulyás (goulash). Start from Moszkva tér and take tram 59 five stops. The Kiss István is open from noon till midnight every day, except Sunday when things close down two hours earlier.

The **Arnyas Nyirfacska,** at Diosarok út 16 (tel. 351-120), is an excellent but completely undiscovered restaurant. Only about four or five people serve local patrons in the small garden and two indoor rooms. It is a real budget value—most of the entrees cost less than $2. To get here, take bus 28 or 128 six stops from Moszka tér. The restaurant is open from noon till 11 p.m. daily. Since it's such an informal place you should call before riding all the way out here; it might be closed.

CAFÉS: Clustered around the squares of Pest are most of the famous cafés, among them the **Café Gerbeaud,** at Vörösmarty tér 7 (tel. 186-823). The Gerbeaud retains some of the Hapsburgian elegance that once graced this city. Its menu offers the finest confections, ice creams, and coffees in all of Hungary. Open every day from 9 a.m. till 10 p.m., it's the premier café in Budapest. Vast green drapes, polished dark woods, and veined green marble provide just the right atmosphere for mid-afternoon coffee at 24 Ft (50¢) for an after-theater pastry at 10 Ft (20¢) to 25 Ft (50¢) or ice cream at 70 Ft ($1.45) to 120 Ft ($2.50).

Another oldtime café in Buda is the **Ruszwurm,** at Szentháromsag 3 (tel. 161-431). The building has been declared a national monument, and in the summer (because of its proximity to Castle Hill) it should be declared a heavy traffic zone as well—there's a tourist crush here. But if you really want to sample an era gone by, try a cup of their excellent coffee and a slice of pastry. Open from 8 a.m. to 10 p.m.

4. The Sights of Budapest

In this section we have listed and briefly described the major points of interest in Budapest. We recommend that you spend at least three full days here. This won't tax your patience—Budapest is one of the most exciting Eastern European capitals.

The two centers of Buda and Pest are roughly opposite each other across the Danube at the Chain Bridge. Public transportation, however, connects them only at their northern and southern sections. Therefore it's best to do your sightseeing first on one side of the Danube and then the other. The Castle District, which is both the geographic and historic high point of Budapest, is the traditional starting point.

THE CASTLE DISTRICT: Situated on a hill over a mile long that rises in places to 200 feet, the Castle District has one historic monument after another. You can avoid walking up Castle Hill by taking bus 16 from Moszkva tér or Engels tér, or special bus V from Clark Adam tér.

The Southern End

Castle Hill was severely damaged during World War II. One result of the wholesale destruction was that most of the 15th- and 16th-century structures were blown off the hill, exposing even earlier sites. Some of the best examples can be found in the **Budavári palota** (Buda Palace), the residence of Hungarian kings since the 13th century. The bulk of the palace that is visible was built in the 18th and 19th centuries. It contains the **Hungarian National Gallery, the Museum of the Hungarian Labor Movement,** and the **Budapest History Museum,** open Tuesday through Sunday from 10 a.m. to 6 p.m.; closed Monday. The National Gallery has Hungarian art objects from the 11th century to the present. In the Budapest History Museum's permanent collection are 2,000 years of Budapest history and the 13th-century Gothic architectural relics. Concerts are held here every Sunday at 11:30 a.m. The Museum of the Hungarian Labor Movement is perhaps of more interest to "fraternal" or "comradely" visitors, but there are some interesting, if often anti-Western, posters.

The Northern End

The year following the Mongol invasion of 1241, King Béla IV began the first defensive works on the hill. Work continued intermittently, and many new buildings were added in Hungary's "Golden Age" under King Matthias Corvin (1458–1490). He had the **Mátyás-templom (Matthias Church)** built for his own wedding to Beatrice of Aragon. The Turkish invasion and subsequent 150-year occupation saw the church turned into a mosque. The Loreto Chapel, in the southwest corner of the church, is known for the red-marble statue of the Virgin Mary. The Turks had walled up the statue, but during the siege of 1686 it was reexposed. The "miraculous" reappearance (and certainly also the bombardment that accompanied it) of the statue is said to be one of the causes of the Turkish surrender. On the third story of the spire you can see a coat-of-arms marked with a raven, symbol of the heroic Hunyadi family. The church museum is located in the crypt. The church was damaged again during the Hungarian Uprising of 1848–1849, but it was restored rather quickly. The post–World War II reconstruction took much longer.

At the northern end of Castle Hill is the **Bécsi kapu (Vienna Gate),** which is largely a reconstruction. On the northwestern corner of the hill, the **Hadtörténeti Múzeum (Military Museum)** displays a collection of Turkish battle regalia. The **Budapest Hilton Hotel** incorporates the remnants of a 13th-century abbey as well as the 17th-century Jesuit College. Right behind the Hilton is the Halász bástya (Fisherman's Bastion), designed by Frigyes Schulek. Built in 1903 in neo-Romanesque style, it's not a reconstruction of anything. At the north end of Úri útca is the unadorned **Magdolna-torony,** all that remains of the Church of St. Mary Magdalene, the only church that the Ottomans let Christians worship in. Catholics and Protestants prayed together in this church—one of the good things to emerge from the Ottoman occupation.

GELLÉRT HILL: In Buda, two major hills sit right at the Danube. The northern one is Castle Hill, and the southern one is Gellért-hegy (Gellért Hill). Dominating the summit of Gellért Hill is a **Winged Victory** dedicated "To the heroic Soviet liberators from the grateful Hungarian people," as well as the **Citadella**

(Citadel). The Citadel was built only about 130 years ago and now, nestled in its ten-foot-thick walls is a hotel, café, and restaurant complex.

ALONG THE DANUBE:
Leaving Castle Hill and heading down toward the Danube, you are presented with an array of bridges. The oldest, the **Chain Bridge** (Széchenyi lánchíd) was designed by Adam Clark, a Scottish engineer, and completed in 1849. The Széchenyi lánchíd was the first step toward a united Buda and Pest. During the six-week siege at the end of World War II, the Germans destroyed all the Danube bridges, including the Széchenyi lánchíd. Farther north, near the **Margaret Bridge** (Margit híd) is the statue of Joseph Bem, a general in the uprising of 1848–1849. In 1956 this was the site of one of the first demonstrations that led to the Hungarian Uprising. North and up the hill from Joseph Bem's statue is the **tomb of Gul Baba,** the so-called Father of the Roses, a holy man and a poet. His tomb has been the goal of Muslim pilgrimages for centuries, even after the Ottomans lost control of Budapest.

MARGARET ISLAND:
Margaret Island (Margitsziget) has long been the refuge of those weary of the urban rush. From Romans and Esterházys to party members, the island has always been a resort area. About 1½ miles long and several hundred yards wide at the middle, it's green with trees, formal gardens, and meadows. A theater, a stadium, and a gargantuan swimming pool are among the island's attractions.

HOUSES OF PARLIAMENT:
Built when Budapest was a part of the Austro-Hungarian Empire, the Parliament was one of the largest buildings then in existence. The architect, Imre Steindl (1839–1902), must have had the British Parliament building on his mind when he designed this, as the similarity has provoked more than one traveler to make the comparison. Tourists are admitted to the building only in escorted tour groups. The present regime has placed a red star atop the spire.

CENTRAL PEST:
Pest is formed by a series of concentric ring boulevards. Like the rings of a tree, which indicate their age by their distance from the center, the oldest boulevards are closest to the Belváros, the city center. Crossing over the Chain Bridge from Buda, you enter Roosevelt tér, a square that has been home to many of Hungary's greatest patriots. Here the statues of Count István Széchenyi and Kossuth Lajos face each other as the two men so often did in life. Moving south from Roosevelt tér you'll come to the famous **Corso,** or promenade, that borders the Danube on the east bank. At Március 15 tér (15th of March Square) is one of Pest's most important churches. One of the oldest surviving structures in Pest, the **Inner City Parish Church** (Belvárosi plebania templom) has parts dating from the 12th century. Snuggled close to the **Elizabeth Bridge** (Erzsébet híd), its primarily 18th-century exterior is not at first remarkable. Like many old structures it has served many masters; the Ottomans carved a prayer niche or mihrab facing Mecca on the inside of the church. Liszt played the organ here, and his "musical Sundays" concerts were often attended by Richard Wagner.

AQUINCUM:
Óbuda was built near the ruins of the original Roman settlement of Aquincum. Though almost flat, the **Military Amphitheater** (Katonai Amfiteátrum) is one of the largest outside the Italian peninsula. Here, up to

16,000 spectators at a time could enjoy circuses and gladiatorial combat in the arena. Not far away, the **Roman camp museum** displays artifacts found in the area. Many of the best pieces have been removed to the National and other museums, and except for the ruins, Óbuda is an unremarkable neighborhood.

SHOPPING: East of Március 15 tér, but not too far south of Kossuth Lajos út, is the main shopping area in Budapest. **Váci út** is the best street to begin any search for Hungarian goods, as the largest Hungarian folkwares shop is here.

5. Nightlife

OPERA AND CONCERTS: Opera became popular in Budapest in the 17th century. At that time Italian and German companies performed for the Esterházy princes. Haydn presented his own compositions in Budapest in a small theater he managed. The official opening of the **Hungarian State Opera House** at Népköztársaság út 22 (tel. 320-126), on September 27, 1884, was attended by Franz Joseph I, then emperor of Austria-Hungary. Today opera is still very much a part of the city's cultural life; check with IBUSZ or the town guide for programs and schedules.

The oldest concert hall in Budapest, the **Vigadó,** was built in the last century at Corvin tér 8 (tel. 388-122). Many concerts are held in the Main Hall of the **Academy of Music** on Liszt Ferenc tér 8 (tel. 420-179).

The main ticket office of the **Hungarian National Philharmonia** is at Vörösmarty tér 1 (tel. 176-222).

BARS: Practically every restaurant we have listed has a perfectly passable, or better, bar. The bars in the Hilton, Atrium Hyatt, and Forum Hotels are all very tasteful, well stocked with Western spirits, but they're patronized primarily by tourists and are very similar to what most Americans will find at home.

Gabor Dobrentei and Laszlo Komma own Budapest's first **English-style pub,** located at Molnar utca 26 on the corner of Molnar and Pinter utca (tel. 189-997), open weekdays from 10 a.m. to midnight, on weekends from 3 p.m. to midnight. The beer is German brewed and served very cold. Laszlo tells us that he's trying to transplant a bit of old England to Hungary. He serves stuffed, grilled chicken livers at 10 Ft (20¢), sausages, and calves' feet along with the beer but there's no formal restaurant dining. The place used to be a flooded dungeon, but herculean effort and a lot of patience turned it into one of the finer bars in Budapest in less than four months. Everything from the beautiful wood decor to the dart boards with a clear line of fire was conceived by Laszlo and Gabor. Magyar and Soviet champagne, three types of English gin, and seven types of whisky round out the well-stocked bar. They hope to have dark English-brewed beer by 1987. On Monday and Thursday there's a calypso/Latin band and several times a month a ragtime group stops by. The place is packed practically every night with trendy, professional Hungarians.

The bar above the **restaurant Bájkal** (Baikal), at Semmelweiss utca 1–3 (tel. 176-839), is an interesting spot to while away the evening. Named for a very deep lake in the eastern half of the Soviet Union, it's a good place to plunge into some icy imported vodka. The Bájkal's modern plasto-ambience is not to be missed for those with a true affinity for futuristic architecture.

NIGHTCLUBS: The **Disco Úi Várklub,** at Irinyi utca 42 (no telephone), is seasonal, open only in the summer. It seems to just make it from one summer to the next, so look for posters if you're in Budapest between June and September. Entrance is 30 Ft (65¢) with any student ID; otherwise, Monday through Thursday admission is 40 Ft (85¢), and Friday through Sunday, 50 Ft ($1.05). Casual dress is fine, and if you're reasonably civil the husky Magyar plains boys will let you mingle. The crowd ranges from young modish university types through those in their late 20s. While the terms "singles scene" or "pickup" are perhaps too strong, there's definitely a good chance to meet someone of the opposite sex here. A vigorous, if unprofessional, floor show takes place randomly on the lower level. Upstairs is a packed disco and bar serving the traditional overpriced drinks. The Disco Úl Várklub is open from 7:30 p.m. to midnight (sometimes later) every day of the week. The overall feel is that of an oversized, yet reasonably under control, college party.

For the more mature, the **Maxim variety show** at Akacfa út 3 (tel. 227-858), is billed as "the most charming cabaret in Middle Europe." The Revue à la Parisienne at 8 p.m. and 11 p.m., every day except Sunday, will not be new to any connoisseur of floor shows, but it's colorful and lively, and far above many other Eastern European floor shows that we attended.

GAMBLING: One of the finest establishments in which to risk your vacation dollars is the **Budapest Casino,** in the Hilton Hotel at Hess András tér 1–3 (tel. 868-859; Telex 224083). Only Westerners with hard currency can gamble, so bring your passport. This is a rather formal establishment: men must wear a jacket and tie and women must also dress appropriately (the floor captain shudders even at the mere thought of blue jeans). The gambling is done in Deutsch marks (West German currency), though the house will cash any other hard currency into chips in DM denominations. The exchange rates are almost competitive with banks, so there's no real need to import stacks of DM just to play. There is a 5-DM ($2) cover charge. The games include roulette, blackjack, baccarat, and slot machines. Minimum bet for roulette is 2 DM (80¢), for blackjack it's 4 DM ($1.50), and the one-armed bandits will spin for 1 DM (40¢). If you wish to familiarize yourself with all the rules and odds of the different games, ask for the free multilingual "Gaming Guide." The casino is open from 5 p.m. to midnight and later, every night.

6. The ABCs of Budapest

BANKS: As in all other Warsaw Pact countries, you cannot get a cash advance on your credit card. However, you may pay for goods and services with your card where it is so advertised. Going to a bank is unnecessary, as almost all hotel exchange desks can change your money at the same rate as a bank. The only time you may lose on an exchange is if you change currency during or as part of a particular purchase—buying international train tickets, for example.

BATH HOUSES AND SPAS: Bathing has been a part of Hungary's history since the Roman Empire. Tiberius Nero ordered the first baths built, and they were merely expanded under Ottoman Turkish control. Today there are 123 springs catalogued and enjoyed in the Budapest area. The best baths are at the **Gellért Hotel** on Szent Gellért tér (tel. 460-700) and **Széchenyi Baths** at Allatkeri tér 11. One of the older public baths is the **Casszar Baths** at Frankel Leo utca 35, built by the Ottoman Turks in the 16th century. There's a small (less than 30¢) entrance fee.

BUSES: The bus station on Engels Tér is the home of **Volán,** the national bus company (tel. 172-562). Open weekdays from 6 a.m. to 6 p.m. and on Saturday to 4 p.m.; closed Sunday. They go practically everywhere in Hungary and are a practical alternative to the radial constraints placed on the traveler by a Budapest-centered railway system. The baggage check is open from 5:30 a.m. to closing time.

EMBASSIES: The U.S. Embassy at Szabadság tér 12 (tel. 126-450) always has someone on duty. As elsewhere, the embassy's function is primarily diplomatic. They can and will help you, but as one official said, "We can only point you in the right direction." They cannot lend you money, drive you around, or accompany you in your search for lost luggage. At the embassy you can catch up on current events by watching a recent telecast of the evening news every Wednesday afternoon at 3:30. On Monday you can see a recent documentary, and on Friday a feature film. If you lose your visa it will take at least three or four business days for them to replace it. The embassy *cannot* shorten the wait; it's the Hungarians who make the rules. Office hours are 8 a.m. to 5 p.m., with an hour break between 1 and 2 p.m. The embassy will also hold your mail for up to two weeks.

The **Canadian Embassy** is at Budakeszi út 55/d (tel. 365-738, 365-728, 165-949, or 165-858).

The **British Embassy** is at Harmincad utca 6 (tel. 182-888).

EMERGENCY NUMBERS: You can use the nationwide emergency telephone numbers in Budapest as well: dial 04 for an ambulance, 05 for the fire department, and 07 for the police.

FILMS: There are several movie theaters in Budapest, all of which post their programs around town and in the very useful "Programme in Hungary." *Szinkronizalt* means that a film is dubbed in Hungarian; otherwise, most films are subtitled.

LAUNDRY: Laundry can be done in the automat located on the north side of Ráckóczi utca, one block east from the Kossuth subway stop on Line 2. It's open weekdays from 7 a.m. to 8 p.m., on Saturday to 4 p.m.; closed Sunday. Only Hungarian is spoken here, so bring your phrasebook and a large dose of patience. One machine will hold a maximum of five kilograms (12 pounds) of laundry, and costs 50 Ft ($1.05). A dryer for a half hour is 19 Ft (49¢). If you're in a rush or just don't want to sweat the day away, the women working there will do your laundry for a negotiable price.

MAIL AND TELEPHONE: The main post office, at Petőfi Sándor 17, is open weekdays from 7 a.m. to 9 p.m., on Saturday to 8 p.m., and on Sunday from 8 a.m. to noon. The mailboxes on the street are red and are "emptied almost every day." There are two 24-hour post offices: Office No. 62 at Lenin krt. 105-107, and No. 72 at Baross tér 11/c.

Any international phone calls you want to make should be placed in Budapest—the connections in the smaller towns are tenuous. It costs 150 Ft ($3.15) per minute to call New York. Calling from the U.S. to Eastern Europe is less expensive; you can dial directly and will usually get a connection immediately. To cut down on costs, go to the main post office at Petőfi Sándor 17, place a one-minute call to North America, and tell the party to call you right back by dialing 011 (international long distance) + 36 (country code for Hungary) + 1 (city code for Budapest) + either 177-853 or 177-964 (these are booths 7 or 8, reserved for incoming calls; if you get one, you'll be paged).

You can also send and receive Telexes at the main post office. The post office will hold Telexes for you for 10 Ft (20¢). The Telex number for the main post office is 225375.

TIPPING: Give taxi drivers 10 Ft (20¢) or 20 Ft (40¢) above the bill, more if the driver carried your luggage around or was otherwise helpful. Tipping in restaurants is usually 10%. You can add or subtract from that amount, depending on the restaurant. Always check to see if service charges were added already. All taxes are included and should be marked as such on the bill. If you feel that the bill is too high, check to see if you've been taxed twice, and always keep a copy of your bill.

TOURS: IBUSZ and many of the other tour agencies offer group and private tours of varying lengths by bus, boat, or on foot. If you prefer sightseeing on a tour, these may be worth your while.

We also suggest that you go into one of the larger bookstores and look for a detailed English-language guidebook. These books are written by natives of Budapest and cover the monuments of the city in far more detail than is possible in the space available here. The advantages of a guidebook are that you can go at your own pace, stop a tour in the middle and resume it after lunch, it's a good souvenir, and it costs much less than a flesh-and-blood guide.

TRAIN STATIONS: In addition to **Keleti pu.**, two other train stations serve Budapest: **Nyugati** (mostly east-west lines) and **Déli** (rail traffic heading south).

7. Excursions from Budapest

THE BUDA HILLS: In the green heart of Budapest, the Buda Hills, you'll see some of the most charming and beautiful countryside in the entire land—and right in the backyard of the city! To get here, take tram 5, 22, or 56E heading west from Moszkva tér for about five to ten minutes to the cog-wheel railroad. On this railway, also known as the Pioneer Railway (Uttörővas út), everything except the engines themselves is run by schoolchildren. The almost eight-mile-long line will bring you right through the heart of the Buda Hills.

For those with a real need for altitude, you can take the chair lift up to the top of the 1,735-foot János-hegy (János Hill). You can get on the chair at Zugligeti út 93, and it goes up to the foot of the lookout tower.

SZÉKESFEHÉRVÁR: Though not technically a day trip from Budapest (unless you have a car), Székesfehérvár (pronounced *Say*-kesh-fe-hair-var) is between Budapest and the Lake Balaton region, and worth a detour. Székesfehérvár was the capital of Hungary for over 500 years, beginning in the reign of Stephen I, the first king, and ending in 1526 with the Ottoman Turkish victory at Mohács. Throughout this period coronations and other regal celebrations took place here. As happened in so many Hungarian cities, the town was totally destroyed by the Ottoman Turks in the 16th century. Today the history of Székesfehérvár is better preserved than the sights. There are still some quaint sections and interesting museums, but, sadly, many new constructions as well.

The Sights

At the **Garden of Ruins** at Szabadsád tér, you can see the 11th-century remains of the Royal Basilica where King Stephen and so many other Hungarian kings were crowned and, in due time, buried.

The Roman ruins in this area of Hungary are in better shape than the medieval relics, which were largely destroyed by the Ottoman Turks. To see the display of ancient Roman ruins, as well as additional historical and archeological finds, check out the **King Stephen Museum,** off Gagarin tér.

Another interesting sight in the heart of the old town is the **Black Eagle Apothecary,** an 18th-century pharmacy. Its well-preserved rococo interior contains original decorations and objects from a drugstore of that time.

Getting Around Székesfehérvár

From the train station, follow Lenin út, which begins to the left of the station. The street eventually turns into Népköztársaság út. After a 15-minute walk you'll see the Hotel Alba Regia; turn left and you'll arrive at the heart of the old town.

The **old town** consists of several pedestrian malls. You enter the area on Szabadság tér; to your right is the Garden of Ruins, the remains of the former Royal Basilica. After one block, turn right on **Március 15 utca,** the town's main street, with many tourist offices and stores.

Albatours, the main tourist office in Székesfehérvár, is at Szabadság tér 6 (tel. 128-18; Telex 021235). They offer maps and information on the town, as well as private rooms for 100 Ft ($2.10) to 600 Ft ($12.50) per day. They usually have shorter lines than IBUSZ, down the street. Albatours is open Monday through Friday from 8 a.m. to 4:30 p.m.

Accommodations

The two-star **Hotel Velence,** at Március 15 utca 10 (tel. 112-62 or 112-63; Telex 21293), at the end of the pedestrian walk in the town center, is our pick for the town's best budget hotel. It's an older place with some nice touches, such as a large stone bannister leading up the stairs. Rooms here are clean but somewhat worn, with very high ceilings. Singles without bath are 300 Ft ($6.25); doubles run 400 Ft ($8.35) without bath and 500 Ft ($10.40) with a private bathroom. There's an inexpensive restaurant downstairs, open from 6:30 a.m. to midnight, that has a menu in English.

Another excellent budget pick in town is **Ket Góbé Vendegfogado,** at Fö utca 7. This is a private house with such friendly and informal owners that you feel you're staying with some old friends. Only seven attic double rooms are offered, but each comes with a private bathroom at an incredible price: only 450 Ft ($9.40). There's a simple but inexpensive restaurant as well. The house is two kilometers (1½ miles) from the town center, but easily accessible by bus 24, 27, or 32.

The six-story glass-and-concrete **Hotel Alba Regia,** Rákóczi utca 1 (tel. 134-84; Telex 21295), is the town's most modern hotel, each room equipped with modern facilities and bathrooms. Despite the appealing facilities, we suggest leaving the Alba Regia as one of your last choices because of its relatively high price: singles rent for 1,200 Ft ($25) and doubles go for 1,260 Ft ($26.25). The Alba Regia (named after the easier-to-pronounce Latin name of Székesfehérvár) is just across the street from the pedestrian malls of the town center.

Private Rooms: In addition to **Albatours** (listed above), **IBUSZ,** at Ady Endre utca 2 (tel. 115-10), has private rooms for 120 Ft ($2.50) single and 200 Ft ($4.15) double. The office is open Monday through Friday from 8 a.m. to 4 p.m., to noon on Saturday.

Dining

A simple private restaurant, **Ket Góbé Vendegfogado,** at Fö utca 7, has two small rooms and a nice terrace, which, unfortunately, overlooks a major roadway. The inexpensive entrees here are always tasty. Cimbalom music plays from 7 p.m. every day except Tuesday. The restaurant is open from 5 a.m. to midnight Sunday through Thursday, to 2 a.m. on Friday and Saturday; closed Monday.

Chapter XVII

WESTERN HUNGARY

**1. Tata
2. Győr and Pannonhalma
3. Sopron, Fertőrákos, and Fertőd
4. Kőszeg
5. Szombathely, Ják, and Herend
6. Pécs and Southwestern Hungary**

SMALL VILLAGES TUCKED AWAY among verdant hills, a balmy Mediterranean climate, and a culture dating from Roman times make western Hungary one of the most attractive regions in the entire country. Rich in history and poor in tourists, western Hungary boasts some of the friendliest people and most fascinating sights that we encountered. Western Hungary shares the Danube River with Czechoslovakia in the north, an extended western frontier with Austria, and the Mura and Drava Rivers with Yugoslavia in the south. More varied in its landscape than the Great Plain, western Hungary has numerous lakes, hills, rivers, and forests.

TRAVELING AROUND WESTERN HUNGARY: We have listed the simplest and best way first—if you have one or enough money to rent one, a **car** is far and away the preferred way to see the towns of western Hungary. The road system is probably one of the best maintained in all of Eastern Europe, and excellent maps of the Hungarian road network are available in the West as well as from IBUSZ. If you are renting, we recommend first traveling to Budapest and renting the car only for your visit to the outlying areas of Hungary. If you are traveling from Austria to Hungary, all the towns (except for Pécs) are on or not far from the main Vienna–Budapest route.

Traveling by **train** in western Hungary presents some difficulties. The rail lines radiate out from Budapest, much like the spokes of a wheel, and do not link up in the western part of the country. The towns of Tata, Győr, and Sopron are on the same "spoke" from Budapest, with Pannonhalma and Fertőd located off it but accessible by bus. Szombathely and Pécs are located on their own "spokes." Kőszeg is on a spur line that runs north from Szombathely and is roughly equidistant from Szombathely and Sopron. Because some of the towns are so remote, and the rail system is inconveniently structured, at some point you will have to travel by bus.

Buses are the staple mode of transport for locals as well as tourists in western Hungary. As a result, buses are often crowded, especially in the summer and in the mornings and early evenings (rush hour—just like at home). You should arrive at least a half hour before the scheduled departure time, and confirm all departure times with the driver as well (after all, the bus driver's watch always has the correct time as far as all departures are concerned). Most bus prices are equivalent to, or slightly less than, the cost of traveling the same distance by train. There isn't much difficulty choosing a bus company as the national bus line, Volán, runs to over 200 cities throughout Hungary. You can get a schedule and more information at the main bus terminal in Budapest on Engles tér (tel. 182-122).

1. Tata

Only 45 miles from Budapest, Tata is a charming baroque village on the shores of Lake Öreg-tó. Surrounded by hills and forests, Tata has been known as a hunting and riding center since the Middle Ages. The village was at its peak under the reign of King Sigismund in the 15th century, and the Hungarian Diet (parliament) met here under King Matthias in 1510. Tata is far enough away from the major routes along the Danube to have escaped some of the destruction that was the lot of many other towns in the course of Hungary's turbulent history. There is a palace built for the ruling Esterházys in the 18th century by the famous architect Jakob Fellner on November 7 tér. There's also an excellent riding school and stud farm in the neighborhood.

ORIENTATION: Tata is situated along the northern shores of Lake Öreg-tó. From the **bus station** to Szabadság tér, take bus 5 for three stops, or walk east on Vár alja út and then south on Ady Endre út. From the **railway station** to Szabadság tér take bus 1 or 3 four stops till you reach the town center—Ország Gyűlés tér. Most of the sights are within walking distance along the lakeside. The telephone area code for Tata is 34. There is a **tourist** office at Ady Endre út 24 (tel. 10), open from 8 a.m. to 4 p.m. weekdays, to noon on Saturday. They don't speak English and don't have much to say to tourists, but they may have maps.

ACCOMMODATIONS IN TATA: There are two hotels that we recommend in Tata, the Hotel Malom and the Hotel Pálma, both are on Szabadság tér, a street about 250 yards south of the town center, Ország Gyűlés tér.

The **Hotel Malom,** at Szabadság tér 8 (tel. 815-30), right behind the Hotel Kristály, is set back from the main road and shaded by trees. Much cleaner than the other hotels on the main strip, it has doubles for 260 Ft ($5.40) and triples for 330 Ft ($6.90) per night. Unfortunately, it's often filled with tour groups from other Eastern European countries, but if you're staying for a short period the genial manager may have room—especially on Sunday and Monday.

Our favorite in Tata is the **Hotel Pálma,** on Szabadság tér (tel. 805-77, ext. 99), in an elegant building surrounded by a beautiful park. Formerly a private estate, this pleasant hotel has a baroque terrace in front and a public pool in back. The rooms are small but clean, and best of all, the hotel is very quiet. A single room costs 374 Ft ($7.80), a double runs 476 Ft ($9.90), and a triple with a private bath goes for 618 Ft ($12.90). All prices include breakfast. On a hot day, cool off in the pool for an additional 8 Ft (15¢).

DINING: The restaurant we recommend in Tata is the **Fényes Grill** (tel. 801-82), less than a mile south of Szabadság tér on Ady Endre út (which turns into utca Vértesszölösi). Decorated in tones of orange, with a large shaded terrace overlooking the Öreg-tó, it's a good place for lunch or dinner. The food is well prepared and filling. Try the Tatai betyártál kettö szemelyes—steak grilled with potatoes and onions for two people, for 200 Ft ($4.15). Most of the other dishes cost around 85 Ft ($1.75) without wine.

A Splurge Choice

One of the reasons we come to Eastern Europe is to sleep in palaces and dine where the princely Esterházy family once did, and you can too, at the **Hotel Diana** (tel. 803-88; Telex 27237). It consists of the castle (actually more of a manor house), built in the 15th century, and the touring hotel, a new construction. In the castle there are only double rooms with baths for 1,330 Ft ($27.70) per night; but the touring house has doubles with or without bath for 930 Ft ($19.40) and 700 Ft ($14.60) respectively. The furnishings are not antique originals but are far superior to those in most other hotels in Eastern Europe. The excellent restaurant is open all week from 7 a.m. till 10 p.m., and the bar stays open till 3 a.m. The Diana usually has rooms available, but it's a long trip out here, so call or Telex first. A cab from either of the stations should cost around 100 Ft ($2.10). Horseback riding at the Diana costs 150 Ft ($3.15) per hour including all equipment, though you should bring a pair of sturdy boots or shoes with heels.

2. Györ and Pannonhalma

Situated on the Mosoni River, not far from the Danube, Györ is almost exactly midway between Budapest and Vienna. Known as Arrabona by the Romans, the town is called "city of waters," as it is astride the confluence of the Mosoni-Danube, Rába, Rábca, and Holt-Marcal Rivers.

Györ is an industrial city, but there are several points of interest for tourists. The most important is the **cathedral** on Martinovics tér. Sitting on a foundation that dates from the 11th century, the church was destroyed and rebuilt several times. It is the home of one of the greatest masterpieces of Hungarian goldsmithing—the **reliquary of (King) St. Ladislaus,** who reigned in the latter half of the 11th century. The reliquary is much like a gold bust with the stoic face of the king adorned by his symetrically coiffed hair and beard. Györ also has an impressive **Carmelite church** dating from the early 18th century on Köztársaság tér, and the **Old Town Hall** at Rákóczi Ferenc utca 1, built a few years later. One of the more elaborate baroque structures in town is the U-shaped **Town Hall** on Szabadság tér. The streets of the old town are well preserved and a delight to walk in on a summer's morning or afternoon.

ORIENTATION: Almost enclosed by rivers, Györ presents little difficulty in navigating around. The old town is cradled in an elbow at the confluence of the Mosnoi-Danube and the Rába Rivers, north of the bus and train stations. To reach both the city center and the old town, walk north over Lenin híd, the big bridge crossing the railroad tracks, and then straight up Lenin út.

Györ's telephone area code is 96.

ACCOMMODATIONS: There is only one hotel in Györ, the **Rába.** It's unexceptional, if comfortable, modern pile with singles for $12 to $15 per night and doubles from $19 to $38, depending on the plumbing. The staff is friendly and helpful, and since this is the largest hotel in Hungary outside Budapest (almost 200 rooms), there is always a room available.

If you have a tent or a car, try the **campground** (tel. 189-86; Telex 24458) at Kiskút-liget, near Hwy. E5 (M1) on the eastern edge of town and also about 100 yards from a canal that empties into the Danube. There are pretty good fishing opportunities practically right in the backyard, and the Danube isn't far away either. It's open from April 15 to October 15. The cost is less than 100 Ft ($2.10) for a spot. To get here, take bus 8 or 8Y east from Szabadság tér, across the Lenin bridge and in front of the Town Hall.

DINING: The restaurant **Vaskakas** ("Iron Rooster"), right by the Carmelite church on Köztársaság tér (tel. 226-55), is a good choice on a hot summer day. The arched vaults and old brickwork keep the cool air in and the dust out. This restaurant extends far back into the old building occupying most of the cellar. It was used repeatedly as a refuge both during Ottoman Turkish bombardments and in other times of trouble. We recommend heading for the Vaskakas for an afternoon repast or something to wet your whistle. You can eat here for less than 250 Ft ($5.20). It's open daily from noon to midnight (to 10 p.m. on Sunday and Monday). On Saturday night there's dancing until the wee hours, and usually things break up at 2 a.m.

Right on the corner of Lajos út and Rózsa Ferenc utca, in the old town, is the restaurant **Halázcsárda** (tel. 248-76), where you can eat well for less than 65 Ft ($1.35). Red shelves contain a collection of pottery in the entranceway to this fish-specialty restaurant. Try the baknyi, carp cooked with mushrooms, buttermilk, and liberally sprinkled with paprika for 45 Ft (95¢); or the cut beefsteak served with liver and chopped onions for 66 Ft ($1.40). Open Monday to Saturday from 10 a.m. till 10 p.m., on Sunday from noon to 9 p.m.

The budget-minded seeking to eat where the locals do should give the restaurant **Új Kálász** a try. The restaurant is just west of the old town on Munkácsy M. utca, about the middle of the block on the west side of the street. If the crowd in the front room is too boisterous, simply ask to be taken into the backroom, which is usually much cooler. The arched brick ceilings are low, and wooden bottles hang on the walls. Meals are usually less than 60 Ft ($1.25), well prepared and filling. The Új Kálász is open every day from 10 a.m. to 11 p.m.

A SIDE TRIP TO PANNONHALMA: Pannonhalma was once a powerful Benedictine Abbey and still serves as a spiritual and academic center. It's located in the hills about nine miles south of Győr on Hwy. 82 heading toward Veszprém and Lake Balaton. Parts of the abbey are over 1,000 years old. One of the few remaining examples of early Hungarian monastic architecture, it's also the earliest remaining Gothic church in Hungary. The church was transformed into a mosque during the Ottoman Turkish occupation, but generally has been held as a sanctuary. During World War II both the Nazis and the Soviets respected, to a degree, the sanctity of the abbey.

There is an extensive collection of relics, from Stone Age artifacts to carvings taken from beneath the Forum in Rome and given to the abbey by Mussolini's foreign minister. The archives contain over 300,000 volumes, including several priceless 11th- and 12th-century documents, such as a deed for an abbey on the Tihany peninsula on Lake Balaton. This founding deed, dating from 1055, is important because it is one of the first documents to contain a large number of Hungarian words sprinkled throughout the text.

The abbey commands a magnificent view down the valley and across the surrounding hills.

3. Sopron, Fertőrákos, and Fertőd

SOPRON: Sopron is one of our favorite towns in western Hungary. Not difficult to get to, it's small yet has a lot to see and several good budget hotels and restaurants. Not far from the Austrian frontier, Sopron is even worth a day trip from Vienna if you have a car. If not, you can spend the night here quite comfortably.

Sopron dates back to the Romans, who founded the settlement and called it Scarbantia. Much of the town's present layout is owed to the 400-year Roman presence. The name Sopron first appeared in documents in the 10th century, when King Stephen founded a municipality here. Originally three villages, they were all united in 1277 under King Ladislaus IV. In the 16th century much of the city was destroyed in the Ottoman Turkish invasion. In the 18th century the city flourished, though the outer walls were removed to reduce its effectiveness as a fortress. The city played unwilling host to about 25,000 French soldiers during the Napoleonic Wars, and the series of conflicts had a less than beneficial effect on the town's fortunes. Although it suffered some damage in World War II, Sopron is still one of Hungary's best-preserved towns.

Sights in Sopron

When you arrive you can't miss the **Firetower (Tűztorony)**, the symbol of Sopron, and one of the tallest structures in the town. Built first in the Romanesque style, the tower was totally destroyed in the fire of 1676; after its reconstruction it became the graceful baroque spire you see today. Moving south on **Fő tér**, the main square, you'll see the **Holy Trinity column**. Built between 1695 and 1701, it's one of the most beautiful baroque votive columns in all of Hungary. Also on Fő tér is the fine **Fabriczius House**, with a baroque exterior and a Gothic interior. Today it's home to part of the **Franz Liszt Museum**. Next to it is the 17th-century home of Mayor Kristóf Lackner. There are many other impressive baroque, rococo, and classical houses, but don't miss the former **Benedictine church** (1280–1300) on the south side of Fő tér. Under the tower (built in the 14th century) five national assemblies were held and three kings and queens were crowned. Also on Fő tér is the **Renaissance Palace,** adorned with corner turrets and home to the Storno collection of fine art.

Practically all the streets south from the Fő tér are veritable museums of medieval architecture. Down Új út are two **synagogues** from the 13th century, and nearby on Szent György utca is the rococo **Erődy Palace.**

Out of the old city (but not far) to the north is **St. Michael's Church (Szent Mihály-tempelom).** To get there, just walk under the tower in Fő tér and then north on Pozsonyi út for about five minutes. Inside the church are some beautiful wall paintings and sculptures, and out back in the old cemetery is the **St. James Chapel (Szent Jakab-kápolna);** built in the early 13th century, it's the oldest building in Sopron.

Orientation

You might think that Sopron was designed for sightseeing, since most of the sights are within the confines of the old city where no automobile traffic is allowed. **Lenin krt.,** the street that circles around the old city, follows the same path as the old moat that once surrounded Sopron.

The **bus station** is just two blocks west of the Firetower on Lackner Kristóf utca. To get to Fő tér, turn right (east) and walk on Lackner Kristóf utca till you reach the Lenin krt. It's just a block farther, if you keep to the left.

The **railroad station** is south and west of the old city at the end of Mátyás király utca. To get to the old town, walk north (the only way you can go) on

Mátyás király utca to Lenin krt. Keep going straight and everything on your left (west) side is the **old city.** Or you can take bus 1, 1M, 2, 4, 9, 12, or 12M for three stops.

If you come by car, remember that no traffic is allowed in the old town. Parking lots are conveniently located all around the old town off Lenin krt.

The **telephone area code** for Sopron, Fertőd, and the surrounding area is 99.

Accommodations

If they have a room available, the **Hotel Palatinus,** at Új út 23 (tel. 113-95), is worth the bit more you pay. Right in the heart of the old town, this hotel is well integrated into the surrounding historical structures. The interior is clean and very well kept, with simple modern furnishings. A single room costs $18 with a private bath, and a double runs $35 (subtract about $10 for rooms without private bath). The restaurant on the first floor serves fine food—Hungarian and some Austrian dishes—and is open from 7 a.m. to 11 p.m. daily.

The **Pension Barbara,** at Lenin krt. 53 (tel. 114-00), has doubles for 450 Ft ($9.40), and one triple room for 500 Ft ($10.40). From July to August they are usually heavily booked, but give the pension a try anyway. All rooms have a toilet and shower, and a complimentary breakfast is served in the quaint, very cool basement kitchen. The building is set back from the street, and the place is very quiet and clean. The owner, Mr. Börzsei Imre (remember that in Hungary the family name comes first), and his wife run this recommended establishment. Just walk right through the unmarked garage door.

Just on the outskirts of town is the **Hotel Locomotiv,** about two miles from Fő tér on József Attila utca (tel. 141-80). A very modern structure, its reception area is on the third floor. The rooms (all doubles) are large and reasonably clean. A room with bath costs 580 Ft ($12.10) nightly, and a bathless room is 400 Ft ($8.35); breakfast is included in these rates. You should have no trouble getting a room here, but come early as it can fill up. Behind the hotel are six tennis courts, rented for 100 Ft ($2.10) an hour. There's a restaurant open from 7 a.m. to 11 p.m. every day. To reach the hotel, take bus 2 to the fifth stop from the railroad station.

Private Rooms: Private rooms are not difficult to find in Sopron. Begin at **Ciklámen Turist,** right on the corner of Lackner Kristóf utca and Lenin krt. (tel. 120-40 or 120-41). The friendly staff will offer you one of their 200 rooms. Though they usually have rooms available, in the height of summer the choices can get pretty slim, so stop by here as early in the day as possible. Single rooms rent for 160 Ft ($3.35), double rooms go for 320 Ft ($6.65), and triple rooms run 500 Ft ($10.40). Breakfast is not included, but all rooms have a private bath. There's a 30% surcharge (which we've included in the listed rates) for stays of less than three days. Ciklámen Turist can also give you information about, and arrange tours to, Fertőd, Fertőrákos, and a variety of other locations in the area. The office is open Monday through Thursday from 7:30 a.m. to 4 p.m., on Friday and Saturday to 8 p.m., and on Sunday to 1 p.m.

Dining

There are several recommendable establishments in Sopron. One we especially liked was the wine restaurant **Voros kakos** ("Red Rooster"), on Lenin krt. To get here, walk out of the old town under the tower, across and slightly to the left on Lenin krt., where you should see the sign of the red rooster easily; walk back through a rather murky corridor to the restaurant. Though small, it has a rear terrace with a pleasant view of the neighborhood. The food is good and filling for less than $5 a meal, without wine. This restaurant is paid the ultimate compliment in Hungary (as in many cultures)—many families come here for a night out.

If you want to evade your tourist compatriate, then head for the hills and the restaurant **Alpesi,** about three miles out of town—you'll need to allow a little time to get here. Drive west from the old town on Ady Endre út, cross the tracks, and then take the second left on Szabadság krt. at the Erzsébet café. Keep going straight and then bear right on Hársfa sor; stay on Hársfa sor (it makes a hard right), and about 150 yards farther on is the restaurant. The atmosphere is very relaxed, and most of the activity takes place outside under the trees. We recommend the pork cutlet Alpesi, an interesting variation on the Cordon Bleu theme, for 50 Ft ($1.05).

FERTÖD: "There is, outside of Versailles, no place in France that could be compared with the magnificence of this one." So wrote the well-traveled French nobleman, the Baron of Riesbeck, in 1788 about the fantastic baroque palace built here by the Esterházy family, initially constructed in 1720 as a 26-room structure with two major outbuildings. Four architects oversaw the later expansion into a 126-room palace that was not completed until the 1780s. Though damaged in World War II, the palace was skillfully restored and all 126 rooms appear much as they did when the Baron of Riesbeck visited them. The small hamlet of Fertöd (pop. 3,000) was once known as Esterháza in honor of the palace. However, research indicates that in the 13th century the village was known by the name of Süttör. There is an extensive collection of porcelain, much of it from Herend, and beautiful antique furniture. The palace's formal gardens should not be missed.

Orientation

Fertöd is about three miles north of Hwy. 85 between Sopron and Györ; follow the signs. It's a small town, and everything of interest is well within walking distance.

The **Esterházy Palace** at Fertöd is open from 8 a.m. till 5 p.m. between April 1 and September 30, with a one-hour lunch break between noon and 1 p.m. In the winter it closes an hour earlier.

Food and Lodging at Fertöd

The restaurant **Haydin** (tel. 459-77) is the only listed dining establishment in Fertöd. Only about 300 yards from the castle, the restaurant is flanked by a gravel parking lot with a small terrace out back. There's a delicious kettle goulash for 26 Ft (55¢); most main dishes are less than 50 Ft ($1.05). Open Monday from 11 a.m. to 3 p.m., Tuesday through Friday and Sunday to 9 p.m., and on Saturday till 10 p.m., the Haydin is often filled with tour groups.

It's actually possible to sleep in the Esterházy Palace at Fertöd, though finding space may be a problem since many tour groups stay here. The **Kastélyszálló,** as the hotel is known (tel. 459-21 or 459-22), is much more like a dorm or hostel than a hotel. Although there are no private baths, everything is well kept and extremely clean. In the two large rooms which each have 12 beds, you'll pay 40 Ft (85¢) for a bed for one night. There are also a few double rooms, also with no private bath, for 250 Ft ($5.20) per day; an extra bed is an additional 50 Ft ($1.05). None of the original furnishings are in this part of the palace, but we feel that the price, cleanliness, and the fact that you'll sleep *in* the palace make it worth your while to stay here.

FERTŐRÁKOS: About three miles north of Sopron out Pozsonyi út is the small village of Fertőrákos. The most interesting sight at Fertőrákos is the quarry, where limestone has been mined for over 2,000 years. In Roman times the quarry was extremely important, and most of the old city walls of Scarbantia (the Roman name for Sopron) were built with its stone. Now it's an interesting and deliciously cool place to visit. Concerts are given fairly regularly in the quarry concert hall, which can hold more than 800 people. The old village of Fertőrákos has the only public pillory in all of Hungary, as well as several interesting baroque buildings.

For tour information, private accommodations in Fertőrákos, and concert schedules at the quarry, contact **Ciklamen Turist Sopron** at Ógabona tér 8, in Sopron (tel. 120-40 or 120-41; Telex 249174). The local bus 6, which you can catch just north of the Lenin krt. on Pozsonyi út in Sopron, will take you to Fertőrákos.

4. Kőszeg

Another jewel in the crown of western Hungary, Kőszeg is a town that we highly recommend visiting. People have been living in this area since at least the early Bronze Age, as Celtic remains attest. It was the Romans, however, who established a settlement here and, among other things, planted vineyards—a tradition continued to this day. King Stephen I built a fortress here in the 10th century to protect the border against frequent Germanic attacks. The fortress was built on the hill of Kőszeg, and a village of the same name was founded in the valley. As a border town, Kőszeg changed hands several times in the last millennium, and was also known under the German name Güns. In 1328 the town had grown large enough to be granted municipal status under King Robert-Karl I.

The town blazed its way permanently into the history books in 1532, when a very small Hungarian garrison under Capt. Miklós Jurisics held off a vastly superior Ottoman Turkish army under Sultan Soliman II for two to three weeks. To separate fact from legend is not always easy; the number of defenders varies from "around 1,000" down to "Miklós' hundreds," and the attacking Ottoman Turkish force was anywhere from "around 100,000" to "over a quarter of a million." An important battle and a heroic fight, this stand did slow the Ottoman Turks long enough for the Hapsburgs to prepare a successful defense of Vienna. In any event, Sultan Soliman II was delayed and subsequently defeated at the very gates of Vienna. Later, as a result of the attempted uprising against the Hapsburgs in 1710, retiring troops under Ádám Baloghs put much of Kőszeg to the torch.

Rebuilt under "German" control, the region regained its fame as a wine-growing area. Never heavily industrialized, the old town has changed little since the middle 1700s, as you'll see when you walk through its small but extremely well-preserved precincts. Gaze over the battlements, as "Miklós' hundreds" once did, and imagine the waving forest of Ottoman Turkish steel that once greeted their eyes.

ORIENTATION: Geographically the highest town in Hungary (850 feet above sea level), Kőszeg lies in the very easternmost foothills of the Alps. To get to Kőszeg, take the train north from Szombathely or the bus from either Sopron or Szombathely. By car from Vienna take Hwy. 87 south, or from Szombathely, Hwy. 87 north.

The **bus and train stations** are right next to each other at the end of Rákóczi Ferenc utca. To reach the town center, either walk north for about 15 minutes or take any bus three stops. There's a convenient **car park** located just behind the castle at the end of Fürst Sándor utca. Because of a newly opened border crossing, less traffic and fewer tourists pass through Kőszeg, making the town all the more peaceful.

There's an **IBUSZ** tourist information desk (tel. 336) at the Hotel Írott-kő, at Kőztársaság tér 4, open from 8:30 a.m. till 5 p.m. weekdays, to 1 p.m. on Saturday; closed Sunday.

THE SIGHTS:
There are numerous baroque and classical buildings in Kőszeg. Worthy of note is **St. James Church (Szent Jakab-tempelom)** built on the site of an ancient Minorite church, which dates from the 13th century. It's one of the most magnificent of Kőszeg's baroque buildings, with an altarpiece dating from 1693. Almost all the buildings on **Jurisics tér** are of historic interest. The most famous of Kőszeg's historical monuments is the **castle** in which Captain Miklós made his stand. The two medieval towers (the oldest surviving section of the castle) are flanked by two Renaissance wings, one of which contains a museum detailing the history of the castle and town.

ACCOMMODATIONS:
The **Hotel Irott-kő** at Kőztársaság tér 4 (tel. 333; Telex 37419), is just a few steps west of Jurisics tér, the main square. Very conveniently located, the hotel has a large but very stark atrium. Their phone number is shared with the local post office—you'll have to ask to be connected to the hotel (pronounced Eer-*ot*-koo). The rooms are clean and modern, but somewhat dark. All rooms are equipped with a private bath, and the price includes breakfast. A single room costs 470 Ft ($9.80), a double runs 860 Ft ($17.90), and a triple goes for 1,180 F ($24.60). This is the largest hotel in Kőszeg and almost invariably has rooms available. There is also a tourist information desk here (see "Orientation").

The **Hotel Strucc,** at Várkőr 124 (tel. 281), right next to the church and just across from the Hotel Írott-kő, is also well placed. With only 18 rooms, this hotel is often full, but by all means stop by and ask. We consider this one of the best hotels in Hungary! Built in 1663, it has always been an inn or hotel. As a result of the building's age some of the rooms don't have private toilets, but everything here is scrupulously clean and well run. The furniture is by far some of the nicest we encountered in Eastern Europe, though the furnishings are only a shadow of their former glory, according to the proprietress. A bathless single costs 300 Ft ($6.25) and a similar double is 520 Ft ($10.85); a double room with a bath costs 650 Ft ($13.55). All these rates include breakfast.

More Choices
Things do fill up in town or available rooms may be out of your price range. If that's the case, take bus 2 two stops from Kőztársaság tér to this group of hotels.

With no private bathrooms and no singles, the **Hotel Park** (tel. 322; Telex 37278) looks like—and is, in fact—much like a dormitory. The hotel is in a red-brick building; clean, it's by no means exceptional. A double room, single occupancy, costs 352 Ft ($7.35), and double occupancy is 424 F ($8.85) per night; a four-bedded room costs 596 Ft ($12.40) total. All prices include breakfast.

You have to take bus 2 another three stops (for a total of five from Kőztársaság tér) to reach the **Hotel Panorama** (tel. 280; Telex 37278). The bus ride is worth the wait, for this reasonably priced hotel is perched on a hillside with an excellent view of Kőszeg and the surrounding countryside. The exterior is somewhat forbidding, a real concrete pile, but the rooms are clean and well lit. Happily, the building has plenty of trees around it. There's almost always something available here, so even if you don't have a car you can risk the ride out here. There are no single rooms. A double room costs 400 Ft ($8.35) per day and a four-bedded room costs 600 Ft ($12.50); all rooms have private bath. There is an additional 60 Ft ($1.25) for breakfast and the 12-Ft (25¢) tourist tax per day per person.

Private Rooms

The **tourist information** folks on Rákóczi Ferenc utca, just south of Köztársaság tér, reputedly have some private rooms for less than 300 Ft ($6.25) a night. They're open weekdays from 7:30 a.m. till 4:30 p.m.

DINING: There's an excellent, if very Austrian, beer restaurant **Bécsi-kapu,** at Rajnis József utca 5 (tel. 254), not far from the castle entrance. The straight-backed wooden chairs won't impede your enjoyment of the old favorite, wiener-schnitzel, for 49 Ft ($1), usually accompanied by beer. It's open from 9 a.m. to 10 p.m.

You have to take bus 2 five stops from Köztársaság tér to reach the **Turista** (tel. 72), a large restaurant with a terrace overlooking Kőszeg some miles distant. The specialties are vasi kanászpecsenze sült burgonzával (roast pork with liver) for 66 Ft ($1.40), and Örségi töltolt comb hagymas (stuffed pork Örségi style) for 59 Ft ($1.25). The food is excellent here, and the prices ideal for budgeteers. The decor is subdued, but on the weekends a local band arrives and the place really jumps. Occasionally a large tour bus will crowd, if not liven up, things. The Turista is open from 10 a.m. till 10 p.m. daily.

5. Szombathely, Ják, and Herend

SZOMBATHELY: Much larger than most of the other towns in western Hungary, Szombathely has several points of interest. In Roman times the settlement was known as Savaria, and it was one of the largest and most important towns in the area.

Orientation

Most of the tourist sights are located within walking distance of Berzsenyi Dániel tér. The **bus and train stations** are right next to each other on Gábor Andor utca. To walk to the city center, head south on Gábo Andor utca till you reach Tolbuhin út, then west, and bear to the right (north) for about 10 to 15 minutes till you reach **Berzsenyi Dániel tér.** Or you can take practically any bus (except the 12A) from the station for two or three stops and you're there. By car you can just follow any of the three major roads—Hwy. 86, 87, or 89—straight into town.

The **telephone area code** for Szombathely is 99.

The Sights

Today's visitors come to see the **Franciscan church** on Savaria tér, a 14th-century Gothic building that was rebuilt in the 17th and 18th centuries in the baroque style. The **Dominican church** on Tolbuhin út is a beautiful baroque structure completed in 1670. And the **cathedral,** on Berzsenyi Dániel tér, is one of the most significant buildings from the Louis XVI era in Hungary.

Despite all these beautiful baroque buildings, Szombathely is best known for its Roman ruins. The most spectacular are the **Garden of Ruins** (Járdányi Paulovits István Romkert), right next to the central (local) bus station off Petőfi

Sándor utca. There are the remnants of an old Roman road, the Quirinus Basilica, and fragments of the old city walls; nearby is a museum detailing the ruins, first discovered in 1938. The much-heralded **Temple of Isis** will probably be of most interest to those knowledgeable in the field of Roman archeology. The ruins are so fragmentary and weathered that they do not present an impressive spectacle to the uninitiated. They're unquestionably important, but nonprofessionals will visit them for their historical interest rather than their visual value.

Accommodations

A 10- to 15-minute walk west from Berzsenyi Dániel tér is the **Hotel Tourist** on Jókai Mór utca (tel. 141-68), the only building in the Jókai park. Primarily for students, the clean and inexpensive institutional arrangements are open to everyone. Absolutely no English is spoken here, so bring your dictionary; the staff is friendly and patient, and you should be too. A tourist bed for 48 Ft ($1) in an eight-bedded room, is about the cheapest we found in all of Hungary. Singles, doubles, and suites are 180 Ft ($3.75), 430 Ft ($8.95), and 870 Ft ($18.15) respectively. It's one of the best buys in (any) town, and, happily, there's almost always a tourist bed available. Don't forget the 12-Ft (25¢) tourist tax.

For the slightly more upscale set, the brand-new **Hotel Savaria,** on Mártirok tér, is just two blocks north and east of Berzsenyi Dániel tér. A single with bath is 880 Ft ($18.35); without bath, 580 Ft ($12.10). A double room with bath costs 1,220 Ft ($25.40), and a double without, 820 Ft ($17.10). All rates include breakfast. Usually there are rooms available in this well-kept establishment. The hotel opened in July 1985, so everything is still agleam—in fact, the smell of wet paint was in the air when we visited. Try the restaurant, which is open daily from 6:30 a.m. till 11 p.m.

Dining

The two restaurants we selected in Szombathely are not near the center of town. However, we think they're worth the ride.

The **Kispityer Halászcsárda,** on Vasvári Pál utca (tel. 121-24) is one of the premier fish specialty restaurants in town. No English is spoken here, but just take the fish of the day—it's quite good and you won't have to do much talking. In any event, this is a good place to put your dictionary to work. Though the Kispityer Halászcsárda specializes in fish, the selection can vary tremendously, depending on supply and season (sometimes they may not have any fish). There's a large open terrace off a quiet residential street that makes for pleasant dining. To get here, take bus 1 south and get off just after Rózsa Ferenc krt. The average meal (fresh fish) price will run over 100 Ft ($2.10), without wine. Open from 11:30 a.m. till midnight, they also feature some of the best music in town.

West of Szombathely, on Dolgozók út, is another of our favorites, the restaurant **Pászdor Chardu.** You can reach the restaurant via bus 5 from the center, a ten-minute ride. The walls are covered with old farm implements, hunting weapons, and deer, fox, and wild goat trophies. The specialty of this restaurant is lamb prepared in a variety of ways for 45 Ft (95¢) to 60 Ft ($1.25) a dish. In season there's also delicious wild boar stuffed with herbs and served with potatoes for 85 Ft ($1.75); szarvascomb burgundi, venison in a burgundy sauce, for 79 Ft ($1.65); and a delicious wild boar goulash for 29 Ft (60¢). Open from 11 a.m. to 11 p.m., the restaurant Pászdor Chardu is heartily recommended.

JÁK: South and west of Szombathely is the Romanesque **Basilica of Ják,** originally part of a Benedictine abbey. The massive size of the church and the wealth of internal and external detail are in marked contrast to the sleepy little hamlet nestled below it. Even today there are scarcely more than 2,500 people in the entire surrounding village. The solitude seems only to enhance the powerful effect that this perfectly preserved church has on even the most casual visitor.

Little is known about the family that founded the church. Earlier it was believed that they were descendants of Vencellin, one of the Germanic knights attached to the military retinue of King Stephen I, the first king of Hungary. Now it is believed that its founders stem from the Csák family, descendants of the Szabolcs, a clan second only to the Árpád, the first family of Hungary. Márton, the first recorded founder, appears on deeds dated between 1221 and 1230. His power was measured not by his military prowess but by the fact that he was able to build this fantastic church right smack in the middle of his estate—which was, even then, in the middle of nowhere. The accepted date for the founding of the church at Ják seems to be 1220. However, in a 17th-century document the following interesting calculation appears: $1651 - 1214 = 437$. Modern scholars assume that the long-dead scholar who wrote that may have had access to a deed long since destroyed. Whatever the actual founding date, 1214–1223 will certainly include most of the likely possibilities.

These early churches were designed to withstand enemy attack. Therefore the plan of a large central gallery and towers with a single, solidly constructed entrance was actually born of necessity. When Ják was built, Hungary had just repulsed one Mongol invasion and King Béla IV feared another (and rightly so). However, the next invasion did not reach Ják, and given several more peaceful years, the builders were able to pay attention to aesthetics as well as military necessity. The architect set the towers over the first bay and gallery, leaving the nave proper open and airy. Though the church at Ják is not the largest or oldest Romanesque basilica in Hungary, its out-of-the-way location spared it from the worst ravages of war, and it remains one of the best examples of early medieval architecture in the world.

The church is about ten miles southwest of Szombathely. The only way to get here is by car or on one of the IBUSZ organized tours. The ticket office next to the church sells an excellent guide, in English, with black-and-white photographs. There is a 20-Ft (10¢) entry fee, and the church is open from 8 a.m. to 4 p.m. daily except Sunday.

HEREND: Actually, Herend is part of the Balaton region, but it lies directly between Szombathely and Budapest, and also on the way to the lake. The **porcelain factory** is very interesting to visit, but if you want to tour the factory you must make reservations through IBUSZ in Budapest. Note that it's not possible to buy porcelain directly from the factory. All transactions, we were told, are handled solely through their Western dealers; thus you can't buy in Herend and avoid the substantial markup. If you're traveling to Herend just to see the sights, fine—but don't bother to come here to avoid any dealer surcharges.

The Intourist Shop here is not a dependable source of fine pottery. They have only extras or rejected orders; it's all in perfect condition, but there's a very irregular selection with few complete sets. The only way to get around the dealers is to place an order and then return in five or so months to pick it up. Intourist cannot send you anything except (same old refrain) through their dealers. The cost of Herend porcelain is best described by the old adage: "If you have to ask, you can't afford it." Single dinner plates of the lowest grade start at $10. There is also a museum of pottery (closed Monday).

6. Pécs and Southwestern Hungary

Pécs and the surrounding countryside south of Lake Balaton make up a pleasant and fertile region. The temperate climate is one of the mildest in all of

Hungary, with comfortable summers and warm, but not too wet, winters. The major town of the region, Pécs is the third-largest city in Hungary.

Known as the "2,000-year-old city," Pécs was the site of a major Roman settlement, called Sopianae, which was at the junction of several major trade routes. From A.D. 433 to 455 Pécs was occupied by the Huns, from 455 to 470 by the Ostrogoths, and after them the Byzantines established control over the city. It was not until late in the first millennium that Pécs became a Hungarian town.

August 23, 1009, marked the founding of the first bishopric in the region. Though the documented claim that Christianity had been present at Pécs for almost 1,000 years may be exaggerated, religion has played an important part in the city's history. Hungary's first university was founded here in 1367 (unfortunately, very little is known about it, as the names of the teachers and students have been lost over time).

The Ottoman Turkish control of Pécs lasted from 1543 until 1686. In this 143-year period Pécs took on the appearance of a Turkish city—baths were built, churches were converted to mosques, and the whole face of the city was altered. Quite large by medieval standards, Pécs' town wall enclosed more terrain than did Vienna's at the time. By 1620, despite the occupation, Pécs had a population of over 5,000 people.

Following the liberation there was great hunger and suffering, but the populace managed to rebuild the city. Libraries were opened, and by the outbreak of the American Revolution in 1776 the first girls' school was founded in Pécs. By the middle of the 19th century one chronicler, János Náray, described Pécs as a city that "lies at the foot of the mountains and prospers from day to day."

You'll also find Pécs a good base for any side trips to the rest of southwestern Hungary.

ORIENTATION: The center of town is the **Széchenyi tér,** a large square with the main IBUSZ office at its southern end. The old city is surrounded by a major ring boulevard and is bisected by the east-west Sallai utca/Kossuth Lajos utca and the north-south Hunyadi János út / Bem utca. The **bus and train stations** are right next to each other at the south end of Jókai Mór utca, a street that runs directly to Széchenyi tér. There are several city buses that run to the center; simply ask before you get on and ride for about ten minutes.

The **IBUSZ** office, at the south end of Széchenyi tér at no. 8 (tel. 121-48; Telex 12234), can help you with most of your queries and has all the tour information. It's open from 8 a.m. to 5 p.m. weekdays, from 8:30 a.m. to 1 p.m. on Saturday; closed Sunday.

The **telephone area code** in Pécs is 72.

THE SIGHTS: On the northern end of Széchenyi tér is the mosque of Pasha Gazi Kassim, the largest Turkish building still extant in Hungary today. No longer a mosque, it is now the **Inner City Parish Church** of Pécs. Nearby, in front of the Ignorantine Church (1721–1731), is the eosine **fountain,** symbol of Pécs.

About a five-minute walk west from Széchenyi tér on Janus Pannonius utca is another interesting historic area. You'll see the famous four-towered Romanesque **Cathedral of Pécs,** built in the 11th century and destroyed and rebuilt several times over. The towers were built over a 100-year period between the 11th and 12th centuries, and the restored baroque façade was primarily the creation of Mihály Pollack. The interior remains primarily Gothic with some baroque additions; most of this rebuilding was completed before the end of the 19th century. Next to the cathedral is the **Bishop's Palace,** built in the neo-Renaissance style in the 13th century. It too has been destroyed and rebuilt several times—most recently between 1838 and 1853. The castle garden offers a pleasant respite on a hot day. The ruins of the old town walls are still visible here; the **Barbican,** just west of the Bishop's Palace, is the best-preserved segment.

There are numerous history museums here. Most of them have a small gallery off Széchenyi tér, with other buildings scattered around the city. One of the best cool-off spots is not the pool, but the **Geology Museum,** in the basement across from the **Vitz Béla Museum**—very pleasant if not overwhelmingly interesting.

ACCOMMODATIONS: The recently renovated **Hotel Nádor** is right on Széchenyi tér (tel. 107-79; Telex 12200). There are usually some vacancies here, and the rooms are well furnished and large. A double without bath costs 820 Ft ($17.10), and with a bath, 1,140 Ft ($23.75). Though the traffic outside can sometimes be annoying, the hotel's excellent location is a boon to any traveler. Open from 7 a.m. to 11 p.m. daily, the restaurant and bar cater to the many German and Austrian visitors here. We recommend that you steer clear of the overpriced "foreign" drinks and stick to the Hungarian stuff.

Just north of Széchenyi tér is the **Hotel Fönix** ("Phoenix") (tel. 116-80). Done in what can only be called revivalist Hungarian art deco, it's unlike anything we've ever seen. A fantastic stairway leads up to the reception area past quite a collection of odd angles and planes. The rooms are spotless, very modern, but somewhat cramped. All have showers but no toilet, except the suite. A single room costs 780 Ft ($16.25), a double runs 830 Ft ($17.30), and a triple goes for 880 Ft ($18.35)—plus 50 Ft ($1.05) for the obligatory breakfast. The 14-room hotel was completed in June 1985.

Private Rooms

There are two private-room agencies in town, both on Széchenyi tér. The ever-present **IBUSZ** is on the south end at Széchenyi tér 8 (tel. 121-48; Telex 12234), open weekdays from 8 a.m. to 5 p.m., to 1 p.m. on Saturday; closed Sunday. **Idegenforgalmi Hivatal,** at Széchenyi tér 1 (tel. 133-00; Telex 12213), is open weekdays from 8 a.m. to 4:30 p.m., to noon on Saturday; closed Sunday.

DINING: The **Hotel Minaret,** not far from the center of town at Sallai utca 35 (tel. 133-22), is usually booked solid with Polish worker tour groups, but there's a good restaurant here. Open from 10 a.m. to 10 p.m., the restaurant is often filled with hotel guests. Though the company is not Hungarian, the food is very inexpensive, although the service is not top-drawer. You will have to work your way through the poorly mimeographed Hungarian menu; most main dishes are less than 70 Ft ($1.45). There are several terraces and a pleasant courtyard.

The recommended restaurant in town is the **Eléfant söröző,** just south of Széchenyi tér on Jókai Mór utca (no phone). This restaurant has excellently prepared Hungarian specialties and some wild game in season. You won't escape for less than 200 Ft ($4.15) for a complete dinner, but the service and food are worth it. The decor is done in marble and wood; a marble elephant stands guard at the foot of a marble stairway that leads from the downstairs café to the restaurant upstairs. Considered by many locals to be the finest establishment in Pécs, the restaurant is open from noon to midnight, the café from 8 a.m. to midnight.

If you're looking for one of the best budget bargains and want to meet some student types at the same time, try the **Xavier söröző** at Alkotmany út 43 at the corner of Petőfi Sándor utca. A very modern concrete structure, the restaurant has an interesting latticework interior and a cool, shaded terrace. Pork filet and vegetables for two at 133.60 Ft ($2.80) and various beef dishes starting around 105 Ft ($2.20) make this a favorite with students. You'll get much larger portions here than in many of the restaurants near the center. After September and during the school year, you can mingle with the many Commonwealth, African, and Arabic students who gather here.

Chapter XVIII

THE DANUBE BEND AND NORTHEAST HUNGARY

1. The Danube Bend
2. The Northern Highlands
3. Eastern Hungary and the Great Plain

TO THE EAST OF BUDAPEST, the delightful towns along the Danube Bend make easy day trips from the capital or rewarding destinations on their own. Northeast Hungary, famous for wines and a green landscape of rolling hills, is a decided contrast to the Great Plain of the east.

1. The Danube Bend

About 25 miles north of Budapest the mighty Danube makes an abrupt swing south. This beautiful and strategically located region has been the source of strife for hundreds of years and the site of human settlements for thousands. Under the Roman Empire the Danube marked the end of "civilized" lands and the main northern line of defense. A millennium later, Hungarian kings ruled and dictated to the rest of the country from this natural east-west gateway. The constellation of nobility that inhabited the towns of Esztergom, Visegrád, and Szentendre led the Hungarian Renaissance and built numerous monuments to their power in these towns. Their downfall and the subsequent Ottoman Turkish invasion resulted in an era of decline and devastation that lasted for the 150-year-long occupation. But many of the ruins, castles, and churches still remain, and the proximity to Budapest makes the Danube Bend ideal for day trips or one-night stopovers.

ESZTERGOM: Astride the Danube River, Esztergom stands at the western entrance to Hungary. It is the first major Hungarian town you will enter if you travel by river, and not more than a morning's train ride from Vienna. Hungary's greatest king, Stephen I, founder of the Árpád Dynasty and later canonized, was born, raised, and ruled here in the 10th century A.D. He was not the first to take advantage of Esztergom's excellent location, however; the Romans had built one of the primary bastions of their trans-Danubian frontier here. Esztergom is regarded by many Hungarians as one of the first Christian municipalities in Hungary. During his reign Stephen I began the construction of a basilica on the Várhegy, the hill where the new basilica now stands. Esztergom is also the seat of the cardinal-primate of Hungary. Unfortunately, as in much of the rest of Hungary, the Ottoman Turks ravaged the city and destroyed the old Várhegy basilica during their occupation.

The Sights

If you're going through Esztergom or spending a night here, you won't want to miss the **Cathedral of Esztergom** and the Cathedral Treasury of Esztergom. The cathedral is the largest church in Hungary. Begun in 1822 on the ruins of the old basilica, it was completed just before the outbreak of the American Civil War, in 1860. On the southern side of the church is the much older Bakócz Chapel (1506), which was incorporated into the newer cathedral.

The **Cathedral Treasury** contains over 60 stunning gold objects and other regalia and is definitely worth a visit. The centerpiece of the collection is the Corvinus-Ceremonial Cross, also known as the Cavalry Cross of Matthias Corvinus. Fashioned by the premier goldsmiths of Paris, it was originally intended as a New Year's gift for the Burgundian noble, Philip the Bold, from his consort in the year 1402. There are also several beautiful drinking horns, including one that may have been used to slake the thirst of Corvinus himself.

Next to the church are the ruins of the old Royal Palace as well as ruins from Roman times.

Orientation

As important as Esztergom once was, time moves a little slower here now. The town center is at the southern foot of the Várhegy, the principal attraction of Esztergom. The bus and train stations are south of the city center. The Danube is to the west, shielded by a small island, the Esztergom-sziget, created by a loop of the river.

The train station is small and the railroad information office is extremely relaxed; don't rush them and they might be able to help you—then again, maybe not. To get to the center of town, take bus 1 four stops; if the bus ticket-seller is closed, the bus driver will take your money directly—4F (8¢). The bus station is within easy walking distance of the city center; walk north on Zalke Máté út for about 10 or 15 minutes.

Taxis are extremely rare here as the town is so small; ask at the desk of the Hotel Fürdő for any taxi services.

The ferry dock is on the Esztergom-sziget, not far from the Kossuth bridge that leads to the Várhegy.

The **tourist information center**, on Széchenyyi tér (tel. 484), one block southwest of the center of town, and the **IBUSZ** office, on Kossuth Lajos utca (tel. 100), one block south of the center, are open from 8:30 a.m. to 5 p.m. on weekdays, to 12:30 p.m. on Saturday; closed Sunday. If you arrive on the weekend or late at night, stop in at the desk of the **Hotel Fürdő**. English is not a strong point in any of these offices, and maps seem to be in short supply.

Accommodations

The small number of hotels in Esztergom is offset by the fact that most visitors come only for the day. We recommend the Hotels Fürdő and Volán for all but the rock-bottom traveler. Reservations are recommended—if these places fill up, there's nowhere else to go.

The **Hotel Fürdő,** at Bajcsy-Zsilinszky út 14, one block north of the center (tel. 292; Telex 226558), is our first choice in Esztergom. Connected to the hotel are a restaurant and café, both with outdoor terraces. There are a few singles for 190 Ft ($3.95) without bath, but most rooms are doubles with bath for 450 Ft ($9.40) per night; there are also a few triple rooms for 550 Ft ($11.45). Breakfast is an additional 50 Ft ($1.05) per person, and there's also a mandatory 12-F (25¢) tourist tax, per person per day. Subtract 180 Ft ($3.75) for a bathless room. The hotel is clean and newly renovated, though somewhat dark. The garden restaurant is open from 7 a.m. to 10 p.m. and serves nicely prepared Hungarian dishes. Behind the Fürdő is a noisy, if welcome, public pool.

The **Hotel Volán,** at József Attila tér 12 (tel. 271; Telex 224508), near the river, is a modern affair. While the Fürdő can fill up with tour groups, the Volán usually has rooms available and for slightly less: about 20 Ft (40¢) to 30 Ft (65¢). The rooms are clean and quiet, with shower stalls that seem to be made out of a single piece of plastic.

The budget choice in Esztergom is behind the green door of the Tourist Hotel, **Turistaház,** at Dobozi M. út 8, just north and west of the Várhegy (tel. 484). No one here speaks English, and the elderly (if spry) proprietress, while pleasant, is extremely difficult to talk to. However, for 56 Ft ($1.15) per person we feel you can afford to be patient. Each room has from six to eight beds and a common bathroom, all scrupulously clean.

Private rooms can be had for extended periods of time; ask at the IBUSZ office.

Dining

Right across from the IBUSZ office on Kossuth Lajos út is the restaurant **Kis Pipa,** one of the better places in town. There's a great luncheon menu for 31 Ft (65¢), along with a relaxed and very slow-paced atmosphere. At night the place really jumps with the mostly local and very friendly crowd. The food is simple and not exceptional, but filling. There is one friendly waiter here, János, who speaks excellent English and uses it to laud his country's way of doing things. He also knows several good swimming places and a couple of good fishing spots. János surprised us by also giving us a few culinary tips about New York (he lived in the States for a while).

The restaurant **Uszó halászcárda,** on the Esztergom-sziget just west of the Bottyan híd (bridge), is one of our favorites in Esztergom. Primarily a fish restaurant, it also serves traditional Hungarian specialties, all for less than 120 Ft ($2.50). The outdoor, canopied terrace is delightfully cool in the summer. When the weather isn't so obliging, head inside to the wood-paneled bar where they play rock music and keep things moving until midnight most nights. The restaurant is open from noon to 10 p.m.

Excursions

On a hot, sunny day even dedicated sightseers might want to relax, take a swim, and have a picnic. **Lake Palatinusz** is a beautiful place with nothing of interest except the local countryside, and peace and quiet to enjoy it in. Since it's about seven miles from town, if you don't have a car, take the Volán bus heading toward Dorog (Dorog is primarily an industrial town and not a particularly interesting tourist destination). Ask one of your fellow bus passengers to tell you when to get off for the lake. There is a bus stop so you can easily catch the bus coming back.

VISEGRÁD: Visegrád, a minute town of only 3,000 inhabitants, is set back into the actual bend of the Danube River. Throughout history its importance was far greater than its current population statistics indicate. In Roman times Visegrád was a vital strategic point in the Roman frontier fortifications. During the Hungarian Renaissance in the 15th century Visegrád was at its zenith; in the reign of King Matthias during that century, a royal palace was completed here. This majestic palace attracted political visitors from across Europe—a tribute to the growing Hungarian influence in Europe. Soon after, however, the Turks invaded the region and destroyed whatever came in their path; Visegrád never fully recovered.

How to Get There

Boats arrive at Visegrád from Vigadó tér in Budapest, at a cost of 40 Ft (85¢) per person. It takes about three or four hours to make the scenic trip. Buses also arrive frequently from Engels tér in Budapest.

Orientation

The main road from Budapest follows the Danube River. One block inland, parallel to the river, lies Fő utca, site of the Royal Palace. Boats arrive at the foot of Rév utca, a street perpendicular to the river. Local buses leave from this street for the Citadel.

The **tourist office** is at Fő utca 3/a (tel. 283-30; Telex 224180), on the riverfront (at this point of the road Fő utca merges into the main riverfront road). They can assist you with information on the Danube Bend region, or in arranging a hotel or a guide. The office is open Monday through Thursday from 8 a.m. to 4 p.m., to 3:30 p.m. on Friday, and from 9 a.m. to 1 p.m. on Saturday.

The Sights

You'll want to visit two royal sites which date back to the heyday of the Hungarian kingdom. The first is the **Royal Palace Palota,** off Fő utca in the center of town, once the seat of the mighty King Matthias. The palace was one of the showcases of Europe, boasting two elegant fountains (one of red marble and the other of white), as well as ornate carvings and coats-of-arms of the royal family. After centuries of war the palace today is largely in ruins; in fact, it was not until World War II that the palace was rediscovered and excavated. Despite the extensive damage, a dedicated excavation effort has revealed such interesting remains as the steambath; here, coals were heated in an area beneath the floor and then water was thrown on the pavement, creating steam. After visiting the palace, you will have an idea of the opulent life led by Hungarian royalty. May 1 to September 30 the palace is open from 9 a.m. to 5 p.m., from 8 a.m. to 4 p.m. October 1 to April 30; closed Monday.

A crucial part of any royal settlement in the Middle Ages and Renaissance era was the **Citadel,** and Visegrád's sits atop a hill overlooking the town. From the 13th to the 15th centuries important congresses were held here, state documents were stored, and other political matters transpired. In addition, of course, the Citadel served as the town's primary defense against attack. Better preserved than the Royal Palace, the mighty Citadel is Visegrád's most worthwhile sight. Besides showing off one of the region's most interesting castles, a visit to the Citadel gives you a splendid view of the Danube.

Accommodations

The **Hotel Silvanus,** H-2025 Visegrád (tel. 281-36 or 283-11), situated high up on a remote hilltop, is Visegrád's nicest hotel. The 75 attractive rooms have quaint furniture and balconies with panoramic views of the mountains or the Danube. A bathless double room costs 946 Ft ($19.70); with bathroom, 1,084 Ft ($22.60) to 1,184 ($24.65), depending on the view. There's a rustic-looking restaurant with game specialties downstairs. A bus from in front of the boat dock comes here; the bus has no number, but "Nagyvillám" is written on the front.

Turista-Szálló, Salamontorony utca 5, one block inland from the river, has hostel-style rooms with three to eight beds per room. A bunk for the night costs 62 Ft ($1.30).

There's also a budget **Hotel Var** on the waterfront, but check with the tourist office to see if it's open; during our visit it was closed for repairs.

Private Rooms: Opposite the ferry station at Rév utca 13, a kindly old woman, **Istvanne Nadler,** rents out two bedrooms in her house from April to October. She charges 300 Ft ($6.25) for a double.

The **tourist office,** at Fö utca 3/a (tel. 283-30; Telex 224180), also rents out private rooms (180 in all): 110 Ft ($2.30) to 150 Ft ($3.15) for a single and 220 Ft ($4.60) to 280 Ft ($5.85) for a double.

Dining

Fekete Hollo ("Black Crow"), at Rév utca 12 (tel. 261-66), is an appealing private restaurant. Here you can eat good spicy home-cooking (it really is home-cooking—the owner, Laszlo Cseke, and his family live above the restaurant) in either a small vaulted brick dining room or an outdoor area with picnic tables. The limited menu is in German or Hungarian only. Two recommended dishes are the knochensuppe mit nudeln, a broth with long, thin noodles and a chunk of pork in the bowl, for 13.50 Ft (30¢); and the schweinsschnitzel mit thymian und kartoffeln, a light slice of pork with thyme and pepper, for 48.70 Ft ($1). A complete and delicious meal will cost only $2 to $3. It's open daily except Tuesday from 9 a.m. to 9 p.m.

SZENTENDRE: Undoubtedly Hungary's most charming town, Szentendre has narrow cobblestone streets with one- and two-story houses. The town was settled by Serbian merchants (from what is present-day Yugoslavia) in the 17th century; over the years many artists settled in Szentendre. Today the artistic community continues to thrive, and many of the local merchants try to keep up the old colorful atmosphere of the town by using antiques in their stores and restaurants. It's a town that should not be left off your Hungarian itinerary.

The Sights

The most interesting sight of Szentendre is the town itself, and you'll enjoy spending several leisurely hours wandering through the pedestrians-only cobblestone streets. Those with an eye for contemporary art can also stop at one of Szentendre's **14 galleries and museums.** We enjoyed the **Open-Air Ethnographical Museum,** which documents living conditions of Hungarian peasants by showing reconstructions of peasant houses and working areas. The museum is located in Szabadság forrás, three kilometers from the town center.

In addition to art exhibits, there are frequent **concerts** and other cultural events. Inquire at the tourist office.

How to Get There

Only 12 miles from Budapest, Szentendre can easily be visited on a day trip. Fast suburban trains leave from Batthány tér in Budapest and arrive in Szentendre 40 minutes later. During rush hour, these trains leave every 5 to 10 minutes; during the rest of the day they leave every 20 minutes. Buses leave every hour from Engels tér in Budapest (and also take 40 minutes). Finally, boat rides down the Danube from Vigadó tér in Budapest take about an hour and 45 minutes.

Orientation

The **Dunatours Tourist Office,** Somogyi Bascó part 6, on the riverfront (tel. 113-11; Telex 225423), has maps and information on Szentendre; they can also arrange for private rooms in town. The office is open Monday through Thursday from 8 a.m. to 6 p.m., on Friday to 5:30 p.m., and weekends from 9 a.m. to 1 p.m. The manager of this office, János Kádár, shares the same name as the president of Hungary.

Accommodations

If you want to stay in Szentendre and enjoy its relaxing pace, we recommend the **Pensione Coca Cola,** at Dunakanyar krt. 50 (tel. 104-10). A single-story house, the pensione features attractive modern double rooms: eight are equipped with bathrooms for 700 Ft ($14.60) to 800 Ft ($16.65), and four share two bathrooms at 600 Ft ($12.50) to 700 Ft ($14.60) each. A friendly owner adds to the pleasure of a visit here. When we arrived, we were promptly served— what else?—a cool Coca-Cola! Those with a car can park in the pensione's private lot.

Hotel Party, Ady Endre utca 5 (tel. 124-91), is the next best choice if Pensione Coca Cola is full. The hotel offers unique (for Eastern Europe) loft-style doubles, with a desk and chair below and the bed up a dozen steps. Many rooms also have a small terrace overlooking the hotel's small park and picnic tables, and you can see the Danube in the distance. Doubles with bathroom rent for 744 Ft ($15.50), and those without for 544 Ft ($11.35). You can also rent boats at the hotel for a ride on the Danube for 150 Ft ($3.15). The Hotel Party also rents four bathless doubles in their tourist hostel, called the "B" building, located next door, for 200 Ft ($4.15). Guests in the "B" building have two clean public bathrooms at their disposal. The Hotel Party is about a ten-minute walk from the town center.

Save as your last pick the **Hotel Danubius,** at Ady Endre utca 28 (tel. 125-11; Telex 224300). Shoe-box-shaped rooms, without bathrooms but with a sink, are rented here for 462 Ft ($9.65) for a single; doubles cost the same price unless you choose to have a private shower, in which case you'll pay 624 Ft ($13). From October to May prices drop about 100 Ft ($2.10). Our hesitation to recommend this hotel stems from the public bathrooms, which are not always as clean as they should be. Bicycles are rented on the premises for only 90 Ft ($1.90) for the day.

Dining

In the **Rab Ráby Vendéglő,** Május 1 utca 1/a (tel. 108-19), hundreds of antiques, ranging from a full suit of armor to three trumpets hanging from the ceiling, make an attractive and unusual setting. A quaint garden area in the back is surrounded by old farm tools. Specialties here include a chicken goulash plate (kopjas csipos somogyi kakasporkolt) for 62 Ft ($1.30), and stuffed turkey with pineapple (hawai toltott pulykamellfile ananasszal) for 95 Ft ($2). Many locals consider this restaurant to be the town's best. Reserve on weekends. It's open Tuesday through Sunday from noon to 10 p.m.; closed Monday.

Aranysárkány ("Golden Dragon"), Vöröshadsereg utca 2 (tel. 116-70), is another excellent restaurant that tries to maintain the culinary traditions of the past; for example, seltzer bottles are still used to serve mineral water. From the dining room, you can see the well-known chef preparing your meal (he has authored a cookbook, *Spring in the Golden Dragon Inn*). The menu changes frequently here, but each type of meat has only one dish per day. Always try to reserve; open noon to 10 p.m. daily.

Nosztalgia Kávéház, Vöröshadsereg utca 2 (tel. 116-60), is a cute little café, with seating in a courtyard or indoors. The café's lively owner, Éliás Tibor, has lined the inside walls with mementos from the life of Jószef Dobos, the first man to add butter cream to cake in 1884. The famous Dobos cream cake is made fresh here every day. While eating your cake, ask Mr. Tibor about cultural happenings in town. In addition to running this café, he's the head of the local art lovers association, and he also sings in and organizes opera performances across town (including one every Saturday evening in his own café courtyard). The café is open from 10 a.m. to midnight in summer, to 10 p.m. in winter; closed Monday.

2. The Northern Highlands

The Northern Highlands range from the Danube Bend along most of the northern frontier. At the center of this area, which includes the caves at Aggtelek and the Mátra and Bükk mountain ranges, is the town of Eger. None of the mountains here is as impressive as Czechoslovakia's Tatras or Yugoslavia's sub-Alps but the rolling forested hills have the majestic Great Plain stretching before them, offering magnificent vistas across the flat lands to the east. It is in these hills that the scant mineral wealth and the more abundant natural game of Hungary are concentrated.

GETTING TO THE NORTHERN HIGHLANDS: The area is accessible by train from Budapest; both Eger and Miskolc are on the main line. Aggtelek and Tokaj are connected by Volán bus with Miskolc. By car, take Hwy. 3 or 25 to Eger and eastward.

EGER: Eger is most famous for the wines grown in this region, notably the red Egri bikavér (bull's blood of Eger), and the numerous thermal baths that bubble naturally up to the surface. Settled very early in Hungarian history, it was, along with Pécs, one of the first five bishoprics founded by King Stephen I in the 11th century. After the Mongol invasion in 1241, construction began on the castle whose ruins tower over the town. The initial Ottoman Turkish invasion that captured Budapest was repulsed here in 1552 by a garrison led by István Dobó. Unfortunately the Ottoman Turks were persistent and eventually captured the town about 35 years later.

The Sights

Today you can look at the impressive ruins of the **castle**, the gun ports and underground passages, and understand how a small force could resist for a long time here. The **castle museum** detailing the town's history is located on the hill in a Gothic building that was once the Episcopal Palace.

There are several well-preserved streets in Eger. The best is **Kossuth Lajos utca,** which is practically lined with baroque and rococo buildings. The **basilica** on Szabadság tér is the second-largest church in all of Hungary. Completely rebuilt in the classical style in the early 19th century its façade boasts a tympanum resting on Corinthian columns. Not far away on Dobó István tér is the **Minorite church,** a fine example of the baroque architecture that Eger is justly famous for. Across the square is the 14-sided **Minaret Mosque,** with its minaret jutting over 110 feet into the air, one of the most telling reminders of the Ottoman Turkish invaders.

Orientation

Eger is roughly circular in shape, with the Vár (castle) on the east side. The **old town** is centered on Dobó István tér, bisected by the east-west Kossuth Lajos utca and north-south Széchenyi utca. The **train station** is not more than a 15-minute walk from Dobó István tér, or if you'd rather not walk, take bus 3 three stops and walk east on Bajcsy Zsilinszky utca for two blocks. The **bus station,** just north of the basilica on Felszabadulás tér is no more than a five- to ten-minute walk east to the old city center. On summer weekends Eger can be very crowded, so if possible, arrive on a weekday.

The **IBUSZ** office is on the small foot passage north of Bajcsy Zsilinszky utca (tel. 114-51 or 124-56; Telex 63336). They are open from 7:30 a.m. to 4 p.m. weekdays only; however, they do change money on Saturday, and in September they-are open Sunday mornings as well.

Eger's **telephone area code** is 36.

Accommodations

Private Rooms: Private rooms in Eger are the best way to stay on a budget. However, the demand for these rooms on summer weekends far exceeds their capacity—be forewarned. Make reservations or try to arrive on a weekday.

Most room arrangements for the entire Northern Region and (of course) Eger are made through the **IBUSZ** office on the small foot passage north of Bajcsy Zsilinszky utca (tel. 114-51 or 124-56; Telex 63336). The room-service office is open from 7:30 a.m. till 4 p.m., weekdays only. First-class private rooms, the only kind they seem to offer, are 300 Ft ($6.25) to 400 Ft ($8.35) for doubles and 400 Ft ($8.35) to 500 Ft ($10.40) for triples; all rooms have a bath. There are luxury apartments available for as much as 1,000 Ft ($20.85) to 3,000 Ft ($62.50) per day. In the high season, if there is good weather, reservations are a must. The IBUSZ office is generally well organized and usually will make a determined effort to find you something.

Another private-room service is **Egertourist,** right on the corner of Bajcsy Zsilinszky utca 9 and the west end of the foot passage (tel. 117-24 or 132-49; Telex 63378). They have some rooms in Eger, in Gyöngyös, and around the countryside in the Mátras. Open from 8 a.m. to 8 p.m. on weekdays, they have about 300 rooms available in the summer and about half that in the winter.

Mátratourist, at Szabadság tér 2 (tel. 115-65; Telex 25285), has a good geographical distribution and offices throughout the Mátras. If you're looking for a hideaway for a day or two, this is the best place to start. Despite the crowds they are very professional, if not friendly. They're open weekdays from 11 a.m. to 2 p.m. and again from 3 to 5 p.m., on Saturday from 9 a.m. to 1 p.m.; closed Sunday.

Cooptourist recently moved to Dobó István tér 3 and had not gotten new telex and telephone numbers when this book went to press. They rent double rooms for 220 Ft ($4.60), plus 50 Ft ($1.05) per extra bed; all rooms have private bath. Their rooms fill up on weekends (just like everybody else's), so try them early and on weekdays, if possible. Cooptourist also sells tickets for a variety of concerts and tours as well as a red coupon good for a 10% reduction at all Hungar-Hotel restaurants (they'll provide a list of these establishments). The office is open from 9 a.m. to 4:30 p.m.

A Hotel Near the Park: For the more upscale traveler we recommend the **Park Hotel,** right near the park on the south side of the old town at Klapka György utca 8 (tel. 132-33; Telex 63355). The lobby is clean and slightly worn, but was being redone as this book was going to print. The rooms are clean but unspectacular, with very comfortable beds; most rooms have balconies. A bath-less single room costs 402 Ft ($8.40), and a double with bath, 1,094 Ft ($22.80); all prices include breakfast. Though the hotel is quite large, it too can fill up on summer weekends.

Dining

Less than a year old, the privately owned **Talizmán** restaurant, at Kossuth utca 23 (no phone), is reputedly one of the finest in Eger. Down in a basement, it's a simple, unadorned spot with wood-paneled walls and soft lighting. This is a good restaurant for lunch or dinner; the customers are usually non-Hungarian, and the prices reflect this. Reservations are a good idea on Friday and Saturday nights. Since there is no phone, drop by on your way up to the Vár (castle). The house specialty is alföldi bojtáravató, pork with liver and garnished with dill and potatoes, for 65 Ft ($1.35). You can eat well here, with some of the fine Egri bikavér, for less than 150 Ft ($3.15) per person. Open from noon to 10 p.m. daily except Monday.

The **Fehér Szarvas Vadásztanya** ("White Stag"), Klapka utca 8 (tel. 132-33), has a large selection of game specialties, including wild boar, filet of deer, and venison stew. Many of these dishes are given a tangy flavor through generous use of onions, paprika, and other spices, and most entrees are served with french fries on the side. The long restaurant has a decor that parallels the menu: the walls are lined with dozens of antlers, a large deerhead, some old guns, and other hunting paraphernalia. A good jazz and folk duet play in the evening. It's open from 6 p.m. to midnight, seven days.

TOKAJ: If you know of Tokaj's international reputation for excellent wine, you may be surprised to find just a small peasant town here when you visit. In fact, much like Plzeň in Czechoslovakia, where beer is the only "sight," the local wine museum and the wine selection is Tokaj's only attraction.

Situated between a hill on one side and a river on the other, the town is just a few blocks of low-scale houses. The famous wine fields of Tokaj lie in the surrounding area. Few tourists are ever seen here; when we visited, we saw only one foreign couple during the day. The bottom line on Tokaj is—visit only if you want to stock up on wine or enjoy the slow pace of a peasant town.

Accommodations

Hotel Tokaj, Rákóczi út 5 (tel. 58; Telex 62741), is the town's only hotel. Of modern cement-block construction, the Tokaj can be easily noticed by its distinctive rainbow-colored roof and bubble windows on the top floor. Doubles cost 430 Ft ($8.95) without bathroom, and 570 Ft ($11.90) with private bathroom.

The **private room bureau** at Ovar utca 6 (tel. 104) has 46 private rooms in town. Actually the office is the manager's home, and when you stop in, you may meet the whole family—as we did when we visited. Rooms cost 133 Ft ($2.75) to 250 Ft ($5.20) a night.

The Sights

The **Town Museum** at Bethlen Gabor utca 7 chronicles the development of the 900-year-old wine industry in Tokaj, and has documents on aspects of Tokaj's history. Sample displays include old wine presses and vintage bottles of Tokaj's wines. It's open from 9 a.m. to 5 p.m.; closed Monday.

Shopping

What should you buy among Tokaj's large wine selection? Our favorite pick is Tokaj-Aszu, a delicious sweet dessert wine that sells for about 80 Ft ($1.65) a bottle, or 110 Ft ($2.30) for an older vintage.

AGGTELEK: Known as one of the most famous cave systems in Europe, Aggtelek is that and more. The caves (*barlang,* as they are known in Hungarian) have been inhabited, or at least visited, since Neolithic times. Remains of the first explorers were found in the 14 miles of the main cave. In the last 2,000 years or so, more cave systems have been discovered. There are guided tours, unfortunately usually only in Hungarian, but you can request (in advance) an English-speaking guide from the IBUSZ people. There is no way to describe the fantastic underground scenery here, but we're sure you'll find the caves worth the visit. Temperatures are a constant 50° to 52° Fahrenheit and it's very damp, so bring appropriate clothing and sturdy shoes. The caves are well lit, and the guides and marked trails have removed the danger from spelunking here.

3. Eastern Hungary and the Great Plain

The Great Plain, or Puszta as the Hungarians call it, covers more than half the country. Once a wild land of swamps and prairie, now it is largely farmland that produces much of Hungary's food. This is the area that most people associate with the Magyar people and their small but sturdy horses that thundered across the plains of the Rhine and the Moselle. Today you can rent horses and ride placidly across the plains—which stretch as far as the eye can see.

SZEGED: World famous for its paprika, Szeged (pop. 170,000) is one of Hungary's most important university towns, as well as an industrial and cultural capital of southern Hungary. Unfortunately, much of Szeged's old-town charm was literally washed away in a flood in 1879. The town was reconstructed in the style of the time with two- and three-story buildings in the center, and subsequently modernized with larger concrete-and-steel apartment houses.

Szeged's old magic comes alive every year from July 20 to August 20 during the **Szeged Summer Festival.** During this month, ballets, dramas, folk dances, concerts, and other events take place in front of Szeged's Votive Church, as well as throughout the town. If you do plan on visiting Szeged, we strongly recommend that you come during the festival for a rich and exciting spectacle of Hungarian culture.

If you're unable to come during this time, try at least to attend one of the frequent organ performances in the town's impressive **Votive Church,** a brick building with two tall narrow clock towers flanking the façade. On many days the two clocks on these towers both actually tell the correct time.

Orientation and Important Addresses

The **Tisza River** divides Szeged in the center, with residential districts on both banks. If you arrive at the **train station** (tel. 109-06), take tram 1 to the town center. If you prefer to walk, go straight one block and then turn right on Április 4 út. After about 15 minutes you'll reach **Dóm tér,** slightly to your right, and the town's large **cathedral.**

If you continue straight past the cathedral, you'll reach the **Szeged Tourist Office** at Victor Hugo utca 1 (tel. 117-11 or 119-66). This office is very helpful in providing information on the latest cultural events, and they can arrange a 50-minute taxi tour of the city's major monuments for 200 Ft ($4.15). Ask to see Zsuzsanna Tóth in this office; she speaks excellent English. Open Monday through Thursday from 7:30 a.m. to 4:30 p.m., on Friday to 4 p.m.; closed weekends.

For more information on cultural events, the monthly **Szegedi Müsor,** at newsstands and the main tourist office, gives you some understanding of what's happening in town, even if it's written in Hungarian.

If you stand outside the tourist office with your back to the Tisza River, the heart of town will be just two blocks straight ahead.

If you're interested in postcards, posters, or art books, drop by **Kepesbolt** at Oskola utca 19.

If you need a **taxi** to take you around, call 133-33.

Accommodations

Perhaps the town's best hotel buy is the **Hotel Tisza** at Wesselényi utca 1 (tel. 124-66). It's located right on Széchenyi tér, a large square in the center of town planted with trees and shrubs; Szeged's main shopping streets are just a few blocks away. The 180 rooms have radios and telephones, and some also feature refrigerators. Singles rent for 422 Ft ($8.80) without bathroom, and 652 Ft ($13.60) with; doubles run 844 Ft ($17.60) without bathroom and 1,104 Ft ($23) with one.

Two blocks north of the Tisza you'll find the **Hotel Hungária,** Komócsin tér 2 (tel. 212-11; Telex 82408), a modern concrete-block building. This three-star hotel offers 132 modern doubles with TV, refrigerator, balcony, and bathroom for 1,110 Ft ($23.15). From your balcony you'll enjoy an attractive view of the river and town center. The town center itself is just a few minutes' walk away.

You'll find the **Hotel Royal,** Kölcsey utca 1 (tel. 129-11; Telex 82403), just a block and a half from Dóm tér, site of the town cathedral. The medium-sized rooms each offer TV, radio, and a living plant; doubles also have refrigerators. The Royal charges 520 Ft ($10.85) for singles without bathrooms; doubles rent for 950 Ft ($19.80) without bath and 1,150 Ft ($23.95) with one.

If you strongly value proximity to the train station at a bargain price, pick **Sarkany Fogadö,** Indóhaz tér 1 (tel. 105-14). The double rooms here are well worn and without bathroom, but very inexpensive at 350 Ft ($7.30).

Private Rooms: The government tourist agency **IBUSZ,** at Klauzal tér 12 (tel. 111-88 or 115-33), has private rooms for rent: singles cost 200 Ft ($4.15) and doubles run 300 Ft ($6.25). The office is open Monday through Friday from 8 a.m. to 4 p.m., on Saturday to 1 p.m.

Szeged Tourist, at Klauzal tér 7 (tel. 117-11 or 119-66), has private rooms at 150 Ft ($3.15) to 200 Ft ($4.15) for singles and 350 Ft ($7.30) for doubles.

The **Express Office,** at Kigyo utca 3 (tel. 113-03 or 113-10), will place students in one of the many student dorms during the summertime. Rooms have two to eight beds each, and bunks go for 50 Ft ($1.05) to 60 Ft ($1.25) per night.

The **Viking Bureau** at Teleki utca 9 (no phone) is the town's only private agency that rents out rooms. It's a very casual place, and may seem disorganized, but the rooms are a real bargain, starting from 50 Ft ($1.05). The office is open from 2 to 6 p.m. weekdays.

Restaurants

Alabárdos, at Oskola utca 13 (tel. 129-14), is the town's nicest restaurant: arched brick ceilings and a few medieval weapons add a decorative touch to the walls; the romantic lighting and a violin and cimbalom musical duet help create the mood. Try the delicious "Alabárdos Dish," a thin beefsteak with onions, peas, paprika, rice, tomato sauce, and french fries. There are also many flambé dishes served in a dramatic fashion: the lights are turned off, the musicians play the equivalent of a drum roll, and the waiter emerges from the kitchen with a long shish kebab of flaming meats. Prices are moderate: entrees cost 50 Ft ($1.05) to 200 Ft ($4.15). Reservations are suggested. The Alabárdos is open Monday through Thursday from 6 p.m. to midnight, on Friday and Saturday to 2 a.m.; closed Sunday.

Starvation Budget: Those with a tight wallet, or with an interest in seeing a typical local spot not frequented by tourists, should go to the **Fasor Vendéglo,** at Marostoi utca 4 (tel. 135-07). It's made up of two bare rooms; a large television dominates the corner of the back (and more popular) room. This might be the Hungarian equivalent of "Archie Bunker's Place," a restaurant-bar where locals come to drink beer or just watch TV and relax. You'll hear people refer to this restaurant as the Sanyi, after the waiter who still works there and is known for his legendary good heart. The food entrees cost only 30 Ft (65¢) to 50 Ft ($1.05) for straightforward dishes. Take bus 71 from Nagy Jano utca in the town center. "Sanyi" is open from 9 a.m. to 11 p.m. Monday through Saturday, on Sunday to 10 p.m.

KECSKEMÉT: The southern Great Plain is for Hungary what the Old West is for the United States: the wide-open spaces where man worked with nature. At the center of this region is the medium-sized city of Kecskemét. There isn't much to see here in term of tourist attractions (though there are some churches from the 17th to 19th centuries, and an interesting Town Hall), but there is a slow-paced charm about this city with its 19th- and early-20th-century buildings, its wide squares and pedestrian promenades, that's hard to convey in words. It's the small things that make a stay here enjoyable. We recall one evening at 6:08 the Town Hall bells unexpectedly sounded, playing a beautiful, mysterious tune, followed by Beethoven's "Ode to Joy." We recommend Kecskemét to the traveler who is seeing Hungary at a relaxed pace and who may be moving on to another destination on the Great Plain after a day or two.

Orientation

From the train station, walk straight down Rákóczi út, a long two-way street with trees lining a pedestrian path in the middle of the street. At Szabadság tér the street widens into a pedestrian-only mall, thus beginning the center of town. About two blocks farther on you'll reach Kossuth tér, with the Town Hall to your left.

Also on this square at Kossuth tér 1, you'll see the **Tourist Information Office** (tel. 223-88). They will provide you with materials about Kecskemét and the southern Plain. They're open Monday through Thursday from 8 a.m. to 5 p.m., on Friday to 4:30 p.m., and on weekends to noon.

Kecskemét's most charming section is the quiet pedestrian mall and the surrounding area from Kossuth tér to Szabadság tér.

Accommodations

The only hotel in town is **Hotel Aranyhomek,** a two-star establishment at Széchenyi tér 3 (tel. 200-11; Telex 26327). It's a modern structure in the center of town overlooking Kossuth tér. Many of the medium-size doubles offer balconies overlooking the pedestrian mall. Doubles cost 670 Ft ($13.95) without bathroom, and 1,110 Ft ($23.15) with bathroom. The hotel also offers a restaurant specializing in regional dishes.

Private Rooms: From the office at Széchenyi tér 1/3 (tel. 229-55), **IBUSZ** rents private rooms for 150 Ft ($3.15) for a single and 200 Ft ($4.15) to 250 Ft ($5.20) for a double. It's open from 7:30 a.m. to 4 p.m. Monday through Friday, to noon on Saturday, and from 8 a.m. to noon on summer Sundays. **Cooptourist,** at Kétemplom alley 9 (tel. 203-57), a small street off the main square, also rents rooms at similar prices. Its hours are 9 a.m. to 5 p.m. Monday through Friday, to 1 p.m. on Saturday.

Dining

Bugazer Csárda, Munkács utca 10 (tel. 241-74), has typical Hungarian food and atmosphere, at less than $4 for the average meal. There are several small rooms here, each with pottery, furs, and other folk objects on the walls. Lively Hungarian music adds to the pleasant atmosphere. The cuisine itself is very good, with pork and veal specialties. For dessert, try the tasty thin palacsintas. Open noon to midnight, seven days.

For a good budget lunch, drop by the **Hary Etelbar** at Két templom köz 3 (tel. 255-67). It's a small café with outdoor tables on a quiet street just a minute off the main square. They offer a limited selection of meat dishes for about 50 Ft ($1.05) each. Open Monday through Friday from 7:30 a.m. to 8 p.m., on Saturday to 3 p.m.; closed Sunday.

To add to the relaxing pleasant pace of Kecskemét, we suggest that you sample a local specialty called *palinka*, a powerful peach brandy.

Chapter XIX

LAKE BALATON

1. Balatonalmádi
2. Balatonfüred
3. The Tihany Peninsula
4. Keszthely
5. Balatonföldvár
6. Siófok

A LONG, NARROW LAKE in western Hungary, Lake Balaton serves as the summer playground for Hungarians, Germans, Austrians, and thousands of other Central Europeans. The attraction of Lake Balaton for readers of this book is not that it has the bluest waters, the most golden sands, or the least crowded beaches—it doesn't. Its appeal is that it offers an excellent budget value with good facilities, and it's an enjoyable place to break up a few days of sightseeing with some good summertime fun.

Lake Balaton, though long and narrow, is rather shallow—even in the center it's only 40 feet deep. It has attracted inhabitants of this region for thousands of years. Settlements were established around the lake in the Iron Age, and during the Roman Empire a number of villas were constructed here.

People continued to enjoy Lake Balaton for hundreds of years, but it was not until the construction of a railroad in the area in the 19th century that Lake Balaton became one of Central Europe's most popular summertime destinations. In the late 19th and early 20th century many aristocrats maintained summer houses on the lake. After World War II many hotels were built. Since then the towns on the lake have grown rapidly and now much of the entire 120 miles of coast has been developed.

Today these modern resort towns offer a full range of summer activities, all at very reasonable prices. For example, for just $1 or $2 you can rent a bicycle or a water raft for a day, or a windsurfer or a tennis court for an hour. At these prices it's a great place to learn how to windsurf or to brush up on your tennis forehand. Adding to the fun are a number of excellent restaurants and budget hotels. In all, you're likely to enjoy a carefree holiday in the sun at Lake Balaton!

And in case you arrive in winter, you won't be left out of all the fun. Wintertime activities include skating, ice sailing, and other cold-weather sports.

HOW TO GET THERE: Frequent buses and trains transport visitors from Budapest to the various towns on Lake Balaton. If you're going to one of the most popular resorts, try to catch an express train to your destination. Between the various towns on the lake, frequent buses, trains, and ferryboats carry visitors about (local tourist offices can give you the latest schedules of the different transportation connections). A fair number of travelers have also reported success in hitchhiking between resorts on Lake Balaton.

WHERE TO GO: In general, the northern part of Lake Balaton offers a physically beautiful area of lush hills and mountains that rise behind the lake. The atmosphere in the north tends to be more family oriented and quieter than in the south. The best-known resorts on the north coast are Balatonalmádi, Balatonfüred, the Tihany Peninsula, and Keszthely.

By contrast, the south doesn't feature as dramatic a landscape, but it does offer more facilities, ranging from sports to concerts. Famous southern-coast towns featured in this chapter are Siófok and Balatonföldvár.

BEFORE YOU GO: To prepare for your visit to Lake Balaton, we recommend that you stop off at a tourist office in Budapest (such as the Tourinform office at Petőfi Sándor utca 17/19) to pick up maps and cultural information on the lake area. These offices give out two maps of the region, one for the north and another for the south. Each provides street maps of the most important towns, a useful tool in orienting yourself when you arrive at each new town.

THE ORGANIZATION OF THIS CHAPTER: What follows is a town-by-town description of our favorite resort areas on Lake Balaton, beginning with Balatonalmádi in the north and moving counterclockwise around the lake.

1. Balatonalmádi

Although it's the fourth largest of Lake Balaton's resort towns, Balatonalmádi, on the north coast of the lake, is small enough to offer a few quiet beaches away from the strip in the center of town. The town itself is on a small hill, and the streets climb up the hill as you move inland.

Settlers since the Romans have enjoyed Balatonalmádi, but it was not until the 1860s that summer villas were built here and the town developed. Over the years it has become a favorite of middle-class Hungarian families, thanks to its proximity to Budapest.

ORIENTATION: The town's main square and center of tourist activities is **Marx tér,** off József Attila út, which runs along the water. The main **tourist office** is at Lenin utca 36 (tel. 381-31). Look for a sign outside reading "General Tours, Zimmer Vermittlung." They offer maps of the town, and rent private rooms at 200 Ft ($4.15) for a single and 400 Ft ($8.35) for a double. Hours are 10 a.m. to 9 p.m.

ACCOMMODATIONS: The **Villa Pax Corporis,** Bajcsy-Zs. utca 8 (tel. 383-71 to 383-73), is an excellent hotel buy. An attractive, quiet villa with 13 rooms, it's situated in the hills a few minutes' walk up from the lake. All the medium-sized rooms here have private bathrooms and small balconies. From July 6 to August 31 doubles cost $22 and an apartment for two is $33. In the off-season doubles cost $18 and the apartment runs $27. When we visited, the kind manager was cooking up some delicious-looking scrambled eggs for the morning breakfast— just one of the extras that make the Villa Pax Corporis a special place.

If the Villa Pax Corporis is full, the **Hotel Tulipán,** on Marx tér (tel. 380-84), is the next best choice. Located on the town's main square, the Tulipán offers 57 Class B doubles, some with a balcony overlooking the lake. Guests can use the private beach of the Hotel Auróra free of charge. In high season rooms cost 737 Ft ($15.35) without bathroom, 838 Ft ($17.45) with a shower only, and 972 Ft ($20.25) with a complete bathroom.

Another choice in town is the **Hotel Auróra,** Bajcsy-Zs. utca 14 (tel. 380-90; Telex 32347), Balatonalmádi's most modern hotel. The steel-and-glass façade frames rooms with tiny bathrooms, balconies, and refrigerators. From June 29 to August 31 singles cost 1,307 Ft ($27.25) and doubles run 1,441 Ft ($30). In low season the same rooms are 938 Ft ($19.55) and 1,074 Ft ($22.40) respectively.

Private Rooms: For private rooms, try the **IBUSZ** office at Petőfi Sandór utca 21 (tel. 383-40), which has some 700 rooms available at 120 Ft ($2.50) to 140 Ft ($2.90). Hours are 8 a.m. to 5 p.m. weekdays, 9 a.m. to 4 p.m. on Saturday, and 9 a.m. to 1 p.m. on Sunday. The main **tourist office** at Lenin utca 36 (tel. 381-31) also offers private rooms, for 200 Ft ($4.15) for a single and 400 Ft ($8.35) for a double. Hours are 10 a.m. to 9 p.m.

DINING: The nicest area restaurant for an evening of dinner, music, and dancing is **Pinkóczi Csárda.** It's two or three kilometers (less than two miles) into the hills on a country road with no name and is accessible only by car (signs on the road show the way) or by taxi (which you can call at 384-71). When you get here you'll find an attractive, peaceful country area. Outside are picnic-style tables covered by a large straw roof; indoors is a large room, again with wood tables and benches. Specialties are richly garnished grilled beefsteak, lamb, and chicken, at a cost of 50 Ft ($1.05) to 150 Ft ($3.15) per entree. The restaurant has both good food and a pleasant atmosphere. It's open from noon to midnight, May to October only.

Another good choice for lunch or dinner is **Paprika Csárda,** back in town at Hunyadi utca 25. The small, one-story white stucco restaurant is run by a local family, who see to it that guests enjoy tasty Hungarian specialties at budget prices: entrees cost 43 Ft (90¢) to 64 Ft ($1.35). It's open daily from 8 a.m. to 10 p.m.

SPORTS: The Pinkóczi Csárda restaurant (see the travel directions above) also runs a **riding school.** A 30-minute lesson costs 150 Ft ($3.15); an hour of riding costs 230 Ft ($4.80).

Guests of the Hotels Tulipán and Auróra can use a **tennis court** for 100 Ft ($2.10) an hour.

2. Balatonfüred

Balatonfüred is one of the best known of the Lake Balaton towns and has some of the best facilities of all the lakeshore resorts. It is favored with some of the better beaches on the lake and also, on the hills behind, some of Hungary's best vineyards—you are literally surrounded with good things here. Not as provincial as some of the other, smaller spots, Balatonfüred has bars with live music, dancing, and some of the most active nightlife we found around the lake.

ACCOMMODATIONS: We recommend the **Panorama Panzio** at Kun Béla út 15 (no phone) as the town's best budget buy. It's a small private white stucco home that offers basic rooms and private bathrooms. From June 15 to August 20 singles cost 325 Ft ($6.75) and 650 Ft ($13.55) for a double. In low season prices drop to 250 Ft ($5.20) to 500 Ft ($10.40).

If you prefer a modern, larger hotel, check into the **Hotel Margaréta,** Széchenyi út 29 (tel. 408-21; Telex 32241). The Margaréta offers a feature we particularly like: each room sports small kitchens with refrigerators, hotplates, and pots and pans. With these facilities, you can save money by cooking an occasional meal if you so choose. The rooms also feature private bathrooms. Rooms rent for 1,570 Ft ($32.70) from May 25 to August 31, for 1,190 Ft ($24.80) from September 1 to 30, and 945 Ft ($19.70) from October 1 to May 24.

Private Rooms

For bargain-priced private rooms, visit **Balatontourist Nord** at Blaha L. utca 5 (tel. 402-81). Their rooms rent for 100 Ft ($2.10) to 150 Ft ($3.15) for a single, and 200 Ft ($4.15) to 1,200 Ft ($25) for a double. The office is open from 8:30 a.m. to 6:30 p.m. Monday through Saturday, to 12:30 p.m. on Sunday.

Another, slightly more expensive, option for private rooms is **IBUSZ**, at Petőfi Sandór utca 4/a (tel. 401-07). Doubles cost 250 Ft ($5.20), 300 Ft ($6.25) for triples, and 400 Ft ($8.35) for apartments. IBUSZ is open Monday through Friday from 8 a.m. to 6 p.m., on Saturday from 9 a.m. to 4 p.m.; and on Sunday from 9 a.m. to 1 p.m.

DINING: The **Panorama Panzio** recommended above also offers good fare in a small restaurant downstairs. A few tables surround a bar indoors, and on a small patio outside there are several tables underneath umbrellas. While the selection of dishes is small, portions are large. We enjoyed pork and chicken entrees for only 49 Ft ($1) to 224 Ft ($4.65) each. Open daily from 10 a.m. to 10 p.m.

SPORTS: The **Tenisz Centar,** opposite the Hotel Margaréta, rents courts for 150 Ft ($3.15) to 180 Ft ($3.75) an hour, depending on the season. You can use their racquets and balls free of charge. Tennis lessons are also given here at reasonable rates. You can make reservations at the Hotel Marina, Margaréta, or Annabella, or at the courts themselves.

In front of the Marina Hotel, a group of West Germans rents modern and well-maintained **windsurfers** for 10 Deutsches marks (about $3.50) an hour. They also give windsurfing lessons.

NIGHTLIFE: For some gaming activities at night, you can take a bus free of charge to the Héviz **casino** on the other side of Lake Balaton. In July and August buses leave from the Marina Hotel at the lake on Széchenyi utca 26 (tel. 408-10) at 7 p.m. Bring your passport and your good-luck charm.

3. The Tihany Peninsula

Roughly midway along Lake Balaton's northern coast and surrounded by hills, the Tihany Peninsula boasts the area's lushest beaches and most beautiful scenery. The beauty of Tihany was known as far back as the Iron Age, when people lived on the peninsula, and during the Roman Empire a number of villas were constructed in the Tihany hills. Today Tihany is one of the Balaton region's most popular destinations.

Unlike most newer Lake Balaton towns, Tihany offers a worthwhile artistic site, the Romanesque church of a Benedictine abbey first founded in 1055. King Andrew, one of Hungary's earliest kings, has been buried in the church since 1060. The monastery's dedication plaque (1055) is the first written example of the Hungarian language.

To get to Tihany you'll have to take a bus, or a ferry from the other side of the lake; trains don't pass in this direction. The ferries across the lake from Szántód rév leave every 20 minutes from 6 a.m. to 8 p.m. and then every hour until midnight.

ORIENTATION: From the ferry landing, our hotel pick at Tihany lies to the left and the **Balatontourist Office** lies ahead at Kossuth utca 20 (tel. 440-52). They rent private double rooms for 300 Ft ($6.25). In July and August the office stays open from 8 a.m. to 6:30 p.m. Monday through Friday, to 1 p.m. on Saturday; the rest of the summer the office closes at 4:30 p.m. on weekdays, and from October 1 to April 15 it's closed altogether.

ACCOMMODATIONS: You'll find some of Lake Balaton's most attractive accommodations at **Club Tihany,** on Club Tihany Rt., Rév. utca 3 (tel. 441-70; Telex 2232272). This "club" consists of 166 Danish-built bungalow apartments. Three different models of bungalows are featured; we recommend the two-story atrium houses, loft apartments with a bedroom upstairs. All houses come equipped with modern bathrooms and kitchens, designed as only the Danes know how. From June 22 to August 31 apartments cost $29 to $36, and in low season they cost $22 to $29. Unfortunately, as the Club Tihany becomes discovered by more and more people, we're sure the prices are destined to rise.

4. Keszthely

Lake Balaton's second-largest town, on the northwest corner of the lake, Keszthely (pop. 21,000) is home to Europe's first agricultural college, opened in 1797.

THE SIGHTS: Of special note in Keszthely is the **Festetics Palace,** on Szabadság utca, an ornate 1750s baroque structure with huge spacious rooms. Once home to princes and counts, the Festetics Palace now houses a library of some 52,000 volumes. You'll enjoy seeing the period furniture and art in the palace.

Visitors to Keszthely can also drop by the **Balaton Museum** at Múzeum utca 2, which has displays outlining the geological and natural history of the Lake Balaton region.

ACCOMMODATIONS: When you first walk into the **Hotel Amazon,** Szabadság utca 11 (tel. 122-48), you'll be reminded of your old university dorm—down to the dimly lit hallways that are rarely repainted. The public toilets date back to a previous age, one with wooden seats. Nonetheless, the toilets are clean and the rooms are rather large. Price is the greatest attraction here, though: singles cost 330 Ft ($6.90), and doubles run 360 Ft ($7.50). Although the hotel is about a ten-minute walk from the beach, it's just a few minutes to the Festetics Palace and a number of good restaurants in town.

Keszthely's fancy modern hostelry is the **Hotel Helikon,** Balatonpart, just off the beach (tel. 113-30; Telex 35276). The eight-story building features balconies which overlook the water. Guests can sunbathe on a private beach in front of the hotel. The rooms are quite comfortable, all with private bathroom and terrace. From June 15 to September 14 doubles cost $33; from April to June 14 and September 15 to November 1 prices fall to $21.

The **Hotel Phoenix,** Balatonpart (tel. 126-30; Telex 35276), has a large attractive lobby with brick walls and a tall raw-wood roof. The rooms here are small with natural-wood furniture, and all have tiny bathrooms with shower. From July 1 to September 15 singles are 915 Ft ($19.05) and doubles run 1,030 Ft ($21.45); from May to June 30 and September 16 to October 1 singles are 515 Ft ($10.75) and doubles are 630 Ft ($13.15).

Private Rooms

Several agencies in town offer private rooms. **Zalator,** Fö tér 1 (tel. 125-60), has singles for 160 Ft ($3.35) and doubles for 180 Ft ($3.75). It's open in summer from 8 a.m. to 5 p.m. Monday through Friday, to 4 p.m. on Saturday, and to noon on Sunday.

IBUSZ, Széchenyi utca 1-3 (tel. 129-51), has singles for 160 Ft ($3.35), and doubles for 330 Ft ($6.90). Open from 8 a.m. to 6 p.m. weekdays, from 9 a.m. to 4 p.m. on Saturday, and from 9 a.m. to 1 p.m. on Sunday.

Cooptourist, Tanácskóztársaság 16 (tel. 124-41), maintains the longest hours of all these bureaus: 8 a.m. to 8 p.m. seven days a week. Singles cost 150 Ft ($3.15), and doubles cost 300 Ft ($6.25) to 500 Ft ($10.40).

Solar Utazasi Iroda, Fö tér 1, offers singles for 150 Ft ($3.15) to 200 Ft ($4.15), and doubles for 200 Ft ($4.15) to 400 Ft ($8.35). It's open weekdays from 9 a.m. to 7 p.m., weekends to 3 p.m.

DINING: We highly recommend the **Vadaskerti Csárda** ("Wildgarden Inn"), located on the Napfeny sor road between Keszthely and Héviz (tel. 127-72). The Wildgarden Inn is one of an increasing number of Hungarian "semiprivate" restaurants, whereby someone rents an establishment for a number of years and takes in a profit above payment of his expenses. Magyar Laszlo, an intelligent and kindly man who speaks some English, has done an admirable job of running the Wildgarden Inn. The interior, with its antlers and skins on the walls, will remind you of a mountain hunting lodge, and the menu reflects that same hunting spirit: roe, deer, wild boar, and fogash fish from Lake Balaton are the house specialties. Outside the restaurant is an attractive terrace where music is played every evening from 5 p.m. The restaurant stays open from 10 a.m. to 10 p.m. seven days a week from March to November, but it's closed on Tuesday in winter. The bus that goes between Keszthely and Héviz stops just down the road from the restaurant.

Hungária Gösser Sörözö, Kossuth Lajos út 35 (tel. 122-65), is an expansive beer garden restaurant with a large courtyard and an indoor dining room patronized by 90% German and Austrian clientele. Surprisingly, for a beer garden the food here is rather good. Try the veal medallions Hungarian style (belsz inermek magyarosan) for 139 Ft ($2.90). They also have good fresh strudels for dessert. It's open from 9 a.m. to 11 p.m. daily; there's dance music from 7 p.m.

TRANSPORTATION NOTE: If you're going from Keszthely to other destinations in the north part of Lake Balaton, note that the bus is almost always quicker than the train, since the train detours to the north. Take the bus from the Fö station. You pay for your ticket as you get on the bus.

A SIDE TRIP TO HÉVIZ: If you're anxious to get in an outdoor swim in the spring, fall, or winter, you need not test the cold waters of Lake Balaton; rather, head for the 14-acre thermal lake at Héviz. Located just 15 minutes away by bus from Keszthely (buses leave every 20 to 30 minutes), Héviz boasts the second-largest thermal lake in the world (the largest is in remote New Zealand). Throughout the year the lake temperature remains a stable 86° to 95° F.

It's not only tourists who enjoy Héviz's facilities. When we visited after closing hours one summer afternoon, the director of the lake facilities was in the water soaping himself in his regular afternoon swim. The lake stays open from 8 a.m. to 5 p.m.; guests must leave by 6 p.m.

Another attraction of Héviz is its casino, the only one in the Lake Balaton area, and only the second one in all of Hungary (the other is in Budapest).

Accommodations

If you want to stay in Héviz and make extensive use of the thermal lake and spa facilities, stay at the attractive, modern **Thermal Hotel** at Kossuth 9 (tel. 111-90; Telex 35296). This popular hotel first opened in 1976, and since then has hosted many guests who want to take advantage of the hotel's therapy facilities. Each of the 203 rooms in the hotel offers a TV, radio, refrigerator, and private bathroom. The lobby features marble floors and a helpful staff. From April to November 1 and December 28 to January 1, a single costs $28.40 and a double rents for $40.40. During the rest of the year, a single is $24.40, and a double is $34.40. Those who wish to take part in the hotel's therapy program should write ahead of time for supplementary prices and information.

Nightlife
In the Thermal Hotel there's also a **casino,** open from 4 p.m. to midnight every day. Here you can play roulette, blackjack, and slot machines with West German marks (you can change money here). The atmosphere is relaxed, especially in the early evening, but it begins to pick up and get more formal after 9 p.m. Those with an observant eye will notice that there are no double zeros on the roulette wheel, and so you have slightly better odds than in the U.S. Remember to bring your passport; otherwise you won't be allowed in.

5. Balatonföldvár
Across the lake from the Tihany Peninsula and slightly to the south lies another popular resort, Balatonföldvár. A wilderness up to the end of the 19th century, Balatonföldvár today offers many sports facilities in its hotels, a feature which attracts a youthful group of visitors.

ACCOMMODATIONS: The **Hotel Festival,** Rákóczi út 40 (tel. 403-71 or 403-72; Telex 227398), a tall modern concrete structure with a long series of balconies on every floor, offers visitors a wide variety of summer sports. You can choose between soccer, badminton, basketball, and volleyball, all free of charge. For 100 Ft ($2.10) you can play an hour of tennis, and for 120 Ft ($2.50) you can go windsurfing for an hour. The Festival offers 320 doubles with private bathroom. From June 28 to September 1 rooms rent for a very reasonable $22. From May 27 to June 27 the price drops to $14, and in September it's an even lower $10.50.
    Hotel Juventus, József A. út 9 (tel. 403-79), is a bargain student hotel where nonstudents can stay as well. The rooms have bright-red furniture and bold blue floors, and terraces but no private bathrooms. Singles are 588 Ft ($12.25), 341 Ft ($7.10) for students; doubles cost 628 Ft ($13.10), 402 Ft ($8.40) for students; and triples run 817 Ft ($17), or 563 Ft ($11.75) for students.

Private Rooms
Cooptourist, at Hajóállomás (the pier) rents villas and apartments. From July 6 to August 15 they cost 1,100 Ft ($22.90) to 1,680 Ft ($35), from June 22 to July 5 and August 16 to 30 they cost 730 Ft ($15.20) to 950 Ft ($19.80), and from May 5 to June 21 and August 31 to September 20 they cost 500 Ft ($10.40) to 700 Ft ($14.60).

DINING: The **Patko Vendéglö,** Moricz zs. utca 73/g (tel. 313-06), is an attractive private restaurant with three different dining areas: indoors, a terrace, and outdoor picnic tables; the latter two overlook a huge empty field. The menu is moderately to expensively priced, with wild game and meat entrees costing 100 Ft ($2.10) to 300 Ft ($6.25). The house special is goose liver Hungarian style for 300 Ft ($6.25). We vividly remember the crêpes dessert, richly adorned with whipped cream. Service is from noon to 4 p.m. and 6 to 10 p.m.

6. Siófok
The largest and most popular resort on Lake Balaton, Siófok (pop. 22,000) is Balaton's undisputed center of activity, offering everything from sports to discos. You'll see people everywhere in Siófok; this is not the place for privacy.

But the crowds of vacationers looking for summer fun create a friendly atmosphere where you easily meet people. When we visited, we met an American from Long Island who preferred Lake Balaton to Coney Island, a French couple en route to Romania, and numerous Germans and Austrians on their annual trek to the "seaside."

Siófok's boom dates back to the opening of the southern railway through town in 1861. Since then the town grew rapidly and today Siófok can accommodate thousands of visitors on any given summer day.

ACCOMMODATIONS: Our preferred budget hotel in town is the **Hotel Vénusz,** Kinizsi utca 12 (tel. 106-60). It's located just one block from the beach, and yet it's considerably less noisy than the larger hotels right off the beach. As you walk in, you'll pass a bar on your right, and the small reception area lies straight ahead. Rooms here are Class B quality, each with a refrigerator, balcony, and private bathroom. In high season, doubles cost 1,302 Ft ($27.15); in low season prices are 20% to 30% less.

Another excellent choice in town is the private **Oazis Pansio,** Szigliget utca 5 (tel. 120-12), a family-run pension a few blocks from the center. The 24 medium-sized rooms in this two-story house are administered by Józsefné Sereg, a kind and lively woman who speaks Hungarian, German, and Russian. She welcomes all readers of this book to her establishment, both for lodging and for the excellent restaurant downstairs (see our recommendation below). All rooms have a private bathroom and cost 500 Ft ($10.40) *per person.* In all, this is one of Lake Balaton's best budget values.

If the above two choices are full, then consider the **Hotel Napfény,** Petőfi sétány 2 (tel. 114-08). It's just a block from the sea and at the start of Siófok's main street. Many rooms sport small balconies overlooking a park. The rooms here are standard Class B doubles, much like those of the Hotel Vénusz, for 1,060 Ft ($22.10) in high season.

Finally, another reasonably priced establishment is the **Touring Hotel** at Fokihegy-Siófok (tel. 106-84), about a 20-minute walk outside the town center on the Fö road in the direction of Balatonföldvár. Here, small double rooms with sinks and large windows, but no bathrooms, cost 800 forints ($16.65) in high season. It's a few minutes' walk to the beach. The excellent Piroska Csárda restaurant is next door.

The Lakefront Hotels

There are four hotels along the lakefront in Siófok on the Petőfi sétány— the **Balaton** at no. 9 (tel. 106-55), the **Lidó** at no. 11 (tel. 106-33), the **Hungária** at no. 13 (tel. 106-77), and the **Európa** at no. 15 (tel. 114-00). They all have 137 rooms with bathrooms and balconies, and are almost identical. The Európa is slightly nicer, as well as slightly more expensive, than the other three. The Hotels Balaton, Lidó, and Hungária charge 782 Ft ($16.30) for a double room from April to May 25 and September 21 to October 2, 1,230 Ft ($25.65) from May 26 to June 28 and August 31 to September 20, and 1,522 Ft ($31.70) from June 29 to August 30. You pay more here for the lakeside location.

Private Rooms

Siótours, Szabadság tér 6 (tel. 108-00), has doubles for 220 Ft ($4.60) to 450 Ft ($9.40). **IBUSZ,** at Fö utca 174 (tel. 111-07; Telex 226075), has doubles costing 220 Ft ($4.60) to 300 Ft ($6.25), as well as some apartments.

On the streets named Batthyány, Lajos, and Ferenc you'll see a cluster of private rooms for rent which you can contact and pay for directly there. Look for the signs reading "Privatenzimmer" outside.

DINING: The **Oazis Pansio,** Szigliget utca 5 (tel. 120-12), is an attractive restaurant with clean white walls and a small terrace area. The cooking featured is home-style (the entire family works in this restaurant), and dishes such as gulyás have that classic taste that made goulash famous the world over. The moderately priced house specialties (featuring a variety of pork dishes) are so hefty we suspected that either a mistake had been made or that they were going out of their way to impress us. But when we looked around the restaurant, we noticed that everyone there was enjoying large platters stacked with slices of meat and delicious vegetables! When a fierce summer rainstorm suddenly erupted, the staff moved the guests on the terrace inside in a flash. To help us get to our hotel during this storm, the owner's daughter tried to call a taxi; when none could be found, one of the waiters offered to drive us home. As you can see, a guest at the Oazis Pansio savors not just good fare, but a friendly family ambience as well!

You can't miss the **Piroska Csárda,** Balatonszéplak-felsö, just off Fö utca (tel. 106-83), a very large, rustic restaurant built of logs with a straw roof, where you can dine indoors, in the courtyard, or at a table outdoors in front of the restaurant. The setting re-creates the *csárda* style of 150 years ago in both the old-style architectural materials and in the cuisine, which features only classical Hungarian dishes. This is a lively place, serving good food at moderate prices. In season it's open from 7 a.m. to 1 a.m. daily; off-season, from 10 a.m. to 10 p.m. daily (sometimes a bit later on weekends). Bus 1 from the center of Siófok passes here about every 20 minutes.

SPORTS: One of the great things about Siófok is the many sports facilities available. You can rent **bicycles** for only 60 Ft ($1.25) a day or 200 Ft ($4.15) for an entire week, as well as rafts and badminton racquets at a stand off Petöfi street, about a block away from the Napfény Hotel.

The four lakefront hotels rent **windsurfers** for about 60 Ft ($1.25) an hour, and also boats for equally low rates.

Part Five

ROMANIA

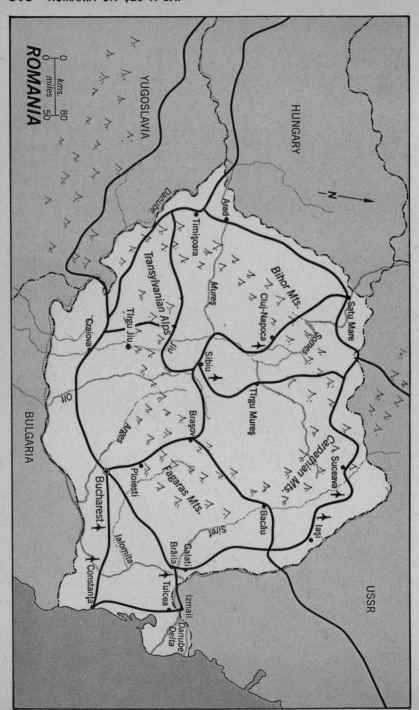

Chapter XX

INTRODUCING ROMANIA

1. About Romania
2. Planning Your Travels
3. Getting There
4. Getting Around
5. Accommodations
6. Food and Drink
7. The ABCs of Romania

A TRIP TO ROMANIA (pop. 23 million) is somewhat like an expedition to the Arctic: both cost a lot and combine few comforts with many challenges. In return for your money and explorer's spirit you'll see sights rarely encountered by Westerners. Consider what Romania offers: picturesque towns nestled among a mountain range where peasants continue to thrive much as they did a hundred years ago in Transylvania; beautiful monasteries built in the Middle Ages and richly decorated with colorful frescoes in Moldavia; and remote swamps filled with wildlife in the Danube Delta.

In many ways Romania differs from Eastern Europe's other countries—everything from language (a Romance, not Slavic, tongue) to economic development (it is Eastern Europe's least well-off country). Most notably, progress and modernity have come slowly to many parts of the country. From the peasants whose way of life seems unchanged for hundreds of years to the beautiful medieval towns, you're in for many rewarding glimpses of the past. You may even feel as though you've traveled through a time machine!

Despite Romania's varied charms, we recommend the country mostly for experienced and adventurous Eastern European travelers. Taking into account the scarcity of budget hotels, often mediocre dining and transportation facilities, and tourism officials who are not always willing or able to help, a visit to Romania can prove a trying, though always unique, experience.

SUGGESTED ITINERARY: If you plan to visit Romania for a week, we suggest that you spend one day in Bucharest, Romania's capital, and one day in Braşov, a picturesque Transylvanian town with cobblestone streets and small houses set at the foot of a mountain three hours north of Bucharest. Count Dracula's castle also lurks near Braşov. From Braşov, continue on to Suceava, which lies at the center of several extraordinary, not-to-be-missed medieval monasteries. To allow for travel time, spend two nights in Suceava. Then continue south (by plane if you can afford it) for two days in Constanţa, an important ancient Greek and Roman port town full of historical monuments that is a flourishing resort today.

If you have additional time for Romania, we suggest spending a day at each of two other Transylvanian towns. Sibiu, two or three hours by train from Braşov, offers several interesting museums of art and history, as well as medieval fortifications. Mountaineers will also enjoy hiking in the Fǎgǎraş Mountains near Sibiu. Cluj-Napoca, with its picturesque churches and unique ethnographic museums, is also worth adding to an extended tour of Romania. Finally, lovers of the great outdoors should consider a day or two in the Danube Delta, a swamp and forest wildlife preserve.

Although most of Romania's cities can be seen in a day or two, allow yourself plenty of time for traveling between destinations. Trains are quite slow and tiring, so don't plan too rigorous a schedule or you'll wear yourself out.

1. About Romania

A CAPSULE HISTORY: Romania's great differences with the rest of Eastern Europe are rooted in the Roman colonization of the area (called Dacia at the time) by the Emperor Trajan in A.D. 106. You can still see scenes from the glorious Dacian campaign on Trajan's Column in Rome and on numerous other Roman public monuments. An intense Romanization of the area over the next 200 years had a strong influence on the language, customs, and other aspects of Dacian life. In A.D. 271 barbarians drove away the Romans, but even under subsequent Slavic invasions over the next several hundred years the Dacians retained the language and customs of the Romans.

In the early Middle Ages the three states that make up Romania—Transylvania, Wallachia, and Moldavia—each set up their own kingdom. After the 15th century, however, continual Turkish attack limited the independence of these provinces for several hundred years.

Despite frequent Turkish victories, Romania was not without its heroes, most notable of whom is Prince Vlad Ţepeş (1456–1476), also known as "The Impaler," and better known as Count Dracula. In contrast to the vampire image bestowed upon him by Irish novelist Bram Stoker in the 19th century, Romanians consider Vlad Ţepeş a great national hero who effectively battled against the invading Turks. His distinctive method of finishing off his enemies, by impaling their heads on a stake, gave him his nasty reputation.

In 1600 the three Romanian states were briefly united, but it was not until 1881 at the Congress of Berlin (after the war in which Romania joined Russia against Turkey) that Wallachia and Moldavia were united as the nation of Romania, with full independence as a monarchy under King Carol. After World War I, in the reign of King Ferdinand (Carol's nephew) and Queen Marie, Transylvania joined Wallachia and Moldavia in the new state. During World War II the fascist Romanian Iron Guard deposed another King Carol and Romania entered the war alongside the Axis.

In 1947 King Carol's son, Michael, formally abdicated and Romania became a socialist state. Under socialism, Romania has been greatly industrialized, much like the rest of Eastern Europe. However, Romania has been unique among Eastern European nations in its independence within the Warsaw Pact. For example, Romania has not participated in Warsaw Pact military maneuvers since 1962, and no Soviet bases are allowed within the country. In 1984 Romania sent athletes to the Los Angeles Olympics even though the rest of the Warsaw Pact boycotted the games. According to official publications, this "genuine independence and national sovereignty" seeks a "policy of détente, disarmament, and peace."

In the opinion of many observers, the Warsaw Pact has allowed such independence because of Romania's fidelity to a rigid internal socialist policy. One result of Romania's economic policy has been great financial problems. Although Romania boasts rich energy supplies, the oil glut of the 1980s combined with low industrial output have contributed to a faltering economy. Much of the country's goods (including food supplies and oil) is exported, which has resulted in erratic shortages of consumer products. As in other developing countries, the traveler to Romania is not immune from these economic problems.

RELIGION: About 80% of the population is Greek Orthodox, and 16% is Roman Catholic. Calvinists, Lutherans, and other minority religions also exist in Romania.

GOVERNMENT: A president and Grand National Assembly (MAN) run the Romanian socialist state. As of this writing, Nicolae Ceausescu has served as president of Romania since 1965, as well as general secretary of the Communist Party, supreme commander of the armed forces, president of the State Council, and so on. With Ceausescu's likeness often seen in newspapers and on television and banners, Western observers have remarked that his personality cult is the most developed in Eastern Europe. Many Romanians do indeed see Ceausescu as a great figure, thanks to his independent foreign policy stance and his strong Romanian nationalism.

LANGUAGE: Romanian, naturally enough, is the language of Romania. Of all Romance languages it is Romanian—not Italian, French, or Spanish—that is the closest to Latin. Even with its Slavic and Turkish influences, Romanian is a fairly accessible tongue for Westerners. Travelers with a smattering of French, Spanish, or Italian will understand some of the language, and those who speak only English will find Romanian much easier to pronounce than Eastern Europe's other languages. As you can see from our capsule vocabulary in the Appendix, many words in Romanian are actually pronounced just as they appear!

Hotel tourism personnel in the larger cities often speak some English; in smaller towns expect to hear French, German, or Russian in addition to Romanian.

The Romanian Leu:

The Romanian national currency is called the leu (plural: lei), made up of 100 bani. Banknotes come in denominations of 10, 25, 50, and 100 lei; coins are issued in 5, 10, 15, and 25 bani, as well as 1, 3, and 5 lei. In this book all rates have been calculated at 11.76 lei = $1 U.S. Thus 1 leu = about 8½¢ and $10 = about 118 lei.

---

2. Planning Your Travels

OVERSEAS TOURIST OFFICES: Romania maintains a National Tourist Office in North America at 573 Third Ave., New York, NY 10016 (tel. 212/697-6971 or 697-6972). Although they offer little detailed practical information (for instance, the best budget hotel in Brașov), they are quite helpful in answering general questions about travel in Romania. Their office in New York is also well stocked with tourist pamphlets and group tour advertisements. Romania's tourist office in England is located at 98-99 Jermyn St., London S.W.1 (tel. 01/930-8812; Telex 262107).

Within Romania, unfortunately, you are likely to find that the tourism industry offers little assistance to foreign visitors. Personnel in tourism offices, restaurants, etc., move so slowly that they may even seem unhelpful. You'll need lots of patience to extract the smallest item of information.

PACKAGE TOURS: Offering few services for individual travelers, Romania presents many challenges to independent travelers. Thus, if you're anxious to see Romania, consider joining a group tour, as Romania's tourism infrastructure is best set up to accommodate groups. Several group travelers we met within Romania reported that they were quite happy and relatively worry-free in their travels—something we rarely heard from individual travelers.

For descriptions of several tours to Romania, write, call, or drop by the Romanian Tourist Office for pamphlets. Tours offered vary from visits to cities important in Dracula's life to spa and beach holidays. One particularly inexpensive tour operator is **Balkan Holidays Limited.** If you don't see their pamphlet in the Romanian Tourist Office, write to Balkan Holidays Ltd., 19 Conduit St., London W1R 9TD (tel. 01/491-4499 or 493-8612; Telex 262923).

If you don't want to join a group, consider at least getting pre-paid hotel vouchers and bookings from the Romanian Tourist Office in the U.S. Although this plan may cost you a little extra money, it will save some difficulties when you arrive.

Another option for those who don't want to join a full-fledged tour is to join a several-day tour once in Romania. The Romanian Tourist Office offers three-day tours for $98, five-day tours for $150, and seven-day tours for $210, all per person. Ask for their "Tour Romania" pamphlet for further information.

COST ESTIMATES: On the whole, Romania's tourist industry provides the least bang for your buck in all of Eastern Europe. Hotels, restaurants, taxis, and other tourist services often prove expensive without exceptional service or quality. Budget hotels are often in poor condition, and transportation in the country, at any price level of ticket, can prove a grueling experience. To a great extent, a grossly unrealistic rate of exchange set by the Romanian government lies behind these high prices. When the dollar was making great gains against most European currencies in recent years, it actually fell against the Romanian lei. Expect to spend between $20 and $35 a day for a very basic standard of living with few frills.

WHEN TO COME: Long and bitter winters reign over Romania. Many hotels as well as private homes lack heating because of oil shortages. In fact, shortages over the past few years have prompted a series of jokes about conditions. According to one, apartment dwellers shouldn't open their windows in winter lest a passerby catch cold. Limited supplies of food compound the problem. Unless you are the most intrepid sort of traveler, we strongly discourage visiting Romania during this time of year.

By March, however, the situation improves. Minimal heating exists and food is more plentiful, so spring can be a pleasant time of year to visit, as can fall. Those bothered by hot weather might avoid Bucharest in July and August, as air conditioning is almost nonexistent.

Average temperatures in Bucharest range from a high of 86° in July and

August, through the 50s and 60s in spring and fall, to a low of 20° in January. Generally the sea coast has warmer winters and cooler summers, while the mountains are cooler in summer and about the same in the winter.

VISAS: Unlike every other country in this book except Yugoslavia, you do not need to apply for a visa before arriving in Romania. Rather, you can procure a visa at the border or at the Bucharest airport. Border officials issue visas for $18 after you have exchanged a minimum of $10 for every day you intend to stay in Romania. Visitors who have pre-paid accommodations and tourist services do not need to exchange this $10 minimum.

If you arrive at the airport, you must first exchange your minimum daily currency amount right after two complete baggage inspections; then at another window you'll receive your visa. If you arrive by train, you get off the train to receive a visa. We recommend that train travelers obtain their visas prior to arrival, as it will save you from dealing with the sometimes fierce Romanian border officials.

Should you prefer to obtain your visa before you go, write to the Embassy of the Socialist Republic of Romania, 1607 23rd St. NW, Washington, DC 20008 (tel. 202/232-4747 or 232-4748), or to 655 Rideau St., Ottawa, ON K1N 6A3 Canada (tel. 613/232-5345).

3. Getting There

Romania is somewhat remote from Europe's most frequented gateway cities. Whereas all the other countries covered in this book are within a few hours of Berlin, Vienna, or Istanbul, Romania borders Eastern Europe's least-visited areas: eastern Hungary, northern Bulgaria, eastern Yugoslavia, and the Ukraine in the Soviet Union.

BY AIR: From the U.S. you can fly Lufthansa to either Frankfurt or Munich and take a connecting Lufthansa flight to Bucharest. In Frankfurt, Lufthansa can also put you on a connecting Tarom Romanian Air Transport flight to Timisoara in western Romania, near the Hungarian and Yugoslavian borders.

For information or assistance while in Bucharest, contact Lufthansa at: Boulevard Magheru 18 (tel. 50-67-66/50-69-83).

Flying to Bucharest

In the chart below First Class and Business Class fares allow unlimited stopovers. The Excursion fare is limited to two stopovers in each direction for a charge of $25 each. The APEX fare permits no stopovers and has a 21-day advance purchase requirement and a $75 penalty fee for cancellation. All fares (subject to change without notice) are subject to a $5 departure tax plus a $5 Custom User fee.

Round-Trip Fares to Bucharest

From:		New York	Anchorage	Atlanta	Boston	Chicago	Houston/ Dallas- Ft. Worth	San Francisco/ Los Angeles	Miami	Phila- delphia
First Class	All Year	3378	4504	4066	3378	4028	4110	4740	3820	3598
Business Class	All Year	1984	2906	2372	1984	2428	2314	2894	2306	2148
10 Day – 3 Month Excursion	Sept. 15–May 14	1050	1488	1178	1050	1160	1178	1233	1196	1113
	May 15–Sept. 14	1214	1652	1342	1214	1324	1342	1397	1360	1277
7 Day – 3 Month APEX	Sept. 15–May 14	840	1278	968	840	950	968	1023	986	903
	May 15–Sept. 14	994	1432	1122	994	1104	1122	1177	1140	1057

BY TRAIN: Train travelers face a lengthy, crowded, and often uncomfortable journey. The 558-mile ride from Budapest to Bucharest takes almost 18 hours; the 450 miles from Belgrade to Bucharest lasts about 14 hours.

BY CAR: From all reports, traveling by car offers the least-appealing possibility for entering Romania. Tough border guards conduct very lengthy inspections, making visitors wait for hours at a time.

4. Getting Around

BY AIR: Tarom flies to many Romanian cities, including Bucharest, Cluj-Napoca, Constanţa, Iaşi, Sibiu, Suceava, and Tulcea. Fares are moderate—Bucharest–Tulcea for 190 lei ($16.15), Bucharest–Suceava for 292 lei ($24.85), and Bucharest–Sibiu for 199 lei ($16.90). Children under 12 receive a discount.

For complete departure times, ask Tarom for their timetable (*orar* in Romanian), which you can obtain from any foreign office. This red timetable also includes the latest domestic fares in the back. To buy tickets, go to the Tarom office listed in the Bucharest section, or to any local office listed in this chapter or in Tarom's timetable.

BY TRAIN: No train system in all of Europe (with the possible exception of Albania, where we have not traveled) bewilders and frustrates travelers like the Romanian State Railways (CFR). To minimize your difficulties, try to follow these guidelines:

(1) Always buy tickets at least one day in advance, and several days in advance if possible (you can buy tickets up to ten days ahead of time). Due to a very bureaucratic system of ticket distribution, train stations only sell tickets a few hours before departure. As a result, long lines and a chaotic situation almost always prevail. Sometimes we have arrived at the train station an hour before departure time and been unable to purchase tickets as the lines were so long.

You can obtain train tickets before the day of departure from the local CFR train office. The Carpaţi Tourist Office sometimes also sells train tickets for hard currency only. Note that advance tickets *cannot* be bought at the train station itself.

The one exception to this rule of advance purchase is for international trains that are just passing through Romania (for example, the *Orient Express,* the *Pannonia Express,* and several others). These train tickets can be bought only at the train station, one hour before the scheduled departure. Keep in mind that tickets for international trains often sell out, so you cannot always count on catching these trains.

You can also purchase tickets from an origination point different from the city you are in, but you must go two or three days ahead of time to the local train bureau and then return the next day so that they can process the tickets.

(2) Purchase seat reservations along with your ticket. In many instances Romanian travel offices give out several reservations for the same seat. We asked a conductor for his response to this problem and he replied, "Sit anywhere there's a free seat." So are reservations worth getting? We say yes, because they're always useful in defending your seat from a challenger who has the same reservation. For all long train rides a reservation is a must, although no guarantee of a seat.

(3) Try to buy first-class tickets. Romanian trains are poorly maintained, making lengthy rides both crowded and unpleasant. First-class tickets can be purchased in separate lines (which are often shorter), and allow you to ride in more comfort for a few dollars more. Although Romanian first-class seats are

less well maintained than most European second-class facilities, they do make the journey more bearable.

(4) Always take the fastest possible train. *Rapid* trains move the most quickly, followed by *accelerat*. *Personal* are by far the slowest trains. If at all possible, limit yourself to *rapid* and *accelerat* trains, and never take a *personal* train. *Personal* trains are so slow and crowded (the list of horror stories associated with these trains is endless) they almost make walking a viable option.

(5) Never ride without a ticket. You might think, since lines are so long, "I'll just buy my ticket on the train and pay a supplement." Unfortunately, such behavior is usually construed by the conductor as fare shirking. If you board the train without a ticket, you'll be hit with a stiff fine of at least $20 and then be kicked off the train—no exceptions.

BY BUS: As difficult as train travel is within Romania, you're going to want to save bus travel for smaller routes where trains don't go. Try to book in advance, and always arrive early to get on to the bus and maybe even find a seat.

BY CAR: Car rentals are quite pricey in Romania: a basic car costs about $320 a week with unlimited mileage, not including insurance. All foreign car-rental agencies represented in Romania charge the same price.

Unfortunately, Romania does not boast a high standard of road construction, and so driving can prove somewhat rigorous. We recommend avoiding nighttime driving as unlit roads make it difficult to see pedestrians, bicycles, horse carts, and other unlit vehicles. According to Romanian law, if you hit anyone on the road, you are assumed guilty and will be assessed a stiff penalty.

Cars can drive up to 60 km/h (37 mph) within cities, and 80 to 90 km/h (50 to 55 mph) outside of cities. You must have either your regular driver's license or an international driver's license, as well as a Green Card for third-party insurance. Never mix drinking and driving. In case of an accident, try to reach the **Automobil Clubul Roman (ACR)** for assistance. Their central office is at 27 Rue Beloianis in Bucharest (tel. 59-50-80).

Local police have the authority to assess small fines to drivers breaking traffic rules. If you refuse to pay, your passport will be confiscated until a court reviews the matter. Needless to say, we'd rather have our passport then a few spare lei.

HITCHHIKING: With great gas shortages limiting the number of cars on the road, you can't always be sure of getting a ride. A tip in hand, such as cigarettes (Kent 100s are best), can greatly increase your chances of getting a ride. One Iraqi student who lived in Romania for several years suggested that waving a U.S. passport is the best way to ensure a ride. Women should keep to public transportation only.

5. Accommodations

HOTELS: Hotels, even those in the budget category, cost the individual visitor a pretty penny due to a rigid system of state pricing. Very basic singles usually cost $12 to $15 and often more; doubles listed in this chapter will most often rent at $30 to $40 for small plain rooms.

Romania's hotels are broken down into three categories: deluxe, first class, and second class. Deluxe hotels are much like the deluxe hotels of other countries; first-class hotels (which are further divided into subdivisions of "a" to "f") offer rooms comparable to B* and B category rooms detailed in the other countries of this book. Second-class rooms are much like Class C rooms of other countries, complete with aging facilities, some of which do manage to maintain a quaint charm about them. Private bathrooms usually do not come with second-class rooms. Public bathrooms vary greatly in quality; we've noted any that are suitable only for hearty, no-comfort-needed travelers.

PRIVATE ROOMS: Unless you have immediate family in Romania (mother, father, sister, or brother), you are not allowed to stay in private rooms, even if the host is a Romanian friend. The Romanians who host you stand to be fined if they're caught accommodating a foreigner.

CAMPING: Camping offers the most inexpensive choice for accommodations, but keep in mind that facilities are crowded and basic indeed. For a list of Romania's 150 campsites, contact the Romanian Tourist Office before you go.

6. Food and Drink

After many months of sampling the various cuisines of Eastern Europe, we have to report that Romanian fare rates low on our comparative scale of regional food. Because of sometimes severe food shortages, most restaurants you will come across serve few Romanian specialties; rather, they concentrate on international dishes of mostly pork and veal, enhanced with bay leaf, garlic, pepper, and other spices. If shortages are particularly acute, your meal might consist of bread, white cheese, and cold cuts. Vegetables do not figure prominently in these restaurants, and there are times when the visitor can go for days without seeing any vegetable dishes whatsoever. In general, international specialties served in restaurants are adequate, though unexceptionally prepared.

When you can find them, Romania does offer some appetizing local dishes, featuring Turkish and Hungarian influences. Expect a hearty soup to begin your meal, such as thick goulash soups, and **ciorbă,** a popular Ukrainian soup with sausages and cream, and other ingredients which vary from place to place.

For an entree, Romanians enjoy **mititei** (short meatballs of chopped sausage), **sarmale** (spiced meat wrapped in cabbage leaves), **tocană** (a stew of pork, beef, or ram meat flavored by onions), and **musaca** (chopped-up meat and vegetable pie); these dishes are often accompanied by **mamaliga,** a corn mush polenta. Grilled dishes are also quite popular in Romania, such as **mici** (meatballs prepared on a grill), and roasted lamb or chicken. The Danube Delta and Black Sea resort towns serve tasty carp, grilled sturgeon, and other fish.

Good **wine** will do wonders to enhance a Romanian meal. Our favorite labels include **Riesling, Muscatel** and **Pinot-Negru.** Another favorite local drink is **tzuică,** a plum brandy. And at the end of your meal, order one of Romania's good dessert wines, such as **Murfatlar.**

For dessert, you can savor several Turkish pastries, such as **baklava** and **kadaif,** both made from dough and richly anointed with honey or sugar, or local pies, called **plăcintă.**

Restaurant Tips

Always ask to see a menu so you have an idea of the prices you'll be charged. Closely check the bill and see that an extra zero has not been added.

Tip generously if you expect to return to a restaurant. You'll receive excellent service the next time around.

Even if it's a sweltering hot summer day in Bucharest, men should not wear shorts or they won't be seated in a restaurant.

Most restaurants add a 10% to 15% service charge to the bill.

7. The ABCs of Romania

BANKS: Exchange rates are uniform across Romania, so you might as well change money in your hotel to save time. Banks usually remain open from 8 a.m. to 3 p.m. Monday through Friday, to noon on Saturday.

BLACK MARKET: We strongly recommend that you avoid all black market currency exchanges in Romania (even if you get five or six times the official rate). Romania's socialist system is one that does not look kindly upon such activity!

There's one curious form of black market trading that at least deserves mention. Among many Romanians, Kent 100 cigarettes serve as the country's unofficial currency. Travelers have reported using Kents to pay for taxis (two packs from the airport to the center of town), for tips, for gifts, etc. If, however, you try to use another Western cigarette brand, you'll earn only blank stares from the locals. Kent 100s can be bought in the hard-currency stores for $1.40 a pack; if you intend on giving some gifts, buy a carton in a duty-free shop on the trip over and you'll save some money.

You may be curious as to why Kent 100s, and no other brand, has become Romania's unofficial currency. Although we didn't find a conclusive answer, we did hear one interesting account. According to this version, Kent 100s became popular after Romania suffered an earthquake in 1977. During this time, the U.S. extended emergency assistance, including Kent 100 cigarettes. For many Romanians, this aid provided the first opportunity to sample good Western cigarettes, and out of gratitude to the company for these free Kents, Romanians continue to prefer them to this day.

CREDIT CARDS: Most budget hotels and restaurants listed in this chapter do *not* accept credit cards.

CRIME: Westerners occasionally encounter petty theft and rip-offs from savvy, street-smart locals. Just be on the lookout and nothing should happen.

CURRENCY: Romanian **lei** (leu in the singular) is the national currency; 100 bani make up each leu. Banknotes come in denominations of 10, 25, 50, and 100 lei; coins are issued in 5, 10, 15, and 25 bani, as well as 1, 3, and 5 lei. You may change money in banks, hotels, and travel bureaus; all give identical rates. Change only a little at a time as you can never be completely sure of getting dollars back for your excess lei. As of this writing, 11.76 lei = $1 U.S. All export and import of lei is illegal. Remember to conserve all currency-exchange slips, both for changing lei back into dollars, and for Customs on your way out.

CUSTOMS: According to a U.S. Embassy paper, "Romanian Customs regulations, while often difficult to understand, are strictly enforced." You are allowed to bring in two cameras, ten rolls of film, two liters of alcohol, four liters of wine, 200 cigarettes, and other personal items. You may also bring in gifts worth up to 2,000 lei ($170); items above this value are taxed. Declare all your valuable items—furs, jewelry, and electronic devices, for example—or you may not be allowed to take them out of the country when you leave.

Before making any large purchases inside Romania, make sure that you can export the item. If export is permitted, you may take out 1,000 lei ($85) worth of goods duty free; purchases above that amount are subject to Customs duty.

ELECTRICITY: As in the other Eastern European countries, Romania's electrical sockets punch out 220 volts, 50 cycles, A.C.

EMBASSIES AND CONSULATES: The U.S. Embassy is located in Bucharest at Strada Tudor Arghezi 7-9 (tel. 11-45-93, 10-40-40, 12-40-40, 12-40-48, or 12-40-49), open Monday through Friday from 8 a.m. to 1 p.m. and 2 to 5 p.m. There are no U.S. Consulates in Romania.

The **Canadian Embassy** is in Bucharest at Nicolae Iorga 36 (tel. 50-61-40), and the **British Embassy** is also in Bucharest at Strada Jules Michelet 24 (tel. 11-16-34).

EMERGENCY PHONE NUMBERS: Dial 061 for an ambulance, 055 for the police, and 081 for the fire department.

GAMBLING: If you enjoy taking risks, head over to Romania's only casino, in Mamaia on the Black Sea Coast.

GAS: Gas is a rare commodity in Romania. We have seen lines that last for six hours and more. Tourists, however, are permitted to cut in front of these nightmarish lines. In order to get gas, you must purchase petrol coupons for about $2.50 a gallon (with hard currency, of course) from a hotel or tourist office before you go to the gas station. At the station, drive up to the special pump for hard-currency coupons. Most stations stay open from 10 a.m. to 10 p.m.

HOLIDAYS: Romanians celebrate the New Year on January 1 and 2, International Worker's Solidarity Day on May 1 and 2, and Romania's National Day on August 23 and 24.

MAIL: Our advice on mail is plain and simple: Don't send or receive mail in Romania. We sent off quite a few letters from Romania to the U.S., and it took several months for *less than half* of the correspondence to arrive. Both Romanians and Westerners have voiced their suspicions to us that all mail to and from the West is closely monitored. You'll do better to wait until you reach another country for both sending and receiving mail.

MOVIES: Most English and American movies play in the original language with Romanian subtitles. Always check beforehand just to make sure.

NEWSPAPERS: The only English-language publication you're likely to see in Romania is the *Romania News,* available at many newsstands.

OFFICE HOURS: Offices usually stay open from 7:30 or 8 a.m. until 4 or 4:30 p.m.

PHOTOGRAPHY: Do not photograph airports, airplanes, border installations, railway stations and tracks, roads, bridges, military camps, electrical and gas plants, waterworks, soldiers on duty, any object of any military use, government buildings, and spots where you see a "no photography" sign (a red slash over a black camera). With those exceptions, Romania does permit photography in the country.

RADIO: On the Black Sea coast, "Radio Holiday" broadcasts every hour in five languages, including English, with news and information. Inquire at your hotel reception for broadcast frequencies.

REGISTRATION: You do not need to register with the Romanian authorities, as the hotel will register you when you check in.

SHOPPING: Best buys include folk jackets and dresses, pottery, woodcarvings, and records with traditional Romanian folk music. These items are available in both local Romanian stores, and in **Comtourist** shops which accept only hard currency. Many hotels also maintain a hard-currency store or counter where you can buy Western cigarettes, chocolate, and other goodies. Shops in larger towns stay open from 7 or 8 a.m. to 7 or 8 p.m., though many stores close for a few hours in the afternoon.

SPAS: One of Romania's claims to tourist fame is its 160 spas, a few of which have operated since Roman times. Although most people come to these spas to cure a specific ailment, some visitors frequent them just to relax and feel better. The Romanian Tourist Office offers many materials on spa programs as well as package tours.

STUDENT TRAVEL: Romania offers few benefits for students traveling on their own. If you have an IUS card, you should receive a discount on train tickets, but not on planes or buses.

TELEPHONE: For local calls, use a l-leu coin, which gives you three minutes. For long-distance calls, go to the international post office.

TIME: Official Romanian Time is two hours ahead of Greenwich Mean Time and seven hours ahead of Eastern Standard Time.

TIPPING: Give waiters 10%, barmen 10%, and bellhops 5 lei (43¢) per piece.

WOMEN ALONE: We've heard from women traveling alone in Romania that some Romanian men maintain a not-always-welcome Latin tradition and try to pick up female visitors (reading a map in public is a sure way to draw attention). A resolute "no" and walking away will usually be enough to deter such types, but if they persist in following you, you can threaten to call the much-feared militia.

Chapter XXI

BUCHAREST

1. Orientation
2. Accommodations
3. Dining
4. Sights and Daytime Activities
5. Nightlife
6. The ABCs of Bucharest

THE FASCINATION OF BUCHAREST lies both in its politics and in its museums. From Bucharest (pop. 2,000,000) you get a picture of what Eastern Europe must have been like during the cold war in the early 1950s, complete with the ubiquitous photos and banners of the nation's leader plastered on walls and across streets. Large, imposing gray buildings line Bucharest's wide boulevards; stores, darkened in an attempt to save energy, stock few items; locals wear clothing of the early 1950s. Beyond this gray façade you can enjoy some rich museums filled with art and the relics of both ancient and modern Romanian history. And Bucharest also boasts some very beautiful parks.

Unless you have a great interest in the politics and history of Romania, a day or two will suffice for Bucharest before you head out into the countryside, a thickly forested region of southern Romania between the Carpathian Mountains and the Danube River.

1. Orientation

When you arrive at the train station or airport your first priority is getting into town. Once in the city center you should be able to find your way around after a short time.

GETTING INTO TOWN: The buses from **Otopeni International Airport** to the city center (near the main tourist office) run sporadically—for 15 lei ($1.28)—with gaps of several hours at a time. Thus you may have to take a taxi. Although a **taxi** driver may quote a price in dollars, be warned that while you may save money by paying in hard currency, such transactions are *illegal*.

Train travelers arrive at the main station—**Găre de Nord** (tel. 052). Stop by the station's ONT Tourist Office (open from 7 a.m. to 9 p.m. Monday through Saturday, to 2 p.m. on Sunday) to see whether they will assist you in finding a hotel room. Otherwise you can call the hotels yourself, or head for the main tourist office in the center of town.

To reach the center, take bus 133 or 179 to Piața Romana, or tram 74 through Piața Romana and then down Bulevardul Magheru. Most of the hotels listed here, as well as those recommended by the Tourist Information Office, are within five or ten minutes of these stops (tram 74 goes right to the main tourist office). You may find it most convenient to take a taxi to your hotel; public transport with its crowded aisles and curving routes can be confusing at first.

The area around the train station is not the best place to stop and ask advice or to accept offers for private rooms (or anything else, for that matter). Nor should you walk north to Calea Griviţei Street, which is being torn up for the new metro and is frequented by some unsavory types.

PUBLIC TRANSPORTATION: We recommend that you do a lot of walking in

Bucharest. Buses tend to fill up rapidly, and on a bus you risk not only being hot and crowded, but also losing your wallet. If you take the bus, refer to the map that the central tourist office gives out (it's also sometimes sold at newsstands) as it includes bus and tram routes. Buy tickets at newspaper stands; as of this writing, buses cost 1.75 lei (15¢), trolley buses cost 1.50 lei (13¢), and trams cost 1 leu (9¢).

The city has recently opened up a metro system—at a cost of 1 leu (9¢) per ride—but it doesn't cover the center of town, and thus it's unlikely that you'll need to use it.

NAVIGATING YOUR WAY: At Piaţa Romană begins the city's main shopping

avenue, **Bulevardul Magheru,** which becomes **Bulevardul Bălcescu;** stores, shops, airline offices, and hotels line this wide street. Parallel to this avenue one block south you'll find **Calea Victoriei,** Bucharest's other major avenue of interest to tourists and home to several museums, hotels, restaurants, and government buildings. In the middle of Calea Victoriei sits the **Piaţa Gheorghiu-Dej,** site of the city's art museum and Communist Party headquarters. Most of the hotels and sights recommended in this chapter are located on these two boulevards or on nearby sidestreets.

TOURIST INFORMATION: For Bucharest information and maps, as well as

other tourist assistance, drop by the **Carpaţi National Tourist Office,** Magheru Boulevard 7 (tel. 14-77-91). Waiting for service here can sometimes be like waiting for Godot, but, with time, you can get useful information. This Carpaţi office also offers packages for an evening of dinner and folklore entertainment at a cost of $13 per person. The office is open from 7:30 a.m. to 8:30 p.m. Monday through Saturday, and from 8 a.m. to 2 p.m. on Sunday.

2. Accommodations

You will have to pay a sizable sum of money for very low quality in Bucharest. Many of the budget hotels we visited have reasonable rooms but bathrooms that run from poorly maintained to a real health risk. In order to get clean toilets, it seems that you have to pay more than $25 per person per day. In many instances we must list hotels that would not be mentioned in any other country simply because that's all that exists in anything even near budget prices.

A SPLURGE CHOICE: Like a rainbow on the horizon of drab Bucharest hotels stands the **Hanul Manuc,** Strada 30 Decembrie no. 62 (tel. 13-14-15; Telex 10795). No other hotel in town can even compare to its charm and character. First built as an inn in 1808, the hotel retains its historic past with old wooden furniture in the rooms, electric lights that look like old gas-burning lamps, and

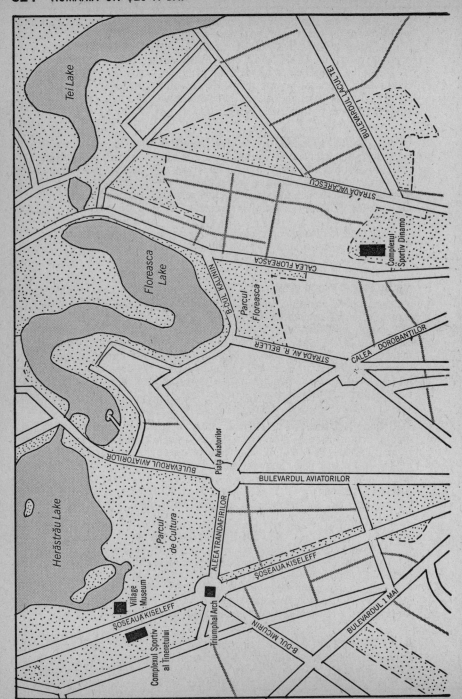

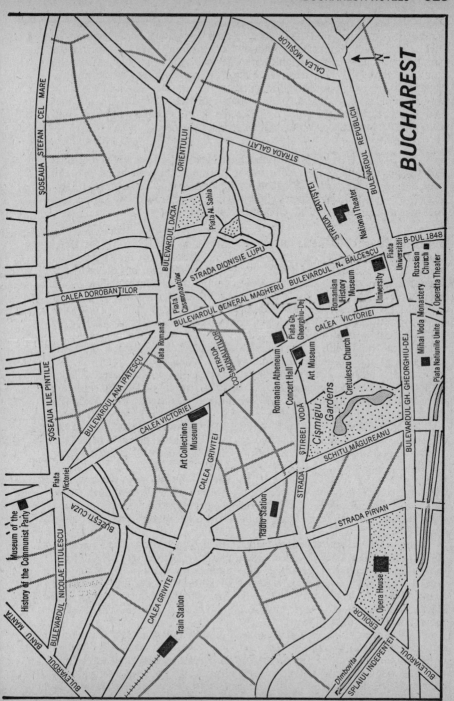

BUCHAREST

SOSEAUA STEFAN CEL MARE

CALEA MOSILOR

STRADA GALATI

BULEVARDUL REPUBLICII

ORIENTULUI

BULEVARDUL DACIA

Piata N. Sahia

STRADA BATISTEI

National Theater

CALEA DOROBANTILOR

STRADA DIONISIE LUPU

Piata Cosmonautilor

BULEVARDUL GENERAL MAGHERU

BULEVARDUL N. BALCESCU

B-DUL 1848

Piata Universitații

Russian Church

Operetta Theater

Romanian History Museum

University

SOSEAUA ILIE PINTILIE

Piata Romană

STRADA COSMONAUTILOR

Piata Gh. Gheorghiu-Dej

CALEA VICTORIEI

Mihai Voda Monastery

Piata Natiunile Unite

BULEVARDUL ANA IPATESCU

Romanian Atheneum Concert Hall

Art Museum

Cretulescu Church

BULEVARDUL GH. GHEORGHIU-DEJ

CALEA VICTORIEI

STIRBEI VODA

Cișmigiu Gardens

Art Collections Museum

CALEA GRIVITEI

STRADA

SCHITU MAGUREANU

Piata Victoriei

BUZESTI CUZA

Museum of the History of the Communist Party

BULEVARDUL NICOLAE TITULESCU

BANU MANTA

BULEVARDUL

Radio Station

STRADA PIRVAN

Opera House

CALEA GRIVITEI

Train Station

Dimbovita

EROILOR

SPLAIUL INDEPENTEI

BULEVARDUL

wooden ceilings supported by large wooden beams. Each of the 32 rooms has two areas: a small parlor at the entry, and then beyond a door, a bedroom. In each room the only thing that looks new is the bathroom. The rooms surround a large courtyard filled with the tables of a beer-hall restaurant. Across from the hotel you can see the ruins of the Old Princely Court, and just a block from the hotel you'll find a busy outdoor food market. Prices for this delightful hotel rate as slightly splurgey; singles with bathroom rent for 443.75 lei ($37.75), and doubles go for 612.50 lei ($52.10). From October 30 to December 16 prices drop somewhat for low season. Write or Telex to reserve a room.

A FIRST-CLASS HOTEL: For an unbeatable location, check into the first-class **Hotel Negoiu,** Strada 13 Decembrie no. 16 (tel. 15-52-50), one block from the large Bălcescu Boulevard. Its 93 small rooms all come with a sink and a TV set, and many have a balcony. Singles without bathroom cost $15.50 to $21.50, and doubles with bathroom and large bathtub cost $35 to $39.

SECOND-CLASS HOTELS: Of second-class hotels in Bucharest, the **Hotel Rahova,** Calea Rahovei 2 (tel. 15-26-17), offers the best value for your money. As in other second category hotels, the 47 rooms look old, but they're fairly large; the bathrooms also have aged over time, but are cleaner than those in many second-class hotels. You'll find the hotel's location convenient, right off Bulevardul 1848, a continuation of Bulevardul Bălcescu. Singles without bathroom cost 194 lei ($16.50); doubles without bathroom run 312 lei ($26.55), or 412 lei ($35.05) with private bathroom.

Another hotel with a fine location off Boulevard Bălcescu is the **Hotel Muntenia,** Strada Academiei 21 (tel. 14-60-10), a second-class hotel with 123 rooms. The rooms show years of wear, but prices are low for Bucharest. Singles without private bathroom cost $15.50; doubles rent for $25 without private bathroom, $29 with a shower, and $33 with a complete private bathroom. The desk clerks here speak no English.

The **Hotel Bucegi,** on Strada Witing 2 (tel. 49-51-20), has some of the cleanest public bathrooms we found. Very little English is spoken here and the small cramped lobby might put you off. A single room costs 206 lei ($17.50) per night; a double room, 355 lei ($30.20); a triple, 495 lei ($42.10); and a four-bedded room, 560 lei ($47.60) per night. None of the 58 rooms has a private bathroom but it is not a big problem here thanks to the well-maintained public bathrooms. The Bucegi is especially convenient for visitors just spending one night in Bucharest before changing trains, as the train station is only two blocks away.

Also in the budget range is the **Hotel Opera,** Strada Brezoianu 37 (tel. 14-10-75), a side street off Bulevardul Gheorghiu-Dej. Like many of Bucharest's second-class hotels, the Opera's 63 small rooms show signs of aging, and the hotel's facilities look old. For those not looking for modernity, the Opera charges 169 lei ($14.35) to 194 lei ($16.50) for a single without bathroom, and 269 lei ($22.85) with a bathtub only. Doubles rent for 313 lei ($26.60) without bathroom and 413 ($35.10) with.

West of the city center and about a 15-minute walk southeast of the train station is the **Hotel Veneția,** at Piața Kogălniceanu 2 (tel. 15-91-49). Though noisy, the 46 rooms are clean and tourists are greeted in a friendly and helpful way. The rooms overlooking the Piața are also quite sunny. The Veneția usually has rooms free. A single room costs 215 lei ($18.30) per night, a double runs 354 lei ($30.10), and a triple goes for 495 lei ($42.10). All prices include breakfast, and none of the rooms has a private bath; the public bathrooms, however, are suitable for not overly fussy visitors only.

3. Dining

Throughout Bucharest you should make reservations for dinner. Places fill up quickly with locals, and once seated, they don't quickly move on. As a result, you can be left standing for a long time if you don't reserve ahead.

TOP CHOICE: At Strada Edgar Quinet 1, off Victoriei, **Casa Capşa** (tel. 13-44-82) serves Bucharest's best fare in an elegant salon reminiscent of the last century. At the Capşa (built in 1852) you'll be seated at a long banquette or on brocade chairs underneath three chandeliers. Decorations on the walls, as well as flowers and attentive waiters in black tie, all add to the appealing ambience. The specialties in this restaurant include beef Wellington, schnitzel Cordon Bleu, and escalope Cordon Bleu, all for $2 to $7. And for an all-out splurge, you can enjoy caviar as an hors d'oeuvre. Service is from noon to 10 p.m.

HOTEL RESTAURANTS: You'll find several good, though slightly splurgey restaurants in the **Intercontinental Hotel,** Bulevardul N. Bălcescu 4 (tel. 13-70-40 or 14-04-00). Of the hotel's several restaurants, locals rate the attractive Madrigal Restaurant as the city's best. The Madrigal's dining room is decorated in a light purple throughout, and French specialties are served. If you prefer international specialties such as wienerschnitzel, veal chop, etc., to French cuisine, go upstairs to the restaurant on the 21st floor, where you can enjoy a panoramic view of Bucharest during your meal. A full three-course meal will cost about $10; if you choose selectively you can certainly eat for less.

For good food served promptly in an attractive setting, drop by the restaurant at the **Hotel Continental,** Calea Victoriei 56 (tel. 16-65-96 or 14-53-49). The hotel's architects designed the large dining room in a pseudo–Louis XIV style, complete with high decorative ceilings and ornate furniture. Breaking with this classical design, however, a small disco with flashing lights and a live band playing rock music is at the side of the restaurant. When we visited, we enjoyed a tasty chicken Cordon Bleu for 38.90 lei ($3.30); other entrees run from 38.90 lei ($3.30) to 73.20 lei ($6.20). The Continental adds a 15% service charge to these prices. Open from noon to 5 p.m. and from 7 to 11 p.m.

OUTDOOR DINING: Bucharest's most pleasant dining ambience can be found at **Parcul Trandafirilor** ("Rose Park"), Calea Dorobanti 9 (tel. 11-22-44). During the summer visitors eat in a large quiet garden coolly shaded from the heat by large trees with shrubbery separating every two tables. During inclement weather you can dine in one of several lovely neo-baroque halls rich with ornate decorations and chandeliers. A large menu of fish and meat specialties (at a cost of $1 and up) is shown to guests, but only a few dishes are actually stocked. Service is slow and food is average, but you can't find a more attractive place for a summer's lunch. Open 10 a.m. to 10 p.m. seven days a week.

For a more vivacious garden restaurant, visit **Restaurantul Cina,** Strada C. A. Rosetti 1 (tel. 14-02-17) off Athena Square. In the evening guests here enjoy a lively local band consisting of an accordion, drums, violin, guitar, and a vocalist who sings Romanian songs. Meat specialties such as pork cutlet cost 25 lei ($2.15) to 50 lei ($4.25); fish entrees will cost you 55 lei ($4.70) to 80 lei ($6.80). The food is pretty good. Hours are 10 a.m. to 10 p.m. You really must make reservations in the evening otherwise the maître d' will send you away or make you wait indefinitely.

4. Sights and Daytime Activities

Bucharest was established in the 15th century under the rule of Vlad Țepeș (Count Dracula) as a bulwark against invading Turks. Over the next several hundred years Bucharest thrived as an important trading post among the various states of Romania. Despite its past economic prosperity and history, few historic structures have survived. As a result, Bucharest wears a modern socialist face of gray buildings. However, in the city's fine museums you'll see preserved relics of Bucharest's art and architecture from its earliest days. Most museums are open from 10 a.m. to 6 p.m.; closed Monday.

MUSEUMS: The **Museum of History of the Socialist Republic of Romania,** Calea Victoriei 15, houses great historical treasures; among the exhibits are art, sculpture, gold, precious stones, and other artifacts from the Neolithic and Roman eras, medieval religious manuscripts and secular art, and a room exhibiting the "proofs of love, friendship, and deep gratitude felt by the party and the entire people for comrade Nicolae Ceausescu."

The **Art Museum of Romania,** Strada Știrbei Vodă 1, offers a varied collection of both Romanian and international artists in the former Royal Palace. Foreign artists include Titian, Tintoretto, El Greco, Rembrandt, Monet, and Renoir.

The **Central Military Museum,** Strada Izvor 137, shows 30,000 displays on military history, with everything from Roman weaponry to the uniforms of today's Romanian soldiers.

The **Museum of the History of the Communist Party,** Calea Kiseleff 3. In a country where the socialist struggle plays such an important part of everyday life, you may be interested to see how they view their own past and revolution.

If you want to see one of the houses that Vlad the Impaler built, stop by the **"Old Princely Court" Museum,** the remains of a 15th-century palace and walls on Decembrie Street.

PARKS: As we mentioned previously, Bucharest is quite famous for its lush parks, and in the summertime you won't want to miss out on a trip to the parks' large lakes. From the center of town, take bus 131 or 331 to **Parcul Herăstrău,** one of the area's largest parks, surrounding a lake. At the park you can go for a leisurely stroll, meet locals, rent a boat for the lake, go swimming, or visit the **Village and Folk Art Museum,** Calea Kiseleff 28-30, on the shore of Herăstrău Lake. This fascinating museum is a collection of 300 peasant houses and artifacts from across Romania, and it offers a great inside view of peasant life in Romania. It's open from 9 a.m. to 6 p.m.; closed Monday.

Another inviting park 40 km (25 miles) north of Bucharest is at **Snagov.** Locals throng here by the thousands in the summer to enjoy the lake-swimming and the well-forested countryside. Voyagers on the trail of Count Dracula will be interested in the small island in the lake—Vlad Țepeș is buried in the island's Snagov Monastery.

SHOPPING: You'll find one of Bucharest's most colorful areas at the **outdoor food market,** located on Strada Halelor right off Piața Natiunile Unite. Here you'll see peasants offering their produce to a busy crowd of Bucharest women. Next door there's a huge food shopping store called **Piața Unirii.** If you want to buy anything, remember that lines tend to move slowly. **Strada Lipscani,** one block away, is another lively area for shopping and people-watching.

5. Nightlife

Unless you meet some locals, you'll probably retire early most evenings in Bucharest as the city offers little in terms of Western nightlife. The almost total absence of lighting on the streets (to save money, of course) does little to electrify the evening action. Locals do stay up late on occasion, but mostly to eat and drink at a restaurant for several hours and maybe dance to the restaurant's live band. Hotels featuring a band and dance floor include the Continental, Athena, Palace, Bucharesti, and several others; a few of these hotels also sponsor nightclub acts.

If you're interested in going to a concert or other cultural event, buy the magazine **Saptâmîma** ("This Week"), available at newsstands and large hotels. This weekly guide lists symphony orchestra concerts, opera, ballet, and other performances in town. Once you decide what you'd like to see, you can go directly to the theater box office to buy tickets. Major concert halls include the grandiose **Romanian Athenaeum** at Strada Franklin 1 on Piaţa Gheorghiu-Dej (tel. 15-68-75), the **Opera House** at Bulevardul Gheorghiu-Dej 70 (tel. 13-18-57), and the **Operetta House,** Piaţa Natiunile Unite 1 (tel. 14-80-11).

If you do go out at night, take a taxi back to your hotel unless you're sure of the way. Finding your way home in the pitch black can prove a rigorous challenge. Dial 053 for a cab.

6. The ABCs of Bucharest

AIRPORT AND AIRLINES: When leaving Romania, take the airport bus to **Otopeni International Airport** from the main Tarom office on the corner at Strada Brezoianu 10, or from Bulevardul Magheru 18 in front of a large pharmacy; 40 minutes later it arrives at the Otopeni Airport. The frequency of this bus changes often: in 1984 they ran every hour; as of this writing, they run every two hours between 5:30 a.m. and 9:30 p.m. For up-to-date bus times, either ask at Tarom (tel. 633-46), at Bucharest's main tourist office, or at the airport (tel. 33-31-37 or 33-66-02).

Tarom has its main office at Strada Brezoianu 10 (tel. 16-33-46 for information and 15-27-47 for reservations). For domestic tickets, go to Tarom's other office at Strada Mendeleev 14 (tel. 59-41-56 or 59-41-85). Domestic flights depart from Băneasa Airport (tel. 33-00-30), near Otopeni.

The **Lufthansa** office, at Bulevardul Magheru 18 (tel. 50-40-74, 50-69-83, or 50-67-66), is open Monday through Friday from 8 a.m. to 6 p.m. **Austrian Airlines,** at Bulevardul N. Bălcescu 7 (tel. 14-12-21 or 14-18-31), stays open the same hours. **Pan Am** has an office at Bulevardul N. Bălcescu 4–6 in the Hotel Intercontinental (tel. 13-63-60).

AUTO REPAIR: For repairs and information, drop by or call the **Romanian Automobile Club,** Strada Nikos Beloianis 27 (tel. 59-50-80).

EMBASSIES: If you run into any troubles at all, call the **U.S. Embassy,** Strada Tudor Arghezi 7–9 (tel. 11-45-93 or 10-40-40), open Monday through Friday from 8 a.m. to 1 p.m. and 2 to 5 p.m. The embassy also invites visitors staying over a week in Romania to register with them; that way if an emergency occurs or if you lose your passport, they already have you on file.

You'll find the **Canadian Embassy** at Nicolae Iorga 36 (tel. 50-61-40), and the **British Embassy** at Strada Jules Michelet 24 (tel. 11-16-34).

EMERGENCIES: If something drastic happens, call the U.S. Embassy duty officer at 10-40-40 at any time of day or night. The Romanian police are at 055, and the emergency number is 061.

TELEPHONES: You can try to make international phone calls at the post office at Calea Victoriei 37.

TRAINS: In order to buy a ticket for train travel from Bucharest, go to one of three places: the National Tourist Office, the Railway Travel Office (tel. 13-26-44) in town, or the train station. To save a lot of frustration, purchase your ticket from the National Tourist Office. You must pay in hard currency, but the lines are considerably shorter. The second best option is to go to the Train Office at Brezoianu 10, inside a building with a "Tarom" sign outside. The office is open from 7 a.m. to 8 p.m. Monday through Saturday, to 1 p.m. on Sunday. Expect long lines at all hours.

The train station offers the most confusing and frustrating option of all. You can only buy tickets for trains on the day of departure; go to the information desk on the right as you walk in and ask which window you must buy your ticket from. First-class tickets are sold in a different, adjacent hall. To get an idea of the bedlam and long lines of the Bucharest station, imagine what Grand Central Station in New York would be like if word got around that tellers were handing out free $10 bills. Please—do yourself a favor and buy your ticket ahead of time!

VISA EXTENSION: To extend your visa, make the required minimum daily currency exchange ($10) for the number of days more you want to stay in Romania. Then, with receipt in hand, go to the passport department of the local police at Nicolae Iorga 27, a five-minute walk from Piaţa Romana. The office is open on Monday and Wednesday from 9:30 to 2 p.m., on Tuesday from 5 to 8 p.m., on Thursday from 9:30 a.m. to 2 p.m. and 5 to 8 p.m., and on Saturday from 9:30 a.m. to 1 p.m. On Friday and Sunday they're closed. As the men in the passport office aren't the most jovial types we've ever met, we recommend that you get your original visa for a day or two longer than you expect to stay in Romania. This way, you'll exchange another $10 or $20 for the minimum daily exchange (money you'll easily spend anyway), but you'll avoid a large hassle and a $10 service fee for extending the visa. Remember—always arrive early if you do need to extend your visa, as hours often change.

Chapter XXII

TRANSYLVANIA AND MOLDAVIA

1. Braşov
2. Sibiu
3. Cluj-Napoca
4. Suceava
5. Iaşi

EVERYONE FROM SMALL CHILDREN to adults has had visions of Transylvania as one of the world's spookiest, most mysterious places. Home of Count Dracula, Transylvania almost seems to be one of those fictional regions like Atlantis that doesn't exist outside of books. In reality, though, Transylvania is home to Romania's most charming towns. In places like Braşov, Sibiu, and Cluj-Napoca, medieval churches and old town halls tower over two- and three-story buildings; pedestrians crowd the cobblestone streets and peasants sell their wares in large outdoor markets. Indoors, museums chronicle the long history of Transylvania that began even before Roman colonization of the region. Modernity has come slowly to these towns, and few places in Europe can rival them for unchanged medieval charm. The local peasants, whom you will see in great numbers, are also unique for Europe in this day and age.

Although not as famous in Western folklore as Transylvania, Moldavia contains Romania's most impressive sights in a chain of medieval monasteries spread out across the countryside. Several of these difficult-to-reach but amazing monasteries are centered around Suceava. When you finally do make it to these sights, you'll agree that the brightly colored frescos on the walls are a moving testament to man's religious devotion.

The picturesque towns of Transylvania and Moldavia should be your prime destinations in Romania. After all, how many opportunities will you have to visit the land of Dracula?

1. Braşov

Travelers discouraged by the somber grays of Bucharest will welcome Braşov's 19th-century setting—old white buildings with red tile roofs, busy pedestrian cobblestone streets, and lush green mountains towering on the horizon. Although Braşov (pop. 200,000) offers only a handful of "sights," it's a great place to begin to appreciate the slow pace and relaxed charms of Transylvania.

Braşov's written history extends back to the 13th century. From that time on Braşov has been a town of traders and merchants. On many a medieval morning horse carts filled with locally produced cloth, metal, and wax would leave town. Several days later the merchants might return with grain and meat obtained from neighboring towns in Wallachia and Transylvania.

Many of Braşov's buildings from the Middle Ages and Renaissance era still exist, thanks to the diplomatic skill and military foresight of town leaders. Even during the many Turkish attacks in the region from the 15th to the 18th centuries, Braşov, with its strong town fortifications, escaped major war damage. Today Braşov remains a center of trade, but local industry has shifted to such products as tractors, furniture, and fabrics.

ORIENTATION AND IMPORTANT ADDRESSES: The train station lies in the heart of modern Braşov. To reach the **Old Town,** take bus 3 or 4; if you prefer to walk for about 25 minutes, go straight down the wide **Bulevardul Victoriei,** and continue to the right down **Bulevardul Lenin.** When the street turns into **Gheorghiu-Dej,** you've arrived in the old section of town.

After you've settled into your hotel, walk down **Strada Republicii,** a wide pedestrian avenue. After three blocks, you'll come to **Piaţa 23 August,** the Old Town Square. The town's principal sights all lie within a block or two of this square.

At Bulevardul Gheorghiu-Dej 9 (tel. 4-28-40), inside the Hotel Carpaţi, you'll find the **National Carpaţi Tourist Office,** which can assist you with information on Braşov and can arrange folklore evenings. They stay open from 7:30 a.m. to 9 p.m. seven days a week.

To buy a train ticket for your next destination, drop by the **CFR Railway Agency,** Strada Republicii 2 (tel. 4-12-18), open from 7 a.m. to 8 p.m. Monday through Saturday, to 1 p.m. Sunday.

If you want to make an international phone call, go to the **Telephone Bureau** at the corner of the Capitol Hotel off Bulevardul Gheorghiu-Dej. We managed to make a call to the U.S. within minutes, and collect at that! The office is open from 6:30 a.m. to 10 p.m.

ACCOMMODATIONS: We recommend that all budget travelers to Braşov stay at the **Hotel Postăvarul,** Strada Republicii 62 (tel. 4-43-30). All 167 rooms in this first-class hotel feature at least a bathtub, and many also have private toilets. Recent renovations at the hotel have further improved facilities. Singles cost 206.25 lei ($17.55) with a bathtub but no toilet, and 293.75 lei ($25) with a complete bathroom. Doubles cost 346.25 lei ($29.45) with a bathtub only, and 433.75 lei ($36.90) for a complete bathroom. Hotel Postăvarul is ideally located, just off the Old Town's main street, Strada Republicii.

An unexciting though fairly low-priced accommodation can be found at the **Hotel Carpaţi Sport,** Strada V. Maiakowski 3 (tel. 4-28-40). The 33 small rooms of this second-class hotel show signs of age; all sport a sink, but no private bathroom. Fortunately, the public bathrooms are reasonably clean for a second-class hotel. Hotel Carpaţi Sport charges 170 lei ($14.45) for a single and 269 lei ($22.85) for a double. Showers cost 22 lei ($1.85) extra.

Save the second-class **Hotel Turist,** Strada Karl Marx 32 (tel. 1-92-85), for your last pick in town. Although the 24 rooms are pretty much standard second class, the private bathrooms don't provide the latest in comfort. Singles cost 170 lei ($14.45); doubles go for 273.75 lei ($23.30).

DINING: If you've always dreamed of guards in armor lowering a drawbridge over a moat so that you could savor a sumptuous banquet of food and wine in a castle, then don't miss the **Restaurant Cetate,** on top of Cetăţuia Hill (tel.

1-76-14). The Cetate is situated inside the 15th-century Braşov Fortress. On your way to the main dining hall you pass several medieval rooms filled with crossbows, axes, suits of armor, and other artifacts from the Middle Ages. As you sit down to dine, a small orchestra performs classics of Renaissance music. Waiters in green-and-red medieval dress quietly serve a fixed menu of tasty international and Romanian specialties. After dinner, several opera singers join the band to finish the evening in rousing song. An evening at the Cetate rates as a splurge, with dinner and entertainment costing $15. If you want to spend less than this, come for lunch when the musicians don't perform. Another surprise at the Cetate is the clientele. When we visited we saw two large tour groups from the U.S.—the only Americans we saw during our entire time in Romania! The Cetate is open from 10 a.m. to 10 p.m. seven days a week; the musical evening begins at 7:30 or 8 p.m. and lasts until 10 p.m. For the evening, you must reserve and pay in advance through the Carpaţi Tourist Office, or through your hotel.

Another appealing local restaurant is the **Cerbul Carpatin** ("The Merchants' Hall") at Piaţa 23 August no. 13 (tel. 4-39-81 or 4-28-40), a 16th-century building on the main town square. You can choose among several of the restaurant's huge spaces: two long thin rooms with tall A-shaped roofs, or a long cellar with a stucco ceiling and walls lined with many wine jugs. In each room you'll notice a lively, spirited atmosphere, spurred on by good food and wine. Fish entrees include carp and filet of sole for $3 to $5, and meat entrees include grilled veal and pork for $1 to $3. With your meal, be sure to sample the restaurant's fine wine from their huge wine cellar. Open 10 a.m. to 10 p.m. A 10% service charge is added to the bill.

For standard but good fare with fast, efficient service, dine at the **Hotel Carpaţi Restaurant,** located in the deluxe hotel at Bulevardul Gheorghiu-Dej 9 (tel. 4-28-40). A large selection of meat and fish specialties is available. Perhaps the best buys at the Carpaţi are the two fixed menus. One of these meals features a fish appetizer, grilled pork cutlet, a salad, rolls, and dessert pancakes, all for less than $5. The modern dining room is open from noon to 4 p.m. and 7 to 10 p.m. A brasserie restaurant stays open continuously from 7:30 a.m. to 10 p.m. A 12% service charge is added to your bill.

THE SIGHTS: Braşov's most famous sight, the **Black Church** (Biserica Neagra), lies just off the main town square at Curtea Bisericii Vechi. This large 14th-century structure earns its distinctive name from the smoke of a fire in 1689 which darkened the church walls. The late Gothic church also houses a huge organ with some 4,000 pipes and a collection of 15th- to 18th-century ornamental carpets.

One block away on the Piaţa 23 August you'll see the 15th-century **Council Hall** (Casa Sfatului), where town leaders once decided Braşov's trade and diplomatic policy. Today the Council Hall also serves as the **Braşov History Museum.** The trading and historical past of Braşov and all of Transylvania is featured. Closed Monday.

Those with a particular interest in Romanian art can also consider a stop at the town **Art Museum,** Bulevardul Gheorghiu-Dej 21. You can marvel at works such as icons painted on glass and wood, as well as many 19th-century Romanian oil paintings.

And if you want to enjoy a panoramic view of both modern and ancient Braşov, you can effortlessly ride to the top of the **Tîmpa Mountain,** 950 yards above town, on a cable car. Rides depart from Strada Aleea Filimon Sirbu at the foot of the mountain.

EXCURSIONS FROM BRAŞOV: All of the Tourist Office's day trips depart from Poiana-Braşov, a large winter-sports capital 13 km (eight miles) from Braşov, but you can make arrangements from their central Braşov office.

One popular destination is the 14th-century **Castle of Bran**, 28 km (17 miles) to the southwest of Braşov, said in legend to be the former home of Vlad (Count Dracula) Ţepeş. Two groups a week leave for this mysterious castle, one with an English-speaking guide and one with a German speaker. The inside of the castle displays a collection of medieval art in its 20 rooms. The half-day trip to Bran trip costs $7.

Unfortunately, getting to the Castle of Bran on your own, not with these infrequently scheduled, organized tours, proves quite a challenge. If you do set out on your own, take the train from Braşov to Rîşnov 20 minutes away; then from in front of the Rîşnov train station, catch a bus to Bran (a 30-minute ride). Before you depart from Braşov, however, check with the tourist office to find out when the bus leaves from the Rîşnov train station and back; connections are not always that great.

If you do believe in vampires or their spirits, of course you'll remember to bring along some garlic—the only effective repellent against vampires!

2. Sibiu

Municipal center of the surrounding area, Sibiu is one of the oldest towns on the Transylvanian Plateau. Some 2,000 years ago the Roman city of Cedonia was established, and the town has been a political and economic center ever since. In the 12th century the town of Cibinium was built on the remnants of the older Roman city, and in 1326 the first major series of fortifications was completed. Sibiu soon became an important center for crafted items as well as a cultural center. A library was established in the 14th century, followed in the 15th century by the Universitas Saxonum and a printing house in 1528.

Today the old town center of Sibiu looks just like what you'd expect from a medieval Transylvanian town: winding cobblestone streets, low houses with red-tile roofs, and an interesting collection of municipal and religious architecture from the Middle Ages. Around the core of the Old Town lie Sibiu's important industrial plants, which produce much of Romania's beer, automobiles, candy, and furniture. Visitors to Sibiu receive the added bonus of proximity to the beautiful Făgăraş Mountains, a hiker's paradise.

IMPORTANT ADDRESSES: The main **ONT Tourism Agency** is located at Strada Bălcescu 53 (tel. 1-25-59). **Tarom Romanian Airlines** maintains an office at Strada Bălcescu 10 (tel. 1-11-57), and the **CFR Railway Ticket Agency** (the easiest place to buy train tickets) is located just down the street at Bălcescu 6 (tel. 1-20-85).

You'll find the **railway station** at Gării Piaţa (tel. 1-11-39), about a ten-minute walk down the Strada Magheru to the town center. Buses depart from Gării Piaţa as well as from Lemnelor Piaţa (tel. 1-70-16). For a **taxi**, dial 053.

Should your car run into difficulties, drop by the **auto repair shop** on Alba-Iulia-Chaussee (tel. 1-48-38).

ACCOMMODATIONS: Sibiu's two main hotels offer attractive facilities constructed in the 18th and 19th centuries but subsequently modernized; both are somewhat splurgey in price.

The **Hotel Împăratul Romanilor**, Strada N. Bălcescu 4 (tel. 1-64-90), is right in the center of town with an unbeatable location. Since it's off a square reserved entirely for pedestrians, it's also reasonably quiet. The Hotel Împăratul Romanilor was built in the 18th century as an inn for Moldavian and Wallachian traders roving from Europe to the Orient. The first two floors were built in 1790 but the hotel has been extensively remodeled in this century. A double costs $29 per night without a shower, and $37 per night with a private bath.

Another good choice is the **Hotel Bulevard,** at Piaţa Unirii 10 (tel. 1-21-40). Built 150 years ago, it has been extensively modernized and is clean. During the summer and on the weekends it's often the spot where wedding receptions and feasts are held. All the rooms have private baths and are decorated in one color —we hope you like orange. A single room is no bargain at 306 lei ($26) per night, and a double costs 512 lei ($43.55) per night. Breakfast is included in the price of the room.

To reserve a room in either hotel, contact the central ONT Tourism Agency, Strada Bălcescu 53 (tel. 1-25-59; Telex 12559). Unfortunately, most of the other hotels are either not open to Westerners or not worth the few dollars you save over the above hotels.

Starvation Budget

For maximum savings, try the **Pădurea Dumbrava** camping grounds (tel. 1-75-91), three kilometers south of Sibiu. To get there, take bus T1 south to the Dumbrava Motel (tel. 1-75-90). The camping area is right nearby and costs 100 lei ($8.50) per site per night. The motel at the campgrounds is extremely no-frills, but a double is an affordable 200 lei ($17). The showers are public and are shared by 10 to 15 people.

DINING: For availability and service, it's best to choose from the restaurants in Sibiu's three main hotels.

The restaurant in the **Hotel Împăratul Romanilor** is the best place to dine in Sibiu, and though it serves a variety of dishes, fresh vegetables are sometimes lacking. The dining room is quite large and is often used for local wedding receptions and parties on weekends. Locals out for a night on the town enjoy the live music and dancing here most nights till closing. The restaurant is open from 7 a.m. to 10 p.m.

The **Hotel Continental,** Calca Dumbrăvii 4 (tel. 1-69-10), which is easy to spot since it's one of Sibiu's few tall buildings, has a restaurant on the second floor. Choices may be limited and quality can vary. We had some rather stringy lamb one evening, but the roast pork was tasty.

The restaurant in the **Hotel Bulevard,** Piaţa Unirii 10 (tel. 1-21-40), is another favorite of locals, who gather here in great numbers on the weekends.

THE SIGHTS: Sibiu is best known for the famous **Brukenthal Museum,** on Piaţa Republicii 3–5, one of Romania's first museums. It's located in the palace of Samuel von Brukenthal, governor of Transylvania from 1781 to 1785, and the building has served as a museum of Transylvanian history and folk culture since 1817. Boasting one of the largest collections on peasant and folk culture in Europe, the museum is a must for anyone interested in folk art. In addition, the Brukenthal Museum contains paintings of such world-renowned masters as Titian, Rubens, Van Dyck, and Lucas Cranach.

Across Piaţa Republicii you'll view the picturesque **Old Town Hall Tower** (1470) with its pointy A-shaped roof and narrow façade. Today this building houses the **Sibiu City History Museum.** Other interesting buildings on the Piaţa Republicii include the baroque **Catholic** church (1726–1728), and the beautiful Gothic and Renaissance **Haller House** at no. 10, built in the 14th century by Mayor Petrus Haller. The building still maintains its distinctive façade complete with original vaults and frame.

Some of Sibiu's most interesting sights are the **medieval fortifications** that once protected the town from enemy attack. You'll find one of the oldest, a defense tower from the 13th century, at Grivița Piața 3. At 6 Martie Piața you can see two other towers (at nos. 1 and 24); the first, known as the **Council Tower,** defended the entrance to the Town Hall. In walking around the town center you'll see almost a dozen towers, bastions, and other remains of the old fortifications from the 12th to the 15th centuries, including our own personal favorite, **Tanners' Tower,** on Strada Zidului.

Two other museums of interest in town are the **History of Pharmacy Museum** at 6 Martie Piața, no. 26, located in a pharmacy that operated from the 16th to 19th centuries, and the **Museum of Folk Technology,** located in the Dumbrava Sibiului Forest. The latter museum demonstrates traditional Romanian folk techniques of processing wood, textiles, food, and other folk traditions in a re-created area of old peasant houses.

A SIDE TRIP TO THE FĂGĂRAŞ MOUNTAINS: The spectacular peaks of the

Făgăraş Mountains offer some of the best hiking in the Balkans, with stunning views in practically every direction. Though the elevation doesn't compare to the Alps and there are not many exposed rock faces, you'll still enjoy this alpine environment.

The highest peak in the range, **Mount Negoiu** (8,365 feet), is only 30 feet short of being the highest peak in the country. In all, over 30% of the Sibiu region is what the Romanians term mountainous. "The Transylvanian Alps," as the Făgăraş are also known, extend almost 45 miles; they are generally steeper from the southern side (Bucharest approach) than from the north (Sibiu approach). Most of the hikes involve nothing more difficult than trail walking.

Camping out in these mountains is quite easy—if you have the necessary equipment. In fact, the excellent system of mountain huts makes a tent largely superfluous. There are 18 different cabins scattered over the mountains at several altitudes; the lowest is the Valea Aurie ("Golden Vale") Hut at 1,485 feet; the Podragu is the highest at 6,930 feet.

Be prepared for the hiking trip. As in all mountain regions the weather can change very abruptly with heavy storms seemingly appearing out of nowhere. Be sure to bring warm clothing and raingear with you no matter what the weather is like when you leave camp. It goes without saying that you should only begin any serious hike with the proper footwear—hiking boots, not sneakers or sandals—and certainly not high-heeled shoes. The temperatures are cool at night during the summer and biting cold in the winter. If you plan to camp out, be sure to bring a sleeping bag.

Getting to the Făgăraş Mountains

South of Sibiu, the Făgăraş Mountains extend east and westward. You can reach them several ways. We prefer to go by train and then walk up. It's not the fastest way, but it's more dependable than the bus. The train runs almost every day.

If you want to get to the **Suru Hut** at the base of Mount Suru (7,535 feet), take the train from Sibiu to Sebeşu de Sus; the hut isn't more than a four-hour walk up. However, you can reach three other huts only by bus. Buses go from Sibiu to the **Poiana Neamţului Hut** for 19 lei ($1.60); from there you can continue to **Bîrcaciu** and **Avrig Huts;** the higher of these two huts is not more than an hour and a half away from the bus stop. A new road has been built all the way up to the **Bîlea-Lac Hut** (6,930 feet) and on to the **Curtea de Argeş,** one of the Făgăraş' most beautiful valleys.

The bus runs from June to October, leaving in the morning and returning to Sibiu in the evening. Be certain to ask the bus driver what time he thinks the bus is leaving. Not all buses run every day, so be certain to check the schedule at Sibiu's ONT office or at one of Sibiu's hotels before you set out. If you go by train, you'll find the Sibiu schedule posted in the train station. Unfortunately, it's impossible to take a day trip by train; so if you go by rail, be prepared for a night out.

Camping is allowed practically anywhere and, amazingly enough, you're allowed to light a fire anywhere you can find enough wood. Needless to say, you must be very careful when lighting one as the terrain gets tinder-dry in the summer; be extra careful when you cover up the remnants of your fire as you leave. Also remember to bring water; there are few springs in the Făgăraş.

The only detailed guide to the Făgăraş Mountains with a map inside is in Romanian, so pay attention to the signs posted along the trails. West of the Făgăraş Mountains are the Munţii Cindrel (Cindrel Mountains). They are lower, tamer, and wooded, and though beautiful, are not as spectacular as the much higher Făgăraş.

Emergency Services

The mountain rescue service in the Făgăraş is not as well developed as such facilities are in other European countries that have extensive mountainous terrain. However, a volunteer rescue service (composed of amateur alpinists) patrols the mountains all through the year to keep an eye on the hikers. If you need to find them in a hurry, they're always on duty at the Suru, Negoiu, Podragu, Caltun, and Bîlea-Lac huts. Their headquarters is at Vistea, at the base of Moldoveanu Peak, outside the Sibiu district.

3. Cluj-Napoca

Cluj is one of Romania's foremost university towns, with a student population of over 24,000. Long under Hungarian control, Cluj shows a distinctive Magyar influence, which extends from the Opera House to the spicy food. A substantial Hungarian minority lives in the area and many of the people still speak or understand Hungarian. One of the most charming cities in Romania, Cluj is in the middle of an area rich in Roman and pre-Roman artifacts.

A CAPSULE HISTORY: Cluj was founded on gold and salt. Since the Transylvanian plateau is rich in both, miners and merchants have flourished here for thousands of years. The first traces of habitation were left by scattered paleolithic tribes, followed by the Thracians. The Thracian civilization was overwhelmed by successive invasions of Scythian and Celtic tribes. Also during this period a people emerged called the Dacians, an offshoot of the Thracian tribe, the claimed forefathers of modern-day Romanians.

The Dacian name of Cluj-Napoca, as recorded by Ptolemy, was simply Napoca. The city's name is hyphenated today for political reasons. When the Hungarians, and then the Hapsburgs, administered the city it was called Cluj. By stressing their Dacian roots and the early history of the town rather than the last 400 years, the Romanians justify their present control. In this section we refer to Cluj-Napoca as Cluj—not for any political reason, but for simplicity.

Even the Romanians admit that the arrival of the Romans brought much good to the area. Under the Roman Emperor Hadrian (A.D. 117–138) the town was granted municipal status, and Antonius later raised it to the rank of colony. As the Roman Empire came under increasing attack from migrating barbarian tribes, the Emperor Aurelianus withdrew most of the Roman soldiers and civil servants south of the Danube in the year A.D. 271.

No one ruler controlled the area until the Middle Ages, when individual nobles became powerful enough to carve out petty kingdoms. Cluj eventually regained its municipal status, and by 1405 was encircled by an impressive new belt of fortifications, covering an area of more than 45 hectares (111 acres). Commerce began to play a greater role in the town, and by 1506 Cluj was holding its own markets and fairs. A plague and two great fires in the 17th century marked a period of stagnation for the town. But by the end of the 18th century Cluj, with a population of 10,660 people, became an important city in Transylvania.

Even with its growing importance, capitalism came slowly to Cluj, and at the time of the 1848 revolution serfdom was still commonplace in Transylvania. Today the city is modernized and, though retaken briefly by Hungary in 1940, is now an integral part of Romania.

ORIENTATION AND IMPORTANT ADDRESSES: The town is divided by the Someşu River which flows roughly west to east. To get from the railroad station to the town center, take either tram T35 or any bus for about five minutes or until you see a large church (St. Michael's) in the middle of a square. The bus costs 1 leu (9¢) and the tram 1.35 lei (12¢) per ticket. You can walk to the city center from the train station in about 15 to 20 minutes; go straight ahead (south) on Strada Horea, cross the bridge, and continue until Piaţa Libertăţii.

The **ONT Tourist Office** is at Strada Gh. Şincai 2 (tel. 2-17-78; Telex 031286), open from 8 a.m. till 6 p.m. Monday through Friday.

You'll find **Tarom** at Piaţa Mihai Viteazul 11 (tel. 1-22-12), and the **Romanian Automobile Club** at Strada 30 Decembrie (tel. 1-23-45).

Buy your train tickets at the **CFR agency** at Piaţa Libertăţii 9 (tel. 1-22-12).

ACCOMMODATIONS: The best bet for affordable living is the **Hotel Continental** on Strada Napoca 1 (tel. 1-14-41). Though not the only choice, and not really inexpensive, it's the best located and run of all the nondeluxe hotels in Cluj. Decorated in a rather exhausted classical style, it is well maintained by Romanian standards. A single room with bath costs $25 per night, and a double room goes for $33 per night. Ask for a window facing the garden because the streetside rooms are very noisy. The hotel restaurant downstairs is open from 10 a.m. till 10 p.m., with dancing most evenings.

If you want to save a few dollars, try one of the 35 second-class rooms of the **Hotel Central** on Piaţa Libertăţii 30 (tel. 2-25-73). The Central is less inviting than the Continental, but is conveniently located. If the Central is full, stop by the second-class **Astoria Hotel** at Strada Horea 3 (tel. 3-01-66).

Camping

For low-budget travelers this may be the town to unroll the tent. If so, try **Kamping Făget,** seven kilometers south on the E15 (also marked DN1 on some maps). There are bungalows for two to four people that cost 152 lei ($12.95) per night and camping places for a trailer or tent cost 36 lei ($3.05) to 40 lei ($3.40) per person per night. Reportedly, there is a city bus that runs out to Feleacu, the closest stop to the campground.

DINING: We found the variety of foods available here more interesting than in other Romanian cities. The best bet is the restaurant in the **Hotel Belvedere,** Strada Călăraşi 1 (tel. 3-44-66), on top of the large hill across the Someşu River from the city center. The restaurant is overpriced and not exceptional, but the location on top of the hill, shaded by trees, can't be beat. This an excellent place for lunch as you can escape the heat with cool breezes and a stunning overview of the city. The food isn't bad, with the average main dish costing around 25 lei

($2.15). Sit and eat while the locals put away a few mid-morning beers; if the day promises to be a real scorcher, consider joining them. One of Cluj's best bands plays at the restaurant on most nights.

Snacks and Fast Food

There is a department store, the **Central,** in Cluj that has a fast-food place as well as a couple of folk goods shops. A modern concrete-and-glass pile, you can't miss it, right off Strada Gn. Doja near the city center.

For those in a hurry, another pick is the **Apertitiv** snackbar at Strada Petru Groza 18. Open from 9 a.m. to 7 p.m. (closed Sunday), this is Romanian fast food at its finest. Walk right up to the counter to order, pay your bill, and eat for about $1.50 to $2 per person.

For a leisurely drink or bite to eat at the middle or end of the day, drop by the **Carpaţi,** one of Cluj's better cafés, conveniently located on the south side of Piaţa Libertăţii. Here you can consume delicious cakes, coffee, juices, and ice cream for under $1.50 a person. Open from 7 a.m. to 8 p.m. Monday through Saturday, and from 8 a.m. to 6 p.m. on Sunday.

THE SIGHTS: Given the often turbulent history of the city, there are many historical monuments of interest in Cluj. Foremost among them is the Roman Catholic **Church of St. Mihail** (St. Michael). Located in Piaţa Libertăţii, at the center of town, the church is a veritable catalog of architectural styles. Begun sometime in the mid 14th century, the building has suffered numerous disasters, such as a fire in 1489 and an earthquake in 1764; each time it was rebuilt in the style of the time. The reconstruction job is stunning and this is the only structure in Cluj that still has fragments of its original medieval decorations.

Out in front on the Piaţa Libertăţii is the gargantuan **Statue of Matei Corvin** (Matthias Corvinus) accepting homage from many of Romania's greatest statesmen. Though Matei Corvin was of Hungarian origin, he did much to unite Transylvania and rout the invading Turks. Designed by John Fadrusz, a resident of Cluj, the statue was dedicated on October 12, 1902.

Also on the Piaţa is one of the most important baroque buildings in Romania, the **Banffy Palace** (1774–1785) at Piaţa Libertăţii 30. It is home to Cluj's art collection and features many famous Romanian as well as Western artists.

Cluj maintains two interesting ethnographic museums. The **Ethnographic Museum of Transylvania,** at Strada 30 Decembrie no. 21, stores 65,000 exhibits on clothes, tools, folklore, music, pottery, and other aspects of peasant life. The **Ethnographic Museum in the Open,** in Hoia Forest, demonstrates typical peasant dwellings and wooden churches in a reconstructed outdoor area.

A must-see for those curious about the mysterious past of Transylvania is the **History Museum of Transylvania** at Strada Emil Isac 2. This museum chronicles the region's history from Roman through medieval times to the present with 100,000 exhibits.

If you'd like to get a feel of what Cluj's old defenses must have been like, visit the **Tailor's Bastion** on Strada Sandór Petőfi. This is the last surviving tower named after the guild that was obligated to maintain and defend it. In the 15th century there were many of these towers, each manned by a different guild, such as the cobblers, the butchers, etc. Now only this tower remains.

EXCURSIONS FROM CLUJ: On a pleasant day, you should consider spending the day hiking in the beautiful local countryside around Cluj. A vast series of country chalets in the area managed by the Cluj ONT office provides a good base to stop off and rest every few hours. They are reasonably well maintained, though crowded. Before you set off into this area, pester the ONT office for maps and information until they provide you with something (they seem to treat maps in particular as a very rare commodity). Signs posted in the countryside are usually rather confusing.

There is a **mineral bath complex** at Băiţa, about 48 km (29 miles) from Cluj, the largest and best known in Romania. There are several others in the area, the closest being the Someşeni Spa, about three kilometers (two miles) outside town.

4. Suceava

The medieval monasteries scattered across Moldavia's Bukovina region in northern Romania are without doubt the most impressive sights in the whole country. Bold red and blue frescos of religious scenes painted almost 500 years ago adorn the façade of these religious structures. Travelers who wish to see these impressive sights should make their way to Suceava, the central town for all exploration in the Bukovina region.

The first traces of civilized habitation in this area were left by Dacian tribes, not under Roman domination, in the 2nd to 3rd centuries A.D. The old capital of Moldavia, Suceava was first mentioned in 14th-century documents. A major commercial and cultural center in the 15th and 16th centuries, the city was repeatedly destroyed by attacks and fire, culminating with the destruction of most of the town by the Turks in 1675. In 1775, just as the American Revolution was beginning to simmer, Suceava was occupied by the Hapsburgs. Since its return to Romania in 1918, the city has experienced increased importance as a commercial center. Although Suceava itself is not as interesting as the surrounding monasteries, their remote location from the rest of Romania neccesitates your setting up base in Suceava.

ORIENTATION AND IMPORTANT ADDRESSES: Suceava is not a large city: its population is less than 70,000. Located on the north side of the Suceava River, the city is flanked to the east and west by hills; the ruins of once-impressive castles and fortifications crown each hill. Piaţa 23 August lies at the center of the city.

There are two **train stations** which service the town: Suceava Station and Suceava Nord (north). To reach the city center from Suceava Nord at Strada Gării 4 (tel. 1-00-37), take any bus for about 10 to 15 minutes. To get to the center of town from Suceava Station at Strada N. Iorga 7 (tel. 1-38-97), take bus 3, 4, 26, or 29 for about 15 minutes. Between the hours of 5 a.m. and 8 p.m. the buses run about every 30 minutes or so, but in the evening the bus service slows down, and stops about 10 or 11 p.m.

The **Suceava County Tourist Office** is on Strada N. Bălcescu (tel. 2-12-97 or 1-09-44); some English is spoken here and it's a good place to ask about any tours they might have to the monasteries. This office has no tour vehicle directly at their disposal, but they often know of other foreign tour groups headed for the monasteries that may be able to fit a couple of people in their bus. (Read the section on "Getting to the Monasteries," below, before you seek out any groups.) The Tourist Office does have a reasonable map of Suceava, though whether they will part with it for nothing is another matter. The office stays open every day except Sunday, from 8 a.m. till 5 p.m.

Tarom has an office at Strada N. Bălcescu 8 (tel. 1-46-86). Motorists in difficulty should go over to the **Auto Club** at Ştefan cel Mare 25 (tel. 1-09-97). Buy train tickets at the same address as Tarom (tel. 1-43-35).

ACCOMMODATIONS: All of Suceava's hotels are within a ten-minute walk from Piaţa 23 August, the city center. Unfortunately, there isn't much choice in Suceava as to where you can sleep. The best deal among the four first-class hotels in town is the **Hotel Balada** at Strada .V. I. Lenin 3 (tel. 1-07-45). The hotel charges $27.50 per person per night in single or double rooms, all with private bath. The place is clean and not too noisy, and is the best hotel in Suceava that's likely to have a free room in the summer. There's a bar but no restaurant; breakfast is included in the room price.

The budget choices are few since there are only two hotels in that category and they're usually filled with large tour groups of Romanians. Cleaner than most Romanian hotels in its category is the 30-room **Hotel Parc,** Bulevardul Ana Ipătescu 6 (tel. 1-09-44). Rooms cost 168 lei ($14.30) to 234 lei ($19.90) per person. The only other second-class hotel in Suceava is the **Casa Tinretului,** at Strada V. I. Lenin 5 (tel. 1-31-92).

Camping

The best and only camping in Suceava is at **Suceava Kamping** on Strada Ilie Pintilie (tel. 1-22-15), about three kilometers (two miles) from the center of town. To get here, take bus 1, 19, or 30 heading toward the Suceava Nord railway station for about 15 minutes.

RESTAURANTS: Although there is a national law that forbids any public establishment, restaurant, disco, or bar to be open later than 10 p.m., this law seems to be broken more often in the Suceava district than in most places in Romania. We have no explanation why—we surmise that it's impossible to keep those fun-loving Moldavians at home.

The **Hotel Arcaşul,** at Strada Mihai Viteazul 4/6 (tel. 1-09-44), has one of the two best restaurants in Suceava; the other is in the **Hotel Bucovina,** Strada Ana Ipătescu 5 (tel. 1-70-48). The fare at both leans heavily on pork, though there was some good lamb stew at the Arcaşul when we visited. A meal for two with wine will cost about 150 lei ($12.75). Both restaurants have a large dining room with a staff too small for the patronage. Patience is the key to ulcer-free dining. Both restaurants are open from 10 a.m. till 10 p.m., unofficially till midnight.

NIGHTLIFE: In the basement of the **Hotel Arcaşul** is one of the better nightspots that we found in Romania. A disco-bar with a reasonably good sound system, it's open every day from 6 p.m. till midnight. This place has a surprisingly good record collection and the tour groups that come here really like to pull out the stops after a hard day on the road. The club is usually filled with foreign tourists; it depends on what bus is in town, but you could find yourself dancing with European tourists from anywhere on the continent!

THE SIGHTS: Suceava is a very modern town with few historical relics extant. The **Folk Art Museum,** at Strada Ciprian Porumbescu 5, the oldest civil building in Suceava County, was an inn in the 16th century. Now it's home to an impressive collection of peasant and folk artifacts. Open from 10 a.m. till 7 p.m.; closed Monday.

On the outskirts of the city lie most of the ruins of the medieval fortifications. Of most note, the **Princely Citadel,** at Parcul Cetăţii 3/14, stands on a high plateau on the east edge of town not more than a 15-minute walk from the city center. It was originally built in 1388 as the fortified home of Prince Petru Muşat **I,** the man who moved Moldavia's capital from Siret to Suceava. Things heated up and, about 25 years later, King Alexandru the Kind began to improve the fortifications, a process later continued by Stephan the Great. "It was impregnable until its destruction" is how our tour guide described the castle. The fragments still remaining show how much damage the Turks were able to cause prior to their departure in 1675. Most of the other town fortifications are in similar condition—primarily just ruins. The one complete set of structures is the Zamca buildings, erected in 1606. On the west side of the city on Strada Zamcii, they offer a glimpse of the once-immense fortifications that the city boasted.

As for the rest of Suceava, well, it's not a particularly interesting place; the city is composed mostly of concrete apartment blocks. The local party headquarters is situated in a large white building called "the White House," a local joke of sorts. The local wags also refer to the buses with the huge natural-gas fuel tanks on their roofs as "Helena Gays," after the *Enola Gay,* the plane that dropped the first atomic bomb. "Helena" refers to Helena Ceausescu, wife of the Romanian Communist Party general secretary, Nicolae Ceausescu. The long gas tanks on the buses do resemble a bomb, and Helena is reputed to have a very "fissionable temperament"—hence the joke.

THE MONASTERIES IN BUKOVINA: One of the reasons to come to Romania is to see the incredible monasteries of Bukovina. Literally illustrated Bibles, these buildings are painted both inside and out—covered everywhere with the most intricate and detailed biblical representations. There are 14 of these monasteries scattered throughout the province, but we detail here the five principal ones—**Voroneţ, Humor, Suceviţa, Arbore,** and **Moldoviţa.** Most of the monasteries are west or northwest of Suceava and are far from any public transportation. Some mode of private transportation is absolutely necessary to reach any of the monasteries (see "Getting to the Monasteries," below). Do *not* try to hitchhike unless you plan to spend a night (or two) out under the stars.

These monasteries were built in the 15th and 16th centuries, beginning during the reign of Stefan the Great, the unifier of Romania. During his peaceful reign, which lasted almost 50 years (1457–1504), many of the Transylvanian and Moldavian villages grew into real municipalities which were able to defeat the Turkish Ottoman armies quite handily. The successful defense of Transylvania and Moldavia by Stefan and his successors was commemorated by the construction of a monastery after every victory over the Ottoman forces.

The monasteries are painted in a Byzantine-Gothic style that emerged from the fusion of Byzantine and early Moldavian cultures. Decorated entirely with frescos, the monasteries are a monument to this method that Michelangelo called "the most difficult and daring form of painting." The whole area has been declared a national monument, and in 1975 was awarded the golden Pomme d'Or by the International Federation of Writers and Journalists on Tourism (FIJET).

Voroneţ

The first and the most important monastery is the Voroneţ. Located in the middle of a small whitewashed village, surrounded by fir trees and set against the green, rolling Moldavian hills, it was built in three months and three weeks by King Stefan the Great in 1488. The frescos were added later, during the reign of Prince Petru Rareş. The frescos here are the equal of any in all of Europe. The magnificent colors, now newly restored, are the hallmark of all the monasteries; but the Voroneţ Monastery is famous for its stunning blue background. Found nowhere else in the world, this singular and intense color has garnered a name for itself—Voroneţ blue.

As you look at the scenes, notice that the archangels blow a bucium, the favorite instrument of Moldavian shepherds to this day. The souls being carried heavenward are wrapped in towels decorated in Moldavian peasant styles; those doomed to hell wear turbans like the Ottomans, the most hated of Moldavia's foes. The western façade is covered with scenes from the Last Judgment; it is the simplest and most dramatic of the frescos. The wild animals return pieces of people who have been torn apart by wild beasts. Only the deer carries no gory trophy, as the deer stands for innocence in Romanian folklore. The sinners broiling in the coals at Jesus' feet present a veritable Moldavian rogues' gallery. Practically every foreign enemy or king is represented, and the ranks of the sinners are filled with Turks and fierce Tartars. On the south wall is the genealogy of Christ arrayed as a huge tree and set against a background of wondrous Voroneţ blue.

Humor

Founded by Vovoide Petru Rareş and Chancellor Theodor in 1530, the church at **Humor** is quite small. Not far from the village of Gura Humorului (six kilometers, or 3½ miles), this monastery looks as though it was brought forth from an illuminated manuscript. Many of the peculiar Moldavian details found at Voroneţ can be found here as well. Of note is the southern façade covered with a composition in 24 scenes created from a poem written by Patriarch Serghie. The poem is dedicated to the Virgin Mary who, it was felt, saved the city from a Persian attack in 626. The Moldavians equated this intervention with their own desire for victory over the Ottomans. So fervent was the artist's hatred of the Turks that both here and at Moldovita Monastery the representations of victory are imagined scenes of good and evil which bear little relation to actual historical events. In another scene the devil is represented as a fat, jocular old woman, an image so comic that it inspires laughter. This monastery was, as early as the 15th century, a workshop for some of Romania's most gifted calligraphers and miniature painters.

Arbore

Smallest of all, dimly lit, and with no cupola, the building at the Arbore Monastery was built by a boyar (a lesser noble) and not a prince. Unlike the Voroneţ Monastery, Arbore is done in green—five shades of it blended with reds, yellows, blues, to give a very different tonality to each shade. The western wall is the most valuable, and on it are numerous miniature scenes from the Book of Genesis as well as scenes from the lives of saints. The figures are painted in motion, their faces glow a healthy pink, and they wear elegant cloaks and gowns; everything is done with the attention to detail and the delicacy that is usually associated with miniatures. In the courtyard you can still see the heavy stone slabs with 15 small hollows cut in them. These slabs were the palettes on which the colors were mixed.

Suceviţa

Much higher up in the hills, the Sucevita Monastery looks much more like a citadel than a place of quiet religious introspection. There is a thick stone wall with several imposing towers, and a stout gatehouse guards the monastery entrance. There are several legends connected with this monastery; one involves a woman who, for 30 years, hauled stone in her ox-drawn wagon for the monastery construction. In memory of her faithful toil a likeness of her head was carved in black stone and set under the eaves. The western wall remains undecorated because, according to legend, a workman fell and died of injuries here. Suceviţa has the greatest number of images of all the monasteries. On the northern wall is the fantastic Scale of Virtues, and on the southern wall is, again, the genealogy of Christ in the shape of a tree. Next to this is the Procession of Philosophers, with Pythagoras, Sophocles, Plato, Aristotle, and Solon all clad in beautiful Byzantine robes. The rest of the building depicts the hierarchy of heaven in intricate detail.

Moldoviţa

The last of the five famous monasteries is the Moldoviţa, the largest of all of them. Built in 1532 and painted five years later, the whole structure is covered with hundreds of pictures. In the open porch you can enjoy the Last Judgment —beautiful, though not considered as dramatic as the one at Voroneţ. On the southern wall is the Prayer to the Virgin and the genealogy of Christ painted against a dark-blue background. Perhaps the most valuable scene here is the Siege of Constantinople, painted 100 years after the event. The fresco is the only monumental representation of the siege. The artist gave a panoramic view of the battle with the Constantinople soldiers resisting mightily. Inside the actual monastery buildings there is the Princely Chair of Prince Petru Rareş as well as an excellent collection of 16th-century ornamental art.

Getting to the Monasteries

The local ONT office in Suceava does not sponsor transportation to the monasteries (for tours, inquire at the ONT Tourist Office in Bucharest). Therefore, unless you have a car, your resourcefulness will be tested to its utmost. In the summer the best and most comfortable way to see the monasteries is to "hitch" a ride with a foreign tour group. If you arrive in the evening, search the lobbies of the Hotels Arcaşul and Bucovina for any groups of foreigners. Once you spot a likely individual you'll have to see if there is any possible way to communicate; put your language skills to work. Most of the groups that come through are French, Italian, and German, though occasionally Spanish, Greeks, Belgians, or Dutch will make an appearance. Ask to speak to the tour organizer ("take me to your leader"), not the group's Romanian guide, who will probably either say no or ask for a bribe. Offer to pay for your place, for gas, or some such to offset any costs that the foreign guide may incur by letting you tag along. We talked to several guides and the consensus was that $5 to $10 per person for the often ten-hour-long tour is not unreasonable. Lunch is usually not included unless the tour leader really likes you. This sum is not payable to anyone in an official capacity and should be offered only after a thorough assessment of the situation has been made. Again, under no circumstances should you talk with the Romanian personnel attached to the tour; talk only with the *Western* tour leaders. Most tours leave the hotels between 8 a.m. and 9 a.m.

5. Iaşi

Iaşi (pronounced ee-*ahsh*), the former capital of Moldavia, is set among the gently rolling hills of the broad expanse between the Moldavian tablelands and the Jijia Plain. It's always been considered an "upland" town, and the residents of Iaşi consider themselves apart from, if not slightly better than, their fellows from the "Lower Country." The first recorded mention of the town occurs in 1408, and from then on Iaşi was host to practically every important Romanian including Stefan the Great (1457–1504). As early as the 16th century Iaşi was also home to schools of higher learning. The large number of polytechnic universities in Iaşi are only a continuation of a tradition begun in the early 1600s when Vasile Lupu established the Vasilian Academy.

THE SIGHTS: Today the town is a modern, growing city most famous for the **Palace of Culture,** and the Church of the Three Hierarchy (1638–1639). Built early in this century in an outrageously flamboyant Gothic style, the Palace of Culture at Piaţa Palat 1 is built on the site of the first Princely Court of the Moldavian Vovoides (1437). Inside the palace are several museums including the principal city art collection, the archives, and the Polytechnical Museum. The **Polytechnical Museum** contains one of Europe's most fascinating collections of old music boxes, mechanical pipes, mechanical pianos, gramophones, mechanical pianolas, and orchestrons. Orchestrons are mechanical orchestras with wind instruments, keyboards, and percussion instruments as well as pastoral scenes painted on a loop of canvas that churns around; they're powered by the arm of the matron who guards this section of the museum.

The town's second major sight, the **Church of the Three Hierarchy** (Trei Ierarhi) at Ştefan cel Mare 62, is covered with such delicate and intricately carved stonework that it can be said to be embroidered. Built by Vasile Lupu in 1638, it was an important center of medieval culture, having both a school and a printing press. Prince Vasile Lupu, the founder of the church, is buried within. The church is open most days from 9 a.m. till 4 p.m., though it's occasionally closed during services on religious holidays.

ORIENTATION:

Iaşi runs along a roughly north-south line with the **Bahlui River** cutting along its southern edge. To reach the center of town from the **railway station,** walk straight ahead (east) up the main street as you leave the station, till you reach Strada Arcu, not more than a five- or ten-minute walk away, and then turn right (south). The town's main square, **Piaţa Unirii,** is just 100 yards farther on.

Iasi's three main tourism offices are in Piaţa Unirii. The **County Tourist Office** is at Piaţa Unirii 12 (tel. 4-30-37). **Tarom** (tel. 1-52-39) and the **CFR Railway Ticket Agency** (tel. 1-36-73) are just a few doors down.

ACCOMMODATIONS:

There are several modern luxury-class hotels in Iaşi, all of which charge well over $25 per person. The one reasonably priced hotel that we found in Iaşi is the **Hotel Continental,** Strada Cuza Vodă 4 (tel. 1-43-20; Telex 22270). This hotel offers both first- and second-class accommodations (the latter are only on the fourth floor). The second-class rooms are clean with no private baths. The first-class rooms are definitely inferior to those in first-class hotels, but all rooms at the Continental are rather quiet. A second-class single costs $11.50; a double, $17.50; and a triple, $26.50 per night. A first-class single with private bath costs $16.50 and a double costs $25 per night.

If the Continental is full or if you arrive late at night, try the **Hotel Unirea,** at Piaţa Unirii 12 (tel. 4-21-10). Again, this is more of the same: a tall concrete structure—impossible to miss—clean but unspectacular. In the late summer and winter it's usually packed with foreign students. In the evening, even during the summer, the bar and game room are often filled with students, many from Arabic countries. A single costs $20.50, a double runs $29.75, and a suite goes for $49 per night; breakfast and private bathrooms come with the room.

Starvation Budget

On the budget end is the **Ciric Tourist Complex** (tel. 1-43-74), located about two miles north of the city center in the beautiful Ciric Forest overlooking several large lakes. On weekends this is where many of Iaşi's families come for the day. There are four-bed bungalows of dubious quality for about $15, as well as numerous places to pitch a tent. To reach Ciric, take bus T45 from the city center two stations and change to bus 15 for another 15 to 20 minutes. The buses stop running at 10 p.m. and hitchhiking at night is very difficult because traffic is sparse.

RESTAURANTS: The **Restaurant Select,** right off the Piaţa Unirii in a two-story yellow building, is a good bet for lunch or dinner. There is an omelet for 10 lei (85¢) and a pork cutlet for 30 lei ($2.55). Downstairs at the bistro are small cakes and buns for 5 lei (45¢) to 7 lei (60¢) as well as soup and other light fare. The interior is quite impressive, with several private banquet rooms and dancing every night. The restaurant is open from 10 a.m. to 10 p.m. and the bistro opens at 8 a.m.

On the top floor of the **Unirea Hotel** at Piaţa Unirii is a café/bistro with ice cream, cakes, and liquor. You enter the bistro from an elevator on the side of the hotel facing the Hotel Traian. The cuisine is average but is compensated for by the excellent view of the whole city. Open from 10 a.m. to 4 p.m. and again from 5 to 11 p.m.

Chapter XXIII

THE BLACK SEA COAST

1. Constanţa
2. The Black Sea Beaches
3. Tulcea and the Danube Delta

ROMANIA'S BLACK SEA COAST is about as diverse as a landscape can be, with bold contrasts between the beauty of nature and the destructiveness of man. The north part of the coast in the Danube Delta is a beautiful region of swamps and forests populated by birds and wild animals undisturbed but for the occasional passing of a tourist boat. South of the Danube Delta, however, large petrochemical factories spew out waste into the sea, making many miles of the coast uninhabitable.

Eventually, the industry ends near Constanţa, an ancient town founded by Greeks in the 5th century B.C. and later settled by the Romans. One former Roman resident here was the poet Ovid, who was banished to Constanţa by an angry Augustus Caesar. Although you won't hear any "Ave Caesars" coming from the ancient marketplace (you probably wouldn't have heard them in Ovid's time either, for that matter), you'll be astonished by the beautiful and well-preserved shopping center of ancient Constanţa as well as by the Roman artifacts inside Constanţa's museums.

South of Constanţa begins a chain of beach resorts. Although not the most attractive in Europe, they make for a decent summer afternoon's swim.

1. Constanţa

Constanţa (pop. 275,000) is the oldest city in Romania. Founded in the 6th century B.C. by Greek traders, Constanţa has been the site of uninterrupted habitation for over 26 centuries. First called Tomis by its Grecian founders, in the 4th century A.D. it was renamed in honor of Constantine the Great and probably called Constantiana. The most famous resident of Constanţa was the great Roman poet Ovid, who was exiled here in the 1st century A.D. He viewed the city as a hostile outland post far away from the cosmopolitan and cultural center of his home. Today the city is a showplace of ancient ruins as well as a gateway to the Romanian Riviera and the principal seaport of the nation.

ORIENTATION: Constanţa is shaped roughly like a fan, with the **Old City** as the base at the southwest corner. The major boulevards run northwest from the Old City for quite a distance. The streets in the small old section of town run in haphazard directions; the rest of Constanţa is very symmetrical and it's easy to get around. Most of the restaurants and hotels are located on or near **Bulevardul Tomis,** which runs northwest from the Old City.

From the Train Station

The **train station (Gara Feroviară),** at Piaţa Victoriei 1 (tel. 1-67-25), is not more than a 20-minute walk from the Old City straight along Bulevardul Republicii. If you don't feel like walking, take any bus heading east from the station along the boulevard.

From the Airport

The **Aeroportul International Mihail Kogălniceanu** (tel. 1-52-76) is classi- fied by the Romanian tourist board as an international one. In the light of terror- ist attacks in European airports, the extensive security surrounding and inundating the airport should comfort some visitors. An **airport bus** for 5 lei (45¢) meets every plane and heads into the city center.

By Car

Constanţa is connected with Bucharest by a two-lane highway that passes through some beautiful Romanian pastoral scenery, which is just as well as traf- fic can be heavy, giving you ample time to view the countryside.

GETTING AROUND: Constanţa offers only surface transportation as there is no metro or plan of building one in the near future. All connection with other beach areas is by bus or, if you have the money, cab. The buses are as crowded here as in the rest of Romania. The cabs in Constanţa will stop if you signal them directly on the street, though they usually expect a tip for this service. The best place for "cab catching" is along Bulevardul Tomis.

IMPORTANT ADDRESSES: The main tourist agency in Constanţa is the **Agency of Domestic Tourism (Agenţia de Turism Intern),** at Bulevardul Tomis 69, a block and a half north of Bulevardul Republicii (tel. 1-71-81 or 1-71-27). Open during regular business hours, they should be able to provide maps and answer some basic questions. We found the staff of the **Hotel Continental,** Bule- vardul Republicii 20 (tel. 1-56-60), also helpful in giving information and maps. At neither place do all staff members speak English.

The **Tarom Airlines** office is at Strada Ştefan cel Mare 15 (tel. 6-05-08). The **automobile club** runs an office at Bulevardul Tomis 26 (tel. 1-18-31). And to avoid the long lines at the train station, buy your rail tickets at the **Agentia CFR,** at Bulevardul Tomis 79 (tel. 1-79-30, ext. 271).

ACCOMMODATIONS: Constanţa is the main Romanian seacoast city and as such suffers from overcrowding and scarce accommodations in the summer. As no one bureau directs tourists to available rooms, it's best to contact hotels di- rectly after an early-morning arrival. This is not difficult to do because most trains from the west (Bucharest) run overnight and generally arrive at Constanţa in the morning. You'll find most of Constanţa's hotels in the Old City, or just north in the vicinity of Bulevardul Tomis.

On the budget side of the scale is the **Hotel Constanţa,** located not far from the Old City at Bulevardul Tomis 46 (tel. 1-77-20), with single rooms for 121 lei ($10.30), doubles for 186 lei ($15.80), and extra beds for an additional 66 lei ($5.60). The hotel hallways are sunny, the bathrooms are not clean, and the water sometimes fails. If not the nicest place to stay in, it is centrally located and inexpensive, and above all, there's almost always a room available.

Located right across from the Continental Hotel, the **Hotel Victoria,** on the busy Bulevardul Republicii at no. 7 (tel. 1-76-22), is noisy but clean. The corner rooms have a good view along the intersection, as well as a small terrace. There are no private bathrooms but the public facilities were very clean when we visited. Unfortunately, since this hotel is located so close to the Continental, it fills up with travelers who go first to the Continental only to find they can't afford it. Rates at the Hotel Victoria are identical to those at the Hotel Constanța.

More expensive, but worth it, is the first-class **Hotel Intim** at Strada Nicolae Titulescu 9, right by the Catholic church in the Old City (tel. 1-78-14; Telex 14243). The Intim is usually filled with groups, and you might consider Telexing in advance if you plan to stay in Constanța for a couple of days. The Hotel Intim is modern, clean, and very quiet, and a single room costs less than $20.

Included more for its location and almost guaranteed vacancies than its facilities is the **Hotel Continental,** the only "international" hotel in Constanța, right on the corner of Bulevardul Tomis at Bulevardul Republicii 20 (tel. 1-56-60 to 1-56-69; Telex 14237). A single room costs $33 and a double room runs $59 per night with breakfast and private bath. By far the best deal is the double room without a bath for $27; the public toilets are reasonably clean here.

DINING: For budget watchers we recommend the **Lacto-Vegetarian** at Bulevardul Tomis 78, not far from the Hotel Continental. This is a good clean snackbar, best for breakfast and lunch, where you can get a sandwich for 10 lei (85¢) and fill up for less than 20 lei ($1.70) to 30 lei ($2.55). You won't be the only one eating on a budget here during lunchtime as office workers from nearby government buildings also frequent the Lacto-Vegetarian. Open from 7 to 11:30 a.m. and again from 1 to 9 p.m., it offers good inexpensive fare with beer available after 10 a.m.

For dinner we recommend the **Casa cu Lei** ("House of the Lions") at Strada Dianei 1 (tel. 1-80-50). The Casa cu Lei offers a bar, a salon, and a restaurant all decorated in an eclectic mix of Spanish, Venetian, and medieval Romanian styles. There is a limited menu, usually about four dishes, all of which are well prepared and in stock. The mixed grill at 42 lei ($3.55) is available most nights; other dishes cost between 27 lei ($2.30) and 40 lei ($3.40). The Casa cu Lei restaurant is open from 10 a.m. to 9:30 p.m. and, in the summer, is cool and quiet inside. Unfortunately no English is spoken here, but the menu isn't hard to decipher if you bring your dictionary or the menu translator in this book. You'll find Casa cu Lei on the west side of the Old City, just south of the marketplace and not far from the Hotel Intim.

NIGHTLIFE: Constanța's nightspots are the hotel bars and restaurants; though touristy, the premier restaurant in the evening is in the **Hotel Continental** at Bulevardul Republicii 20 (tel. 1-56-60). It features the largest menu and has the best food availability in town. Reservations are a must for dinner. The average main dish will set you back 30 lei ($2.55) to 45 lei ($3.85) with service charge included (no need to tip unless the service was outstanding) of no more than 10%. There is live music and dancing every night.

For dessert, try the **sweetshop** on the corner of Bulevardul Tomis and Bulevardul Republicii, a convenient place for ice cream.

THE SIGHTS: There are two sights of primary importance in Constanța: the National History and Archeological Museum, and the rediscovered Roman shop and market complex. Both are located right off the main square (Piața Ovidiu) in the Old City.

The **National History and Archeological Museum,** at Piața Ovidiu 12, contains artifacts from the Stone Age to the present; by far the best part of the museum is the collection of antiquities from the Dacian, Greek, and Roman eras. The treasury boasts an impressive array of Greek statuary, primarily busts, from the 4th through 2nd centuries B.C. The jewel of the collection is the Glykon, an oddly disturbing composite of man, serpent, lion, and wild antelope. Known as the Goddess of Fortune and protector of the ancient city of Tomis, the Glykon dates from the 2nd or 3rd century A.D.

The nearby **Roman market complex** must be seen to be believed. Originally discovered as workers were bulldozing foundations for a new roadbed in 1959, the whole complex is now protected by a roof. The colorful mosaic floor is made up of thousands of small tiles covering an area of more than 2,000 square yards. An altar where human sacrifices were once offered to the gods stands at one end of the market.

Other interesting museums in Constanţa include the **Museum of the Romanian Navy** at Strada Traian 53, which details "the age-old interest in seafaring" by Romanians, and the **Museum of the Sea,** on Strada Remus Opreanu, a collection of life from the Black Sea as well as other seas around the world.

Those interested in Constanţa's most famous resident may want to visit the **Statue of Ovid** in Piaţa Ovidiu. The work was designed by the Italian sculptor Ettore Ferrari in 1887. In case you were wondering what offended Augustus Caesar so as to banish one of Rome's greatest poets, refer to Ovid's work the *Art of Love,* which supposedly provoked the emperor's anger.

2. The Black Sea Beaches

Romania has developed its coast south of Constanţa into one continuous chain of large resort hotels, equipped with modern restaurants and summer-sports facilities. Although this coast offers clear waters and sandy beaches, we advise dedicated beachgoers to continue on to the Bulgarian Black Sea coast. The landscape off the Romanian coast lacks the dramatic mountains and cliffs that make the Bulgarian coast so breathtaking. Furthermore, Romania's coast has been so developed with large hotels that it's difficult to find a spot on the beach with any natural beauty or privacy. By contrast, quiet natural spots can be found across Bulgaria's coast. Finally, a vacation on Romania's coast costs considerably more than one in Bulgaria.

If you want to spend only a day or two at the beach after a visit to Constanţa and not go all the way to Bulgaria, you will certainly enjoy yourself. You'll find that the coast is the most efficiently run part of Romania, and many of the difficulties of travel in Romania are less evident here. At the same time, however, remember that even better beaches lay over the border in Bulgaria.

In case you were wondering, the coast north of Constanţa offers little for the sun-worshipper. Directly to the north, industrial plants line the coast; nearer the Soviet border you'll find some more natural scenic beaches, but they're very difficult to reach and have no hotels.

ACCOMMODATIONS: In each coastal resort town, hotels keep 20% of their rooms set aside for individual travelers. In order to book into these rooms, you must go to the local tourist office, called the **Literal ONT Office,** where rooms are held until 6 p.m. every day. At the ONT office you make the room reservations and pay for them as well.

If ONT doesn't have any available rooms, you can go directly to a hotel, for each hotel manager maintains a "special reserve" which he gives out as he pleases. Use all of your charms to convince the manager to give you one of these special rooms.

EXCURSIONS: Those interested in ancient history and archeology should not miss a visit to **Istria,** north of Constanța. Intrepid Greek merchants settled in Istria in 657 B.C. and built up a small colony. These Greek pioneers thrived on the import of such products as wine, olive oil, and weapons. Then, hundreds of years later, the Roman Empire gained control of this important port town, and the city continued to flourish until the 7th century A.D.

In a visit to Istria today, you can see a small museum filled with both Greek and Roman relics, and you can visit the impressive remains of several of Istria's town walls, different neighborhoods, and religious temples, such as one to Aphrodite.

The easiest way to see Istria is on an ONT half-day tour. The entire outing from Constanța takes about four hours, which includes an hour and a half of driving, two hours in the museum, and half an hour enjoying drinks at a restaurant in Constanța. We took this tour with a guide during our stay at the coast and we remember the visit as one of the highlights of Romania.

3. Tulcea and the Danube Delta

Imagine a swampy, marshy region with 300 species of birds flying through the skies. Wild boars, foxes, wolves, wildcats, flamingoes, and snakes are at home among the tall weeds of the marshes or within thick forests. Is this region in the heart of South America or Africa? No, you'll find this exotic area in Romania's Danube Delta, where the mighty Danube River splits into three branches and empties into the Black Sea after journeying all the way from Germany through eight countries.

Every year this large region goes through great ecological changes; thanks to the continual flow of water and sand deposits from the Danube, the land of the Delta extends some 120 feet into the sea. With this natural evolution, mostly unhampered by man, a great variety of wildlife continues to live here as it has for many thousands of years. In addition to the above-named animals, the Danube Delta boasts singing swans, tawny owls, sea eagles, and sturgeon, the source of the black caviar that is prized throughout the world. In summer the region hosts dozens of new species of birds which migrate from West Africa, the Nile, the Persian Gulf, and the Soviet Union. In all, lovers of wildlife in its natural setting won't want to miss out on the Danube Delta, an unspoiled dream world of nature.

TULCEA: At the center of the Danube Delta lies the pleasant town of Tulcea, a small port that is the center of Romania's canned-fish industry. Although Tulcea was first inhabited by Greek and then Roman settlers, it offers little in terms of exciting sights today. However, many travelers visit this pleasant town because it serves as a springboard for travel into the Danube Delta. And before you set out into the Delta, you'll want to stop by the **Danube Delta Museum,** Strada Progresului 32, a natural history museum which previews the wildlife of the Delta; the museum is open from 9 a.m. to 5 p.m. Tuesday through Sunday, from 8 a.m. to noon on Monday.

You can get to Tulcea by plane or train. Tarom flies regularly from Bucharest, a 45-minute journey. You can also take a train from Bucharest or Constanța, but make sure to get the express and not the snail-paced local!

Orientation and Important Addresses

When you arrive at Tulcea's **train station,** walk straight along the **Dunarea Canal** (on Strada Portului) for ten minutes to reach the center of Tulcea and the town's two hotels. First you'll see the Hotel Delta, and one block to the right you'll find the Hotel Egreta.

To buy railway tickets in advance, visit the **CFR Railway Office** on Strada Babadag, open from 7:30 to 8:30 a.m. and from 9:30 a.m. to 2 p.m. Monday through Saturday.

You'll see the **Main Post and Telegraph Station** at Strada Păcii 20. The telephone bureau here operates from 7 a.m. to 9 p.m. seven days a week.

Accommodations

Tulcea's most comfortable accommodations are at the first-class **Hotel Delta,** Strada Isaccei 2 (tel. 1-47-20). It's located just off the docks in the center of town. The 117 modern rooms all provide balconies, telephone, and private bathroom, but only doubles are available. Rooms rent for 396.25 lei ($33.70) to 412.50 lei ($35.05). The restaurant downstairs serves standard hotel fare with efficient service.

If you're looking to save more money, or if you're traveling alone, then choose the **Hotel Egreta,** located just a block from the Hotel Delta at Strada Păcii 1 (tel. 1-71-03). In this modern first-class hotel every two rooms share a bathroom with toilet and shower in a mutual hallway. All of the 116 small rooms have a telephone, and some also have a TV. Singles cost 185.65 lei ($15.80) and doubles are priced at 280 lei ($23.80). Doubles with completely private bathrooms are available for 296.25 lei ($25.20). Breakfast in the hotel's restaurant costs an additional 23.75 lei ($2). Downstairs in the hotel lobby you'll see a list and timetable of Danube Delta boats conveniently posted.

EXCURSIONS INTO THE DELTA:

As with everything else in Romania, you can either explore on your own or with an organized tour.

If you prefer to go off on your own, head for **Crişan,** an outpost situated around a hotel in the middle of the Delta. Many large boats of the Navrom company leave for Crişan and other destinations from Tulcea's river landing stage on Strada Portului. At Crişan you're likely to find a local fisherman who will take you on a tour through the canals in his rowboat to see the abundant wildlife. The National Tourist Board Carpaţi (see address below) sells vouchers for $1 an hour; you give the vouchers to local fishermen should you not care to bargain with them directly.

If you're so overwhelmed by the beauty of the Delta that you want to spend the night, you can stay at the **Hotel Lebăda** in Crişan (tel. 1-47-20 and ask for the Hotel Lebăda). This hotel, with its stucco façade and straw roofs, offers 148 rooms with shower and toilet, breakfast included. Doubles cost 321 lei ($27.30) to 337.50 lei ($28.70). Small apartments with two rooms cost 437.50 lei ($37.20). Hot water is only available from 6 to 9 a.m. and from 6 to 10 p.m. Screens guard the windows against mosquitoes, and the reception is always well stocked with bug repellent, just in case. The hotel also runs a fairly good restaurant with a terrace overlooking a canal. A complete meal here costs 55 lei ($4.70).

If you prefer a simpler tour without the worries of heading out on your own, then the **National Tourist Board Carpaţi** in the Hotel Delta, Strada Isaccei 2 (tel. 1-47-20), can help out. This small desk organizes group excursions into the Delta region. You might choose an eight-hour trip (starting at 10:30 a.m.) at a cost of $32 for transportation, lunch (at the Hotel Lebăda in Crişan), and dinner. If you lay out $48, you can embark on a two-day trip, which also includes a night's accommodations. Carpaţi also makes arrangements for fishing expeditions into the Delta. The one drawback to the organized tour is that the motors of the large boat often scare away the very birds and animals that you're hoping to see in your explorations.

If you prefer to set out into the Delta with your own private skipper and just your family or friends, the National Tourist Board Carpaţi will rent a little motor boat, along with a pilot and gas, for $15.50 an hour.

Whether or not you join a Carpaţi tour, make sure to ask Carpaţi for their Danube Delta map, which includes a lot of interesting information in English about the region's wildlife.

Part Six

BULGARIA

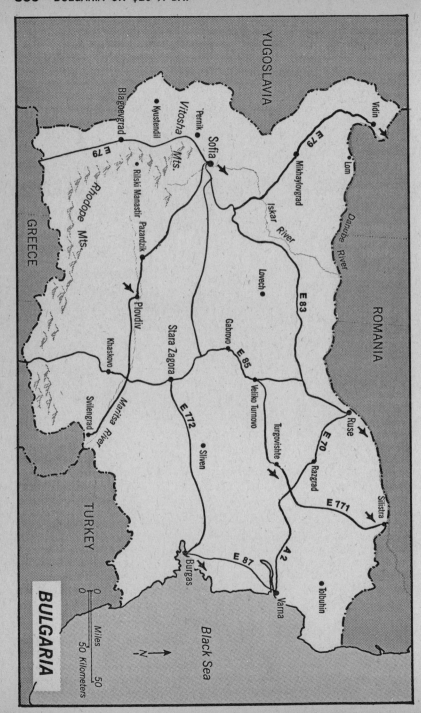

Chapter XXIV

INTRODUCING BULGARIA

1. About Bulgaria
2. Rules and Regulations
3. Getting There
4. Getting Around
5. Accommodations
6. Food and Drink
7. The ABCs of Bulgaria

EASTERN EUROPE'S LEAST-KNOWN country, Bulgaria (pop. 9,000,000) offers visitors surprise after pleasant surprise. A land of great natural beauty, Bulgaria boasts ancient monuments dating back thousands of years, a distinctive urban architectural style of the 18th and 19th century which makes for some of Europe's most charming city neighborhoods, and a coastline that rivals the French Riviera.

On Bulgaria's Black Sea coast you can lie in the hot sun beside bold blue waters on an isolated beach; several miles away, you can go parasailing in one of Europe's most popular beach resorts, and just beyond the largest Bulgarian resort you can visit a dozen medieval churches. In Plovdiv or Veliko Turnovo you can climb up a small hill to find an unchanged world of the 19th century, complete with winding cobblestone streets and ornately painted houses. In the Valley of the Roses you can visit the international rose market in June and make all of your romantic fantasies come true!

What all of these places in Bulgaria hold out to the visitor is unspoiled beauty. Of course Bulgaria has its share of unimaginative modern block constructions, but in many parts of the country changes have come slowly; for some Bulgarians, an early-20th-century—or even 19th-century—way of life continues. Rich with historical sights, breathtaking natural scenery, and a growing chain of tourist facilities, Bulgaria is definitely worth including in your Eastern European travels.

SUGGESTED ITINERARY: We have divided this chapter into inland cities and coastal cities, but in a visit to Bulgaria, we suggest seeing as much of both as possible. Begin your travels with at least two days in Sofia, Bulgaria's capital, which serves as a proud example of Bulgarian culture, complete with the impressive Aleksander Nevski Cathedral, the National History Museum (with a collection of art and historical objects from ancient Thracian to modern times), and other museums. Then spend a day to the south of Sofia visiting the Rila Monastery, a bastion of religious devotion since the beginning of Bulgarian Christianity.

Continue on toward the Bulgarian seaside with a day stop in either Veliko-Turnovo or Plovdiv, depending on whether you're headed to the northern or southern part of the coast. Veliko-Turnovo in the north shows off interesting medieval fortifications and typical Bulgarian homes of the 18th and 19th centuries. Plovdiv also offers a charming 19th-century quarter that has hardly changed in 125 years.

Spend a few days enjoying the clear waters of the Bulgarian Black Sea coast, an inviting stretch of smooth sand beaches punctuated by small inlets and rocky cliffs. Your actual destination will depend on what type of beach resort you seek (we discuss the options in Chapter XXVI). We do recommend one city in particular to all visitors to the coast: Nesebar, a tiny town on a spit of land (a former island) whose lovely medieval churches stand side by side with 18th- and 19th-century architecture.

Bulgaria produces 70% of all roses on the international market, and early June is "harvest" time. If you want to be inundated with fragrant red roses, visit Karlovo or Kazanluk, two cities in central Bulgaria about an hour from Plovdiv.

1. About Bulgaria

A CAPSULE HISTORY: Recent archeological finds have shown that as early as 4000 B.C. skilled and innovative goldsmiths and metalworkers were practicing their crafts in Bulgaria. In ancient Greek times, Bulgaria was inhabited by the Thracians, who, according to the ancient Greek historian Herodotus, "would be invincible and by far the most powerful of peoples" if only they were united by a strong leader—but they weren't. The Black Sea coast was later attacked and conquered by Phillip II of Macedonia and his son, Alexander the Great. In the 1st century A.D. the area was seized by the Romans and incorporated into their empire. You can still see Roman ruins in several locations in Bulgaria today.

In A.D. 681 the Bulgarian state was founded when seven Slavic tribes in the area joined together. In the 13th century the state of Bulgaria was at the height of its power, and its territory extended into almost all of present-day Albania, half of present-day Greece and Romania, and small parts of present-day Turkey and the Soviet Union. By 1396, however, the Ottoman Turks had invaded the country, beginning five centuries of domination. Turkish rule in Bulgaria finally ended in 1877 when Russia intervened to route the Ottomans. During World War II the Bulgarians fought with the Germans; in 1944 the Soviets declared war on Bulgaria and again "liberated" the country, ushering in socialism. According to official government statements, postwar development in Bulgaria has been marked by "enormous positive achievements."

The two Russian liberations have formed a very strong bond of friendship between Bulgaria and the Soviet Union unparalleled in the rest of the Warsaw Pact.

RELIGION: Although exact statistics are not available, the predominant faith in Bulgaria is the Eastern Orthodox church; the second-largest religious group, the Muslims, comprise about 10% of the population.

GOVERNMENT: Bulgaria is a "people's republic." The National Assembly holds legislative power. Georgi Dimitrov was the first leader of socialist Bulgaria, and is often revered as the modern father of Bulgaria.

The Bulgarian Lev

The official unit of Bulgarian currency is the lev (plural: leva), made up of 100 stotinki. The official exchange rate as we went to press was 1.010 leva = $1 U.S. However, travelers on tourist visas get an 80% bonus for all currency exchanged at a Balkantourist office, which brings the exchange rate to 1.829 leva = $1 U.S.—and this is the exchange rate we used for price conversions in this guide. At that rate, 1 lev = about 55¢, and $10 = about 18 leva.

Note: Don't exchange currency at banks in Bulgaria, because they will not give you that 80% bonus.

LANGUAGE: Bulgarian is a close cousin to Russian and both use the Cyrillic alphabet. Almost all Bulgarians we met spoke at least some Russian, and a number also spoke German. On the Black Sea coast many tourist offices and hotels have English-speaking personnel. Road signs and public notices are often written in Roman as well as Cyrillic lettering; larger hotels often have English menus in their restaurants. However, in the smaller towns, English and Roman lettering are rare indeed.

COST ESTIMATES: As Bulgaria does not enforce a daily minimum currency exchange, the country is a budget traveler's dream. If you stay in private accommodations (which are available throughout most of Bulgaria) you'll spend only $2 to $3 a day on housing, so together food and housing are likely to cost less than $10 a day. If you stay in a hotel you'll spend closer to $25 a day, possibly less, especially if you're traveling with a companion. Domestic transportation is also inexpensive. The only two things that cost a great deal are international transportation and car rentals.

2. Rules and Regulations

Balkantourist, the national travel board, can answer questions about travel to Bulgaria, and provide Bulgarian pamphlets and maps. In the U.S., write or call the Bulgarian Tourist Office at 161 E. 86th St., New York, NY 10028 (tel. 212/722-1110). In Canada, contact the Bulgarian Trade Mission, Tourist Department, 1550 De Maisonneuve West, Montréal, Québec (tel. 514/935-7494). In England, it's the Bulgarian National Tourist Office, Regent Street, London, W1 126 (tel. 01/437-2611). Once in Bulgaria, Balkantourist offices offer assistance in almost every town.

VISAS: All travelers must get a visa before they go to Bulgaria. Unless you live in Washington, D.C., or nearby, send your passport, visa application form (which the embassy or Bulgarian tourist office will give you), one photograph, and a self-addressed, stamped envelope to the nearest Bulgarian Embassy. We recommend sending all this by certified mail. Also include the visa fee of $14 (double-check the price at the Bulgarian Tourism office). A transit visa for 30 hours or less in Bulgaria, by contrast, costs $9 (you'll need a transit visa, for example, if you plan to travel by train from Yugoslavia to Istanbul). Note that only money orders, certified checks, and cash are accepted. The visa will be valid for six months from the date of issue.

In Washington, the **Embassy of the People's Republic of Bulgaria** is at 1621 22nd St. NW, Washington, DC 20008 (tel. 202/387-7969). In Canada, the address is 325 Steward St., Ottawa, Canada (tel. 613/232-3215). There is also a Bulgarian Consulate General at 100 Adelaide West, 1410 Toronto, ON M5H 1S3 (tel. 416/363-7307).

When filling out the visa form, always put down that you will be staying 30 days even if you plan to spend only two days there. The price is the same, but it will save you a lot of trouble if you decide to spend more time in Bulgaria and would otherwise have to extend your visa.

Expect the whole process to take at least two weeks. Also note that Bulgarian embassies in Europe are not particularly helpful, and you will have to wait one week to get your visa there, so you are better off taking care of the visa before you leave home.

3. Getting There

BY AIR: The best, most frequent connections from the U.S. to Sofia are offered by Lufthansa German Airlines. Transatlantic flights connect with flights to Sofia four times a week in Frankfurt, and four times a week in Munich. In addition, Lufthansa connects in Frankfurt with Balkan Bulgarian Airlines for another three flights weekly.

From the U.S., it is more expensive to fly to Sofia than to any other Eastern European city. The lowest Lufthansa fare is the midweek 7 day–3 month Excursion fare: $849 round trip between November 1 and March 31. For information or assistance while in Sofia, contact Lufthansa at: Blvd. Al. Stamboliski 9 (tel. 88-23-10/88-42-23).

Flying to Sofia

First Class and Business Class fares allow unlimited stopovers. The Excursion fare is limited to two stopovers in each direction for a charge of $25 each. The APEX fare permits no stopovers and has a 21-day advance purchase requirement and also a $75 penalty fee for cancellation. Fares (subject to change without notice) are subject to a $3 departure tax plus a $5 Custom User fee.

Round-Trip Fares to Sofia

		From:	New York	Anchorage	Atlanta	Boston	Chicago	Houston/ Dallas- Ft. Worth	San Francisco/ Los Angeles	Miami	Phila- delphia
First Class	All Year		$4182	$5308	$4870	$4182	$4832	$4914	$5544	$4624	$4402
Business Class	All Year		2294	3216	2682	2294	2738	2624	3204	2616	2458
10 Day–3 Months	Sept. 15–May 14		1216	1654	1344	1216	1326	1344	1399	1362	1279
Excursion	May 15–Sept. 14		1427	1865	1555	1427	1537	1555	1610	1573	1490
7 Day–3 Months	Nov. 1–Mar. 31	Midweek	849	1287	977	849	959	977	1032	995	912
		Weekend	899	1337	1027	899	1009	1027	1082	1045	962
•	Apr. 1–May 31	Midweek	899	1337	1027	899	1009	1027	1082	1045	962
	Sept. 16–Oct. 31	Weekend	958	1396	1086	958	1068	1086	1141	1104	1021
•	June 1–Sept. 15	Midweek	958	1396	1086	958	1068	1086	1141	1104	1021
		Weekend	1028	1466	1156	1028	1138	1156	1211	1174	1091

Midweek = Mon–Thurs
Weekend = Fri–Sun
All airfares are quoted as round trip fares, and are subject to change without notice.

BY TRAIN AND BUS: Trains connect Bucharest and Belgrade with Sofia. Both rides take about ten hours. The slightly longer train ride from Istanbul costs $27 on the old, but now unexceptional, *Orient Express* (the glamorous *Orient Express* you may be thinking of is another special train).

BY CAR: You can also drive to Bulgaria across a number of border checkpoints from Yugoslavia, Romania, Turkey, and Greece. Note that certain countries (such as Turkey) forbid the use of their rental cars in Bulgaria. Make sure that the company you rent from outside Bulgaria allows travel into Bulgaria before you plan a tour by car.

BY BOAT: Some luxury cruise liners dock in Bulgaria, but no regularly scheduled international boats service the coast.

4. Getting Around

BY AIR: BalkanAir operates inexpensive flights from Sofia to Burgas, Varna, and a number of other cities. For a complete flight schedule, write or call Balkan Airlines, 50 E. 42nd St., Suite 1501, New York, NY 10017 (tel. 212/661-5733).

BY BUS AND TRAIN: Trains are the most convenient transportation in inland Bulgaria, though they're often crowded. Trains don't run along the Black Sea coast, however, but you can rely on the extensive bus connections. Both buses and trains are very inexpensive, although buying tickets sometimes proves a challenge (you encounter fair-sized lines). Try to purchase the ticket a day or two before your planned departure if possible to ensure getting a ticket, and always arrive with plenty of time to spare before departure.

BY CAR: Car rentals are quite expensive in Bulgaria, starting at about $250 a week for the bottom-of-the-line Soviet Lada with unlimited mileage and insurance. If you drive in Bulgaria, all you need is your national driver's license. However, you must have "civil liability" insurance (the Green Card). If you don't have this insurance document, you can buy it at the Bulgarian border for 20 leva ($10.95) for six days of insurance.

You may drive up to 120 km/h (80 mph) on Bulgarian highways, 80 km/h (50 mph) outside of cities, and 60 km/h (37 mph) in populated areas. One final note: It is absolutely forbidden to mix drinking and driving. For roadside assistance, call the Union of Bulgarian Motorists at 146.

For further information on seeing Bulgaria by car, ask Balkantourist for their pamphlet "Motoring Across Bulgaria."

BY TAXI: Taxis are very reasonable in Bulgaria, and the drivers are usually honest. Most rides within a city will cost less than $1.

HITCHHIKING: Hitchhikers may have some luck in Bulgaria with the many trucks on Bulgaria's main highways. These drivers see few Americans and are often curious to meet them. Women should not hitchhike alone.

5. Accommodations

HOTELS: Hotels are graded from five (the best) to one stars. As a point of reference, think of two-star hotels as the standard class B hotels of other Eastern European countries. Most hotels listed in the Bulgaria chapters have two or three stars. One-star hotels are usually for the more adventurous, starvation-budget traveler since facilities, especially public bathrooms, may not be very clean.

PRIVATE ROOMS: Staying in a private room in a Bulgarian home is Bulgaria's best budget buy, usually costing just a few dollars. Private accommodations are divided into three categories and priced according to location and facilities. Our own experience with private accommodations in several towns on the Black Sea coast proved rather pleasant as we stayed in the center of town and enjoyed large clean rooms with pristine public bathrooms.

In smaller Bulgarian towns, the staff at the tourist bureau that rents out private rooms may not speak any Western language. To tell them you want a private room, say: "Bich iskal chasna kvartira za [number of nights you want to stay] noshchti."

Registration

If your stay in a private home has not been arranged by a local tourist bureau, you must register at the local passport office for foreigners. In Sofia, you'll find this office at 9 Narodno Subranie Square, next to the Grand Hotel Sofia.

6. Food and Drink

Bulgarian cuisine is neither the most interesting nor the dullest in Eastern Europe, but it's certainly the region's most economical. Greek, Turkish, and Central European cuisines have influenced Bulgarian cooking. As in other Eastern European countries, the Bulgarian diet emphasizes hearty meat dishes such as lamb, pork, sausages, and meatballs; and, as in Greece and Turkey, these meats are generally grilled or prepared on a skewer (like a shish kebab).

Two Bulgarian specialties among their many meat dishes are *kebapcheta,* a dish of minced lamb (usually from the ribs or the shoulder) with onions and spices, and *gyuvech,* a vegetable-and-meat stew served in a clay casserole pot. Nonmeat specialties include *banitsa,* a cheese pastry; yogurt; *fasul,* white beans in tomato sauce served either hot or cold; *tarator,* cold soup of yogurt and chopped cucumbers with garlic; and *chopska salad,* a mixed salad of lettuce and tomato with thickly grated cheese on top. The more daring can quench their thirst with *ayran,* a popular drink of yogurt mixed with water (without sugar, of course!).

Although Bulgaria's geographic position in southern Europe favors growing fresh vegetables, you'll find few in Bulgarian restaurants, thanks to a vigorous export policy. Furthermore, not all items listed on menus are always available. One thing's for certain though: Bulgarian restaurants always have plenty of good, cheap wine! Try the Trakia label for both white and red wine.

As in other Eastern European countries, many of Bulgaria's best restaurants are in large hotels, usually devoid of any charm. When possible, more colorful local places have been recommended in this guide.

7. The ABCs of Bulgaria

BLACK MARKET: As of this writing, the black market rate is about 3 to 4 leva per dollar, around twice the official rate with bonus. However, Bulgaria is a country where you do *not* want to be on the wrong side of the law, and such transactions should be avoided.

CIGARETTES: You can buy Western brands of cigarettes at low cost in the Corecom hard-currency stores.

CLIMATE: On the Black Sea coast the temperature averages in the 70s in May, June, September, and October, and in the 80s in July and August. For up-to-date information, Radio Varna broadcasts the weather and news in the summertime in English from 11:30 a.m. to noon at 774 kHz. The broadcast times change, so check at Balkantourist.

CREDIT CARDS: They are accepted in Bulgaria at some of the larger hotels and stores, especially on the Black Sea coast.

CURRENCY: The lev (plural: leva) is the currency of Bulgaria; 100 stotinki make up 1 lev. If you have a tourist visa (as opposed to a business visa or a visa to visit friends) you will be given an 80% bonus above the so-called official rate if you exchange at Balkantourist. Thus as of this writing the official exchange rate is 1.016 leva per dollar, but with the bonus the tourist gets 1.829 leva per dollar. Dollar price conversions given in this guide's Bulgaria chapters include this bonus. Only when paying for international transportation will you not get this premium. *Never* exchange money in a bank in Bulgaria because banks do not give you the 80% tourist bonus.

There is a 1% exchange fee when changing cash, and a 1% plus 50 stotinki (27¢) fee when changing checks. As in the other socialist countries, it is forbidden to import or export Bulgarian currency. Keep all receipts, even though it's doubtful that you will get any Western money back for your leftover leva when leaving Bulgaria.

CUSTOMS: You are allowed to bring in two quarts of wine and one of alcohol, 250 ounces of cigarettes or tobacco, as well as personal possessions. On your way into Bulgaria, register any item worth more than 50 leva ($27.35), especially electronic equipment and antiques, to ensure that you'll be allowed to take it out of the country.

You may take out Bulgarian products as long as you show that you have officially changed money to buy the item, or if you have purchased the item in a hard-currency Corecom store. Remember to save all receipts! Before making large purchases, always check with the embassy.

ELECTRICITY: The electric power is 220 to 240 volts, 50 cycles, A.C.

EMBASSIES AND CONSULATES: The U.S. Embassy is in Sofia at Alexander Stambolijski 1 (tel. 88-48-01 to 88-48-05), just west of Lenin Square in the heart of the city, open from 8 a.m. to 5 p.m. weekdays (to 1 p.m. on Wednesday).

The **British Embassy** is in Sofia at Al. M. Tolbuhin 65 (tel. 87-83-25 or 88-53-61). To get here, take tram 2, 12, 14, 18, or 19 from the city center three stops to Al. M. Tolbuhin; walk southwest on this road and the embassy is in the middle of the third block from the tram stop.

Citizens of **Canada** use the U.S. Embassy, and all other Commonwealth nationals use the British Embassy.

FIRST AID: The number to call for help throughout Bulgaria is 120. In Sofia, there is a hospital for foreign citizens at 1 Akad E. Pavlovcki, Mladost 1 (tel. 72-00-52).

GAMBLING: You can gamble in the Grand Hotel in Varna, in the Drouzhba resort on the Black Sea coast, and at the Vitosha–New Otani Hotel in Sofia.

GAS: As of this writing, gas costs about $1 a liter, and sometimes (but rules change frequently on this) you can get a 20% discount if you buy coupons from a Balkantourist office or a large hotel and pay in cash (in Western currency, of course).

GROUP TOURS: A surprisingly large number of American travel companies include Bulgaria on their tours. Ask Balkantourist for their "List of Some Tours to Bulgaria in 1987," a compilation of almost 30 such tour operators.

HOLIDAYS AND SPECIAL EVENTS: January 1 (New Year's Day), May 1 (Labor Day), May 24 (Day of Slavonic Literacy, Education, and Culture), September 9 (National Day), and November 7 (Day of Victory of the Great October Socialist Revolution).

From late May to June, Sofia celebrates the **Weeks of Music,** when orchestras from across Europe come to perform. Other special events include several summer festivals on the Black Sea coast such as the **Burgas International Folklore Festival** at the end of August, and the **International Chamber Music Festival** in Plovdiv in September.

NEWSPAPERS AND MAGAZINES: A Bulgarian English-language paper is available in larger hotels.

OFFICE HOURS: Offices are open Monday to Friday from 8 or 8:30 a.m. until 5 p.m., with a break for lunch.

PHOTOGRAPHY: Although not nearly as strict as the Romanians in enforcement of their rules, the Bulgarians forbid photos of all military installations, transportation stations (air, sea, and land), communications facilities such as radio and TV stations, industrial enterprises, mines, laboratories, and reservoirs. Taking photos from airplanes is also off-limits to Western photographers. Pay special care not to photograph border installations, especially near the sensitive Bulgarian-Turkish frontier. If a uniformed official asks you to surrender your film for any reason, don't argue with him.

REGISTRATION: If you stay in a hotel, private room, or campground, your visa will be stamped to account for every day in Bulgaria. If you arrange accommodations other than hotels, private rooms, or camping set up by a local tourist bureau, register with the local police.

SHOPPING: Stores are usually open from 9 a.m. to 12:30 p.m., then from 3 to 8 p.m., but on major shopping streets stores often stay open all day. The Corecom chain of stores sells chocolate, cigarettes, alcohol, and other goodies for hard currency.

Favorite tourist buys include embroidery, tablecloths, place mats, napkins, ceramics, and dolls in national costumes.

SPAS: The two most popular mineral spas are at **Hissarya,** 25 miles north of Plovdiv, and **Kyustendil,** west of Sofia. There is also a spa at **Pomorie** on the Black Sea coast, as well as in other cities. Inquire at Balkantourist.

SPORTS: The Black Sea coast offers a wide variety of summer sports; **hunting** and **fishing** (both individual and group) can be arranged through Balkantourist. You can **hike** in the mountains; ask Balkantourist for their brochure "Mountaineering in Bulgaria." Pamporovo, 85 km (50 miles) from Plovdiv, and Vitosha, just 20 km (12 miles) from Sofia, are two popular **ski** resort areas.

STUDENT TRAVEL: Bulgaria offers few discounts to students traveling on their own. The national student organization, Orbita, offers student discounts only to organized groups. Try to use the IUS card for discounts on international transportation, but don't be surprised if no discounts are given.

TELEPHONE AND TELEGRAM: Within the same city, you can talk as long as you want with a 2-stotinki (1¢) coin. Some telephones also accept two 1-stotinki coins. The quality of connections between cities is often poor.

TIME: Bulgaria is one hour ahead of Central European Time; two hours ahead of Greenwich Mean Time in winter and three hours ahead in summer; and seven hours ahead of Eastern Standard Time in the U.S.

TIPPING: Bulgarians don't tip very much, which leaves things mostly up to your discretion. You should tip a waitress or waiter, a bartender, or a bellhop if you are very pleased with the service.

TOILETS: Many public bathrooms charge 10 stotinki (5¢). Should you forget to pay as you walk in, an attendant will loudly remind you.

Chapter XXV

SOFIA AND THE INLAND CITIES

1. Sofia
2. The Rila Monastery
3. Veliko Turnovo
4. Plovdiv

BULGARIA'S INLAND CITIES offer visitors a wealth of historic monuments, from the remains of ancient kingdoms to picturesque old towns. The museums of the capital city of Sofia boast beautifully detailed Thracian gold pieces dating back to 4000 B.C. At the Rila Monastery, to the south of Sofia, you can follow Bulgarian Christianity from its earliest roots in the 10th century. Veliko Turnovo, the medieval capital of Bulgaria, has the remains of fortifications that once protected the heart of a great empire. And in both Veliko Turnovo and Plovdiv you can admire untouched neighborhoods showing off the picturesque architecture of the 18th and 19th centuries, the period of Bulgaria's "National Revival" after 500 years of Turkish domination. With the great range of historic and artistic sights, Bulgaria's inland cities simply can't be ignored in a visit to the Balkans.

1. Sofia

Bulgaria's capital, a city with clean wide avenues and bustling crowds, Sofia (pop. 1,000,000) provides a fitting introduction to the impressive culture of the country. Sofia is largely a modern town, although it has been inhabited for thousands of years, first by the Thracians and then by the Romans. Today's Sofia dates from only the late 19th and early 20th centuries. In fact just a century ago fewer than 15,000 people lived in Sofia, then an important provincial town in the Turkish Empire. Today Sofia is an attractive modern capital city, where you can see the evolution of Bulgarian culture in its great museums and relax in the parks and cafés that testify to the city's mild climate.

ORIENTATION AND IMPORTANT ADDRESSES: Surrounded by mountains, Sofia is roughly in the central axis of Bulgaria, not far from its western border. The city is bounded by the **Vladajska Reka** (river) to the north and by an extensive range of parks to the south. The cultural center of the city is located along **Al. Georgi Dimitrov** on the southernmost edge and **Al. Marsal Tolbuhin** on the north. **Al. Ruski** runs from 9 Septemvri Square through the center of town. All of the major sights are within easy walking distance of 9 Septemvri Square.

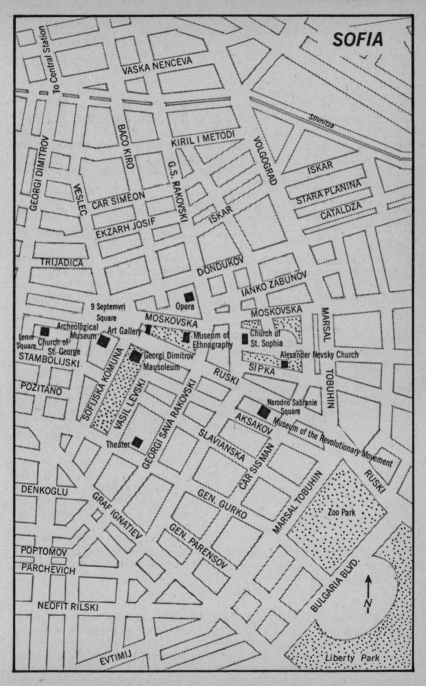

SOFIA

To Central Station

VASKA NENCEVA

GEORGI DIMITROV

BACO KIRO

KIRIL I METODI

VOLGOGRAD

Stivnitza

ISKAR

STARA PLANINA

CATALDZA

VESLEC

CAR SIMEON

G.S. RAKOVSKI

ISKAR

EKZARH JOSIF

TRIJADICA

DONDUKOV

IANKO ZABUNOV

MOSKOVSKA

9 Septemvri
Square

Opera

MOSKOVSKA

MARSAL

Archeological
Museum

Art Gallery

Museum of
Ethnography

Church of
St. Sophia

Lenin
Square

Church of
St. George

Georgi Dimitrov
Mausoleum

Alexander Nevsky Church

STAMBOLIJSKI

SOFIJSKA KOMUNA

RUSKI

SIPKA

TOBUHIN

POZITANO

VASIL LEVSKI

Narodno Sabranie
Square

GEORGI SAVA RAKOVSKI

Museum of the Revolutionary Movement

Theater

SLAVIANSKA

AKSAKOV

CAR SISMAN

RUSKI

DENKOGLU

GRAF IGNATIEV

GEN. GURKO

MARSAL TOBUHIN

Zoo Park

POPTOMOV

GEN. PARENSOV

PARCHEVICH

BULGARIA BLVD.

NEOFIT RILSKI

N

EVTIMIJ

Liberty Park

You'll find the main **Balkantourist** office at 37 Dondukov Blvd.; several major hotels also run tourist information desks.

The **U.S. Embassy** is located on Al. Stambolijski 1, just west of Lenin Square in the heart of Sofia (tel. 88-48-01 to 88-48-05). The embassy recommends that U.S. travelers register with them so they can be contacted if an emergency should arise. The embassy also gives out a useful 18-page pamphlet on Sofia which includes advice for U.S. travelers in Bulgaria. Hours are 8 a.m. to 5:30 p.m. weekdays (on Wednesday to 1 p.m.).

The **British Embassy** is located on Al. Marsal Tolbuhin 65 (tel. 87-83-25 or 88-53-61). To get here, take tram 2, 12, 14, 18, or 19 from the city center three stops to Al. M. Tolbuhin. Walk southwest on this road and the embassy is in the middle of the third block from the tram stop.

Citizens of **Canada** use the U.S. Embassy, and all other Commonwealth nationals use the British Embassy.

TRANSPORTATION TO AND FROM SOFIA: You have a number of options for getting to Sofia.

By Air

Several public buses run directly from the airport to the center of town, including buses 84 and 284. For airport information, dial 7-12-01 to 7-12-05.

Balkan Airlines has their international office at 12 Narodno Sobranie Square (tel. 88-44-93 or 88-44-33). For domestic tickets, go to the office at 10 Sofiiska Communa St. (tel. 88-44-36 or 88-13-94).

By Train

Buy international train tickets at the **Rila Railway Bureau,** 5 Gourko St. (tel. 87-07-77).

To get from the train station to town, simply follow the clearly indicated signs to the tram station and take tram 1, 7, or 15 for three stops east across the river to Lenin Square. If you walk, it won't take more than 20 to 25 minutes east and then south along Al. Georgi Dimitrov till you reach Lenin Square.

By Bus

Three main bus terminals serve all of Bulgaria. Buses to Plovdiv, Svilengrad, and Borovice leave from the East Terminal; to get here, take tram 14 from Lenin Square. Buses to Blagoevgrad, Planik, and the Rila Monastery leave from the West Terminal on Deveti Septemvri Street; take tram 5 to get here. The bus terminal on Pirdop Square serves all of northern Bulgaria; take tram 3 to the last stop and then walk in the same direction for about five minutes, past the railroad tracks.

GETTING AROUND: The major sights of Sofia are located in the center of town, but should you need to use public transportation or taxis, you'll find both very inexpensive.

Buses and Trams

All public transportation in Sofia—and throughout Bulgaria—costs 6 stotinki (3¢) per ticket, and each ticket is good for one ride on a bus or tram. Tickets are punched and canceled on the bus or tram; if you transfer you must use another ticket. As in all of Eastern Europe these prices are so low that it's ridiculous to risk a fine by riding without a ticket. Buy all tickets from the small booths located near most major stops. City maps diagram the transport system with buses in red and trams in black. The system begins at 4 a.m. on weekdays and closes at 12:45 a.m. every night. Service is very slow past 10 p.m. or before 5:30 a.m.

Taxis

You can catch a taxi at hotels, train or bus stations, and marked taxi stands. It's difficult to flag down cabs—officially they are only supposed to load and unload passengers at the taxi stands. Prices for taxis are quite reasonable, less than 2 leva ($1.10) for most rides in the city.

ACCOMMODATIONS: You'll find that almost all the hotels listed here are in the city center area. Although there has been a hotel building boom in recent years, it has only added more hotels in the upper price range, and so most hotels in Sofia are quite pricey. The old adage "You get what you pay for" holds especially true in Sofia; some low-budget hotels are so rundown that all Western travelers should avoid them.

One well-maintained hotel that usually has rooms available is the **Hotel Serdika** on Levsky Square (tel. 44-34-11). The summer of 1985 saw this hotel under reconstruction, but things should be cleaned up by now. The rooms are attractive, and have a small shower cubicle. The hotel is on a major thoroughfare and the noise level is quite high. There are no single rooms, only doubles. Single occupancy costs 40 leva ($21.85) per night; add another 3 leva ($1.65) for double occupancy.

A Splurge Choice

We recommend the **Grand Hotel Bulgaria,** situated right in the center of town on 9 Septemvri Square (tel. 87-19-77), as the best deal in town for its style, location, and price. Most of the rooms look out at the Georgi Dimitrov Mausoleum, in full view of the red star atop the Bulgarian Communist Party headquarters! The Grand's elegance of days gone by has faded, but some fine details still remain. The hotel is clean and has recently been renovated; traffic on 9 Septemvri Square is restricted so the rooms are very quiet. A single room costs 59 leva ($32.25), and a double room runs 107 leva ($58.50). All rooms have private bathrooms and the room price includes breakfast. The one possible problem with this hotel is that it's almost always full. Ask. When we stopped in there were a couple of rooms available.

Student Accommodations

In the low-budget range is the excellent **Orbita Student Service,** right off Al. Alexander Stambolijski on ul. Car Samuil 45A (tel. 87-95-52; Telex 22381). Although the Orbita Hotel in Sofia will not be built for another couple of years (1988 maybe), the Orbita office controls several student dorms between July 1 and September 15, and charges only $4 per person per night, double occupancy. If you're traveling alone you probably will have to share a room with a stranger. The Orbita chain is well run and they usually have rooms available. If you plan to do a lot of traveling in Bulgaria it makes sense to stop in with an itinerary and reserve all, or at least some, of your Orbita hotels in advance. The Orbita office is open only on weekdays from 8:15 a.m. to 5:30 p.m.

A Last Resort

The **Hotel Slavijia,** at U. Sofijski geroj 2 (tel. 52-55-51), is listed here in case the hotels in the center of town are booked solid—the Slavijia always has openings. A frequent choice of budget-conscious visitors from the Middle East, the hotel has managed to stay pretty clean despite occasionally rowdy guests. The hotel is located in a quiet neighborhood; from Lenin Square, walk two blocks south and catch tram 5 west for six stops; the hotel is on the left side of the tram. A single room costs 26 leva ($14.20) and a double runs 37 leva ($20.25) per night. All the rooms have a private bath and the room price includes breakfast.

DINING: Sofia offers many excellent budget dining opportunities in local "folk-style" restaurants. Every Bulgarian has his or her own favorite hangout, so if you have friends in Sofia, ask for their suggestions. Regardless of who recommends them, all of these folk-style establishments seem to have several features in common. Located in basements cool even in summer, they seem to be frequented more by urban professional types and couples than anyone else. Most of these establishments also feature some form of live music and dancing.

Local Favorites

Many locals enjoy the **Strandjata,** in the basement of the Church Museum right on Lenin Square, on their spirited evenings out on the town. The Strandjata serves Bulgarian specialties including a very flavorful gyuvech for 1.50 leva (80¢), a meat-and-vegetable stew whose recipe varies from place to place. Unfortunately, noisy reconstruction on Lenin Square has affected the Strandjata adversely. By the time you arrive things should have returned to normal. Open from 10 a.m. to 11 p.m. or midnight every day.

As we headed to the **Tirolska Sreshta Restaurant** at Vitosha 94, we witnessed the installation of the new lion statues in front of the National History Museum. This proved to be a good omen indeed, as we enjoyed some of the best food in Sofia. The sirene po'shopshi for 1.68 leva (90¢), a baked cheese dish, was sublime, and the gyuvech stew was thick, hearty, and filling at 1.50 leva (80¢). Though the Tirolska Sreshta can fill up, it's not quite as hectic as the Strandjata—a pleasant place to sip a little slivovitz (plum brandy). Open from 10 a.m. to 11 p.m.

Overlooking the park across from the Central Army House is the restaurant **Krystal,** at Aksakov 10 (tel. 87-20-85). The interior is pleasantly lit in the evening and the restaurant features some of the better bands in Sofia. The service is attentive and the food is well, if not imaginatively, prepared. Most main dishes won't cost more than $3. The meals we had were filling, but the beef filets were a bit overcooked. Given the price and the music, the Krystal is not a bad choice for dinner.

An Italian Restaurant

The restaurant of choice for the native of Sofia is the Italian restaurant **Rubin,** right on Lenin Square (tel. 87-47-04). One of the favorite places of Bulgarians in the fast lane, the Rubin serves good food with excellent service. Obviously an Italian restaurant in Bulgaria won't be the best Italian restaurant you could visit during your stay in Europe, but it's a pleasant change of pace. It's always full, so make reservations, especially for dinner. The average main course will cost over 10 leva ($5.45), but the pasta is much cheaper.

A Splurge Choice

The **Restaurant Bulgaria,** in the Grand Hotel on 9 Septemvri Square (tel. 87-02-02), offers some of Bulgaria's best food in an impressive split-level dining room with a large dance floor. An extensive menu lists several foreign dishes as well as Bulgarian specialties; the average main dish costs less than $4—

expensive by Bulgarian standards. Though the sheer size of the Bulgaria restaurant prevents it from filling up, the headwaiter does recommend reservations for dinner on the weekends. There's dancing every night. Service is from noon to 3 p.m. and from 6 to 11 p.m.

CAFÉS: Overlooking the park across from the Central Army House is the café **Krystal,** at Aksakov 10 (tel. 87-20-85). Actually a modern concrete-and-glass restaurant/café complex with indoor and outdoor cafés, and a bar and a restaurant upstairs, the Krystal stays open from 10 a.m. to 11 p.m. The outdoor café is located under the overhanging upstairs restaurant and, though not very airy, is quite cool in summer. Close to the theaters, the Krystal is often filled with the evening theater crowd. The café serves ice cream and assorted cakes for about 2 leva ($1.10) a portion.

For those with a persistent sweet tooth, try **Café Magura,** at Vitosha 80 (tel. 51-30-65). Not far from the National History Museum on Al. Vitosha off Lenin Square, it's a good place to stock up on calories before tackling the museum's extensive collection.

SHOPPING: The **Sredets Shop** and the **Souvenir Shop** right next to each other on U. Legue 7/10 are two of Sofia's best souvenir shops. You can buy a variety of tooled leather and wood objects as well as traditional folk costumes. Some interesting and very inexpensive leather and fur clothing can be found in three different stores at U. Slavyanska 4, Al. Ruski 2, and U. Tzar Kaloyan 5.

You'll also find a number of **Corecom** hard-currency shops in town. The one at 8 Tsar Kaloyan St. sells food, alcohol, and cigarettes; another Corecom at 3 A. Zhdanov St. also sells alcohol and cigarettes.

NIGHTLIFE: Sofia is not a center of late-night activity. Even so, the quality and number of contemporary bands is much greater in Bulgaria than in many of the other Eastern European countries, except for Hungary. As locals are friendly and very curious about Westerners, especially Americans, you'll find the residents of Sofia a fun-loving and entertaining lot.

Some interesting things to do include an evening at the **Bulgaria Concert Hall** at 1 Aksakov St., where the Sofia Philharmonic plays.

For other nighttime entertainment, try the two **variety shows** in the Hotels Grand and Moskva Park—not the best we have encountered, but a show can make for an amusing evening. The cover charge is less than $1 and, as expected, the drinks are overpriced.

The disco crowd should try the **Orient** (no, don't head for the airport), at Al. Stambolijski 2 (tel. 88-19-57), a nightclub that has dancing most evenings from 9 p.m. to midnight.

Another good bet if you have a car are some of the folk-style restaurants on the outskirts of town. The **Chernata Kotka** ("Black Cat Inn"), about eight miles southeast of Sofia on Hwy. E80, features authentic Bulgarian dining and a "folk show" most nights with a more elaborate show on the weekends. Balkantourist runs evening tours to this and other restaurants, but we prefer the independent route. Some of the most epic bouts of food and alcohol consumption ever related to us by reputable Bulgarians have allegedly taken place at the Chernata Kotka.

THE SIGHTS: Housed in the former Judicial Building right off Lenin Square, the **National Museum** surprised us with one of the most impressive collections of gold artifacts that we saw in all of Eastern Europe. Important relics from every major site across Bulgaria, including the magnificently carved doors from the Rila Monastery and weapons from Veliko Turnovo, are also on display here. It's a very large museum with a lot to see, and you can easily spend a long afternoon here.

The heart of Sofia—and perhaps all of Bulgaria—is the **Alexander Nevsky Church,** right in the middle of Ruski Boulevard. It is a monument to Russian soldiers who died in the war to free Bulgaria from Turkish domination. Built at the turn of the century, the church was designed by a Russian architect in the style of the grandest churches in Russia. The huge cupola, extensive giltwork, and three massive altars (one done by a Czech, one by a Russian, and one by a Bulgarian artist) contribute to the awe-inspiring sense of sacrifice that the church was built to enshrine. Times may have changed, but the Alexander Nevsky Church embodies a debt that many Bulgarians feel is owed to the Russian people. It's a symbol for one of the fundamental pillars of Bulgarian-Soviet friendship.

Across from the Alexander Nevsky Church is the considerably smaller **Church of St. Sophia.** Originally built in the 6th or 7th century on the site of two smaller Roman churches, under Ottoman rule St. Sophia was converted for a time into a mosque. Much of the remaining church has been reconstructed to repair earthquake damage. Still, you'll see rich mosaics lining the floor and the typical shape of basilicas in the Balkans and Asia Minor, a symmetrical cross with a dome above.

Perhaps the most interesting Roman relic in Sofia is the **Church of St. George.** A Roman bathhouse in the 3rd and 4th centuries A.D., the structure was converted into a church centuries later. Today you'll admire several frescos from the 11th and 12th centuries. As if the structure had not been altered enough times, in the 15th century St. George was made into a mosque, only to be changed into a church again. In front of the church you'll see the remains of a Roman street.

Museum Hopping

Museum hopping is particularly easy in Sofia as almost all museums are located between Lenin Square and Boulevard Ruski along 9 Septemvri Square.

On 9 Septemvri Square you'll find the **National Archeological Museum,** located in the former Great Mosque from the 15th century. Four sections detail Bulgarian events from prehistoric times to the Middle Ages. Of particular interest is the gold treasure of Vulchi Trun, a masterpiece of Thracian workmanship on 13 vessels of gold. The museum is open from 10 a.m. to 5 p.m.; closed Monday and Tuesday.

One block down from the Archeological Museum is the **Georgi Dimitrov Mausoleum.** A memorial to the Bulgarian Communist leader who rose to prominence in the Reichstag Fire Trials in 1933 and died in 1949, the structure contains Dimitrov's embalmed body. Every hour a small changing-of-the-guard ceremony takes place in front of the mausoleum. During important socialist holidays, Bulgarian party leaders review parades from the top of the mausoleum.

Across the street, art buffs may want to see the **National Art Gallery.** Bulgarian art from the National Revival period of the 18th century—the first real expression of Bulgarian art in 500 years—highlights the collection. It's open from 10:30 a.m. to 6:30 p.m.; closed Tuesday.

Housed with the National Art Gallery in the former Royal Palace is the **Ethnographical Museum.** The collection displays typical Bulgarian folk costumes, national art and architecture, and social and cultural trends in Bulgarian society. Open from 9 a.m. to 5:30 p.m.; closed Monday and Tuesday.

Farther down the road at Boulevard Ruski 14 we come to the **Museum of the Revolutionary Movement in Bulgaria.** Students of history will be interested in the photographs and historic documents that show how Bulgarians view their socialist struggle. It's open from 9:30 a.m. to 6:30 p.m.; closed Monday and Tuesday.

Two other museums nicely complement the Revolutionary Museum; the **Central Army Museum,** at 23 Boulevard Skobelev, and the Museum of Bulgarian-Soviet Friendship, at 4 Boulevard Klement Gottwald. The army museum houses Bulgarian weapons, uniforms, and other military paraphernalia from the wars for liberation from the Turks in the 19th century and from the fascists in World War II. The Army Museum is open from 9:30 a.m. to 7 p.m.; closed Monday and Tuesday.

The **Museum of Bulgarian-Soviet Friendship** contains three sections which, according to one Bulgarian guide, detail "the revolutionary roots of the friendship, the impact of the Russian Revolution on Bulgaria," and the development of socialism in Bulgaria. It's open from 9:15 a.m. to 6:30 p.m. weekdays only.

If these museums only whet your appetite for more socialist museums, you can choose between the Soviet Army Memorial, the Monument and Ossuary to the Soviet Soldiers, and several other possibilities.

Outside Town

Just six miles from the center of Sofia lies the small **Boyana Church.** In a small village at the foot of Mount Vitosha, this 13th-century church contains some of the most notable examples of Bulgarian medieval art. The wall murals have unusually lifelike faces for medieval art, as they were based on actual people in the 13th century. This technique of realism predated similar developments in the Italian Renaissance by a century.

2. The Rila Monastery

The Bulgarians say that the Rila Monastery, one of Bulgaria's most important historical monuments, is as old as Bulgarian Christianity, and they cannot imagine one without the other. Founded on the site where John of Rila (Ivan Rilski) lived and prayed, the monastery was well established by the 10th century. At the time of the first Bulgarian kingdom it was an acknowledged center of learning and church power. The Ottoman Turk invasion in the 14th century did not initially affect the Rila Monastery. Thanks to the monastery's quasi-independence during Turkish rule (the fantastically ornamented documents sent by the pasha are still at Rila) the monastery is well preserved. Despite a mid-15th-century attack during the reign of the still-hated Sultan Murad II that laid waste most of the surrounding countryside, much of the monastery standing today is from the 14th century. The last of the resident monks left in the early 1960s, so now Rila just serves as one of Bulgaria's largest tourist attractions.

High in the Rila Mountains (3,785 feet), the monastery looks more like a fortress than a church from the outside. Monasteries were usually protected with fortifications as the wealth of the monastery attracted bandits, and in those days the preferred method of settling arguments was often with a sword. The whole complex was given a thorough reworking during the National Revival period in the 19th century, as evidenced by the incredible woodwork across the monastery. The **Tower of Hrelyu,** over 40 feet high, dominates the monastery and contains a small chapel decorated with 14th-century frescoes. The **monastery church,** with its five domes, was entirely redone in the spirit of the National Revival, and is covered inside and out with a fantastic array of frescos. The four ceremonial guest rooms are also lavishly decorated and each is named after the town that donated the funds: Koprivshtitsa, Teteven, Samokov, and Chirpan.

The **library** of the Rila Monastery has 134 manuscripts dating from the 10th through the 19th centuries.

The **Historical Museum** at Rila features a valuable collection of jewelry, coins, and weapons, as well as a silver bishop's throne. One of the centerpieces of the collection is the original monastery charter granted by the last king of the Second Bulgarian Kingdom in 1378. Written on leather in Old Bulgarian, the document carries the signature of the king and his gold seal. Probably one of the most spectacularly carved wooden objects ever made, the famous **Rila Cross** is alone worth the trip. The cross is not more than 16 inches high yet it contains 140 biblical scenes with over 1,500 human figures, each no larger than a grain of rice. The cross took the Monk Raphael over 12 years to carve; the strain on his eyes caused him excruciating pain and eventually blinded him.

The Rila Monastery is located in some of Bulgaria's most beautiful mountain terrain and is a good starting point for hikes. Ask in the monastery gift shop for maps of the area. You should be able to find someone at the monastery who speaks English who can answer questions and may even be hired as a tour guide.

GETTING THERE: Unless you have a car, the visit to the Rila Monastery is a very long one-day excursion from Sofia. The monastery is about 85 miles south of Sofia in the Rila Mountains. To get there, take the Sofia–Athens highway to the town of Kocherinovo, and then continue up a well-marked winding road for about another 18 miles.

There's a bus from Sofia that leaves from the Western Bus Terminal; a round-trip ticket costs less than 3 leva ($1.65). Be certain to ask the driver when he/she is going to return lest you miss the bus. Hitchhiking to Kocherinovo is a possibility, but traffic from there up the valley is exceedingly sparse.

FOOD AND LODGING: There are two **campsites** near the monastery, the Bor and the Rila; both are open all summer. The bathing facilities are somewhat limited and in the high season they can get crowded.

The **Druzhba ("Friendship") Restaurant** is probably the most common name for any establishment in Bulgaria, but in Rila the Druzhba is the best bet for lunch. Tourists and pilgrims rub elbows with the local farmers at the often-crowded Druzhba; a lot of spirit flows—both liquid and otherwise. We recommend the famous Rila bone soup and the mixed grill platter; both can be had for less than $2.

3. Veliko Turnovo

Capital of Bulgaria during the greatest years of the Bulgarian empire, Veliko Turnovo has had 600 years to adjust to its status as a beautiful, quiet provincial town. Situated on three hills, Veliko Turnovo's charming 19th-century streets wind back and forth up the mountainside. The National Revival–style buildings of Veliko Turnovo are older and more beautiful as you ascend the hills.

GETTING THERE: The central Veliko Turnovo station is not on Bulgaria's main train route and involves changing trains. When you arrive at the Veliko Turnovo station, take bus 4, 6, or 8 *south* (seemingly away from the city), or *right* as you exit the train station, for five stops. As with all other local buses in Bulgaria, the bus costs only 6 stotinki (3¢).

If you're coming from Romania, take the train to Gorna Orechovitza on the primary international route. Go out the main entrance at Gorna Orechovitza and walk straight ahead; keep to the right past a small market to the first main road that you intersect—not more than a five- to ten-minute walk. To your right is the bus stop where you buy your ticket; it's 50 stotinki (27¢). Take bus 10, marked in Cyrillic "V. Turnovo," to the last stop, about a 15- to 20-minute ride; don't get off until after you climb up a long hill and enter a clearly metropolitan area.

Veliko Turnovo is serviced by narrow but adequate roads and is approximately in the center of Bulgaria. Because of the hilly terrain there is only one north-south highway that runs through the town. Parking is sometimes a difficulty, so either park by the 16-story Hotel Etur on Ivailo Street or at the train station and take the bus into town.

There is no commercial airport in the area.

ORIENTATION: The early Bulgars who founded Veliko Turnovo chose a well-protected site for the castle and town walls, on a point of land that is almost entirely surrounded by the steep cliffs bordering the **Yantru River.** The rest of Veliko Turnovo has expanded west from the Old City as best it could, and spreads over what little flat valley bottom there is.

You can think of the town as a sideways "S" if you put north at the top of the page. The main commercial district is in the westernmost side of the "S," followed, as you move east, by the main park, more restaurants, the older part of town, and finally the fortifications. This description is not all-inclusive as Veliko Turnovo has monuments from various historical periods in more than one area. The main street is **Vasil Levski,** which turns into **Georgi Dimitrov;** then for a short distance it becomes **Dimitir Blagoev,** and finally **Ivan Vazov.** As confusing as its name changes may seem, the street is one of the few that buses can navigate, so it's not difficult to find.

At **Balkantourist,** located just off Memorial Square, as of this writing no one speaks English and no maps are available.

For city maps (in Cyrillic for 33 stotinki, or 18¢), head for the tourist shop in the lobby of the **Hotel Etur** on Ivailo Street. The staff at the desk at the Hotel Etur is much better prepared to help tourists, though their English is extremely limited. Ask here about any tours of the city.

GETTING AROUND: In Veliko Turnovo getting around is simple: walk. There's no real need to take a bus or taxi anywhere as the town is so small. If you think you can't make it up or down the hill, take any bus along the main street. The buses run from 6 a.m. to 10 p.m. Cabs are almost nonexistent—there's no need for them. If you must have one, ask your receptionist or the desk at the Hotel Etur to call one for you.

ACCOMMODATIONS: The best buy in town is the new 16-story **Etur Hotel** at ul. Ivailo 2 (tel. 2-16-17). There's almost always a room available here: singles with a private shower cost $13, and doubles with private bath are under $30. The reception staff is friendly and helpful, but no one speaks much English. The manager, who does speak some English, is in during business hours, though he may be difficult to find. The views from the hotel, especially on the upper floors, can't be beat, and you can also flag down a passing night breeze.

Private Rooms

The small glass-enclosed office on Dimitir Blagoev Street right on the small square of the same name—on the lateral "S" about midway on the right (eastern) curve—operates a private-room service, open weekdays from 2 to 9 p.m. They should be able to find you a place for less than $6 per person per night.

Although the **Orbita Youth Complex** at 15 Hristo Botev St. is often full, many people in Veliko Turnovo offer private rooms of their own. This is okay if you are only staying one night; but be certain in any case to register with the police. The people who are most likely to have something to offer are older people living on a pension or student types living on a stipend. Simply ask where you can find a *soba* (room); prices should not be more than 8 leva ($4.35) to 10 leva ($5.45).

DINING: There are several good places to eat in Veliko Turnovo, none of which will seriously threaten the budget of even the poorest traveler.

Our favorite spot in Veliko Turnovo is the **Balkan Restaurant,** on Dimitir Blagoev Street. Done in what can only be described as parasol-pink, the restaurant features a very small terrace with an excellent view out over the city and the river valley. The food is excellent and the beer is cold. Try the mixed grill for 5 leva ($2.75), which comes with small cutlets and shashlik or shish kebab.

At the restaurant **Rodina** at 17 Dimitrov St., not far up the hill from the center of town, you can eat very well for less than $3 per person. It's open from 6 a.m. to 9 p.m.

A good splurge choice is the restaurant in the Hotel Etur. Though unremarkably furnished, the Etur offers excellent lamb steak or kebabs for less than $5 per person. Open from 6 a.m. till 10 p.m.; there is music and dancing most evenings from 8 p.m.

THE SIGHTS: Veliko Turnovo is one of the most important historical and archeological sites in all of Bulgaria. Principally known for the **fortifications** and building done while the city was capital of the Second Bulgarian Kingdom (1185–1396), the city also has extensive ruins dating from much earlier, as well as a wealth of medieval and baroque buildings.

The most famous and the oldest of the fortifications is the **Tzarevetz,** or Castle of the Tzar; today the impressive battlements and numerous ramparts and gates are under extensive (if not excessive) reconstruction. The ruins you see have already been built up from rather vague foundations and there seems to be no intention of halting the restoration work. There are some really impressive panoramas here, and the site rivals any defensive positioning anywhere in the world. When the fortifications were intact, the only access was across a narrow ridge and over a drawbridge. The tallest restored tower is named after Baldwin of Flanders, a Crusader who was imprisoned and died here after his capture in 1205. A second important defensive ridge in Veliko Turnovo is the **Trapezitza,** from which you can see ruins of palaces and chapels of the boyars, the Bulgarian nobility.

Veliko Turnovo was the capital of Bulgaria and its fall in 1393 to the Ottoman Turks marked the beginning of almost 500 years of subjugation. One cannot view these fortifications and the broad expanse of the river-valley cliffs without immediately noticing the immense difficulties any attacker would have faced. The Ottoman Turk siege in 1393 was a brutal one, and after its capture, Veliko Turnovo was burnt to the ground.

Veliko Turnovo has a long history of opposition to foreign invaders besides the 1393 fight against the Turks. In the Church of St. Dimitur the brothers Piotr and Assen began a successful insurrection against the Byzantine Empire in 1185; only a fragment of the church remains. As you wander about the town you'll see numerous plaques commemorating the victims of some failed uprising.

Although Veliko Turnovo was seriously damaged in an earthquake in 1913, fortunately many of its beautiful Bulgarian National Revival houses survived. One of the most beautiful, the **Nikoli Han** building, is now a museum, aptly of the National Revival, open from 9 a.m. to 4 p.m.; closed Monday.

SHOPPING: Veliko Turnovo is a great place to pick up some wonderful souvenirs, especially along picturesque Georgi Sava Ranovski Street, which is lined with fantastic 18th- and 19th-century homes. The charming narrow old streets that wind upward from Georgi Sava Ranovski boast several interesting shops. Travelers who aren't too concerned about weight restrictions should look at the store selling copper and iron cooking utensils as well as pottery. The shop is open from 9 a.m. to 7 p.m., with a lunch break between noon and 2 p.m. There are small items and trinkets from 5 leva ($2.75) to large copper platters for 60 leva ($32.90). Next to the metal shop are several others selling wood, glass, and some excellent woven items, utensils, statues, plates, and more. These stores are generally open from 8:30 a.m. to 6 p.m., with a lunch break from noon to 1 p.m.

4. Plovdiv

At first glance Plovdiv seems like an unlikely tourist destination. As you drive into Bulgaria's second-largest city (pop. 300,000), you pass modern socialist housing complexes galore. However, once you reach the heart of the Old Town you'll come upon one of Bulgaria's most romantic old quarters, built in the National Revival style of the 18th and 19th centuries. In this old part of town, called Trimontium (Three Hills), cobblestone streets free of cars wind up the three hills. Lining the streets are Bulgarian homes of the 19th century with their typical second floor overhanging the street.

The pace in Trimontium is so slow and relaxed, and the beauty so unspoiled, that you might forget you're in Bulgaria's second-largest city! In addition to this charming glimpse of 19th-century Bulgarian life, Plovdiv offers visitors two museums with Thracian pieces from 4000 B.C., as well as Roman ruins around town.

ORIENTATION: The **Marica River** divides Plovdiv into a modern section to the north and the historic section to the south. **Georgi Dimitrov** is a major avenue which connects the two sections across a bridge. On the south side of town, **Trimontium** lies to the east of Dimitrov Avenue, or to your right when facing the river. You'll notice that Trimontium really is located on three green hills, so you'll have to hike up to find Plovdiv's most charming section. Two blocks parallel to Dimitrov Avenue to the west lies **Vasil Kolarov** Street, the town's main shopping mall and promenade, which is usually crowded, especially in the evening.

Balkantourist has an office for foreigners at 34 Moskva Blvd. (tel. 5-28-07), across the Marica River from the Old Town. They have maps and information on Plovdiv, but they only rent private rooms during Plovdiv's trade fairs in May and October. The office is open from 7 a.m. to 9 p.m. Since it's far from the train station, you should try to find a hotel before going to Balkantourist.

ACCOMMODATIONS: The **Hotel Leipzig**, Blvd. Ruski 70 (tel. 3-24-70), just a ten-minute walk to Trimontium, has small rooms with tiny bathrooms in a typical modern style. Singles with bathroom cost 22.80 leva ($12.45), and similar doubles run 33 leva ($18.05). The room price includes breakfast. To get here from the train station, walk straight ahead two blocks. A fair number of European visitors to Plovdiv stay at the Hotel Leipzig.

The **Hotel Bulgaria**, Blvd. Patriarch Evtimij 13 (tel. 2-60-64), built in a 1950s modern style, is today slightly rundown. Centrally located at the beginning of Plovdiv's main shopping street, the Hotel Bulgaria charges 28.96 leva ($15.85) for singles with bathroom and 20.18 leva ($11.05) per person for similar doubles.

DINING: In Trimontium you'll come across a number of charming old-style restaurants. At **Trakiyski Stan,** 9 Puldin St. (tel. 2-45-10), we enjoyed some of the best food we sampled in all of Bulgaria. At this appealing establishment you can dine in one of several different outdoor areas framed by wooden walls. The best seats of the house are on a small narrow balcony romantically overlooking Trimontium; as you dine here, you may be amused to see the waiter cautiously making his way in the limited space between the table and the wall. The food at Trakiyski Stan is excellent, featuring tender meat in tangy sauces, all at moderate prices (just a few dollars each), and the service is efficient. A charming extra here is the piano and violin music in the evening. Try to reserve.

Puldin, 3 Kniaz-Tseretelev St. (tel. 3-17-20), is another good restaurant in Trimontium with an ornate, almost Arabic decor. As you walk in, you first pass an enclosed area with a fountain in the middle before you enter a bar with small, low wooden tables. To one side is a disco (open 8 to 11 p.m.) that looks like a mosque with its tall ceiling and hanging copper lamps. Also off the central bar is an outdoor courtyard for dining, and a small indoor room with a peaceful view of Trimontium. Medium-priced ($3 to $5), typical Bulgarian veal and pork specialties are served, and there's a menu in English. It's open from 10 a.m. to 11 p.m. Try to reserve; a lot of groups come to Puldin.

If all you want is a quick snack, you can find tasty **pizza** at 20 Rajko Daskalov. A small pizza costs 84 stotinki (45¢).

IMPORTANT ADDRESSES: For train tickets, go to the **Rila Bureau of Voyage** at 47 Vasil Kolarov St. International train tickets are sold from 8 a.m. to 12:30 p.m. and 1 to 4 p.m. Monday through Friday, from 1 to 4 p.m. on Saturday. For domestic tickets it's open from 7:30 a.m. to 7 p.m. Monday through Friday. One woman who works at the international ticket counter speaks excellent, almost flawless idiomatic English; as a child, she lived in Washington, D.C. when her father worked in the embassy there.

The **post office and telephone bureau** is located off Dimitrov Boulevard at the start of Kolarov Street.

For **dry cleaning,** go to Dimitrov 30 (tel. 5-18-40), across the river from the center. A sign outside reads in English "same-day cleaning." It costs 1.50 leva (82¢) to clean a pair of trousers. Open from 7 a.m. to 7 p.m.

The **Bulgarian Airlines** office is at 4 Dimitrov St. (tel. 2-20-03 or 3-30-81). For a **taxi,** call 5-27-36.

THE SIGHTS: You should start your sightseeing by wandering in the **Trimontium** area up the hill from Georgi Dimitrov Street. In what is certainly the town's most interesting section, you'll see typical houses and neighborhoods of 18th- and 19th-century Bulgaria. As we mentioned earlier the distinctive feature of 18th- and 19th-century Bulgarian architecture is the projection of the second floor over the first. On the first floor you'll observe large old stones cemented together, and on the second, painted stucco façades in such colors as pale yellow or dark gray. On the houses of the more affluent, ornate patterns or decorations adorn the second floor. By allowing the second floor eaves to overhang, the Bulgarians were able to construct more living space on narrow streets.

Other sights in Plovdiv include the **Archeological Museum,** 1 Suedinenic Square, which displays an interesting collection including gold masterpieces dating back to the 3rd century B.C. The star attraction is the Panagurishte gold treasure, a wine set from the 3rd century B.C. illustrating scenes from Greek mythology.

The **Ethnographic Museum,** at 2 Doctor Tchomakov, housed in an ornate home dating from 1847, displays mostly 18th- and 19th-century Bulgarian National Revival art, although there are a few older pieces here as well.

You'll find a similar collection at the **Museum of the National Revival and the National Liberation Struggles,** on Lavrenov Street in Trimontium. Here you'll see displays on National Revival art as well as on the struggles for freedom from that period up to the Balkan War in 1912.

In 1833 the French Romantic poet Lamartine stopped in Plovdiv for a few days en route from the Far East. In commemoration of his stay, the Bulgarians have opened a **Lamartine Museum** at 19 Knyaz Tsretelev in Trimontium. The Bulgarians are particularly proud of his mention of this Balkan country in his book *Travel to the East,* and so have endowed the museum with articles and photographs on Lamartine.

Those interested in ancient Roman history should consider visiting the ancient **Theater of Philippopolis** at Djoumaya Square, near the entrance to the Georgi Dimitrov tunnel. Roman buffs will enjoy these well-preserved remains of a 2nd-century marble theater built during the rule of the Roman Empire. Another Roman amphitheater is on the 19th of November Square in Trimontium.

Chapter XXVI

BULGARIA'S BLACK SEA COAST

**1. Varna
2. North of Varna
3. South from Varna to Burgas
4. Sozopol, Duni, and the South Coast**

ONE OF THE MOST PLEASANT surprises in researching this guide came in discovering the Bulgarian Black Sea coast. We had often heard Eastern Europeans extoll the virtues of Bulgaria's eastern coast, but we remained skeptical—until we arrived in Bulgaria. Lo and behold, we discovered a long stretch of sand complete with mountains majestically rising behind the shore! White stucco houses with red-tile roofs stand out on the hills overlooking clean aquamarine-colored water that gradually blends into a dark blue out at sea.

Bulgaria's coast offers not just good beaches, but also tourist facilities at excellent budget prices. In fact, if you follow some of the budget tips offered in this chapter, your visit to the Bulgarian coast could well be the least expensive, as well as one of the more memorable, summer holidays at the sea that you may ever enjoy.

You can think of Bulgaria's coast as divided into two parts: resorts and typical Bulgarian towns. Since World War II the Bulgarian government has invested heavily in seacoast resorts, building up dozens of modern hotels at a time in select areas. You'll find thousands of visitors, mostly Eastern Europeans, at these large resorts, as well as many restaurants, sports facilities, and other tourist amenities. Sports available include waterskiing, tennis, billiards, volleyball, parasailing, and bicycling.

Today resort towns make up about 20% of the Bulgarian coast. Some of Bulgaria's most popular modern resorts are Albena, Golden Sands (Zlatni Pyassutsi), and Sunny Beach (Slunchev Bryag). If one of them appeals to you, we suggest booking a package hotel plan, for the savings can be substantial. For instance, Balkan Holidays Limited offers a round-trip flight from London to Varna, a week's hotel, and full board for a very reasonable $210 to $400, depending on the time of year. Two-week packages cost $250 to $500. You can pick up their pamphlet "Balkan Summer '87 [or '88] Holidays" at any Balkantourist office, or you can write to **Balkan Holidays Limited,** Sofia House, 19 Conduit St., London W1R 9TD England (tel. 01/491-4499; Telex 262923).

Bulgaria's coast also offers many peaceful undeveloped areas where small towns exist as they did before World War II. In a number of these villages, fishermen still take their boats out to sea in the early morning, and in the afternoon you can see them at the docks untangling knots from their nets. We generally prefer these quieter, typical villages to Bulgaria's largest resorts because these are unique to Bulgaria—large beach resort towns can be found the world over.

Some of Bulgaria's seacoast towns contain great riches in Bulgarian art. For example, Nesebar provides a glimpse of magnificent Bulgarian medieval churches and 19th-century domestic architecture. Varna offers a collection of museums with pieces dating back to the ancient Greek colonization. Other towns such as Balchik show the coast at its most charming, with an easy pace of life rarely encountered in the West.

OUR FAVORITE BEACHES: Although locals debate Bulgaria's most attractive beaches, we prefer the northern third of the coast above Varna. In this area the cliffs are the most dramatic and the waters seem to be the clearest. At the same time the area to the south holds out a special appeal for adventuresome travelers seeking undeveloped beaches and rocky coves where few other visitors are seen.

We strongly recommend three beaches in particular, which feature both modern facilities at budget prices, and a relaxed, uncrowded atmosphere: Club Med at Roussalka in the northern third of the coast, Holiday Village Elenite in the central part of the coast, and Holiday Village Duni in the southern third of Bulgaria's coast. Each of these is detailed in the subsequent sections of this chapter.

WHEN TO COME: The best time to visit the Black Sea coast is in June and September. During this time splendid sunny weather prevails with temperatures averaging in the mid 70s, yet the crowds are about half of the July and August levels. During July and August Bulgaria's coast becomes the playground for all of Eastern Europe and the Soviet Union. It's best to avoid this high season, but even then, the enterprising traveler can find a quiet beach outside the major resorts. May and October are often quite pleasant as well, with temperatures averaging in the mid 60s to 70°F.

HOW TO GET THERE: If you're already in Bulgaria, the easiest way to reach the Black Sea coast is to fly to Varna from Sofia. The flight takes 40 minutes and costs 68 leva ($37.20) round trip. Contact BalkanAir at 10 Sofiiska Communa St. (tel. 88-44-36 or 88-13-94) in Sofia.

The train ride for this 469-km (282-mile) route is less expensive, but it takes eight to ten hours.

If you want to fly directly via charter from London, contact Balkan Holidays Limited, Sofia House, 19 Conduit St., London W1R 9TD, England (tel. 01/491-4499; Telex 262923).

TRANSPORTATION ALONG THE COAST: The easiest and most economical way to get around the coast is by **bus**, since frequent service connects the major coastal cities in summer. Whenever you plan to travel by bus, buy your tickets as far in advance as you can (a day or two before). At the very minimum, arrive 30 minutes before departure time to get your ticket. Lines are often long and buses fill up quickly.

The Kometa line also operates **hydrofoils** that stop at Varna, Nesebar, Burgas, Pomorie, Sozopol, and Primorsko near the Turkish border. Tickets go on sale one hour before departure (remember to bring your passport); ticket windows close 15 minutes prior to departure. The fares are low: for example, the ride from Varna to Nesebar costs only 5.50 leva ($3), not including a slight charge for luggage. Although the hydrofoils run less frequently than the buses, they are a fun alternative.

Finally, a **train** runs between Varna and Burgas to the south, taking about an hour to an hour and a half. As the line veers inland after both Varna and Burgas, the train is not an option for other towns along the coast.

1. Varna

Travelers to the Black Sea coast are likely to begin their visit in Varna (pop. 250,000), a lively modern port town which has been an important trade center for thousands of years. It was first inhabited around 600 B.C. by Greek settlers who called it Odessos; later the Romans took over and commanded much of their regional trade from this port. In the early Middle Ages, under Bulgarian rule, Varna handled much of Bulgaria's foreign trade to Constantinople, Venice, and Dubrovnik. In A.D. 1393 Varna was captured by the Turks; they used the port as a major military installation for hundreds of years.

Today Varna is a much-frequented destination both for its rich history and for its excellent transportation connections to the rest of the Black Sea coast. The city's museums, including the Archeological Museum and the Naval Museum, display many relics from Varna's long history. Other monuments in town include the Roman public baths from antiquity. Aside from its tourist sights, Varna offers a lively holiday resort atmosphere, bustling with visitors from Eastern and Western Europe. A modern shopping mall runs through the center of town, and when it's full with vacationers, you'll see Bulgaria at its most cosmopolitan.

We recommend that travelers visiting the coast at a leisurely pace spend a day sightseeing in Varna. Those anxious to move right on to the Black Sea coast's finest beaches should quickly pass through, however, as a modern port town can only offer crowded and less than pristine beaches.

ORIENTATION: The streets in the center of old Varna resemble a haphazardly prepared mosaic, but thanks to a number of large avenues framing this mosaic of streets it's possible to orient yourself without too much trouble. The city borders the Black Sea, and near the port lie the train and boat stations. **Chervenoarmejski Boulevard** runs along the port in the center of town. If you walk about a dozen blocks down Chervenoarmejski Boulevard from the train station, you'll come to **Dimitrov Boulevard,** a wide pedestrian avenue perpendicular to the sea. Follow Dimitrov Boulevard for four blocks; a mall continues to the left on **Lenin Boulevard.** Varna's major museums, hotels, tourist agencies, and stores are all situated on and around these three major avenues.

Getting into Town

If you arrive at Varna's airport, west of the city, take bus 15 to the center. It costs 10 stotinki (5¢) and takes 20 to 25 minutes.

If you roll into the train station at Slavejkov Square (just off the Varna port), walk for about ten minutes down Vapcarov Street, past Slavejkov Square after you exit from the station (ask to make sure you're on the right street). After two blocks, Vapcarov veers slightly to the left; continue walking along this street to reach Lenin Boulevard.

While you're on Vapcarov Street before you come to Lenin Boulevard you'll see the **Balkantourist** office for foreigners at 3 Moussallah St. (tel. 2-55-24 or 2-08-07). In addition to providing information on Varna, this office can find you a private room for only 3.60 leva ($1.95) per person. From about July 20 to August 20 these rooms usually fill up, so you might want to write or call ahead for this period. Balkantourist can also reserve hotel rooms in other cities on the Black Sea coast. The office is open from 7:30 a.m. to 1 p.m. seven days a week in summer and 8 a.m. to 7 p.m. in winter.

Important Addresses

The **Balkan Airlines** office is at 15 Lenin Blvd. (tel. 2-29-48). For flight arrival and departure information, you can also call the airport at 42-32. If you're going westward by train, there are several places to buy tickets: go to 3 Shipska St. (tel. 2-62-73) for international railway tickets, and to 27 Juli Street, no. 13 (tel. 2-11-37) for domestic tickets. For general information, call the railroad station at 2-25-51.

For information on transportation up and down the coast, refer to the "Transportation Along the Coast" section at the beginning of this chapter.

ACCOMMODATIONS: Surprisingly for a large modern town, Varna offers only four hotels, one of which is an expensive deluxe choice. If the following picks don't appeal to you, consider finding a hotel in a nearby resort town and visiting Varna on a day trip.

For our money, the best choice in town is the **Hotel Orbita,** 25 Vasil Kolarov Blvd. (tel. 2-51-62). Run by the country's student organization, Orbita, the hotel accepts all travelers. Attractive rooms with private bathroom in a modern building are 24.60 leva ($13.45). Students with the Eastern European IUS card may also get some reduction on this price. The Hotel Orbita is located about ten minutes away from Lenin and Dimitrov Boulevards.

Hotel Odessa, 1 Georgi Dimitrov Blvd. (tel. 2-53-12 or 2-83-81), is a standard "B" category hotel built just two minutes from the beach. The receptionist sits isolated behind a long glass window and greets guests through slots in the glass; this description should give you some idea of the measure of friendliness you can expect from the staff. The staff aside, you may meet some interesting people at the Odessa; many of the guests are Russian. Singles with bathrooms are about $20, and doubles run $30. You'll find a restaurant and coffeeshop downstairs off the lobby.

A Starvation-Budget Pick

Next door to the central Balkantourist office for foreigners is the **Hotel Moussallah,** 3 Moussallah St. (tel. 2-39-25), a very basic, rather rundown hotel with singles for 8.50 leva ($4.65) and doubles for 6.50 leva ($3.55) per person. As the public bathrooms are poorly maintained, we recommend this hotel only as a last resort. It must be said, however, that the location, just off Lenin Boulevard and ten minutes from the train and port station, is excellent.

DINING: Situated in Varna's Primorski Park right off the beach north of the old town, the **Restaurant Horizont** (tel. 8-25-33) offers some of Varna's best fare. The restaurant is divided into two rooms, one an attractive patio with large windows overlooking the park and sea. The gregarious staff at the Horizont is especially well disposed to Americans; when we visited, they all assembled to ask questions and observe their unique Western visitors. The menu features a wide variety of Bulgarian food, including pork goulash for 3.21 leva ($1.75), veal hunter's style for 3.23 leva ($1.77), and a tasty mixed grill Horizont, with pork, meatballs, potatoes, vegetables, and spices, for 5.12 leva ($2.80). It's open from 6 a.m. to 11 p.m. daily; reserve if you're coming after 7 p.m. Luckily, you'll find a menu with English translations here.

Varna's largest hotel, **Cherno More,** at 35 Georgi Dimitrov (tel. 3-50-66 or 3-40-88), offers good fare in a large modern dining room on the second floor. The long restaurant has a stage where a band plays in the evening. A wide variety of guests frequent the Cherno More: when we visited, we saw some Soviet athletes, an English tour group, and two African exchange students, one of whom had also lived for a while in Washington, D.C. A large selection of Bulgarian and international specialties features fish, steak, veal, pork, and lamb dishes at a cost of 3.65 leva ($2) to 6.57 leva ($3.60).

THE SIGHTS: Varna's most interesting sight is the **Archeological Museum,** at 5 Sheinovo St. off Lenin Boulevard. More than 40,000 archeological objects highlight the settlements in Varna from the earliest inhabitants in the Paleolithic era until the end of Ottoman Turkish rule in the 19th century. One room also displays coins.

Since Rome once administered Varna, it's only logical that Varna should be host to the **Roman Public Baths,** 15 Chervenoarmejski Blvd. These remains, dating back to the 3rd and 4th centuries A.D., will give you an idea of the central role public baths played in the Roman era.

Because of Turkish rule, the influence of the Renaissance appeared rather late in Bulgaria, but when it finally did come, it produced some interesting architecture, writing, and art, as the **Museum of the Bulgarian Renaissance,** 27 Juli no. 9, testifies. On display are old textbooks, newspapers, journals, and documents. The museum itself is housed in a typical construction of the Bulgarian Renaissance style (also known as the "National Revival") from 1861.

Another popular museum in town is the **Naval Museum,** at 2 Chervenoarmejsky Blvd. right off the shore. The naval forces of Varna from ancient to modern times, both merchant and military, are displayed. The Bulgarians are particularly proud of one exhibit, the hull of the *Druzky* (the *Intrepid*), a mine-layer that blew up a Turkish ship in 1912.

Especially if you won't have the opportunity to visit the Revolutionary Museum in Sofia, you'll get a good sense of the Bulgarian revolutionary fervor from the **Museum of the Workers' Revolutionary Movement,** November 8 Street no. 5. A natural complement to this museum is the **Memorial to Those Who Fell in the Struggle Against Fascism and Capitalism,** in Primorski Park.

Sights Outside Varna

About ten miles away from Varna are the remains of the **Aladzha Monastery,** carved into a rock mountain in the 13th century. Little is left of the original monastery, for the outside walls have collapsed. Nonetheless, it's still fascinating to see this structure painstakingly carved into solid rock by devoted monks, the only such site in Bulgaria. Outside the monastery you can also look at some medieval prints in a small museum.

2. North of Varna

From Varna, most sun lovers will want to move north to an area that combines Bulgaria's most beautiful beaches with modern facilities.

ZLATNI PYASSUTSI (GOLDEN SANDS): After a 30-minute bus ride to the north of Varna we come to the largest and most popular resort town in the northern half of the coast, Zlatni Pyassutsi (Golden Sands). The beach here is some two miles long; the shoreline boasts some 67 hotels, enough to accommodate almost 15,000 visitors, as well as dozens of restaurants. For our tastes, it's too crowded, but it does offer good sports and recreation facilities. If you'd like to spend time in this active resort, your best bet is to reserve a one-week package ahead of time, as you'll save considerably on the hotel rate.

Accommodations

Those arriving in town without prearranged accommodations should drop by the **Balkantourist** accommodation office (tel. 6-57-88); as most of the streets here have no visible name, this office, located just a block from the beach, has no formal address, so ask for directions. It's open from 7:30 a.m. to 10 p.m. They arrange *all* hotel bookings in Golden Sands. If you go straight to a hotel, you'll be sent back to Balkantourist.

Dining

Golden Sands boasts one of the coast's best restaurants—the **Vodenitsata** ("The Watermill"), on a street with no name next to the Diana Hotel (tel. 85-53-77). Tables are spread out in two garden areas of this romantic outdoor restaurant (the tables in the back garden overlook a functioning wooden watermill). For dining in inclement weather, you can also eat inside on rustic tables beside a fireplace in an old stone building. The moderately priced specialties (for just a few dollars each) include delicious chicken on a skewer and grilled game sausages. You'll find an appealing atmosphere with very good regional specialties. In fact, we like this restaurant so much that we suggest that visitors to the north coast stop in even if they're just passing through town.

ALBENA: Quite different in atmosphere from Golden Sands, Albena, our favorite of Bulgaria's modern resort towns, is just 18 miles north of Varna (but almost an hour away by bus). While many of Bulgaria's other resorts are populated by families, Albena attracts many young singles from Eastern Europe. In addition to its visitors, Albena's innovative modern architecture, which often uses oval and triangular shapes rather than rectangles for its buildings, gives the town a more contemporary look than the 1950s high-rise design of hotels featured across much of the Bulgarian coast. At the same time, with only 38 hotels, almost half as many as in Bulgaria's largest resorts, Albena allows a little more space to move around in, and almost everything is accessible by foot. For meeting Eastern Europeans in a holiday resort, Albena may offer the best atmosphere on the whole coast.

Another advantage of Albena is its proximity to isolated beaches. Just to the north, quiet, virtually unpopulated beaches welcome adventurous travelers in search of a tranquil place to rest by the seaside for the day.

Orientation

As in most Bulgarian beach resorts, you'll find it simple to get around. The main road in town runs parallel to the shore, and hotels and restaurants are located on either side, the budget hotels on the far side from the shore. One town landmark which you can use to orient yourself is the **Dobrydzha Hotel**, Albena's tallest hotel, which sweeps upward toward the sky like a wave from its base.

Accommodations

If you arrive in town without accommodations, go to the main **Balkan-tourist** complex (tel. 21-52 or 23-12; Telex 74567), located half a block away from the Dobrydzha Hotel. You *must* book and pay for your hotel room in this bureau. Keep insisting on the cheapest hotel; only your determination will prevent the staff from placing you in an expensive hotel right off the shore. Ask for the hotels up on the hill from the beach; these are generally the cheapest. The Balkantourist office is open 24 hours a day in the summer.

Dining

Many of Albena's hotels have restaurants, but after dining in quite a few of them, we've found that they all offer virtually the same menu and decor with pretty good food. In other words, you'll enjoy your meal, but you probably won't want to ask the chef for the recipe.

Of the town's many hotel restaurants, we suggest the one in the **Hotel Dobrydzha**, open from 11:30 a.m. to 11 p.m. You'll find modern hotel decor here with the usual hotel band occupying a stage at the center of the restaurant in the evening. Service is polite and attentive, and adds to the pleasure of choosing from Albena's most extensive menu. The best surprise about the restaurant is that the prices are about the same as in the rest of Albena's hotels; a tasty dinner can be enjoyed for less than $5.

Sports

One of the great advantages of staying in a resort town like Albena is the wide variety of sports. For example, you can lay down a few aces in a **tennis** game at the Hotels Kaliopa, Kardam, Prague, Zvezda, and Ralitsa. Daring souls can go **parasailing** (a boat pulls you while you're suspended mid air by parachute) outside the Dorostar and Gergana Hotels. Or you can rent surfboards, waterskis, and boats at many beachfront hotels.

At the south bazaar across from the Dorostar Hotel, you can rent a **bike** for the day for less than $1. Many hotels also rent roller skates, flippers, snorkels and masks, and guitars. As you can see, there's a lot to do in Albena!

Transportation and Important Phone Numbers

Buses depart from the **bus terminal** (tel. 28-60) about every 15 minutes to Balchik and Golden Sands, as well as every 30 minutes to Varna, and every two hours to Kaliakra in the north. You'll find the Albena's bus stop down the main road in town a few minutes past the Hotel Dobrydzha.

For **tourist information** call 23-12, 23-89, or 20-48. For the **police**, dial 20-02; the **fire department** is at 160. **Lifeguards** stand ready at 22-11, and for **first aid** dial 23-06.

BALCHIK: Balchik is a beautiful example of an older town that has not lost its character through tourist modernization. Balchik was first settled 25 centuries ago. Today the town has a typically Mediterranean ambience with white-washed houses and red-tile roofs. Among the homes lining the coast at Balchik is the former palace of Romanian Queen Marie (prior to World War II, Balchik and the coast to its north was part of Romania and that country's most fashionable resort area). Balchik also sports a lovely botanical garden which stays cool even in the height of summer. Visitors to Balchik include many of the Bulgarian intelligentsia.

On the whole, Balchik is an attractive vacation destination for those who prefer beautiful beaches in a quiet atmosphere—something the big resort towns don't offer.

Accommodations

The **Balkantourist** office, 33 Dimitrov St. (tel. 24-10), rents private rooms for only 2.50 leva ($1.35) to 4.50 leva ($2.45)! They also have a pamphlet in English about Balchik. The office is open from 7 a.m. to 10 p.m., seven days a week.

If you prefer to stay in a hotel, choose the **Balchik Hotel,** September 9 Square (tel. 28-09). This hotel offers 72 beds in attractive rooms with tiny bathrooms. Singles run 10 leva ($5.45) and doubles go for 20 leva ($10.95). Since the Balchik is a fairly small hotel and one of the few places to stay in town, it's a sage idea to reserve beforehand. It's just five minutes away from the beach. If you stay at the Balchik Hotel, you'll probably meet many Czechs, as they are the hotel's most frequent visitors.

ROUSSALKA: If we could soon return to any spot on the Black Sea coast for a vacation, we'd go to Roussalka, one of the Bulgarian coast's most breathtakingly beautiful areas. Situated on the north coast not far from the Romanian border, Roussalka hosts one of the least-known and most inexpensive Club Meds—**Club Méditerranée,** Roussalka Par Tolboukine (tel. 345; Telex 74577).

Three small beaches surrounded by rocks make up the Club Med's shore; off in the distance you can see Nos Kaliakra, where cliffs rise 200 feet above the water and down below frolics Bulgaria's only seal colony! On land, small one-story white houses dot the landscape, providing quiet romantic accommodations for all. Many of these rooms have a small terrace overlooking the sea, and all have a private bathroom.

As you may know, at Club Med you get more than just a splendid setting. You can also enjoy a wide variety of activities, including tennis, waterskiing, sailing, volleyball, and other sports—all at no extra charge. The vast array of food (which you serve yourself, so you can take as much as you wish!) rates as the most impressive and delicious on the whole coast. Another plus about this Club Med is that the facilities are rarely crowded—only about half of the rooms are rented, except perhaps during a peak week or two in July. Full room and board costs about $30 a day per person from June 5 to 19 and from August 15 until the middle of September, $33 from June 20 to July 2 and from July 7 to 30, and $37 from July 3 to 6 and July 31 to August 14. If you reserve in advance from the U.S., they'll pick you up in Varna free of charge.

NORTH OF ROUSSALKA: North of Roussalka, you begin to near the Romanian border. You'll find attractive camping facilities at Durankulak, just six kilometers from the border, but we suggest that you don't cross over onto the Romanian coast, as prices in Romania are higher and the food is not as good.

If you want to explore more beaches and coastal towns, why not go to some of the Bulgarian cities to the south? Here are the highlights of the coast from Varna to Burgas.

3. South from Varna to Burgas

BJALA AND OBZOR: The first towns you encounter driving south down the main road from Varna are Bjala and Obzor, two small villages about 50 km (30 miles) south of Varna and popular among Bulgarian and Eastern European vacationers. The facilities are more basic than in the resort towns; if you want to stop here you'll have to stay in a private home, a great opportunity if you want to see typical Bulgarian life and enjoy the sandy beaches and clear waters in a casual atmosphere at very minimal cost.

Important Addresses

In Bjala, the **Tourist and Information Office** is at 3 A. Premianov St. (tel. 264). They have private rooms for 2.90 leva ($1.60) to 3.50 leva ($1.90). The office is open June 1 to September 13 from 7:30 a.m. to 8 p.m., seven days a week. In Obzor, the **Balkantourist** office is at 36 Dimcho Katsarov Blvd. (tel. 23-06). They rent private rooms for 2.80 leva ($1.55) per person, and they have information on the town's simple **Motel Obzor,** which offers rooms with private bathrooms for 10 leva ($5.45) per person. The office is open from 7 a.m. to 10 p.m.

SUNNY BEACH: The next stop on the coast, Sunny Beach (Slunchev Bryag), greatly contrasts with the above towns. The coast's largest and most popular resort, Sunny Beach boasts over 100 hotels, enough for 25,000 people! The beach at Slunchev Bryag stretches for five miles, but as you might imagine, 25,000 bodies spread out over even this distance leaves little room to move about. Restaurants are often overwhelmed with people, leaving a fair number of guests waiting around for tables at any given time. We think that the resort has been overdeveloped; it's simply too big and crowded. Another disadvantage of such widescale development is that the local color of Bulgaria has been lost in the town. Things have become so sanitized in Sunny Beach that you might almost be sitting on the Florida coast! Of course the advantage of a large resort is the wide variety of sports offered, ranging from rollerskating to parasailing.

Accommodations

Since Sunny Beach attracts more visitors than any other Bulgarian seacoast location, it has also become the most expensive town on the Black Sea. A one- or two-week package provides for the only affordable way to stay at Sunny Beach. Contact Balkantourist (see addresses in the introduction) for further information.

Once in Sunny Beach, you can obtain information and accommodations from the Balkantourist office off the main road from the highway leading to the beach (it has no name).

Transportation

The charming town of Nesebar is only 5 km (3 miles) away, and buses leave about every ten minutes for 6 stotinki (3¢). Burgas is 45 km (27 miles) to the south, and buses leave about every 30 minutes for 1 lev (55¢). Within Sunny Beach, a mini-train runs from the center at the Hotel Kuban to both ends of the resort for 50 stotinki (27¢).

ELENITE: Since hotels are so expensive and crowded in Sunny Beach, we strongly recommend staying at either Nesebar, 5 km (3 miles) to the south (see below), or at the virtually unknown **Holiday Village Elenite,** 11 km (6½ miles) to the north (tel. 41-13; Telex 83581). This wonderful holiday village is 5 km (3

miles) past Vlas, a small city north of Sunny Beach. Unlike the mass of hotels across the Bulgarian coast, the Elenite is an imaginative modern hotel complex built by Finns and opened in 1985. The rooms are in small houses spread out on a hill overlooking the seaside. Half of the 465 rooms have small kitchenettes and private bathrooms. Several food stores, restaurants, and discos operate in the village complex, helping take care of all your vacation needs. On the hotel's private beach you can rent windsurfers and umbrellas, or take a short walk down the beach to find a quiet area to yourself. Rooms here cost an amazingly low 10 leva ($5.45) per person without kitchen, and 11 leva ($6) per person with kitchen, much less than you'd pay at crowded Sunny Beach!

To get here, take a taxi from Sunny Beach (it will cost only a few dollars). We highly recommend Elenite for excellent facilities with some privacy and quiet, all at an excellent budget price.

NESEBAR: In case you're wondering where it is that the Bulgarian Black Sea coast's history manifests itself, visit Nesebar, the coast's most charming and romantic town. Founded by Greek settlers on an island (today connected to the mainland by a small strip of land) in the 6th century B.C. and called Messambria, Nesebar was already minting its own gold and silver currency by the 5th century B.C. Hundreds of years later the Romans administered Nesebar, although it didn't figure prominently in their global plans. Few ancient monuments can be seen in a visit to Nesebar today; still, you'll be quite impressed by the fascinating combination of small medieval churches and National Revival houses, the architectural style that developed in the Bulgarian "Renaissance" of the 19th century.

The Sights

Perhaps of most interest are the **medieval churches,** several of which managed to survive despite the 500-year Turkish occupation of Bulgaria. Starting in the 10th century, 40 churches were built in Nesebar, and today the remains of eight of them can be seen (the Turkish invasions and a big earthquake in 1913 destroyed the others). Most of these churches were built in a combination of stone and brick, a common technique for Bulgarian-Turkish architecture. In one or two of the churches, such as at Sveti Stefan (the town's principal church since the 15th century), you can still see beautiful mosaics and frescos.

The second charming aspect of Nesebar comes in its typical 18th- and 19th-century Bulgarian National Revival architecture. The hallmark of this style is the two-story house, the first floor made of stone and the second story of wood overhanging the first. The first floor was used for storage (often for fishing nets) and the second story as living quarters. These houses still standing throughout most of the town almost make you believe that you're part of a scene from 100 years ago!

Accommodations

Balkantourist, at Jana Laskova 18 (tel. 28-55), can arrange a private room for 3.30 leva ($1.80) to 4.50 leva ($2.45). The one catch is that from June 7 through August 25 groups usually fill all the rooms, so you have to hope for an odd spare room. The office is open from 7 a.m. to 10 p.m., seven days a week.

If you have no luck at the Balkantourist office, try the **Hotel Messambria,** Ribarska 2 (tel. 32-55), a good budget hotel with tiny private bathrooms. The most appealing quality about the Messambria is its location, right smack in the middle of the old part of Nesebar. Unfortunately, the hotel is not carefully administered; when we first arrived, the only receptionist was away from the desk for quite some time. Even if the staff is less than attentive, the hotel does offer great budget prices: singles cost 10 leva ($5.45) and doubles run 20 leva ($10.95).

Dining

For a typical Bulgarian meal in a picturesque restaurant with an enclosed outdoor area and a small dining room, visit the **Lozarska Kushta** ("The Vinegrower's House"), on Emona Street (tel. 36-28). To start out with, try the unusual appetizer of lentils in a delicious creamy tomato sauce for 48 stotinki (25¢). Then continue on with the house specialty, Lozarska kaschta, a pork dish garnished with onions, mushroom sauce, ham, and cheese, all served in a big casserole dish, at 9.67 leva ($5.30) for two. Mostly Western tourists come here, but it certainly deserves a hearty recommendation. Service is from 11:30 a.m. to 2:30 p.m. and 6 to 11 p.m.

Kapitanska Sreshta, on Cajka Street (tel. 34-29), is a good fish restaurant in a typical 150-year-old Bulgarian house. In the upper floor of this two-story restaurant the furniture and decorations are as they were when the building was someone's home, and it looks almost like a period museum. Waiters in naval dress serve delicious fish dishes (which depend on the catch of the day) for only 4 leva ($2.20) to 8 leva ($4.35) each. A four-man band plays folk music in the evening; add some good regional white wine and this makes for a very enjoyable time out. The restaurant is open from 11 a.m. to 3 p.m. and 5 to 11 p.m. Many people come here from Sunny Beach for dinner, so try to reserve.

POMORIE: Although it lacks the historic charm of Nesebar and the glorious beaches of the north coast, Pomorie offers some of the coast's most famous health-spa facilities. (Using techniques unknown to many Americans, the Bulgarian doctors at Pomorie apply mud cures for a variety of gynecological, skin, and rheumatic diseases.) Despite an ancient history dating back to the 4th century B.C., the town Pomorie of today has been all modernized, holding no real historic sights of interest to the visitor. Outside the center of town, Pomorie processes most of Bulgaria's salt supply. Thus we recommend Pomorie (located 18 km, or 11 miles, south of Sunny Beach) only to those who wish to take advantage of the health facilities in town.

Accommodations

If you want to take part in a health-cure program, stay at the **Hotel Pomorie**, on Yavorol Boulevard (tel. 24-40; Telex 83531). A concrete-block and stone construction with yellow balconies, the Pomorie features in its spacious lobby an unusual configuration of lamps that resembles a strand of DNA. The medium-sized rooms at the Pomorie offer a quiet environment with balconies and private bathrooms perfect for holiday relaxation. Singles rent for 48 leva ($26.25), and doubles go for 54 leva ($29.50).

A much cheaper alternative for accommodations in Pomorie is to stay in private lodgings for 3.50 leva ($1.90) per person. Go to **Balkantourist** at Nikolai Luskov 49 (tel. 21-01 or 21-03) to make the arrangements.

The Best Beach

From the center of Pomorie, follow Professor Stojanov Street, which leads to a strip of beach surrounded by a salt lake on one side and the Black Sea on the other. If you continue walking past the Bulgarian workers' holiday cabins, after about 15 minutes you'll arrive at a long strip of black sand beach with far fewer bathers than in the town center.

BURGAS: Huge ship cranes dominate the port skyline of Burgas, Bulgaria's second port town and largest ship producer. The modern city of Burgas has little in terms of tourist sights and its beaches are not as attractive as others on the coast. However, Burgas may be a good base from which to make day trips to the rarely visited beaches to the south. Apart from the Duni Holiday Village (see the next section), Burgas marks the last cluster of hotels on the south coast.

Accommodations

We recommend the **Hotel Primorets,** L. Dimitrova 1 (tel. 4-31-37 or 4-41-17), as the town's best budget buy. Despite a drab, gray cement exterior, inside you'll find a modern-style hotel with 120 appealing rooms. Singles with bathroom cost 18 leva ($9.85) and doubles are 25 leva ($13.65). All guests must also purchase 10 leva ($5.45) worth of food coupons a day, but these can be used in any Balkantourist restaurant. Downstairs you can relax at one of two bars or dance the night away at the hotel disco. The Primorets is just a few minutes from the train station across Vasil Kolarov Square.

Hotel Briz, Vasil Kolarov Square, at Ivan Vazov Street (tel. 4-31-90 or 4-31-91), a simple hotel offering no frills, is one block from the train station. Singles cost 11.80 leva ($6.45) without bathroom and 18 leva ($9.85) with; doubles cost 9.80 leva ($5.35) per person without bathroom and 12.80 leva ($7) per person with bathroom.

Dining

The restaurant **Cherno More,** at Parvi Mai 58 (tel. 4-38-29), features a 1950s-style interior and outdoor café tables on one of Burgas's main malls. The limited menu offers Bulgarian dishes for 2.15 leva ($1.20) to 5.22 leva ($2.85). One specialty is kavarma, pieces of lamb with onions and vegetables, for 3.40 leva ($1.85). Open from 8 a.m. to 11 p.m., seven days a week.

Transportation Addresses

The **BalkanAir** office is at Parvi Mai 24 (tel. 4-50-36, 4-56-85, or 4-56-05). The **airport** telephone number is 4-21-89. The passenger harbor for **hydrofoil** boats (tel. 4-27-38), **buses** (tel. 4-56-31), and **trains** is at 4 Vasil Kolarov Square. For a **taxi,** call 4-54-51.

HEADING SOUTH FROM BURGAS: If you're in Burgas, you'll certainly want to explore some of the south coast's beautiful beaches. Here are our favorite towns.

4. Sozopol, Duni, and the South Coast

The 75 km (45 miles) of coast south of Burgas are the least developed in Bulgaria, and have long been a favorite of campers. The problem for the traveler is that it's harder to get around here than in the north, as less frequent public transportation services the area (though buses and hydrofoils do come to some cities). Roads are also not as well maintained as those in the north. Also, the facilities are inferior to those in the north; for example, restaurants are often mediocre, and with the exception of Duni Holiday Village, there are no suitable hotels for the general public.

Thus we recommend the south coast to more adventurous travelers willing to travel in less comfort. The rewards for these sacrifices can be great: imagine soaking up the hot sun in the busy months of July or August on a sparsely populated, sometimes even deserted beach. To find these isolated seaside outposts, randomly explore the coast by walking, public bus, or hitchhiking; you're bound to come across a cove or beach to your liking.

SOZOPOL: The first town you'll pass, 32 km (19 miles) to the south of Burgas is Sozopol, a pleasant fishing village with a population of 4,000. Houses built in the National Revival style make up the heart of the town, and around the harbor you'll see fishing boats and fishermen.

For a private room in Sozopol, go to the **Balkantourist** office at 2 Chervenoarmejska St. (tel. 378) in the center of town.

Two restaurants in Sozopol deserve mention. The **Vinarska Izba,** on a street with no name—you must ask (tel. 553)—has a large, pleasant outdoor dining terrace with standard food and music in the evening. Entrees cost 2 leva ($1.10) to 8 leva ($4.35). It's open from noon to 3 p.m. and 5 p.m. to midnight.

Another good choice is the smaller **Vyaturna Melnitsa** on Morski Skali Street (tel. 844). From the patio of this attractive, inexpensive restaurant you overlook the small island of Sveti Ivan, off Sozopol's coast. When we visited, we enjoyed a hearty bowl of goulash. Hours are 7 a.m. to 11 p.m.; during the middle of the afternoon, however, they often take a few hours off to relax.

KAVACITE: Many people crowd the beaches in the immediate vicinity of Sozopol, so you may prefer to explore the coast to the south near the next town, Kavacite, five kilometers away. A small bus-train transports visitors to Kavacite from Sozopol.

In Kavacite you can spend the night in one of 50 double rooms (all with private bathroom) of the **Motel Kavacite.** The motel charges 12.60 leva ($6.90) per person. If you want to stop here, it's best to seek a room early in the day as the motel fills up quickly.

DUNI: The next beach south of Kavacite is one of our favorite resort areas on the coast, the **Duni Holiday Village.** Like the Elenite Holiday Village to the north, the Duni was built by Finnish engineers. The complex of modern little houses scattered on the hillside just opened in the summer of 1986, and offers a quiet, uncrowded beach in front. Guests also enjoy modern restaurants and other facilities right on the premises. The Duni is the perfect spot from which to continue explorations of the south coast. For more details and reservations, contact a Balkantourist office in the U.S. or in Bulgaria.

FARTHER SOUTH: Just south of Duni flows the **Ropotomo River,** an unspoiled area with very lush, almost tropical vegetation. From 8:30 a.m. to 6 p.m. every day a tourist boat takes travelers on a one-hour tour of this beautiful and quiet area for 1.80 leva ($1). If you're coming by car from the north on the E87 highway, take the first left after the bridge. This will bring you down a dirt road to the boat.

A few more villages mark the south coast after the Ropotomo River before the Turkish border, notably **Primorsko, Kiten, Michurin,** and **Ahtopol.** Each of these small towns rents private rooms from its local tourist bureau. If you find that the beaches are fairly crowded in the town itself, go slightly outside of town and you'll see that the number of people quickly thins out, and if you're lucky, you'll find an area all to yourself.

EASTERN EUROPE

Miles 0 ——— 300
Kilometers 0 ——— 300

N

U.S.S.R.

Baltic Sea

EAST GERMANY (GDR)

East Berlin • Potsdam
Magdeburg •
To Frankfurt →
Leipzig •

WEST GERMANY

POLAND

Gdynia • Gdańsk

Poznań •
Warsaw •
Łódź •
Lublin •
Wrocław •
Częstochowa •
Kraków •

Karlovy Vary •
Prague •
Plzeň •
Tábor •
Brno •
Želina •

CZECHOSLOVAKIA

Vienna • Bratislava
Sopron •
Győr •
Szombathely • Budapest •

AUSTRIA

HUNGARY

Pécs •

Trieste •
Ljubljana •
Zagreb •

Opatija •

Zadar •
Split •

ITALY

Adriatic Sea

Belgrade •

YUGOSLAVIA

Dubrovnik •

Rome •

ALBANIA

Iaşi •

Cluj •

ROMANIA

Sibiu • Braşov •

Bucharest • Constanţa

BULGARIA

Varna •
Burgas •
Sofia •

Black Sea

Plovdiv •

Istanbul •

TURKEY

GREECE

Athens •

Mediterranean Sea

Part Seven

YUGOSLAVIA

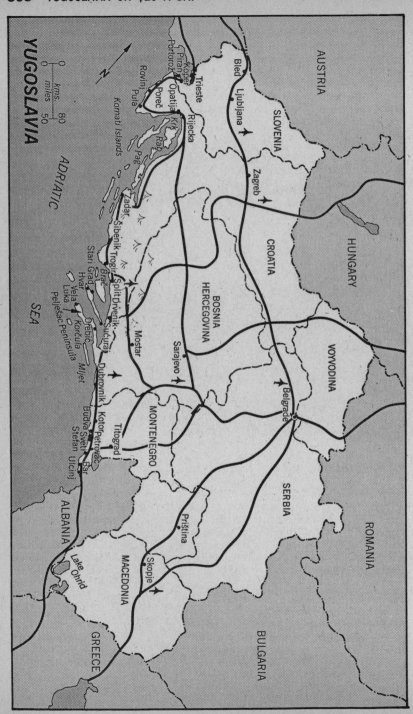

Chapter XXVII

INTRODUCING YUGOSLAVIA

1. About Yugoslavia
2. Rules and Regulations
3. Getting There
4. Getting Around
5. Accommodations
6. Food and Drink
7. The ABCs of Yugoslavia

YUGOSLAVIA IS BOTH OLD AND NEW. When the Greeks first established colonies in the 4th century B.C., they encountered an ancient Ilyrian civilization that was perhaps 2,500 years older. And yet the country did not exist as a unified nation until after the First World War. The very name Yugoslavia was not coined until 1928; before that it had been known as Serbia or the Kingdom of the Serbs, Croats, and Slovenes. Old and new, the country has a mix of some of the most varied and attractive countryside in all of Europe. From Yugoslavia's slice of the Alps in the north to the dry hills in the south, from the narrow ridges and valleys of inland Yugoslavia to the rugged Adriatic coast of sand and pebble beaches and offshore islands, there are a multitude of different and exciting places to visit.

The citizens of Yugoslavia are as diverse as the landscapes they inhabit. There are several major ethnic groups—Croatian, Bosnian Muslim, Macedonian, Montenegrin, Serbian, and Slovene—and numerous smaller groups, including Hungarians, Turks, Bulgarians, Albanians, and many others. The culture of modern-day Yugoslavia is a composite and yet, on the whole, harmonious one. Yugoslavia boasts some of the friendliest people, the cleanest and most sun-drenched beaches, and some of the best food in all of Europe.

SUGGESTED ITINERARIES: Yugoslavia is too large to detail all the possible itineraries, so we mention here only our top choices—what, in our opinion, are the "must see" sights of the country. We recommend that you spend at least a week here. The inland region is worth at least three days and the coast perhaps more.

The Inland Region
We have totaled our daily minimums for inland Yugoslavia and the sum is in excess of six days. Ljubljana is the gateway to Yugoslavia's slice of the Alps

and is a fascinating city in its own right. Spend at least a day here and another day to explore the mountains, a short ride away. Zagreb, transportation hub of the north, is a city you'll probably pass through, and it warrants a day's stopover at least. If you're just going to see Sarajevo, then it's possible to get a feel for the old city in one day. There are numerous other inland wonders, detailed later, which you can add to your itinerary as you see fit.

The Coast

The Adriatic coast has some of the most spectacular scenery in all of Europe. Though it is entirely rocky, with sandy beaches only in the south, it has some of the clearest and warmest water to be found anywhere in the Mediterranean. You'll want to spend at least two days on the Istrian Peninsula, where many of the towns are best seen with a car. Piran, Poreč, and Pula are some of the most picturesque towns of the peninsula. We hope you'll also visit the backcountry—a climb up Učka Mountain will give you quite another perspective of Istria. The Croatian coast north of Zadar is best enjoyed on the Kvarner Islands off the coast. Though difficult to reach except by car or ferry, the islands provide a relaxed pace. Plan to stay at least one night.

Moving southward, we come next to our favorite islands on the coast, Hvar and Korčula. Fortunately, these islands have not been discovered by the great crowds of people who vacation along the Yugoslavian coast. Thus what awaits you on these islands is beautiful medieval towns (also called Hvar and Korčula) built under Venetian rule, basking in the hot, seemingly eternal sunshine of the Adriatic. Whether you're an active sports buff or a beach-loving sun worshipper, you'll find plenty to do on both islands. At Hvar you can rent motorboats or scooters and ride around all day long; or, if you prefer, at Korčula you can swim out to a nearby deserted island to lie in the sun undisturbed for the day. Another advantage of Hvar and Korčula is that both are fairly easy to reach, as frequent ferries connect these islands with the mainland. Those in search of perfect holiday resorts can hardly do better than to spend several days at Hvar and/or Korčula.

Perhaps the most rewarding sight in all of Yugoslavia lies farther south at Dubrovnik. A medieval walled city poised over crystal-clear waters, Dubrovnik is like a fairytale city come to life. Buildings with chalk-white walls and red-tile roofs, Venetian churches with outstanding works of religious art, and moats and wooden drawbridges all make for one of Europe's truly great cities. Allow at least two days to admire the immeasurable charms of Dubrovnik.

1. About Yugoslavia

A CAPSULE HISTORY: The country as we know it today came into existence after World War I. Each of its component provinces was settled by a different ethnic group, as we detail below.

Early History

Yugoslavia has known civilization for over 5,000 years, ever since the Ilyrians first settled in the area. The Greeks followed in the 4th century B.C., setting up trading cities that later became colonies. By the 1st century A.D. the Romans had arrived, and by A.D. 117 they controlled all of the Balkan peninsula, calling what is today Yugoslavia, Dalmatia. What had been Ilyria furnished more and more manpower for the empire, until even emperors, such as Claudius Gothicus, Aurelian, Probus, and Diocletian—whose palace at Split still survives—claimed Ilyrian descent. The Slavs and many of the peoples that now inhabit this area had not yet arrived on the scene. In A.D. 395 the Roman Empire was divided along the Drina River, through what is now Bosnia and Montenegro. This division left the area open to repeated barbarian invasion.

Appearance of the Slavic Peoples

The barbarian invasions, which had begun in the 3rd century, and the division of the empire was followed by the fall of the Roman Empire. Numerous barbarian tribes raided the Balkan peninsula but it was not until the 6th century A.D. that Slavic tribes settled here: the Slovenes and Croats in the north and the Serbs in the south. In time the northerners became more oriented toward the West and adopted the Western forms of Christianity, whereas the Serbs, heavily influenced by the Byzantine Empire, eventually became part of the Orthodox or Eastern form of Christianity. In the Dark Ages numerous feudal kingdoms arose but were unable to unite effectively. Ottoman Turkish domination of the area was firmly established following their victory over an allied Balkan force on the Kosovo plains in 1389.

Ottomans and Hapsburgs

From 1389 on, most of modern Yugoslavia was controlled by the Ottoman Empire. This has left a distinctly Eastern flavor to life in Yugoslavia, especially in Bosnia, where a sizable percentage of the population converted to Islam. The one power rival to the Turks in the region over these years was the Venetians, who controlled many of the islands and towns along the Yugoslav coast. Much Venetian architecture and many symbols of the rule of this maritime republic are still visible today along the Yugoslav coast.

By the end of the 17th century the European powers successfully began to challenge Ottoman Turkish control, and by 1699 most of the area was ceded to the Hapsburgs by the Treaty of Karlowtz. Even though the treaty gave Dalmatia to Venice, the Hapsburgs gained control of the area at the Congress of Vienna in 1815 in exchange for what is now Belgium. By then so many different ethnic groups had settled in the region and so many competing empires laid claim to the same area that Serbia, as Yugoslavia was then known, became a boiling cauldron of racial, religious, and political tensions.

World War I and After

In 1914 the armed camp that all of Europe had become needed only one spark to set it off. On June 28, 1914, in Sarajevo, Archduke Franz Ferdinand, heir to the Austro-Hungarian Empire, and his wife were assassinated by a Bosnian student, Gavrilo Princip, a member of an independent Serbian nationalist group. The spark was struck, and as the great German leader Bismarck had predicted, war came as the result of "some damn foolish thing in the Balkans." Following the carnage and horror of the "war to end all wars," a new Southern Slavic State (Jugoslovenski Drzava) was founded. Unfortunately World War I had not solved the state's ethnic problems, nor had the Italians given up their territorial ambitions. As a result of worsening political and ethnic tensions, the democratic state was dissolved in 1929 by King Alexander, who proclaimed a "royal dictatorship," outlawing all opposition and renaming the country Yugoslavia (Jugoslavija). The depression in the early 1930s hit Yugoslavia particularly hard, and on a state visit to France, King Alexander was assassinated by a man working for Macedonian and Croatian separatist groups. Weak and wracked by economic hardships and internal violence, Yugoslavia desperately attempted to walk a neutral path through an increasingly militant Europe.

World War II and Postwar Yugoslavia

Following rebuffed overtures to an alliance, Hitler ordered the invasion of Yugoslavia in the early summer of 1941. The royal government capitulated in two weeks, but the campaign disrupted German plans to invade the Soviet Union. Many Yugoslavs feel that the two-month delay the invasion of their country caused slowed the Germans long enough for the Russian winter to grind the Axis offensive to a halt. If the Royal Yugoslavian Army was not capable of stopping the Germans, several newly organized partisan armies began fiercely to resist the invaders. The most powerful and best organized were the Communist partisans under Josip Broz Tito. By 1943 he was proclaimed president of the National Liberation Committee and later leader of the Yugoslavian Communist Party. Expelled from the Soviet alliance in 1948 for his "nationalistic" views, Tito led Yugoslavia down an increasingly independent path. A point critical in understanding present-day Yugoslavia is that the Yugoslavians successfully won their own Communist revolution. Led by Tito, the country steered an independent course. It is not a part of the Soviet-sponsored Warsaw Pact or the American-sponsored NATO. In the 1950s the country was not exempt from Stalinist-style terror tactics, but Tito managed effectively to unite Yugoslavia as no other leader had since the Romans. Following Tito's death the country is examining his legacy; it remains to be seen if the different ethnic groups can resolve their differences and the country's economic problems without the strong leadership of Tito at the helm.

Yugoslavia Today

Not at all the repressive police state that some Americans believe it to be, Yugoslavia is very different from all the other Eastern European countries. While Tito was at times overbearing, he spent the late 1970s actually distributing power to the federal government. The result is a nation that is in many respects quite similar to the Western European countries. Though outspoken criticism of the state is still largely forbidden, there are real democratic freedoms in Yugoslavia.

You do need a visa to enter Yugoslavia, but otherwise there are no special obligations that the Western tourist need fulfill. Enjoy your vacation in Yugoslavia, one of the sunniest and by far the most relaxed of all the Eastern European lands.

PEOPLE: Unlike any of the other Eastern European countries, Yugoslavia has never had one dominant nationality. There are several major ethnic groups and a smattering of practically every minor ethnic nationality to be found in the Balkans. The population of almost 23 million is divided into six major "peoples of Yugoslavia": Serbs, Croatians, Slovenes, Montenegrins, Macedonians, and Bosnian Muslims. There are, however, numerous other groups representing a sizable chunk of the population, including Albanians, Austrians, Bulgarians, Czechs, Germans, Greeks, Gypsies, Hungarians, Italians, Jews, Poles, Russians, Ruthenians, Slovaks, Turks, Ukrainians, and Vlachs, to name most, but not all, of Yugoslavia's ethnic minorities. The major religions are about as diverse; the north is primarily Catholic, and Serbian Orthodox and Bosnian Muslim are the major religions in the rest of the country.

In short, make no generalizations about Yugoslavia, a land rich in cultural diversity.

GOVERNMENT: Yugoslavia is a federation composed of six republics and two autonomous provinces. Five of the republics—Serbia, Croatia, Slovenia, Montenegro, and Macedonia—have somewhat homogeneous ethnic majorities. The sixth, Bosnia-Herzegovina, is divided among Serbs, Croats, and Muslims, and no single ethnic group has a clear majority. The two autonomous provinces, Vojvodina and Kosovo, were created in response to large Hungarian and Albanian ethnic minorities, respectively.

The League of Communists of Yugoslavia is the only official political party. In addition, however, each republic has its own party structure, which often competes with those of the other republics and the central party organization.

LANGUAGE: You'll find more locals who speak English than in any other country in Eastern Europe, thanks in part to the large number of English-speaking tourists who visit Yugoslavia. This does not mean that everyone understands English. On the coast many in the tourism industry speak English, but inland very few Yugoslavs speak any foreign languages. On the coast, German and Italian can also help you get around.

Although Serbo-Croatian, a fairly difficult Slavic tongue, is the language of Yugoslavia, a sizable number of people, especially inland, speak different languages such as Slovenian (in the northwest), Macedonian (in the southeast near Greece), Albanian (in Kosovo near Albania), and other languages. Equipped with a Berlitz *Serbo-Croatian for Travelers* or any other Serbo-Croatian phrasebook, however, you should be able to communicate basic messages with any Yugoslav, as almost all understand Serbo-Croatian.

Inflation Alert
Of all the countries listed in this book, Yugoslavia is most likely to see changing prices because of inflation. Over the past few years the government has reported an inflation of 50% to 60%; some locals think the figure is actually higher than reported. As a result, you should refer to the dollar prices given in this chapter, for they will prove more accurate than fluctuating dinar prices, especially in the second year of this book (1988).

---

2. Rules and Regulations

The Yugoslavs operate their **North American tourist office** at 630 Fifth Ave., Suite 210, New York, NY 10111 (tel. 212/757-2801). Their highly professional office can provide you with many pamphlets and maps and answer any questions you may have about travel to Yugoslavia. Their address in England is 143 Regent St., London W.1 (tel. 01/439-0399 or 734-5423).

In addition to the tourist office, a large Yugoslavian travel agency, **Kompas,** can give you information on Yugoslavia and can also reserve private rooms for a $10 Telex fee (a very useful service, especially for July and August). They maintain offices at 630 Fifth Ave., Suite 1658, New York, NY 10111 (tel. 212/265-8210), and in California, c/o Douglas Aircraft Co., International Mail Code 200-36, 2500 E. Carson St., Lakewood, CA 90712 (tel. 213/593-9818 or 593-

4635). The foreign office of **Atlas Ambassador** at 60 E. 42nd St., New York, NY 10165 (tel. 212/697-6767), can also reserve private rooms, but only in Dubrovnik.

VISAS: Americans and Canadians need visas to travel in Yugoslavia (British subjects do not). We recommend always getting a visa beforehand just to be sure, but as Yugoslavia is the most relaxed of the nations covered in this book, 90-day visas can easily be obtained at the border for free. One instance where you may find it convenient to obtain your visa before you go, however, is if you plan to travel on a night train to Yugoslavia, since you will have to get off the train in the middle of the night to procure the visa.

Yugoslavian Consulates issue visas within a day or two. There are consulates at 767 Third Ave., 17th Floor, New York, NY 10017 (tel. 212/838-2300); 307 N. Michigan Ave., Suite 1600, Chicago, IL 60601 (tel. 312/332-0169); 1375 Sutter St., San Francisco, CA 94109 (tel. 415/776-4941); and 2410 California St. NW, Washington, DC 20008 (tel. 202/462-6566). The Yugoslavs also have consulates in Pittsburgh and Cleveland. All consulates are open from 10 a.m. to 1 p.m. Monday through Friday.

The Yugoslavian Dinar

The national currency of Yugoslavia is the dinar, made up of 100 para (which are rarely seen these days). Banknotes come in denominations of 10, 20, 50, 100, 500, and 1,000 dinars, and there are also coins issued worth 1, 2, 5, and 10 dinars.

As of this writing, 292 dinars = $1 U.S., and this is the exchange rate used in this guide. Thus 1 dinar = ⅓¢, or $10 = about 2,900 dinars.

Note that this exchange rate is expected to change dramatically by the time you arrive in Yugoslavia. Because of the expected fluctuation in the exchange rate, many hotels quoted us prices in dollars only. In the accommodations sections throughout Yugoslavia we cite whatever rates hoteliers gave us, whether dinars and dollars, or only dollars. But even if the dinar figures change, the rates cited in dollars will still be approximately the amount you'll pay.

---

3. Getting There

BY AIR: Lufthansa's transatlantic flights to both Frankfurt and Munich make regular connections to Belgrade and Zagreb. Lufthansa also connects in Frankfurt with JAT Yugoslavian Airlines flights to Dubrovnik, Ljubljana, and Split. For information or assistance while in Belgrade, contact Lufthansa at: Terazije 3/ VI (tel. 32-49-76/78). For information or assistance while in Zagreb, contact Lufthansa at: Hotel Intercontinental Krsnjavoga 1 (tel. 44-56-55).

Flying to Zagreb or Belgrade

Lufthansa's First Class and Business Class fares allow unlimited stopovers. Excursion fare is limited to two stopovers for $25 each. The APEX fare permits no stopovers and has a 21-day advance purchase requirement and also carries a $50 penalty for cancellation. All fares are subject to a $3 departure tax plus a $5 Custom User fee.

Round-Trip Fares to Belgrade and Zagreb

From:		New York	Anchorage	Atlanta	Boston	Chicago	Houston/ Dallas- Ft. Worth	San Francisco/ Los Angeles	Miami	Phila- delphia
First Class	All Year	$3386	$4512	$4074	$3386	$4036	$4118	$4748	$3828	$3606
Business Class	All Year	1844	2766	2232	1844	2288	2174	2754	2166	2008
14 – 90 Day Excursion	Sept. 15–May 14	1035	1473	1163	1035	1145	1163	1218	1181	1098
	May 15–Sept. 14	1239	1677	1367	1239	1349	1367	1422	1385	1302
14 – 45 Day APEX *	Nov. 1–Apr. 14 All Week	729	1167	857	729	839	857	912	875	792
	Apr. 15–May 14 Midweek	739	1177	867	739	849	867	922	885	802
*	Aug. 15–Oct. 31 Weekend	769	1207	897	769	879	897	952	915	832
	May 15–Aug. 14 Midweek	849	1287	977	849	959	977	1032	995	912
	Weekend	909	1347	1037	909	1019	1037	1092	1055	972

Midweek = Mon-Thurs All fares are subject to change without notice.
Weekend = Fri-Sun

BY TRAIN: Overland travelers can arrive in Yugoslavia by train from Italy, Austria, Hungary, Romania, Bulgaria, and Greece. If you travel at night, remember that you'll be awakened for border formalities, but travelers from Austria, Italy, and Greece should be able to get more rest than night voyagers from Eastern Europe.

BY BOAT: Travelers from Italy and Greece have the romantic option of sailing to Yugoslavia by boat. The Yugoslavian company **Jadrolinija** transports travelers several times a week during the summer between Zadar and Ancona (in Italy), and between Vela Luka (in Korčula), Stari Grad (in Hvar), Split, and Ancona. Passage only costs $25 to $40 depending on the route and time of year, and a bed in a cabin costs an extra $13 to $25. If you prefer to travel southward, Jadrolinija offers one or two ferries a week from Rijeka and other major Yugoslav port towns to Korfu and Igoumenitsa in Greece. The fare from Dubrovnik to Corfu along the coast of Albania, for example, is $25 to $28 for passage, and takes about 18 hours. Accommodations with meals included cost an additional $46 to $54 per person.

For complete details of these and other ferries, write to Jadrolinija's main office at Obala Jugoslavenske Mornarice 16, Rijeka (tel. 051/22-356). For reservations for your car on a ferry, contact Adriatica Extra Value Travel, 437 Madison Ave., New York, NY 10022 (tel. toll free 800/223-1980, or 212/750-8800).

Another Yugoslavian company, **Jadroagent,** operates ferries between Bar in Yugoslavia (south of Dubrovnik) and Bari in southern Italy. The route takes nine hours and costs $25 to $35 for passage (depending on season), and $35 to $45 extra for a bed. They have offices at Gruška Obala 46 (tel. 050/23-469) in Dubrovnik, and Obala 13 Jula no. 4A (tel. 22-366) in Bar.

The Italian line **Adriatica** has the most connections between Yugoslavia and Italy. Yugoslavian ports of departure include Dubrovnik, Split, and Zadar, and Italian destinations include Trieste, Venice, Rimini, Ancona, Pescara, and Bari. Fares range from $24 to $50, depending on the route and time of year. A bed for the ride will cost you anywhere from $35 to $60 extra in basic cabins. For a complete schedule and fares, write to Adriatica, Head Office, Zattere 1411, Venice, Italy (tel. 041/781-611).

4. Getting Around

BY AIR: The Yugoslav national airlines, JAT, offers domestic flights to Belgrade, Sarajevo, Zagreb, Dubrovnik, Ljubljana, Zadar, Pula, Titograd, Split,

Rijeka, Ohrid, and a number of other cities. Inquire at any JAT office for prices and a complete schedule.

BY TRAIN: Travelers will find that trains in Yugoslavia often do not meet their travel needs. The principal line extends from Austria through central Yugoslavia to Bulgaria and Greece in the south. From this line several routes go to the coast, but no trains run on the coast itself. Secondary routes are fairly comprehensive in the northern part of Yugoslavia in Croatia and Slovenia, but on the coast and in the southern part of the country you must rely on buses or a rented car. When reading train schedules, remember that *dolazak* means arrival and *polazak* means departure.

BY BUS: Yugoslavia offers extensive bus connections in the country, especially on the coast where train connections are poor. To travel by bus, just remember to buy your tickets ahead of time (to ensure a reservation for the exact time you want to leave); try to arrive well ahead of departure time—buses on shorter routes don't take reservations and fill to capacity.

Local intercity buses usually cost about 45 dinars (just 15¢).

BY CAR: Travelers to Yugoslavia, especially to the Adriatic coast, may find it convenient to rent a car. The two most economical firms we have come across in Yugoslavia are Unis Turist Europcar (a division of National Car Rental), and AI Putnik Internationa. Both offer a Renault 4 for $168 per week with unlimited mileage, but keep in mind that the price will actually be about $250 a week when you add tax and insurance.

Unis Turist Europcar maintains offices in Belgrade (Cara Uroša 10; tel. 011/634-766), Zagreb (Gajeva 29a; tel. 041/447-500), Sarajevo (JNA 4; tel. 071/24-555), Dubrovnik (Masarikova 9; tel. 050/25-593), Zadar (Benkovacka bb; tel. 057/30-048), and several other cities. You can reserve Europcar autos from the U.S. by calling the toll-free number: 800/CAR-RENT.

AI Putnik International has offices in Belgrade (Kneza Miloša 82; tel. 011/641-566), Sarajevo (at the Holiday Inn; tel. 071/214-593), Zagreb (in the Hotel Esplanada, Mihanovićeva 1; tel. 041/275-777), Dubrovnik (in the Hotel Dubrava, Babin Kuk; tel. 050/32-300), Zadar (Natka Nodila bb; tel. 057/33-834), and four other cities.

You may find one or two companies with similar rates, but be aware that many companies charge considerably higher rates.

If you do rent a car, remember that driving on the coastal roads always seems to take longer than you might expect, as the often-curvy and mountainous roads demand caution from even the most experienced driver. Also keep in mind that getting from one island to another takes a fair bit of time, so don't schedule yourself a rigorous island-hopping itinerary, otherwise between the driving, waiting for and taking ferries, and finding a place to stay, you may have no time to relax on the beach!

If you plan to explore some of Yugoslavia's islands by car, make sure to arrive at the car-ferry station early, especially if the ferries leave infrequently (only once or twice a day). Lines for the car-ferries do grow long, and sometimes the first ferry fills up and you'll have no other option but to wait for the next one.

BY FERRY: **Jadrolinija** operates the domestic ferries which sail to various ports up and down the Yugoslavian coast. Their schedules are posted in most tourist offices, and in the Yugoslavian newspaper, *Slobodna Dalmacija*. You can buy tickets at travel agencies, or at the Jadrolinija office located near the port of most coastal towns. Both Jadrolinija and local travel agencies charge the same price for ferry tickets. For sample fares and sailing times, see the "Ferryboats" section "The ABCs of Dubrovnik" in Chapter XXX.

HITCHHIKING: The ultimate budget route is hitchhiking. You might think that the restricted number of possible routes (on the coast there's usually only one road) and the extensive tourist traffic would make the entire Yugoslavian coast a hitchhiker's paradise. Unfortunately, this is not the case. First, there are many Yugoslav youths competing for rides. Second, many of the cars are foreign (non-Yugoslav) tourists who either don't want to bother with hitchhikers on their vacation or who simply don't have the room. And last, in a part of the world where a VW Rabbit is considered a medium-sized car, there are few cars that have the room for an extra person and his or her baggage.

If you plan to hitchhike at all, it's best to do it for day jaunts or when you don't have much luggage. No more than two people at a time should hitchhike; three people together will almost never get a ride. Women should never hitchhike alone. Be certain to stand in a place where you can be seen and where there's room for a car to pull over. This isn't as easy as it may sound, especially along the coast where the winding road has a sheer drop to the sea on one side and rocky cliffs on the other. If you're hitching in the summer, bring a hat and drinking water; there are few trees or shady nooks, especially on the coast.

5. Accommodations

HOTELS: Hotels are classified as "L" (for deluxe), followed by A, B, C, and D categories. As with the other countries in this book, we usually recommend Class B hotels, for they represent the best budget value: Class B rooms usually offer private bathrooms and clean, medium-size rooms. Class C and Class D rooms are considerably more basic, and without private bathroom.

Hotel prices vary greatly, depending on location and season. For example, hotels at the seaside are usually more expensive than those inland, especially at such popular coastal towns as Dubrovnik. Conversely, in less frequently visited Yugoslavian towns, savings on hotels will be greater. Hotel rates rise considerably in the summer, above all on the coast. Shoestring-budget travelers will find maximum savings by avoiding the peak months of July and August on the coast.

Keeping in mind the above factors, you can roughly estimate your hotel expenses by figuring that Class A rooms cost $20 and up per person; B category rooms run $10 to $25 per person, and C and D category rooms are less than $15 or $20 per person.

When you arrive at a Yugoslavian hotel, most clerks will tell you the price of your room in U.S. dollars or West German marks, not dinars. However, when you check out of the hotel, you pay in dinars at the current exchange rate. Why this unusual system? Since the dinar exchange rate fluctuates so often (commanding less Western currency all the time), pegging prices to Western currency ensures stable prices all year long.

Nonetheless, in smaller hotels frequented by Yugoslavs, you may be quoted a price in dinars. In this guide we quote just dollar prices when only these were given to us, and dinar prices with dollar equivalents if dinar rates were given to us.

PRIVATE ROOMS: We strongly recommend that you consider private rooms for your stay in Yugoslavia—you just can't find a better travel bargain! As in many Eastern European countries, private rooms are much like Italian pensiones, where you rent a room *(soba)* in someone's house. More often than not, you'll hardly ever see the owner, except on the first day when you arrive and the last when you depart. In addition to this privacy, many rooms may remind you of standard Class B hotel rooms, with clean, attractive public bathrooms.

In general, prices of private rooms range from $3 to $25. Most rooms on the coast cost around $7 to $10 per person during the height of the summer.

For maximum savings, stay four nights in private accommodations; travel bureaus charge a 20% to 30% supplement on the price for stays of three nights or fewer. For the latest private room prices, pick up the pamphlet "Jugoslavija '87 [or '88] Private Accommodation Rates," available in travel agencies. Most of our city listings cite several travel agencies where you can rent private rooms; just remember to arrive during the agency's business hours or you'll have to stay in a pricier hotel, at least for the night!

In many cities, you may be approached by locals who want to rent you rooms in their homes. In most cases these rooms prove just as suitable as those rented from a bureau. However, you do run the risk that the room is in a distant location, has unpleasant facilities, etc., so we suggest that you not pay until you see the room.

If you feel like bargaining, try for a 30% discount on the private room rates listed in this book. We suggest this figure because those who rent their rooms off the street don't pay the 31% commission required of homeowners operating through travel agencies. Once you explain that you understand they're saving this commission, you may be able to get a lower price.

One final word: Many who rent out private rooms do not give you a towel unless you ask specifically for one, so ask for a *peskir za kupanje*.

CAMPING: If you're interested in camping in Yugoslavia, ask the Yugoslavian National Tourist Office for their brochure "Camping Yugoslavia 1987 [or 1988]." This helpful 24-page pamphlet lists camping grounds, facilities, and prices.

6. Food and Drink

Yugoslavia boasts an excellent cuisine, one which, to our mind, rivals Hungarian fare as the best of Eastern Europe. Italian, Austrian, Hungarian, Greek, and Turkish cooking have all influenced Yugoslav cuisine, giving it an assorted selection of specialties.

The Turkish influence in Yugoslavia has endowed the national diet with many tangy grilled meat dishes, such as *ćevapčići*, small spicy patties of ground pork or veal; *ražnjići*, chunks of pork or veal on a shish kebab; *djuveč*, meatballs prepared with rice, green peppers, carrots, potatoes, and cheese, baked in a clay bowl; *sarma*, cabbage filled with meat and rice; *punjene paprike*, green peppers stuffed with rice and meat with tomato sauce; or *sogan dolma*, onions stuffed with meat, rice, and pepper.

Seafood lovers also have a great deal to look forward to, including bass, San Pietro (a light flavorful fish of the Adriatic), dentex (a more pronounced taste), and other fish, usually prepared on a grill over hot coals, as well as shellfish like delicious shrimp *(skampi)*, crab, and lobster.

Even before you sample these fine entrees, you'll want to enjoy some of Yugoslavia's appetizers. Don't fail to try Dalmatian ham *(Dalmatinski pršut)* along with Kajmak cheese, a white cheese made from the top layer of milk.

To finish up your meal with sweet delights, order *baklava*, a pastry with nuts and honey; *kadif*, a thin dough pastry that looks like spaghetti, often covered with honey; or *palačinke*, the sweet crêpe popular across Eastern Europe.

And of course you shouldn't miss Yugoslavia's fine inexpensive wines. Try Grk for a strong white from the island of Korcula, Žilavka from Herzegovina for a lighter white, or Dingač for a rich red wine. Thirst-quenching Yugoslav beer is also widely available. At dessert, the hearty can finish off their meal with Šljivovica, the country's famous (and strong) plum brandy.

7. The ABCs of Yugoslavia

AUTO REPAIR: In most cities you can telephone the **Yugoslav Automobile Association** at 987 for information and assistance on the road.

BANKS: Many banks in major cities have the wonderful hours of 7 a.m. to 7 p.m. Monday through Friday, and 7 a.m. to 1 p.m. on Saturday, although some banks, especially those in smaller towns, close much earlier. Note that you can exchange money more quickly in tourist offices, and at the same rate of exchange. Remember to bring along your passport when you exchange money.

BLACK MARKET: Almost nonexistent in Yugoslavia. Although some locals do prefer payment in dollars, they will rarely give you a special rate for your greenbacks.

CLIMATE: In the inland cities the average temperature varies from about 50° Fahrenheit in the winter to about 85° in summer. Along the coast the summer temperatures average 85°, but the winters are warmer, averaging in the low 50s.

For summer weather reports along the coast, tune in on Radio Zagreb (at 90.5, 93.9, 96.9, 98.1, 98.5, 98.9, and 99.7 MHz on the FM dial) between 8 and 8:10 a.m. and between 11 and 11:10 a.m. for broadcasts in English, German, and Italian.

CREDIT CARDS: Many restaurants and hotels accept the major credit cards, especially American Express and Diner's Club, but in the small establishments you must pay in cash. You cannot use your credit cards to get a cash advance in Yugoslavia.

CURRENCY: The national currency of Yugoslavia is the **dinar,** made up of 100 para (but because of inflation these coins are rarely seen anymore). Banknotes are issued in denominations of 10, 20, 50, 100, 500, and 1,000 dinars, and coins worth 1, 2, 5, and 10 dinars are also circulated.

As of this writing, 292 dinars = $1 U.S., but this figure is expected to change dramatically by the time you arrive in Yugoslavia. Because of the expected fluctuations in the exchange rate, many hotels will quote you prices in dollars only; you will have to pay in dinars, but at the rate of exchange for that day.

Yugoslavia does not require you to make a minimum daily currency exchange (a common feature in other Eastern European countries), but dinars *cannot* be changed back into Western currency, so we recommend that you exchange only a little at a time so that you aren't left with a lot of dinars. You're allowed to bring 2,500 dinars ($8.55) into Yugoslavia for your first trip of every year.

In addition to dinar banknotes, many hotels, restaurants, car-rental agencies, and other tourist establishments accept **Yugoslav National Bank Checks,** and give a 10% discount if you use these checks! We haven't been able to figure out why the Yugoslavs offer discounts for these checks, but why argue with a good thing? Places offering these discounts will have a sign prominently displayed on the window or on the sales counter; you can buy the bank checks in banks or in travel offices. In the future, the authorities have plans to expand the use of these checks to shops and other public institutions; as of now, however, you can only get discounts in hotels, some restaurants (public ones only), and travel agencies. Checks come in 100-, 200-, 500-, 1,000-, and 2,000-dinar denominations. Unlike dinar currency, these bank checks *can* be changed back into foreign currency when you leave the country.

CUSTOMS: Customs inspections usually proceed with more calm in Yugoslavia than in other Eastern European countries. You are allowed to bring in personal possessions, 200 cigarettes, a bottle of wine, and a pint of spirits. You can take "souvenirs" out of the country without paying extra duty, but if you plan on making any large purchases, check with your embassy or a tourist office for complete guidelines on duty taxes.

DRIVING AND TRAFFIC REGULATIONS: Foreigners need their national (or U.S. state) driver's license in Yugoslavia, as well as proof of insurance in the form of a Green Card, which you can get at the border or when you rent a car. The speed limit is 120 km/h (75 mph) on highways, 100 km/h (62 mph) on major roads, and 60 to 80 km/h (35 to 50 mph) on other roads. You must always wear seatbelts when in the front seat. Remember to drive with great caution on the sometimes hair-raising coastal roads.

ELECTRICITY: U.S. appliances need adapters before use since Yugoslavian plugs deliver a strong 220 volts, 50 cycles, A.C.

EMBASSIES AND CONSULATES: The U.S. Embassy is in Belgrade at Kneza Miloša 50 (tel. 645-655, 645-622, or 645-465), and there is a U.S. Consulate General in Zagreb at Braće Kavurica 2 (tel. 444-800).

The **British Embassy** is in Belgrade at Generala Zdanova 46 (tel. 645-055, 645-034, or 645-087). There are British Consulates in Zagreb at Ilica 12 (tel. 445-522) and in Split at Titova Obala 10 (tel. 41-464).

The **Canadian Embassy** is in Belgrade at Kneza Miloša 75 (tel. 434-524), down the street from the American Embassy.

EMERGENCIES: Call 92 for the police, 93 for the fire department, and 94 for an ambulance.

GAS: Gas costs about $2.25 a gallon. Coupons are no longer necessary to buy gas, but if you do purchase coupons at the border or at any foreign Yugoslav Tourist Office, you'll get a 10% discount on your gas purchases.

HOLIDAYS: Yugoslavs celebrate the New Year on January 1 and 2, Labor Day on May 1 and 2, Veterans' Day on July 4, and Days of the Republic on November 29 and 30. The six republics of Yugoslavia all have regional holidays in addition to these national holidays.

MAIL DELIVERY: You'll find it most convenient to receive your mail at **American Express,** which maintains offices in Belgrade, Dubrovnik, Split, Sarajevo, Zagreb, and a number of other cities. See our city listings or contact American Express for addresses.

MEDICAL CARE: British subjects are entitled to free care when in need, but travelers from the U.S. and Canada must pay for all medical bills.

MOVIES: Most movies on the coast are shown in their original language, but inland, movies are usually dubbed over. Make sure to check whether the film is dubbed before buying tickets and sitting down in the theater.

NEWSPAPERS AND MAGAZINES: You can find Western newspapers and magazines such as *Time, Newsweek,* and the *International Herald Tribune* at most large hotels in popular tourist areas in Yugoslavia.

PACKAGE TOURS: Yugoslavia is a big tour destination for American (and obviously Yugoslavian) tour operators. You can choose anything from an active town-a-day "Grand Tour" of Yugoslavia, to a relaxing week flight/hotel package at the beach. For further information, contact the Yugoslav National Tourist Office, where you can pick up a briefcase full of tour descriptions.

PHOTOGRAPHY: You can photograph everything in Yugoslavia except military installations; such outposts will usually be clearly designated (a sign with a camera and a red slash over it). For maximum savings, remember to stock up on film before you go, as it's more expensive to buy abroad.

POST OFFICES: Post offices usually remain open from 8 a.m. to 2 p.m. and 4 to 6 p.m. Monday through Friday, as well as 8 a.m. to 2 p.m. on Saturday. Large post offices are sometimes open for extended hours.

SHOPPING: Souvenir hunters relish the country's folk items, such as handmade embroidery, fine lace, leather goods like wallets and handbags, woodcarvings, jewelry, national costumes, etc. Stores that sell folk crafts, called *narodna radinost,* can be found in many tourist towns.

In summer shops usually stay open from 9 a.m. to 1 p.m. and 4 to 7 p.m. Monday through Friday, to 4 p.m. on Saturday; in the winter, from 8 a.m. to noon and 5 to 8 p.m. weekdays, to 3 p.m. on Saturday. Large department stores often remain open from 8 a.m. to 8 p.m.; food stores usually stay open from sunrise to sundown.

SPORTS: Yugoslavia is a veritable paradise, offering great swimming, snorkeling, scuba-diving, boating, fishing, hunting, skiing, and other sports. For detailed information on any one sport in Yugoslavia, ask at the nearest overseas office of the Yugoslavian National Tourist Office before you depart.

STUDENT TRAVEL: Yugoslavia's national student travel organization, **Naromtravel,** Moše Pijade 12 in Belgrade (tel. 011/339-030), runs several good student hotels which we have listed in this guide. These hotels recognize the ISIC student card and the FIYTO card (Federation of International Youth Hostel Travel Organizations youth card; it's available to anyone under 26 years old). Students will also find many youth hostels across the country. Consult the International Youth Hostel Federation directory, which you can buy from student offices in the U.S., for addresses.

Students receive some discount on museums, as well as on train travel to other Eastern European countries if you have the socialist IUS (International Union of Students) card. JAT gives students a 10% discount on domestic flights, and Naromtravel offers some discounts on international charter flights. See our Belgrade student section in Chapter XXXII for more details.

TELEPHONE: You can always save money on international phone calls by going to the post office, as hotels add extra charges to the already-inflated telephone rates. When making local calls, note that Yugoslavia has two sizes of coins (old coins are large; new ones are smaller), so you may have to change your new coins for the larger old coins in order to make a call if you come across an older phone.

TIME: Yugoslavia, along with most of Europe, is on Central European Time: five hours ahead of New York in the summer during daylight savings, or six hours ahead in the winter.

TIPPING: The Yugoslav National Tourist Office told us that Yugoslavs tip waiters 30 to 60 dinars (10¢ to 20¢) or more if they are very satisfied with service, 10 to 20 dinars (3¢ to 6¢) for bartenders and bellhops, and 20 to 30 dinars (6¢ to 10¢) for taxis. Service personnel in frequent contact with Westerners may expect more, however.

Chapter XXVIII

THE ISTRIAN PENINSULA AND CROATIAN COAST

1. The Istrian Peninsula
2. Portorož and Piran
3. Opatija to Mošćenička Draga
4. The Croatian Coast

BORDERING THE ADRIATIC SEA on the northern shore of Yugoslavia, the Istrian Peninsula and Croatian coast, including their numerous associated offshore islands, provide some of the most attractive, and most secluded, vacation destinations for Westerners and Eastern Europeans alike.

1. The Istrian Peninsula

The Istrian Peninsula is a rocky headland at the northern end of the Adriatic Sea, not far from Italy and Austria. Its excellent ports, protected by rocky inland terrain, have made Istria attractive to seafaring civilizations since history was first recorded.

Settled by the Greeks and then the Romans, the area was firmly controlled for over 400 years by Venetians. Today the Greek and Roman ruins are found among well-preserved medieval towns—all set against the rugged shoulders of the Dinaric Alps. The clear water and ruggedly dramatic beaches make Istria one of Yugoslavia's most beautiful tourist destinations. Its proximity to Italy, Germany, and Austria makes Istria the low-cost get-away choice for other Europeans also. Especially in July when the Germans visit, and in August when the Italians arrive, Istria is filled with vacationers in pursuit of the perfect tan.

The most beautiful towns on the peninsula—Piran, Portorož, Pula, and Poreč—are also the most popular, so you'll have to allow time to find rooms, or even better, make reservations whenever possible. Istria's interior is largely ignored by tourists, so one need only go a mile or so inland to find beautiful and almost untouched landscapes.

> **Fire Warning**
> In summer the grasses and shrubs throughout the country are tinder dry. On the coast, access roads are few and far between, and water supplies—except for drinking—are restricted, so a fire could be disastrous. Always be *extremely* careful with all open flames—matches, cigarettes, and all campfires.

GETTING THERE: Known as the "gateway to the Adriatic," Istria is most easily reached by bus or car; there are few train lines on the peninsula. The tourist authorities have recently constructed a single-strip airfield at Portorož capable of handling smaller (no larger than 50 seats) commercial passenger aircraft. There are much larger airports at Pula and Rijeka; contact JAT for schedules and information.

If you have your own boat, the town is also home to the largest marina on the Istrian peninsula—indeed, one of the largest on the whole Dalmatian coast. In short, Portorož is the gateway to the "gateway of the Adriatic."

If you're coming (or going) by ferry, Rijeka—headquarters of Yugoslavia's leading carrier, Jadrolinija—is connected with both the Dalmatian and trans-Adriatic ferry system.

Train travel to Istria is perhaps the most difficult. The western edge of the peninsula is best reached from Trieste, though there are infrequent trains to Pula from the Yugoslavian interior. On Friday afternoon around 3 p.m. you can battle with the locals in Ljubljana to catch the last coast-bound train of the day.

GETTING AROUND: If you don't have a car you'll have to depend on buses or your thumb. Many of the accommodations along the coast are quite far from each other. This makes finding a good budget room that much harder, as it takes time to move from place to place.

Buses link almost every town on the peninsula; however, the inland spots are serviced much less frequently than is the coast. There are two types of buses, intercity and local routes. Many of these small resort towns are well connected with local buses. In the summer the bus lines run generally every half hour from 4 a.m. till midnight. Intercity buses are scheduled (usually posted on all the stops) also in this time period, though less frequently. Local buses cost 45 dinars (15¢) and intercity buses run anywhere from 100 dinars (35¢) to 500 dinars ($1.70), depending on the distance. You pay on the bus.

Driving is the option that we recommend, if you can afford it. In the summer coastal traffic is very busy, so allow extra time if you have a schedule to meet.

Hitchhiking is an alternative, though not as good as you might think. (See the "Hitchhiking" section in Chapter XXVII.)

ISTRIAN CUISINE: Before we launch into the actual sights of the area, a brief introduction to the Istrian kitchen is in order. The most famous Istrian contribution to cooking is *kraski pršut*, a "mountain ham" well salted and then dried for several months. Often served as an hors d'oeuvre with the succulent local olives, it's a meal in itself. The fish dishes are not to be missed, but of special note are the grilled crayfish Buzara style. There is also an Istrian *jota*, a hearty tripe or sometimes fish goulash. The coastal region is also home to several wine-producing areas. While the whites generally come from inland there are several superior red wines grown in Istria, notably Teran, Refošk, Merlot, a cabernet, and Barbera, as well as two good white wines, Malvasia and Rebula.

2. Portorož and Piran

PORTOROŽ: The "City of Roses," known in Venetian times as Portorose, this is one of the most modern of the Dalmatian resorts. If you come by air, you'll see the sun glistening on salt pans near the airstrip. As you approach, the boot-shaped form of the Piran-Portorož peninsula emerges from the brilliant blue of the surrounding Adriatic.

The one sight in Portorož is the salt pans, which have been worked for over 700 years. They once generated a sizable income for the town, but now it's the beaches that are truly valuable. Many of the best hotels and restaurants in Slovenian Istria are here, and its proximity to Piran (1½ miles) makes it a good base. The nightlife here is by far the best in the area.

Orientation

The town is quite small with numerous hotels and restaurants arrayed along the main strip, next to the beach. The center of town is roughly around the **Grand Hotel Palace.** The **airstrip** (tel. 79-617) and **marina** are about two miles farther east along the shore (you can walk or take the bus).

The **main tourist office** is at Obala 14a (tel. 73-155), and you can write them for reservations at 66320 Portorož. If you get a private room, it might be in the hills behind the resort, usually not more than a 15-minute walk from the beach.

There are **trains** from the interior to Koper in the morning and evening, and **buses** from Koper every 1½ hours between 6 a.m. and 11 p.m. Taxis can be had at any of the large hotels. A ride to Piran is 220 dinars (70¢), and to Koper, 550 dinars ($1.90). You can also call for a cab (tel. 73-555 or 76-000).

The **telephone area code** is 066.

Accommodations

There are numerous hotels and several private-room services along the main street in Portorož. Almost all are within walking distance of each other.

Hotels and Inns: Our favorite hotel is the Barbara; not far from the beaches, it's one of the more reasonably priced and best kept in Portorož. There are, however, at least another 16 first- or second-class hotels in Portorož. In the high season these hotels are part of the Greater Portorož Tourist Authority, a well-run organization dedicated to providing excellent service.

If you're arriving at short notice with no reservations, it's best to stop first at the **Turist Biro** (tel. 76-562), not far from the central bus stop near the main pier. Here they can find private rooms as well as quickly check to see which hotels have vacancies and for how long; they can also check for accommodations in Piran. The staff is friendly and multilingual so language should not be a problem. The office is open from 8 a.m. to 9 p.m., to noon on Sunday.

There are also several inns or boarding houses that offer a pleasant, very informal atmosphere, great Istrian cooking, and low prices. The best is the **Boarding-house Valeta** (tel. 73-145). Located above Portorož, this inn has 16 double rooms for $10 to $15, depending on the room and season. There is live folk music most nights in the summer and great views of the harbor all year round.

Private Rooms and Apartments: The offices of **Generalturist** (tel. 73-449), **Globtour** (tel. 73-356), and **Kvarner Express** (tel. 75-190) all have some private rooms to offer at $15.50 for first-class doubles and $14 for second-class doubles, per night. There's also a new tourist tax to be added on—about 30 dinars (10¢) per person per night.

Apartments are available but you must reserve them. The average apartment rents for $33 for a three-day stay with a room-cleaning service. Most of the rooms and apartments are in houses located up the hill, usually not more than a 15-minute walk from the shorefront.

These offices are open from 8 a.m. to 9 p.m., on Sunday from 9 a.m. to noon.

Budget Dining in Portorož

If you walk into any of the hotels along the main promenade you'll be able to dine well for a reasonable amount. However, one of our favorites, the **Jadran** restaurant, has both self-serve and excellent sit-down dining. Open for breakfast and till 11 p.m., the Jadran is across the main promenade right on the beach. They serve a delicious pork steak for about $2 and some excellent fresh fish, priced by weight, usually not more than $4 a serving. But the specialty of the Jadran, and indeed the whole resort, is the sto (pronounced shtoe), or in Slovenian, rož (rawsh) cocktail. Roughly translated as the "100 years drink," this bluish concoction is one quarter gin, one quarter dry masti (any dry white wine will do), and one half a light, locally produced blue liquor called Adria Blu (you can substitute any mild—but not sweet—blue-colored liquor). Mix these ingredients together and then add any chilled sparkling wine (champagne) in one part wine to two parts base. Serve chilled. The Portorož Tourist Bureau makes a 2,200 liter (580-gallon) rož cocktail once a summer and sells you a commemorative glass that they will keep filled with "the blue stuff," as rož cocktails are referred to, for as long as supplies last.

A Splurge Choice: The **Marina** restaurant (tel. 76-973) is one of the best in the area, and air-conditioned to boot. It's open from noon to 3 p.m. for lunch and 7 to 11 p.m. for dinner daily. The building is an unspectacular brick structure at the marina, two miles east of Portorož, but the interior is tastefully decorated in brick and dark wood, with an abundance of plants and panoramic windows. The food and service are excellent, with fresh fish delivered at least once a day. There's an extensive Italian menu and several changing fish specialties for 4,400 dinars ($15.05) to 4,900 dinars ($16.80) a kilogram; surprisingly, shrimp is the cheapest fish entree, at 2,500 dinars ($8.55).

In Dvori: Far from the coast on the road from Portorož to Izola is the small town of Dvori. Accessible only by car, the untouristed restaurant at Dvori has an excellent Istrian kitchen with some of the most delicate smoked ham we've yet tasted. A meal here will cost less than $3 per person, but serving times are a bit difficult to pin down. The locals who eat here know where the place is and when it opens; tourists will have to chance it. The restaurant's hilltop location is often visited by cool breezes in summer and has a good view year round.

Nightlife

At Portorož the bar and disco scene is quite lively. Mostly the crowds are German, Austrian, or Italian, with a smattering of other European nationalities thrown in. A disco in the Hotel Jadran and two nightclubs, one in the Hotel Bernardin and the other in the Hotel Metropol, attract a fun-seeking crowd with no particular age demarcation. For the underground-pleasure seekers there's a disco under the swimming pool at the Hotel Palace and the Bau-Bau in the basement of the Hotel Riviera.

PIRAN: Known under the Venetians as Pirano, the town actually dates back to Greek (and earlier) times, when watch fires (in Greek, the word for fire is *pyros*) were lit to keep ships safe from the rocks off Punta Maria. Today there's a lighthouse that still shines, though with an electric beam and not wood fires. Displaying much of its original Venetian charm, Piran is one of the most beautiful towns on the Adriatic coast. In the 6th century A.D. Piran was sacked, along with most of the Roman world, despite the best efforts of the Emperor Justinian. In the early Middle Ages the harbor, which today contains nothing more threatening than various pleasure craft, was home to a pirate fleet. In fact many of the walled towns on both shores of the Adriatic were built to defend against the depredations of buccaneers from Piran and other, similar, bases. Piran's history as a pirate's lair was ended by the ascendency of Venice as a city-state in the 13th century. The town, though nominally under the control of Venice, maintained a certain degree of autonomy. Italy controlled Istria until 1945, when the province was given to Yugoslavia.

Sights

The comparison of Piran to Venice is not an idle one, for almost 500 years Piran was under Venetian rule. Notice the stunning **St. George's Church** (Sveti Juraj), with its surprisingly sunny interior, on the ridge overlooking the town. Its bell tower was copied from the one in the Piazza San Marco (St. Mark's Square), and many other parts of the town were designed by architects of the same period. The center of town, the **Tartinijev trg.**, was named after the Pirano-born composer Giuseppe Tartini (1693–1770). Also of interest are the theater, an aquarium, and a small nautical museum with some interesting models of locally built sailing craft from an earlier era in Istria's history.

Orientation

The town of Piran is on a point of land only about two miles west of Portorož and a 25-minute bus ride from Koper, where the nearest train station is located. Because of limited space only people with hotel accommodations in Piran are allowed to drive their cars past the traffic-control gate. All other visitors must park their cars in the lots slightly east of the town. The town center, Tartinijev trg., about a 10- to 15-minute walk from the traffic-control gate and the parking lots, is right on the inner harbor.

Accommodations

If you arrive in July or August without a reservation there will probably be nothing available in Piran, one of the most popular resorts on the Dalmatian coast. However, you can inquire at the **private-room bureau (THP)** on Tartinijev trg., 66330 Piran (tel. 73-630; Telex 34154), located in a red building that, the locals maintain, was built by a wealthy Venetian merchant for his illicit love. The merchant was obviously not worried about his reputation, as the words "Let them talk" are set in stone above the lintel. Today the staff are friendly, and they'll do their best to find you a space in Piran. With over 500 beds at their disposal, they recommend that you reserve in May in order to ensure that you can get the accommodation you want. The office is open from 8 a.m. to 9 p.m. daily (except Sunday, when they take a break from noon till 5 p.m.). The people at the bureau can also check for vacancies at any of the three clean and well-located hotels in Piran. Prices range from $12 to $18 for a double room, including utilities and cleaning service. There's a 50% reduction for every day after the third, and an inclusive one-time fee of $3 for insurance and registration.

Budget Dining

Right on the ocean, the **Tri Vdove Piran** is our pick of the numerous restaurants that line the ways. An awning shields the crisped sun worshippers and troglodytes alike from the strong Mediterranean sun. We recommend the Tri Vdove fish platter for two (or one if you're really starving). A generous portion of several different types of grilled seafood, it makes an excellent meal for 3,300 dinars ($11.30). Open from 10 a.m. to 11 p.m.

High above the town, next to the old city walls, is the restaurant **Obzidje,** a small establishment with an excellent Istrian kitchen. They serve some delicious smoked ham and a goodly selection of fresh seafood as well, all for about $3 a meal. Open from 4 to 11 p.m., it's quite a walk up the road behind St. George's Church, but the view is worth it. If you get lost (hard to do unless you jump off the cliff), just ask someone where the soccer ("food-bal") field is; the restaurant is right nearby.

PULA: According to legend Pula was founded by seamen who, failing to capture Jason (of Golden Fleece fame) and Medea (the lead in the play by Euripides), jumped ship and settled here. However it was founded, Pula was a bustling town by the time the Romans arrived and conquered it in the 2nd century B.C. The town grew to around 30,000 (a good size considering that Paris had only 20,000 people in the 15th century) and was one of the principal Roman bastions on the Adriatic. The main sight of Pula is the **Roman arena,** one of the best-preserved examples extant. The usual "games," including combats between man and beast and the infamous gladiatorial contests, were standard fare here for the 20,000-odd spectators the arena could hold.

3. Opatija to Mošćenička Draga

Across the Istrian peninsula to the southeast is a stretch of curved pebble beaches and glorious baroque buildings, all backed by some of the region's highest mountains. Opatija, named after a Benedictine abbey founded in 1453, was once the resort of Austro-Hungarian nobility and still retains an atmosphere of that by-gone elegance. To the north is a section of old fishing villages and beautiful pebble beaches well connected by a coastal highway, known as the Opatija Riviera. The area is justly famous for its clear water and well over 2,000 hours of sunshine yearly. Only slightly more than 100 years ago this whole area consisted of simple fishing villages, often with no connection to the rest of Istria except by boat.

OPATIJA: In Opatija a small hotel was opened and guests first came in 1844, but it was not until the arrival of the railroad in the latter half of the 19th century that tourism really took off. No more than a two-day train journey from the twin imperial capitals, Vienna and Budapest, Opatija fast became one of the Hapsburgs' favorite wintering spots. The stunning 19th-century buildings, beautiful four-mile-long promenade, and the sculptured formal garden give today's visitor a glimpse of Opatija's imperial past. If you tire of the sun and sand you can always retire to the cool, forested slopes of Mount Učka (4,579 feet). Here you can wander in peace or play hide and seek with a few other hikers and the youthful Yugoslav army recruits who occasionally exercise in the woods.

Opatija, like the resorts in the West, is very crowded in July and August. According to the locals the best time to visit, both in terms of weather and crowds (or lack thereof), is in May or September. We tend to agree, because the crowds are sometimes overwhelming in the high season. Also in late February or early March the locals kick out the stops with a carnival. If you can only visit in the high season, reservations are a must. Since the beaches are generally rocky and very narrow, one item that would prove very useful to have is an air mattress. Easily carried and then inflated, it's useful not only for cushioning the rocky beaches, but also, if space is short on shore, for floating on at sea.

Orientation

The steep slopes and sea cliffs left only a narrow strip for development. Along the Opatija Riviera there is one road and one bus line. In Opatija this road becomes two, with the east-bound lane running above the town and the west-bound lane running along the shore. The Opatija Riviera runs west from Opatija to Ika, Lovran, Medveja, and much farther on to the village of Mošćenička Draga. The main street in Opatija, **M. Tito Avenue,** is where you'll find many of the hotels, all the tourist offices, and the bus routes. The other villages on the Opatija Riviera are so small that orienting yourself shouldn't be a problem.

Each small village has a tourist office right near the center. Opatija has several along M. Tito Avenue. The **tourist bureau** people are usually very friendly and helpful with a good supply of excellent maps. Office hours in the summer are usually from 8 a.m. to 8 p.m., with shorter hours on Sunday. Generalturist, Kompas, and Kvaner Express tourist bureaus have varied tour programs and special events, everything from dinner parties and party boats to various excursions.

Getting Around

Bus 32 runs from Rijeka all the way to Lovran every 15 to 20 minutes; there's another bus that continues on to Mošćenička Draga every hour. The transportation network is open from 5 a.m. till midnight daily.

If you don't have a car, you might wish to use taxis, especially if you rent a room up the mountainside. Taxis are available until 1 a.m. most nights, sometimes later on weekends. All the hotels along the Opatija Riviera have access to cabs, so simply ask any receptionist to call for you. The average cab ride should not be more than 150 dinars (50¢) to 200 dinars (70¢), though you could spend as much as 1,000 dinars ($3.45) to take a taxi up the mountainside.

Hitchhiking is an option, but not really necessary given Opatija's excellent bus system. If you need to hitchhike, be aware that on the very narrow and twisting coastal road there are not many places where cars can stop at all. Otherwise, with all the traffic, prospects are good.

There is a train station in Rijeka, and a good-sized airport on the Isle of Krk, about eight miles outside Rijeka.

Opatija's **telephone area code** is 51.

Accommodations

Many of the older hotels have been extensively remodeled and much of the original decor is gone. However, almost all the hotels are clean and comfortable. Between July 15 and August 15 reservations are a must. For reservations and any other inquiries, Telex the **Turistički Savez Opatija** (tel. 711-710; Telex 24163).

If you don't have reservations, the best places to begin are the two **Kvarner Express** offices, one on M. Tito Avenue and the other right by the Continental Hotel. The office on M. Tito Avenue is small and open only in the summer; it handles all the private rooms to the east of their office, and the main office near the Continental Hotel handles all the rest of the Opatija Riviera. They are open daily from 8:30 a.m. to 8 p.m. (on Sunday to 5 p.m.). Most of the rooms are doubles, with prices from $13 to $19. If you don't have a car you may be forced to use taxis to get back and forth to your rooms. This isn't so bad, as the taxi ride will rarely cost more than 900 dinars (around $3). Generalturist, Kompas, and Kvaner Express can all check for hotel vacancies all along the Opatija Riviera.

High above the Opatija Riviera, on the slopes of **Mount Učka,** is the pension of the same name (tel. 713-450). A small, relatively new building with an excellent view down the whole coast, the Učka pension sometimes has available rooms even in the high season. Though the facilities are unspectacular it is quiet and pleasantly cool, a refreshing change from the beach. Only accessible by car, it's at least a half-hour drive on narrow, twisting roads from Opatija up the mountainside.

Camping: There are two campsites in the area, **Preluka** and **Ičiči.** To get to Preluka camping, take bus 32 toward Rijeka; to Ičiči, take the same bus in the other direction. Both campsites are often very crowded in the summer. Because the houses extend miles up the hillsides and the landscape is so steep, it's not really practical simply to head to the hills in search of a suitable campsite. You'll be walking a long way.

Budget Dining

The choices are almost endless, as all the hotel and restaurant kitchens have access to the same excellent seafood practically all year round. We recommend the following.

The **Plavi podrum,** east of Opatija in the town of Volosko (tel. 713-629), is one of the restaurants that is less frequented by the tourist hordes, though all of the area's restaurants are busy in the evening. Done up in traditional Istrian manner, the Plavi podrum serves a variety of meat and fish dishes, at prices averaging less than $7. It's a good 20- to 30-minute stroll from the city center along the promenade east, or take bus 32 up the hill and out of town for about 10 to 15 minutes.

The **Vila Anston,** just before the town of Ičiči on the coastal highway (tel. 711-379), is another of the better local restaurants. Reservations are necessary in the evening, but the atmosphere is very relaxed and it has an excellent kitchen. We enjoyed some delicious fish during our visit—grilled with herbs, it cost around $6 for a healthy serving. Parking is also sometimes a problem here, so bus riders do have an advantage. The Vila Anston is open till 11 p.m. on weekdays, and weekends till midnight.

One of our favorites is an eatery just above Opatija on the road up to Mount Učka. The **Anfora** restaurant (tel. 711-246) is within easy walking distance of M. Tito Avenue. It is informal and generally less crowded than the restaurants on the main strip. Though they have fish dishes, we recommend trying the delicious smoked ham and lamb dishes. The Anfora is a place where many of the people who work in the tourist bureaus during the day eat and relax at night.

There are many restaurants all along the Opatija shorefront, where the Class A and B hotel restaurants do not differ greatly, and all have excellent seafood.

4. The Croatian Coast

About 10,000 years ago the Croatian coast and offshore islands were a series of mountain ranges flooded by melting glaciers. To visualize the geography today it is best to think of the numerous little islands as mountaintops peeking above the sea, and the narrow inlets and fjords as flooded valleys.

Until the 19th century the convoluted coast and island maze provided a home to pirates. Once the region was well forested, but centuries of shipbuilding have long since cleared the area along the sea. Now the barren, rocky coast stands exposed to the sun, a very different place from when the Ilyrians and Greeks first settled the wooded shores.

For tourists, the area south of Rijeka to Senj, including Cirkvenia, does not compare to many of the other stretches of coast. It's better to head out for the three large and most hospitable Adriatic islands of Krk, Rab, and Lošinj, or go inland to the stunning Vinodol Valley. With the Dubracina River flowing in the valley, the green countryside is a welcome change from the very arid coast. South of Senj, which is a major port town with a ferry terminal, the coast is steep and barren but with beautiful rocky shoreline and crystal-clear water. Here there are several beautiful coves that are relatively quiet, even in the high season.

The Adriatic islands are considered some of the cleanest and most secluded places to go; however, there is not a lot of organized activities, and transportation is often a problem. If you're really looking for an absolutely quiet vacation, then the Adriatic islands are for you. Hotels are not clustered together, which reduces crowding but makes a car a necessity.

The coast between Karlobag and Ravanjska is also stunning, though the large towns of Tribang and Sibuljina can become overcrowded. Access through the coastal mountains to the interior is limited as there are only a few roads over the passes. Therefore most of the resorts are spread along the shore rather than clustered in one area, as they often are in Istria and south of Zadar.

WATER-SHORTAGE WARNING: The semi-isolated and very dry Croatian coast often suffers from water shortages in the summer. Especially in late summer, water is often rationed, and many of the second- and third-class accommodations limit water use to cooking and drinking.

ORIENTATION: Most of the coast south of Rijeka and north of Ravanjska is separated from the interior by the nearly 100-mile-long Velebit mountain range. There are major roads inland at Senj and Karlobag, but only three or four other, smaller roads. In the north the beautiful Vinodol Valley parallels the coast between Bakarac and Novi Vinodolski.

Tourist Offices

Tourist offices, usually clearly marked along the roadside, handle everything from directions and room finding to tours and other organized programs. Basically every town larger than 2,000 people has a tourist office. In the summer these offices are open daily from 8 a.m. to 9 p.m. (on Sunday to 1 p.m.). The smaller offices in the more remote areas basically set their own hours.

If you are entering the area from the north, we recommend that you stop at Rijeka, where most of the tourist bureaus have their main offices. Just a short walk (ten minutes) east of the main station in Rijeka, on—or just off—Obala Jugoslavenski Moranice, are the main offices for **Autotrans,** the biggest bus carrier, at Žabica 1 (tel. 25-33; **Jadrolinija,** the main ferry carrier, at Obala Jugoslavenski Moranice 16 (tel. 22-356 or 25-203); **JAT,** Yugoslavian Air Transport, at Trg. Republike 9 (tel. 30-207); **Croatia-Express,** a major tour and transportation operator, at Borsia Kidriče 1 (tel. 23-304); and Rijeka's own central tourist office, **TIC,** in the same building as JAT (tel. 33-909).

Getting Around

Without a car, getting around the coast may be a problem as bus lines do not always connect and the **buses** are always crowded in summer. However, this is somewhat offset by their low cost; a ride from Rijeka to Zadar costs less than $5. Your best bet is to check schedules carefully and begin bus trips at the major towns where it's possible to buy a reservation. In Rijeka is a central office that handles much of the bus transportation in the area. A short walk (ten minutes) east of the main station, the **Autotrans** office, at Žabica 1 (tel. 25-335), is just off the main street, Obala Jugoslavenski Moranice. Here you can get schedules and purchase tickets.

There are no **trains** along the coast. There are train terminals at Rijeka and Zadar, but nowhere else on the shore between the two cities.

Hitchhiking is possible, but not as easy as you might think. The conditions in the day are very dry, desert-like in fact, so pay special attention to the "Hitch-hiking" section in Chapter XXVII.

Given that the Adriatic islands have some of the most beautiful beaches and that traveling on land can be so difficult, the best bet for the traveler without a car is the **ferry.** Rijeka is the headquarters of **Jadrolinija,** at Obala Jugoslavenski Moranice 16 (tel. 22-356 or 25-203), just across the street from the TIC, the Central Tourist Bureau. Here the multilingual staff can give you schedules and advice as to possible itineraries using their ship lines, and sell you tickets.

Closer to the rail station is **Croatia-Express,** a major tour and transportation operator, at Borsia Kidriče 1 (tel. 23-304). They have ferry services around the Kvarner Islands, including the many Kornati Islands to the south. Prices vary but are generally less than $7 per person for hops around the islands, or $10 to $15 for intercity travel. Reservations are an absolute must in the summer, though most boats will let you stand for the trip (if all the seats are sold out) for about a 15% to 20% reduction.

ACCOMMODATIONS: There are numerous pensions perched right along the coast with access to a private or semiprivate beach. Sometimes these beaches are not much bigger than a patio and the way down can range from a well-built metal staircase to a rope ladder. The parking facilities are also often limited, and before pulling into a pension or small hotel to see if there are vacancies, make certain that you can get back on the road again.

What you get varies from secluded, sunny pensions with separate white-washed outbuildings to dorm-like accommodations with no showers. Much of the quality of service is based on local water supplies. State standardization is finally creeping up the coast—there are few places where you can avoid the tourist tax (probably none by next summer). As a result all private accommodations are being classified. Class A or first category costs $12.50 and includes a private shower; second class runs from $8 to $10 and has a bathroom for every three or four rooms; third class is less than $7.50, and is generally dorm-style accommodations, sometimes without showers. Prices are fixed in Western currency, and are actually increased if you pay in dinars.

DINING: Take time when traveling these shores to sample the fish, usually very good and always fresh. Menus are limited in the small towns, and if you don't care for fish, you'll have to live on the excellent cured hams or lamb. At every eatery, no matter how lowly, there are always one or two specialties of the day. Try to order these as they usually are fresh and well prepared, but always ask the price first. (Asking ahead of time shows that you don't own any oil wells and are concerned how much you spend. It also prevents any nasty surprises.) For tourists, everything is extra—bread, pommes frites, etc.—so order with that in mind. With care, not too much to drink, and a few inquiries before ordering, you can eat for less than 1,100 dinars ($3.75).

Surprisingly enough, some of the shorefront pensions do not always serve fresh fish. Even though you can practically fish out your bedroom window, the owner or cook doesn't always have time to run into town or to go out and catch dinner. So . . . ask first or look at somebody else's plate. Most of the food is extremely cheap. Some room-and-board deals average out to $6 a day, including two complete meals.

RAB: Not far from Rijeka, the Isle of Rab is one of the lushest of the Dalmatian Islands. The main village, called Rab, is reminiscent of both Venice and Dubrovnik, its larger cousin to the south. Settled since at least the 3rd century B.C., the town has changed little. The New Town (Novi grad) was built between the 14th and 17th centuries, and there is a small Romanesque basilica, the Cathedral of St. Mary Minor (Sveta Marija Velika), built in the 12th century. To eat, there is fish, fish, and more fish, all of it excellently cooked. The nightlife is fairly lively as the different nationalities seem to fraternize on Rab with little or no difficulty.

Chapter XXIX

THE CENTRAL COAST

1. Zadar
2. The Kornati Archipelago and Šibenik
3. Split
4. Side Trips from Split
5. Hvar
6. Korčula

THE ISLAND GEMS in the Adriatic Sea off Yugoslavia's central coast are outstanding, even in this area known for its appealing islands. In the Kornati Archipelago to the south of Zadar you can rent a fisherman's shack and live in isolation for a week among barren and starkly beautiful islands. At Hvar, a large island first inhabited by Greek settlers in the 4th century B.C., you can enjoy modern tourist facilities and more sun per day than at any other island in the Adriatic. At Korčula, to the south of Hvar, wander by morning around a picturesque Venetian town said to be the birthplace of Marco Polo, and go snorkeling in crystal-clear waters in the afternoon.

The mainland coast offers its own share of unique sights. When the great Roman Emperor Diocletian was looking over the entire empire for a place to retire to, he chose Split, and the remains of his palace form the core of the town to this day. Our first stop on the central coast is Zadar, a town much visited for its excellent transportation links with Italy and Yugoslavia's Dalmatian coast.

1. Zadar

Although Zadar lacks the charm of many of the coast's other cities, it serves as an important transportation hub for both Yugoslavian and Italian destinations. Zadar was an important city as long as 2,000 years ago when the Roman Empire set up a colony here; traces of this Roman settlement can still be seen in the Old Town. During the Middle Ages, Zadar (called Zara in Italian) was a prime rival of Venice. In 1202 during the Fourth Crusade, Venice insisted that the Crusaders stop in Zara to defeat the Turks, her principal enemy of the time (later on that same crusade, Venetian forces in Constantinople looted the four bronze horses that now adorn the Basilica of San Marco). For many of the years between 1202 and 1797 the Venetians continued to dominate Zara.

In 1920 Zadar became part of Italy in accordance with the Treaty of Rapallo, and it was not until 1944 that the city was returned to Yugoslavia. You'll still find traces of the old rule in the fluent Italian spoken by many of Zadar's older residents.

Unfortunately, the war years were not kind to Zadar. In fact, it earned the title of "most bombed city" in Yugoslavia. Thus we suggest that upon your arrival you avoid the many unexceptional postwar sections of Zadar, and instead head straight for the Old Town, a peninsula off the central part of the city. Here you can walk among buildings built in the Venetian Gothic style, which include parts of the Old Town walls (note the Lion of San Marco, the symbol of Venice at the town gates at Pred grad. vratima), and several interesting Romanesque and Gothic churches.

As modern constructions devoid of charm make up the greater part of the city, we do not recommend a lengthy visit to Zadar; however, we list the following information for those who are passing through town en route to other destinations on the coast.

IMPORTANT ADDRESSES: The **Tourist Information Office** (Turisticko Drustvo Liburnija), at Omladinska ulica 1 in the Old Town (tel. 22-146), offers visitors information on Zadar and its nearby islands, as well as private rooms (for $7.15 to $11.65 per person in summer and $5.25 to $9.05 during the rest of the year). From June 15 to September 15 the office stays open from 7 a.m. to 11 p.m.; during the rest of the year the hours are 7:30 a.m. to 12:30 p.m. and 5:30 to 7:30 p.m.

The helpful **Atlas Office** (tel. 33-39), which acts as the representative for **American Express,** can be found at Branimirova Obala 12, a street across the port from the Old Town.

The **train station** is located on Prilaz Oslobodenja, a 15- to 20-minute walk south of the Old Town. Coastal ferries and boats to Italy leave from Istarska Obala on the north side of the Old Town. **Buses** depart from Radnička Obala, right next to the ferry terminal in the old part of town.

ACCOMMODATIONS: Zadar's only hotel in the Old Town area is the **Hotel Zagreb,** ulica Borisa Kidriča bb (tel. 24-266; Telex 27157), overlooking the Adriatic Sea. Rooms are simple B category, with bare white walls, two small tables, a fair-sized window (about half the rooms overlook the Adriatic), and a private bathroom. Room prices are set according to one of four seasons: July and August; June and September 1 to 15; May and September 16 to October 31; and the rest of the year. Over these four periods, single rooms will cost 6,336 dinars ($21.70), 4,400 dinars ($15.05), 3,520 dinars, ($12.05), and 2,530 dinars ($8.65) respectively; doubles, over the same four periods, rent for 9,400 dinars ($32.20), 6,919 dinars ($23.70), 5,360 dinars ($18.35), and 3,740 dinars ($12.80).

A pleasant choice for visitors seeking modern facilities and comfort is the **Hotel Kolovare,** on Šetalište Nenada Parente, a road that leads south from the old part of town (tel. 33-022 or 33-947). The hotel offers compact rooms with a private bathroom, as well as a pool and small strip of beach across the road from the hotel (note, though, that the water in the Zadar area is not as clear as in many other Yugoslavian coastal towns). Singles rent for $23.05 to $23.75 and doubles go for $35.25 to $36.60 in July and August; in June and September, rates fall to $16.30 to $16.95 for singles and $24 to $25.25 for doubles; during the rest of the year prices are even lower.

DINING: The **Restaurant Maestral,** at the town marina on Koruška Street, across the bay from the Old Town (tel. 30-549), offers delicious food in elegant surroundings. You'll find the restaurant on the second floor overlooking the town marina, so throughout your meal you can admire the impressive yachts in the port. Inside, you'll see an attractive modern blue interior and waiters decked out in colorful sport shirts. The menu features both meat and fish dishes at moderate prices, costing from about $3 to $4.50 an entree. We enjoyed the tasty "hot platter marina," consisting of grilled sirloin of beef, fried bacon, mushrooms, onions, and vegetables in a creamy butter sauce; if you're more adventurous, try one of their several flambé dishes. In all, we highly recommend the Maestral for both lunch and dinner.

One of the plainest-looking restaurants we visited in all of the Yugoslavian coast, **Gostionica Primošten,** Jurja Barakovića 3 (tel. 33-935), also serves exceptional fresh fish prepared on the grill. The restaurant's half a dozen tables are set along a narrow backstreet in the center of town; at the end of the block you see a tiny kitchen, from which clouds of smoke billow up to the sky. Despite its simplicity, you may find a certain appeal to the place; however you feel about the decor, though, you're sure to enjoy the food. The restaurant features large portions of tender grilled fish in delicious buttery sauces, all for only $3.50 a plate! During inclement weather you can dine in the equally bare indoors, which resembles a basement recreation room. As you walk over to the restaurant, just remember not to let the decor scare you away; the place serves some of the best fish on the coast! It's open from 10 a.m. to 11 p.m. seven days a week in summer; during the winter it's closed on Sunday. From October 15 to November 15, the owner goes on vacation and the restaurant is closed.

ISLAND SIDE TRIPS: During July and August, local travel agencies sponsor daily trips to the **Kornati Islands** (see the next section, "The Kornati Archipelago and Šibenik," for more description). Day-trippers can also visit the islands right off Zadar, which include **Ugljan, Dugi Otok, Sestrunj, Molat, Olib,** and others. Ugljan is particularly well situated for side trips since it sits just across from Zadar in the Adriatic. Boats depart approximately every half hour in summer for Ugljan, and once a day for the area's other islands. Inquire at the Zadar Tourist Office or other travel bureaus for more details.

2. The Kornati Archipelago and Šibenik

Travelers seeking an oasis of quiet after the active, crowded shores of Yugoslavia's northern coast will find the unspoiled islands of the Kornati Archipelago or the picturesque Gothic town of Šibenik the perfect answer to their quest.

THE KORNATI ARCHIPELAGO: Can there still be a group of 150 *uninhabited* islands anywhere in the Adriatic? Yes, there are, in Yugoslavia's **Kornati Archipelago,** a group of rocky, largely barren islands, scattered from north to south like a string of pearls, offering visitors a world of perfect natural beauty. The islands were discovered long ago, and archeological finds show that people lived on the Kornati islands during the Stone Age, some 4,000 to 7,000 years ago. Thousands of years after the first settlements the Romans constructed several impressive summer villas on the Kornatis. Since then fishermen and shepherds have occasionally inhabited the islands, but in the last century the Kornati Archipelago was struck by a vicious fire which, according to a local guidebook, lasted 40 days and left the islands barren.

Today you'll find a few dozen houses (which are inhabited only part of the year) on the various islands. They belong to shepherds whose sheep graze here, and to fishermen who catch almost all of the Yugoslavian coast's scampi and lobster. (If a restaurant in Dubrovnik tells you that their shrimp are fresh and caught locally, chances are that the truth of the matter is that the shrimp are frozen Kornati scampi!).

The rich undersea life of fish and shellfish makes the Kornati area a prime attraction for snorkelers and scuba-divers. Above water, the inspiring limestone cliffs of these islands (some as high as 300 feet), the caves, grottos, and other natural formations all attract lovers of natural beauty who desire seclusion from the modern world.

Staying on the Kornati Islands

You'll find the gateway to the Kornati on **Murter,** a small fisherman's island located between Zadar and Šibenik and connected to the main coastal highway by a bridge. The **Kornatturist Biro,** Trg II Dalmatinske, 59243 Murter (tel. 75-215 or 75-058), organizes day boat trips around the Kornati Islands, but they also offer quite an extraordinary vacation possibility: during the summer they rent out some of these fisherman's cottages on the small Kornati Islands.

After you make the arrangements through Kornatturist, you'll start your journey to the cottage along with a local fisherman, who will take you by boat to his house (for $37.65, round trip) and set you up in his primitive fishing home. Once he leaves, you can enjoy an entire island, practically in the middle of no-where, all by yourself, or perhaps with a few other families. Of course these houses lack comfort: there is no running water or electricity, but there is a cis-tern which is refilled with fresh water by local fishermen from time to time. Every two or three days a fisherman will bring fresh fish and other food prod-ucts, for which you pay about 20% more than you might on the mainland.

If you prefer to have your own motorboat to explore the Kornatis and be less dependent on the occasional passing fishing boats (after all, you can't just order in food from the mainland by telephone!), the Kornatturist office will rent a boat for $22.60 for a full day, or $15.05 for a half day. Even if you don't stay on the islands, a day cruising the area by private motorboat will be quite a memora-ble experience.

In order to rent one of these private homes, you must write Kornatturist ahead of time, and plan to stay a minimum of seven days. Cottages cost $28.25 a day for two from June 29 to August 24, $22.60 from June 1 to 29 and August 24 to September 14, and $17.70 during the rest of the year. Kornatturist rents houses on the islands of **Levrnaka,** which has the most beautiful sandy beach of the Kornati Islands; **Piškera,** an old fishing settlement where only a church and a few houses remain; **Žut,** the archipelago's second-largest island, where live-stock is put out to pasture; **Lavsa,** a fair-sized island which is home to some Roman ruins; and several other islands. Of course these cottages won't appeal to everyone, but for outdoor types who want to relax in the quiet and beauty of nature, we can think of nothing more exciting!

For further information on the Kornati Archipelago, buy the guide by Mladen Friganović called *National Park: The Kornati Archipelago,* available at tourist offices in Šibenik, Murter, and Zadar.

ŠIBENIK: Among the many picturesque medieval towns on the Adriatic, Ši-benik (pop. 30,000) is relatively unfrequented by travelers, thus affording visi-tors a more tranquil stay than in many Yugoslavian coastal towns. First founded in the 10th century A.D., Šibenik is best remembered by historians as a bastion in the 17th- and 18th-century battles against Turks.

The Sights

Today Šibenik features many 15th- and 16th-century stone buildings in the Venetian Gothic style. The town's most noted monument is the beautiful **Cathe-dral of St. Jacob** (Sveti Jakov), a 15th-century masterpiece of Yugoslav religious art which exemplifies the glories of the floral Gothic style (note, for example, the 71 portrait head sculptures of 15th-century locals on the cathedral frieze). Across from the cathedral are the Renaissance **Town Hall** to the north and the **Rector's Palace** to the south, now home to the town museum (it includes exhibitions of archeological finds from Danilo, a nearby settlement dating back to the Stone Age). In all, Šibenik offers visitors a pleasant respite before continuing on north or south.

Accommodations

The only hotel in the old part of Šibenik, the **Hotel Jadran,** on Obala Oslobodenja (tel. 23-925; Telex 27389), is located right on the seafront. The modern rooms offer Danish design furniture and pleasant bathrooms which, we think, merit more than the hotel's class B category rating. Singles cost $18.10 to $18.85 in July and August, $15.80 to $16.95 in June and September, and $13.20 to $14.30 during the rest of the year; doubles rent for $32.40 to $33.90 in July and August, $28.25 to $30.15 in June and September, and $22.60 to $24.50 during the rest of the year.

Travelers looking for sportier, more beach-oriented hotels should stay at the **Hoteli Solaris** (tel. 23-844 or 26-889; Telex 27326-YU-SOLAR), a modern seafront complex of four different hotels about five kilometers (three miles) south of Šibenik. At the Solaris you can enjoy the hotel's beach, go waterskiing, play tennis, or engage in numerous other activities. Double-room rates with full board run about $30 per person in July and August, $25 in June and September, and $16.50 during the rest of the year.

Private Rooms: The **Tourist Bureau** (Turisticki Savez), at V. Lisinskog 1 (tel. 22-075), across from the Cathedral of St. Jacob, rents private rooms to visitors for $7.50 to $12, depending on the time of year and category of the room. The bureau is open from 8 a.m. to 2 p.m. and 4 to 10 p.m.

Dining

If you have any doubts about the superlative quality of Yugoslavian seafood, visit the **Restaurant Uzorita,** Rade Končara 58 (tel. 23-660). This private restaurant, not well known to tourists, which features outdoor courtyard tables or quiet indoor dining, has long been a favorite of locals. Of the many restaurants we visited in Yugoslavia, we shall long remember our visit here with two Yugoslav friends. The waiters served us a huge bowl of scampi, prepared in a delicious white wine sauce. The truth is that we continued to devour these incredible scampi in seemingly endless quantity for a good half hour! If you prefer, you might sample the San Pietro, eel, bass, shellfish—none costing more than $4.50 to $5.50 a plate. Several delicious meat entrees are also available. You'll find the restaurant outside the center of town right across from the large town stadium. Open noon to midnight, seven days a week.

Side Trips from Šibenik

Probably more popular than Šibenik itself is the Krka River and its impressive **Krka Falls,** located 12 km (7¼ miles) from Šibenik. These beautiful waterfalls, a rare example of a European cascade, flow along lush green unspoiled countryside and limestone and travertine rocks to their final destination, the sea next to Šibenik.

Although several different waterfalls mark the path of the Krka River to its source, you'll find the most impressive waterfall at **Skradinski Buk,** a multilayered 300-foot-wide cascade framed by dark-green vegetation and trees. In addition to being a tourist attraction, the Krka River region serves as home to two monastic orders (one on a small island in the middle of the river), and several hydroelectric power plants.

You can visit the Krka region on a tour organized by one of Šibenik's travel agencies, or you can take a bus from the station in Šibenik at Obala Jugoslavenske mornarice on the waterfront.

3. Split

Starting in A.D. 295 the great Roman Emperor Diocletian began building a huge summer palace on the Dalmatian shores where he was born. Ten years later he stepped down as emperor. Leaving the power and problems of the Roman Empire behind, he settled into his completed palace in what is now the city of Split. Diocletian died 11 years later, having enjoyed what present-day Yugoslavs claim is the mildest climate on the Adriatic coast.

After Diocletian's death his palace was used by exiled Roman emperors. After the fall of the Roman Empire, the palace was no longer used and local squatters began to settle within the palace walls. In A.D. 614 3,000 to 4,000 people moved from nearby Salona into the palace, soon after that ancient town was overrun by invading Avar tribes. With these migrations into the palace of Diocletian begins the modern history of Split.

In subsequent years the city flourished inside the remains of Diocletian's Palace, and then eventually outside the walls as well. The once-large avenues within the transformed palace became smaller as new buildings were put up, and every inch of space was used to the fullest; even pagan Roman temples were transformed into houses of Christian worship. After Venice took over the Dalmatia area in 1420, the city experienced an architectural expansion (as well as an economic boom thanks to increased trade), blending the stately quality of the Roman constructions with the flamboyant Gothic of the Venetian style.

This amazing architectural mix (which also incorporates later Renaissance buildings, as well as modern reconstructions, TV antennas on roofs, etc.) still remains, and creates a thoroughly charming Old Town, which bustles with pedestrians throughout the year (cars are not allowed in the historic center). The ancient center of Split, along with the town's modern sections, make up the second-largest Yugoslavian city on the Adriatic (pop. 200,000); today Split serves as Dalmatia's center of finance, industry, and culture. Although the big-city architecture of Split's new sections (modern apartment buildings and colorless office buildings) may disappoint, the Old Town of Split offers visitors an exciting area certainly worth an interruption of your sunbathing and swimming.

ORIENTATION: Split is rather large, but you'll end up spending most of your time in **Grad,** the historic Old Town, half of which is contained within the walls of Diocletian's Palace. If you arrive by bus, train, or boat, you'll find yourself at **Obala Bratstva I Jedinstva,** a wide avenue on the harbor just a five-minute walk to Grad. With your back to the sea, walk left down Obala Bratstva I Jedinstva; the street soon becomes **Titova Obala,** and to your right you will see the façade of **Diocletian's Palace.** The area inside the old palace walls boasts not only the most charming and interesting sights in town, but also most of Split's travel agencies.

Travelers arriving by plane at Split's **airport** at Kaštel Štafilić, 20 km (12 miles) outside town, can take a JAT bus to the air terminal at Obala Lazareta, a street right off Obala Bratstva I Jedinstva.

Once you arrive in Grad, stop first at the **Split Tourist Office** at Titova Obala 12 (tel. 42-142; Telex 26177-YU-TURIST). This office rents private rooms in town and offers a wide selection of guidebooks in English about Split and its environs. The helpful personnel can also answer whatever questions you

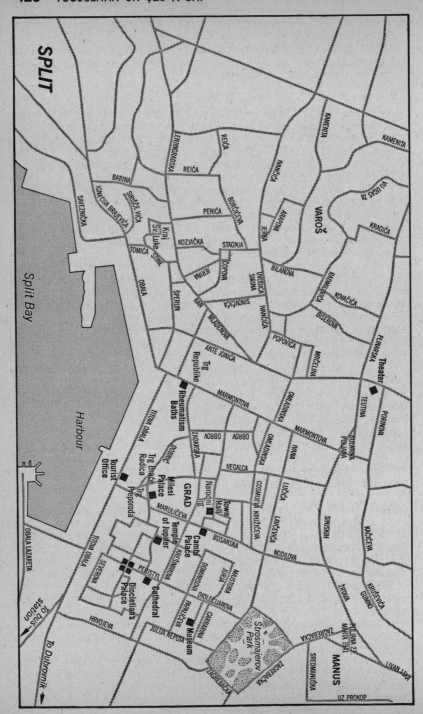

may have about Split. During the summer they're open from 7 a.m. to 10 p.m. seven days a week; during the rest of the year their hours are 7 a.m. to 9 p.m. Monday through Saturday and 8 a.m. to 1 p.m. on Sunday.

ACCOMMODATIONS: The **Hotel Bellevue,** Ante Jonića 2 (tel. 47-175 or 586-615; Telex 26443-YU-BELLEVUE), offers visitors comfortable facilities in an excellent location, just outside Grad, right off Trg Republike. Rooms all come equipped with private bathroom and old-style furniture. We offer one warning about this pleasant hotel: light sleepers should avoid rooms facing the noisy Trg Republike. Rooms are priced according to season: from June 1 to October 1, singles rent for $33 and doubles cost $45.10; in April, May, and October, singles cost $29.10 and doubles run $40.10; during the rest of the year, singles cost $25.80 and doubles are $36.80.

Hotel Srebrna Vrata ("The Silver Gate"), Poljana Kraljice Jelene 3 (tel. 46-869), draws its name from the eastern gate to Diocletian's Palace, adjacent to the hotel. There are no signs outside with the hotel's name, so make sure to ask someone where it is. Once inside, you won't find a reception, rather just a small room to the left that resembles a night watchman's room. You've probably got the idea now that the 12-room Srebrna Vrata offers only basic facilities: the rooms are small and bare with a bed just six inches off the ground; public bathrooms merit just an "okay" rating. Conversely, the hotel offers visitors an excellent location minutes from all the monuments in Diocletian's Palace at an inexpensive rate. A single costs $14.30, and a double, $19.80; breakfast comes with the room.

A similar hotel featuring very basic facilities (it's rated in the D category) in an excellent location is the **Hotel Central,** Narodni Trg 1 (tel. 48-242). Again you won't see a large sign outside the hotel, but it's easy to find as it's right on the town's main square. Facilities are clean, but rooms are not quiet, due to the bustle of shoppers and locals who congregate in the evening on the main square. Rooms cost $16.50 for a single and $22 for a double.

If the Bellevue is full and if these last two choices don't appeal to you, consider staying at the **Hotel Split,** Trstenik (tel. 522-888), located outside the center of the city on the south coast. The modern rooms all offer private bathrooms, and half also have small balconies overlooking the hotel's private strip of beach. It's a fine place to be if you're looking for more comfort and quiet than the town center can offer. In July and August, singles cost $22.60 and doubles run $36.25. During the rest of the year, singles rent for $16.80 and doubles go for $27.30. Take bus 7 or 17 from the beginning of Prvoboraca Street (just south of Grad) to the last stop (which, fortunately, is right in front of the hotel).

Student Lodgings

In July and August students can stay at the **Studenski Dom Ljubo Uvodic Razin,** at Spinutska bb (tel. 42-822), in the Spinut district in the northeast part of town. The Student House rents out single, double, and triple rooms, all for only $8.80 a person, complete with private bathroom. Call ahead before going, as rooms fill up quickly. Take bus 17 from the beginning of Prvoboraca just south of the Old Town, off Titova Obala. Make sure to ask the driver to let you know when to get off.

Private Rooms

Your best budget buy in Split is undoubtedly a private room, which you can rent at several local travel bureaus. Prices range from $9 to $15.40 in July and August, and $7 to $12.30 during the rest of the year. Go to the **Split Tourist Office,** Titova Obala 12 (tel. 42-142); **Dalmacijaturist,** at either Titova Obala 5, open from 7 a.m. to 8:30 p.m. (tel. 44-666), or at Obala Bratstva I Jedinstva 8, near the transportation stations, (tel. 45-065); or one of Split's other travel bureaus.

DINING: Most locals speak of the **Restaurant Mak,** on the top floor of the modern Koteks Shopping Center, Maslešina bb (tel. 523-645), as the town's number one restaurant. The interior resembles a Japanese steakhouse, with large windows and ornate red-and-black wood tables and chairs. A distinguished crowd frequents the Mak, often Yugoslavian businessmen in sharp-looking suits and ties. The excellent menu features mostly meat entrees, such as veal escalope prepared in one of four different styles, the "gypsy spit" of pork, lamb, bacon, kidney, and green peppers prepared on the grill, or several different steak dishes. If you prefer, you can also order fish, such as the delicious scampi. Prices for a restaurant of this elegance and quality offer exceptional value. Most meat and seafood entrees will cost $2 to $3, a truly incredible budget find. The only thing you need do to ensure this fine meal is to reserve beforehand. They're open from noon to 5 p.m. and 7 p.m. to midnight; closed Sunday.

For a good Yugoslavian meal in a rustic setting, try the **Ero Restaurant,** Marmontova 7 (tel. 46-161). Wood beams support the ceiling in this small restaurant, and wood chairs and tables accommodate guests at the restaurant. Folksy red, white, and black tableclothes cover the tables. The restaurant offers a large selection of mostly meat dishes. In particular we highly recommend the "Curasko Specialty Ero," a large plate for two of two tasty, slightly spicy grilled steaks, prosciutto crudo, tomatoes, onions, and many home-style fries. You can feast at the Ero at very reasonable prices, ranging from $1.25 to $4.50 an entree. And don't forget to add a fine bottle of local wine to your meal for only $3 to $6. You can save more on these prices by paying with Yugoslvian National Bank Checks, for which you receive a 10% discount.

Another good rustic restaurant is the **Sarajevo,** Ilegalaca 6 (tel. 47-454), inside the Old Town walls in an old nunnery hundreds of years old. Sturdy stone walls and subdued lighting create a quiet ambience. The menu offers mostly Yugoslavian meat specialties, but a few fish entrees are also available, all for $1.50 to $4.25 a dish. The restaurant is open from 8 a.m. to 11 p.m. seven days a week; reservations are a good idea.

If you're in the mood for some good fresh fish, visit the **Arkina Riblja Konoba,** Vl. Srečko Jelićić Radmilovićeva br. 2 (tel. 589-200). The menu features fish soups, rice with squid or fish, and entrees such as grilled scampi. The cozy interior has white stucco walls and is perfect for an intimate, quiet dinner. Fish entrees cost about $4 a plate. It's open from 9 a.m. to 11 p.m.; reservations are recommended on weekends. You'll find the restaurant a five- to ten-minute walk outside Grad. Go down Titova Obala, past Trg Republike, and take a right down Ante Jonića. After one block, turn left on Jenka Ivančića; then take the second right and you'll see the restaurant.

We suggest the **Restaurant Adriana,** Titova Obala 7 (tel. 44-079), more for its fine location overlooking the town harbor than for its average cuisine. Dozens of the restaurant's outdoor tables line Titova Obala, Split's busiest promenade in the evening, and so while eating you can people-watch or observe the ship traffic in the port. The Adriana offers such simple international specialties as beef goulash and roast pork for only $1.50 to $2.50 an entree. Open from 7 a.m. to midnight, seven days a week.

Another establishment featuring a special location is the **Luxor** (tel. 46-768), a unique outdoor café between the ancient Roman columns of the Peristyle in the heart of Diocletian's Palace. As you enjoy a drink or an omelet, you can admire the majestic Roman structures around you and imagine the ceremonies that once took place here. Diocletian himself received his guests from the small balcony at the port end of this square. The café is open from 7 a.m. to midnight, seven days a week.

NIGHTLIFE: In the evenings, pedestrians and shoppers crowd Split's streets, especially on **Titova Obala** along the harbor, and at Narodni Trg, right in the center of the Old Town. After you have joined this evening procession, you can then attend a performance at the **Dalmacijakoncert Concert Hall,** Trg Republike 1 (tel. 42-999). From July 15 to August 15 you can enjoy the concerts, opera, and ballet of the **Split Summer Festival;** many of these events are performed in the majestic Peristyle of Diocletian's Palace.

IMPORTANT ADDRESSES: The **bus station,** at Obala Bratstva I Jedinstva 12 (tel. 45-047), the **train station,** on Obala Bratstva I Jedinstva (tel. 48-588), and the **marine terminal,** at Gat Španskih Boraca 4 (tel. 43-366), are all located on the south side of Split's harbor, a five- to ten-minute walk from the Old Town (Grad). The train station runs a baggage check office around the clock; the bus station has one open from 4:30 a.m. to 10 p.m.

The **JAT** office at Titova Obala 9 (tel. 45-666) stays open from 6:30 a.m. to 8 p.m. Monday through Friday, to 2:30 p.m. on Saturday; closed Sunday. They can also give you information on departures to the airport by bus from the air terminal.

If you want a private **guided tour** (for an hour and a half) of Split's central monuments, go to the **Ured Vodica** (Guides' Office) at the port side of the Peristyl Piazza (tel. 42-190 or 581-751). A guide for one or two people costs about $10; if you're in a larger group, you pay by the person, starting at $4 each for a group of three, and then less for more people. The office assists travelers from 9 a.m. to 7 p.m. Monday through Saturday, from 9 a.m. to noon and 4 to 7 p.m. on Sunday and holidays.

If you run into automotive troubles, call 987 or visit the **Auto Moto Društvo** (Touring Club of Split) at Obala Lazareta 3 (tel. 41-646).

Your dirty clothes piling high in your luggage? Go to the **Galeb Dry Cleaners** at Rade Končara 57 (tel. 522-641), a street on the south side of town.

THE SIGHTS: The **Old Town** within the walls of Diocletian's Palace contains Split's most important monuments and museums.

Diocletian's Palace

Begin your sightseeing by entering the palace's **Brass Gate** on Vestibula Street, facing the port. On this street you'll pass under the brick **Vestibule,** the only part of Diocletian's living quarters which shows the same colossal space it had in the 4th century A.D. You'll also see a very large circular opening at the top of the domed roof which allows natural light to illuminate the room.

After continuing through the Vestibule you'll reach the noble **Peristyl,** one of the best surviving remnants of Diocletian's Palace. During his days at the palace, Diocletian would receive foreign VIPs and adoring admirers in the square. To impress his visitors, the Roman emperor imported many of the huge columns from Egypt to build this structure, as well as a small black-granite sphinx from the 15th century B.C. which you'll see on the side of the Peristyl.

Walk a few steps to your right under the Peristyl columns to **Diocletian's Mausoleum.** Not surprising since he approved the design of the palace, Diocletian's burial place was the largest of the palace's four temples. The mausoleum features a design similar to that of the Pantheon in Rome, and sports busts of Emperor Diocletian and his wife, Prisca, inside. During the Middle Ages the mausoleum was converted into the **Cathedral of St. Domino** (Sveti Dujam), a structure rich in Gothic and Renaissance decorations. In the 13th and 14th centuries the town planners also added a graceful **campanile** to the church. Ever since then this Romanesque-Gothic campanile has towered over Split's skyline. Energetic travelers can climb to the top for a panoramic view of the city.

Now, backtrack straight across the Peristyl Square and continue down Kraj sv. Ivana half a block to the **Temple of Jupiter,** a Roman temple in excellent condition, albeit without the statue of Jupiter. In the Middle Ages this pagan temple was also converted into a Christian building, in this case in the form of a baptistery. If the building is closed when you pass by, inquire at the tour guide office in the Peristyl office as to how to gain entrance.

If you want a better idea of how large Diocletian's Palace was, visit the **Underground Halls** at Titova Obala 20. Although you can only visit the Western section of the basement, you'll get a sense from the 17 huge vaulted stone-and-brick rooms of the scale and grandeur of Diocletian's Palace. It's certainly the largest basement we've ever seen! Because waste material and rubble was stored in these halls since the Middle Ages, they were in remarkably good condition when the town uncovered them in 1956—and remain so today. The basement is open from 8 a.m. to noon and 4 to 7 p.m.

Museums

The picturesque 15th-century Gothic mansion at Papalićeva 5 (inside the old palace walls) houses the **City Museum.** The collection displays the town's weaponry from the 15th to the 18th centuries and documents the history of Split. It's open from 9 a.m. to 1 p.m. (on Thursday to 4 p.m.); closed Sunday.

The **Archeological Museum,** at Zrinjsko-Frankopanska 12, displays some of the best-preserved remains from the Roman era at Split and nearby Salona. Open from 9 a.m. to 1 p.m. and 4 to 6 p.m. Tuesday through Saturday, on Sunday from 10 a.m. to 1 p.m.; closed Monday.

The **Maritime Museum,** Trg Braće Radića 7, chronicles the great seafaring tradition of Split. It's open from 9 a.m. to noon; closed Sunday.

4. Side Trips From Split

Using Split as a base, day-trippers can choose between the majestic Roman ruins of a once-great society at Solin and the inspiring medieval churches and houses of Trogir.

SOLIN: Long before Diocletian made his home at Split, **Salona** (called today Solin) served as the economic and political center of the Roman Empire in Dalmatia. As many as 60,000 people lived in this city during that time, as compared with only 6,000 today. During Diocletian's residence in nearby Split, Salona reached its financial and cultural zenith. From the 5th to the 7th centuries it was attacked and sacked by barbarian tribes, who destroyed many of the buildings and caused the Salona residents to take refuge in the unoccupied palace of Diocletian.

Those interested in Roman relics will find several sights to enjoy today in Solin, including the ruins of a **Roman theater** (2nd century A.D.), remains of the **public forum** (1st century A.D.), and an **amphitheater** (2nd century A.D.) that once could seat 18,000 people. On your way to Solin, you'll pass impressive **Roman aqueducts,** some of which are still used to bring water to Split from the nearby hills!

We recommend that visitors to Solin buy the guide *The Yugoslav Coast 3* (available in the Split Tourist Office), which contains a useful map of the ruins and some detailed description.

You can drive to Solin on the road that leads north from Split, or you can take a bus from Sukoišanska ulica in Split (note that this station is *not* the main bus station in Split listed earlier).

TROGIR: A tiny island with cobblestone streets and truly impressive Gothic churches and art, Trogir should simply not be missed! First colonized by Greeks, the town became prominent during Roman times when it served as an important trading town. During the Middle Ages Trogir flourished architecturally under the tutelage of the Venetians, who took over in 1420, and many of Trogir's romantic buildings still impart the aura of the Venetian period. Most buildings were constructed of large gray stones, and quite a few are adorned with family crests and other rich details, as well as red-tile roofs.

The most impressive sight in town is the **Cathedral of St. Lawrence,** a 13th-century artistic gem. Students of art will want to spend time analyzing the cathedral's portico (called **Radovan's Portal,** after the 13th-century artist), a very detailed sculpture work with dozens of religious scenes on several layers. Inside you'll see a 14th-century altar and a pulpit from the same era. In the sacristy, you can also admire paintings by Gentile Bellini, brother of Giovanni Bellini (the most important 15th-century Venetian painter). The cathedral stands on the picturesque **town square,** across from the Town Hall and diminutive clock tower, all fine examples of Gothic architecture.

For further information on Trogir, visit **Dalmacijaturist** in town (tel. 73-550); there you can buy (supplies permitting) a useful guide by Ivo Babić called *Trogir: An Illustrated Guide.*

Motorists can drive the 26-km (15½-mile) route from Split by heading north on the main coastal road; other travelers can take the bus from Sukoišanska ulica in Split. You'll want to spend at least half a day exploring the artistic treasures of Trogir.

HEADING SOUTH: Travelers from Split setting their sights on the coast's most beautiful city, **Dubrovnik,** face a four- or five-hour drive along the **Makarska Riviera,** an area of pine forests, pebble beaches, and small resort towns. So don't rule out a quick stop for a little swimming and sunning to break up the drive.

If you look forward to truly splendid beaches, however, we highly recommend a visit to the fun-loving island of **Hvar** or the medieval wonder of **Korčula,** our next ports of call.

5. Hvar

According to countless Yugoslavian publications, Hvar is blessed with more sunshine than on any other island in the Adriatic—an average of 7½ hours of sun a day for 365 days a year! In addition to its balmy climate, Hvar offers visitors good tourist facilities at some of the most unspoiled beaches and waters of the Adriatic. As one British student described the island to us, with just a touch of hyperbole, "It's just like heaven on earth!" After a day of swimming, sunning, and boating in the exceptional climate of Hvar, you can then spend the evening at the cafés, strolling around the harbor, eating ice cream, or drinking in local bars on the port while enjoying a summer zephyr from the sea.

Adventurous Greek colonists first discovered and settled this wonderful island in the 4th century B.C. By the 3rd century B.C. the Romans decided they wanted the island, so they successfully fought the Greeks for it. For much of the past thousand years Venice administered Hvar, up until 1797. During that time Venice's fleet of warships wintered in the Hvar harbor. Two Turkish attacks in the 16th century not only were able to penetrate the harbor, but also destroyed many of the island's most historic buildings. Today, islanders live a charmed traditional life; most locals rear livestock (mainly lambs); grow lavender, rosemary, olives, figs, and grapes; go fishing; build boats; and welcome many tourists.

GETTING TO HVAR: Travelers without a car will welcome the frequent ferry connections from Split and Dubrovnik to the town of Hvar and to Stari Grad, 12½ miles away. (By contrast, many other Adriatic islands offer ferry connections to uninteresting port towns far from the central city, as in Korčula.) The two-hour ride from Split costs about $2 per person, and $10 for a small car.

Motorists driving up from the south can take the ferry from Drvenik on the coast to Sućuraj on the far-eastern tip of skinny Hvar, for about $3 for a small car, and 50¢ for each person. Be prepared for a long, demanding drive when continuing on from Sućuraj to Hvar or Stari Grad, more than 50 miles away; the narrow road runs above many steep cliffs and often curves abruptly.

THE TOWN OF HVAR: We highly recommend the town of Hvar (pop. 4,500) to travelers looking for active, exciting summer fun. From Hvar, you can cruise to one of a dozen nearby flat and forested islands; you can rent a private motorboat or scooter to ride at your own pace; you can dine in one of several dozen good restaurants; or you can just sit at a portside café and sip some good local wine. You are sure to be amused in Hvar!

The town offers much more than just extensive tourist facilities, however. A busy shipping port throughout history, like so many other Yugoslavian cities, Hvar developed under Venetian influence in the Middle Ages, and many of the town's old stone and marble buildings reflect this. You'll see 13th- and 14th-century **walls** surrounding the town and impressive medieval monuments, such as a 15th-century **Franciscan Monastery** (open from 9 a.m. to noon and 4 to 6 p.m.), which houses paintings by Tiepolo and others, and the 17th-century **Hvar Theater** (open from 9 a.m. to 1 p.m. and 8 to 10 p.m.), said to be the oldest theater in all of Europe.

Accommodations

The town's four centrally located hotels are somewhat pricey for the budget traveler, so we strongly suggest private rooms as the best option. If you still prefer a hotel, try the **Hotel Bodul** (tel. 74-049; Telex 26235-YU-HVAR). You'll find the hotel about a ten-minute walk from the main port, in a scenic location overlooking the Križna Luka bay. All 150 modern rooms come equipped with private bathroom and terrace, many of which overlook the sea. The Bodel charges $25.50 for a single and $22.50 per person in a double from July 1 to September 15; $21.50 for a single and $18.50 per person in a double in June and the last half of September; and $14.50 for a single and $12.50 per person in a double in April, May, and October.

The town has three other class B hotels: the **Dalmacija** (tel. 74-120; Telex 26235-YU-HVAR), at the end of the town's main port; the **Delfin** (tel. 74-168; Telex 26235-YU-HVAR), one block behind the main port; and the **Pharos** (tel. 74-028; Telex 26235-YU-HVAR), a few blocks inland from the main port. Each rents fairly modern rooms with private bathroom for the following rates: $23.50 to $27.50 single and $20.50 to $24.50 per person double from July to September 15; $19.50 to $23.50 single and $16.50 to $20.50 per person double in June and the last half of September; $13.50 to $16.50 single and $11.50 to $14.50 per person double in April, May, and October; and $10.50 to $12.50 single and $8.50 to $10.50 double during the rest of the year.

Private Rooms: At the center of the town's harbor area, the Hvar Tourist Board (tel. 74-956; Telex 26235-YU-HVAR) rents private rooms for $5.95 to $10.40 single and $3.95 to $7 per person double from July to September 15; $5.20 to $9 single, and $3.40 to $5.95 per person double in June and the last half of September; and $4.50 to $8.10 single and $3.05 to $5.40 per person double during the rest of the year. Remember that a 30% surcharge to these rates will be added for stays of three days or fewer.

Dining

Hvar features many small restaurants, most of which offer good seafood and national specialties at very fair prices. It seems that every local frequents a different favorite restaurant, and no one restaurant seems to tower above the others. Believe it or not, you can dine well, in an attractive setting, at literally dozens of different restaurants.

Our one culinary tip in town is for pizza-starved travelers who don't want another good seafood meal, but some tangy tomato sauce and thick mozzarella lavished on a well-baked slice of pizza dough. If this sounds like you, try **Pizza Miko,** a small indoor restaurant with stone walls just one street off the main port, open from 11 a.m. to 1:30 p.m. and 6:30 to 11 p.m.; on Sunday though, the restaurant stays open only from 6 to 11 p.m.

Sports and Island-Hopping

Most locals and visitors to Hvar go swimming on the many islands off the coast, for local beaches are small and quite crowded. We prefer the sandy beaches at **L. Palmižana** and **Vala** on the St. Klement Island. The nude beaches (for "naturalists," as the locals call them) are at **U. Stipanska** and **Jerolim.** Boats to these destinations leave from the main port about every half hour between 8 and 11 a.m., and then return 3 to 7 p.m. The ride to Palmižana costs $1.50 round trip, and to Jerolim only 75¢ round trip. The nearest and most accessible of all these islands is Jerolim, which swarms with so-called naturalists. If you seek a flat rock to lie out on and some beautiful clean waters, then you'll find Jerolim to your liking.

If you prefer to navigate the waters on your own, you can rent a little motorboat from several travel agencies or private operators around the bay. Daily rates run about 5,500 dinars ($18.85) for the boat and two or three liters of gas. You might think this a somewhat splurgey expense, but once you're out on the high seas exploring the coves and beautiful islands near Hvar, you'll find the money well spent.

If riding to a nearby beach on a motorscooter appeals to you, local operators will rent a vehicle for the day, complete with a full tank of gas, for about $11. Inquire at **Dalmacijaturist** (tel. 74-021 or 74-105), open from 7:30 a.m. to 9:30 p.m. seven days a week, or one of the private operators on the town harbor.

IMPORTANT ADDRESSES: Call **Jadrolinija** for ferry information at 74-132 or 74-036. Local travel agencies can also provide information on ferries to and from Hvar, and on local buses.

STARI GRAD: As its name suggests (Stari Grad means "old city" in Serbian), Stari Grad was the site of Hvar's first Greek settlement, called Pharos, in the 4th century B.C. Although little of the Greek and Roman settlements remain, you can view impressive artwork from the Renaissance, such as Tintoretto's *Christ's Burial* in the 15th-century **Dominican Monastery** (aside from this painting, the rest of the church is rather uninteresting due to a 19th-century restoration). Art buffs can also visit paintings of St. John the Baptist and St. Laurence by Titian (or perhaps Veronese—the artist's identity is disputed) in the nearby village of **Vrboska** in the baroque church of Sveti Lovrinc.

In contrast with the town of Hvar, life in Stari Grad moves more slowly. A smaller community lives around the long narrow port, and just beyond this settlement you can see miles of uninterrupted green countryside. You can't zoom around on a rented motorboat or scooter here, but if you're looking to relax in an easy-going town and enjoy tranquil beaches nearby, then you should visit Stari Grad.

Accommodations

Hotel Helios, situated slightly inland on the right side of the harbor (tel. 75-822; Telex 26205-YU-HELIOS), offers 214 modern, though slightly worn, rooms with private bathroom for the following rates: $24.50 single and $38 double from July to September 15, $19.50 single and $28.80 double in June and the last 15 days of September, and $14.70 single and $22 double in April, May, and October. The Helios also rents attractive bungalow apartments which include a small kitchen with supplies, living room, small bedroom, and private bathroom. We highly recommend that you stay in one of these 25 bungalows if one is available, for they provide comfortable accommodations at an excellent budget value. Over the same time periods listed above, the bungalows for two cost $29.70 in high season, $24.20 in middle season, and $18.70 in low season.

Next door you'll find the more modern and well-maintained **Hotel Adriatic** (tel. 75-822; Telex 26205-YU-HELIOS), which also offers visitors a private beach. Rooms cost about 10% more than those at the Hotel Helios.

Private Rooms: Located on the harbor, **Dalmacijaturist** (tel. 75-825) rents private rooms to Stari Grad's visitors. From July 1 to September 15 rooms rent for $4.50 to $6.40 per person; during the rest of the year, $3.75 to $5.25 per person. The office is open from 8 a.m. to 1 p.m. and 5 to 8 p.m.

Dining

Two unlikely restaurateurs, Bojana and Vladimir Mitic, own and run the excellent **Feral Restaurant,** Ciklopska 21 (no phone). Bojana, a dentist by training, and Vladimir, a lawyer, operate the restaurant during the summer, and then spend the winters in the U.S., where Vladimir works as a real estate agent and Bojana continues her studies of dentistry. Why, then, do they own a restaurant? It's a good investment, they say. But they're not people to take the money and run; they serve visitors a huge, memorable meal at very reasonable prices. You'll find the locale simple and unpretentious, with stone and stucco walls and low ceilings in the restaurant's two small rooms; disco and pop tunes play in the background. During the summer you can also dine in a small garden in the back. The house specialty is the "Feral," which imitates the shape of an old-fashioned lamp. Beef chunks and ground meat shaped into patties with ham and cheese inside, or several different types of fish such as squid, are skewered onto four shish-kebab poles; along with more meat and vegetables below, all this forms a large culinary "feral." A feast for two costs 2,400 dinars ($8.20) with meat and 2,800 dinars ($9.60) with fish. If you prefer something less ostentatious, you can order several other, more moderately priced grilled meat and fish dishes. Don't miss the huge salad generously covered with grated goat cheese, or the delicious appetizer of fried cheese with a crispy crust, a local specialty. The Feral is open from 11 a.m. to 3 p.m. and 5 p.m. to 1 a.m., seven days a week; from October 15 to May 1 the restaurant is closed.

6. Korčula

Those skilled in the art of island-hopping will be hard-pressed to find a more charming and romantic island than Korčula. Located roughly between Split and Dubrovnik in the Adriatic, Korčula offers visitors beautiful unspoiled beaches, a densely covered countryside of fig groves and vineyards (which produce a wonderful local wine, Grk), and the medieval walled city of Korčula, built in the ornate Venetian architectual style.

Settled by the Greeks in the 4th century B.C., Korčula was ruled by the Romans after 35 B.C. From A.D. 1000 to 1779 the mighty Venetians controlled Korčula in four separate eras, some lasting for several hundred years at a time, most notably from 1420 to 1797. According to local legend, Marco Polo was born on the island; perhaps more historically documented was his detention on the island in 1298 after Korčula defeated the Venetians in a large naval battle.

The long island stretches from east to west in the Adriatic; Vela Luka, a major port town, is situated at the west end; the city of Korčula, the island's "must-see," lies at the east end.

Note: As in many small Adriatic islands, Korčula's towns do not use specific addresses, so to find a hotel or restaurant listed in this section, ask for directions.

GETTING TO KORČULA: Several times a week **boats** depart from Dubrovnik, Rijeka, Split, and Hvar for Korčula. **Buses** also leave twice a day from the main bus station in Dubrovnik.

If you're traveling by car, you can take a car ferry from Split every day to Vela Luka on the west end of the island, or you can take a ferry first from Kardeljevo on the mainland to Trpanj on the Pelješac Peninsula (cost for the one-hour ride: about $5 for the car, and $1 per person), and then from Trpanj you can drive across the thin Pelješac Peninsula to Orebić and catch the ferry to Korčula (cost for the 15-minute ride: about $2 for the car and 40¢ per person). If you're driving up from the south, you can drive directly to Orebić on the Pelješac Peninsula.

THE TOWN OF KORČULA: Even the most dedicated sun worshipper will enjoy an afternoon away from the seashore in the picturesque town of Korčula (pop. 3,000). The small walled city with its marble buildings and Gothic churches is somewhat reminiscent of Dubrovnik; both cities were built under Venetian rule in the Middle Ages. Unlike Dubrovnik, however, Korčula is not crowded with tourists and so you can enjoy the town's sights by yourself on a quiet summer afternoon.

The Sights

Walking up the steps leading to the Old Town, you'll see the winged Lion of San Marco, the symbol of Venice, above the stone tower which forms part of the town's **fortifications.** The Venetians did not want any doubts as to who ruled Korčula! Inside the town walls, many splendid examples of Venetian architecture remain along the pedestrians-only cobblestone streets. In particular, be sure to visit the **Cathedral of St. Mark** (Sveti Marko), a church begun in the 13th century which features a large altarpiece by the prolific painter Tintoretto (his thousands of paintings are displayed in churches and museums all across Europe), as well as the 14th-century **Abbey's Palace** (Opatska Palace), which houses a collection of church art from the 15th to the 20th centuries. In the heart of the Old Town at Ul. Marka Pola, you can also visit the house where the intrepid Venetian explorer, Marco Polo, was purportedly born.

Weekly from April to October a special dance called the **moršeka** is performed outdoors in Korčula to celebrate the victorious battles against the Turks. Two groups of traditionally dressed knights from the Middle Ages, symbolizing the evil Turks (in black) and the local islanders (in virtuous red) sing, talk, and fight over a beautiful maiden in this island ritual. Although this symbolic dance was once performed all across Europe, today it continues to be performed only in Korčula. Inquire at any town tourist office for more details.

After exploring the churches, palaces, and streets of the town, you can relax at the peaceful and wonderful beaches, all of which overlook majestic silhouettes of nearby islands and peninsulas; if you have a car, you might also consider visiting one of the nearby fishing villages or the breathtaking cove at Pupnatska Luka (read on for more details).

Accommodations

We heartily recommend the attractive, modern **Hotel Bon Repos** (tel. 81-019 or 81-102; Telex 27556-YU-HOTKOR), whose rooms have private bathrooms and balconies. Located just a short walk down the road from the Korčula ferry landing and about half a mile from the town center, the Bon Repos is the perfect place to spend a restful vacation. The hotel maintains its own small private sandy beach, as well as an outdoor swimming pool and a tennis court. If you tire of the hotel's strip of beach, they'll transport you to the nearby nudist island of Stupe on their own motorboat. All this comes at an excellent price. Singles cost $24.20 in July and August, $17.60 in June and September, and $11 to $12.65 the rest of the year. Doubles rent for $36.30 to $41.80 in July and August, $23.10 to $27.50 in June and September, and $17.60 to $20.90 the rest of the year. You can also dine in a fine restaurant downstairs.

Another attractive, modern hotel is the **Hotel Marko Polo,** located on a small peninsula overlooking the Old Town (tel. 711-100; Telex 27556-YU-HOTKOR). Many of the 109 rooms offer panoramic views of the Old Town, in addition to modern facilities such as telephones, large bathtubs, and even two elevators in the hotel! Like the Bon Repos, the Marko Polo offers a small private beach and rides to the island of Stupe. Unfortunately, the Marko Polo, for all its positive features, also costs more than most of Korčula's other hotels. In July and August singles rent for $30.80, and doubles run $44 to $49.50; in June and September single rooms rent for $24.20 and doubles for $33 to $37.40; during the rest of the year prices are a considerably more reasonable $13.20 to $16.50 single and $22 to $26.40 double.

Visitors without the luxury of a car should consider staying at the **Hotel Korčula** (tel. 711-078; Telex 27556-YU-HOTKOR), Korčula's only hotel in the Old Town area. Although not located on a beach like the town's other hotels, the Korčula (and many of its 20 small, modern rooms) overlook a peaceful bay on the northwest side of the Old Town. To reach the hotel, walk on the left side of the Old Town along the harbor; you'll arrive after a few blocks. Rooms with bathroom cost $19.80 to $26.40 single and $37.40 to $44 double in July and August; $13.20 to $17.60 single and $25.30 to $29.70 double in June and September; and $10.45 to $13.20 single and $18.70 to $22 double in May and October.

If Korčula's other hotels are full, then try the **Hotel Park** (tel. 711-004; Telex 27556-YU-HOTKOR). You'll notice that rooms in the Park look slightly older than those in Korčula's other hotels; nonetheless the hotel does feature a private beach as well as windsurfing lessons for about $4 an hour in front of the hotel (from 9 a.m. to 5 p.m.). The 153 rooms with private bathrooms cost exactly the same as those at Hotel Bon Repos. You'll find the Park next door to the Hotel Marko Polo, just a few minutes' walk outside the Old Town.

Private Rooms: One block before the town walls on the left side of the harbor (signs reading "Tourist Bureau" point out the way) the **Turist Biro Marko Polo** (tel. 711-067) rents private rooms for $11.50 to $13.50 per person in high season, $9 to $11 in low season. The office is open from 7 a.m. to 9 p.m., seven days a week.

If you prefer to find a room on your own, many locals advertise their rooms between the ferry landing and the town center with signs that read "Sobe, Zimmer, Room," or perhaps just "Sobe." When inquiring about the price, make sure you understand whether the price is per person or for the entire room.

Dining

Don't leave Korčula without dining in the charming **Restaurant Adio Mare**, Ul. Marka Pola 91 (tel. 711-253). This restaurant features home-cooking in a real family atmosphere. The middle-aged father, Ante Cuitković, distinguished by his happy smiles and large apron, presides at the grill; his daughter and other relatives serve the restaurant's few tables. You'll see the grill in the restaurant's first area, a small courtyard with wooden picnic tables; to the right is an intimate indoor space with many locally made decorations on the walls. In this colorful ambience you can savor excellent local specialties such as "Dalmation pržolica with cabbage" (beef roasted on the live coals with cabbage), and barbecued baby beef (a beef filet grilled and served on a wooden plate with red peppers and mustard). These dishes are remarkable both for their very tender beef and for the distinctive flavor imparted by the grill technique that Mr. Cuitkovic has truly mastered. You can also enjoy good fresh fish prepared over the open fire. Prices are very reasonable, ranging from $2.50 to $5 for a filling entree. Service is April to October only, from 11 a.m. to 2 p.m. and 6 p.m. to midnight.

Many locals highly recommend the **Gradski Podrum,** Trg Maršala Tita, right inside the town walls (tel. 81-222), a restaurant featuring both attractive sidewalk tables in a small piazza, and indoor dining. Inside, Gradski Podrum looks somewhat like an American diner, with white stone walls, processed-looking wood paneling, and modern lamps hanging from the ceiling. The restaurant offers both national and international specialties at very reasonable cost, from $1.50 to $4 a plate. We found their local specialties such as scampi (for a bargain $2) far better than their attempts at international dishes, such as spaghetti.

Important Addresses

Atlas (tel. 81-231, 81-061, or 81-062) located right in front of the entrance to the Old Town, sells ferry tickets and offers day trips to areas in and around Korčula, but it doesn't rent private rooms. The office is open from 8 a.m. to 1 p.m. and 5 to 9 p.m.

The **bus station** is located just one block outside the entrance to the Old Town (tel. 711-216 or 711-106 for information).

LUMBARDA: If you're looking for a peaceful fishing village where lush green countryside surrounds the town and few signs of the 20th century can be found, consider visiting Lumbarda, located just four miles southeast of Korčula on a small cape. Founded by Greek colonists is the 4th century B.C., today the town is inhabited by only 1,000 people, mostly fishermen. For visitors, Lumbarda offers pebble beaches and 20 small islands off the shore, a few of which are accessible to the strong swimmer, who can then pretend to be Robinson Crusoe for the day. (One suggestion to make the swim more enjoyable: bring along your mask and snorkel, so you can marvel at the vast undersea world as you paddle along.) Travelers less interested in vigorous swimming can relax in the slow, easy-going pace of the town, and maybe brighten up the afternoon and evening by sipping some wine from the Lumbarda region, such as the dry white wine Grk.

You can reach Lumbarda by bus from Korčula; your first stop in town should be the **Hotel Lumbarda** (tel. 50-262 or 50-263), the central hotel reception for Lumbarda's three hotels, as well as its private-room-finding service. A modern room with private bathroom in the Lumbarda or the town's other two hotels costs approximately $19.10 for a single and $27.10 to $28.25 for a double in July and August, $14.50 for a single and $19.85 to $21 for a double in June and September, and $10.30 for a single and $16.05 to $17.20 for a double in April, May, and October. The higher double-room prices indicate a room with a balcony overlooking the sea.

If you prefer a private room in Lumbarda, the hotel reception will rent a single or double for $4 to $7 per person from July 15 to August 15, or $3 to $6 per person during the rest of the year.

PUPNATSKA LUKA: If you have a car on Korčula, consider visiting Pupnatska Luka, perhaps the most scenic and impressive beach on the island. Here a small strip of beach lies at the foot of lush mountains surrounding the entire long narrow bay; in the distance you can see gray silhouettes of islands. It's a hideaway where you will soon forget the outside world.

To get to Pupnatska Luka, drive toward Vela Luka on the island's main road. At Pupnat, follow the signs to Pupnatska Luka, and you'll end up on a hair-raising road precariously poised above tall cliffs. Soon you'll see the bay far below and a tiny sign indicating the path to the beach. From this point you must continue by foot 500 feet down on a small dirt path. We must warn that this trip is only for the adventurous; but once you reach the beach, we think you'll agree that this is one of those places that makes the Yugoslavian coast special.

RAČIŠĆE: Another secluded fishing town is Račišće, eight miles north of Korčula. This tiny town (pop. 500) encircles a small bay that serves as the port; the peninsula of Pelješac lies in the distance. It's the type of town where the children playing by the port and the fishermen bringing in their boats from an early-morning outing will all notice the arrival of strangers to their little town.

Your only hotel choice in this peaceful town is the 11-room **Hotel Mediteran** (tel. 710-813). All the rather bare rooms feature private bathrooms and balconies that face the sea. There's a restaurant downstairs. You'll find the prices at the Mediteran very reasonable: $20.90 for a single and $33 for a double in July and August, $14.30 for a single and $22 for a double in June and September, and $11 for a single and $17.60 for a double in May and October.

VELA LUKA: You can take a boat from Hvar or Split to Vela Luka on the far-western side of Korčula. The town (which means "Big Port" in Serbian) is the largest on any Adriatic island, with almost 5,000 inhabitants, mostly fishermen, wine growers, and shipbuilders. Although the city offers some attractive beaches in the environs, you may want to continue on to the town of Korčula, as Vela Luka cannot match the charm of Korčula's Venetian-style houses and churches.

If you do decide to spend some time in Vela Luka, try the 170-room **Posejdon** (tel. 82-226), an attractive hotel near the beach with a private swimming pool. Rooms come with private bathroom, and many are also equipped with a terrace overlooking the town harbor. Singles cost $16.95 to $18.85 in July and August and $9.40 to $15.80 the rest of the year; doubles cost $26.35 to $33.90 in July and August and $15.05 to $26.35 the rest of the year.

You can also rent rooms from the **Turisticki Biro** (tel. 82-042; Telex 27559) or **Atlas** (tel. 82-078) for $7.55 to $12.45 per person in July and August, $5.65 to $9.80 the rest of the year.

Buses leave several times a day from Vela Luka for travelers continuing on to Korčula.

Chapter XXX

DUBROVNIK AND THE SOUTHERN COAST

1. Dubrovnik
2. Montenegro and the Southern Coast

FEW VISITORS TO YUGOSLAVIA can resist the charms of Dubrovnik and the Montenegrin coast to its south. Of all the Adriatic coast's enticing cities, Dubrovnik stands foremost in preserving the picturesque cityscape of the Middle Ages. Huge chalk-white walls surround the Old Town, which presents ornate buildings and architectural details at every corner. It's almost as though the Dubrovnik of the 15th century had been frozen in time, only to be brought to life again in the 20th century!

To the south of Dubrovnik are some of Europe's most beautiful and unspoiled beaches, many situated at towns as old as Dubrovnik. The buildings and layout of many towns in Montenegro show a great similarity to Venice; in places such as Kotor, this distinctive Venetian architecture is in an incredible natural setting of mountains and a bold blue lake in front of the port. To the south at Ulcinj lies Yugoslavia's longest sand beach, a blessing to travelers not accustomed to pebble beaches.

1. Dubrovnik

No tour of the Yugoslavian coast is complete without a visit to Dubrovnik (pop. 35,000), the medieval walled city that has been aptly called "the Pearl of the Adriatic." Originally known as "the Republic of Ragusa," Dubrovnik developed into a major trading capital between East and West in the Middle Ages, and the city accumulated great wealth. With its riches, Dubrovnik built up a glorious town of narrow streets filled with ornate off-white marble architecture, completely surrounded by high stone walls to protect against foreign invasion. Miraculously, the city remains to this day as it was in the 15th century, with original palaces, churches, moats, drawbridges, and defensive walls all intact. As in Venice, you cannot drive in the town center; and we feel that Dubrovnik, along with Venice, certainly ranks as one of the most romantic and exciting cities in all of Europe!

A CAPSULE HISTORY: Established in the 7th century A.D., Dubrovnik had already built up a fair-sized navy of 300 boats by the 10th century. Although it continued to trade with countries across the Mediterranean from that time,

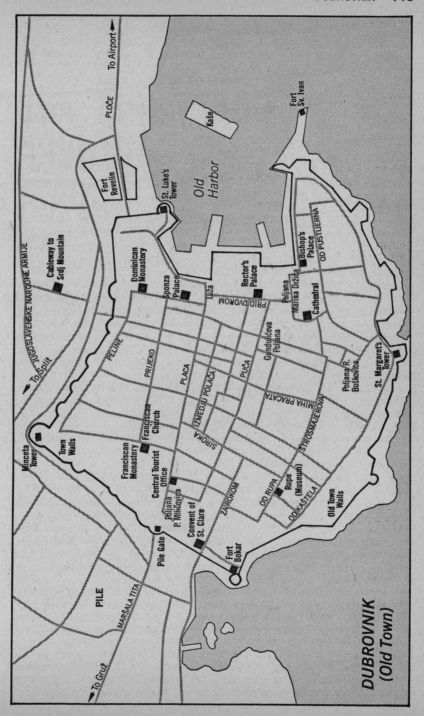

DUBROVNIK (Old Town)

To Airport

PLOCE

To JUGOSLAVENSKE NARODNE ARMIJE

To Split

Cableway to Srdj Mountain

Fort Revelin

St. Luke's Tower

Old Harbor

Kaše

Fort St. Ivan

Dominican Monastery

Sponza Palace

Luža

Rector's Palace

PRID DVOROM

Poljana Marina Držića

Bishop's Palace

OD PUSTIJERNA

Cathedral

PELINE

PRIJEKO

PLACA

Gundulićeva Poljana

PUCA

Poljana R. Boškovića

St. Margaret's Tower

SIROKA

IZMEDJU POLACA

MIHA PRACATA

STROSMAJEROVA

Minčeta Tower

Town Walls

Franciscan Monastery

Franciscan Church

Central Tourist Office

Poljana P. Miličevića

Convent of St. Clare

ZAROKOM

OD RUPA

Rupe (Museum)

OD KAŠTELA

Old Town Walls

Pile Gate

Fort Bokar

MARSALA TITA

PILE

To Gruž

Dubrovnik's development was retarded by the rule of the iron-fisted Venetians, who subjugated Dubrovnik from 1205 to 1358 (although it may be said that the Venetian influence on local architecture was a positive one). In 1358 the considerably more liberal Hungarian-Croatian kingdom took control and allowed Dubrovnik to evolve into a free and independent state. When Turkish invasions threatened in subsequent years, Dubrovnik worked out a deal whereby they could live and trade in peace, in exchange for gold and silver "gifts" to the Ottoman Empire. Thus by the 15th and 16th centuries, the Republic of Dubrovnik had reached the height of its power and economic success, thanks to the thriving shipping industry. But the slump in the shipping industry in the 17th century (due to a change in sailing routes), followed by a severe earthquake in Dubrovnik in 1667, marked a downturn in the city's fortunes. In 1806 the French under Napoleon's command sacked the city; by 1808 the Dubrovnik Republic ceased to exist. From 1815 to 1918 (when Yugoslavia was formed), Dubrovnik was administered by the Austrian Empire.

ORIENTATION: Today the historic medieval **Old Town (Stari Grad)** of Dubrovnik makes up only a small part of the entire city. You are likely to arrive in **Gruž,** where all public buses and boats come in, a district about a 30-minute walk to the northwest of Stari Grad. Before you hurry with bags in hand to Stari Grad, keep in mind that you'll find many of the town's hotels in Gruž. To the west of Gruž is **Lapad,** a large peninsula where many of Dubrovnik's summer beach hotels are found. If you walk south of Gruž and Lapad, after about 20 to 25 minutes you'll pass **Pile,** a smaller district right outside the Stari Grad town walls. From Pile you cross a drawbridge (of course, just like you've always dreamed about!), and then you've reached the glorious core of Dubrovnik, in Stari Grad. The main street, **Placa,** with its marble pavement worn smooth from hundreds of years of pedestrian use, continues on to the other end of the walls, where you'll find the second entrance to the Old Town (we describe this walk in our sights section). The last section of town to the south of Stari Grad is called **Ploče.**

ACCOMMODATIONS: With a building code (in effect since 1292) that closely regulates construction in Stari Grad, you can hardly expect the small Old Town to be dotted with hotels. Thus most of Dubrovnik's hotels are located in the Gruž and Lapad districts, with a few in Ploče and only one hotel in the Old Town itself. If you prefer to stay in the Old Town or its immediate surroundings, we recommend that you rent a private room and ask specifically for a central location. If you are choosing between Gruž and Lapad, we recommend Gruž to those visitors who prefer a lively port atmosphere (Gruž handles most of Dubrovnik's shipping and tourist boats). If, conversely, you plan to do a lot of swimming and prefer a beach area, then you should choose a hotel in Lapad to be within walking distance of the shore.

In Stari Grad

Dubrovnik's one and only hostelry within the walls of Stari Grad is the **Hotel Dubravka,** Ulica od Puća 1 (tel. 26-293). Although a basic Class C hotel, it's unlikely to have a vacancy since it's located one minute from Placa, and everyone wants to stay here. According to the receptionist, you should reserve during the spring to stay at the Dubravka in the summer. Once in a blue moon a vacancy opens up because of a cancellation, but the chances are very slim. From June 1 to October 1, doubles cost $39.60 and singles run $17.60. During the rest of the year, doubles fall in price to $27.50 and singles drop to $15.40; most rooms do not have private bathrooms.

In Gruž

The Class B **Garni Hotel Petka,** Gruška obala 76 (tel. 24-933), offers visitors pleasant modern rooms that overlook either the bay of Gruž or the mountains behind Dubrovnik. You can walk to the Petka in 10 to 15 minutes from the bus/airport terminal by walking along the port with the bay to your left. Despite its central location in the Gruž district, the hotel's rooms are well insulated against noise and you'll sleep like a baby here. From July 1 to September 30 the Petka charges $18.70 for bathless singles and $24.40 for singles with bathroom; you'll pay $35.30 to $42.90 for doubles without bathroom and $48.40 with. You receive a fair reduction on these rates during other times of the year.

If the Petka is full, or if you're looking to save as much money as possible, walk down the street to the **Hotel Gruž,** at Gruška obala 26 (tel. 24-777). You'll recognize the hotel by its distinctive façade, which looks like an antitank barrack, with thick white stone walls and small windows. Inside, the rooms are equally bare and slightly worn (the public bathrooms are in decent condition, however). The Gruž charges correspondingly low prices: $16.50 to $22 for singles and $27.50 to $33 for doubles from July to September, $13.20 to $16.50 for singles and $19.80 to $25.30 for doubles in May and June, and $11 to $13.20 for singles and $14.30 to $17.60 for doubles during the rest of the year. Some doubles come with private bathrooms, but singles do not.

Those nostalgic for their university dormitory might consider staying at the **Hotel Stadion,** M. Tita 96 (tel. 23-449), right behind the train station. This unique Class D hotel with 110 rooms along very long corridors offers guests the use of an Olympic-size swimming pool—an offer which attracts many students and sports groups. From July to September singles cost $22 to $24.20 and doubles run $29.70 to $38.50, in May and June singles rent for $15.40 to $17.60 and doubles go for $24.20 to $28.60, and in April and October singles cost a bargain $11 to $12.10 while doubles run $16.50 to $22. The upper end of these price ranges is for a room with a private bathroom.

The considerably more modern **Hotel Lero,** at Iva Vojnovića 18 (tel. 325-55 or 247-34; Telex 27599-YU-HOLER), also attracts many young people; when we visited, an attractive group of Swedish coeds was checking into the hotel. You can reach the Old Town from the Lero in about a 20- to 25-minute walk, or in less time by bus 4. Just down the road you can swim and sun at a small beach in front of the Hotel Bellevue. July to September high-season rates are $29.70 to $36.30 for singles and $41.80 to $46.20 for doubles, May and June rates are $23.10 to $24.20 for singles and $31.90 to $37.40 for doubles. The rest of the year, rooms rent for $15.40 to $16.50 single and $20.90 to $25.30 double. All 155 rooms have a private bathroom.

Just down the block is the attractive **Hotel Bellevue,** Pera Čingrije 7 (tel. 250-76 or 247-34; Telex 27599-YU-HOLER), a 56-room hotel poised on the top of a cliff with a beautiful cove beach below. We particularly like the Bellevue for its combination of a relaxing beach with proximity to Stari Grad, only a 15- to 20-minute walk away, or five minutes by bus. Many of the modern rooms (from 1970) overlook the hotel's little cove at the beach. If you arrive during July and August you'll pay $31.90 to $36.30 for a single and $41.80 to $52.80 for a double; in May and June the rates fall to $23.10 to $26.40 single and $31.90 to $39.60 double. Finally, if you visit in April or October you'll receive the super-discount rate of $16.50 to $18.70 single and $20.90 to $25.30 double.

In Lapad, Near Sumratin Bay

The following hotels are about three kilometers (two miles) away from Stari Grad, but you can swiftly reach the center from Lapad by bus 2, 4, 5, or 6.

The great advantage of staying in Lapad is that you can walk to a small beach with beautiful clear water in just minutes.

The only hotel we know of in all of Europe that operates its reception on the ninth floor is the **Hotel Kompas**, Aleja I. L. Ribara 50 (tel. 23-776 to 23-778; Telex 27630-YU-HOKUM). The 129 modern rooms offer private bathrooms and attractive small balconies overlooking the mountains or the sea. You'll especially enjoy the Kompas if you intend to do some relaxing in addition to your sightseeing in Dubrovnik: the hotel also boasts an indoor and outdoor swimming pool, a solarium, a massage parlor, and a hairdresser. Singles run $33 from July to September, $26.40 in May, June, and the first 15 days of October, and $23.10 during the rest of the year; doubles cost $46.20 to $58.30 in high season, $33 to $44 in mid-season, and $26.40 to $35.20 in low season.

The 48-room **Hotel Jadran**, Stonska 4 (tel. 23-276), offers guests slightly older rooms with a nice view of the bay or of the thickly forested hills nearby. Singles rent for $28.80 to $38.40 from July to September, $20.40 to $26.40 in May and June, and $13.20 to $16.80 in April and October. Doubles cost $43.20 to $50.40 from July to September, $31.20 to $38.40 in May and June, and $20.40 to $25.20 in April and October. Price differentials reflect the room's view (sea or mountain), and whether the room comes with private bathroom.

Hotel Zagreb, I. L. Ribara 27 (tel. 25-642), a few blocks inland from the bay, looks like an old colonial mansion, but in reality it only rents 25 slightly rundown rooms, most with private bathroom. If you're willing to do away with the more modern facilities of many of Dubrovnik's other hotels, the Zagreb will give you an excellent budget value. Singles cost $20.90 from July to September, $15.40 in May and June, and $12.10 in April and October. During the same time periods, doubles cost $38.50 to $41.80, $27.50 to $31.90, and $22 to $24.20.

Next door to the Zagreb and also a few minutes away from the sea is the **Hotel Sumratin**, I. L. Ribara 31 (tel. 24-722). Here you can rent attractive, fairly modern rooms with private bathroom for $28.60 to $40.70 single or $34.10 to $46.20 double from July to September. In May and June, prices drop to $23.10 to $29.70 for a single and $24.20 to $35.20 for a double; finally, in April and October, prices fall even further to $14.30 to $19.80 in a single and $15.40 to $23.10 in a double. Tennis players will appreciate the added bonus of several courts right near the hotel.

In Lapad, in the Babin Kuk Area

Those who plan to combine their sightseeing with a lot of sun and surf might consider the **Hotel Neptune**, XIII J. D. Brigade (tel. 23-755; Telex 27523-YU-HD), a 210-room hotel offering a private beach, tennis court, swimming pool, and other resort amenities. All rooms have large terraces, and more than half face the sea, thanks to the hotel's position on a peninsula. From July to September single rooms rent for $29.70 and doubles go for $41.80 to $48.40; in May and June prices are $26.20 single and $31.90 to $37.40 double; in April and October prices reach their best value of $17.60 for a single and $22 to $25.30 for a double. The hotel is somewhat far from Stari Grad, but nearby buses 5 and 6 cover the distance in only 10 or 15 minutes.

Splurge Choices

If you want to relieve your wallet of some extra dollars and live in style, stay at the **Hotel Excelsior**, F. Supila (tel. 23-566; Telex 27538-YU-EXCEL), located in Ploče less than a ten-minute walk from Stari Grad. As you step into the lobby you'll see a panoramic view of the island of Lokrum, the crystal-clear water down below, and Stari Grad in the distance; if you're willing to go all out in your splurging, you'll be able to gaze at the impressive scenery from your balcony.

The spacious rooms with furniture from the 1960s are priced strictly on location (all rooms come with private bathroom); you'll have to lay out some extra bucks for that great view of the sea, but you can save by facing a mountain. In July and August singles rent for $27.50 to $55 and doubles go for $44 to $92.80, in May and June as well as from September 1 to 15 singles cost $22 to $44 and doubles run $33 to $70.40, and the rest of the year prices fall to $17.60 to $33 single and $22 to $46.20 double.

For those who agree that Dubrovnik merits a splurge, we also highly recommend the 108-room **Grand Hotel Imperial**, M. Simoni 2 (tel. 23-688 or 23-689; with the suggestive-sounding Telex 27639-YU-HOT-IMP), an elegant hotel just minutes way from the Old Town walls. Many British and French visitors stay at the Imperial, and relax in the handsome rooms with older furniture suggesting prewar European hotels. Many rooms also have balconies where late-night romantics can admire the stars over the Adriatic. From July 1 to September 30 the Imperial charges $46 for a single and $69 for a double; during the rest of the year, rooms cost $23 to $35 for a single and $40 to $55 for a double. According to the reception manager, Andrija Seifried, the hotel also rents a few bathless rooms on a first-come, first-served basis at a 40% discount. "We don't advertise these rooms," he says, but if you go see Mr. Seifried, he'll offer one if it's available.

The Youth Hotel

Students with the ISIC card, or youths under 26 with the FIYTO card, can take advantage of one of Dubrovnik's best budget buys, the **Karavan International Youth Hotel**, ulica Ivanska 2 in Lapad (tel. 23-841). For only 1,320 dinars ($4.50) per person—the same price applies all year long—you can rent two- or three-bed bungalows in a 16th-century castle's gardens. The rooms are completely bare and the private bathrooms are really worn, but you won't find a cheaper deal anywhere in Dubrovnik. You can take bus 2 or 4 to the Old Town from here. From 7 p.m. to 2 a.m. a small outdoor disco attracts many of the students staying in the youth hotel.

Private Rooms

After a stay in one of Dubrovnik's private rooms, you'll certainly agree that no other accommodations can match the charm and authenticity of living with the locals. When we visited Dubrovnik we stayed in a delightful private room just outside the Stari Grad walls; during the evening we could watch the summer sun set over the ramparts of the castle walls and then beyond the Adriatic Sea.

Several travel agencies offer private rooms to foreigners, and in theory all charge the same price for first-class rooms (although you may notice nominal differences from office to office): 3,396 dinars ($11.65) for a single room and 4,958 dinars ($17) for a double in July and August. During the rest of the year those prices fall to 3,000 dinars ($10.25) for singles and 4,200 dinars ($14.40) for doubles. Don't forget, however, that if you plan on spending fewer than four nights in Dubrovnik, you'll pay a 30% surcharge on these rates; but if you convince them to give you a second- or third-class room (in a worse location with more basic facilities), you can save some money as well.

To arrange your private room, go to one of the following agencies, or to almost any tourist office in town:

Atlas, Pile 1 (tel. 27-333 or 27-122; Telex TUD 27565), is open from 7 a.m. to 8 p.m. If you want to reserve a room beforehand, write Atlas at Tiha Ulica, Dubrovnik.

Turisticki Informativni Centar (TIC), Poljana Paska Miličevića 1 (tel.

26-354 to 26-356; Telex TUD 27565), is right inside the Stari Grad walls, entering from Pile. The TIC often can offer you a room when others have exhausted their supply. They also operate an office in Gruž at Gruška obala 64 (tel. 23-748) and in Lapad at Batala bb (tel. 25-044).

General tourist is at F. Supila 29 in Ploče (tel. 23-554 or 23-556).

You also have the possibility of skipping a visit to these tourist bureaus entirely by renting a room directly from the owner. Often, upon your arrival with luggage in hand at the Gruž bus station or port, a number of middle-aged women will descend upon you with room offers. Some rooms may indeed offer you a savings over the price you might pay at a tourist bureau, but check out the location and room before you say okay. Remember that the closer to Stari Grad you are, the better; so although a nearby Gruž accommodation may be tempting at the moment, you'll be far happier in Stari Grad when you wake up the next morning. Renting a room on your own will be particularly to your advantage if you plan on spending fewer than four nights in Dubrovnik; that way you won't have to pay the 30% "extra" fee the travel agencies charge.

DINING: In researching this book, we were often told by locals that Restaurant X served good steaks and meat; we would try the place and always come away convinced of the superiority of American steakhouses. We finally came across a steakhouse that could give its American counterparts a run for their money in the **Restaurant Domino,** Od Domina (tel. 32-832). Its decor is perfect for downing a hearty steak. Dim lighting flickers on heavy stone walls and hardwood tables and chairs. If you prefer less striking environs while you eat, sit outside at one of the two dozen sidewalk tables. Domino offers visitors a virtual plethora of steak-related entrees, including beefsteak, T-bone, rumpsteak, filet mignon, steak tournedos, and hamburgers! Not only does the restaurant give you a large selection of steaks, it also serves you a mouthwatering, very tender piece of meat which you'll long remember. You'll find prices very reasonable as well, considering the high quality of the meal: steak entrees cost 935 dinars ($3.20) to 1,540 dinars ($5.25). You'll probably be tempted to return to Domino more than once during your stay in Dubrovnik; many locals feel that this is Dubrovnik's best restaurant, and we have no reason to argue with them. It's open from 11 a.m. to midnight, seven days a week; closed in December and January. Try to reserve.

Another fine addition to Dubrovnik's culinary scene is the **Nimfa Restaurant,** Frank Supila 6, just outside the town walls in Ploče (tel. 23-678). This restaurant, built in 1985, is the perfect place to go for a romantic evening out. Candlelight illuminates the long stone walls, a striking blue cloth drapes the ceiling, and a skilled pianist plays mellifluous jazz classics in the background. An elegant waiter in black tie will serve excellent, memorable dishes, all at very reasonable prices for the quality and quantity of the food. To start, you can sample one of several spaghetti or soup appetizers for $1 to $2, followed by one of many meat and fish entrees, ranging in price from $2.50 to $7 each. Portions are huge; the delicious and tender steak Nimfu, served with potatoes and vegetables, could easily feed two people. Although the restaurant lacks local color (mostly Westerners dine here), the food is truly special; we highly recommend this restaurant along with the Domino as two of the town's best. It's open from 11 a.m. to 4 p.m. and 6 p.m. to 3 a.m. Reserve during the summer.

To sample some fine seafood in an appealing ambience, try the **Riblji Restoran,** Široka Ulica 1 (tel. 27-589). Upstairs, you can dine in a pretty terrace garden decorated with vines that hang from a trellis. If you prefer a more nautical atmosphere, eat downstairs where nets, stuffed fish, and other marine objects adorn the walls. The entrees of carefully prepared fish (often sautéed with light spices) include scampi, dentex, squid, and several other dishes, costing an average of $4 or $5 each. Reserve during the high season (July to September); it's open from 10 a.m. to 11 p.m., seven days a week.

As you enter the Old Town gates from Pile, to the right you'll pass the entrance of **Jadran,** P. Miličevića 1 (tel. 29-325 or 23-547), a good restaurant picturesquely housed in a 13th-century convent. In the summer you dine in the colonnade encircling a large medieval courtyard. According to legend, a small marble figure in the back of the courtyard offers good luck to those who touch it; it was blessed by a nun who ran away from the convent to marry her lover, and she wanted to make everybody's secret wish come true by giving special powers to this statue. If your secret wish is to dine in style that evening, you won't be disappointed; the menu offers a wide selection that should please everyone. You can order tasty fresh fish for about $4 a plate, international specialties such as veal, steak, and chicken dishes for $2.50 to $5, or Yugoslavian national specialties, such as čevap (mixed meats grilled on a skewer and served with rice in a savory tomato sauce) for less than $3! A skilled rock and pop band plays in the evenings after 8 p.m.

You're unlikely to meet a more energetic and enterprising family anywhere in Eastern Europe than the Rudenjak clan, owners of **Ragusa 2,** Zamanjina 12 (tel. 22-435). Now in their third generation of restaurateurs, the young Rudenjaks actually seek out guests for their restaurant by handing out copies of their menus to passersby. After traveling for months through countries whose restaurants had a much less friendly atmosphere, we welcomed the Rudenjak's friendly family-owned place! You can choose to dine either at attractive sidewalk tables on a typical Dubrovnik street, or inside an equally colorful restaurant with cozy low ceilings and a wide variety of Yugoslavian paintings on the wall. Ragusa offers a small selection of fish specialties including scampi, squid, the catch of the day, and lobster, at prices ranging from about $5 for a plate of fish or scampi to about $12 for a pound of lobster. You'll find the restaurant one block to your right after walking six streets down Placa from the town belltower. Open from 10 a.m. to midnight, seven days a week.

To sample some delicious breakfast and dessert pastries, go to the **Labirint Bar,** at Domenico 3, behind the main square toward the south drawbridge.

DUBROVNIK AT NIGHT: Most Dubrovnik locals and visitors spend their evenings strolling up and down Placa, Stari Grad's main street. Young locals take the evening promenade with special seriousness; they don their best clothes, and then after strolling a few times up and down Placa, they stand idly against a building to await their friends. As you join this promenade, in addition to people-watching you can also listen to street musicians, admire street artists, and rest at a local café, all making for a relaxed, typically local evening.

After your evening stroll you may be able to attend one of Dubrovnik's frequent musical performances. If you visit Dubrovnik during the crowded months of July and August, you can spend the evening at a ballet, concert, opera, theater, or other recitals of the **Dubrovnik Summer Festival (Dubrovačke Ljetne Igre),** which begins on July 10 and ends August 25. During the festival virtuoso musicians and artists from all over the world perform several different events each day; for those who love the performing arts, it's certainly an ideal time to visit Dubrovnik. Almost all travel agencies and hotel receptions can provide a schedule of events and sell tickets, which cost anywhere from $1 to $8.

At other times of the year you can attend concerts of the **Dubrovnik Symphony Orchestra,** held twice weekly; the **Colegium Musicum Ragusinum,** given once a week; or the **Lindo–Folk Dance Company,** who perform twice a week. To pick up a schedule (for free) of upcoming symphony orchestra concerts, go to

Kovačka 3 on the third floor anytime between 9 a.m. and 2 p.m. Drop by any local tourist information office for details on performances of the latter two groups.

Those who are "slave to the rhythm" should head to the **Bakhos** disco at F. Supila 6 in the Ploče district's Lazareti. At Bakhos you can dance between the old stone walls of the town lazareti (the quarantine area) with a crowd of mostly 18- to 25-year-olds, although some older travelers do make appearances. Bakhos stays open from 10 p.m. until 3 a.m. seven days a week, and charges a very reasonable 250 dinars (85¢) to get in.

SEEING THE OLD TOWN (STARI GRAD): Begin your sightseeing by wandering through Stari Grad's narrow streets with their Gothic buildings and smoothly worn pavements, as Stari Grad is one of the world's greatest living museums of medieval culture.

After an hour or so of serendipitous wandering you may want to walk around the perimeter of Dubrovnik atop the one-mile-long **city walls.** These massive walls were first built in the 12th and 13th centuries when Ragusa realized that it needed protection from the onslaught of foreign invasions. Although defensive walls were common in the Middle Ages, Dubrovnik's walls constitute one of the world's best remaining examples of such military architecture (the walls we see today date from 1453–1660). At some points the walls extend to a 30-foot width and rise up some 80 feet. Once the city's wooden drawbridges (two over land, two over water) were closed and guards were on alert in the wall's 15 towers, access to Dubrovnik was virtually impossible. Make sure to climb the Minčeta Tower on the northwest corner; from here you can enjoy the best view of the city afforded along the entire length of the walls. You can go to the top of these walls for 100 dinar (35¢) at either the Pile or Ploče gates to the city, open from 9 a.m. to 6:30 p.m.

If you want an even greater panoramic overview of the Dubrovnik area, take the cable car to the top of the **Srdj Mountain.** The rides operate from 9 a.m. to 9 p.m. May to October, and 9 a.m. to 4 p.m. during the rest of the year at a cost of 330 dinar ($1.15). Rides depart from Od Srda behind Stari Grad, not far from Ploče.

MORE DUBROVNIK SIGHTS: Art aficionados will have a lot to appreciate in addition to the beautiful city walls and façades of the town buildings. As you enter Stari Grad from the Pile drawbridge, you pass the 14th-century **Franciscan Monastery** immediately to your left, one of Dubrovnik's most beautiful examples of Gothic architecture. Next door you can visit a pharmacy from the 14th century (the third oldest in all of Europe), which displays the original objects of an apothecary from the Middle Ages.

Continuing down Ploče, you soon arrive at **Luža,** Stari Grad's main square. To the left you'll see the 15th-century **Sponza Palace,** the site of Dubrovnik's Customs House (a crucial building for a city totally reliant on trade), and a state mint later in history. Today the building houses the **Museum of the Socialist Revolution** and a modern art gallery.

Behind this building as you walk toward Ploče, you pass the **Dominican Monastery** (Samostan Dominikanaca), a monastic complex built in the 14th century which contains paintings by Titian, Paolo Veneziano, and others. Beyond this monastery lies the town's second drawbridge (complete with attached chains), and then the **Old Harbor,** from which countless shipments arrived and departed in the glory days of the Republic of Ragusa.

Now backtrack to the Luža square, but this time turn left and walk down

Prid Dvorom and you'll find two more sights worth a visit. Down the block on the left is the **Rector's Palace** (Knezev Dvor), the residence and official chambers of the rectors who ruled the Republic of Ragusa for 1,000 years. (Interestingly, Dubrovnik's rector served only a one-month term; the various aristocrats of the town would take turns in this prestigious office, thus preventing abuses of power.) Today you can visit the council rooms, the rector's personal work rooms, and exhibitions on the history and glorious lifestyle of old Dubrovnik. If you attend a concert of the Dubrovnik Symphony Orchestra, you'll return again to the palace as the concerts are performed in the building's atrium.

Finally, on your tour of Dubrovnik's most important sites, go across the street from the Rector's Palace to the **cathedral,** a rare baroque church in Dubrovnik built in the 17th century. Architecturally the building is not nearly so interesting as the works of art contained inside. In the church treasury, see the large painting of the Assumption (attributed to Titian), a rich collection of gold and silver church objects, and Raphael's *Madonna della Seggiola.*

EXCURSIONS FROM DUBROVNIK: As you might have noticed by looking at a map, several enticing islands lie off the Dubrovnik shores. The only one you can visit on your own in a day trip is **Lokrum,** located just off the Old Town. According to legend, the English King Richard the Lion-Hearted was shipwrecked here in the 12th century on his return from the Third Crusade. In the 19th century Austrian Archduke Maximilian maintained a royal summer palace on the island. Today thick forests cover most of the island, but on the side opposite Dubrovnik you'll find small cliffs with flat stone tops where you can sunbathe and reach the water, albeit carefully. Should you grow hungry during the day, you can choose between two island restaurants for lunch. Boats leave every day from 9 a.m. to 7 p.m. from the Old Harbor, for a fare of 240 dinars (80¢) round trip, 120 dinars (40¢) for children.

Unfortunately, the larger islands off Dubrovnik—**Koločep, Lopud, Šipan,** and farther up the coast, **Mljet**—cannot be visited in a day trip unless you join an organized tour by one of Dubrovnik's many travel offices. Lopud, a favorite home of captains and sailors in the Dubrovnik navy, is more developed than the other islands (more restaurants, etc.) but it also offers beautiful beaches. Our favorite of the group is Mljet, a romantic island covered with pine forests, vineyards, and olive groves, that has been inhabited by the Ilyrians, the Greeks, the Romans, and many others. Some residents even claim that Odysseus landed here after his return from Troy and was thoroughly enchanted.

Ferries leave for these four islands once a day from Dubrovnik, with no returning connections until the next day. The ride takes 25 minutes to Koločep, an hour to Lopud, 2½ hours to Šipan, and four hours to Mljet; the ride all the way to Mljet will cost you about $1. For information on organized day tours to these islands, inquire at Atlas, Generalturist, or one of the other travel agencies in town.

THE ABCs OF DUBROVNIK: The following miscellaneous information should be helpful.

Airlines

You'll find the **JAT** main office at Pile 7 (tel. 20-055, 23-575, or 23-576). The local Atlas office represents **Pan Am** at Pile 1 (tel. 27-333).

Airport

Dubrovnik's **International Airport Čilipi** lies 24 km (14½ miles) to the south of Dubrovnik. The JAT airport bus goes into town for 130 dinars (45¢).

You'll see the bus right in front of the airport exit, and you pay the driver directly on the bus. The ride takes about 25 minutes, but if your plane arrives after about 9 p.m. you may have to find a taxi, which will cost you a considerably steeper 4,000 dinars ($13.70) or so. The bus will take you to the JAT Terminal at Put Maršala Tita in the Lapad section of Dubrovnik; several hotels are located within fair walking distance of this terminal. Buses leave from this same terminal about every half hour to the airport, with the last bus leaving according to the flights scheduled—but be sure to check with JAT for exact times, lest you miss the last bus and be forced to take a taxi. For airport flight information, call 77-122 or 77-177.

American Express

The versatile Atlas travel agency also houses the American Express office in the back right-hand corner of their office at Pile 1 (tel. 27-333). They're open from 7 a.m. to 8 p.m., seven days a week.

Auto Repair

For aid or information, call **Proleter,** N. Tesle 5 (tel. 987 or 23-368). For repairs, contact Proleter or **Dubrovkinja,** Masarykov Put 3 (tel. 23-178 or 28-940).

Buses

The town's **main bus station** (autobusni kolodvar) is in Gruž at Put Republike 1 (tel. 23-088), just across from the JAT air terminal where you catch the bus to the airport. If you're continuing on to Kardeljevo to catch a train, figure that the bus takes two hours and costs about 297 dinars ($1); the bus south to the train station in Bar takes 3½ hours at a cost of 660 dinars ($2.25). To continue northward to Split, prepare to spend about 800 dinars ($2.75) and 4½ hours. Finally, if you want to go all the way north on the Yugoslavian coastline to Rijeka, it will take 12 hours and cost 2,156 dinars ($7.40). Should you want to check some luggage, the station's garderoba is open from 5 a.m. to 10 p.m. every day.

Crowds

Tourists flood Dubrovnik in July and August, so we offer these tips: if possible, arrive in the off-season. Even in June the number of visitors has yet to reach its peak, and many hotels offer off-season rates. If you do come during the high season of July, August, or even September, try getting a really early start. The idea of rising at 7 a.m. may seem debilitating, but once up, you'll be glad. At 7:30 or 8 a.m. you can wander peacefully through Dubrovnik's lovely streets; you can even go shopping or visit travel agencies without waiting on lines as many stores open at 8 a.m. Then, like clockwork, at 9 a.m. the group tourists hit the street and everything becomes bedlam again.

Emergency Numbers

Dial 92 or 33-333 for the police (there's a police station at Put M. Tita 75), 93 for the fire department (at Put JA 5), or 94 for first aid or an ambulance.

Ferryboats

Jadrolinja ferries depart from Dubrovnik to cities in the north about ten times a week, although local routes from Dubrovnik run more frequently.

This sample schedule of ferry stops (allowing for a short time between arrival and departure) should give you a rough idea of how long the trips take and how much they cost (fares are from Dubrovnik):

Dubrovnik to Korčula: departs at 10 a.m.; 1,698 dinars ($5.80) per person, 4,731 dinars ($16.20) per car.
Korčula to Hvar: departs at 1:15 p.m.; 2,045 dinars ($7) per person.
Hvar to Split: departs 3:53 p.m.; 2,481 dinars ($8.50) per person, 6,743 dinars ($23.10) per car.
Split to Šibenik: departs 5:15 p.m.; 2,661 dinars ($9.10) per person.
Šibenik to Zadar: departs 9:40 p.m.; 3,365 dinars ($11.50) per person.
Zadar to Rab: departs 12:50 a.m.; 3,887 dinars ($13.30) per person.
Rab to Rijeka: departs 4:30 a.m.; 4,510 dinars ($15.45) per person, 12,871 dinars ($44.05) per car.
The ferry on the return trip from Rijeka departs at 7:45 a.m.

After September 15 these fares go down for the off-season; students do *not* receive discounts on ferries.

For further information and tickets, go to either the **Jadrolinja Shipping Lines** office at Gruška obala 31 in Gruž (tel. 23-068) or to the **Atlas** office at Pile 1.

Gambling
You can wager your splurge funds at casinos in the **Libertas Hotel,** Lav-čeviča 1 (tel. 27-444), from 8 p.m. to 2 a.m.; the **Imperial Hotel,** at M. Simoni 2 (tel. 23-688), from 9 p.m. from June 1 through September 30 only; or the **Hotel Croatia** (tel. 78-022) in Cavtat south of Dubrovnik on the coast.

Information
Although all the town's tourist agencies can answer questions about Dubrovnik, the official **Tourist Information Office (TIC)** is located at Poljana P. Miličeviča (tel. 26-354 or 26-355), the first office to your right after you enter the Pile Gates to the Old Town. You can also telephone 985 for general information.

Laundry
Jugoplastika at Uz Jezuite, behind the market square, will clean jackets, pants, etc., in one or two days for only 100 dinar (35¢) a shirt, 190 dinar (65¢) for pants, and 210 dinars (70¢) for a jacket. They're open from 7 a.m. to noon and 5 to 7 p.m. Monday through Friday, to noon on Saturday. They don't speak English, but they'll understand what you want.

Market
You can shop for fruits and vegetables in the mornings in Gunduličeva Poijana Square, right behind the main square, Luža, at the end of Ploče.

Newspaper
For a 35-dinar (12¢) investment in the Serbian newspaper **Slobodna Dalmacija** you'll get a fairly complete listing of weekly boats, buses, and trains that service the Dalmatian coast. For help in reading the schedules, ask your hotel reception.

Post Office
The main post, telegraph, and telephone office is at 22 Maršala Tita, a few minutes from Stari Grad toward Gruž, open from 7 a.m. to 10 p.m.

Public Transportation

As of this writing, a local bus ride costs 50 dinars (15¢), which you must pay on the bus in exact change. Keep some extra change in your pocket in the likely event the fare increases by the time you visit Dubrovnik.

Rental Cars

You can rent a car at most Dubrovnik travel agencies, including **Alpe-Tour** (tel. 23-747) and **Autotehna-Avis** (tel. 26-477) at F. Supila 3 and 27; **Dubrovnikrent** (tel. 32-860) and **Globtour-Interrent** (tel. 33-393) at Gruška obala 98 and 53 in Gruž; **Inex** at F. Supila 24 (tel. 26-917); and **Kompas-Hertz,** at I. L. Ribara 50 (tel. 23-799).

Taxis

You can find a taxi at the Pile and Ploče entrances to the Old Town (tel. 34-343 for Pile), or at the coach terminal (tel. 28-499) and at the port in Gruž (tel. 24-799).

Telephone Area Code

To call Dubrovnik from another city or town in Yugoslavia, the area code is 050.

Tours

Many of Dubrovnik's travel agencies sponsor group day trips by bus or boat. Some popular destinations include **Montenegro** (Budva, Sveti Stefan, and Kotor), **Sarajevo,** a cruise through **Koločep, Lopud,** and **Šipan** (costs about $15), and a cruise to **Mljet** (costs about $20). Inquire at **Atlas,** Pile 1 (tel. 273-33), **Generaltourist,** Frana Supila 29 (tel. 23-555), or other local travel agencies.

Trains

Unfortunately, trains do not run to Dubrovnik. The nearest stations are at **Kardeljevo,** 110 km (66 miles) to the north of Dubrovnik, and **Bar,** 140 km (84 miles) to the south; you can take a bus from Dubrovnik to both cities. From Kardeljevo you can visit Sarajevo in about three hours for 529 dinars ($1.80) for a second-class ticket; from Bar, you can continue on to Beograd, a seven-hour journey, for 1,028 dinars ($3.50) for a second-class ticket. Express trains zip across these routes more rapidly, but at a substantially higher cost. The Atlas office in town can give you timetable information and sell you tickets.

2. Montenegro and the Southern Coast

According to many cognoscenti of the Yugoslavian coast, the Adriatic shores south of Dubrovnik have no rival. Although virtually devoid of the many islands that characterize most of Yugoslavia's coast, Montenegro offers dramatic cliffs, scenic lakes, and some of the most magnificent beaches, both pebble and sand, in all of Europe. Unfortunately, a 1979 earthquake gravely damaged two of Montenegro's most charming medieval cities, Kotor and Budva. Nonetheless, the remains of these two towns, the charming peninsula of Sveti Stefan, and the wide sand beach at Ulcinj, the last Yugoslavian outpost before Albania, all make worthwhile destinations after a visit to Dubrovnik. Descriptions of our favorite towns along the coast follow.

SOUTH TO THE BAY OF KOTOR: The beautiful **Bay of Mlini** will catch your eye first as you drive south of Dubrovnik. You'll see a small town at the foot of a pebble beach, overlooking several small rocky islands close to the shore. On the south side of the bay lies **Cavtat,** where the ancient Greek town of Epidaurus stood until it was overrun by Slav invaders in the 7th century A.D. After Cavtat the road veers inland, and the next body of water you'll see is the **Bay of Kotor.** If you are hurrying southward, you can take a car (or bus) ferry at **Kamenari** to **Plavda** for 375 dinars ($1.30) for a car, and 33 dinars (11¢) for each person, thus skipping the long drive around. If you have some extra time, however, we highly recommend that you make the drive around the scenic Bay of Kotor (about an hour's excursion).

Throughout history European nations have used the well-protected Bay of Kotor to anchor their warships; the strongest powers of the day have also fought many long battles over this bay, and consequently it has changed hands many times. Past owners include the Greeks, Romans, Slavs, Venetians, Austrians, French, Russians, Turks, Germans, and Italians! Today you'll find it a minor battle just to drive successfully along the bay as it features quite a few hairpin curves, but daring travelers will be rewarded with a breathtaking sight of dark-blue waters surrounded by steep rugged mountains rising into the clouds. In the middle of the lake you'll also notice a tiny island, built by sailors in the 15th century to house a small church.

Kotor

The most interesting town on the Bay of Kotor is Kotor itself, an important port settlement in the Middle Ages, and a Venetian colony between 1420 and 1797. In 1979 the two large earthquakes that struck Montenegro had their epicenters near Kotor, and as a result much of the town remains eerily deserted. Although rubble continues to lie along several streets in Kotor, some sections of this small town are slowly coming back to life. Unlike in Budva, here you are allowed to enter the town (although a sign at the entrance warns: "As visit to the old town is dangerous, entrance on own responsibility"). Once inside the town walls, you'll enjoy such architectural reminders of Venice as the 12th-century **Cathedral of Sveti Tripan,** which features paintings by Veronese and Bassano.

The town's most impressive sight, the three-mile-long medieval **defensive walls,** remain fully intact despite recent earthquakes. These 16th-century walls protected Kotor mainly from sea attack; most interestingly, they also zigzag up the steep one-mile-high mountain behind Kotor, sometimes extending as high as 30 feet, to provide protection from a mountain invasion.

BUDVA: Much of Budva, a picturesque medieval city built under Venetian supervision in the Middle Ages, came tumbling down in two earthquakes in April and May of 1979. Of 187 houses in the Old Town, the earthquake destroyed or damaged 182 of them. Some 1,000 inhabitants were transferred to housing complexes in nearby towns and only a handful of people remain. A sign on the massive 15th-century town walls warns away curious visitors: "Because of the possibility of new falling objects," it reads, "it is severely prohibited to enter the old city." Workmen continue to labor on the reconstruction of old Budva, but for the foreseeable future (locals estimate that repairs won't be finished until 1990) the Old Town will remain closed. At the same time modern Budva remains completely intact, and the town continues to be a favorite resort spot with beautiful pebble beaches.

Accommodations

Kompas, Nova ul. bb (tel. 41-908 or 41-365; Telex 61365), rents private rooms for $5.70 to $7 per person in a double from June 15 to September 15; during the rest of the year the price drops to $2.45 to $3.25 per person in a double. You can also rent an apartment for two from Kompas for $14.30 to $16.50 per person, depending on the season. Kompas is open from 7 a.m. to 9 p.m.

Monday through Friday, to 10 p.m. on Saturday, and 7 a.m. to noon and 5 to 7 p.m. on Sunday.

Both **Montenegro Express,** 13 Mai Ulica (tel. 41-696 or 41-116), open from 7 a.m. to 10 p.m., and **Mogren Tourist,** Maršala Tita 23 (tel. 41-983 or 41-414), open from 7 a.m. to 9 p.m., rent private rooms at similar prices. All three travel agencies sponsor hydrofoil rides to Dubrovnik, a 100-minute trip, for about $20.

Student Hotels: Naromtravel, Yugoslavia's youth travel agency, runs a youth hotel **Karavan** at Bečići, a beach town about two miles away from central Budva (tel. 41-685). Three people share each basic room and a private bathroom in one of six modern pavilions located right off the beach. The Karavan also makes sure that its students will be entertained: it offers sports activities during the day and a disco by night. Full room and board in this active resort costs $15.80 per person in July and August, $11.35 in June and September, $10.40 in May and October, and $9.35 in April. If you prefer to rent a room with two beds rather than three, there's an additional $4 charge per person.

Dining

Even if you're just driving through town, try to stop at the **Restaurant Jadran,** Slovenska Obala 10 (tel. 42-986), a charming restaurant that serves excellent food. The energetic owner, Nikanović Krsto, will do everything possible to ensure that you fully enjoy your visit to the Jadran. Mr. Krsto divides his time between tending the large outdoor grill and serving tables with spirited good humor. His grill features good fresh fish and tender meat dishes—all for $2 to $5 an entree. Along with a tasty grill, this restaurant offers visitors an attractive outdoor garden shaded by a trellis and grape vines. The Jadran is open daily from 7 a.m. to 11 p.m., but closed in December and January.

SVETI STEFAN: Just five miles south of Budva lies Sveti Stefan, a spectacular island, connected to the mainland by a thin strip of land, that houses one of Europe's most unique resorts. The entire fishing village has been converted into one large, immaculately clean (some say *too* clean) resort complex, with each house accommodating a guest. The island was first inhabited by the Paštrović family in the 15th century as they sought protection from Turkish attacks. The Paštrović clan lived a charmed life on the island, ruling over the local fishermen, often independent of local political authority, until 1929. In 1960 the hotel opened on the island.

The **Hotel Sveti Stefan** (tel. 41-333 or 41-411; Telex 61188-YU-SVSTF), constitutes a super-splurge, for that once-in-a-lifetime experience. A double room costs $36.30 per person in May and October, $47.30 in June and September, and $66 in July and August. The rooms are furnished with 19th-century pieces; many rooms also have an enchanting view of the sea through a small window. Modern facilities include a swimming pool, two tennis courts, and a restaurant that charges about $15 per person for dinner.

If you prefer to enjoy the scenic environs of Sveti Stefan at considerably less cost, you can stay in a private room in a nearby village. The **Montenegro Express** office at the beginning of the Sveti Stefan peninsula (tel. 62-262; Telex 61455), rents 800 beds at the cost of 1,920 dinars ($6.60) to 2,400 dinars ($8.20) per person from June 15 to September 16; in the off-season, prices fall by more than half.

If you're not a guest but want to visit the Sveti Stefan island hotel, they'll charge you 660 dinars ($2.25); open from 11 a.m. to 7 p.m.

SOUTH TO PETROVAC: After combing the beaches across the Yugoslavian coast, we have found that the six miles of beachfront from Sveti Stefan to Petrovac are some of the most picturesque, and undiscovered, on the Adriatic. This coastline boasts many rocky beaches, an undeveloped area with beautiful bays, forbidding cliffs, and enchanting crystalline waters. From Sveti Stefan, a rugged dirt road continues down the coast. Soon you'll pass through a nudist camp, and then the road continues above some stunning vistas of Sveti Stefan and the larger coastal area. It's definitely a trip for the adventurous and daring, but the rewards are large: small steep paths lead down from the road at several points, and if you're able to make it down without mishap, an entire cliff, cove, or small beach can be yours for the day.

If you prefer to stay in a hotel in the small town of **Petrovac** and explore these beaches from the south (rather than staying in a private room in Sveti Stefan), choose the **Castellastva** (tel. 85-199; Telex 61199-YU-PALAS), the **Riviera** (tel. 85-135; Telex 61199-YU-PALAS), or the **Vile Oliva** (tel. 85-121; Telex 61199-YU-PALAS), three large Class B hotels with comfortable facilities and private bathrooms. Singles in all three hotels cost a reasonable 2,200 dinars ($7.55) in April, May, and October; 3,520 dinars ($12.05) in June and September; and 4,950 dinars ($16.95) in July and August. Doubles cost 4,180 dinars ($14.30) in April, May, and October; 6,600 dinars ($22.60) in June and September; and 8,250 dinars ($28.25) in July and August. Petrovac itself also offers a fine sandy beach.

ULCINJ: If you've been wondering where you can find wide strips of sandy (not pebble or rock) beaches, then come to Ulcinj, Yugoslavia's last outpost before the Albanian border. In Ulcinj you'll enjoy seven miles of long sandy beaches (Yugoslavia's longest sand beach, called Velika Plaža) and clear waters. At the far end of the beach, a small island for "naturalists" lies just before the river that divides Yugoslavia from Albania.

Ulcinj itself was a 15th- and 16th-century Venetian colony captured by the Turks in 1571. Under the command of Eulag-Ali, 400 pirates were brought from Algiers, and voyagers by sea in the vicinity were subject to ruthless attacks. These bold pirates later established a slave market in Ulcinj, and it was not until the beginning of the 19th century that their operations ceased. Today the Turkish influence can be seen in the unique blend of medieval Venetian architecture, along with minarets and mosques.

Your best bet is to rent a private room in or around Ulcinj. You'll see many signs outside houses along the Velika Plaža reading "Sobe" or "Zimmer," indicating room rentals. Alternatively, you can rent from **Montenegro Express** (tel. 81-834) right in Ulcinj for only about $5 a person in high season.

Chapter XXXI

SLOVENIA AND CROATIA

1. Ljubljana
2. Touring Slovenia
3. Zagreb and Inland Croatia
4. Sarajevo

IF WE WERE TO SELECT an area most likely to please the novice traveler to Eastern Europe, Slovenia and central Croatia would be our first choice. The big cities—Ljubljana in Slovenia and Zagreb in Croatia—are by far the most Western European of all the major Eastern European cities. The whole area is clean and safe, with an abundance of consumer goods. In the big cities the young people are as "up" on the latest fads as the rest of Western Europe, and the tourist officials are efficient and friendly. Both Slovenia and much of central Croatia spent several hundred years under Venetian and Hapsburg control. The culture simply reflects these influences and continues in its own vibrant fashion.

A CAPSULE HISTORY: First settled by the Ilyrians, present-day Slovenia and central Croatia were part of the Roman Empire for some 400 to 500 years. The people who inhabit these regions today are the descendants of Slavic tribes who entered the area after the final collapse of Justinian's Empire in the 6th century A.D. Though the Croats and Slovenes managed to remain, it was not without a fight. Successive waves of migratory peoples plowed southward down the Balkan Peninsula, and later Middle-Eastern empires surged northward. The Croats and Slovenes were not above a little rampaging themselves: Slovene warriors helped to bring down the Roman Empire and Croat sailors were the terror of the Adriatic for centuries.

Ottoman Turks and Hapsburgs
Though an allied Balkan force fell before the Ottoman Turkish armies at the battle of Kosovo in 1389, Slovenia and central Croatia never were truly a part of the Ottoman Empire. Slovenia had been under the control of Charlemagne, and later, parts of central Croatia were ruled by various Germanic nobles. Following the Hungarian defeat at the battle of Mohács in 1526, most of Slovenia and Croatia fell to the Hapsburg Empire. While Venice eventually gained a certain measure of control over the coastal areas, Slovenia and central Croatia remained firmly in the Austro-Hungarian Empire.

The Coming of Napoleon

Following Napoleon's victory over the "Holy Alliance" at Austerlitz on December 2, 1805, the Austro-Hungarian Empire lost control of Slovenia and Croatia. By 1809 Slovenia and much of Croatia were part of the Ilyrian Provinces under French military mandate. But by 1814, upon the defeat of Napoleon and the Congress of Vienna, the Hapsburgs returned. Oddly enough, Napoleon, who effectively ended the French Revolution, is considered a hero and liberator in Ljubljana. Many Slovenian and Croatians have felt that things were never as bad under the French as they were under the Hapsburgs. As one Slovenian comrade declared, "Napoleon may have crushed the French Revolution, but he brought many bourgeois-revolutionary ideas with him."

Today

Not heavily damaged during World War II, Slovenia and Croatia have become the two richest republics in all of Yugoslavia. Though both republics are best known for their sun-drenched coasts, we found the history, culture, and stunning scenery of the interior more than enough reason to cap the suntan oil and roll up the beach towel. Though they would never admit it publicly, some Yugoslavians are a bit put off by tourists who come merely for the beaches and ignore the rest of their country. As we mentioned before, much of inland Yugoslavia is largely unexplored by foreign visitors and is a treasure trove of natural and man-made wonders.

1. Ljubljana

Ljubljana is a thoroughly modern city of 300,000 people situated on both banks of a branch of the Sava River. In the Ljubljana History Museum artifacts found in the area date back to 3000 B.C. The tireless Romans established a settlement here, and in the 6th century A.D. invading Slovene tribes took over and began to cultivate the land. Long a part of the Austro-Hungarian Empire, Ljubljana shows its imperial past both in its architecture and in its layout. Ljubljana was severely damaged by an earthquake in 1895 and an extensive reconstruction of its baroque buildings was carried out. The city was again damaged, but not heavily, during World War II. Today Ljubljana is a thriving metropolis and capital of one of Yugoslavia's most productive republics.

THE SIGHTS: On both sides of the Ljubljanica (as this branch of the Sava River is known) the **Old City** of Ljubljana lies north of Karlovška cesta and south of the old market. Right by **Prešernov trg,** the main square, you'll see the **Franciscan church,** dating from the 18th century. The beautiful baroque square is also worthy of note. Across the Lekarna Tromostovje, a triple-span bridge, and on the way to the baroque cathedral, built in the early 18th century, is the **Vodnikov trg,** the market square. There is an incredible variety of produce and other items for sale at the Ljubljana market, as well as several folkware shops off the square. Continuing back south there is F. Robba's fountain of the Carniolan Rivers (Robbov Vodnjak) and the **Town Hall,** which was initially erected in 1484; the original structure was destroyed and the Town Hall was rebuilt in 1718. The dark, arcaded interior is cool in summer and houses some Roman and early medieval relics. Note the carving of a mounted horseman, an early knight we were told.

Back across the river on the southern edge of the Old City stand the monumental **Ursulinen Church** and the old university buildings. Near the old **university complex,** on Dvorni trg, is the **Slovenian Philharmonic Hall;** the orchestra has a history dating back to 1701. Nearby is the **Križanke,** a complex of restored buildings including a monastery. Perched above the whole city is the **castle;** recently restored, it also has a lovely panorama of the city.

ORIENTATION: The main street, **Titova cesta,** runs north and south through the city. Along it are the main stores, offices, and the TIC, the central tourist office. The city is centered on the **Partisan Monument (Spomenik ilegalca)** and east toward the river, on Copova ulica, is **Prešernov trg,** the main square and true heart of the city. Across the river is the **market square** and more of the Old City.

At the foot of, but not in, Ljubljana's Skyscraper (Nebotičnik) at Titova cesta 11, is the always-welcome **TIC, Tourist Information Office** (tel. 23-212). It's open from 8 a.m. to 9 p.m. daily (on Sunday from 8 a.m. to noon and 5 to 8 p.m.); in winter the office closes one hour earlier. The TIC will supply you with plentiful information about Ljubljana and all of Slovenia as well, plus some genuinely good advice for travelers. There are English-speaking guides who can be hired for three to four hours for about 4,400 dinars ($15). The office can help you with getting private rooms or student accommodations (see the "Accommodations" section, below).

Ljubljana's **telephone area code** is 061.

Arriving by Air

The closest airport is at **Brnik,** some 15 miles to the north of Ljubljana. Inquire at the TIC office about the new airport bus service.

Arriving by Bus or Train

The bus and train stations, not more than a 10- to 15-minute walk from Prešernov trg, are located four blocks east of Titova cesta to the north of the city center. Ljubljana is on the main rail line and is a major terminus for bus traffic.

Arriving by Car

There is a highway system under construction from Zagreb and good two-lane roads throughout Slovenia. The border crossings with both Italy and Austria are extremely crowded in July and August, and there is heavy north-south traffic in the western part of the republic.

ACCOMMODATIONS: Unlike many resort areas, Ljubljana usually has some accommodations available, though not always within easy walking distance of the city center. Student and budget rooms are generally much easier to find here than in Zagreb.

Hotels

All the following hotels are in or near the city center:

The **Pri Mraku,** at Rimska ulica 4 (tel. 223-412 or 223-387), is a clean modern establishment. Be certain to get here as early in the day as possible, as it usually fills up by afternoon. The day receptionist speaks English. A double room with a bath costs 6,300 dinars ($21.60); without bath, 4,530 dinars ($15.50). A triple room with a bath costs 7,300 dinars ($25); without bath, 5,200 dinars ($17.80). All prices include breakfast.

The **Hotel Turist,** at Dalmatinova ulica 15, is one of the few hotels in town that has an affordable single room. The guardian angel of tourists stands watch above the door leading into the rather spartan lobby. The rooms are very clean but, again, unadorned. A single room costs 5,170 dinars ($17.70), a double runs

7,590 dinars ($26), and a triple room costs 10,890 dinars ($37.30); all rooms have a private bath. Ask for a room facing the quiet courtyard in the back, as the street side is somewhat noisy.

A Splurge Choice

The **Grand Hotel Union,** at Miklošičeva cesta 1 (tel. 24-507; Telex 31295), is right up from Prešernov trg, the main square. The Union is a well-appointed hotel that usually has space for travelers without reservations; however, during trade fairs or other big events they do fill up. All the high-ceilinged rooms are clean and well lit. There are no singles; a double costs $34 per night. All the rooms have private bathrooms, but ask for a room with a bathtub—they are generously built and spotless (no water shortage here). Though the furnishings are not spectacular, we feel that this hotel has both a good location and staff, and is worth the price. The very efficient staff at the reception desk speaks English and will try to make your stay in Ljubljana an enjoyable one.

Budget Best

A budget bargain not far outside the city center is the **Hotel Bellevue,** on Celovška cesta (tel. 313-133). A small operation, there are only 11 rooms, though generally they have one available. The bathrooms, at the end of each floor, are shared. Still, a single room costs 2,530 dinars ($8.65), a double runs 4,048 dinars ($13.85), and a triple room costs 5,560 dinars ($19); breakfast is included. The Bellevue is about a 20-minute walk from the TIC office, or you can catch bus 7 south and, after it turns right, get off at the first stop after the railroad bridge; the hotel is on the left side (south) of Celovška cesta and a bit of a walk up a hill. There is also a delightful terrace restaurant, open from 9 a.m. to 11 p.m. daily in the summer. The hotel is on a hill facing east and does have a "belle vue" of Ljubljana.

Private Accommodations

The **TIC** people at Titova cesta 11 (tel. 23-212) handle private rooms and can direct you to the closest youth hostel with space available. They have plenty of private rooms, but only 12 or 15 of them are in the city center, so you may have to take the bus to your room. Prices are $8 to $12 per person, depending on the type of room, location, and plumbing. The student accommodations are only available from May through August. Though technically the TIC does not rent any rooms at all, they can call around and quote you a price. The friendly English-speaking staff at the TIC office makes it a good place to start.

DINING IN LJUBLJANA: Eating well is no problem in Ljubljana. We found a couple of restaurants on the south side of Ljubljana near the old university buildings.

The **Pri Virezu** (tel. 218-303) is perhaps the most done-up restaurant in Ljubljana. It's right on the river, just north of Karlovška cesta, and has a front terrace. Inside, the vaulted ceilings and exposed stonework adorned with shields, swords, bardiches, and spears set the tone. The restaurant's specialties are veal, beef, and game: try the čevapčiči, wild boar (in season), for 1,210 dinars ($4.15). You won't escape for less than this, especially if you sample some of the local wines. English is spoken by the very proper waiters; reservations for dinner are necessary. Open from noon to midnight; closed Monday.

Not far away—but completely different—is the **Pod Skalco,** at Gosposka ulica 19 (tel. 211-816). Recognizable as a university hangout, it's a good place to sit outside on nice days—and there are a lot of them in Ljubljana. We recommend the baked mushrooms for 440 dinars ($1.50). If you're not sure what to order, you can go indoors and point to the smoked fish and cold salads, from 800 dinars ($2.75) to 1,000 dinars ($3.40), that are on display in the large steel-and-wood bar. There's also a good wine celler; try the Šipon or Beli pinot, both locally grown sweet, white wines, or the Briski cabernet for the red wine drinkers. Open from 11 a.m. to 12:30 a.m. daily.

In the courtyard of the old university complex right next to the Ljubljana Music Festival building is the **Plečnikov Hram.** The beautiful terrace is right off Trg Francoske Revolucija (Square of the French Revolution, which has a column honoring Napoleon, liberator of Ljubljana). The restaurant has no printed menu, and you'll find the menu terms in the Appendix of help in being understood. English is not spoken here. However, you can eat here for less than 500 dinars ($1.70). Indoors, the reinforced bar has supported many a graduate student till he or she was in the right frame of mind to continue his or her research. The Plečnikov Hram is open from 8 a.m. to 10 p.m.; closed Sunday. At night it's crowded with students till well past 1 a.m., on most nights until 2 a.m.

A Meal with a View

High above the city, on the corner of Titova cesta and Kidričev ulica, is the bar and café atop the **Skyscraper (Nebotičnik).** Depending on the weather the view is indeed spectacular, with an occasional glimpse of the mountains. Take the elevator to the 12th floor; the center one is an express. The service is somewhat lackadaisical, but who cares when the weather's nice?

2. Touring Slovenia

Perhaps the best way to begin to describe Slovenia is to use the exact words of the official tourist pamphlets: "Slovenia is a small country in the middle of Europe."

The capital of Slovenia, Ljubljana, is geographically closer to both Vienna and Milan than it is to Yugoslavia's capital, Belgrade. Though not as high as their Austrian and French counterparts, the Julian Alps excel in natural beauty and the friendliness of the people.

Although generalizations that try to sum up a region's qualities run the risk of oversimplifying, we feel it's fair to say that Slovenia is a mixture of Austrian cleanliness and efficiency, Hungarian passion, and the determination and friendliness characteristic of its own citizens. Not a sovereign territory, Slovenians still have a fervent national pride; they often think of themselves as a separate country. National pride aside, Slovenia, set in the heart of south-central Europe, is one of Yugoslavia's most beautiful regions.

AROUND SLOVENIA: The **Julian Alps** are certainly a must. The beautiful town, and nearby lake, of **Bled,** with its stunning castle, is one of the most photographed Slovenian sights—and rightly so. **Triglav Park,** right near the Austrian border, is Slovenia's largest mountain playground. To the south and west is the karstic (limestone) terrain dotted with caves; the most extensive are the **Postojna Caves.** Nearby is the **Castle of Predjama,** and practically on the Italian border are the **Lipica** stables, home to the famous "Lipizzaner" stallions. Farther west is the Slovenian layer of Istria, detailed in Chapter XXVIII. In northeastern Slovenia, the ancient town of **Ptuj** is at the foot of the hilly Slovenske Gorice wine-growing district.

POSTOJNA: About 32 miles south of Ljubljana on the highway to Trieste and the Istrian coast is the impressive **cave complex of Postojna.** With nearly 15 miles of discovered passageways, Postojna is a vast, self-contained underground world. The seemingly numberless caverns and grottos defy description, but water has been at work here for hundreds of thousands of years, slowly sculpting and carving. Unlike some of the "dry" caves in parts of the western United States, many of Postojna's passages are water galleries—flooded tunnels. The caves are so damp that they are also home to a diminutive fellow, *Proteus anguinus*. These little critters are "an endemic biological curiosity"—Postojna is the only place you will find this particular kind of newt. This leads us to remind you that no matter how hot it is outside, the temperature in the caves is very cool and damp; bring warm clothing.

You can see the caves on foot or in the comfort of an electric train. There are three major areas open to tourists, all of which are electrically illuminated (in fact Postojna has been electrified longer than most of Yugoslavia; in 1983 the 100th anniversary of Postojna's electrification was celebrated). In no case are visitors allowed to roam around unescorted—the tour guides are strict on this point. There is an entrance fee of less than 30¢ per person.

While you're in the neighborhood you can visit the **Castle of Predjama,** a Renaissance cave/castle and now a museum. The castle is only about five or six miles west and north of the cave entrance. Nestled against the slopes of Mount Hrusica, the old cave fortress of Predjama was once the lair of the rebel knight Erasmus Predjamski, a figure quite unlike Robin Hood.

There are several tours from Ljubljana and from Istrian towns to the Postojna area. Access is much easier with a car, though summer tourist traffic can make the 30-mile trip from Ljubljana a very long one. If you cannot make it any farther, there are several pensions and hotels within walking distance of the cave entrance area. There is also an overcrowded campground nearby. The **Postojna tourist office,** where you can get more information, is in town at Tržaška ulica 4 (tel. 21-841).

LIPICA: Set among lush pastures bordered by 100-year-old oaks, the landscape of the **Lipica stables** has been basically unchanged for the last century or so. A few new buildings to accommodate tourists and a beautiful new hotel are the only additions. Home of the world-famous Lipizzaner, a breed of horse, Lipica was first established in 1580 by the Austrian Archduke Charles, the son of Emperor Ferdinand. The Lipica stables provided the Imperial stables with some of the finest show horses the world has ever seen. Perhaps you've seen pictures or an actual performance of the Spanish Riding School in Vienna—horses standing and walking on their hind legs with a rider, precision riding that would put a watchmaker to shame, and other such feats. For over 400 years these horses have been bred and trained here at Lipica.

It is possible to ride some of these regal beasts, and the fees are reasonable: basically $15 for three hours and a group lesson in the ring. There are also trail riding and group trips around the surrounding fields. Riders must have a trainer accompany them at all times.

Staying in Lipica

There are also organized tours to Lipica, but it makes the most sense to spend at least a night here. The hotel is overpriced, but there are a few pensions in the nearby town of Lokev, or you can stay in Trieste (the Yugoslav-Italian border is less than four miles away). You can see the cleared border zone from the farm, and emblazoned on a nearby hill in 100-foot-high letters is the word "TITO." Camping is a problem as you are not allowed to simply set up a tent anywhere, certainly not on the Lipica farm. Some of the local farmers may be more inclined to say yes, but ask first.

For tour information and reservations, contact **Kobilarna Lipica,** 66210 Sezana (tel. 73-009, 73-541, or 73-781; Telex 34217).

3. Zagreb and Inland Croatia

Croatia is a vast U-shaped province controlling about one-fifth of the total land area of Yugoslavia and most of the Dalmatian coast. Zagreb, located approximately at the bend of the U, is the capital of this very diverse province. There is so much to see in Croatia that we described the coastal areas in Chapters XXVIII, XXIX, and XXX. In this chapter we cover only Zagreb and the inland sights of Croatia. There are numerous natural and historical monuments here—everything from Kumrovec, the birthplace of Josip Broz Tito, to the magnificent waterfalls at Plitvice. Zagreb is also the first major city you will enter if you're coming to Yugoslavia from anywhere except Trieste.

Almost everybody coming to Yugoslavia passes through Zagreb at least once—it's the main transportation hub in the northern part of the country. Located between the Sava River and the slopes of the Medvednica peaks, Zagreb enjoys a Mediterranean climate tempered in summer by cooler continental weather. Its population of over 800,000 makes it the second-largest Yugoslavian city, after Beograd (Belgrade). The Upper Town of Zagreb is the oldest section, the Lower Town was built at the turn of the century, and the modern Novi (new) Zagreb was built after the Second World War.

The city is host to several major international cultural events, such as the Music Biennale, an international festival of modern music, as well as the World Festival of Animated Film, one of the most prestigious of its kind. There are also two international trade fairs, one in the autumn and the other in the spring.

A CAPSULE HISTORY: Around A.D. 615 the first Croatian tribes stormed into the area, destroying the Roman settlement of Andautonia on the site of the present-day village of Šćitarjevo. Following the victory of the Croatian noble-man Demetrius Zvoimir over the Byzantine forces, a bishopric was established in Zagreb in 1094. Later, in 1242 Béla IV, known in Hungary as a Hungarian king and by residents of Zagreb as a Croato-Hungarian king, granted the city royal privileges. Hungarian or not, Béla IV was busy trying to piece back together the Árpáds kingdom, which had fallen apart in the wake of the Mongol invasion of 1240–1241; Zagreb was part of that kingdom.

The area was long associated with Hungary, though generally Croatia was allowed a degree of autonomy under local leadership; in 1557 Zagreb was first mentioned as the capital of Croatia. Following the Austro-Hungarian victories over the Ottoman Turkish Empire, Zagreb and Croatia fell into the Hapsburgs' orbit. Though there was oppression under the Hapsburgs, technological development did follow. In 1862 Zagreb was linked by railway with the rest of the Austro-Hungarian Empire. The city did not suffer much damage during the war and Zagreb has since been incorporated into Yugoslavia as the capital of Croatia, one of the most productive republics.

GETTING TO ZAGREB: Zagreb, the hub for both domestic and international traffic, has an estimated 40 million people pass through its stations and roadways during the course of a year.

By Car

There's an excellent four-lane highway that is not yet completed between Ljubljana and Zagreb, and there are plans to extend the highway south to Beograd (Belgrade) sometime in this century. Roads are generally in repair and traffic inland is usually not heavy. Traffic information and road maps are available at the **Automobile Club of Croatia** (AMSH) Information Center at Siget 17 (tel. 522-522). Also try the Tourist Service Department at Draškovićeva 46 (tel. 449-816).

By Train

There is almost always a layover of some sort in Zagreb. On the international trains from Budapest and points north, the layover is at least three hours. You must change in Zagreb for practically any other destination in Yugoslavia. The information office at the **Central Railroad Terminal** at Tomislavov trg 12 (tel. 272-244 or 272-245) does have a rather harried English-speaking staff who can answer most of your rail-travel questions.

By Air

There is an **international airport** about ten miles from the city proper. A JAT-operated **shuttle bus** runs back and forth between the airport and the Hotel Esplanade every hour from 4 to 6 a.m., and then every half hour till 7 p.m. The trip takes about 20 to 25 minutes and costs 145 dinars (50¢) per person. JAT, Aeroflot, Air France, Alitalia, CSA, INEX ADRIA, KLM, Lufthansa, SAS, Swissair, and several other major airlines fly out of the Zagreb international airport. The very well-organized **JAT** office at Trg N. Zrinjskog 17 (tel. 443-322) can help you with most of your domestic Yugoslavian flight needs.

ORIENTATION: Zagreb is divided into three main sections: the Upper Town, the Lower Town, and the New Town. The Upper Town, the oldest section, contains most of the historical monuments. The Lower Town was built at the turn of the century and has wide boulevards and several imposing edifices built in different styles. The Lower Town is also known for the impressive array of linked squares. These are three squares or parks, one after the other, stretching north from the railroad station. These squares are also paralleled by another three squares to the west. Zagreb's New Town is across the Sava River and of little interest to the tourist.

The center of town is the **Trg Republike** (Republic Square), which is the hub of many buses and trams and is roughly midway between the railroad station and the Upper Town.

Getting into Town

To get from the **railroad station** (Glavni kolodvor) to the center of town, walk north (straight ahead) as you leave the station building on Praska. Continue for about 10 to 15 minutes on Praska until you reach the Trg Republike. If you don't want to walk, take tram 6 or 13 for two stops. The **bus station** (Autobusni kolodvor) is on Avenija Marina Držića, about eight blocks east of the railroad station down Branimirova Street. To get to the Trg Republike from the bus station, take tram 6 for four stops.

Tourist Information

The main **tourist information office** is at Trg N. Zrinskog 14 (tel. 441-880). However, there are over 20 other tourist offices, including all the major Yugoslavian tour operators. All the offices have at least one branch within easy walking distance of the Trg Republike. Also, a walk north along Praska from the railroad station will yield many different tourist offices.

Important Addresses

The **U.S. Consulate General** is at Brace Kavurica 2 (tel. 444-800), and the **British Consulate** is at Illica 12 (tel. 445-522).

Public Transportation

There is an excellent **tram** system running from 5:30 a.m. to 10 p.m. and a local bus system as well.

THE SIGHTS: There's a whole lot to see in Zagreb, especially in the Upper Town. Expect to spend at least a day exploring all the things the city has to offer.

The Upper Town

Kaptol and the Upper Town, formerly known as Gradec (Grič in Croatian), were two adjacent settlements that were joined when the bishopric was founded in A.D. 1094. They have been mentioned under a common name, Zagreb, since the middle of the 16th century. Kaptol, meaning "Chapter" in old Croatian, was the see of the bishop and deans, the political center, while Gradec was the mercantile and crafts quarter.

The Kaptol

In the Kaptol is **St. Stephen's Chapel** in the Gothic cathedral of the same name, parts of which date from the 13th century. **St. Stephen's Cathedral** is famous for representing the easternmost spread of Gothic architecture. Here also are the 15th- and 16th-century walls and towers that have become the symbols of Zagreb. The main square, **Trg Kaptol,** is lined with several notable 17th- and 18th-century buildings. Between the two towns of Kaptol and Gradec was a stream running roughly down Tkalčićeva Street, that has now been covered over and diverted. Across the stream was a bridge, now a street, known as the **Bridge of Blood** (Krvavi most) for all the feuds that ended in bloodshed between the two municipalities.

Gradec

Up the hill from Krvavi most, just off Radićeva Street, is the most famous sight in Gradec, the old **stone gate,** the former eastern gateway, dating from the 13th century. Farther along, on Katarinski trg, is the wonderful baroque **Church of St. Catherine,** for the nobility. Nearby, on Radicev trg, is the Gothic **Church of St. Mark,** for commoners, and the old grammar school (1607) that was once the seat of the oldest university in Yugoslavia (1669). The oldest surviving tower in Zagreb is the **Lotrščak Tower,** on Strossmayererovo šetalište (promenade). Every day at noon to mark the hour a cannon is fired from the old tower, which has been converted into an art gallery and museum. The old **Jesuit Monastery,** at Jezuitski trg 4 (tel. 444-465), is now an art gallery and museum.

Also of note is the wonderful baroque palace, **Vojković-Oršić-Rauchova,** on 9 Matoševa. Built in 1764, the palace now is home to the **Croatian Historical Museum** (tel. 277-991). At the northern end of Gradec is the **Priest's Tower** (Popov toranj), dating from the 13th century. At the begining of the 20th century an astronomical observatory was added to the tower. Next to the Priest's Tower, at Opatička 20, is the oldest girls' school in Zagreb, now the **Town Museum of Zagreb** (tel. 274-642). There are also numerous interesting 17th- and 18th-century buildings throughout the Upper Town.

The Lower Town

This part of Zagreb was developed in the late 19th and early 20th century and is the business and commercial center of the city. Of particular interest are the **three linked squares or parks,** running north from the railroad station. These parks are paralleled by three similar squares to the west. The main square and the center of Zagreb is the **Trg Republike,** located at the north end of the arcade formed by the three linked squares in front of the railroad station.

ACCOMMODATIONS: There are *big* problems for the budget traveler in Zagreb. There is a shortage of private rooms. There are few student accommodations. Camping possibilities are limited. Two factors combine to create even more of a crush on the already overburdened budget-accommodation scene in Zagreb. First, Zagreb is a major crossroad for Italian, Hungarian, and Yugoslavian traffic. The city is the primary choke point through which the vast majority of all the coast-bound traffic passes. The result is that there are many, many people waiting four, five, or six hours for their train connections. Second, there is no easily available budget housing, and the police certainly are not about to let people sleep in the nearby parks.

For the medium- to upper-bracket traveler more accommodations are becoming available as more class A and class B establishments are being built.

If you're a budget traveler and just passing through, schedule your transportation to avoid a stopover in Zagreb; there is really very little in the way of budget accommodations. Either continue your trip with no layover in Zagreb or make a reservation in one of the establishments we list. Almost all of the proprietors of these the hotels assured us that there's a 99% chance of success if you call three or four days in advance to reserve a room for a single night.

You can also stay in Ljubljana, which has plenty of budget accommodations, and is only 2½ hours away from Zagreb by train. You then can return to Zagreb for a day visit.

Hotels

Almost all the Class C hotels are being closed or renovated to Class B standards and prices. There are two hotels we can recommend for the budget traveler.

The **Central Hotel,** at Branimirova 3 (tel. 272-300), one of the few Class C hotels left, has bathless doubles for less than $14. Not well maintained, the Central nevertheless is often crowded with starving artist types attending the several yearly conferences. Located just across from the railroad station, it's always worth a try. Whether or not the Central will still be here when you arrive is still up in the air. While officially it is not scheduled for renovation and "recategorization," the manager was not certain as to the hotel's fate.

Farther away from the city center and the railroad station is the **Hotel Jadran,** at Vlaška 50 (tel. 414-257). It has been newly renovated and is now a Class B hotel. The prices have increased substantially, but a double room with a shower is still under $25. There are also a few rooms without private bath for about $15 double. To get here from the Trg Republike, take tram 11 or 12 east for three stops to Kvaternikov trg, and then walk back west for two or three minutes.

A Splurge Choice

Hotel Dubrovnik, Gajeva 1 (tel. 424-222; Telex 21670-YU-HOTBK), offers attractive modern rooms right in the center of town, just off the Trg Republike. Despite the central location, the medium-sized rooms are very quiet, and they come equipped with modern bathrooms. Prices are slightly splurgey, but a fair value for the comfort and location of the hotel: 7,480 dinars ($25.60) for a single and 13,178 dinars ($45.15) for a double.

Private Rooms

A law was passed in the summer of 1985 affecting the registration and classification of private rooms. The upshot of these new registration procedures for those natives of Zagreb who wish to rent out rooms is that the whole system is in a shambles. There are few private rooms and poor coordination and management of the available resources. We hope that by the time you arrive they will have sorted everything out.

There are three main private-room services: **Croatiaturist,** at Tomislavov trg 17 (tel. 710-410), right on the corner to the north of the railroad station; **Generalturist,** at Trg N. Zrinjskog 18 (tel. 445-299), about two blocks farther north; and **TD Novi Zagreb,** at Trnsko 15e (tel. 521-523).

Student Accommodation

Sad to say, but in Zagreb, a city flooded with young student travelers and other "rock-bottom" budget travelers, there is only one student hotel and it's very poorly equipped. There are no plans to increase the number of student accommodations in the 1987 fiscal year. The office that handles all student accommodations is the **Omladinski turistički centar (Youth Tourist Center)** at Gajeva 25 (tel. 447-701). The office at Petrinjska 73 (tel. 441-738 or 447-503) handles all other student affairs and has information on hostels and student discounts.

Camping

Camping opportunities are just as bad. There is one campsite on the outskirts of the city, but it's not connected directly by public transportation (though there may be a bus by 1987). The single camping ground is **Mladost camp,** at the very end of the Slavski most (bridge) tram line, but not across the Sava River; stay on the north (Zagreb) side of the river. There is about a ten-minute walk west. To get here from Trg Republike, take tram 14 west, and from the railroad station take tram 4 west to the Slavski most end station.

DINING IN ZAGREB: Zagreb boasts some of the finest Croatian cooking as well as fresh and abundant seafood and freshwater fish. Here are our favorites.

Near the Trg Republike

For a good meal in a cozy, attractive setting with hanging bronze lamps and plants in the windows, visit the **Restaurant Drina,** Preradoviceva 11 (tel. 447-859). At the Drina you can choose among national specialties of Serbia, many of them prepared on the grill. We recommend sogan dolma, a delicious dish of onions stuffed with meat, rice, spices, and tomato sauce. Entrees are inexpensive, averaging between $1 and $3. The menu comes in Italian, German, and Serbian only, but the waiters can help translate. The Drina is open from 8 a.m. to 11 p.m., seven days a week.

Fish lovers will delight in the **Korčula Restaurant,** Nicola Tesla 17 (tel. 422-658). The interior displays an assortment of sea paraphernalia, including a copper bell, lifejackets, a steering wheel, and ropes, all surrounded by white stucco walls and plants. You can order a wide range of fish entrees from the Serbian-, Italian-, and German-language menu, including delicious scampi prepared in a tomato and garlic sauce for $3.75 to $5.65, depending on the portion. Most fish entrees (which they boast are fresh every day) cost less: only $1.30 to $1.95. It's open from 8 a.m. to midnight daily. Reservations are a good idea, except in July and August when locals head out of town to the seaside and you should have no trouble getting a table.

Good wild game can be enjoyed at **Lobacki Rog,** Ilica 14 (tel. 425-246). Our favorite part of this popular restaurant is the attractive garden in the back, where you can dine underneath many tall trees which shade you from the heat, and the walls are covered with vines and leaves. Game specialties include medallions of venison ($13 for two), garnished breast of lamb ($3.75), and many grilled items for less, such as čevapčiči (wild boar) with onions for only 385 dinars ($1.30). You can also enjoy a bottle of wine along with your meal for $2 to $3. Try to reserve for the evening, as many groups come during this time. It's open from 9 a.m. to midnight, seven days a week.

The restaurant **Kornat,** at Gajeva 9 (tel. 419-242), has both a self-service area and sit-down service in the pleasant courtyard out back. Reputed to be one of the finest fish restaurants in all of Zagreb, the Kornat has fish brought in fresh daily (except on weekends). The average fish platter will cost 450 dinars ($1.55) to 550 dinars ($1.90) with a salad and french fries. In the summer they serve more freshwater fish, and in the winter saltwater fish are available. The courtyard is very quiet and cool, with a business-luncheon-type crowd in the daytime and a trendier crowd in the evening. The Kornat is open from 9 a.m. to 11 p.m. daily.

A recommended place for summer dining outdoors is the **Gradski Podrum,** A. Cesara 2 (tel. 275-279). The restaurant is in a large courtyard, half-covered with a red plastic roof with the Coca-Cola logo printed all over it. Green plants add to the appealing outdoor atmosphere. The restaurant features Croatian and Serbian dishes, such as grilled ribsteak with marigold and garlic, and muckalica Serbian style, pieces of veal in a tangy tomato sauce with onions and peppers. These memorable entrees cost $2.25 to $4. In cool weather the restaurant opens its large cellar downstairs where you can listen to live piano music (you enter this part of the restaurant around the corner at Trg Republike 10). Open from 9 a.m. to 11:30 p.m., seven days a week.

In the Upper Town

The most attractive restaurant in town is **Stare Vure** ("The Old Watch"), Opaticka 20 (tel. 275-565), next to the Zagreb City Museum. The walls of the restaurant display old photos and memorabilia from the Croatian National Theater of the 19th century, and swinging big-band jazz classics play in the background. Outside the restaurant you can dine in a 16th-century courtyard whose buildings are covered with ivy. Look under the ivy on the left wall and you'll see an old sun dial. The regular customers are an eclectic mix of local musicians, artists, actors, and students, as well as officials from the U.S. Consulate who come to enjoy the tasty beefsteaks for about $3. Other entrees include frogs' legs sautéed with breadcrumbs. In all, it's a fun place for lunch or dinner. It's open from 10 a.m. to midnight; closed Monday. No food is served from July 15 to August 16 every year, though the bar remains open.

You can enjoy fine cuisine in the huge, lively **Kaptolska Klet,** Kaptol 5 (tel. 274-948), across from St. Stephen's Cathedral. You can choose to dine in one of several areas, including a room with white stucco walls, wood beam frames, and a few folk plates on the wall, or a spacious courtyard, half of which is covered by a large hexagonal roof. Begin your meal with some of the excellent Kajmak cheese, made from goats' milk. Then don't miss the incredible mushroom soup Zagorje style, a tomato-based soup with potatoes and mushrooms flavored with bacon. For the main course, hearty meat dishes such as sausage, shish kebab, meat patties, liver, and pork are the specialties. The restaurant is open from 9 a.m. to 11 p.m.

The Railroad Station Area

The **Hotel Esplanade,** at Mihanovićeva 1 (tel. 512-222), is right across from and west of the railroad station. The restaurant has a large terrace surrounded by an ivy-covered wall and serves a wide variety of both Yugoslavian and foreign dishes. If you wish to break the $25-a-day budget and eat excellent food, we recommend that you do it here. Most dishes cost over 740 dinars ($2.55), but in the evening the black-jacketed waiters will provide four-star service by moon- and candlelight.

NIGHTLIFE: Right off the Krvavi most at Tkalčićeva 16 is **Club Z** (tel. 428-888). The red plush interior, the stained wood with brass trim, and a superior sound system are complemented by the works of local artists on the wall. The atmosphere, despite the attempt at an English pub style, is very relaxed and very local. They serve hamburgers at 250 dinars (85¢) along with their large selection of Western liquors. The Club Z is open from 9 a.m. till midnight.

For the younger crowd there's the **Big Ben** disco on Dogovičeva. However, the younger set has to go to school in September so the Big Ben closes down and doesn't reopen until the next summer.

Trendy Zagreb locals often head outside of town for their weekend fun. One place that we heard a lot about was **Club Flash,** in the small village of Samoborska. It's frequented by Zagreb's young professional set, so you may meet a group in a bar or club in Zagreb who have a car and are planning to head out to Club Flash later; otherwise a car is a must. To get to the Club Flash, drive south to Ljubljanska avenija and then west, past the highway on the E-94. Drive for about ten minutes until you see the exit sign for Samobor, then keep straight on into town.

THE MARKET: Zagreb is justly famous throughout Yugoslavia for its huge **open-air market (Tržnica Dolac),** open every day except Sunday from 6 a.m. to 1 p.m. Here on summer mornings before the heat sets in, you can haggle for some of the fantastic kackavalj, a white cheese made from sheep's milk with a delicious tangy flavor. Then work around to the meat stalls where you can find some of the best kolbasa (various sausages) you'll ever eat. Add a loaf of home-baked bread and some fresh garden produce to your haul and enjoy a true feast, Croatian style, in one of the parks. Even though food prices may go up a bit for foreigners, you can buy a good meal at the market for practically nothing. There are also many worked goods and cloth items for sale. Look around, eye everything carefully, and never take the first price offered. The market isn't hard to find—it's both visible and audible from the Trg Republike.

AN EXCURSION TO THE PLITVICE LAKES: The Plitvice Lakes are actually 16 connected glacial tarns or lakes that were created by glaciers. They are an amazing collection of waterfalls, streams, and caves set in the green woods east and across the mountains of the dry coastal terrain. Plitvice is very different from the rocky, almost desert, coastal terrain. The cooler forest temperatures and refreshing spray from the waterfalls will take the edge off even the hottest day. There is a substantial forest around the waterfalls, so bring appropriate footgear if you plan to do some exploring. A lot of effort has gone into keeping the park pristine. No building has been built higher than the trees, and of course, you should not litter, light fires, or in any way endanger or pollute the park.

Fire Warning
In the summer, despite the water, the surrounding forests become tinder dry. Absolutely no campfires are allowed outside designated campsites. All campers using butane stoves should be careful as the head ranger reports that caravans (as trailers or RVs are called here) have had problems with accidental stove fires.

Orientation

There is really no way to get to the lakes unless you have a car. The **information office** is clearly marked at the first entrance (Ulaz 1), open from 9 a.m. to 6:30 p.m. in the summer (tel. 76-314, 76-524, or 76-544). There's an entry fee of about 50¢ per person to enter the park.

Several hotels are in the vicinity, but they tend to be filled with tour groups, so we recommend that you just stop off for the day at Plitvice. There is no camping in the park, only at designated campsites.

Dining

The **Lička Kuća,** one of our all-time favorite restaurants in Yugoslavia, is at the Plitvice Lakes. Built out of hand-hewn pine logs, it's right across the road from the first entrance (Ulaz 1) at the north end of the park. The heavy wooden beams are often wreathed in wood smoke from the large open grills in the center of the single large dining room. This dimly lit establishment, with many little nooks, has some of the most delicious meat dishes you'll find. The headwaiter assured us that only the finest cuts—the best sausages, the plumpest pork, and the tenderest lamb—arrive at the kitchen. We recommend the grill platter for around $2—a hearty helping of all the house specialties—and a frothy cold beer to top it off. The waiters, dressed in traditional peasant costume, serve the food a bit abruptly, but on the whole the service is good. There is live music every night and another dining room with a stage and dancing below.

4. Sarajevo

If all you know about Sarajevo is that it hosted the 1984 Winter Olympics, you might expect to find here a modern sports complex par excellence and little else. But Sarajevo (pop. 450,000) is full of surprises. Consider these typical scenes: a long moaning chant suddenly sounds forth from the town's many mosques, and Sarajevo's Muslims (almost a third of the area's population), many wearing small white caps and fezes, hurry to one of the day's five prayers. Down the street, less religious locals sell copper, leather, and other wares on narrow, crowded streets bustling with shoppers, and just blocks away, other locals pray in the town's Roman Catholic, Orthodox, or Jewish centers of worship.

As these scenes indicate, Sarajevo is a very diverse town full of life and excitement. The old market center is lined with quaint little cobblestone streets, mosques, tiny stores, and picturesque houses. And surrounding the town stand majestic mountains equipped with modern sports facilities. In all, Sarajevo is one of the most fascinating towns west of Istanbul.

Although the area around Sarajevo was long inhabited by Roman legions and then Slavic tribes, the city itself reached prominence in the 15th century when the Turks occupied it. For several hundred years the town served as an important trading point on the route from Constantinople to Dubrovnik and Venice. It was not until 1878 that the city was finally freed from Turkish hands, only to be put under the control of the Austro-Hungarian Empire. Local opposition to this rule culminated in the assassination of the heir to the Austro-Hungarian throne, Archduke Franz Ferdinand, by a young Sarajevo townsman seeking independence for Bosnia in 1914. This assassination triggered World War I.

GETTING THERE: The so-called **express train** from Belgrade to Sarajevo takes about six hours. Buy tickets and seat reservations a day or two before you depart. Travelers by train from the coast face a three-hour ride from Kardeljevo for 529 dinars ($1.80).

To buy tickets when leaving Sarajevo, go to **Unis Turist** at Vase Miskina 16 (tel. 510-150); **Olimpik Turs,** at Vase Miskina 2 (tel. 23-806 or 23-241), open from 7 a.m. to 9 p.m. Monday through Saturday, from 8 a.m. to 1 p.m. on Sunday; or to the train station.

JAT flies to Sarajevo's Butmir airport (tel. 41-844), ten kilometers (six miles) outside the town center; a JAT bus takes passengers to and from the airport to the JAT office at Vase Miskina 4 (tel. 518-077 or 611-326).

ORIENTATION: The train station (tel. 35-330) and bus depot (tel. 38-646) are located in **Stanični Trg,** about a 25-minute walk to the historic center of town. It's best to take tram 1 straight to **Baščaršija,** the old bazaar and center of Sarajevo's principal sights and hotels. On your way to Baščaršija, you'll pass along the small **Miljacka River,** which flows though Sarajevo.

In Baščaršija, the area's major streets all run parallel to the Miljacka River. The town's main shopping street, **Vase Miskina,** which later changes into **Sarači,** is two blocks from the river and runs parallel to it. This street is full of quaint little shops, and an indoor complex of stores called the Gazi-Husrevbeg Covered Market. On these streets, shoppers can purchase leather goods such as moccasins and handbags, and many copper items such as genie vases, magic lamps, and other objects such as Turkish saz guitars. (If you do want to buy something, remember to bargain with confidence; it's part of the game of outdoor markets!) The town's most interesting mosque, Gazi-Husrevbeg, is also found on Sarači.

ACCOMMODATIONS: Right in the heart of town, just minutes from Baščaršija, you'll find the Class B **Hotel Evropa,** Vase Pelagica 5 (tel. 532-722; Telex 41219). At first the rooms in the Evropa may strike you as small with depressingly dim lighting, but after a while the tiny lamps and the decorative curtains on the windows give the rooms a simple charm. The private bathrooms are quite small, and hot water often takes five or ten minutes to warm up, but the receptionist is very helpful and the location is great. Single rooms rent for 7,782 dinars ($26.65) and doubles go for 12,210 dinars ($41.80).

A less expensive choice right in the center of town is the **Hotel Stari Grad,** Maršala Tita 126 (tel. 533-394). Although the hotel is listed as Class D, the rooms are quiet, clean, and well maintained, making it one of the town's best buys. It's also located just off the main market square. Singles without private bathrooms cost $15.05, and doubles without bathroom run $25.40.

You'll find another good budget value at the small **Hotel Central,** Zrinjskog 8 (tel. 33-566). Rooms appear old but clean, and the public bathrooms are also well maintained. The hotel does in fact boast a central location, just minutes from Sarajevo's markets and main mosques. The Central charges 3,582 dinars

($12.25) for singles without bathroom, 8,485 dinars ($29.05) for a double with private bathroom, and 6,175 dinars ($21.15) for a double without bathroom.

Although slightly outside the heart of town, the **Hotel Zagreb,** Valtera Perića 1 (tel. 36-680), provides visitors with a good backup choice if the above hotels are full. Rooms are small but fine for budget travelers who don't expect great luxury. There's also an attractive modern café downstairs. Singles cost $12.10 without bathroom and $13.20 with a shower only. Doubles cost $22 without a bathroom and $24.20 with a shower and toilet. It's about a 15-minute walk to the town center from here.

Students can also stay in the **youth hostel (Dom Ferijalaca),** at Zadrugina 17 (tel. 36-163), which offers rooms with six to eight beds for about $2 per bed.

Private Rooms

A much cheaper alternative to hotels in Sarajevo are private rooms. The **Turist Biro Sarajevo,** JNA 50 (tel. 25-151, 24-844, or 39-203), rents singles for 1,650 dinars ($5.65) to 2,200 dinars ($7.55), and doubles for 2,200 dinars ($7.55) to 4,400 dinars ($15.05). They also can give you information on folk performances and concerts in town. This office remains open from 7 a.m. to 9 p.m. Monday through Saturday, from 8 a.m. to 1 p.m. on Sunday.

Unis Turist, Vase Miskina 16 (tel. 510-150; Telex 41829), also rents private rooms in the center for $4 to $10 per person, and private apartments for $200 a week. The English-speaking department manager, Snežana Dabić, can assist you with any special requests you may have.

Skiers' Accommodations

Visitors who have come to Sarajevo to go skiing can stay in one of a number of hotels in the mountains, about 15 to 30 km (9 to 18 miles) outside the city center. Most of these hotels are in the B category—lodge or pavilion-style houses popular among skiers. For further information on ski accommodations and preparations for a ski trip, inquire at the Yugoslav National Tourist Office.

DINING: Our favorite restaurant in town is **RS,** at Maršala Tita 5 (tel. 26-372), a private restaurant with a simple outdoor garden and an indoor space covered with photographs of old Sarajevo. Hrapović Sarajko, a soft-spoken man of 30, runs this excellent restaurant (popular with both locals and tourists) with careful attention to his clients. A member of the Yugoslav Communist Party, he strongly denies that he is a capitalist, despite the fact that he owns this restaurant. Whatever his personal beliefs, under his supervision you're sure to enjoy a memorable meal at RS. We highly recommend the "RS Odresak," a really delicious slice of veal stuffed with cheese, spices, and a buttery sauce, all covered with a crisp batter outside, for only 550 dinars ($1.90). If you prefer seafood, you can enjoy fresh fish from Lake Skadar on the Yugoslavian-Albanian border. For a side dish, order the tasty grilled mushrooms with cheese on top, for 330 dinars ($1.15). It's open from 9 a.m. to midnight in summer and noon to midnight in winter. Try to reserve.

Demanding travelers from France and Italy often frequent **Šentada,** at Darovalaca krvi 21 (tel. 614-051), for seafood. A father and son operate this small restaurant, which has two small rooms with wood and corkboard walls. The menu features well-prepared, tasty fresh fish every day, ranging from scampi (for only about $2 a portion) to San Pietro (for about $2.50) and lobster (for about $7 a pound). When we visited, we sampled freshwater eel—with some hesitation at first—but it proved quite tender and delicious. Along with your meal you can enjoy wine from the owner's private cellar. It's open from 9 a.m.

to midnight, seven days a week. Reserve for evenings as this is a small restaurant. You'll find the Šentada across from the Hotel Bristol.

To taste Turkish and regional specialties, don't miss the **Restaurant Morića Han,** Sarači 77 (tel. 532-289 or 535-941). Several indoor areas with white stucco walls and an attractive courtyard lined with tables make up this large restaurant. Inside, ancient sayings in Arabic are written on the wall. On one, the 11th-century Persian poet Omar Khayyam advises his readers to enjoy themselves day by day with eating, love, and what he calls "life's greatest pleasure," wine. Subscribers to this bohemian way of life can indulge in a rich flavorful meal combining all of these elements. For good eating, try the sarajevski sahan, a delicious shish kebab with a juicy sauce, along with stuffed onion, stuffed tomato, other vegetables, and a touch of cream. Another popular dish from the Middle East is dolma, a vegetable stuffed with meat. Fine Yugoslavian wine during the meal completes the trio of Omar Khayyam's code of life. For dessert, sample baklava or kadaif, a sweet transparent spaghetti pastry with honey. This entire feast is very reasonably priced, with entrees running about $2 each. Open 9 a.m. to midnight, seven days a week.

How about a New Wave pizzeria? At **Papillon,** Livanjska br. 48 (tel. 33-908), you can enjoy a good European-style pizza (round, but with a thicker crust than most American pizzas) for 330 dinars ($1.15) in an attractive modern interior of red velvet chairs and subdued red lighting. New Wave music plays at a fair volume throughout the meal, a feature which attracts many young Yugoslav locals. Cheap wine, beer, and drinks are available along with the pizza. The only drawback to the restaurant is its remote location in the Koševo district of town, so it's best reached by car; bus 16B also comes here from the Skenderija. It's open from 5 p.m. to midnight Monday through Saturday; closed Sunday.

For an after-dinner drink and some exotic Arabic-sounding music on the weekend, stop by the garden restaurant **Kolobara** at the Letno Kino off Sarači. A local couple performs Bosnian music on a saz (a Turkish guitar) to a mostly Yugoslav audience. The music plays from 6:30 to 9 p.m. on Friday, Saturday, and Sunday.

THE SIGHTS: Don't fail to visit the **Gazi-Husrevbeg Mosque,** the town's largest and most interesting, erected in 1531 (but largely rebuilt after a fire in the 19th century) on Sarači Street. Outside, you see a large 19th-century fountain where Muslims wash themselves before prayer. Inside, you'll view carpets on the floor sent by Egyptian leaders Nasser and Sadat, Libya's Khaddafi, the late Shah of Iran, and others. Behind the mosque is a 16th-century **Clock Tower** (Sahat Kula), which has a lunar calendar (with 125 days per month). If you wander around the Baščaršija area, you can also visit a few more of the town's more than 80 mosques and 78 minarets (see below for more details on Muslim religious practices).

For a look at how a typical Muslim family lived in years past, stop by the **House of the Svrzo Family,** at Jovana dr Kršića 5. In this picturesque house, you can walk through the three different areas of a Muslim home: one for men, one for women, and one for guests.

The **Museum of the City of Sarajevo,** at Svetozara Markovića 54, also details life in Sarajevo in days of old, starting from the Neolithic era to the present.

Museum buffs may also want to visit the **National Museum of Bosnia-Herzegovina,** Vojvode Putnika 7, which has large archeological, natural history, and ethnological exhibits on Sarajevo and Bosnia-Herzegovina, such as folk costumes and art, musical instruments, and other exhibitions.

One of the town's most unprepossessing sights is also its most famous. At the small **Princip Bridge** over the Miljacka River in the town center, Gavrilo Princip assassinated the heir to the Austro-Hungarian throne, the spark that started World War I. A plaque at the bridge reads that Princip "shot for freedom," but it does not even mention World War I.

SOME BACKGROUND ON THE MUSLIM RELIGION: Five times a day—at sunrise, 10 a.m., noon, in the afternoon, and at sunset—you can hear the call to prayer across the streets of Sarajevo. This call, known as the "ezan," comes from the top of a mosque's minaret, and is delivered in a strong and emotional vibrato voice. Soon after, the religious faithful will gather at the mosque for prayer. Before entering the mosque, Muslims wash their feet at a fountain in front of the mosque (a cleansing known as the "abdest"), so that they will be clean before God. Inside the mosque they bow down and pray in the direction of Mecca, in Saudi Arabia. In the mosque, which is cleared of all non-Muslims prior to worship, the imam (leader) stands before the faithful and leads the prayer.

IMPORTANT ADDRESSES: For information on Sarajevo, stop by the **Sarajevo Tourist Office** at Sarači 81 (tel. 535-202). You can also buy small Tito pins in this bureau. It's open from 8 a.m. to 8 p.m. Monday through Saturday, from 10 a.m. to 2 p.m. on Sunday.

Travelers to Sarajevo can receive their mail at the **Atlas** office (they represent American Express), JNA 81 (tel. 532-521 or 533-521; Telex 41243). They're open from 8 a.m. to 7 p.m. Monday through Saturday, to 1 p.m. on Sunday.

The Help and Information Service of the **Auto Association of Bosnia and Herzegovina** assists motorists in need with a towing service, information on road conditions, and legal aid. Call 987; their stations are open from 8 a.m. to 8 p.m.

EXCURSIONS TO THE MOUNTAINS: If you want to enjoy a fine panoramic view of Sarajevo and the breathtaking mountains in the surrounding area, visit **Mount Trebević,** some 5,000 feet above sea level. To get there, cross the river from the town center and make your way to the ski lift at D. Tucovica 32. The lift operates every hour on the hour from 10 a.m. to 9 p.m. on weekdays and 8 a.m. to 10 p.m. on Saturday, Sunday, and holidays, for a fare of 132 dinars (45¢) round trip. The ride to Mount Trebević takes 12 minutes—among other things, you'll see the Olympic bobsled track on the way, and upon your arrival you'll find several little paths on which to wander around in the mountains.

Travelers who prefer to enjoy the grand vista of the mountains from the comfort of a restaurant chair can stop at the **Restoran Vidikovac** (tel. 536-430), located right next to the top of the ski lift. Bosnian grilled dishes are the specialty here, such as lamb roast for 528 dinars ($1.80). The outdoor tables of the restaurant rest on one of the highest spots in the area, and offer a thoroughly enjoyable panorama of the mountains. If you prefer, you can sit at the restaurant and just sip coffee or a drink. It's open from 10 a.m. to 10 p.m.

Chapter XXXII

BELGRADE (BEOGRAD)

1. Orientation
2. Accommodations
3. Dining on a Budget
4. The Sights
5. The ABCs of Belgrade

WITH ITS TALL MODERN BUILDINGS, loud traffic, and bustling streets, Belgrade (pop. 1,500,000) is definitely a capital well suited for city slickers. Some visitors may at first be overwhelmed by Belgrade; it can be difficult to find one's way around, and the city's most charming areas need to be sought out. In fact, when you first arrive, you may conclude that Belgrade is just a modern city with little to offer.

With time, however, you'll discover rewarding sections of town to visit, such as the quiet parks of Kalemegdan, the old town fortress, or Skadarlija, an area frequented by artists and musicians which continues to maintain a 19th-century atmosphere. Belgrade is also home to many of Yugoslavia's largest and most important museums, which detail everything from old Roman settlements in Serbia to the life story of Yugoslavian President Tito. Those willing to look behind the dull urban façade will find an interesting, varied city in Belgrade.

A CAPSULE HISTORY: Belgrade's historians like to boast that the Yugoslav capital has been destroyed 36 times, thanks to the city's strategic position. Celtic tribes first inhabited the Belgrade area in the 3rd century B.C., but by the 1st century A.D. the Romans had taken command of the region. The name Belgrade was given to the area's main settlement by Slavic tribes who ruled from the 8th century on. When the Turks swept through Serbia in the 16th century, however, Belgrade began a period of 350 years under Turkish domination, followed by a shorter Austro-Hungarian rule in the 19th century.

After Belgrade gained independence from the Austro-Hungarian Empire at the end of World War I, the city had a very brief respite before the onset of World War II when the Nazis initiated an aerial-bombing campaign in 1941. Since the war Belgrade has enjoyed a peaceful and prosperous time as capital of the Yugoslavian Socialist Republic and as the country's largest city.

1. Orientation
Travelers arriving at the train and bus stations who want to check their bag-

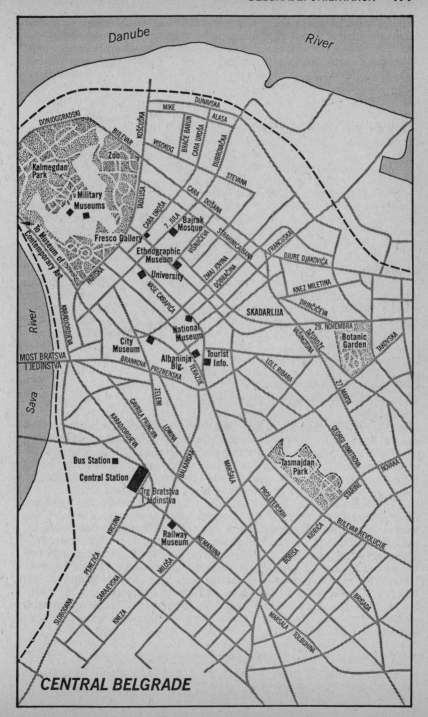

CENTRAL BELGRADE

gage before finding a hotel should cross the street and head for the **Putnik Garderobe** at Karadordeva 83. There's also a baggage check (but no lockers) in the train station, but lines are always long since each and every bag must be personally inspected (a terrorist explosion went off in the baggage checkroom a number of years ago). At Putnik you probably won't see any lines and they will only ask to see your passport. Each bag checked costs 55 dinars (19¢) per day. Open from 5:30 a.m. to 11 p.m.

TOURIST INFORMATION: At a small window on the right before you leave the station, you'll see the **Exchange Bureau,** open from 6 a.m. to 10:30 p.m., but they sometimes close earlier if they run out of money. Next to the Exchange Bureau, a station **Information Office** (tel. 646-240) can supply you with a map of Belgrade and book a hotel as well. It's open from 7 a.m. to 9 p.m.

For additional information, stop by the **Putnik Travel Office** at Trg Bratstva I Jedinstva 1A (tel. 657-995), across from the station. The kind staff can help orient you to the city and give you maps and information. They can also make couchette reservations for you much more quickly than in the train station. The office is open from 7 a.m. to 8 p.m. Monday through Saturday. Ten feet up the street you'll find another Putnik bureau which rents out private rooms (see "Accommodations").

Soon after you settle down, stop by one of the most helpful tourist bureaus we have come across in researching this book, Belgrade's **Tourist Information Office (Turisticki Informativni Centar),** located in the pedestrian underpass below the Albanian building on Terazije Street (tel. 635-343 or 635-622). The staff in this office know their stuff, and when we visited they were helpful on a wide variety of questions that would have left most Eastern European offices stumped. They can also give you materials on Belgrade and Serbia, including the *Beogradscope,* a monthly pamphlet which lists cultural happenings in Belgrade (also look for *Beogradscope* in hotels). They're open from 8 a.m. to 8 p.m., seven days a week including holidays.

FINDING YOUR WAY AROUND: Unfortunately, Belgrade is not the easiest place to find your way around. Compounding the problem are long, zigzagging avenues, and many street signs in Cyrillic lettering (both the Roman and Cyrillic alphabets are used in Serbia). However, most maps have Roman letters, and so with some effort you can indeed get around Belgrade. Before you start out, try to buy a good map from a newsstand (we used "Plan Beograde 1986").

The **train station** lies just east of the Sava River, at **Trg Bratstva I Jedinstva.** To reach Belgrade's largest shopping avenue, **Maršala Tita,** which turns into **Terazije,** walk east for about ten minutes up a hill from the station. If you continue left down Maršala Tita and then Terazije, you will pass the tall **Albania** building (under which you'll find the Tourist Information Office), and then after two blocks you'll reach the town's major square, **Trg Republike.** In Trg Republike you'll see numerous cafés and the National Museum. The road leading slightly left from Trg Republike is called **Knez Mihailova,** a shopping area filled with stores, cafés, and pedestrians, especially in the evening. Continuing down this road you eventually reach **Kalemegdan Park,** site of Belgrade's old fortress. And with this brief review off you go!

2. Accommodations

Even with dozens of small hotels, Belgrade offers visitors very few good budget values. Although most Belgrade hotel rooms come with bathrooms, the rooms appear small and bare—in all, not the greatest value for your dollar. Prices are especially high for single travelers, who often pay more than $25 a night for a room. Private rooms make up one ray of hope on the budget-accommodations horizon, but few of these exist so it's best to reserve Belgrade's private rooms ahead of time.

Hotels right in the center are generally expensive, fairly plain, and often somewhat rundown. The more basic hotels near the train station offer the lowest prices, but not a top location, especially at night when suspicious-looking types can be seen. Hotels outside the immediate center, although not ideally located, offer the most attractive rooms of these three areas.

IN THE TOWN CENTER: The Hotel Kasina, Terazije 25 (tel. 335-574; Telex 11865-KASINA-YU), is on Belgrade's busiest shopping avenue in the center of town. Some of the 99 rooms in this Class B hotel appear slightly rundown, and all rooms lack almost any decoration, but the Kasina offers a location that can't be beat. Try for the rooms in the back of the hotel to avoid noise from the street. Singles with bathroom rent for $31.90; doubles go for $39.60.

Walk down the street and you'll reach the slightly more moderate **Hotel Splendid,** a class B hotel on a side street off Terazije Avenue, Dragoslava Jovanovića 5 (tel. 335-444). Although there are many worse hotels in town, still you are likely to find the hotel name somewhat misleading, as the hotel's 50 rooms are small with tiny bathrooms. Singles rent for $29.70 to $36.30, and doubles run $37.40 to $44.

Minutes from picturesque Skadarlija Street you'll find the 79-room **Hotel Union,** Kosovska 11 (tel. 341-055). Although dull green may not be your first choice as a decorating color, you'll find the rooms spacious, equipped with private bathrooms, and conveniently located in central Belgrade. Singles cost $29.70 to $36.30, and doubles rent for $37.40 to $44.

Most of its rooms are rather pricey, but the Class A **Hotel Palas,** Topličin Venac br. 23 (tel. 637-222, 637-911, or 637-178; Telex 11323), does offer four bare single rooms with shower and toilet for only $19.80—a true bargain for the single traveler in Belgrade. In addition, students get a 10% to 20% discount in the months of July and August. Since there are only four of these bargain rooms, we strongly recommend you write and reserve well ahead of time. Otherwise, normal rates are $44 single (these rooms offer more comfort) and $60.50 double. You'll see the hotel in the center of town, just a few minutes' walk from Belgrade's major shopping streets.

A good choice for those seeking a section of Belgrade quieter than the large shopping avenues is the **Hotel Toplice,** 7 Jula 56 (tel. 626-426). The hotel offers 120 small, attractive rooms with modern bathrooms. Best of all is its location—just minutes from the Kalemegdan Park, one of Belgrade's most beautiful areas which houses many of the city's museums. Singles with breakfast cost $36.30; doubles run $44.

NEAR THE TRAIN STATION: The area around the train station offers the most inexpensive and basic accommodations in town. For travelers not seeking the absolute lowest prices, we recommend the **Hotel Bristol,** Karadordeva 50, two blocks to the left from the train station (tel. 626-063). You'll find that their rooms, equipped with old furniture, a radio, and a telephone, look considerably more attractive than those in many of the town's other hotels in the same price range. Singles rent for $33 with breakfast, and doubles go for $44. Another plus about the hotel is the taxi stand in front, where a number of taxis always seem to be waiting. We advise light sleepers to request the quiet rooms in the back of the hotel.

For an excellent budget hotel that offers 33 medium-sized, worn but clean rooms, check into the **Hotel Pošta,** Slobodana Penezića Krcuna 3 (tel. 642-046). You'll find the Pošta across the street from the right side of the station (to your right with your back to the tracks). Singles with bathroom cost $11; doubles cost $17.60 without bathroom and $22 with. An additional bed in the room costs $5.50.

If you walk straight for one block from the front of the train station and then turn left, in about five minutes you'll reach the **Hotel Prag,** Narodnog Fronta br. 27 (tel. 687-355 or 680-655; Telex YU-12494-HP). Although the room price of $30.80 to $37.40 for singles and $39.60 to $45.10 for doubles may seem excessive for the hotel's 118 bare rooms with private bathrooms, remember that that's what rooms cost in this city, and that the location is quite convenient, right between the train station and the center of town.

Travelers seeking the closest hotel to the station will choose the **Hotel Centar,** Trg Bratstva I Jedinstva 7 (tel. 644-055). Bare rooms sport light-green walls and a sink; the hotel is pretty rundown, and the public bathrooms are not the city's cleanest. What, then, brings travelers to the Centar? The rates are among the lowest in the city: singles without bathroom cost $11, and doubles, $22. From the train station, walk across the street to your right through a park of down-and-out types and you'll arrive in a minute.

For budget travelers not looking for a lot of comfort, we list the **Hotel Astoria,** Milovana Milovanovića 1 (tel. 645-422), a Class C hotel one block from the train station. Public bathrooms are barely acceptable. The hotel's one redeeming feature is its price: the 78 small box-like rooms rent for $22 single without private bathroom; doubles cost $29.70 without bathroom and $34.10 with.

OUTSIDE THE IMMEDIATE CENTER: Travelers seeking some comfort should try two fairly modern Class B hotels (from the early 1970s) about a ten-minute walk from both the train station and the town center: the **Hotel Turist,** Sarajevska 37 (tel. 682-855; Telex 12900), and the **Hotel Park,** Njegoševa 2 (tel. 334-722). Both offer singles with private bathroom for $31.90 and doubles for $39.60.

If you're looking to save as much money as possible, go to Belgrade's absolutely cheapest hostelry, the **Hotel Trim,** at Kneza Višeslava 72 (tel. 559-128). This basic hotel is in a somewhat remote location, but bus 53 from Kneza Miloša (a square about a five-minute walk from the train station) comes here. Singles with bathroom cost 2,531 dinars ($8.65), and doubles run 4,732 dinars ($16.20) —truly a bargain compared to the rest of Belgrade's hotel prices.

Another fairly inexpensive buy about 10 or 15 minutes from the center of town, but slightly farther from the train station, is the **Hotel Taš,** at Borisa Kidriča 71 (tel. 334-507). The Taš only rents 19 small rooms, each with large windows and a big bathroom. Some rooms also overlook an attractive park next to the hotel. Singles with breakfast cost $24.20, and similar doubles run $28.60.

Another great bargain in a distant locale is the **Youth Hostel Mladost,** which rents 120 beds at Bulevar JNA 56A (tel. 465-324 or 463-846). Four or five students share each room for 1,870 dinars ($6.40) with the IYHF card, or 2,310 dinars ($7.90) without. To get to the Mladost, take tram 9 for nine stops from the train station.

PRIVATE ROOMS: You can only rent private rooms from the **Putnik** bureau at Trg Bratstva I Jedinstva 1 (tel. 641-251 or 642-473). Unfortunately, they only offer a total of 80 places in the entire city, but as there's a high turnover of rooms every day, you have a fair chance of finding a room if you arrive early in the day or reserve ahead of time. Singles cost $7.70, doubles are $11.60, and triples run $13.70. The office is open from 7 a.m. to 8 p.m. Monday through Saturday.

3. Dining on a Budget

ON SKADARLIJA: A stroll on Skadarlija followed by a meal in one of this street's picturesque restaurants offers visitors a fine evening out. Paved with cobblestones and graced with tall trees, this famous street has many restaurants and cafés; as you walk down the lane, music wafts out from several of the street's restaurants.

Originally built 200 years ago, Skadarlija has changed little over the years, thanks to a concerted effort by town planners. Thus in addition to attracting many foreign visitors, Skadarlija serves as the favorite hangout for local artists, musicians, and those who favor a bohemian lifestyle. We particularly enjoyed the following restaurants on Skadarlija.

Musicians, artists, and poets, as well as visiting dignitaries (including Margaret Thatcher, George Bush, German Chancellor Kohl), have dined at the **Tri Šešira** ("Three Hats"), Skadarska 29 (tel. 377-501). One plaque inside the restaurant boasts that Tito also ate here, and anyone who sits at the same table he once did will receive a flower in memory of the beloved Yugoslavian president. Tri Šešira has been around for 125 years, and the managers do their best to preserve a 19th-century aura. Wood paneling and off-white walls adorned with old pottery lamps and plates make up the decor. In the back, a small garden accommodates diners in the summer. In this appealing atmosphere, old Serbian specialties from the 19th century (such as a flavorful Serbian grilled beefsteak, pork and veal dishes) are served at reasonable prices. Grill specialties run $1 to $2.25.

The largest restaurant on Skadarlija, **Dva Jelena** ("Two Deer"), at Skadarska 32 (tel. 334-885), gives you a choice of dining on one of several outdoor terraces, or in rooms with wood paneling and fresco paintings overhead, suggesting a 19th-century hunting lodge. Grilled meats are the specialty at Dva Jelena, such as grilled pork or veal, for $1.30 to $3.20. For an appetizer, don't miss the creamy, flavorful veal soup. In the evening, a local folk band plays, for which you pay a 10% supplement on your bill. The restaurant is open from 8 a.m. to midnight, seven days a week.

In keeping with the artistic flavor of Skadarlija, **Ima Dana,** Skadarska 38 (tel. 334-422), serves its visitors in the "salon of Serbian poets," a room whose walls sport portraits of Serbian and Bosnian bards. In warm weather you can also dine in a large outdoor garden. During the evening local musicians perform for guests, but during the day the only music you'll hear is from other restaurants down the street. You may find service a bit slow, but you can enjoy good grill specialties at Ima Dana, including moutchkalitza leskovac style, a pork dish prepared on the grill with onions, tomatoes, and peppers, for 583 dinars ($2), and veal medallions uzice style, a very flavorful dish of veal with cream cheese, onions, and peppers on top, for 825 dinars ($2.85). Open from 11 a.m. to 5 p.m. and 7 p.m. to 1 a.m.

RESTAURANTS AROUND TOWN: We highly recommend the **Dva Ribara** ("Two Fishermen"), Narodnog Fronta 21 (tel. 686-471), for seafood lovers. Waiters dressed in sailors' white shirts over black-and-white striped undershirts serve you in a ship's-cabin decor that includes two buoys and a steering wheel hanging from the ceiling. Appetizers include calamari, fish, octopus, and other tangy seafood salads, mixed with onions and mayonnaise. Entrees feature squid, pike, sole, trout, scampi, and other fish dishes, all for 385 dinars ($1.30) to 1,980 dinars ($6.80). Wine from the Adriatic region (such as the famous Posip) is available along with your meal. The Fishermen serve from noon to 5 p.m. and 7 to 11 p.m.

For another good seafood dinner, come aboard the **Zlatna Lada** ("Golden Ship"), at Kolarceva 9 on Terazije Square (tel. 334-018), a restaurant in the town center (across from the Albania building) with canvas hanging above the tables like a sail and other maritime objects around the restaurant. Service is prompt and efficient, thus adding to the enjoyment of a tasty meal. Prices are very reasonable, with entrees costing $1.70 to $6. It's open from 11 a.m. to 1 a.m., seven days a week.

For a lighter meal in a lively atmosphere, visit the **Aeroclub Beograd,** on 7 Jula no. 36 (tel. 628-281). The walls are plastered with pages from the Sunday *New York Times,* and loud pop music plays throughout the two-story place to the delight of the university-age crowd. Pizzas (for $1 to $2), spaghetti, dessert, and drinks can be enjoyed at the Aeroclub for moderate prices. Open from 8 a.m. to 11 p.m.

ISLAND DINING AT ADA CIGANLIJA: The holiday resort spot for many Belgrade locals lies on a small island up the Sava River from the town center at Ada Ciganlija. As many as 150,000 holiday makers come to this island on hot summer days to swim and sunbathe. For the visitor to Belgrade, the island is more interesting for its restaurants than for its beaches.

On the north shore of the island (the side closest to town), dozens of houseboats gently swaying in the water serve home-cooking to a few tables inside and maybe a few outdoor tables as well. Of course the specialty is fish, which local fishermen bring by almost every day. Although few tourists visit these restaurants, they are immensely popular with locals, and there's no better way of getting away from the city for an evening. Take bus 501 or 511 from the center to the Ada Ciganlija bridge. From the bridge you must walk for about 15 minutes to the north side of the island.

The Yugoslav jet-set often frequents the **Restoran Odisej** (tel. 550-515), one of the shore's most elegant boat restaurants. Red-fabric seats and wood-paneled walls decorate the small interior, which fits only six tables. Fish entrees cost about $2.25 each. It's open from 8 p.m. to the surprisingly late hour of 5 a.m., seven days a week. As the restaurant is so small, don't forget to make reservations.

A more youthful crowd hangs out at the **Laguna Restaurant** (tel. 541-442), a larger place with wood furniture and small quaint tables. New Wave and jazz music plays while you enjoy the restaurant's freshwater fish. Open noon to midnight, seven days a week; it's best to reserve in the evening.

If these two choices don't appeal to you, walk up and down Ada Ciganlija and visit some of the shore's other restaurants until you find one to your liking.

4. The Sights

MUSEUMS: The **National Museum,** Trg Republike 1A, displays a quarter of a million objects detailing the art and culture of Serbia from the earliest recorded history to the present; the museum also houses foreign art as well. Sample displays include Roman jewelry, ancient sculpture, Serbian religious art, modern paintings by Picasso, and many other items. A grab bag with something to please everyone, it's open on Tuesday, Wednesday, and Friday from 10 a.m. to

5 p.m., on Thursday to 7 p.m., on Saturday from 9 a.m. to 5 p.m., and on Sunday from 10 a.m. to 2 p.m.; closed Monday.

The **Museum of the Serbian Orthodox Church,** 7 Jula no. 5, contains old church paintings, frescos, manuscripts, and other religious artifacts. It's open from 7 a.m. to 2 p.m. Tuesday through Saturday, from 11 a.m. to 3 p.m. on Sunday; closed Monday and holidays. For a beautiful collection of religious frescos from the Middle Ages, drop by the **Gallery of Frescos,** Cara Urosa 20, open the same hours as the National Museum.

Fans of modern art may want to check out what Yugoslavian artists have been doing this century in the **Museum of Contemporary Art,** kod Ušća, Novi Beograd. The almost 6,000 pieces in the museum include 20th-century paintings, sculptures, and other art forms. The museum is open from 10 a.m. to 7 p.m. in summer, to 5 p.m. in winter; closed Tuesday.

The **Military History Museum,** in the middle of Kalemegdan Park, displays a diverse collection of weaponry, ranging from ancient swords to modern tanks and artillery. Open 10 a.m. to 5 p.m.; closed Monday.

Anyone confused about the turbulent and bloody history of Belgrade might be interested in visiting the **Belgrade City Museum,** Zmaj Jovina 1, which chronicles the greatest and worst moments in the city's past.

Although it's hard for a Westerner to understand the great impact President Tito had on the Yugoslav nation, you can get a good idea by visiting the **Josip Broz Tito Memorial Center,** in Dedinje at Bulevar Oktobarske Revolucije 92. In this large area, you can visit Tito's tomb, his former residence, and various collections on Tito's role in the Yugoslavian revolution.

SIGHTS AROUND TOWN: Those who think that Belgrade is made up exclusively of large modern buildings should head for **Kalemegdan** (see "Orientation" for directions), a large park on a hill on the north side of town. Belgrade's first settlements appeared here thousands of years ago. In the 1st century A.D. the Romans established a military camp on this hill, and over the years the Serbians, Turks, and Austrians used Kalemegdan as a fortress against attacks. Although many of the old walls have fallen, in a casual stroll through the park you'll come across a number of remaining defensive architectural features, such as tall ramparts from the Middle Ages to the 19th century.

Not everyone goes to Kalemegdan to sightsee; in fact, the park is a favorite of Yugoslavian couples who come here to hold hands away from the bustle of the big city.

Another charming section of town you won't want to miss is **Skadarlija** (mentioned above in our restaurant section). Gypsies originally settled this area in the early 19th century, but soon artisans, merchants, and others moved into the area. By the turn of the century Skadarlija became a favorite of writers and artists, and with its 19th-century flavor still intact, it remains one of Belgrade's most popular and romantic areas to this day.

5. The ABCs of Belgrade

AIRPORT AND AIRLINE OFFICES: JAT operates a bus to and from the **JAT** ticket office at Bulevar Revolucije 17 (tel. 331-042), the train station, and the airport, 16 km (9½ miles) outside the center of town. The ride to the airport costs 130 dinars (45¢).

For information on these buses and on Belgrade at the airport, stop by the **Airport Tourist Bureau,** on the left near the exit (tel. 602-326), open from 7 a.m. to 10 p.m., seven days a week.

For JAT tickets call 331-042 (information) or 413-166 (reservations) for international flights, and 332-179 (information) and 413-022 (reservations) for domestic flights. For airport information, dial 601-424.

Lufthansa has an office at Terazije 3/IV (tel. 324-976), and **Pan Am** has an office in the Hotel Slavija, Svetog Save 1 (tel. 441-484 or 443-470).

AMERICAN EXPRESS: You can send your mail to one of two American Express offices: Zmaj Jovina 10 (tel. 631-974 or 624-858), or Moše Pijade 11 (tel. 341-471 or 332-522). You're likely to find the first office, the larger of the two, to be more helpful. It's open from 8 a.m. to 8 p.m. Monday through Friday, to 3 p.m. on Saturday.

BOOKSTORES: For English-language guidebooks to Belgrade and other sections of Yugoslavia, drop by the **Jugoslovenska Knjiga,** Knez Mihailova 2, in the Albania building at the beginning of Terazije Street (tel. 622-948). They're open from 8 a.m. to 8 p.m. Monday through Saturday.

BUSES AND TRAMS: The complicated fare structure of Yugoslavian buses does not easily lend itself to comprehension by foreigners, but this is as much as you need understand: if you plan on riding the buses, buy a block of 12 tickets at any newsstand; these cost 150 dinars (50¢), as of this writing. When you take a ride between two points in the center, stamp three tickets after getting on the bus. If you are going a particularly long way (perhaps to a distant district), you must stamp four or five tickets (ask the driver to be sure). If you try to buy tickets from the driver on the bus you'll pay two or three times more than the normal price. And if you're caught without a ticket (checks occasionally occur in the beginning of the month), you'll be assessed a 1,000-dinar ($3.40) fine.

CONCERTS AND CULTURAL EVENTS: For tickets to concerts, theater, and other events, stop by the **Bizet Servis Kulturnog Centra** at Kolarčeva 6 (tel. 621-174). They may not speak English, so it's best to find out from the Tourist Information Office what events are taking place before you go by (the concert bureau is just half a block from the information office). Classical concerts usually cost about $2, and rock concerts run $2 to $4. The ticket office is open from 9 a.m. to 9 p.m. Monday through Saturday; closed Sunday.

DRY CLEANING: For dry cleaning, go to Obilićev Venac 10, a small street in the center of town off of Trg Republike (tel. 182-187). They charge about $1 to clean and press a pair of pants or a jacket, and they offer 24-hour service. You'll find a cheaper, though slower, dry cleaners at Mišarska 6 (tel. 332-326). Pants and jackets cost 220 dinars (75¢), and 165 dinars (55¢) for shirts, and take two days to clean.

EMBASSIES: The **U.S. Embassy** is at Kneza Miloša 50 (tel. 645-655, 645-622, or 645-465); the **Canadian Embassy** is down the street at Kneza Miloša 75 (tel. 434-524); and the **British Embassy** is at Generala Ždanova 46 (tel. 645-055, 645-034, or 645-087).

EMERGENCY PHONE NUMBERS: Dial 92 for the police, 93 for the fire department, and 94 for an ambulance. Call 987 for automotive help on the road.

GAMBLING: On summer Sundays, horses race in the **Hippodrome** on Paštrovićeva 2 at 3 p.m. The hotels **Metropol** at Bulevar Revolucije 69 (tel. 330-911), **Majestic** at Obilićev Venac 28 (tel. 636-022), and **Jugoslavija** at Bulevar Edvarda Kardelja 3 (tel. 600-222) also operate **casinos** with roulette, blackjack, poker, chemin de fer, and slot machines for foreigners only, open from 10 p.m. to 4 a.m.

LIBRARIES: On the spur of the moment you may decide to continue on to Greece or any other country. Where should you get more information? The **British Council Library,** Knez Mihailova 45 (tel. 622-492), holds 20,000 English-language books, including 200 periodicals and a fair number of guidebooks (mostly for Europe). The library stays open from 9:30 a.m. to 1:30 p.m. and from 5 to 8 p.m. Monday through Saturday. There's also an **American Reading Room** at Cika-Ljubina 19/II (tel. 630-111), open from 9 a.m. to 5 p.m. Monday through Friday.

NIGHTLIFE: Those anxious to hit the Belgrade club scene should consider the **Duga Disco** at Sredačka 5 (tel. 456-743), a very small club with a few tables and a tiny dance floor. Duga is popular among a wide age group of Belgrade students, actors, and local artists. It's open from 9 p.m. to 5 a.m. seven days a week, but don't come before midnight or 1 a.m. as only then does the action pick up. In any case, this is a club to go with someone rather than to meet someone. Americans usually do not have to pay an entrance fee.

OUTDOOR MARKET: If you'd like to assemble a picnic lunch, shop at the large fruit and vegetable market at Zeleni Venac, located four or five blocks south of the train station. The merchants keep their stands open from roughly 5:30 a.m. to 12:30 p.m. Monday through Saturday, from 6 a.m. to 1 p.m. on Sunday. In winter the market closes slightly earlier.

SIDE TRIPS: Boats for the **Iron Gate,** the largest gorge in all of Europe (in Kladovo near the Romanian border), where the Danube is compressed to a width of only 1,300 feet for over five miles, leave every day at 7 a.m. and return at 7 p.m. for 2,090 dinars ($7.15). You can buy tickets from 6:30 a.m. to 8 p.m. at **Beogradbrod Travel Agency,** Karadordeva 8, Savsko Pristaniste, on the riverbank (tel. 622-279).

STUDENT TRAVEL: Naromtravel-Karavan, Knez Mihailova 50 (tel. 187-822; Telex 11743-YU-NAROMT), offers student discounts for train travel to other socialist countries with the IUS card, 20% discount on some national flights, and various discounts on international charter flights (for example, Belgrade to London, round trip, costs $160, or half that for one way). As most of their international charters are for Yugoslavian students, foreigners usually must wait until a week before departure in order to buy a ticket. The office is open from 7 a.m. to 4 p.m. Monday through Friday.

TAXI: You can telephone a taxi at 417-377 or 443-443. Note that it's more expensive to travel by taxi between midnight and 4 a.m. and on public holidays, as a second fare applies.

TELEPHONE AND TELEGRAPH: It costs about $3 for the first minute to telephone to the U.S., and then about $2 for each subsequent minute. To make an international call, go to the post office at Zmaj Jovina 17 (a few blocks behind Trg Republike), open 24 hours a day.

TOURS: Putnik operates tours of the city from the Hotels Slavija, Metropol, Intercontinental, and Jugoslavija, and from Terazije Square. Tours cost $11 per person. Inquire in your hotel, the Tourist Information Office, or any Putnik office for further details.

TRAIN AND BUS STATION: Belgrade's **train station** at Trg Bratstva I Jedinstva (tel. 645-936, 645-822, or 645-722) ranks as one of Eastern Europe's least appealing; many who wander through the station look like characters out of Rod Serling's television show "The Twilight Zone."

To buy tickets, go to the left wing of the building beside track 1. Windows 3 and 4 sell international tickets, and Window 3 also sells international seat reservations. Window 8 sells tickets for the Sarajevo express, and no. 10 for the Split–Zadar–Šibenik route. Numbers 11 and 12 sell tickets for Bar and Titograd. Other windows sell tickets for other routes. If you want to make couchette reservations, go to the atrium in front of the station: the left atrium window makes couchette reservations for Slovenia, Macedonia, and Athens; the right window makes couchette reservations for other destinations.

For **bus information,** call 624-751 or 627-049.

WEATHER REPORTS: From June 1 to September 1, Radio Belgrade gives a quick report at 12:02 p.m. on 439 MW, and 88.9, 94.3, and 95.3 FM. If you speak Serbian you can also call 983 for a weather report.

WOMEN ALONE: One local woman told us, "I don't walk around alone at midnight," an attitude common among Yugoslavian women (due mostly to tradition). Although the city is usually fairly safe for women, we recommend normal big-city caution, especially at night around the train station area of town.

Appendix

EASTERN EUROPEAN VOCABULARIES AND MENU TERMS

IN THE LARGER CITIES of Eastern Europe, which have more experience dealing with Western travelers, English will not be total gibberish to many of the government officials, tourist information officers, hotel staff, and restaurant waiters you come across. In the smaller cities and towns, however, you'll probably find English a collection of interesting, if unintelligible, sounds to most of these same people.

For each of the seven Eastern European languages treated in this Appendix we begin with a list of the letters in that language's alphabet, followed by a short vocabulary of words and phrases and a rough guide to their pronunciation (accented syllables are shown in capital letters), and then selected menu and food terms.

The vocabulary and menu terms in this Appendix do not constitute a comprehensive phrasebook to each Eastern European language, but you'll find many (we hope) useful phrases and terms to help you get around, get a room, and choose your meals.

1. Polish Vocabulary

The Polish alphabet has a few more letters than English—a total of 33. Most are pronounced somewhat as they are in English:

a	*a*lmost (never as in lace)
ą	mais*on* (French pronunciation)
b	*b*oy
c	lo*ts*
d	*d*ay
e	g*e*t
ę	str*en*gth
f	*f*ool
g	*g*irl
h	*h*ello
i	mar*i*ne
j	*y*oung
k	*k*ey
l	*l*ord
m	*m*om
n	*n*o
o	n*o*r
ó	n*u*clear
p	*p*en
r	*r*un
s	*s*un
t	*t*op
u	n*u*clear (like ó)
w	*v*ery
x	o*x*
y	d*i*d
z	*z*ero

Additional letters and consonant clusters are as follows:

ć	*ch*eese
ch	lo*ch* (Scottish pronunciation)
cz	*ch*oice
dz	a*dz*e
dź	*j*erk
dż	bri*dg*e
ł	*w*eek
ń	on*i*on
sz	*sh*ore
ś	*sh*eer
ź	gara*g*e
rz	plea*s*ure
ż	a*z*ure

Note that Polish distinguishes between genders, hence adjective and verb endings differ for male and female, as in the expression "I would like": chciałbym (male) or chciałabym (female).

EVERYDAY EXPRESSIONS

		Pronounced
Hello, Greetings	Witam, cześć	VEE-tam, Cheshch
Good morning	Dzień dobry	Dzheyn DO-bri
Good evening	Dobry wieczór	DO-bri VYEH-choor
How are you?	Jak się masz?	Yak sheh mash?
Very well	Bardzo dobrze	BAR-dzo DO-bzheh
Thank you	Dziękuję	Dzhyen-KOO-yeh
You're welcome	Proszę	PRO-sheh
Please	Proszę	PRO-sheh
Yes	Tak	Tak
No	Nie	Nyeh
Excuse me	Przepraszam	Psheh-PRA-sham
How much does it cost?	Ile kosztuje?	EE-leh kosh-TOO-yeh?
I don't understand	Nie rozumiem	Nyeh roz-OOM-yem
Just a moment	Chwileczkę	Khvi-LECH-keh
Good-bye	Do widzenia	Do vee-DZEN-ya

TRAVELING

Your passport, please	Proszę o paszport	PRO-sheh o PASH-port
Here is my passport	Tu jest mój paszport	Too yest mooy PASH-port
Here is my bag	Tu jest mój bagaż	Too yest mooy BA-gazh
I am with a group	Jestem z grupą	YES-tem z GROO-pown
I am staying . . .	Będę przebywać . . .	BEN-deh psheh-BI-vach . . .
a few days	kilka dni	KEEL-ka dnee
two weeks	dwa tygodnie	dva ti-GOD-nyeh
a month	miesiąc	MYEH-shonts
I am visiting relatives	Odwiedzam krewnych	Od-VYED-zam KREV-nih
I am visiting friends	Odwiedzam przyjaciół	Od-VYED-zam pshi-YA-choo
Where is the . . .	Gdzie jest . . .	Gdzhyeh yest . . .
bus station	dworzec autobusowy	DVO-zhets ow-to-bu-SO-vi
train station	dworzec kolejowy	DVO-zhets ko-ley-O-vi
airport	lotnisko	lot-NEE-sko

baggage check	przechowalnia bagażu	psheh-ho-VAL-nya ba-GA-zhoo
check-in counter	recepcja, kasa	reh-TSEP-tsya, KA-sa
Where can I find a taxi?	Gdzie mogę znaleźć taksówke?	Gdzhyeh MO-geh ZNA-leshch tak-SOOF-keh?
How much is the fare?	Ile kosztuje przejazd?	EE-leh kosh-TOO-yeh PSHEH-yazd?
I am going to . . .	Idę do [walking] . . . Jadę do [riding] . . .	EE-deh do . . . YA-deh do . . .
One-way ticket	Bilet w jedną stronę	BEE-let w YED-no STRO-neh
Round-trip ticket	Bilet tam i z powrotem	BEE-let tam i spo-VRO-tem
Car-rental office	Wypożyczalnia samochodów	Vi-po-zhi-CHAL-nya sa-mo-HO-doof
Where can I find a gas station?	Gdzie mogę znaleźć stacje benzynową?	Gdzhyeh MO-geh ZNA-leshch STA-tsyeh ben-zi-NO-vo?
Please fill the tank	Proszę napełnić bak	PRO-sheh na-PEL-neech bak

CHANGING MONEY

Where can I change money?	Gdzie mogę wymienić pieniądze?	Gdzhyeh MO-geh vi-MYEH-neech pyeh-NON-dze?
Can you (sir/madam) change traveler's checks?	Czy może Pan/Pani wymienić traveler's checks?	Tchi MO-zheh Pan/PA-nee vi-MYEH-neech traveler's checks?
I would like to change dollars.	Chciałbym/chciałabym wymienić dolary.	KCHOW-bim/KCHOW-a-bim vi-MYEH-neech do-LA-ri.
What is the exchange rate?	Jaki jest kurs wymiany?	YA-kee yest koors vi-MYA-ni?

ACCOMMODATIONS

| I'm looking for . . . a hotel a pension | Szukam . . . hotel pensjonatu | SHOO-kam . . . HO-tel pen-syo-NA-too |

a youth hostel	schronisko młodżiezowe	skhro-NEE-sko mlo-dzheh-ZHO-weh
I have a reservation.	Mam rezerwacje	Mam reh-zer-VA-tsyeh
My name is . . .	Moje nazwisko . . .	MO-yeh naz-VEE-sko . . .
Do you have a room . . .	Czy ma Pan/Pani pokój . . .	Tchi ma Pan/PA-nee PO-kooy . . .
for tonight	na dzislejszą noc	na dzhee-SHEY-shon nots
for three nights	na trzy doby	na tchi DO-bi
for a week	na tydzień	na TI-dzheyn
I would like . . .	Chciałbym/chciałabym . . .	KCHOW-bim/KCHOW-a-bim . . .
a single	jedynke, na jedną osobę	yeh-DIN-keh, na YED-no o-SO-beh
a double	dwójke, na dwie osoby	DVOOY-keh, na dvyeh o-SO-bi
I want a room . . .	Chcialbym/chcialabym . . .	KCHOW-bim/KCHOW-a-bim
with a shower	z prysznicem	sprish-NEE-tsem
without a shower	bez prysznica	bez prish-NEE-tsa
with bath	z łazienka	z wa-ZHEN-ko
without a bath	bez łazienki	bez wa-ZHEN-kee
How much is the room? . . .	Ile kosztuje pokój? . . .	EE-leh kosh-TOO-yeh PO-kooy? . . .
with breakfast?	z śniadaniem?	s shnya-DA-nyem?
May I see the room?	Czy mogę zobaczyć pokój?	Tchi MO-geh zo-BA-chich PO-kooy?
The key	Klucz	Klooch
The bill, please	Poproszę rachunek	Po-PRO-sheh ra-HOO-nek

EATING

Restaurant	Restauracja	Res-tau-RA-tsya
Breakfast	Śniadanie	Shnya-DA-nyeh
Lunch	Obiad	O-byad
Dinner	Kolacja	Ko-LA-tsya
A table for two, please.	Proszę o stolik na dwie osoby.	Pro-SHEH o STO-leek na dvyeh o-SO-bi.
Waiter	Kelner	KEL-ner
Waitress	Kelnerka	Kel-NER-ka
I would like . . .	Poproszę . . .	Po-PRO-sheh . . .
a menu	karte	KAR-teh
a fork	widelec	wi-DEL-ets
a knife	nóż	noozh

a spoon	łyźke	WIZH-keh
a napkin	serwetke	ser-VET-keh
a glass (of water)	szklanke (wody)	SHKLAN-keh (VO-di)
the check, please	poproszę rachunek	po-PRO-sheh ra-HOO-nek
Is the tip included?	Czy napiwek jest wliczony?	Tchi na-PEE-vek yest vlee-CHO-ni?

GETTING AROUND

I'm looking for . . .	Szukam . . .	SHOO-kam . . .
a bank	bank	bank
the church	kościół	KOSH-chyoo
the city center	śródmieście	shrood-MYESH-chyehh
the museum	muzeum	moo-ZEH-oom
a pharmacy	aptekę	ap-TEH-keh
the park	park	park
the theater	teatr	TEH-atr
the tourist office	biuro podróży	BYOO-ro po-DROO-zhi
the embassy	ambasade	am-ba-SA-deh
Where is the nearest telephone?	Gdzie jest najbliższy telefon?	Gdzhyeh yest nay-BLIZH-shi te-LEH-fon?
I would like to buy . . .	Chciałbym/chciałabym kupić . . .	KCHOW-bim/KCHOW-a-bim KOO-peech . . .
a stamp	znaczek	ZNA-chek
a postcard	pocztówke	po-CHTOO-fkeh
a map	mape	MA-pe

SIGNS

No trespassing	Wstęp wzbroniony	Vstemp vzbro-NYO-ni
No parking	Nie parkować	Nyeh par-KO-vach
Entrance	Wejście	VEY-shchyeh
Exit	Wyjście	VIY-shchyeh
Information	Informacja	Een-for-MA-tsya
No smoking	Nie palić, palenie wzbronione	Nyeh PA-leech, PA-len-yeh vzbron-YO-neh
Arrivals (air)	Przyjazdy (Przyloty)	Pzhi-YAZ-di (Pzhy-LO-ti)
Departures (air)	Odjazdy (Odloty)	Od-YAZ-di (Od-LO-ti)

Toilets	**Toalety**	To-a-LEH-ti
Danger	**Niebezpieczeństwo**	Nyeh-bez-pyeh-CHEIN-stvo

NUMBERS

1	**jeden** YEH-den	15	**piętnaście** pyent-NA-shchyeh
2	**dwa** dva	16	**szesnaście** shesh-NA-shchyeh
3	**trzy** tchi	17	**siedemnaście** shedem-NA-shchyeh
4	**cztery** TCHTEH-ri	18	**osiemnaście** oshem-NA-shchyeh
5	**pięć** pyench	19	**dziewiętnaście** dzheh-vyent-NA-shchyeh
6	**sześć** sheshch	20	**dwadzieścia** dva-DZHYEH-shchya
7	**siedem** SHEH-dem	30	**trzydzieści** tchi-DZHYEH-shchee
8	**osiem** O-shyem	40	**czterdzieści** tchter-DZHYEH-shchee
9	**dziewięć** DZHYEH-vyench	50	**pięćdziesiąt** pyen-DZHYEH-shont
10	**dzieslęć** DZEH-shyench	60	**sześćdziesiąt** shesh-DZHYEH-shont
11	**jedenaście** yeh-den-A-shchyeh	70	**siedemdziesiąt** sheh-dem-DZHYEH-shont
12	**dwanaście** dva-NA-shchyeh	80	**osiemdziesiąt** o-shem-DZHYEH-shont
13	**trzynaście** tchi-NA-shchyeh	90	**dziewięćdziesiąt** dzhye-vyen-DZYEH-shont
14	**czternaście** tchter-NA-shchyeh	100	**sto** sto
		500	**pięćset** PYENCH-set
		1,000	**tysiąc** TI-shonts

2. Polish Menu Terms

GENERAL TERMS

soups	**zupy**	ZOO-pi
eggs	**jajka**	YAY-ka
salads	**sałaty**	sa-WA-ti
meats	**mięso**	MIEN-so
fish	**ryba**	RI-ba
vegetables	**warzywa**	va-ZHY-va
desserts	**desery**	deh-SEH-ri
fruits	**owoce**	o-VO-tseh
beverages	**napoje**	na-PO-yeh
condiments	**przyprawy**	pshi-PRA-vi
salt	**sól**	sool
pepper	**pieprz**	pyepsh
mustard	**musztarda**	moo-SHTAR-da
vinegar	**ocet**	O-tset
oil	**olej**	O-ley
sugar	**cukier**	TSOO-kyer

SOUPS

barszcz	Polish beet soup	**chłodnik**	green vegetable soup with veal
botwina	cold beet soup with vegetables	**grzybowa**	mushroom soup

jarzynowa	vegetable soup	zalewajka	onion soup
kapusniak	cabbage soup	zupa	soup
krem pomidorowy	tomato soup	zurek Polski	beef soup with sausages
rybna	fish soup		and sour cream

MEATS

baranina	lamb	kotlet schabowy	breaded pork cutlet
befsztyk Tatarski	steak tatare	kułduny	dumplings filled with meat
bigos	sausages and sauerkraut	kurczę	chicken
cielecina	veal	mieso	meat
comber sarni	venison	pieczen z dzika	roast wild boar
dziczyzna	game	pierozki	large dumplings with meat
escalopki	veal or pork schnitzel	sarnina	roast venison
flaki	tripe with seasoning	stek	steak
ges	goose	szynka	ham
golonka	boiled pork shank	watroba	liver
gulasz wołowy	beef goulash	wieprzowina	pork
indyk	turkey	wołowina	beef
kaczka pieczona	roast duck	zajac	hare
konina	horse		

FISH

dorsz	cod	ryba	fish
karp	carp	sandacz	pike-perch
łosis	salmon	sledz	herring
pstrag	trout	wegorz	eel
raki	crayfish		

EGGS

jaja gotowane	boiled eggs	omlet	omelet
jaja sadzone	fried eggs	z groszkiem	with green peas
jajecznica	scrambled eggs	konserwowym	
		z pieczarkami	with mushrooms

SALADS

mizeria ze smietana	cucumber salad	sałatka zielona	green salad
sałata mieszana	mixed salad	sałatka z pomidorow	tomato salad
sałatka z czerwonej kapusty	red cabbage salad		

VEGETABLES

cwikła	red beets	pieczarki	mushrooms
frytki	french fries	pomidory	tomatoes
groszek	peas	ryz	rice
grzyby	mushrooms	selery	celery
kapusta	cabbage	szpinak	spinach
kluski z ziemniakow	dumplings	zlemniaki	potatoes
marchenka	carrots		

DESSERTS

kompot mieszany	mixed compote	waniliowe	vanilla
lody	ice cream	tort czekoladowy	chocolate cake
kacaowe	chocolate	tort makowy	poppy seed cake
kawowe	coffee (flavor)		

FRUITS

cytryna	lemon	jabłka	apples
gruszki	pears	owoce	fruit

BEVERAGES

herbata	tea	szampan	champagne
kawa	coffee	wino	wine
mleko	milk	białe	white
piwo	beer	czerwone	red
smietanka	cream	woda mineralna	mineral water
sok	juice		

CONDIMENTS AND OTHERS

bułki	rolls	musztarda	mustard
chleb	bread	ocet	vinegar
chrzan	horse radish	pieprz	pepper
cukier	sugar	ser	cheese
lod	ice	sol	salt
masło	butter		

COOKING TERMS

dobrze upieczone	well done	smazona	fried
faszerowany	stuffed	wedzona	smoked
gotowany	boiled	zapiekana	baked
krwiste	rare	z rusztu	grilled

3. German Vocabulary

German pronunciation is largely regular, that is, you pronounce all vowels and consonants, following a regular pattern.

Vowels

a	f*a*ther
	*au*nt
ä	m*e*t
	r*ai*n
e	p*e*n
	p*ai*n
i	b*i*t
	d*ee*d
ie	f*ee*l
o	n*o*t
	n*o*te
ö	hors d'*oeu*vre
u	f*oo*t
	f*oo*d
ü	no English equivalent
	round lips say *ee*
y	like ü above

Diphthongs

ai, ay, ei, ey	cr*y*
au	c*ow*
au, eu	b*oy*

Consonants

c, f, h, k, m, n, p, t, x	as in English
b	ma*p* at the end of a word
	otherwise as in English
ch	Ba*ch*
d	ba*t* at the end of a word,
	otherwise as in English
g	Ba*ch* only in the ending ig
	tac*k* at the end of a word
j	*y*et
Kn	pronounce both letters
qu	kv
s	*z*oo before a vowel
	*sh*oe before p and t
β	me*ss* at the end of a word

B	me*ss*
tsch	Dut*ch*
tz	ki*ts*
v	*f*ur
w	*v*ase
z	ki*ts*

EVERYDAY EXPRESSIONS

		Pronounced
Hello	**Guten Tag**	GOO-ten-tahk
Good morning	**Guten Morgen**	Goo-ten MOR-gen
Good evening	**Guten Abend**	GOO-ten AH-bent
How are you?	**Wie geht es Ihnen?**	Vee gait es EE-nen?
Very well	**Sehr gut**	Zayr goot
Thank you	**Danke**	DANK-eh
You're welcome	**Bitte**	BIT-teh
Please	**Bitte**	BIT-teh
Yes	**Ja**	Yah
No	**Nein**	Nine
Excuse me	**Verzeihung**	Fehrt-SAHY-oong
How much is it?	**Wieviel kostet es?**	Vee-FEEL KOH-stet ess?
I don't understand you	**Ich verstehe Sie nicht**	Ich fehr-SHTAI'i zee nicht
Just a moment	**Einen Augenblick, bitte**	Ahynen OW-gen-blick, BIT-teh
Goodbye	**Auf Wiedersehen**	Owf VEE-der-zai'n

TRAVELING

		Pronounced
Your passport, please	**Reisepaβ, bitte**	RAHYS-eh-pass, BIT-te
Here it is.	**Hier ist ehr**	Heer ist ehr
Here is my bag.	**Hier ist mein Tasche**	Heer ist mayn TA-sheh
I am with a group	**Ich bin mit einer Reisegruppe**	Ich bin mit AHY-neh RAHYS-eh-groop-eh
I am staying . . .	**Ich bleibe . . .**	Ich BLAHY-beh
a few days	**ein paar Tage**	Ahyn pahr TAH-ge
two weeks	**zwei Wochen**	tsvahy VOH-ch'n
a month	**einen Monat**	AHY-nen MO-nat
I am visiting	**Ich besuche**	Ich be-ZOO-cheh
relatives	**Verwandte**	fehr-VAHN-teh
friends	**Freunde**	FROYn-deh
I'm on vacation	**Ich bin auf Urlaub**	Ich bin owf OOR-lahwb
Where is the . . .	**Wo ist . . .**	Vo ist

bus station	der Omnibus-Bahnhof	dehr OM-nee-booss BAHN-hof
train station	der Bahnhof	dehr BAHN-hof
airport	der Flughafen	dehr FLOOK-hahfen
baggage room	die Gepäckaufbe-wahrung	dee Ge-PECK-owf-bev-ahr-ung
check-in counter	der Abfertigensschalter	dehr ahb-FERT-eh-gens-shal-ter
Where can I find a taxi?	Wo kann ich ein Taxi kriegen?	Vo kahn ich ahyn TAK-si KREE-gen?
How much will the fare be?	Wieviel wird es kosten?	Vee-FEEL veerd es KOHST-en?
I am going to . . .	Ich fahre nach	Ich FAH-reh nach
One way ticket	Einfach Fahrkarte	AHYN-fach FAR-kahr-teh
Round trip	Rückfahrkarte	REWK-fahr-kahr-teh
Car rental office	Autovermietlungsbüro	OW-toe-fehr-MEET-lungs-byur-oh
Where can I find a gas station?	Wo kann Ich eine Tankstelle finden?	Vo kahn ich AHYN-eh TAHNK-shtel-le FIN-den?
How much is gas?	Was kostet das Bensin?	Vas KOST-et das ben-TSEEN?
Please fill the tank.	Volltanken, bitte.	FOLL-tahn-ken, BIT-te

CHANGING MONEY

Where can I change money?	Wo kann ich Geld wechseln	Vo kahn ich gelt VEK-sel'n?
Can you change traveler's checks?	Können Sie diese Reiseschecks einlosen?	KEU-nen zee DEE-ze RAHYS-es-checks AHYN-lews-en
I would like to change dollars	Ich möchte Dollars wechseln.	Ich MEU-chte DOH-lar VECH-seln.
What is the exchange rate?	Was ist der Wechselkurs?	Vas ist dehr VECH-sel-kurs?

ACCOMMODATIONS

I'm looking for . . .	Ich suche	Ich ZOO-cheh
a hotel	ein Hotel	ahyn ho-TEL
a pension	eine Pension	AHY-ne pen-ZYOHN
a youth hostel	eine Jugendherberge	AHYne YOO-gend-hehr-behr-ge

I have a reservation	**Ich habe reserviert.**	Ich HAH-be re-zehr-VEERT
My name is	**Mein Name ist**	Mahyn NAH-meh ist
Do you have a room . . .	**Haben Sie ein Zimmer**	HAH-ben zee ahyn TSIM-mer
for tonight	**für heute Nacht**	fewr HOY-te nacht
for three nights	**für drei Nacht**	fewr drahye nacht
for a week	**für eine Woche**	fewr AHYN-eh voch
I would like . . .	**Ich mochte**	Ich MEUCH-te
a single	**ein Einzel**	ahyn AHYN-tsel
a double	**Doppel-zimmer**	dohppel TSIM-mer
I want a room with/without . . .	**Ich möchte ein Zimmer mit/ohne**	Ich MEUCH-te ahyn TSIM-mer mit/OH-neh
bath/shower	**Bad/Dusche**	baht/DOO-she
a view	**Blick**	blik
How much is the room . . .	**Wieviel kostet das Zimmer . . .**	Vee-feel KOST-et das TSIM-mer
with breakfast	**mit Frühstück**	Mit FREW-shtewk
May I see the room	**Kann ich das Zimmer sehen**	Kahn ich das TSIM-mer SAHY-en.
The key	**der Schlüssel**	dehr SHLEWS-sel
The bill, please	**Die Rechnung, bitte.**	Dee REHCH-noong, BIT-te

EATING

		Pronounced
Restaurant	**Restaurant**	Res-taur-ahnt
Breakfast	**Frühstück**	FREW-stewk
Lunch	**Mittagessen**	MIT-tak-ess-en
Dinner	**Abendessen**	AH-bent-ess-en
A table for two, please	**Eine tisch für zwei, bitte**	AHY-ne tish fewr tsvahy BIT-te
Waiter	**Ober**	OH-behr
Waitress	**Fräulein**	FROY-line
I would like . . .	**Ich möchte**	Ich MEUCH-te
a menu	**eine speisekarte**	AHY-ne SHPAHY-ze-kar-te
a fork	**eine Gabel**	AHY-ne GAH-bel
a knife	**ein Messer**	ahyn MES-ser
a spoon	**einen Löffel**	AHY-nen LEUF-fel
a napkin	**eine Serviette**	AHY-ne ser-vi-YEHTE

a glass (of water)	ein Glas (Wasser)	ahyn glas VAHS-ser
the check, please	Zahlen, bitte	TSAH-lehn, BIT-te
Is the tip included?	Ist Bedienung inbegriffen?	Ist Be-DEE-nung IN-be-grif-fen

GETTING AROUND

I'm looking for . . .	Ich suche	Ich ZOO-cheh
a bank	ein Wechsel	ayn VEK-zel
the church	Kirche	KEER-che
the city center	Stadtmitte	SHTAHT-mit-te
the museum	Museum	Moo-ZAI-oom
pharmacy	Apotheke	Ah-poh-TAI-ke
theater	Theater	tai-AT-er
tourist office	Fremdenverkehrsbüro	FREM-den-fehr-kehrs-bew-ro
the embassy	die Botschaft	dee BOT-shaft
Where is the nearest telephone?	Wo ist der nächste Telefon?	Vo ist dehr NECH-ste TE-le-fohn
I would like to buy . . .	Ich möchte kaufen	Ich mewch-teh Kauf-en
a stamp	eine Briefmarken	AHYN-eh BREEF-mahr-ken
a postcard	eine Postkarte	AHYN-eh post-kar-te
a map	ein Stadtplan	ahyn Shtatplahn

SIGNS

No trespassing	Eintritt verboten
No parking	Parken verboten
Entrance	Eingang
Exit	Ausgang
Information	Auskunft
No Smoking	Rauchen verboten
Arrivals	Ankunft
Departures	Abfahrt/Abflug
Toilets (Men, Women)	Toiletten (Herren, Frauen)
Danger	Gefahr

NUMBERS

1 eins ahyns	12 zwölf tsveulf	50 fünfzig FEWNF-tsich
2 zwei tsvahy	13 dreizehn DRAHY-tsehn	60 sechzig ZECH-tsich
3 drei drahy	14 vierzehn FEER'tsehn	70 siebzig ZEEB-tsich
4 vier feer	15 fünfzehn FEWNF-tsehn	80 achtzig ACHT-sich
5 fünf fewnf	16 sechszehn ZECH-stsehn	90 neunzig NOYN-tsich
6 sechs sechs	17 siebzehn SEEB-tsehn	100 (ein) hundert ahyn-hoon-dert
7 sieben ZE-eb'n	18 achtzehn ACHT-tsehn	
8 acht acht	19 neunzehn NOYN-tsehn	500 fünfhundert FEWNF-hoon-dert
9 neun noyn	20 zwanzig TSVANT-sich	
10 zehn tsehn	30 dreißig DRAHYS-sich	1,000 (ein) tausend ahyn-tau-zent
11 elf elf	40 vierzig FEER-tsich	

4. German Menu Terms

GENERAL TERMS

soups	Suppen	ZOO-pen
eggs	Eier	AH-yer
salads	Salate	za-LAH-te
meats	Fleisch	flahysh
fish	Fisch	feesh
vegetables	Gemüse	ge-MEW-seh
desserts	Nachspeisen	NACH-spahy-sen
fruits	Früchte	FREWCH-te
beverages	Getränke	ge-TRAN-keh
condiments	Würze	VEWR-tseh
salt	Salz	zalts
pepper	Pfeffer	PFEF-fer
mustard	Senf	zenf
vinegar	Essig	Es-sich
oil	Öl	eul
sugar	Zucker	TSOO-ker

SOUPS

Aalsuppe	eel soup	**Gulaschsuppe**	a thin beef gulash
Bauernsuppe	sausage and cabbage soup	**Kaltschale**	cold fruit soup
		Königinsuppe	beef soup with sour cream and almonds
Brotsuppe	soup made with black and white bread, apple juice, and spices	**Leberknödelsuppe**	soup with liver dumplings
Erbensuppe	pea soup	**Linsensuppe**	lentil soup with sausage
Flädlesuppe	soup with bits of pancake	**Ochsenschwanzsuppe**	oxtail soup
Fleischbrühe	clear meat broth with with noodles or dumplings	**Zwiebelsuppe**	onion soup
Frühlingssuppe	vegetable soup		

MEATS

Deutsches Beefsteak	—	Wurst	sausage
Filetsteak	steak	Zunge	tongue
Kalbfleisch	veal	Frikadellen	cold meatballs
Kasseler Kotelett	pork chop	Gulasch	spicy beef stew
Kotelett	cutlet, chop	Kalbkotelett	veal chop
Lammfleisch	lamb	Kalbleber	calf's liver
Leber	liver	Kalbrouladen	rolled fillet of veal
Nieren	kidneys		stuffed with ground pork
Schinken	ham	Königsbergerklopse	meatballs in sour
Schnitzel	cutlet		cream and caper sauce
Schweinefleisch	pork	Wiener Schnitzel	fried escalopes of
Spanferkel	suckling pig		breaded veal
Speck	bacon		

FISH

Aal	eel	Krebs	crab
Austern	oysters	Lachs, Salm	salmon
Barsch	freshwater perch	Makrele	mackerel
Flunder	flounder	Matjeshering	salted herring filets
Forelle	trout	Muscheln	mussels/clams
Garnelen	prawns	Rotbarsch	red sea-bass
Hecht	pike	Sardellen	anchovies
Heilbutt	halibut	Schellfisch	haddock
Hering	herring	Seebarsch	bass
Hummer	lobster	Seezunge	sole
Jacobsmuscheln	scallops	Thunfisch	tuna
Kabeljau	cod	Zander	pike / perch
Karpfen	carp		

SAUSAGE

Aufschnitt	assorted sliced sausages	Himmel und Erde	fried blutwurst with
Blutwurst	blood sausage		potato and apple purée
Bratwurst	pork sausage	Knackwurst	thick, short sausages
Frankfurter	sausages served with	Leberwurst	liver sausage
Würstchen	bread and mustard	Mettwurst	red-skinned, smoked
			pork sausage

FOWL AND GAME

Ente	duck	Gans	goose
Fasan	pheasant	Hase	hare

Hirsch	venison	Reh	venison
Huhn	chicken	Taube	pigeon
Hühnchen	chicken	Truthahn	turkey
Kaninchen	rabbit	Wachtel	quail
Rebhuhn	partridge	Wildschwein	wild boar

EGGS

ham and eggs	Schinken und Eier	fried eggs	Spiegeleier
a boiled egg	ein gekochtes	scrambled eggs	Rühreier
soft/hard	Ei weich/hart	omelet	Omelette

VEGETABLES

Auberginen	eggplant	Karotten	carrots
Blumenkohl	cauliflower	Kartoffeln	potatoes
Bohnen	beans	Kohl	cabbage
Bratkartoffeln	fried potatoes	Kopfsalat	lettuce salad
Braunkohl	broccoli	Lauch	leeks
Champignons	mushrooms	Linsen	lentils
Chicorée	endive	Mais	sweet corn
Endiven	endive	Mohrrüben	carrots
Erbsen	peas	Pilze	mushrooms
Erdäpfel	potatoes	Rosenkohl	brussels sprouts
Fisolen	green beans	Spargel	asparagus
Gemischtes Gemüse	mixed vegetables	Spinat	spinach
Grüner Salat	green salad	Tomaten	tomatoes
Gurken	cucumber	Weißkohl	cabbage
Karfiol	cauliflower	Zwiebeln	onions

DESSERTS

Apfelstrudel	apple pastry	Mozartkugeln	chocolate balls with a
Arme Ritter	fried bread cinnamon		rum-flavored filling
	and sugar	Pfannkuchen	pancake
Eis	ice cream	Nusstorte	walnut cake
Faschingskrapfen	deep-fried buns	Rehrücken	chocolate cake with
	filled with apricot jam		blanched almonds
Fruchtsalat	fruit salad	Sachertorte	chocolate cake filled
Kaiserschmarren	white raisin pancake		with apricot jam and covered
Kasnudeln	noodles with fruit		with chocolate icing
	and poppy seeds	Schokoladenpudding	chocolate pudding
Lebkuchen	honey cakes	Schokoladentorte	chocolate cake

FRUIT

Ananas	pineapple	**Kirschen**	cherries
Apfel	apple	**Mirabellen**	plums
Apfelsine	orange	**Melone**	melon
Aprikosen	apricots	**Pampelmuse**	grapefruit
Banane	banana	**Pfirsich**	peach
Birne	pear	**Trauben**	grapes
Erdbeeren	strawberries		

BEVERAGES

Apfelwein	cider	**Orangeade**	orangeade
Bier	beer	**Orangensaft**	orange juice
Kaffee	coffee	**Sprudel**	soda
mit Sahne	with cream	**Tomatensaft**	tomato juice
mit Milch	with milk	**Zitronenlimo-**	lemonade
schwarzen	black	**nade**	
koffeinfreien	decaffeinated	**Zitronentee**	lemon tea

COOKING TERMS

Blutig	rare	**Geräuchert**	smoked
Gebacken	baked	**Geschmort**	braised
Gebraten (im Ofen)	roasted	**Gut durchge-braten**	well done
Gedämpft	stewed, steamed	**Mariniert**	marinated
Gegrillt	grilled	**Mittel**	medium
Gekocht	boiled	**Vom Rost**	broiled

5. Czechoslovakian Vocabulary

There are 32 vowels and consonants in the Czech alphabet, and most of the consonants are pronounced about as they are in English. Accent marks over vowels lengthen the sound of the vowel, as does the *kroužek*, or little circle ("°"), which appears only over "o" and "u."

A, a	f*a*ther
B, b	*b*oy
C, c	ge*ts*
Č, č	*ch*oice
D, d	*d*ay
D', d'	*Di*or
E, e	n*e*ver

F, f	*f*ood
G, g	*g*oal
H, h	un*h*and
Ch, ch	Lo*ch* Lomond
I, i	n*ee*d
J, j	*y*es
Ќ, k	*k*ey
L, l	*l*ord
M, m	*m*ama
N, n	*n*o
N', n'	Ta*ny*a
O, o	*aw*ful
P, p	*p*en
Ŗ, r	slightly trilled *r*
Ř, ř	slightly trilled *r* + *sh* as in cru*sh*
Ş, s	*s*eat
Š, š	cru*sh*
T, t	*t*oo
T', t'	no*t y*et
U, u	r*oo*m
V, v	*v*ery
W, w	*v*ague
Y, y	funn*y*
Z, z	*z*ebra
Ž, ž	a*z*ure, plea*s*ure

EVERYDAY EXPRESSIONS

		Pronounced
Hello	**Dobrý den**	DAW-bree den
Good morning	**Dobré jitro**	DAW-breh YEE-traw
Good evening	**Dobrý večer**	DAW-bree VEH-chair
How are you?	**Jak se máte?**	YAHK seh MAH-teh
Very well	**Velmí dobře**	VEL-mee DAW-brsheh
Thank you	**Děkují vam**	DYEK-ooee-vahm
You're welcome	**Prosím**	PRAW-seem
Please	**Prosím**	PRAW-seem
Yes	**Ano**	AH-no
No	**Ne**	neh
Excuse me	**Promiňte**	PRAW-min-teh
How much does it cost?	**Kolik to stojí?**	KAW-leek taw STAW-ee
I don't understand	**Nerozumím**	NEH-raw-zoo-meem
Just a moment	**Moment, prosím**	MAW-ment, PRAW-seem
Good-bye	**Na shledanou!**	NAH-skleh-dah-noh-oo

TRAVELING

Your passport, please	**Váš pas, prosím**	vahsh-pahss, PRAW-seem
Here is my passport	**Zde je můj pas**	zdeh-yeh-mooy-pahss
my bag	**moje zavazadla**	MAW-yeh ZAH-vah-zah-dlah
I am with a group	**Jsem se skupinou**	sem-seh-SKOO-pee-noh
I am staying . . .	**Zůstanu . . .**	ZOO-stah-noo
a few days	**několik dnů**	NYEH-koh-leek-dnoo
two weeks	**dva neděle**	dvah-NEH-dyeh-leh
a month	**jeden měsíc**	YEH-den-MYEH-seets
I am visiting	**Navštívím**	NAHV-shtvee-veem-
relatives	**příbuzné**	PRSHEE-booz-neh
friends	**přátele**	PRSHAH-tell-eh
I am on vacation	**Jsem na dovolené**	sem-na-DOH-voh-leh-neh
Where is the . . .	**Kde je . . .**	GDE-yeh
bus station	**autobusové nádraží**	AHOO-taw-boos-oh-veh-NAH-drah-shee
train station	**nádraží**	NAH-drah-shee
airport	**letiště**	LEH-tyish-tyeh
baggage check	**úschovna zavazadel**	OO-skohv-nah-ZAH-vahz-ah-del
check-in counter	**[no Czech equivalent]**	—
Where can I find a taxi?	**Kde najdu taxíka?**	GDE-NAI-doo-TAHKS-ee-kah
Where can I find a gas station?	**Kde najdu benzínovou pumpu?**	GDE-NAI-doo-BEN-zeen-oh-voh-POOMP-oo
How much is gas?	**Kolik stojí benzín?**	KOH-leek-STOH-yee-BEN-zeen
Please fill the tank	**Naplňte mi nadrž, prosím**	NAH-puln-teh-mee-NAH-dursh, PRAW-seem
How much is the fare?	**Kolik bude ta cesta stát?**	KOH-leek-BOO-deh-tah-TSES-tah-STAHT
I am going to . . .	**Pojedu do . . .**	POH-yeh-doo-doh
one-way ticket	**jednoduchá jízdenka**	YED-no-dookh-ah-YEEZ-den-kah
round-trip ticket	**zpáteční jízdenka**	ZPAH-tech-nee-JEEZ-den-kah
car-rental office	**půjčovna aut**	POO-EECH-awv-nah-AH-OOT

CHANGING MONEY

Where can I change money?	**Kde dostanu vyměnit cizí valutu?**	gdeh-DAW-stah-noo-VEE-myen-eet-TSEE-zee-VAH-loo-too
Can you change traveler's checks?	**Mužete mi rozměnit cestovní šek?**	MOOSH-eh-teh-mee-RAHZ-myen-eet-TSES-tohv-nee-sheck
I would like to change dollars	**Chci vyměnit dolary**	CHTSEE-VEE-myen-eet-DOH-lahr-ee
What is the exchange rate?	**V jakém pomeru se vyměnuje dolar?**	FYAHK-ehm-pohm-yehr-oo-seh-VEE-myen-oo-yeh-DOH lahr

ACCOMMODATIONS

I'm looking for . . .	**Hledám**	HLEH-dahm
a hotel	**hotel**	HAW-tel
a pension	**penzión**	PEHN-zee-ohn
a youth hostel	**studentskou ubytovnu**	STOO-dent-skoh-OO-beet-ohv-noo
I have a reservation	**Mám zamluvené nocleh**	mahm-ZAH-mloo-veh-neh-NAWTS-leh
My name is . . .	**Jmenují se . . .**	MEH-noo-yee-seh
Do you have a room . . .	**Máte pokoj . . .**	MAH-teh-POH-koy
for tonight	**na dnešek**	NAH-dneh-sheck
for three nights	**na tři dny**	NAH-trshee-dnee
for a week	**na týden**	NAH-tee-den
I would like . . .	**Chci . . .**	chtsee
a single	**jednolůžkový pokoj**	JED-noh-loosh-koh-vee-POH-koy
a double	**dvojlůžkový pokoj**	DVOY-loosh-koh-vee-POH-koy
I want a room . . .	**Chci pokoj . . .**	chtsee-POH-koy
with a bath	**s koupelnou**	SKOH-pehl-noh
without a bath	**bez koupelny**	BEHZ-koh-pehl-nee
with a shower	**se sprchou**	SEH-spur-choh
without a shower	**bez sprchu**	BEZ-spur-choo
with a view	**s pohledem**	SPOH-hlehd-ehm
How much is the room? . . .	**Kolik stojí pokoj? . . .**	KOH-leek-STOH-yee-PAW-koy
with breakfast	**se snidaní**	SEH-snee-dan-nyee
May I see the room?	**Mohu vidět ten pokoj?**	MOH-hoo-VEE-dyet-ten PAW-koy
The key	**Klíč**	kleech

| The bill, please | **Dejte mi učet, prosím** | DAY-teh-mee-OO-cheht, PRAW-seem |

EATING

Restaurant	**restaurace**	REHS-tow-rah-tseh
Breakfast	**snidaně**	SNEE-dah-nyeh
Lunch	**oběd**	OH-byed
Dinner	**večeře**	VEH-chair-sheh
A table for two, please.		
(Lit.: There are two of us)	**Je nás dva.**	yeh-NAHS-dvah
Waiter	**čísník**	CHEESS-neek
Waitress	**slečna**	SLECH-nah
I would like . . .	**Chci . . .**	chtsee
a menu	**jídelní lístek**	YEE-del-nee-LEES-teck
a fork	**vidličku**	VEED-leech-koo
a knife	**nůž**	noosh
a spoon	**lžičku**	lu-SHICH-koo
a napkin	**ubrousek**	OO-broh-seck
a glass (of water)	**skleničku (voda)**	SKLEHN-ich-koo (VOH-dah)
the check, please	**účet, prosím**	OO-cheht, PRAW-seem
Is the tip included?	**Je v tom zahrnuto sropitné?**	yeh-FTOHM-zah-HUR-noo-toh-SPROH-peet-neh

GETTING AROUND

I'm looking for . . .	**Hledám . . .**	HLEH-dahm
a bank	**banku**	BAHNK-oo
the church	**kostel**	KAWS-tell
the city center	**střední město**	STRSHEHD-nee-MYES-toh
the museum	**muzeum**	MOO-zeh-oom
a pharmacy	**lekarnu**	LEK-ahr-noo
the park	**park**	pahrk
the theater	**divadlo**	DEE-vahd-loh
the tourist office	**cestovní kancelař**	TSES-tohv-nee-KAHN-tseh-larsh
the embassy	**velvyslanectví**	VEHL-vee-slahn-ets-tvee
Where is the nearest telephone?	**Kde je nejblizsi telefon?**	gde-yeh-NAY-bleesh-ee-TEL-oh-fohn
I would like to buy . . .	**Chci koupit . . .**	chsee-KOH-peet
a stamp	**znamku**	ZNAHM-koo
a postcard	**pohlednice**	POH-hlehd-nit-seh
a map	**mapu**	MAHP-oo

SIGNS

No trespassing	**Cizím vstup zakázán**	TSEE-zeem-fstoop-ZAH-kahz-ahn
No parking	**Neparkovat**	NEH-park-oh-vaht
Entrance	**Vchod**	fchawd
Exit	**Východ**	VEE-chawd
Information	**Informace**	EEN-for-mah-tseh
No Smoking	**Kouření zakázáno**	KOH-rsheh-nee-ZAH-kah-zahn-oh
Arrivals	**Příjezd**	PRSHEE-jehzd
Departures	**Odjezd**	AWD-jehzd
Toilets	**Záchod**	ZAH-chawd
Danger	**Pozor, nebezpečí**	POHZ-awr, NEH-bez-pech-ee

NUMBERS

1 **jeden** YEH-den	12 **dvanáct** DVAH-nahtst	40 **čtyřicet** CHTI-rshee-tset
2 **dva** dvah	13 **třináct** TRSHEE-nahtst	50 **padesát** PAH-deh-saht
3 **tři** trshee	14 **čtrnáct** CHTUR-nahtst	60 **šedesát** SHE-deh-saht
4 **čtyři** CHTEE-rshee	15 **patnáct** PAHT-nahtst	70 **sedmdesát** SEH-doom-deh-saht
5 **pět** pyet	16 **šestnáct** SHEST-nahtst	
6 **šest** shest	17 **sedmnáct** SEH-doom-nahtst	80 **osmdesát** AW-soom-deh-saht
7 **sedm** SEH-doom	18 **osmnáct** AW-soom-nahtst	
8 **osm** AW-soom	19 **devatenáct** DEH-vah-teh-nahtst	90 **devadesát** DEH-vah-deh-saht
9 **devět** DEH-vyet		
10 **deset** DEH-set	20 **dvacet** DVAH-tset	100 **sto** staw
11 **jedenáct** YEH-deh-nahtst	30 **třicet** TRSHEE-tset	500 **pět set** PYET set
		1000 **tisíc** TYEE-seets

6. Czechoslovakian Menu Terms

GENERAL TERMS

soup	**polévka**	POH-lehv-kah
eggs	**vejce**	VAYTS-eh
meat	**maso**	MAHS-oh
fish	**ryba**	REE-bah
vegetables	**zelenina**	ZEHL-eh-nee-nah
fruit	**ovoce**	OH-voh-tseh
desserts	**moučniky**	MOHCH-nee-kee
beverages	**nápoje**	NAH-poy-yeh
salt	**sůl**	sool
pepper	**pepř**	PEH-prsh
mustard	**hořčice**	HOHRSH-chee-tseh
vinegar	**ocet**	OH-tseht
oil	**olej**	OH-lay
sugar	**cukr**	TSOO-ker

tea	čaj	chye
coffee	káva	KAH-vah
bread	chléba	CHLEHB-ah
butter	máslo	MAHS-loh
wine	víno	VEE-noh
fried	smažený	SMAH-sheh-nee
roasted	pečený	PECH-eh-nee
boiled	vařený	VAH-rsheh-nee
grilled	grilovaný	GREE-loh-vah-nee

SOUPS

bram borová	potato	rajská	tomato
čočková	lentil	slepičí	chicken
gulášová	goulash	zeleninová	vegetable

MEATS

biftek	steak	klobása	sausage
guláš	goulash	králík	rabbit
hovēzr	beef	skopové	mutton
játra	liver	telecí	veal
jehněčí	lamb	telecí kotleta	veal cutlet
kachna	duck	vepřové	pork

FISH

kapr	carp	štika	pike
kaviár	caviar	treska	cod
rybí filé	fish filet	úhoř	eel
sled	herring	ústřice	oysters

EGGS

míchaná vejce	scrambled eggs	vejce na mekko	soft boiled eggs
smažená vejce	fried eggs	vejce se slaninou	bacon and eggs
vařená vejce	boiled eggs	vejce se šunkou	ham and eggs

SALADS

fazolový salát	bean salad	okurkový salát	cucumber salad
hlávkový salát	mixed green salad	salát z cévené řepy	beet salad

VEGETABLES

brambory	potatoes	**květák**	cauliflower
celer	celery	**mrkev**	carrots
chřest	asparagus	**paprika**	peppers
cibule	onions	**rajská jablíčka**	tomatoes
houby	mushrooms	**zelí**	cabbage

DESSERTS

buchta	cake	**jablkový závin**	apple strudel
cukrovi	cookies	**palačinky**	pancakes
čokoládová zmrzlina	chocolate ice cream	**vanilková zmrzlina**	vanilla ice cream

FRUITS

citrón	lemon	**jablko**	apple
hruška	pears	**švestky**	plums

BEVERAGES

čaj	tea	**víno**	wine
káva	coffee	**cervené**	red
mléko	milk	**bílé**	white
		voda	water

CONDIMENTS

chleb	bread	**majonéza**	mayonnaise
cukr	sugar	**pepř**	pepper
hořcíce	mustard	**ocet**	vinegar
kečup	catsup	**olej**	oil

7. Hungarian Vocabulary

Our transcription of the Hungarian language used here is of necessity approximate. Your best bet is to mimic the pronunciation of Hungarians whenever possible.

a	t*au*t
á	b*ah*
e	*e*ver
é	d*ay*
i	t*ee*n
í	t*ee*n
o	b*o*ne
ó	b*o*ne (but slightly shorter)
ö	sub*ur*b or French p*eu*r (shown phonetically below as "ur")
ő	sub*ur*b or French p*eu*r (shown phonetically below as "ur")
u	m*oo*n
ú	m*oo*n
ü	t*ee*n
ű	t*ee*n

Most Hungarian consonants are pronounced approximately as they are in English, including the following: *b, d, f, h, k, l, m, n, p, t, v,* and *y*. There are some differences, however, particularly in the consonant combinations, as follows:

c	ge*ts*
cs	*ch*ill
g	*g*ill
gy	he*dge*
j	*y*outh
ny	as in Russian *ny*et
r	slightly trilled *r,* as in Spanish
s	*sh*eet
sz	*s*ix
z	*z*ero
zs	a*z*ure, plea*s*ure

EVERYDAY EXPRESSIONS

		Pronounced
Hello	**Jó napot**	YOH-naw-poht
Good morning	**Jó reggelt**	YOH-rej-jelt
Good evening	**Jó estét**	YOH-esh-tayt
How are you?	**Hogy van?**	HOJ-vawn
Very well	**Nagyon jól**	NAW-jon YOHL
Thank you	**Köszönöm**	KUR-sur-nurm
You're welcome	**Kérem**	KAY-rem
Please	**Legyen szíves**	LEH-jen see-vesh
Yes	**Igen**	EE-gen
No	**Nem**	NEM
Excuse me	**Bocsánat**	BOH-chah-nawt
How much does it cost?	**Mennyibe kerül?**	MEN-yee-beh keh-reel
I don't understand	**Nem értem**	NEM ayr-tem

| Just a moment | **Egy pillanat** | EJ peel-law-nawt |
| Good-bye | **Viszontlátásra** | VEE-sont-lah-tahsh-raw |

TRAVELING

Your passport, please	**Kérem, az utlevelét**	KAY-rem awz OOT-leh-veh-layt
Here is my passport	**Tessék, az utlevelem**	TESH-shayk awz OOT-leh-veh-lem
Here is my bag	**Tessék, a táskám**	TESH-shayk aw TAHSH-kahm
I am with a group	**Csoporttal utazom**	CHOH-port-tawl oo-taw-zom
I am staying . . .	**Néhány . . .**	NAY-hahn
a few days	**napig leszek itt**	NAW-peeg leh-sek eet
two weeks	**két hétig leszek itt**	KAYT HAYT-eeg leh-sek eet
a month	**egy hónapig leszek itt**	EJ HOH-naw-peeg leh-sek eet
I am visiting relatives	**Rokonaimat látogatom meg**	ROH-koh-naw-ee-mawt lah-toh-gaw-tom meg
friends	**barátaimat**	BAW-ray-taw-ee-mawt
I am on vacation	**Szabadságon vagyok**	SAW-bawd-chah-gon vaw-jok
Where is the . . .	**Hol van . . .**	HOHL vawn
bus station	**az autóbuszállomás**	awz OW-toh-boos-ah-loh-mahsh
train station	**a vasútállomás**	aw VAW-shoot-ah-loh-mahsh
airport	**a repülőtér**	aw REH-pee-lur-tayr
baggage check	**a csomagmegőrző**	aw CHOH-mawg-meg-ur-zur
check-in counter	**kell bejelentkeznem**	kel BEH-jeh-lent-kez-nem
Where can I find a taxi?	**Hol kaphatok taxit?**	HOHL kawp-haw-tok TAWK-seet
How much is the fare?	**Mennyi a viteldíj?**	MEN-yee aw VEE-tel-dee
I am going to . . .	**. . . -ig akarnék menni**	. . . -eeg aw-kawr-nayk men-ee
one-way ticket	**egy útra**	EJ oot-raw
round-trip ticket	**oda-vissza**	OH-daw-VEES-saw
car-rental office	**autókölcsönző**	OW-toh-kurl-churn-zur
Where can I find a gas station?	**Merre van egy töltőállomás**	MEH-reh vawn ej TURL-tur-ah-loh-mahsh

How much is gas?	**Mennyi a benzin?**	MEN-yee aw BEN-zeen
Please fill the tank	**Tele kérem**	TEH-leh kay-rem

CHANGING MONEY

Where can I change money?	**Hol lehet pénzt váltani?**	HOHL leh-het PAYNST vahl-taw-nee
Can you change traveler's checks?	**Utazásicsekket lehet itt beváltani?**	OO-taw-zah-shee chek-ket leh-het eet beh-vahl-taw-nee
I would like to change dollars	**Szeretnék amerikai dollárt beváltani**	SEH-ret-nayk aw-meh-ree-kaw-ee DOHL-lahrt beh-vahl-taw-nee
What is the exchange rate?	**Mennyi az árfolyam?**	Men-yee awz AHR-foh-yawm

ACCOMMODATIONS

I'm looking for a hotel	**Egy szállodát keresek**	ej SAH-loh-daht keh-reh-shek
I'm looking for a pension	**Egy penziót keresek**	ej PEN-zee-oht keh-reh-shek
I'm looking for a youth hostel	**Egy ifjúsági szállót keresek**	ej EEF-yoo-shah-gee SAH-loht keh-reh-shek
I have a reservation	**Foglaltam már szobát**	FOHG-lawl-tawm mahr soh-baht
My name is . . .	**A nevem . . .**	aw NEH-vem
Do you have a room . . .	**Van egy szobája . . .**	VAWN ej soh-bah-yaw
for tonight	**ma éjszakára**	MAW ay-saw-kah-raw
for three nights	**három éjszakára**	HAH-rom ay-saw-kah-raw
for a week	**egy hétre**	EJ HAYT-reh
I would like . . .	**Kérek . . .**	KAY-rek
a single	**egy egyágyas szobát**	EJ EJ-ah-jawsh sho-baht
a double	**egy kétágyas szobát**	EJ KAYT-ah-jawsh soh-baht
with bath	**fürdővel**	FEER-dur-vel
without bath	**fürdő nélkül**	FEER-dur NAYL-keel

with shower	zuhanyozóval	ZOO-hawn-yoh-zoh-vawl
without shower	zuhanyozó nélkül	ZOO-hawn-yoh-zoh NAYL-keel
with a view	szép kilátással	SAYP KEE-lah-tahsh-shawl
How much is the room?	Mennyibe kerül a szoba?	MEN-yee-beh keh-reel aw SOH-baw
with breakfast	a reggelit beszámítva	aw REG-geh-leet beh-sah-meet-vaw
May I see the room?	Megnézhetem a szobát?	MEG-nayz-hem-tem aw SOH-baht
The key	a kulcs	aw KOOLCH
The bill, please	Kérem a számlámat	KAY-rem aw SAHM-lah-mawt

EATING

Restaurant	Vendéglő	VEN-dayg-lur
Breakfast	Reggeli	REG-geh-lee
Lunch	Ebéd	EH-bayd
Dinner	Vacsora	VAW-choh-raw
A table for two, please	Kérek egy asztalt két személyre	KAY-rek ej aws-tawlt KAYT seh-may-reh
Waiter	Pincér	PEENT-sayr
Waitress	Pincérnő	PEENT-sayr-nur
I would like . . .	Kérnék . . .	KAYR-nayk
a menu	egy étlapot	ej AYT-law-poht
a fork	egy villát	ej VEEL-laht
a knife	egy kést	ej KAYSHT
a spoon	egy kanalat	ej KAW-naw-lawt
a napkin	egy szalvétát	ej SAWL-vay-taht
a glass (of water)	egy pohár (vizet)	ej poh-hahr (VEE-zet)
the check, please	fizetek	FEE-zeh-tek
Is the tip included?	A borravaló szerepel a számlában?	aw BOHR-raw-vaw-loh seh-reh-pel aw sahm-lah-bawn

GETTING AROUND

I'm looking for a . . .	Keresek egy . . .	KEH-reh-shek ej
I'm looking for the . . .	Keresem a . . .	KEH-reh-shem aw
bank	bankot	BAWN-koht
church	tamplomot	TEM-ploh-moht

city center	belvárost	BEL-vah-rosht
museum	múzeumot	MOO-zeh-oo-moht
pharmacy	patikát	PAW-tee-kaht
park	parkot	PAWR-koht
theater	színházat	SEEN-hah-zawt
tourist office	turista ügynökséget	TOO-reesh-taw eej-nurk-shay-get
embassy	nagykövetséget	NAWJ-kur-vet-shay-get
Where is the nearest telephone?	Hol van z legközelebbi telefon?	HOHL vawn aw LEG-jur-zeh-leb-bee TEH-leh-fohn
I would like to buy . . .	Kérek . . .	KAY-rek
a stamp	egy bélyeget	ej BAY-eh-get
a postcard	egy levelezőlapot	ej LEH-veh-leh-zur-law-poht
a map	egy térképet	ej TAYR-kay-pet

SIGNS

No trespassing	Átlépni tilos; Belépni tilos
No parking	A parkolás tilos
Entrance	Benjárat
Exit	Kijárat
Information	Tudakozó
No smoking	Tilos a dohányzás
Arrivals	Érkezések
Departures	Indulások
Toilets	Toalettek
Danger	Vigyázat

NUMERALS

1 egy EJ	12 tizenkettő TEEZ-en-ket-tur	40 negyven NEJ-ven
2 kettő KET-tur	13 tizenhárom TEEZ-en-hah-rohm	50 ötven URT-ven
3 három HAH-rohm	14 tizennégy TEEZ-en-nayj	60 hatvan HAWT-vawn
4 négy NAYJ	15 tizenöt TEEZ-en-urt	70 hetven HET-ven
5 öt URT	16 tizenhat TEEZ-en-hawt	80 nyolcvan NYOHLTS-vawn
6 hat HAWT	17 tizenhét TEEZ-en-hayt	
7 hét HAYT	18 tizennyolc TEEZ-en-nyohlts	90 kilencven KEE-lents-ven
8 nyolc NYOHLTS	19 tizenkilenc TEEZ-en-kee-lents	
9 kilenc KEE-lents	20 húsz HOOS	100 száz SAHZ
10 tíz TEEZ	30 harminc HAWR-meents	500 ötszáz URT-sahz
11 tizenegy TEEZ-en-ej		1,000 ezer EH-zer

8. Hungarian Menu Terms

GENERAL TERMS

soups	**levesek**	LEH-veh-shek
eggs	**tojás**	TOH-yahsh
salads	**saláták**	SHAW-lah-tahk
meats	**hús**	HOOSH
meat dishes	**húsételek**	HOOSH-ay-teh-lek
fish	**halak**	HAW-lawk
vegetables	**főzelék**	FUR-zeh-layk
desserts	**tészták**	TAYS-tahk
fruits	**gyümölcs**	JEE-murlch
beverages	**italok**	EE-taw-lohk
bread	**kenyér**	KEN-yayr
butter	**vaj**	VAW-ee

CONDIMENTS

mayonnaise	**majonéz**	MAW-yoh-nayz
mustard	**mustár**	MOOSH-tahr
oll	**olaj**	OH-law-ee
vinegar	**ecet**	EH-tset
salt	**só**	SHOH
black pepper	**bors**	BORSH
paprika	**paprika**	PAW-pree-kaw

COOKING TERMS

fresh	**friss**	FREESH
raw	**nyers**	NYERSH
spicy	**fűszerezve**	FEE-seh-rez-veh
salty	**sós**	SHOSH
baked/fried	**sütve**	SHEET-veh
deep-fried	**zsírban sütve**	ZHEER-bawn sheet-ve
steamed	**párolva**	PAH-rohl-vaw
braised	**dinsztelve**	DEEN-stel-veh
stuffed	**töltve**	TURLT-veh
toasted	**pirítva**	PEE-reet-vaw
boiled	**főzve**	FURZ-veh
rare	**félig nyersen**	FAY-leeg nyer-shen
medium	**közepesen kisütve**	KUR-zeh-peh-shen KEE-sheet-veh
well done	**agyonsütve**	AW-john sheet-veh
hot (peppery)	**csípős**	CHEE-pursh
hot (in temperature)	**forró**	FOHR-roh

cold	**hideg**	HEE-deg

SOUPS

húsleves	bouillon	**paradicsomleves**	tomato soup
zöldborsóleves	pea soup	**gulyásleves**	goulash soup
zöldségleves	vegetable soup	**gombaleves**	mushroom soup

EGGS

tükörtojás	fried eggs	**kemény tojás**	hard-boiled eggs
rántotta	scrambled eggs	**szalonnával**	with bacon
omlett	omelet	**kolbásszal**	with sausage
gombás omlett	mushroom omelet	**sonkával**	with ham
lágy tojás	soft-boiled eggs		

SALADS

fejes saláta	green salad	**uborkasaláta**	cucumber salad
paprikasaláta	pepper salad	**vegyes saláta**	mixed salad

MEATS

marhahús	beef	**kacsa**	duck
borjúhús	veal	**liba**	goose
disznóhús	pork	**bárány**	lamb
csirke	chicken		

MEAT DISHES

pörkölt	goulash	**tokány**	ragoût
bécsi szelet	wienerschnitzel	**nyársonsült**	shishkebab
kotlett	cutlet	**paprikáscsirke**	chicken paprikash
pecsenye	roast	**malacsült**	roast piglet

FISH

ponty	carp	**tonhal**	tuna
csuka	pike	**halászlé**	fish stew

fogas	pike-perch	**csuka tejfölben**	pike with sour cream
pisztráng	trout		

VEGETABLES

burgonya	potato	**lecsó**	pickled vegetables
káposzta	cabbage	**bab**	beans
rizs	rice	**zöldbab**	green beans
gomba	mushrooms	**paradicsom**	tomato
spenót	spinach		

DESSERTS

almás rétes	apple strudel	**csokoládé torta**	chocolate cake
cseresznyes retes	cherry strudel	**lekváros palacsinta**	palacsinta
túrós rétes	cheese strudel		with preserves
		fagylalt	ice cream

FRUITS

barack	apricot	**körte**	pears
cseresznye	cherries	**narancs**	oranges
dinnye	melon	**szőlő**	grapes

BEVERAGES

víz	water	**vörös bor**	red wine
tej	milk	**koktél**	cocktail
narancslé	orange juice	**pálinka**	brandy
kávé	coffee	**sör**	beer
tea	tea	**barna sör**	dark beer
kakaó	cocoa	**pezsgő**	champagne
fehér bor	white wine		

9. Romanian Vocabulary

Romanian vowels are pronounced somewhat differently from the same letters in English:

a	father
ă	ago
â	[same as î; see below]
e	met
i	be
î	like ago, but shorter and tenser
o	go (but slightly shorter)
u	boot

Most Romanian consonants are pronounced quite similarly to their English equivalents, with the following exceptions:

c	cat [except in "ce" or "ci" combinations]
ce	check
ci	cheap
g	goat [except in "ge" or "gi" combinations]
ge	jet
gi	Jeep
ş	sheep
ţ	gets

EVERYDAY EXPRESSIONS

		Pronounced
Hello	Salut	sah-LOOT
Good morning	Bună dimineata	BOO-nah dee-mee-NAH-tsah
Good evening	Bună seara	BOO-nah seh-ah-RAH
How are you	Ce mai faci	cheh mye fahch
Very well	Foarte bine	fo-AHR-teh BEE-neh
Thank you	Mulţumesc	mool-tsoo-MESK
You're welcome	Sinteţ bine venit	SIN-tets BEE-neh veh-NEET
Please	Vă rog; Te rog	vah rohg; teh rohg
Yes	Da	dah
No	Nu	noo
Excuse me	Scuză-mă; Pardon	SKOO-zah mah; par-DOHN
How much does it cost?	Cit costă?	kit KO-stah
I don't understand	Nu inteleg	noo oon-tseh-LEG
Just a moment	Numai cun moment	NOO-mye oon mo-MENT
Good-bye	La revedere	lah reh-veh-DEH-reh
I am sorry	Imi pare rău	oom pah-REH ro

TRAVELING

Your passport, please	Paşaportul dumnevoastră vă rog	pah-shah-POR-tool doom-nah-VAH-strah vah rohg
Here is my passport	Aici este paşaportul meu	ah-EECH ESS-teh pah-shah-POR-tool MEH-oo
my bag	bagajul meu	bah-GAZH-ool MEH-oo
I am with a group	Sint cu grupul	sint koo GROO-pool
I am staying . . .	Stau . . .	STAH-oo
a few days	citeva zile	kit-eh-VAH zee-LEH
two weeks	două săptămini	DO-ah sep-tah-MOON-ee
a month	o lună	o LOO-nah
I am visiting relatives	Imi vizitez rudele	oom vee-zee-TEZ ROO-deh-leh
friends	prietenii	pree-YEH-teh-nee
I am on vacation	Sint in vacantă	sint in vah-KAHN-tsah
Where is the . . .	Unde este . . .	OON-deh YES-teh
bus station	staţia de autobuz	STAH-tsee-yah deh ow-toh-BOOSS
train station	staţia de tren; gara	STAH-tsee-yah deh tren; GAH-rah
airport	aeroportul	ah-eh-ro-POR-tool
baggage check	controlul bagajelor	kohn-TROL-ool bah-GAH-zheh-lor
check-in counter	casa de bilete	KAH-sah deh bee-LEH-teh
Where can I find a taxi?	Unde pot gasi un taxiu?	OON-deh poht gah-SEE oon tak-SYOO
How much is the fare?	Cit este taxa? Cit costul unei calători?	kit YESS-teh TAHK-sah; kit KOSS-tool OO-nay kah-lah-TOH-ree
I am going to . . .	Merg la . . .	mehrg lah
one-way ticket	Tichet numai dus	tee-KET NOO-mye dooss
round-trip ticket	Tichet in circuit	tee-KET in cheer-KWEET
car-rental office	Oficiu de inchiriat maşini	o-FEE-chyoo deh een-kee-ree-YAT mah-SHEEN

Where can I find a gas station?	Unde pot găsi o benzinărie?	OON-deh poht gah-SEE o ben-zee-nah-REE-yeh
How much is gas?	Cît costă benzina?	kit KOS-tah ben-ZEE-nah
Please fill the tank	Te rog umple rezervorul	teh rohg OOM-pleh reh-zeh-VO-rool

CHANGING MONEY

Where can I change money?	Unde pot să schimb bani?	OON-deh poht sah skeemp BAH-nee
Can you change traveler's checks?	Schimbaţi cecuri de calătorie?	skeem-BATCH CHEH-koor deh kah-lah-toh-ree-yeh
I would like to change dollars	Aş dori să schimb dolari	ash do-REE sah skimp do-LAHR-ee
What is the exchange rate?	Care este cursul?	KAH-reh ESS-teh KOOR-sool

ACCOMMODATIONS

I am looking for . . .	Caut . . .	kowt
hotel	hotel	ho-TEL
a pension	pensiunea	pen-SYOO-nah
a youth hostel	cămin studenţesc	kah-MEEN stoo-den-TSESK
I have a reservation	Am o rezervare de loc	ahm o reh-zehr-VAH-reh deh lohk
My name is . . .	Mă numesc . . .	mah noo-MESK
Do you have a room . . .	Aveţi o cameră . . .	ah-VEH-tee o KAH-meh-rah
for tonight	pentru o noapte	PEN-troo o no-AHP-teh
for three nights	pentru trei nopţi	PEN-troo tray NOPTS
for a week	pentru o săptămina	PEN-troo o sep-tah-MUH-nah
I would like . . .	Aş dori . . .	ash do-REE
a single	cameră pentru o persoana	KAH-meh-rah PEN-troo o pehr-so-AH-nah
a double	cameră pentru două persoane	KAH-meh-rah PEN-troo DO-o per-so-AH-neh

I want a room . . .	**Aş dori o camera . . .**	ash do-REE o KAH-meh-rah
with a bath/shower	**cu baie/duş**	koo BAH-yeh /doosh
without a bath/shower	**fără baie/duş**	FUH-rah BAH-yeh /doosh
with a view	**vedere**	veh-DEH-reh
How much is the room?	**Cit costă camera?**	kit KOS-tah KAH-meh-rah
with breakfast	**cu micul dejun**	koo MEE-kool deh-ZHOON
May I see the room?	**Pot să văd camera?**	poht sah vud KAH-meh-rah
The key	**cheia**	KAY-ah
The bill, please	**Nota vă rog**	NO-tah vah rohg

EATING

Restaurant	**Restaurant**	res-tau-RAHNT
Breakfast	**Micul dejun**	MEE-kool deh-ZHOON
Lunch	**Prinzul**	PRIN-zool
Dinner	**Cina**	CHEE-nah
A table for two, please	**O masă cu două locuri**	o MAH-sah koo DO-ah LO-koo-ree
Waiter	**Chelner**	KEL-nehr
Waitress	**Chelnariţa**	KEL-nah-ree-tsah
I would like . . .	**Aş dori . . .**	ash doh-REE
a menu	**un meniu**	oon men-YOO
a fork	**o furculită**	o foor-koo-LEE-tsah
a knife	**un cuţit**	oon koo-TSEET
a spoon	**o lingură**	o LEEN-goo-rah
a napkin	**şerveţel**	SHEHR-veh-tsel
a glass (of water)	**un pahar (de apa)**	oon pah-HAR (deh AH-puh)
the check, please	**nota de plată**	NO-tah deh PLAH-tah

GETTING AROUND

I am looking for . . .	**Eu caut . . .**	YEH-oo kowt
a bank	**o bancă**	o BAHN-kah
the church	**biserica**	bee-SEH-ree-kah
the city center	**centrul oraşului**	CHEN-trool o-RAH-shoo-lui

the museum	**muzeul**	moo-ZEH-ool
a pharmacy	**farmacia**	far-mah-CHEE-ah
the park	**parcul**	PAHR-kool
the theater	**teatrul**	teh-AH-trool
the tourist office	**oficiul de turism**	o-FEE-chool deh too-REEZM
the embassy	**ambasada**	ahm-bah-SAH-dah
Where is the nearest telephone?	**Unde este cel mai apropiat telefon?**	OON-deh YES-teh chel MAH-ee ah-pro-PYAT teh-leh-FOHN
I would like to buy . . .	**Aş vrea să cumpar . . .**	ash vrah sah KOOM-por
a stamp	**timbru postal**	TEEM-broo po-SHTAL
a postcard	**o carte poştala**	o KAR-teh po-SHTAH-luh
a map	**o hartă**	o HAR-tuh

SIGNS

No trespassing	**Nu incălca**	noo in-kahl-KAH
No parking	**Parcarea interzisă**	pahr-KAH-reh-ah in-tehr-ZEE-suh
Entrance	**Intrare**	in-TRAH-reh
Exit	**Ieşire**	yeh-SHEE-reh
Information	**Informaţii**	in-for-MAH-tsee
No smoking	**Fumatul interzis**	foo-MAH-tool in-tehr-ZEESS
Arrivals	**Sosiri**	so-SEE-ree
Departures	**Plecări**	pleh-KUH-ree
Toilets (WC)	**Toaleta (WC)**	toh-ah-LEH-tah
Danger	**Pericol**	peh-REE-kol

NUMBERS

1 **unu** OO-noo	13 **treisprezece** TRAY-spreh-zeh-cheh	20 **două zeci** DO-uh zech
2 **doi** doy	14 **patrusprezece** PAH-troo-spreh-zeh-cheh	30 **tre zeci** trey zech
3 **trei** tray	15 **cincisprezece** CHEENCH-spreh-zeh-cheh	40 **patru zeci** PAH-troo zech
4 **patru** PAH-troo	16 **şasesprezece** SHAH-say-spreh-zeh-cheh	50 **cinci zeci** cheench zech
5 **cinci** cheench	17 **şaptesprezece** SHAP-tay-spreh-zeh-cheh	60 **şase zeci** SHAH-seh zech
6 **şase** SHAH-say	18 **optsprezece** OHPT-spreh-zeh-cheh	70 **şapte zeci** SHAP-teh zech
7 **şapte** SHAP-tay	19 **nouăsprezece** NO-uh-spreh-zeh-cheh	80 **opt zeci** ohpt zech
8 **opt** ohpt		90 **nouă zeci** NO-uh zech
9 **nouă** NO-uh		100 **o sută** o SOO-tuh
10 **zece** ZEH-chay		500 **cinci sute** cheench SOO-teh
11 **unsprezece** OON-spreh-zeh-cheh		1,000 **o mie** o MEE-eh
12 **doisprezece** DOY-spreh-zeh-cheh		

10. Romanian Menu Terms
GENERAL TERMS

soup	supa	SOO-pah
eggs	ouă	O-ah
meat	carne	KAR-neh
fish	peşte	PESH-teh
vegetables	vegetale	veh-jeh-TAH-leh
fruits	fructe	FROOK-teh
dessert	desert	deh-SEHR-teh
beverages	băuture	buh-oo-TOO-reh
salt	sare	SAH-reh
pepper	piper	pee-PEHR
mustard	mustar	moo-SHTAR
vinegar	oţet	o-tset
oil	ulei	oo-LEH-eey
sugar	zahăr	ZAH-har
tea	ceai	chah-ee
coffee	kafea	kah-FEH-ah
bread	pîine	PUH-ee-neh
butter	unt	oont
wine	vin	veen
vodka	vodka	VOD-kah

SOUPS

ciorbă pescareasca	fisherman's borscht	**supa cu taitei**	noodle soup
ciorbă taraneasca	peasant's borscht	**supa de pasare**	chicken soup

MEATS

cirnaţi	sausage	**pui**	chicken
creier	brains	**raţa**	duck
curcan	turkey	**rinichi**	kidneys
ficat	liver	**sarmale**	meat rolled in cabbage
gîscă	goose	**snitel**	pork schnitzel
mici	grilled meat balls	**şunca**	ham
miel	lamb	**vită**	beef
porc	pork		

FISH

pastrav	trout	**şalău**	sturgeon
plachie de crap	carp cooked in the oven with spices	**saramura de crap**	grilled carp

EGGS

ouă fierte	boiled eggs	ochiuri romanesti	poached eggs
ouă jumări	scrambled eggs	cu şunca	with ham
ouă ochiuri	fried eggs	omletă	omelet

SALADS

salata de castraveţi	cucumber salad	salata verde	green salad
salata de cruditati	mixed salad		

VEGETABLES

cartofi prajiţi	fried potatoes	orez	rice
cartofi fierti	boiled potatoes	puré de cartofi	mashed potatoes
castraveti	cucumbers	roşii	tomatoes
ciuperci	mushrooms	salata de cartofi	potato salad
conopida	cauliflower	sfecla rosie	beets
fasole	beans	spanac	spinach
fasole verde	string beans	sparanghel	asparagus
mamaliga	polenta	varza	cabbage
mazare	peas	varza acră	sauerkraut
morcovi	carrots	varza rosie	red cabbage

DESSERTS

baclava	sweet baklava pastry	de ciocolata	chocolate
clătite	crêpes	de vanilie	vanilla
cozonac	Moldavian pound cake	plăcintă	pie
frişca	whipped cream	cu brinza	with cheese
ingheţată	ice cream		

FRUITS

căpsuni	strawberries	pere	pears
cirese	cherries	piersici	peaches
lămpie	lemons	portocale	oranges
mere	apples		

BEVERAGES

apa minerala	mineral water	lapte	milk
bere	beer	sifon	soda
neagra	dark	ţuica	plum brandy
blonda	light	vin	wine
cafea	coffee	roşu	red
coniac	brandy	alb	white

CONDIMENTS AND OTHERS

brinza	cheese	pîine	bread
caşcaval	Cheddar cheese	piper	pepper
chifle	rolls	sare	salt
gheaţă	ice	telemea	feta cheese
muştăr	mustard	unt	butter
oţet	vinegar	zahăr	sugar

COOKING TERMS

copt	baked	la gratar	grilled
fiert	boiled	prajit	fried
fript	broiled	umplut	stuffed

11. Bulgarian Vocabulary

The Bulgarian language is written in the Cyrillic alphabet, not the Latin characters familiar to those who speak English or the other Western European languages. The Bulgarian letters and their pronunciation are roughly as follows:

А, а   *f*a*ther*

Б, б   *b*oy

В, в   *v*ery

Г, г   *g*ood

Д, д   *d*ead

Е, е   n*e*ver

Ж, ж   a*z*ure, plea*s*ure

З, з   *z*ebra

И, и	n*ee*d
Й, й	*y*es
К, к	o*k*ay
Л, л	*l*eave
М, м	*m*other
Н, н	*n*othing
О, о	*o*pen
П, п	*p*ortrait
Р, р	slightly trilled *r*
С, с	*s*ilk
Т, т	*t*ap
У, у	r*oo*m
Ф, ф	*f*ather
Х, х	slightly harder than the *h* in *h*ark
Ц, ц	ge*ts*
Ч, ч	*ch*icken
Ш, ш	*sh*ip
Щ, щ	*shch*, as in fre*sh ch*eese
Ъ, ъ	like "*uh*," but shorter and more gutteral
Ь, ь	much like a fleeting *y* inserted between a consonant and a vowel
Ю, ю	*u*nion
Я, я	*Ya*lta

In addition to these individual letters, certain vowel combinations have specialized pronunciations:

ай	*ai*sle

ей	freight
ий	as in f*ee*t, but more elongated
ой	b*oy*
уй	as in g*ooey*, but shorter

EVERYDAY EXPRESSIONS

		Pronounced
Hello	Здравейте	zdra-VAY-teh
Good morning	Добро утро	DO-bro OO-tro
Good evening	Добър вечер	DO-bar VEH-cher
How are you?	Как сте?	Kak steh
Very well	Добре съм	do-BREH sahm
Thank you	Мерси; Благодаря	mer-SEE; blah-go-dar-YAH
You're welcome	Моля	MOL-yah
Please	Моля	MOL-yah
Yes	Да	dah
No	Не	neh
Excuse me	Извинявам се,	eez-veen-YAH-vahm seh,
	Извинете	eez-vee-NEH-teh
How much does it cost?	Колко струва?	KOL-ko STROO-vah?
I don't understand	Не разбирам	neh rahz-BEE-rahm
Just a moment	Момент само	mo-MENT SAH-mo
Good-bye	Довиждане	do-VEEZH-dah-neh
I am sorry	Извинявам се, Простите	eez-veen-YAH-vam seh, pro-STEE-teh

TRAVELING

Your passport, please	Паспорт, моля	pass-PORT MOL-yah
Here is my passport	Ету го паспорта	EH-too go pass-Por-tah
my bag	моя багаж	Mo-yah bah-GAZH
I am with a group	Аз съм със групата	ahz sum sus GROO-pah-tah
I am staying. . .	Аз живея тук...	ahz zhee-VAY-ah toohk
a few days	няколко дена	NYAH-kol-ko DEH-nah
two weeks	две седмици	dveh SED-mee-tsee
a month	един месец	eh-DEEN MEH-sets
I am visiting relatives	Дойдох да видя роднини	DO-ee-dohk dah VEE-dyah rohd-NEE-nee
friends	приятели	pree-YAH-tel-ee
I am on vacation	Аз съм в отпуска	ahz sum vuh OT-poo-skah
Where is the . . .	Къде е...	kuh-DEH eh
bus station	автобусната гара	ahv-to-BOOSS-nah-tah GAH-rah
train station	гарата	GAH-rah-tah
airport	аерогарата	ah-EH-ro-gah-rah-ta
baggage check	багажната каса	bah-GAZH-nah-tah KAH-sah
check-in counter	штанд за проверка на билетите	shtand zah pro-VEHR-kah na bee-LEH-tee-teh

Where can I find a taxi?	Къде се намира такси?	kuh-DEH seh nah-MEE-rah TAKS-see
How much is the fare?	Колко струва билет?	KOL-ko STROO-vah bee-LET
I am going to . . .	Аз пътувам до...	ahz pah-TOO-vahm do
one-way ticket	Билет в една посока	bee-LET vuh ed-NAH po-SO-kah
round-trip ticket	Билет в две посоки	bee-LET vuh dveh po-SO-kee
car-rental office	Бюро за наемане на колите	byoo-RO zah nah-YEM-ah-neh na ko-LEE-teh
Where can I find a gas station?	Къде е бензинна станция?	kuh-DEH eh ben-ZEE-nah STAHN-tsee-yah
How much is gas?	Колко струва бензин?	KOL-ko STROO-vah ben-ZEEN
Please fill the tank	Пълн резервоар, моля	pah-lun reh-zehr-vo-AHR, MOL-yah

CHANGING MONEY

Where can I change money?	Къде мога да обменя парите?	kuh-DEH MO-gah dah ob-men-YAH pah-REE-teh
Can you change traveler's checks?	Мога ли да обменя пътнишки чекове?	MO-gah lee dah ob-men-YAH PUHT-neesh-kee CHEK-o-veh
I would like to change dollars	Искам да обменя долари	EEZ-kahm dah ob-men-YAH DO-lehr-ee
What is the exchange rate?	Колко струва един долар?	KOL-ko STROO-vah eh-DEEN DO-lar

ACCOMMODATIONS

I am looking for . . .	Аз търся...	ahz TUR-syah
a hotel	хотел	ho-TEL
a youth hostel	студентското общежитие	stoo-DEN-sko-to ob-shteh-ZHEE-tee-yeh
I have a reservation	Имам резервация	EE-mahm reh-zehr-VAH-tsee-yah
My name is . . .	Казвам се...	KAHZ-vahm seh
Do you have a room . . .	Имате ли стая...	EE-mah-teh lee STAH-yah
for tonight	за една нощ	zah ed-NAH nozht
for three nights	за три нощи	zah tree NOZH-tee
for a week	за една седмица	zah ed-NAH SEHD-mee-tsah
I would like . . .	Искам...	EEZ-kahm
a single	с едно легло	suh ed-NO leg-LO
a double	с две легла	suh dveh leg-LAH
I want a room . . .	Искам стая...	EEZ-kahm STAH-yah
with a bath/shower	с баня/душ	suh BAHN-yan/doosh
without a bath/shower	без баня/душ	bez BAHN-yah/doosh
with a view	с хубава гледка	suh KHOO-bah-vah GLED-kah
How much is the room?	Колко струва стаята?	KOL-ko STROO-vah STAH-yah-tah
with breakfast	със закуска	suh Zah-KOO-skah
May I see the room?	Мога ли да видя стаята?	MO-gah lee dah VEE-dyah STAH-yah-tah

| The key | Ключ | klyooch |
| The bill, please | Сметка, моля | SMET-kah MOL-yah |

EATING

Restaurant	Ресторант	res-to-RAHNT
Breakfast	Закуска	zah-KOO-skah
Lunch	Обед	o-BED
Dinner	Вечеря	veh-CHEH-ryan
A table for two, please	Моля маса за двама	MOL-yah MAH-sah zah DVAH-mah
Waiter	Сервитьор	sehr-vee-TYOR
Waitress	Сервитьорка	sehr-vee-TYOR-kah
I would like . . .	Искам...	EEZ-kahm
a menu	меню	men-YOO
a fork	вилица	VEE-lee-tsah
a knife	нож	nozh
a spoon	лъжица	LAH-zhee-tsah
a napkin	солфетка	sohl-FET-kah
a glass (of water)	чашка (вода)	CHASH-kah (vo-DAH)

MENU TERMS

soup	чорба, супа	chor-BAH; soopa
eggs	яйца	yah-ee-TSAH
meat	месо	meh-SO
fish	риба	REE-bah
vegetables	Зеленчуци	zeh-len-CHOO-tsee
fruit	Плодове	plo-do-VEH
desserts	Десерти	deh-SEHR-tee
beverages	Напитки	nah-PEET-kee
salt	Сол	sohl

pepper	Пипер	PEE-pehr
mustard	Горчица	gor-CHEE-tsah
vinegar	Оцет	o-TSET
oil	Масло	MAH-slo
sugar	Захар	ZAH-khar
tea	Чай	CHAH-ee
coffee	Кафе	kah-FEH
bread	Хляб	khlyab
butter	Краве масло	KRAH-veh mah-SLO
wine	Вино	vee-NO
vodka	Ракия	rah-KEE-yah

GETTING AROUND

I am looking for . . .	Аз търся...	ahz TUHR-syah
a bank	Банка	BAHN-kah
the church	черква	CHEHRK-vah
the city center	центъра на града	TSEN-tah-rah na grah-DAH
the museum	музей	moo-ZAY
a pharmacy	аптека	ahp-TEH-kah
the park	парк	pahrk
the theater	театър	teh-AH-tahr
the tourist office	туристическо бюро	too-ree-STEE-chess-ko byoo-RO
the embassy	легация	leh-GAH-tsyah
Where is the nearest telephone?	Къде е най-близкия телефон?	kuh-DEH eh nah-ee-BLEEZ-kee-yah tel-eh-FOHN
I would like to buy . .	Искам да купя...	EEZ-kahm dah KOO-pyah

a stamp	марка	MAHR-kah
a postcard	пощенска карта	POHSH-ten-skah KAR-tah
a map	карта	KAR-tah

SIGNS

No trespassing	Не се влиза!; Входа забранен!	neh seh VLEE-zah; FKHO-dah zah-brah-NEN
No parking	Не се паркира; паркирането забранено	neh seh pahr-KEE-rah; pahr-KEE-rah-neh-to zah-brah-NEH-no
Entrance	Вход	fkhod
Exit	Изход	EEZ-khod
Information	Справки	SPRAHF-kee
No smoking	Не се пуши	neh seh POO-shee
Arrivals	Кацане; иядване	KAH-tsah-neh; EE-dvah-neh
Departures	Излети; тръгване	EEZ-leh-tee; TRAHG-vah-neh
Toilets	Тоалети	toh-ah-LEH-tee
Danger	Опасно!	O-pah-sno

NUMBERS

1	един	eh-DEEN	6	шест	shest
2	два	dvah	7	седем	SEH-dem
3	три	tree	8	осем	O-sem
4	четири	CHEH-tir-ee	9	девет	DEH-vet
5	пет	pet	10	десет	DEH-set

11	единадесет	eh-dee-NAHD-ee-set
12	дванадесет	dvah-NAHD-ee-set
13	тринадесет	tree-NAHD-ee-set
14	четиринадесет	cheh-tir-ee-NAHD-ee-set
15	петнадесет	pet-NAHD-ee-set
16	шестнадесет	shest-NAHD-ee-set
17	седемнадесет	seh-dem-NAHD-ee-set
18	осемнадесет	o-sem-NAHD-ee-set
19	деветнадесет	deh-vet-NAHD-ee-set
20	двадесет	DVAH-deh-set
30	тридесет	TREE-deh-set
40	четиридесет	cheh-TIR-ee-deh-set
50	петдесет	pet-deh-SET
60	шестдесет	shest-deh-SET
70	седемдесет	seh-dem-deh-SET
80	осемдесет	o-sem-deh-SET
90	деветдесет	deh-veht-deh-SET
100	сто	sto
500	петсотин	PET-sto-teen
1,000	хиляда	kheel-YAH-dah

12. Bulgarian Menu Terms

Ordering in a Bulgarian restaurant that has no English translation is a special challenge, since the menu is written in the Cyrillic alphabet. The following is listed as a guide to asking for the most popular Bulgarian dishes:

COLD APPETIZERS

haiver	caviar	**shunka**	ham
kashkaval	yellow cheese	**shpekov salam**	smoked sausage
lukanka	dried sausage	**sirene**	cheese

SOUPS

chorba gulash	goulash soup	**chorba ot riba**	fish soup
chorba ot leshta	lentil soup	**pileshka supa**	chicken soup

SALADS

domati presni	fresh tomatoes	**shopska salad**	mixed salad with grated cheese
krastavitsi presni	fresh cucumbers	**zelena salata**	green lettuce
meshana salata	mixed salad		

EGGS

omlet	omelet	**yatsa na ochi**	fried eggs
yatsa birkani	scrambled eggs		

MEATS

agneshko	lamb	**ramstek**	rumpsteak
biftek	beefsteak	**schnitzel**	schnitzel
kievski kotlett	chicken kiev	**shashlik**	shish kebab
kyufteta	meat balls	**stek**	steak
meshana skapa	mixed grill	**svinsko**	pork
pilye	chicken	**teleshko**	veal

FISH

byala riba	perch	**pirzhena riba**	fried fish
lefer	blue fish	**skumriya**	mackerel
moruna	codfish		

VEGETABLES

domati	tomatoes	**kartofi**	potatoes
gibi	mushrooms	**morkovi**	carrots
grah	peas	**oriz**	rice

DESSERTS

kicelo mlyako	yogurt	**sladoled**	ice cream
kompot asorti	mixed compote	**torta**	cake
palachinka	crêpe		

FRUITS

grozde	grapes	**portokali**	oranges
kryshi	pears	**praskova**	peach
limon	lemon	**yabilka**	apple
plodove	fruits		

BEVERAGES

chai	tea	**beli vina**	white wine
pryasno mlyako	milk	**cherveni vina**	red wine
kafe	coffee	**shumyaschi vina**	sparkling wine
mineralna voda	mineral water	**pivo**	beer
shveps	Schweppes (lemon or orange soda)		

CONDIMENTS

chlyab	bread	**med**	honey
konfitur	jam	**zahar**	sugar
maslo	butter		

COOKING TERMS

file	filet	pirzheni	fried
na gril	grilled	shishcheta	shish kebab
natyur	plain	s limanov sos	with lemon sauce
pecheno	roast		

13. Yugoslavian (Serbo-Croatian) Vocabulary

Serbo-Croatian is written with two separate alphabets, Latin and Cyrillic, each containing 30 letters. Equivalents for the two are given below.

A, a	А, а	*fa*ther
B, b	Б, б	*b*oy
C, c	Ц, ц	ge*ts*
Č, č	Ч, ч	*ch*oice
Ć, ć	Ћ, ћ	*ch*eese
D, d	Д, д	*d*ay
Dž, dž	Џ, џ	*j*am
Đ, đ (Dj, dj)	Ђ, ђ	*j*eans
E, e	Е, е	*ne*ver
F, f	Ф, ф	*f*ood
G, g	Г, г	*g*oal
H, h	Х, х	*h*all (but slightly harder)
I, i	И, и	n*ee*d
J, j	Ј, ј	*y*es
K, k	К, к	*k*ey
L, l	Л, л	*l*ord
Lj, lj	Љ, љ	E*li*ot
M, m	М, м	*m*ama
N, n	Н, н	*n*o
Nj, nj	Њ, њ	Ta*ny*a

O, o	О, о	*o*pen
P, p	П, п	*p*en
R, r	Р, р	slightly trilled *r*
S, s	С, с	*s*un
Š, š	Ш, ш	cru*sh*
T, t	Т, т	*t*op
U, u	У, у	r*oo*m
V, v	В, в	*v*ery
Z, z	З, з	*z*ebra
Ž, ž	Ж, ж	a*z*ure, plea*s*ure

In addition to the above alphabet letters, Serbo-Croatian includes five vowel combinations, as follows:

aj	aj	*ai*sle
ej	ej	fr*ei*ght
ij	иj	like an elongated *ee*
oj	oj	b*oy*
uj	уj	g*ooey*

EVERYDAY EXPRESSIONS

Hello	Dobar dan	DO-bar dahn
Good morning	Dobro jutro	DO-bro YOO-tro
Good evening	Dobro vječe	DO-bro VYEH-cheh
How are you?	Kako ste?	KAH-ko steh?
Very well	Dobro sam	DO-bro sahm
Thank you	Hvala ljepo	HVAH-lah LYEH-po
You're welcome	Molim	MO-leem
Please	Molim vas	MO-leem vass
Yes	Da	dah
No	Ne, Nije	neh, NEE-yeh
Excuse me	Oprostite	o-PRO-stee-teh
How much does it cost?	Koliko košta ovo?	ko-LEE-ko KOSH-tah O-vo

I don't understand.	**Ne razumjem**	neh ra-ZOOM-yem
Just a moment	**Momenat samo**	MO-meh-naht SAH-mo
Good bye	**Dovidjenija**	do-vee-JAY-nyah
I am sorry	**Molim za oprostaj**	MO-leem zah O-pro-shtye

TRAVELING

Your passport, please	**Vas pasoš, molim**	vash PAH-sosh, MO-leem
Here is my passport	**Ovdje je moj pasoš**	OHV-jeh yeh moy PAH-sosh
	Evo moj pasoš	EH-vo moy PAH-sosh
my bag	**moj bagaž**	moy BAH-gazh
I am with a group.	**Ja sam sa grupom.**	yah sahm sa GROO-pom
I am staying . . .	**Stanujem ovdje . . .**	STAH-noo-yem OHV-jeh
a few days	**nekoliko dana**	NEH-ko-lee-ko DAH-nah
two weeks	**dva tjednja**	dvah TYED-nyah
a month	**mjesec**	MYEH-sets
I am visiting relatives.	**Došao sam da vidim rodjaka.**	DO-shah-o sahm dah VEE-deem ro-JAH-kah
friends	**prijatelja**	pree-YAH-tel-yah
I am on vacation.	**Ja sam u raspustu.**	yah sahm ooh RASS-poo-stoo
Where is the . . .	**Gdje je . . .**	gdyeh yeh
bus station	**autobusna stanica**	OW-toh-boo-snah STAH-nee-tsah
train station	**železnicka stanica**	ZHEH-lez-neech-kah STAH-nee-tsah
airport	**aerodrom**	ah-EH-ro-drohm
baggage check	**bagažna priznanica**	BAH-gazh-nah pree-ZNAH-nee-tsah
check-in counter	**štand kontrole bileta**	shtahnd kon-TRO-leh bee-LEH-tah
Where can I find a taxi stand?	**Gdje je taxi stanica?**	gdyeh yeh taxi STAH-nee-tsah
How much is the fare?	**Koliko košta karta [ticket]?**	KO-lee-ko KOSH-tah KAR-tah
I am going to . . .	**Idem u . . .**	EE-dem ooh
one-way ticket	**karta u jedan pravac**	KAR-tah ooh YEH-dan PRAH-vats
round-trip ticket	**karta u dva pravca**	KAR-tah ooh dvah PRAHV-tsah

car-rental office	**radnja za pozamljivanje automobila**	RAD-nyah zah po-zam-LEE-van-yeh ow-to-mo-BEE-lah
Where can I find a gas station?	**Gdje je benzinska stanica?**	gdyeh yeh ben-ZEEN-skah STAH-tee-tsah
How much is gas?	**Koliko košta benzin?**	KO-lee-ko KOSH-tah BEN-zeen
Please fill the tank.	**Molim, pun rezervoar.**	MO-leem, poon reh-ZER-vo-ar

CHANGING MONEY

Where can I change money?	**Gdje ču moci da mjenjam novac?**	gdyeh choo MO-chee dah MYEH-nyam NO-vats
Can you change traveler's checks?	**Dali mogu da mjenjam putnički cekovi (traveler cekovi)?**	da-LEE MO-goo dah MYEH-nyam POOT-neech-kee CHEK-o-vee (traveler CHEK-o-vee)
I would like to change dollars.	**Želim da mjenjam dolare.**	ZHEH-leem dah MYEH-nyam DO-lah-reh
What is the exchange rate?	**Pošto je dolar u dinarima?**	PO-shto yeh DO-lar ooh dee-NAR-ee-mah

ACCOMMODATIONS

I am looking for . . .	**Tražim . . .**	TRAH-zheem
a hotel	**hotel**	HO-tel
a pension	**pansjon**	PAHN-syon
a youth hostel	**omladinski turistički dom**	O-mlah-deen-skee TOO-ree-steech-kee dom
I have a reservation	**Imam rezervaciju**	EE-mam reh-zer-ZO-vem seh
My name is . . .	**Zovem se . . .**	ZO-vem seh
Do you have a room . . .	**Dali imate sobu . . .**	dah-LEE EE-mah-teh SO-boo
for tonight	**za jednu noc**	zah YED-noo noch
for three nights	**za tri noči**	zah tree NO-chee
for a week	**za tjedan**	zah TYEH-dahn

I would like . . .	Zelim . . .	ZHEH-leem
a single	za jedno lice	zah YED-no LEE-tseh
a double	za dvije osobe	zah DVEE-yeh o-SO-beh
I want a room . . .	Zelim sobu . . .	ZHEH-leem SO-boo
with a bath/shower	sa kupatilom/tušom	sah koo-PAH-tee-lom/TOO-shom
without a bath/shower	bez kupatila/tuša	bez koo-PAH-tee-lah/TOO-shah
with a view	sa ljepim vidikom	sah LYEH-peem VEE-dee-kom
How much is the room?	Koliko košta soba?	KO-lee-ko KOSH-tah SO-bah
with breakfast	sa doručkom	sah DO-rooch-kom
May I see the room?	Dali mogu da vidim sobu?	DAH-lee MO-goo dah VEE-deem SO-boo
Key	Ključ	Klyooch
The bill, please	Račun, molim	RAH-choon, MO-leem

EATING

Restaurant	Restoran	REH-sto-rahn
Breakfast	Doručak	DOH-roo-chak
Lunch	Ručak	ROO-chak
Dinner	Večerja	VEH-cher-yah
A table for two, please	Molim stol za dvije osobe	MO-leem stohl zah DVEE-yeh O-so-beh
Waiter	Kelner	KEL-ner
Waitress	Kelnerica	kel-NER-ee-tsah
I would like . . .	Želim	ZHEH-leem
a menu	meni (jelovnik)	MEH-nee (YEH-lohv-neek)
a fork	vilicu	VEE-lee-tsoo
a knife	nož	nozh
a spoon	žlicu	ZHLEE-tsoo
a napkin	salvetku	sal-VET-koo
a glass (of water)	čašu (vode)	CHAH-shoo (VO-deh)

GETTING AROUND

I am looking for . . .	Tražim . . .	TRAH-zheem
a bank	banku	BAHN-koo
the church	crkvu	TSURK-voo
the city center	centar	TSEN-tar
the museum	muzej	MOO-zay
a pharmacy	apoteku	ah-po-TEK-oo

the park	park	park
the theater	pozorište	po-ZOH-ree-shteh
the tourist office	turističko biro	too-ree-STEECH-ko BEE-ro
the embassy	ambasadu	ahm-bah-SAH-doo
Where is the nearest telephone?	Gdje je najbliži telefon?	gdyeh yeh nah-ee-BLEE-zhee teh-LEH-fon?
I would like to buy . . .	Želim da kupim	ZHEH-leem dah KOO-peem
a stamp	poštansku marku	PO-shtan-skoo MAR-koo
a postcard	dopisnicu	do-PEE-snee-tsoo
a map	kartu	KAR-too

SIGNS

No trespassing	Ne ma ulaza (Ulaz zabranijen)	neh mah OO-lah-zah (OO-laz zah-bran-YEN)
No parking	Ne ma parkiranija (Parkiranije zabranijeno)	neh mah par-KEER-an-yah (par-KEER-an-yeh zah-bran-YEN-o)
Entrance	Ulaz	OO-laz
Exit	Izlaz	EEZ-laz
Information	Informacija	een-for-MAH-tsyah
No smoking	Pušenije zabranijeno	poo-SHEH-nyeh zah-bran-YEH-no
Arrivals	Doljetanja [planes] Dolaski [vehicles]	do-LYEH-tan-yah DO-las-kee
Departures	Odljetanija [planes] Odlaski [vehicles]	od-LYEH-tan-yah OD-las-kee
Toilets	Toaleti	toh-ah-LEH-tee
Danger	Opasno	O-pas-no

NUMBERS

1	jedan YEH-dahn	13	trinaest TREE-nah-est	60	šezdeset SHEHZ-deh-set
2	dva dvah	14	četrnaest cheh-tur-NAH-est	70	sedamdeset seh-DAHM-deh-set
3	tri tree	15	petnaest PET-nah-est	80	osamdeset o-SAHM-deh-set
4	četri CHEH-tree	16	sesnaest shess-NAH-est	90	devedeset deh-VEH-deh-set
5	pet pet	17	sedamnaest sheh-DAHM-nah-est	100	sto stoh
6	šest shehst	18	osamnaest o-SAHM-nah-est	500	pet stotina pet STO-tee-nah
7	sedam SEH-dahm	19	devetnaest deh-VET-nah-est	1,000	hiljada hee-lee-YAH-dah
8	osam O-sahm	20	dvadeset DVAH-deh-set		
9	devet DEH-vet	30	trideset TREE-deh-set		
10	deset DEH-set	40	četrideset CHEH-tree-deh-set		
11	jedanaest yeh-DAH-nah-est	50	pedeset PEH-deh-set		
12	dvanaest DVAH-nah-est				

14. Yugoslavian Menu Terms

GENERAL TERMS

soup	čorba	CHOR-bah
eggs	jaja	YAH-yah
meat	mjeso	MYEH-so
fish	riba	REE-bah
vegetables	povrće	PO-vur-cheh
fruit	voće	VO-cheh
desserts	deserti	deh-SEHR-tee
beverages	napitki	nah-PEET-kee
salt	sol	sohl
pepper	biber	BEE-behr
mustard	slačica, sent	SLAH-cee-tsah, sent
vinegar	sirće	SEER-cheh
oil	ulje	OO-lee-yeh
sugar	šećer	SHEH-chehr
tea	čaj	chye
coffee	kafa	KAH-fah
bread	hljeb, kruh	khlyeb, krookh
butter	puter	POO-tehr
wine	vino	VEE-no
vodka	rakija	rah-KEE-yah

SOUPS

dnevna juha	soup of the day	juha od rajcica	tomato soup
goveda juha	consommé	riblja juha	fish soup
juha od gljiva	mushroom soup		

MEATS

biftek	beefsteak	odrezak	veal steak
cevap	minced meat grilled	patka	duck
culbastija	grilled veal or pork	pile	chicken
divljac	game	prsuta	smoked meat
govedina	beef	ramsteak	rumpsteak
jagnjetina	lamb	raznjici	pork on a skewer
jetra	liver	sunka	ham
kobasice	sausages	svinjetina	pork
kunic	rabbit	teletina	veal
meso	meat	vesalica	grilled pork or veal
muckalica	grilled meat dish		

FISH

bakalar	cod	musule	mussels
grgec	perch	pastrmka	trout
hobotnice	octopus	riba svjeza	fresh sea fish
jastog	lobster	Sanpiero	San Pietro fish
jegulja	eel	saran	carp
lignji	squid	skampi	shrimp
losos	salmon	zubatac	dentex

EGGS

jaja	egg	omlet sa sirom	cheese omelet
omlet	omelet	omlet sa sunkom	ham omelet

SALADS

mesana salata	mixed salad	salata od hobotnice	octopus salad
rajcica salata	tomato salad	zelena salata	lettuce

VEGETABLES

gljive	mushrooms	mrkva	carrot
grasak	peas	paprike	peppers
krastavac	cucumber	paradajz	tomatoes
krumpir	potatoes	przeni krumpir	french fries
kupus	cabbage	repa	beets
luk	onions	riza	rice
mahune	french beans	spanac	spinach

DESSERTS

baklava	sweet pastry with syrup	sladoled	ice cream
dnevni kolac	cake of the day	od cokolade	chocolate
kompot mesani	stewed mixed fruit	od vinilije	vanilla
palacinke	crêpes	s vrhnjem	with whipped cream
pita od jabuka	apple strudel	torta od cokolade	chocolate cake
		vocna salata	fruit salad

FRUITS

ananas	pineapple	jagode	strawberries
breskve	peaches	kruske	pears
dinja	melon	limun	lemon
grozdje	grapes	pomorandza	orange
jabuke	apples	tresnje	cherries

BEVERAGES

bijela vina	white wine	pivo	beer
caj	tea	sljivovica	plum brandy
crna vina	red wine	specijalna vina	dessert wine
kava	coffee	vino	wine
mineralnu vodu	mineral water	vocni sok	fruit juice
mleko	milk	voda	water

CONDIMENTS AND OTHERS

biber	pepper	senf	mustard
kruh (hleb)	bread	sirće	vinegar
maslac (puter)	butter	so	salt
secer	sugar		

COOKING TERMS

dobro peceno	well done	nepeceno	rare
filovano	stuffed	przeno	fried
kuvano	boiled	srednje peceno	medium
na rostilju	grilled		

NOW, SAVE MONEY ON ALL YOUR TRAVELS!
Join Arthur Frommer's $25-A-Day Travel Club™

Saving money while traveling is never a simple matter, which is why, over 24 years ago, the **$25-A-Day Travel Club** was formed. Actually, the idea came from readers of the Arthur Frommer Publications who felt that such an organization could bring financial benefits, continuing travel information, and a sense of community to economy-minded travelers all over the world.

In keeping with the money-saving concept, the annual membership fee is low—$18 (U.S. residents) or $20 (Canadian, Mexican, and foreign residents)—and is immediately exceeded by the value of your benefits which include:

(1) The latest edition of any TWO of the books listed on the following page.

(2) An annual subscription to an 8-page quarterly newspaper *The Wonderful World of Budget Travel* which keeps you up-to-date on fastbreaking developments in low-cost travel in all parts of the world—bringing you the kind of information you'd have to pay over $25 a year to obtain elsewhere. This consumer-conscious publication also includes the following columns:

Hospitality Exchange—members all over the world who are willing to provide hospitality to other members as they pass through their home cities.

Share-a-Trip—requests from members for travel companions who can share costs and help avoid the burdensome single supplement.

Readers Ask . . . Readers Reply—travel questions from members to which other members reply with authentic firsthand information.

(3) A copy of *Arthur Frommer's Guide to New York.*

(4) Your personal membership card which entitles you to purchase through the Club all Arthur Frommer Publications for a third to a half off their regular retail prices during the term of your membership.

So why not join this hardy band of international budgeteers NOW and participate in its exchange of information and hospitality? Simply send $18 (U.S. residents) or $20 U.S. (Canadian, Mexican, and other foreign residents) along with your name and address to: $25-A-Day Travel Club, Inc., Gulf + Western Building, One Gulf + Western Plaza, New York, NY 10023. Remember to specify which *two* of the books in section (1) above you wish to receive in your initial package of members' benefits. Or tear out this page, check off any two books on the opposite side and send it to us with your membership fee.

PRENTICE HALL PRESS   Date_____
ONE GULF + WESTERN PLAZA, NEW YORK, NY 10023

Friends, please send me the books checked below:

FROMMER'S $-A-DAY GUIDES™
(In-depth guides to low-cost tourist accommodations and facilities.)

☐ Europe on $25 a Day $12.95	☐ New Zealand on $25 a Day $10.95
☐ Australia on $25 a Day $10.95	☐ New York on $45 a Day............. $9.95
☐ Eastern Europe on $25 a Day $10.95	☐ Scandinavia on $50 a Day $10.95
☑ England on $35 a Day $10.95	☐ Scotland and Wales on $35 a Day..... $10.95
☐ Greece on $25 a Day................ $10.95	☐ South America on $25 a Day $9.95
☐ Hawaii on $45 a Day................ $10.95	☐ Spain and Morocco (plus the Canary
☐ India on $15 & $25 a Day........... $9.95	Is.) on $40 a Day $10.95
☐ Ireland on $30 a Day................ $10.95	☐ Turkey on $25 a Day (avail. Sept. '87) . $10.95
☐ Israel on $30 & $35 a Day $10.95	☐ Washington, D.C. on $40 a Day...... $10.95
☐ Mexico on $20 a Day $10.95	

FROMMER'S DOLLARWISE GUIDES™
(Guides to accommodations and facilities from budget to deluxe with emphasis on the medium-priced.)

☐ Alaska (avail. Nov. '87) $12.95	☐ Caribbean $12.95
☐ Austria & Hungary $11.95	☐ Cruises (incl. Alaska, Carib, Mex,
☐ Benelux Countries (avail. June '87) ... $11.95	Hawaii, Panama, Canada, & US) $12.95
☐ Egypt............................. $11.95	☐ California & Las Vegas $11.95
☐ England & Scotland $11.95	☐ Florida $10.95
☐ France............................ $11.95	☐ New England $11.95
☐ Germany $11.95	☐ New York State (avail. Aug. '87)...... $11.95
☐ Italy.............................. $11.95	☐ Northwest......................... $11.95
☐ Japan & Hong Kong $12.95	☐ Skiing in Europe $12.95
☐ Portugal (incl. Madeira & the Azores) . $11.95	☐ Skiing USA—East $10.95
☐ South Pacific (avail. Aug. '87) $12.95	☐ Skiing USA—West $10.95
☐ Switzerland & Liechtenstein $11.95	☐ Southeast & New Orleans............ $11.95
☐ Bermuda & The Bahamas............ $10.95	☐ Southwest......................... $11.95
☐ Canada $12.95	☐ Texas............................. $11.95

THE ARTHUR FROMMER GUIDES™
(Pocket-size guides to tourist accommodations and facilities in all price ranges.)

☐ Amsterdam/Holland $5.95	☐ Mexico City/Acapulco $5.95
☐ Athens............................ $5.95	☐ Montreal/Quebec City $5.95
☐ Atlantic City/Cape May $5.95	☐ New Orleans $5.95
☐ Boston............................ $5.95	☐ New York.......................... $5.95
☐ Cancun/Cozumel/Yucatán $5.95	☐ Orlando/Disney World/EPCOT $5.95
☐ Dublin/Ireland $5.95	☐ Paris $5.95
☐ Hawaii............................ $5.95	☐ Philadelphia........................ $5.95
☐ Las Vegas $5.95	☐ Rome $5.95
☐ Lisbon/Madrid/Costa del Sol......... $5.95	☐ San Francisco $5.95
☐ London $5.95	☐ Washington, D.C. $5.95
☐ Los Angeles $5.95	

SPECIAL EDITIONS

☐ Bed & Breakfast—N. America $7.95	☐ Shopper's Guide to the Best Buys in
☐ Fast 'n' Easy Phrase Book	England, Scotland & Wales......... $10.95
(Fr/Ger/Ital/Sp in one vol.) $6.95	☐ Swap and Go (Home Exchanging) $10.95
☐ How to Beat the High Cost of Travel ... $4.95	☐ Travel Diary and Record Book........ $5.95
☐ Marilyn Wood's Wonderful Weekends	☐ Where to Stay USA (Lodging from $3
(NY, Conn, Mass, RI, Vt, NJ, Del, Pa). $9.95	to $30 a night) $9.95
☐ Motorist's Phrase Book (Fr/Ger/Sp) ... $4.95	

In U.S. include $1 post. & hdlg. for 1st book; 25¢ ea. add'l. book. Outside U.S. $2 and 50¢ respectively.

Enclosed is my check or money order for $_____

NAME_____

ADDRESS_____

CITY_____ STATE_____ ZIP_____